# THE SECRET INITIATION OF
# Jesus at Qumran

# THE SECRET INITIATION OF
# Jesus at Qumran

## The Essene Mysteries of John the Baptist

— Robert Feather —

Bear & Company
Rochester, Vermont

Bear & Company
One Park Street
Rochester, Vermont 05767
www.InnerTraditions.com

Bear & Company is a division of Inner Traditions International

**Library of Congress Cataloging-in-Publication Data**
Feather, Robert.
  The secret initiation of Jesus at Qumran : the Essene mysteries of John the Baptist / Robert Feather.
       p. cm.
  Summary: "An examination of the early, mysterious Essene community at Qumran that links it with John the Baptist, Jesus, and the beginnings of Christianity"—Provided by publisher.
  Includes bibliographical references and index.
  ISBN 1-59143-044-5 (pbk.)
1. Essenes. 2. Qumran community. 3. John, the Baptist, Saint. 4. Jesus Christ. 5. Christianity—Origin. 6. Dead Sea scrolls. I. Title.

BM175.E8F36 2005
296.8'14—dc22
                                                          2005006310

Printed and bound in the United States by Sheridan Printing

10  9  8  7  6  5  4  3  2  1
Text design and layout by Priscilla Baker
This book was typeset in Sabon, with Oxford and Agenda as display typefaces

# — Contents —

*To Jozef Tadeusz Milik*

# Acknowledgments

Every book on religious history is derivative. In fact, the same can be said for any nonfiction work and almost anything claiming to be fiction. *West Side Story* drew on Shakespeare, Shakespeare drew on the real-life rivalry of two families in Florence, the Ghibellines and Guelphs, who became the Montagues and Capulets of *Romeo and Juliet,* only to metamorphose into the Jets and Sharks of New York.* The Koran drew on the Christian Scriptures, the Christian Scriptures drew on the Hebrew Scriptures, and they all drew on truth, myth, and legend receding into the very dawn of consciousness.

This book is no different for much of its contents, yet there are some revelations of hidden truths to which opportunity and chance have led. Even so, without the guidance of others, those discoveries would never have occurred. Professor George Brooke, Department of Religions, University of Manchester, England, gave generously of his time in commenting on a number of chapters; Robert Shrager, historical consultant, surveyed the entire work despite a full-time role as executive director of major international companies; and Brian Norman, a historian, had direct input into parts of the text. To those others who have helped and inspired me on the way, my gratitude and acknowledgment of their invaluable contributions. They are listed below, in no particular order.

Jozef Milik, Dead Sea Scrolls scholar of the École Biblique, East
    Jerusalem, and Paris
Yolanta Zaluska Milik, art historian, Paris

---

*Shakespeare also drew on Arthur Brooke's poem "The Tragicall Historye of Romeus and Juliet" and the sixteenth-century Italian story *Giuletta e Romeo.*

Professor J. Harold Ellens, University of Michigan (retired)

Robert D. Leonard, Jr., fellow of the Royal Numismatic Society, Fellow of the American Numismatic Society

Robert Morgan, author and explorer, Kansas

Dr. Kenneth Lönnqvist, University of Helsinki

Dr. Minna Lönnqvist, University of Helsinki

Jonathan Williams, curator, Department of Coins and Medals, British Museum, London

Kathryn Phillips, assistant librarian, Arthur M. Sackler Gallery, Smithsonian Institution, Washington, D.C.

Magen Broshi, Israel Museum, Jerusalem

Dr. Gillian Pyke, Egyptologist

Joan Allegro, consultant, Isle of Man

Jeff Edwards, illustrator, Oxford

Sarah Feather, research consultant, London

David Freeman, librarian, West London Synagogue

Tina Elliot, educationalist, West London Synagogue

Mark Winer, senior rabbi, West London Synagogue

Helen Freeman, rabbi, West London Synagogue

Christopher Naunton, librarian and membership secretary, Egypt Exploration Society, London

Dr. Esther Eshel, Bar-Ilan University, Ramat Gan, Israel

Hanan Eshel, professor at Bar-Ilan University, Ramat Gan, Israel

Tuvia Fogel and Marinella Magri, Il Caduceo s.r.l., Milan

Jeanie Levitan, Anne Dillon, Peri Champine, Inner Traditions, Rochester, Vermont

Dr. D. Olav Röhrer-Ertl, Ludwig-Maximilians Universität, Munich

Dr. D. Hahn, Institut für Röentgendiagnostik der Universität Würzburg, Germany

Robert Donceel and Pauline Donceel-Voûte, professors at Louvain Catholic Seminary, Belgium

Wendy Smith, honorary research fellow, Institute of Archaeology and Antiquity, University of Birmingham, England

Charles M. Sennott, Europe bureau chief, *Boston Globe*

# ⌒ Foreword ⌒

New ways of looking at established ideas are always challenging to scholars and exciting to laypersons in any field. Robert Feather is a master at stimulating thoughtful people in both categories with innovative hypotheses for reexamining traditional models of thought and interpretation. He has a remarkably imaginative capacity to operate soundly along the front lines of historical and cultural inquiry. This was the hallmark of his intriguing 1999 book entitled *The Copper Scroll Decoded* (and its 2003 reprint, *The Mystery of the Copper Scroll of Qumran*). Now we have, from his facile and fruitful pen, an equally challenging work called *The Secret Initiation of Jesus at Qumran*. His subtitle indicates that he proposes to unveil John the Baptist's connection to the Essene sect. For most laypersons and many serious scholars, this undertaking is less esoteric, even more interesting, and of substantially greater practical relevance than his stellar research on the Copper Scroll.

When we are presented with such new ways of looking at traditional models as Feather offers us, it is always important to discern the possibility and then the probability of the truth of this new perspective. In an effort to take a constructive view of this work and its innovative hypothesis, I have tried to place myself inside Feather's worldview and model. I have endeavored to analyze what his new insights look like if one views the whole picture of Jesus and the Baptist through them. This is the honest way to test an innovative hypothesis. I have concluded that Feather's work offers a legitimate new proposal that is heuristically sustainable by the evidence he presents, and therefore his work requires serious attention.

Scholarship requires that all the disparate details of a new model be considered as a whole. Individual aspects, taken by themselves, sometimes do not seem clearly persuasive. When all the facets of a model are taken together, however, they frequently paint a new picture on an old canvas, which is more illuminating than traditional or familiar modes of interpretation. In this new book, Feather's hypothesis manages all the data as a coherent whole somewhat better than many previous interpretations of the story of Jesus, John the Baptist, and the sources of Qumran monotheism. Admittedly, the author must fill in large gaps of historical assessment with well-considered speculation or heuristic and phenomenological reasoning, since history is slippery and unstable when we attempt to press it for conclusive empirical information.

The best historians, when looking into the deep well of their historical sources, are always afflicted with the fact that the first picture they see is the reflection of their own image. Feather does not apologize for the fact that the story told in this highly readable book is cast in the image of his own perspective, assumptions, imagination, and rationality. Indeed, not only does he not apologize, but he also announces up front what his assumptions and speculations are. So this is an honest and a good book, and it reads like a novel.

Feather has assembled here numerous strands of argumentation and a variety of data that has not been previously addressed in this comprehensive and holistic way. These strands converge in a fashion that confirms the author's general hypothesis and produces a coherent whole, managing the data quite satisfactorily. This convergence is what makes Feather's proposal persuasive and worthy of careful examination.

He introduces novel ideas that come from unexpected directions, forcing us all to look at the Dead Sea Scrolls, and the Qumran community that produced or preserved them, in a substantially new way. I am convinced that he has thus opened us to patterns of insight and trajectories of inquiry that will, over the long term, be fruitful for our analysis of what was really going on in late Second Temple Judaism and in that isolated Qumran community on the bluffs above the Dead Sea two thousand years ago.

*The Secret Initiation of Jesus at Qumran* is an examination of the nature and historical roots of that Qumran community and the connections that may be discerned between it and the preaching of John the Baptist, the ministry of Jesus, and the origins of Christianity. Through the eyes of scholars like Jozef Milik, who were actually the first to discover the nature of the Dead Sea Scrolls and to analyze them, Feather offers us eyewitness accounts of crucial data on such things as the possible burial site of John the Baptist. He makes a persuasive argument for connections between the roots of Christianity in the Qumran community, or, in its larger ideological context, the Essene movement, and the far more ancient monotheism of the Egyptian pharaoh Akhenaten.

Some mysterious factors in the known history of Second Temple Judaism (500 B.C.E.–300 C.E.) and Christian origins (30–300 C.E.), which Feather addresses in this volume, are as follows. First, the Qumran community spoke of and anticipated the coming of two or three messiahs: a royal messiah in the line of David, a priestly messiah in the line of Aaron, and a suffering servant messiah who seemed to be something of a combination of the prophetic figures of Deuteronomy 18:15 and Isaiah 53. This third messiah may have been seen by the Essenes at Qumran as a characteristic of one or both of the royal and priestly messiahs.

Second, although Paul in 1 Corinthians 11:23–29 seems to make a eucharistic sacrament out of Jesus's Last Supper, doing so on the grounds that the supper was the highly significant Jewish Passover meal, neither Jesus's conduct at that last supper nor Paul's sacralizing of it looks anything like a Passover celebration. Third, there is a string of quotations in the Christian Scriptures that are apparently taken from documents present among the Dead Sea Scrolls discovered in 1947 in the desert caves near the Dead Sea, although a connection between the Jesus movement and the Qumran community has been consistently avoided or neglected in most biblical scholarship, at least until recently. Fourth, there was an apparently significant influence of Essene and perhaps Qumran-Essene ideas on the formation of Jesus's self-concept and on the shape of early Christianity.

Other important and mysterious aspects of this matter of the Essene connection with Jesus and John the Baptist are of even more immediate practical concern. A few specially trained and uniquely committed scholars focused their research on the Qumran community and the Dead Sea Scrolls from the time that the first scrolls came to light, in the late 1940s and early 1950s. Nonetheless, incredible delays in publication of the results; massive losses of the collected data and artifacts that seem to have simply disappeared; dysfunction and lethargy on the part of people entrusted with the administration, preservation, and publication of the papers and research reports of the early DDS research scholars; and the like have raised considerable distress in the general scholarly community and sunk the spirits of many laypersons who cultivated serious historical and religious interest in these matters.

Feather's argument that Jesus's family connection with Egypt, recorded in the Gospels, had much larger significance than has been acknowledged over the last two millennia is linked in his model with Jesus's connection with the Qumran Essenes and with their connection, in turn, with ancient Egyptian monotheism. This line of thought is very new and innovative, largely speculative, and enormously intriguing. Feather weaves this data into his comprehensive hypothesis in a convincing way. If one concedes the relevance and cogency of his hypotheses, his complete argument and comprehensive model has internal integrity, at least at the heuristic and phenomenological level. The strength of his model is his persistent effort at internal consistency. The wisdom in his model is his acknowledgment that it is speculative, although stimulating and intellectually intriguing.

When his argumentation is taken as a unitary whole, Robert Feather's hypothesis works. In that context, the details seem adequately supportive of the whole. The hermeneutical circle is complete, in that he proposes his hypotheses, adduces the data, analyzes and tests that information, expands the sample so as to generalize it, draws preliminary conclusions from the arguments and data, and reviews the hypotheses in the light of the model produced by the process. Thereafter he proposes the consequent worldview, the principal constraints, and the degree of legitimate speculation, and offers us his report. He has done the work he has chosen to do appropriately and thoroughly. So we should take his proposal under serious consideration as one that manages the data adequately in terms of the initial hypotheses. His book should be read widely, get much exposure, and not be overlooked merely because it is novel and innovative in its approach, rather than derived from the prime centers of academe or from mainstream academic authorities.

Every possible way that we can view the roots and origins of Christianity in its Jewish incubation in the first century C.E. should be explored. Every insight that can be imagined or dug up on Jesus, John the Baptist, and their Jewish and Christian associates should be offered. They represent a moment in the ancient world that was generative of all the crucial influences that have shaped the Western world ever since. There was a moment in history, from the return of the Jewish exiles from Babylon in 500 B.C.E. to the established order of Rabbinic Judaism and of Imperial Christianity in 300–400 C.E., and particularly the first century C.E., that has had a greater ethical and religious effect on the whole world than any other era. If that moment can be better explained or understood by a careful study of Feather's work, such attention should be our scholarly imperative.

I commend this intriguing book to your devoted attention. It will reward you.

J. HAROLD ELLENS
NEW YEAR'S DAY 2005
FARMINGTON HILLS, MICHIGAN

J. Harold Ellens, Ph.D., is a retired professor of philosophy, biblical studies, and psychology. He is also a retired Presbyterian theologian and ordained pastor. He is currently a research scholar at the University of Michigan in Second Temple Judaism and Christian Origins and is writing a book for the University of Michigan titled *Jesus as the Son of Man in John's Gospel* and a book for Praeger Press called *Sex in the Bible*. His recent publications include *God's Word for Our World* (two volumes) with T & T Clark; *The Destructive Power of Religion and Violence in Judaism, Christianity, and Islam* (four volumes) with Praeger Press; *Psychology and the Bible: A New Way to Read the Scriptures* (four volumes) with Praeger Press; *Jesus as the Son of Man: The Literary Character* (monograph) with Claremont University; *Pastoral Psychology* (three volumes) with Kluwer Academic/Human Sciences Press; and other related monographs. He is also the author or editor of 106 additional books and 166 professional journal articles. He lives with his wife in Farmington Hills and is the father of seven children and grandfather of eight grandchildren.

*Delegates at a Dead Sea Scrolls Conference in Hereford, June 2000.*

Standing, back row: Timothy Lim (1st from left), E.D. Herbert (3rd from left), Ralph Klein (7th from left), Martin Abegg (9th from left), George Brooke (10th from left), Hans van der Meij (11th from left), Armin Lange (12th from left), D. Parry (2nd from right).

Standing, middle row: Emeritus Professor Geza Vermes (3rd from left), Emanuel Tov (5th from left, with glasses), E. Ulrich (6th from left), S. Talmon (7th from left), Sidney White Crawford (8th from left), Peter Flint (10th from left), H. Scanlin (12th from left), J. Vander Kam (13th from left).

Kneeling: Lika Tov (5th from left), S. Metso (6th from left), Robert Feather (11th from left), S. Daley (13th from left), E. Tigchelaar (3rd from right).

# ⌐ Preface ⌐

This book was originally intended as a sequel to *The Mystery of the Copper Scroll of Qumran,** which dealt with aspects of the Dead Sea Scrolls and, more particularly, one of the scrolls that had been engraved on copper by the strange community of Essenes that inhabited Qumran. I was trained as a metallurgist, and the use of copper by a devout Jewish sect, living by the Dead Sea around the first century B.C.E., had aroused my curiosity—especially as the Hebrew text seemed to be a list of buried treasures, treasures that apparently had never been found.

Identifying the location of some of the treasures described in the Copper Scroll was only one of the claims substantiated in that book; these treasures I identified as being in various museums around the world. Furthermore, a detailed analysis arose from my reading of the name of an Egyptian pharaoh encrypted in the text of the scroll—an interpretation confirmed as "not unreasonable" by both Professor John Tait of University College London and Professor Rosalie David of Manchester University. The profound conclusion was that the Hebrews must have been present at the court of Pharaoh Akhenaten and that the origins of monotheism date back to his time.

For my next book I had planned to take a closer look at the Qumran community's beliefs and way of life, examining how these may have influenced the beginnings of Christianity and its emergence as a daughter religion of Judaism. However, while discussing the project with Jozef Milik, one of the scholars who originally worked on deciphering the Dead Sea Scrolls back in the early 1950s, my research took a strange and totally unexpected twist. Jozef Milik had been the leader of the team of translators

---

*Published by Inner Traditions International, June 2003. An earlier version, *The Copper Scroll Decoded,* was published by HarperCollins in June 1999, and under other titles in Italy, Holland, and Japan.

based at the École Biblique in East Jerusalem; he had also been, at that time, an ordained Catholic priest.

What Monsieur Milik revealed to me, in the course of many intriguing conversations he and I shared about the Essene community, inspired me to write this book and informs a substantial part of it.

*The Secret Initiation of Jesus at Qumran* is not intended to give a detailed description of the evidence relating to the formation, activities, and raison d'être of the Qumran Essenes or the discoveries of the Dead Sea Scrolls. Much of this was covered in *The Mystery of the Copper Scroll of Qumran,* and there are many other sources of information on the subject. Suffice it to say that the Qumran Essenes, a mysterious Jewish sect that suddenly vanished from its habitat by the Dead Sea in Judaea around 68 C.E., was a unique community in Jewish history, and in many ways practiced a form of Judaism very different from that being pursued elsewhere in the Second Temple period.

Qumran has long been a place of controversy and intense discussion—at international conferences, seminars, and in learned publications. No one is certain of the origins of the strange, reclusive sect that wrote and possessed what are now known as the Dead Sea Scrolls. Nor is there agreement as to the degree of influence the sect had on early Christianity, or its relationship to John the Baptist and Jesus.

Such is the intensity of feelings about who exactly these Essenes were that it is not uncommon to see professors shouting across conference rooms at each other as they defend their respective pet theories. Numerous respected scholars have their own individual ideas about what was going on at Qumran; and while there is consensus on many issues, there are also large areas where there are just no accepted answers. Perhaps part of the reason is that there are basic misunderstandings with regard to the *origins* of the community. As Magen Broshi, of the Israel Museum, likes to put it: "There are at least ten different theories about the origins and function of Qumran. By definition, nine of them are wrong."

As our story unfolds, it will become increasingly evident that the *activities* of the Essenes are central to the plot, and of profound significance to Judaism, Christianity, and Islam, as well as many other religions.

The first part of this book surveys the historical setting and the characters involved in shaping the events that occurred in those distant Second

Temple times some two thousand years ago, a period that spanned the activities of the Essenes at Qumran and the life of Jesus. As a corollary, clarification along the way of how close the Qumran-Essene community was to the thinking and practices of Pharaoh Akhenaten is of critical importance in assessing both the revelations of Jozef Milik and the other astounding findings that are forthcoming in the second part of the book.

## Time line from Akhetaten to Qumran (1340 BCE–132 CE)

| Rulers of Holy Land | Date | Event |
|---|---|---|
| Egyptians | c. 1340 | Akhenaten-Nefertiti/Joseph-Jacob (Amarna Period) |
| | c. 1200 | Moses and Israelites in Sinai |
| | c. 1160 | Joshua commences conquest of Canaan |
| | | Period of Judges |
| Israelites | 1050 | King Saul |
| | | King David |
| | 970 | King Solomon builds 1st Temple at Jerusalem |
| | | Period of divided kingdoms of North and South |
| | 740 | Prophet Isaiah |
| | 722 | Assyrians conquer Northern Kingdom, disperse 10 tribes |
| | 700 | Assyrians dominate Southern Kingdom |
| Assyrians | 625 | Jeremiah begins prophecy |
| | 610 | Prophet Habakkuk |
| | 590 | Prophet Ezekiel |
| | 586 | Babylonians capture Jerusalem, destroy 1st Temple, disperse Southern Kingdom of Judah |
| Babylonians | 540 | Persian invasion allows return from Babylon |
| | 516 | Jerusalem Temple rebuilt and rededicated as 2nd Temple |
| Persians | | |
| | 320 | Greek Ptolemy rule |
| Greeks | 198 | Greek Seleucid rule |
| | | Onias IV High Priest (Teacher of Righteousness) |
| | 167 | Maccabees reestablish Jewish rule and Hasmonean reign |
| Israelites | 150 | Essenes settle at Qumran |
| | 63 | Romans conquer Jewish state |
| Romans | 37 | Rome appoints Herod king, 2nd Temple restored |
| Parthians | 4 | King Herod dies, John the Baptist born, Jesus born |
| **BCE** | | |
| **CE** | c. 32 | John the Baptist beheaded |
| | c. 33 | Jesus crucified |
| | c. 64 | Paul executed |
| | 68 | Qumran destroyed by Romans |
| Romans | 70 | 2nd Temple destroyed by Romans |
| | 132 | Revolt against Romans led by Bar-Kochba |

ADAPTED FROM ROBERT FEATHER, *THE MYSTERY OF THE COPPER SCROLL OF QUMRAN*
(INNER TRADITIONS, 2003), 141.

# — 1 —

# Conversations with
# Monsieur Jozef Milik

G reen-painted graffiti match the darker drab color of the massive double doors bordered in faded gray stone. A red circle with angled line forbids vehicle parking—*Prière de ne pas stationner devant cette porte*—adding to the inhibition I feel as I key in the entry numbers Monsieur Milik has given me. The door lock clicks, allowing the heavy guardian of the gloomy high-ceilinged interior hallway to be pushed open and then crunch closed behind me, shutting out the droning vehicles and tired Quartier outside. My eyes take several minutes to become accustomed to the now dim light. I walk through into an open yard littered with debris, an old motorcycle, a broken bedframe . . . huge buildings on three sides, entrances everywhere. I am lost.

Back by the front entrance my eyes are by now adjusted enough to the gloom to see a listing of dozens and dozens of names. Among them I find "J. Milik—Bâtiment 6 Rue3G." Someone enters through the front door. *"Excusez-moi, madame, où est six rue Trois?"* I inquire. I am directed to a set of dusty glass-paneled doors and gain entry using the same digital code. Climbing the steep stone steps loaded down with brandy bottle, cameras, and recording equipment is no easy task. Little wonder Monsieur Milik rarely leaves the confines of this heavy-jowled building. Each feline-odored landing reveals a group of four green-painted, peeling doors, sometimes a nameplate, sometimes nothing; door frames are often barred by several locks and signs of re-sited fasteners. The third floor is little different, with no indication of which door belongs to Monsieur Milik. I ring all the bells and knock. Nothing. I go up a flight, repeat the exercise, and continue to the musty-smelling fifth floor, where I find winding, narrow, decaying corridors with small, heavily

1

fortified doors. Part of it has been condemned for human habitation.

I go back down to the third floor, determined to try every door again. Looking more closely at a faded nameplate, I can just make out the words "Milik *et* Zaluska." I ring and knock more determinedly. There is a shuffling moment before a dark-featured, serious-faced woman, youthful shoulder-length nut-brown hair belying her obvious older years, materializes in the doorway. I hand her a bunch of dark red roses. She perks up and smiles, thanking me. *"Ils sont beaux,"* she murmurs.

Madame Milik ushers me into a long, narrow, untidy, bookshelved hallway and through a room to the left, stacked high with more books, files, papers everywhere. A small black laptop computer sits openly incongruous on a large table. She urges me on into another open-accessed room, where a small brown wooden table and one chair are set by the window. A chaise longue covered in faded, nondescript material sits by the inner wall, a bed on the other side. Bookshelves line every other available centimeter of wall space, reaching back into a darkened cavernous area opposite the window with yet more books and pamphlets. Madame Milik retreats, muttering: "He will be with you soon."

My senses start to race as I stand by the little table, still in my bulging outer coat. What will he be like, this doyen of the Dead Sea Scrolls, who controlled and led the original translation team working on the earliest fragments of material found at Qumran in 1947? He is the most dedicated and revered exponent of ancient Middle Eastern texts; many people didn't even realize he was still alive.

Minutes pass as I wait for the man Hershel Shanks, editor of the U.S. journal *Biblical Archaeology Review,* describes as "intensely shy . . . dour, melancholy . . . the most talented of the scholars," and I recall what John Strugnell, editor in chief of the Dead Sea Scrolls research team until 1990, said of him: "Milik has more intelligence for these materials in one of his hands than any of that group."[1] According to Professor George Brooke, of Manchester University, Jozef Milik has been a relative recluse for many years and does not even reply to letters.

Scuffing footsteps draw nearer, then . . . magically, he's there in front of me: pale, chiseled head, sharp-featured face, wrinkled but with no scars or blemishes, short thinning white hair, stooping frame perhaps five-feet-five or -six, baggy blue trousers, faded blue woolen sweater worn at the elbows. We shake cold hands, and he sits carefully on the wooden chair. I hand him the bottle of brandy, still in its thin white plastic bag. He acknowledges it with a brief *"Merci,"* placing it on the table, where it remains unexamined all through our conversation. It is not important, a mere detail. Why I am there is what matters. That is what he wants to know.

I start telling him why I have called, dropping a few familiar names to reassure him I live in his world. He is still very tentative about who I am, what I am. My visiting card draws some questions, and I respond that the initials after my name indicate I am *"un ingénieur . . . un metallurgiste."* He has not seen many of those recently! He beams interest and peers closely with his better eye at the card, holding it up to catch the window's late-afternoon light. His left eye oscillates between being excessively wide open and almost shut.

I ask if I may take off my coat and put it on the chaise longue. He motions me to do so, and I resume my position standing by the table. To rest my sore feet and to get on a more equal eye level, I kneel by the table, and our conversation continues about why I am in France and about my proposed book. Am I to kneel and pray to this lapsed Catholic priest all through our meeting?

Suddenly his rasping, thin voice, in a blend of Polish, French, and English accents, expresses the realization that I have nothing to sit on. He apologizes and shuffles quite quickly out of the room, returning with a small wooden chair. He is not as incapacitated as I had been led to believe. In the end we talk for nearly one and a half hours. Bit by bit I feel my way into his mind and confidence, eliciting childlike bursts of giggling and serious moods of reflection. (See page 16 of the color insert.)

It was not until my third visit, in October 1999, when I returned to present him with a copy of my book on one of the Dead Sea Scrolls, that Jozef Milik started to talk more freely about his early life and work, volunteered his date of birth as March 24, 1922, and told me why he had left the Catholic Church. Ostensibly it was to marry his rather delightful wife, Yolanta, née Zaluska, but there were other reasons, reasons connected with what he had found and interpreted in the scrolls of the Dead Sea.

Two hours into our conversation he quietly and almost casually spoke of a certain event in a burial place near Qumran. It was one of those nerve-tingling moments; my mind reeled with the impact of what he was saying.

Those dramatic words of Jozef Milik started me on a journey of discovery to determine how the circumstances at the time of Jesus might confirm or disprove his revelation. It was a quest that was to take me from the cold dampness of a Parisian autumn day to the remote dryness of Egypt, to the holy places of Jerusalem, to an offshore haven on the Isle of Man, to catacombs in Rome, to Washington and New York, to a Gothic building in Germany, and back to the barren shores of the Dead Sea in Israel. As my journeys and research progressed, it became increasingly clear that something extraordinary, as yet not revealed, may have occurred at Qumran, and that there were others who were party to this knowledge but were not keen for the evidence to become public.

Since publication of my previous book, *The Mystery of the Copper Scroll of Qumran,* I have come across many further pieces of evidence that confirm a connection between a uniquely monotheistic pharaonic period in Egyptian history and the Essenes of Qumran, who lived a thousand years later and a thousand miles distant. As remarkable as this connection may appear to be, to date the relationship has been criticized but not refuted, and a number of eminent scholars have indicated that it begins to explain some anomalies in their own research. The evidentiary examples that I cite in this book have a considerable bearing on early Judaism and the story of Jesus and his epoch, and as I progressed farther along the "Jozef Milik trail," many more examples came to light that supported my conjectures regarding this link. These are included within the body of this text as they became relevant.

The main thrust of my current search, however, was the nature of the people who lived at Qumran between, perhaps, 150 B.C.E. and 68 C.E., the secrets they kept, their relationship to the earliest followers of Jesus, and the incredible revelations of Monsieur Milik.

You could jump deep into the book and find out what Jozef Milik had confided on that cold drizzly day in Paris, but you would lose the background and atmosphere of how it fits into the cycle of events that occurred two millennia ago around the time when Jesus was born and the Second Temple still existed in Jerusalem.

To set the scene, we need to look more closely at the nature of the Qumran community and what was going on in their isolated settlements within the historical background that encompassed their lives.

# 2

# A Historical Canter through the Intertestamental Years (320 B.C.E. to 132 C.E.)

The early history of Judaea and Palaestina, the names by which the encompassing areas were known in Roman times, is well documented elsewhere, and only the events that relate to our story are highlighted here (see table 1, page 9). We pick up the sequence of events in more detail with the arrival of the Romans in an area previously dominated by Greek and, prior to that, Persian influences, but now under the control of Jewish rulers—the Hasmoneans.

It is 63 B.C.E. A Roman legion under Pompey has swept down from Syria and stormed Jerusalem in Rome's insatiable drive to dominate most of Europe and the countries surrounding the Mediterranean. Hyrcanus, son of Salome Alexandra Yannai, the last ruler of the Jewish Hasmonean kingdom of Judah, had cooperated with the Romans in their conquest, and for his reward was made high priest and ethnarch (governor) of the new dominion. Emperor Julius Caesar, following the usual pattern of appointing proxy rulers, nominated Antipater, the son of an Idumean family that had converted to Judaism under the Hasmoneans' rule, as *apotropos*—head of the state. Antipater's son Phasael was made governor of Jerusalem, and another son, Herod, was made governor of the Galilee in 47 B.C.E.

Roman rule was not secure, however. The son of Aristobolus ben Yannai (brother of Hyrcanus), known as Mattathias Antigonus, wrested control of Judah from Herod in 40 B.C.E. He was aided by the Parthians (Persians), who were still warring with Rome. Once in power, Antigonus got rid of Hyrcanus, made himself high priest, and drove Herod's brother Phasael to suicide. The Jewish population rallied to the new ruler as a true

5

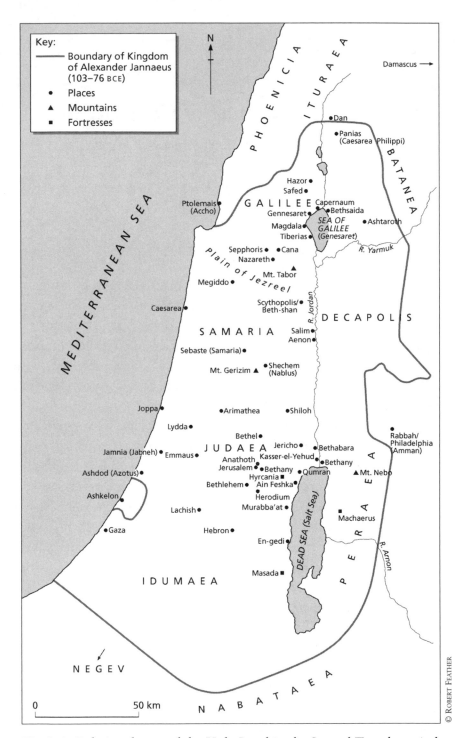

*Fig. 2.1. Relational map of the Holy Land in the Second Temple period.*

descendant of the Hasmoneans, and his victory was commemorated by the striking of a coin bearing a menorah (a seven-branched candelabra kept in the Jerusalem Temple) and the Greek inscription "King Antigonus" and Hebrew words *"Hever ha-Yehudim"*—Mattathias the High Priest—but his reign was to be short-lived.

Once ousted, Herod ran screaming to Rome to elicit the help of Mark Antony and Octavian, barely four years after the chill winds of March and cold steel of Brutus had frozen the life of Emperor Julius Caesar. Herod was ratified by the Roman senate as king of Judah and led a mercenary army back to reconquer Jerusalem and execute Antigonus in 37 B.C.E.

Herod the Great, as he was later to become known, turned out to be a cruel but constructive ruler. He eliminated many of his old Hasmonean enemies, imposed stiff taxes, abrogated the rights of traditional Jewish Law courts, and appointed the high priest himself. Not surprisingly, he thoroughly antagonized the largely Jewish population.

Conscious of his debt to Rome, Herod embarked on an ambitious program of construction. He built a series of fortresses, including the garrison city of Sebaste on the old site of Samaria, and the fortress of Herodium, near Bethlehem. In honor of the Roman emperor, Herod also constructed a complete new city at Caesarea, on the northern coast of his realm, comprising battlements, palaces, market forums, an amphitheater, a hippodrome, Roman baths, and an artificial harbor. New roads and aqueducts were laid down to serve the new establishments.

Herod's most ambitious enterprise, however, was the renovation of the Second Temple in Jerusalem (built in 538–515 B.C.E.), in which he initially followed the strict religious codes, only to mar his monumental work by erecting a huge golden eagle of Rome on the top. The Pharisees, a devout Jewish sect, were incensed and removed the idolatrous symbol. Shortly before his death, Herod took revenge by having many of them killed. After Herod's death in 4 B.C.E., Emperor Augustus Caesar (who changed his name from Octavian) ratified the division of Israel under the control of Herod's children—Archelaus, Antipas, and Philip.

Archelaus commenced his rule over the province of Judah in 4 B.C.E.— a significant date in Christian history—and proved to be even more cruel than his father. Tired of the complaints he was receiving, Emperor Augustus replaced Archelaus in 6 B.C.E. with the rule of prefects drawn from the elite Roman cavalry and subject to the Roman legate in Syria. The harshest of these prefects, who ruled from 26 to 36 C.E., was a certain Pontius Pilate, a man we will meet again later in the story of Jesus.

Nor was Herod Antipas, the ruler of Galilee, the gentlest of creatures. He continued his father's practice of enforcing Hellenization on his subjects and renovated the cities of Tiberias and Sepphoris (the latter several miles north of Nazareth). While the previous Greek rule had prevailed, attractive cultural, religious, and philosophical elements of that civilization had pervaded the entire Middle East. With the arrival of the Romans, it continued to hold sway in many aspects of day-to-day life.

It is against this stormy background of political and social turmoil that, in 5 or 6 B.C.E., Jesus was born.[1]

Simultaneous with the period of the birth of Jesus, the leader of a group of Zealots named Judas of Galilee led some two thousand men against the city of Sepphoris in the north and seized Herod Antipas's palace. Antipas, with the aid of the Roman governor of Syria, Varus, responded by razing the city and crucifying all the Zealots.[2] Antipas rebuilt the city, and it was perhaps this bitter experience that convinced the predominantly Jewish aristocratic population of Galilee, with its minority of Gentile Greeks, to remain relatively neutral in the Jewish revolts that were to follow in 66 C.E. and thus survive a repeat of the lesson.

The atmosphere in which Jesus was brought up was therefore one of group rivalries, conspiracy, and an indigenous fear of the ruling classes. Although according to the Christian Scriptures his father was apparently a craftsman carpenter, Jesus early in his life showed an interest in religion and the Torah (Hebrew Scriptures).

Besides the Zealots—those prepared to fight the Romans—there were several other competing Jewish factions. Most prominent were the Pharisees, or Sages, who emphasized the need to return to the Torah instead of indulging in political agitation. The Sadducees—who represented the wealthier classes and supported the temple high priest and his fellow priests—cooperated even more closely with the Romans for the sake of an easier life. Yet another religious group, the Samaritans—descendants of the tribes of Ephraim and Manasseh—followed their own version of Judaism. There were also minority religious sects, such as the Essenes, a brotherhood of reclusives. All five of these groupings were to cast their influence over the life of Jesus.

**TABLE 1**

**Events in Judaea and vicinity 320 BCE–132 CE and the Roman rulers**

| | Events BCE | Roman Rulers |
|---|---|---|
| **GREEK RULE** | 320 Greek Ptolemy rule, after the death of Alexander the Great | |
| | 198 Greek Seleucid rule | |
| | 175 Zadokite High Priest Onias III deposed and replaced by his brother Jason | |
| | 172 High Priest Onias IV flees to Egypt and is replaced by Hellenist High Priest Menelaus | |
| | 171 Onias III murdered at instigation of High Priest Menelaus | |
| | 167 Hellenization increases; temple at Jerusalem transformed into sanctuary for Olympian god Zeus; Judaism proscribed | |
| **JEWISH HASMONEAN RULE** | 166 Jewish uprising under Judas Maccabee | |
| | 164 Maccabees reestablish Jewish rule, beginning of Hasmonean rule; rededication of Jerusalem Temple | |
| | 161 Judas Maccabee killed in battle; his brother Jonathan becomes rebel leader | |
| | 152 Jonathan Maccabee appointed high priest | |
| | 150 Essenes settle at Qumran | |
| | 143 Simon Maccabee appointed high priest and ethnarch | |
| | 142 Jonathan Maccabee executed in prison | |
| | 135 High Priest Simon Maccabee murdered by his son-in-law | |
| | 135 John Hyrcanus I appointed high priest and ethnarch | |
| | 104 Aristobulus I appointed high priest and king | |
| | 103 Alexander Jannaeus becomes high priest and king | |
| | 88 Plot to overthrow Jannaeus by Pharisees in league with Seleucid King Demetrius III; 800 Pharisees crucified | |
| | 76 King Alexander Jannaeus dies; his widow, Salome Alexandra, becomes queen; their son, Hyrcanus II, becomes high priest | 70 Pompey elected consul of Rome |
| | 67 Hyrcanus II becomes king and high priest; deposed in same year by his brother Aristobulus, who becomes high priest and King Aristobulus II | |

| | Events BCE–CE | Roman Rulers |
|---|---|---|
| **ROMAN RULE** | 63 Romans under Pompey conquer Jewish state; King Aristobulus II deposed; Hyrcanus II reinstated as high priest; Antipater, an Idumean convert to Judaism, made overseer of Judaea | 46 Julius Caesar (110–44 BCE) becomes dictator after defeating Pompey<br><br>44 Julius Caesar murdered; Octavian, Mark Antony, and Lepidus rule as coalition |
| **PARTHIAN RULE** | 42 Antipater assassinated<br>40 Antigonus, son of Aristobulus II, made king and high priest, ousting Romans from control of Jerusalem region, with Parthian (Asian power based by the river Euphrates) support; Hyrcanus II maimed and exiled | |
| **ROMAN RULE** | 37 Rome appoints Herod the Great, son of Antipater, as king, who reconquers Jerusalem for Rome; 2nd Temple restored; Hasmonean dynasty ends<br>30 Hyrcanus II executed<br><br><br><br>4 King Herod the Great dies; Jesus born*<br>4 King Herod's three sons share power; Herod Archelaus appointed ruler of Judaea and Samaria; Galilee and Peraea ruled by his brother Herod Antipas; northeast of Galilee ruled by Herod Philip | 27 Octavian (63 BCE–14 CE) made emperor and Augustus<br>14 Augustus replaced by Emperor Tiberius (42 BCE–37 CE) |

**BCE**

**CE**

| | Events BCE–CE | Roman Rulers |
|---|---|---|
| **ROMAN RULE** | 6 Herod Archelaus deposed by Augustus; direct Roman rule of Judaea by the prefect Coponius; census leads to Zealot uprising<br>26 Pontius Pilate appointed prefect of Judaea; Jesus commences ministry<br>35 John the Baptist beheaded at Machaerus by Herod Antipas<br>c.36 Jesus crucified<br>36 Pontius Pilate and High Priest Caiaphas removed from office | 37 Emperor Tiberius dies; Caligula (12–41 CE) becomes emperor |

**ROMAN RULE**

| | Events CE | | Roman Rulers |
|---|---|---|---|
| 39 | Herodian ruler of Galilee, Prince Agrippa, replaces Prince Antipas | | |
| | | 41 | Claudius (10 BCE–54 CE) becomes emperor |
| 41 | Agrippa I appointed king of Judaea by Emperor Claudius | | |
| 44 | King Agrippa I dies; Roman procurator appointed | | |
| | | 54 | Nero (12–41 CE) becomes emperor |
| 64 | Paul and Peter executed in Rome | | |
| 66 | Zealot uprisings commence | | |
| 68 | Qumran destroyed by Romans | | |
| | | 69 | Vespasian (9–79 CE) becomes emperor[†] |
| 70 | Second Temple in Jerusalem destroyed by Romans under Titus | | |
| 74 | Zealot stronghold at Masada captured by Romans | | |
| | | 79 | Titus (39–81 CE) becomes emperor |
| | | 81 | Domitian (51–96 CE) becomes emperor |
| 132 | Revolt against Romans led by Bar-Kochba | | |

*The conventional date for Jesus's birth is the year zero. Another plausible date, suggested by Hugh Schonfield,[3] is 6 or 7 CE, based on the works of Josephus and the Gospels of John and Luke.

†From 68 to 69 CE there was a period of civil wars in the Roman Empire, with three emperors, all dying in 69 CE, reigning for brief periods in succession, namely Galba (3–69 CE), Otho (32–69 CE), and Vitellius (15–69 CE).

Having looked briefly at the pertinent historical developments in the Middle East, we can now move on to examine the views of writers and scholars on the role of the Qumran Essenes and other religious groupings, and their effects on the early Jesus movement.

# — 3 —

# Scribblers, Squabblers, and Scholars

T he conventional understanding of the emergence of Christianity is that it grew out of mainstream Judaism, Jesus and all his followers having been born Jews and practiced Judaism during their lives. Increasingly, that view is being challenged by studies of the Dead Sea Scrolls, 75 percent of whose material had not been accessible to the general public right up until 1991. Moreover, 5 percent of the textual fragments found at Qumran have yet to be published. As more material has become available, a reassessment of views and theories is ongoing.

Many of the rash of new theories propagated about the Qumran-Essenes and early Christianity over the past fifty years have sought evidence from these emerging texts and from other relatively recently discovered ancient texts. These include the Genizah collection of largely Jewish documents dating back to 900 C.E., found in an ancient Cairo synagogue; the Nag Hammadi Christian-oriented codices, found in northern Egypt; the Rylands Fragment, also found in Egypt, containing the oldest known extract of the Christian Scriptures; and the Dead Sea Scrolls, found at Qumran between 1947 and 1956.

The tidal wave of scholarly and more contentious comment that followed publication of these four sets of documents has been of tsunamic proportions. Much of the commentary has concentrated on Christian issues, and although a relationship to Jesus was obvious in the Nag Hammadi and Rylands material, it was not so obvious in the other two voluminous sets of documents. Initially, some connections to Jesus in the Dead Sea Scrolls were claimed by a few scholars, but then in the period from the 1960s to 1980s, the tendency was to shy away from too close an association.

However, from 1991 onward, as most of the remaining Dead Sea Scrolls material was released, the scholarly tide turned back toward the initial contentions. We will look at these serious scholarly efforts more closely later on, but it is best to first dispose of the more unsustainable theories—some of which nevertheless may contain elements of truth, but generally cloud an understanding of the early Jesus movement.

## The Lemming Theories

Before the exposure in 1991 of most of the outstanding scroll material, I, like most of the uninitiated, had tacitly understood that there was little relationship between the Christian Messiah Jesus and the messianic figures with whom the Qumran Essenes were obsessed. Conventional scholarship, largely dominated in the earlier years by Catholic commentators, insisted that there was little connection between these commentators' own conception of Jesus and the ideas of the Qumran Essenes. Later on, however, some of those Catholic commentators altered their views, largely, I believe, as a result of an enlightened study of the Dead Sea Scrolls.

These views were sometimes obscured by an external layer of fanciful literature that attempted to distance the Jesus of the first century C.E. even farther from his roots by portraying him as a myth whose story was based on legend, or even hallucination.

Much of the early comment on the Genizah, Dead Sea, and Nag Hammadi scrolls sought a great deal more in the texts than was present; we can follow some of these more plausible (although some would say laughable) attempts in chronological order. For convenience, these theories can be lumped together and labeled "lemming" theories, for reasons that will become apparent as we proceed.

No sooner had a translation of the Genizah Cairo-Damascus documents been published in 1910 than the *New York Times* jumped on the bandwagon with a sensational headline in its Christmas Day edition claiming that the texts described Jesus and the apostle Paul. These Damascus documents, found in Cairo, Egypt, among the Genizah texts, turned out to be a copy of a much earlier work, also found among the Dead Sea Scrolls at Qumran.

The next notable sensational claim came from a respected Sorbonne University professor, André Dupont-Sommer, who wrote in 1950 that he saw Jesus in the "pierced messiah" mentioned in one of the Dead Sea Scrolls: "The Galilean Master . . . appears in many respects as an astonishing reincarnation of the Teacher of Righteousness."[1]

When we come to discuss who this Teacher of Righteousness really was, it becomes apparent that Dupont-Sommer was quite wrong in his assumptions about the Teacher as "the exact prototype of Jesus." As an outsider from the predominantly Catholic translation team (he had once been an abbé), Dupont-Sommer was immediately criticized by his peers for jumping to preposterous conclusions. Nevertheless, Edmund Wilson, a respected American literary journalist and columnist for *The New Yorker,* picked up the theme and subsequently published a book entitled *The Scrolls from the Dead Sea*, in which he claimed that Qumran, "with its ovens and its inkwells, its mill and its cesspool, its constellation of sacred fonts and the unadorned graves of its dead, is perhaps, more than Bethlehem or Nazareth, the cradle of Christianity."[2]

A year later John Marco Allegro, the only Methodist among the predominantly Catholic original Dead Sea Scrolls translation team in Jerusalem, broke ranks and claimed that one of the Dead Sea Scrolls included mention of messianic crucifixion and resurrection.[3]

He was undoubtedly a brilliant scholar, but his claims became more extreme with the publication of his book *The Sacred Mushroom and the Cross* in 1970, which claimed that Christianity was born out of Jesus's followers imbibing hallucinatory drugs.[4] In 1979 he went even farther down this hypothetical trail, claiming that Jesus was no more than a fanciful legend developed by the Essenes to extemporize on their own Teacher of Righteousness. Allegro conceived of this Teacher figure as an Exodus-period Joshua/Jesus incarnate who was killed by the Israelite Wicked Priest, Alexander Jannaeus, around 88 B.C.E.[5]

Still, John Marco Allegro figures dramatically in the story of the Dead Sea Scrolls, and his more substantial testimony and the rationale for it will be considered later on.

Within this frenzied arena of scroll commentary there has also developed a subculture of pseudohistorians who continue to feed and substantiate their increasingly outrageous claims by cross-referencing each other.

There has also, however, been a relatively recent spate of highly speculative material from serious scholars.

In the mid-1980s Robert Eisenman, a professor of Middle Eastern religions at California State University, published a number of works attempting to relate the Qumran Essenes to characters in the Christian Scriptures.[6] One of Eisenman's ongoing themes has been the idea that James the Just, the brother of Jesus, was the leader of the Qumran-Essene community. When more of the Cave 4 Dead Sea Scrolls material became available in 1991, Eisenman, together with Michael Wise, associate professor of Aramaic at the University of Chicago, continued the theme in their book *The Dead Sea Scrolls Uncovered*. In this work, they also discuss what they believe is a reference in the Dead Sea War Scroll to a suffering, wounded, and ultimately slain messianic figure.[7]

Two journalist protégés of Robert Eisenman, Michael Baigent and Richard Leigh, expanded on Eisenman's theories in their book *The Dead Sea Scrolls Deception*, published in 1991.[8] In addition, they accused Catholic authorities and the Vatican of a cover-up conspiracy designed to distance the teachings and beliefs of the Qumran Essenes from early Christianity. *Holy Blood, Holy Grail*, by Baigent, Leigh, and Henry Lincoln,[9] was published in 1982, but the authors had already climbed on the bandwagon with their claim that Jesus did not die on the cross but instead lived on to marry and have children.

Nineteen ninety-two saw the publication of a book by Barbara Thiering, of the University of Sydney, *Jesus the Man: A New Interpretation from the Dead Sea Scrolls*. One could almost replace "New Interpretation" with "Rewriting," as Thiering attempts to push the composition of some of the pertinent scrolls forward into the first century C.E. to justify a claim that the person she saw as the leader of the Qumran Essenes was harassed by Jesus—in his role as the Wicked Priest.[10]

Thiering's more recent work, *The Book That Jesus Wrote: John's Gospel*,[11] contends that Jesus was a member of the Essenes, married Mary Magdalene, and did not die on the cross, but rather lived to old age in Rome or Gaul (France). She claims, contrary to accepted scholarship, that Josephus wrote about Jesus, and she dismisses virtually all research on the Gospels as faulty. Another recent author, Laurence Gardner, who claims the title of Chevalier Labhran de Saint Germain, takes up Thiering's thesis in his *Bloodline of the Holy Grail*,[12] tracing the descendants of a surviving Jesus to the Royal House of Stewart in Scotland through the French Merovingian kings and the Celtic kings of Britain.

The list could go on and on, the theories becoming increasingly more fantastic and unsustainable. However, all these leaps in the dark—these attempts to see a contemporary Jesus in the Dead Sea Scrolls texts—collapse given the irrefutable conclusions of carbon dating and paleography, which prove that the pertinent version of the Damascus documents and the relevant Dead Sea Scrolls originated well before the existence of Jesus, John the Baptist, and the apostle Paul. While the Dead Sea Scrolls mention a number of historically verifiable figures of the first century B.C.E., there are none from the first century C.E.

## Overcooking the Books

Although I've just been rather scathing about these peripheral theories, they should not all be dismissed out of hand. Some of these questionable oeuvres are written by people with undoubted scholarship, and there are occasional nuggets of truth that do add to the store of knowledge. Nor should so-called scholarly works be immune from criticism. In many instances reputable scholars have been proved completely wrong in their theories. I cite three examples. Right up to his death in 1976, the eminent American scholar Solomon Zeitlin, of Dropsie College, Philadelphia, an avid contributor to the *Jewish Quarterly Review* and author of numerous books, including *Who Crucified Jesus?*[13] maintained that the Dead Sea Scrolls were a forgery.

In his view, the Zadokite documents were written by the Kairites in the eighth century C.E. John Allegro, one of the original Dead Sea Scrolls research team, contrived an elaborate translation of a scroll fragment that he named 4Q Therapeia. He read into it an account of medical rounds undertaken by a certain Caiaphas. His translation was quoted by another eminent scholar, James H. Charlesworth,[14] in Charlesworth's own translation of same, but was subsequently shown to be nothing more than a scribal practice exercise of jumbled letters.[15]

In another example, Professor Torleif Elgvin, of Lutheran Theological Seminary, Oslo, described how, when working on a section of Dead Sea

Scrolls material from which the last words in a half-dozen or more lines of texts were missing, he interpolated and then published what he thought the words might be. Sometime later a colleague came to him with a scrap of text that exactly fit the missing section. Professor Elgvin generously confessed that in every instance he had put in the wrong words.[16]

Other authors, such as Professor G. Wells of Birkbeck College, London, in *The Historical Evidence for Jesus;*[17] Albert Schweitzer, the German theologian and medical missionary who wrote *The Quest for the Historical Jesus;*[18] Timothy Freke and Peter Gandy, in *The Jesus Mysteries;*[19] Ahmed Osman in his *Jesus in the House of the Pharaohs* and *Christianity: An Ancient Egyptian Religion;*[20] Earl Doherty, *The Jesus Puzzle;*[21] and Alvar Ellegard, *Jesus: One Hundred Years Before Christ,*[22] search anywhere but the contemporary sources to try to demonstrate that Jesus did not exist. For them the Jesus story was based entirely on myths or earlier historical/biblical characters.

More reprehensible is the form of denigration of Jesus and his family that is presented as being probable reality and yet is based on mere speculation. The idea that Jesus's mother was raped by a Roman soldier, as suggested in a BBC TV documentary, *The Virgin Mary,* has no foundation in factual evidence and is a rehash of deliberately distorted polemic created by those who opposed the validity of early Christian teachings.[23]

Strangely enough, a recent novel by the young French author Eliette Abécassis, *The Qumran Mystery,*[24] which makes little attempt to pretend it is anything other than a book of fiction, presents some prophetic realities not unrelated to my allegedly more factual work in the present book. Real personalities, although disguised in name, are relatively easy to identify, and the thrust of *The Qumran Mystery* follows some eerily familiar paths in what may well be reality.

## Conventional Scholarship

When we turn to mainstream views on Jesus, most scholars, many of whom have studied the biblical and nonbiblical evidence for Jesus far more intensely than I and who do not have a Christian bias, conclude that Jesus *did* exist as a revered person sometime during the first third of the first century C.E.

It would not be surprising to find modern Christian authors expressing certainty about the existence of Jesus, but a number of relatively modern Jewish writers have endorsed the view.[25] Those writing commentaries on the Christian Scriptures have included Claude Goldsmid Montefiore, a pioneer of Reform Judaism in England ("What a Jew Thinks About Jesus," *The Hibbert Journal,* 1934–35); Joseph Klausner, an Israeli scholar *(Jesus of Nazareth);* and Samuel Sandmel, professor of Bible and Hellenistic literature, Hebrew Union College–Jewish Institute of Religion in the United States.

So where does conventional scholarship stand on the possibility of a connection between Jesus and other characters from the Christian Scriptures and the Qumran-Essene community? Surprisingly, a number of eminent observers of early Christian history, such as Dr. Matthew Black,[26] Dr. Hugh Schonfield,[27] and Hyam Maccoby[28]—visiting professor at Leeds University until his death in May 2004—make little more than passing reference to the "Qumran Essene effect." Their views can be summarized as follows: "The oldest roots of the Christian movement in 'Galilee' is to be sought in a group of dedicated Nazirites, sectarians who continued the ancient Israelite institution of the lifelong Nazirite."[29]

Even a modernist writer like John Crossan, professor of biblical studies at DePaul University, Chicago, has a virtual blind spot when it comes to considering how the Qumran Essenes might have influenced Jesus or the Christian Scriptures. When he does mention the Dead Sea Scrolls, his facts are questionable.[30]

In all these works, the associations of Jesus and John the Baptist with Qumran are highly contentious, accepted by many scholars but disputed by others, as the following paragraphs point out.

The present state of opinion from authoritative scholars such as Magen Broshi (former curator, Shrine of the Book, Israel Museum), Geza Vermes (professor emeritus, Oxford University), and Professor George Brooke (Manchester University) is weighted in favor of John the Baptist having been a member of the Qumran-Essene community at some period in his life. The tendency, however, is to resist drawing a similar association for Jesus. This resistance, as one would expect, is far stronger from Christian, particularly Catholic, commentators, such as Father Émile

Puech (director of research, CNRS, Paris), Professor Carsten Peter Thiede (minister, Church of England), Father Jerome Murphy-O'Connor (École Biblique, East Jerusalem), and Professor J. Van der Ploeg (University of Nijmegen, Holland).

Nevertheless, according to Douglas Lockhart, a Scottish immigrant scholar now in Australia, the Catholic Church admitted on camera in a recent documentary that the early church must have been influenced by the Essenes.[31] In fact, some earlier scholars, such as Dr. Joseph Klausner[32] in 1925 and Heinrich Graetz[33] in the nineteenth century, were firmly convinced long before the discovery of the Dead Sea Scrolls that John the Baptist was at one time an Essene.

The opinion of these latter scholars is largely based on analysis of the Christian Scriptures and the descriptions of John the Baptist given by Flavius Josephus, a contemporary Roman/Jewish historian (37–c. 100 C.E.). The most relevant quotation from the Christian Scriptures indicating John the Baptist's membership in the Qumran-Essene community comes from Luke 1:80:

> And the child grew, and waxed strong in spirit, and was in the deserts till the day of his showing to Israel.

The Gospel of Luke endorses the probability that John the Baptist attained intellectual and religious maturity elsewhere than at his home when it refers to him spending his early life in the desert. For example, when Luke describes the Baptist as "living in the wilderness and eating a diet of locusts and wild honey," it is understood by most scholars to be a reference to the Qumran Essenes, as anyone banished from membership would have previously taken a vow to eat only prepared food that had been blessed by the leader of the community. Once evicted, they would be forced to eat only wild food.[34] John the Baptist's baptizing ritual was very reminiscent of the ritual immersion practiced by the Essenes; and, as we shall see later, many of Luke's sayings in the Christian Scriptures can be related to sectarian texts in the Dead Sea Scrolls.

In the words of an earlier commentator, Israeli professor Yigael Yadin, "The influence of the sect's teachings is recognizable in the views, practices, ideology and even the very phraseology of the founders of

Christianity."[35] Professor Yadin had little doubt that John the Baptist was a member of the community for a period of his life. Other experts of the Christian Scriptures, like the German Otto Betz and the Frenchman Jean Steinmann, believed that John the Baptist grew up as an Essene, almost certainly in the wilderness at Qumran.[36]

The consensus tendency is, however, to resist the conclusion that John the Baptist was a *long-term* member of the community, or that Jesus had ever been a member. John the Baptist's rebellious character does not seem to be consistent with his remaining very long within the quiescent structure of the Qumran community. This resistance among Christian theologians and historians has almost certainly been motivated by a desire to retain the uniqueness of the Christian message and avoid the implication that another sect might have been the source of many of its beliefs and practices.

However, even staunch Catholic traditionalists, like Father Jerome Murphy-O'Connor (École Biblique, East Jerusalem), were forced to admit as early as 1960, long before much more persuasive information had become available from the Dead Sea Scrolls, that Paul, the architect of Christianity, was definitely in contact with someone who knew Essene teaching thoroughly, and that Timothy, one of Jesus's close followers, belonged to the same circle as John the Baptist.[37]

The more the emerging information is examined and the existing material reevaluated, the more apparent it becomes that the hotbed of spiritual industry bubbling away at Khirbet Qumran on the northwestern edge of the Dead Sea was a cauldron from which were cast many of the templates of early Christian ideas—a background that early Christian writers were readily able to adapt to the experiences of Jesus.

To assess what the relationship of John the Baptist and Jesus might have been to Qumran, it is necessary to understand a bit more about this strange, quirky, secretive, male-dominated, nonconformist community, and why the predominantly Christian researchers involved in early Dead Sea Scrolls studies tended to shy away from linking Jesus and John the Baptist to Qumran.

# ── 4 ──

# Perceived Dangers
# for The Church

lthough all religions tend to distance themselves from their antecedents to highlight their apparent uniqueness, before the discovery
of the Dead Sea Scrolls it was generally accepted that Christianity
grew out of mainstream Judaism—that is, the kind of Judaism that was
being followed by the majority of Jews living under Roman occupation in
Judaea and Galilee at the turn of the zero millennium. The main strands of
Judaism were espoused by the Sadducees, a group attached to the Second
Temple at Jerusalem that adhered closely to the letter of the Law of the
Hebrew Scriptures; and by the Pharisees, a group receptive to a more
humane, practical form of Judaism. It was from this pharisaic strand that
Christianity was traditionally considered to have sprung.

After the discovery of the Dead Sea Scrolls in the late 1940s and early
1950s, it soon became apparent that the type of Judaism that had been
practiced by the authors/possessors of the scrolls—a minority Essene
group that numbered perhaps less than four thousand, or 2 percent of the
Jewish population—was far more similar to early Christian practices and
beliefs than that of any previous group. The worry for modern Christian
authorities was not so much that they had gotten their suppositions wrong
regarding which strand of Judaism had given birth to Christianity but that
it was becoming increasingly difficult to distance Christianity from this
previously little-known new slant on Judaism (Essenism).

If there was, and still is, a motivation behind the alleged conspiracy by
church authorities to delay or even suppress or distort the messages emerging from the Dead Sea Scrolls, it is related to the scrolls' uncomfortably
close parallels to the teachings of Jesus.

In 1953 a team of scholars was brought together by the École Biblique (a Catholic institution that had been established in 1890) to try and deal with, and translate, the huge volume of Dead Sea Scrolls material emerging from the caves near Qumran. The original group of scholars, led by Father Roland de Vaux, then current director of the École Biblique, was composed of:

Father Dominique Barthelemy, École Biblique
Father Jozef Milik, École Biblique
John Allegro, Oxford University
John Strugnell, Oxford University[1]
Patrick Skehan, Johns Hopkins University, United States
Frank Moore Cross, Baltimore University, United States
Claus-Hunno Hunzinger, Germany
Jean Starcky, France

Representing the cream of their generation of biblical scholars, the team comprised six Catholics, two Protestants, and one member often wrongly referred to as an atheist. Much of the early writings of the École Biblique caucus was, in hindsight, clearly designed to deflect any idea that Christianity came out of Essenism, while reluctantly accepting some close parallels.[2]

I don't want to dwell for long on the history of delays and prevarications that have dogged the release of Dead Sea Scrolls texts—what Professor Geza Vermes, in 1977, called "the academic scandal . . . of the twentieth century." These have been well charted by writers in America such as Michael Baigent and Richard Leigh,[3] Robert Eisenman,[4] Professor Norman Golb,[5] and Hershel Shanks,[6] the latter three of whom perhaps had an extra chip on their shoulders because they had been kept out of the inner circle.

Suffice it to say that all the key members of the original translation team (the "Jerusalem team"), including Roland de Vaux, Jozef Milik, and Dominique Barthelemy and their successors—who have dominated release of the nonbiblical material relating to the Qumran-Essene sect (and much of the biblical material) between 1947 and 1991—were Catholics with predominantly French affiliations. To the credit of the Americans, it has been mainly their persistent hammering at the door that has opened up

most of the hidden material and made it, at least in photographic repro-
ductions, available to worldwide scholarship. Nevertheless, some 5 percent of the original Dead Sea Scrolls material still remains officially
unpublished.[7]

Ironically, the earliest attacks on the uniqueness of Christ came from a
French professor and from one of the Jerusalem team's own members, John
Marco Allegro, whom we mentioned briefly before but whose actions we
will discuss in greater detail here. (See page 16 of the color insert.)

## John Allegro

If there is one person who can be said to have caused the greatest angst
among the inner circle of staunch defenders of the uniqueness of Christianity, it was John Marco Allegro. When recruited in 1953 by the École
Biblique to be part of the international translation team of the Dead Sea
Scrolls, he was seconded from Oxford University.

He was generally labeled the atheist on the team. It is dangerous, however, to place a blanket religious label on him—or on anyone, for that matter—as some scholars persist in doing. As his wife, Joan, notes, at one
point in his career John Allegro was a probationer Methodist minister, and
in this early period of his life he almost certainly still believed in the reality of Jesus Christ.[8]

Always an independent spirit and outsider to the École Biblique inner
clique, he was nevertheless initially well respected and was instrumental in
getting the Copper Scroll opened at Manchester College of Technology;
after Professor Wright Baker successfully cut open the Copper Scroll por-
tions in 1955–56, John Allegro was the first to translate them into English.
But such was the perceived dynamite of their contents that he was refused
permission by the Jerusalem team to publish *his* translation under *its* aus-
pices. Impatient and frustrated, he finally published it himself, in English,
in 1960.[9]

This episode added strain to what were his already fraught relations
with the École Biblique's East Jerusalem team. As previously stated,
Allegro had broken ranks with his colleagues by claiming that one of the
Dead Sea Scrolls included mention of the messianic crucifixion of a figure
depicted as the Teacher of Righteousness and this figure's resurrection.

Relations between Allegro and his peers took a further nosedive when five of those peers, on March 16, 1956, published a condemnatory letter about him in the London newspaper *The Times*.

An unprecedented public attack on a scholastic colleague, the letter was related to a series of broadcasts Allegro had done for the BBC in which, they thought, he had implied a close connection between the crucifixion of the Teacher of Righteousness and the resurrection of Jesus Christ. Allegro replied in *The Times* of March 20 (coincidentally the fourth anniversary of the finding of the Copper Scroll), explaining that, while he saw many parallels between the ways in which "the two masters" had met their deaths, he made a clear distinction between the priestly messiah of the Qumran Essenes and the Davidic Messiah of the Gospels. (For the full texts of both these letters, see appendix 1.)

We can only imagine the effect this attack would have on a man whose life and career had been devoted to academic study. To have his scholarship maligned in public by his peers must have been hurtful in the extreme for John Allegro. His position at Manchester University came under severe pressure from his superiors, and he was denied funds to pursue his Dead Sea Scrolls visits to Jerusalem, forcing him to seek financing from private philanthropists.

© ROBERT FEATHER

*Fig. 4.1. Mrs. Joan Allegro and her son Mark at the 1996 University of Manchester Conference on the Copper Scroll.*

Here was a man who for many years had been a painful thorn in the side of the Christian Church, especially the Catholic authorities, and who had stated that he "had enough information to destroy Christianity." There could also be little doubt that John Allegro at one period in his life had come under extreme pressure from outside forces. A letter from Allegro to someone he still counted as a friend in Jerusalem, Frank Cross, dated ten days before the infamous *Times* letter, makes it evident that the strain was telling: "I'm as near a nervous breakdown as I have ever been," he wrote (see appendix 2).

Later, in 1970, Allegro was to write: "The Church and mankind have reached the end of the road. The historical foundation of the Church lies in ruins . . ."[10] Lecturing in 1985 in the United States at the University of Michigan, Allegro's position had solidified to outright antagonism toward the church: "Jesus," he declared, "had nothing at all to do with the crucified Christos of Paul's theology. . . . And to judge from the Church's subsequent history as well as the illegitimacy of its claims to primacy, one cannot help the feeling that the wrong side won."[11] Unsustainable ramblings as these later writings were, they nevertheless needed to be taken seriously, as his earlier work was undoubtedly of scholastic merit.

The threat presented by John Allegro could well have been the motive for the team at the École Biblique to denigrate his published views. In making this statement, it is germane to keep in mind the case that authors Michael Baigent and Richard Leigh make in their book *The Dead Sea Scroll Deception*: that the École Biblique, as a Catholic institution, was controlled by forces in the Vatican through its Pontifical Biblical Commission. The commission, they maintain, was set up as long ago as 1903 with the express remit of safeguarding the authority of the Scriptures and of promoting their right interpretation. They note that since 1956, every director of the École Biblique has been a member of the commission.

## The Shapira Affair

It is ironic that John Allegro expounded upon one of the strangest episodes in the history of the Dead Sea Scrolls,[12] which also involved the early demise of its central character, although he may well have been motivated by the parallels in victimization suffered by a certain Moses Wilhelm

Shapira. A number of aspects of the affair are germane to this present book, so a brief diversion is worthwhile.

On March 9, 1884, Moses Wilhelm Shapira, a Jew of Russian ancestry originally from Kamenets-Podolsk, who had converted to Anglican Christianity, blew his brains out with a gun in a room of the Hotel Bloemendaal in Rotterdam. He had been driven to suicide by ridicule and condemnation following the discovery of what he claimed was a genuine ancient Hebrew Scriptures document. As the owner of an antique shop in Christians Street, Old Jerusalem, he claimed to have acquired from an Arab fifteen strips of dark-stained parchment measuring, on average, three and a half by seven inches. The written text turned out to contain variant passages[13] from Deuteronomy written in a very early form of Hebrew and dating back to the Phoenician ninth-century-B.C.E. period. The lettering was similar to that found on the Moabite Stone, a large black basalt stela unearthed near the Dead Sea in the late nineteenth century C.E.[14]

Moses Shapira communicated the excitement of his discovery to the scholastic world, but he was met with stony silence and rebuttal. Few believed the texts could have survived for so long, and in any case they were not consistent with Holy Writ; moreover, they were composed of extracts from various parts of the Bible. They were denounced as forgeries by a number of world experts, some of whom had never even examined the strips.[15] After Moses Shapira's death, the British Museum sent the Deuteronomy texts for auction, and they were acquired by book dealers Bernard Quaritch Ltd. for approximately eighteen dollars.[16] Unfortunately, they were later apparently destroyed in a fire.

At present, however, reexamination of the evidence in light of the subsequent discovery of the Dead Sea Scrolls has shifted scholarly opinion in the direction of acknowledging that Shapira's strips, wrapped in linen and smeared with asphalt (as some of the Dead Sea Scrolls had been), may well have been genuine.[17] From the Dead Sea Scrolls we now know that the Qumran Essenes sometimes extracted passages from different sections of Pentateuchal works to produce amalgams in a similar manner to that in the Shapira Deuteronomy texts.

The scrolls of the Qumran Essenes also exhibit examples of early Phoenician-style lettering, especially for the name of God. That some of the Qumran Essenes might have fled to the eastern side of the Dead Sea after the destruction of their settlement in 68 C.E. to find refuge in the caves of Wadi Mujib, near Dibon, taking some of their most precious scrolls with them, seems entirely plausible. It was there that Shapira claimed the fragments were discovered.

The areas of interest, from this book's point of view, revolve around the Shapira texts' emphasis (much stronger than that found in the Hebrew Scriptures) on the concept of a "loving God" and "loving one's neighbor." If the Shapira texts were genuine, and at one time in the possession of the Qumran Essenes, the Christian overtones of these two concepts become much more significant; for both Jesus and Paul, these two concepts were the fundamental pillars of the new belief.

Additionally, if the Shapira Deuteronomy texts were genuine, and were once part of the Dead Sea Scrolls library, as now appears to be the case, it pulls the antique connections of the Qumran Essenes back well into the ninth century B.C.E., at least in terms of their knowledge of this ancient orthographic script and certainly in terms of their allegiance to this much earlier period.

Why the particular scribe who wrote the text should choose to use such an ancient font is a curiosity, unless of course the text itself was actually composed as early as the ninth century B.C.E., in which case the Shapira fragments would have been the oldest biblical text ever discovered. A comparison of the fragments' content and paleography to that in some of the Dead Sea Scrolls, Samaritan scrolls, and non-Qumran-Essene Dead Sea Scrolls leads me to conclude that the Shapira strips were authentic and were written by very early ancestors of the Essenes.

# ~ 5 ~

# Was Jesus a Real Person?
# The Literary and Other Sources

Very few reputable scholars, religious or otherwise, doubt the existence of "a Jesus" who can be identified as the platform on which
Christianity was built. When Albert Einstein, one of the world's
most famous Jews, was asked by an interviewer in 1929 whether he
believed in the historical Jesus, he replied: "Unquestionably! No one can
read the Gospels without feeling the presence of Jesus. His personality
pulsates in every word. No myth is filled with such life."

The problem is that the experts' views of who Jesus really was vary
across the entire spectrum of first-century C.E. activists: from the philosophical Greek cynic of Burton L. Mack, to the Galilean mystic of Marcus
J. Borg, to John Dominic Crossan's monk, to James M. Robinson's ascetic, to Bart D. Ehrman's apocalyptic prophet, to the marginal Jew of John
P. Meier, to the charismatic Hasid of Geza Vermes. Unhappily, as retired
professor Harold Ellens, of the University of Michigan—author of many
books on the subject, including *Jesus as the Son of Man: The Literary
Character*—puts it, as the quest for the historical Jesus proceeds, "We
know more and more that we know less and less about the person from
Nazareth."[1]

There are three main literary sources where corroborative information
on the life of Jesus can be found:

1. The Christian Scriptures, the Koran, apocryphal and pseudepigraphic texts.
2. Contemporary historians and writers of the first century C.E.
3. Jewish and other religious sources.

# Christian Scriptures, Koran, and Apocryphal and Pseudepigraphic Texts

Many contradictions and variations relating to Jesus and John the Baptist are evident in the first four books of the Christian Scriptures. This is not surprising, considering the time lapse between Jesus's life and the writing of the Gospels, and the additional time lapse and editing that the Gospels have undergone between the original versions and the ones we read in the Christian Scriptures today. We have only to look at versions of a news report produced by modern-day journalists in four different newspapers to see how they can get their facts wrong and come at the same story with different agendas and from differing angles. Inaccurate reporting, however, does not mean that the original events were necessarily a fabrication.

Bearing in mind the supposed delay in the writing down of these Christian Scriptures' works (Mark c. 70 C.E., Matthew c. 95 C.E., Luke c. 105 C.E., John c. 110 C.E., but parts perhaps pre–second century C.E.); the fact that none of the Gospel authors was an eyewitness to the events surrounding Jesus's life; and the later interpolations that might have been applied to the Gospels, the resultant versions do agree on the essential elements and message of Jesus's and John the Baptist's lives, teachings, and deaths.

A good cross-check on the reliability of the Gospels is to examine whether they report other historical happenings correctly. An analysis of this sort will also give us pertinent and interesting information to help establish the possible dates of Jesus's life. So how do the historical figures mentioned in the earliest works of the Christian Scriptures relate to the known historical facts of the period? Table 2 sets out some of the detail.

**TABLE 2**

**Historical personalities in relation to John the Baptist and Jesus**

| Christian Scripture | Event | John the Baptist | Jesus |
|---|---|---|---|
| According to Luke | Birth | During the reign of Herod the Great, King of Judaea (37 BCE–4 CE) (1:5-14) | Caesar Augustus (27 BCE–14 CE) Cyrenius governor of Syria (2:1–12) |
| | Start of ministry | Fifteenth year of Tiberius Caesar (. . . ?) (29 CE) Pontius Pilate governor of Judaea (26–36 CE) | Not mentioned |

| Christian Scripture | Event | John the Baptist | Jesus |
|---|---|---|---|
| According to Luke | | Herod (Antipas?) tetrarch of Galilee (4 BCE–39 CE) | |
| | | Philip tetrarch of Trachonitus/Lysanius (4 BCE–34 CE) | |
| | | Annas and Caiaphas (18–37 CE) high priests* (18 CE) (3:1-20) | |
| | Death | Not mentioned | Pilate (ruled 26–36 CE) (23:1-25) |
| According to Mark | Birth | Not mentioned | Not mentioned |
| | Start of ministry | Not mentioned | Not mentioned |
| | Death | King Herod Antipas (?) (4 BCE–39 CE) Herodias Philip (tetrarch?) (4 BCE–34 CE) (6:14–28) (15:1–47) | Pilate (ruled 26–36 CE) |
| According to Matthew | Birth | Not mentioned | Herod the King (ruled 37 BCE–4 CE) (2:1) |
| | Start of ministry | Archelaus ruler of Judaea (4 BCE–6 CE) (2:22) | Not mentioned |
| | Death | Herod (Antipas?) the tetrarch's birthday Herodias's daughter Salome† (14:1–12) | Pontius Pilate (ruled 26–36 CE) (27:2) |
| According to John | Birth | Not mentioned | Not mentioned |
| | Start of ministry | Not mentioned | Not mentioned |
| | Death | Not mentioned | Annas (6–18 CE) Caiaphas high priest (18–37 CE) Pilate (ruled 26–36 CE) Caesar (18:12–40; 19:1–42) |

(. . . ?) Assumes that Luke was quoting the wrong Caesar when he cites Tiberius for the date of the start of John the Baptist's ministry, and that he meant Julius Caesar.

(?) indicates name not given in the Christian Scriptures but assumed to be.

*The only year both were high priest, although Annas appears to have exercised power over his son-in-law Caiaphas after losing his office.

†Became Herod's stepdaughter when Herod married his brother Philip's wife.

This analysis of historical figures mentioned in the Christian Scriptures gives the following as the most likely dates for John the Baptist and Jesus:

| John the Baptist | | Jesus | |
|---|---|---|---|
| Birth | 6–8 BCE | Birth | 4–6 BCE |
| Start of ministry | 18–20 CE | Start of ministry | 25–26 CE |
| Death | 26–28 CE | Death | 28–30 CE |

## The Koran

For the Koran (or Quran)—the most important book of Islam—Jesus was a holy prophet and messenger, but not a divine messiah. The traditions embodied in the Koran talk about Jesus, son of Mary, as being part of the proof of Allah's sovereignty (Sura 2:87, 136, 253). Written long after the time of Jesus, in the seventh century C.E., the work nevertheless has no hesitation in confirming the birth of Jesus (Sura 29), recording him as healer, teacher, and worker of miracles (Sura 3), and accepting the Gospels as essentially true. The brief details of Jesus's life given in the Koran do not, however, refer to any external evidence that might be used to corroborate his existence.

For Muslims, the last great prophet, Muhammad, is the supreme model for humankind of God's word, and it is only through him that God can be reached. Jesus is, nevertheless, seen as a great prophet and is revered as Isa ibn Maryam—Jesus the son of Mary (Mary is the only woman mentioned in the Koran). The Koran points to Jesus being born of a virgin, untouched by Satan, and performing miracles of healing and resurrection of the dead. He does not die on the cross, however, but is taken by God directly to heaven.

When the End Days of the world approach, Muslims believe Jesus will descend to defeat Satan and usher in a period of perfection when all faiths will be united. That the Koran, written down soon after Muhammad's death in 632 C.E., takes up many ideas that originated at Qumran is evident from numerous common ideas not found in Rabbinic Judaism or Christianity.[2] This is a factor that will also be considered more fully in relation to the Christian Scriptures.

Light and darkness are a repetitive theme in the Koran and Dead Sea Scrolls. Unlike the Christian Scriptures, however, which also takes up Qumran's "children of light" motif and might be thought of as the exemplar, only in the Koran is the Qumran source used to equate "light" and absolute predestination. The Koran repeatedly uses the idea of Allah misleading the sinner, which seems to parallel the Dead Sea Scrolls' Damascus document concept of "those who He hated, he misled," while the Qumran usage of the term *pesher,* in the sense of interpretative prognosis, is taken up as *tafsir* in Islam.

The Qumran Essenes' habit of deliberately using cryptic letters in

Dead Sea Scrolls material to hide secret knowledge available only to the *cognoscenti* is virtually unknown in biblical literature, but there are a number of examples in the Koran; the cryptic Arabic letters that head several chapters in the Koran, for example, have never been deciphered.[3] One even has to wonder whether the designation of the holy scripts of Muhammad as the Qur'an (meaning "recital") might imply a memory of the name Qumran.

Interestingly, there is currently a hot debate going on in Islam-oriented circles about exactly where and how Muhammad obtained his biblical knowledge. For traditionalists, of course, there is no problem; his knowledge came directly from Allah. Islamic scholars such as Dr. G. R. Hawting and Ibn Warraq,[4] however, want to know how, in the pagan environment of Mecca, where some four fifths of the Koran was revealed to Muhammad, the Hebrew Scriptures and the Christian Scriptures could have been assimilated.[5] Various theories are postulated, but the one garnishing considerable support identifies a Jewish-Christian group that might have survived somewhere in Arabia. No one knows the origins of this apparently influential group. Could they possibly be Essenic? We shall return to this possibility later.

We know that when Qumran was destroyed in 68 C.E. by the Romans, not all the inhabitants were killed, and the survivors must have fled in all directions.

A small number ended up with the Zealots at Masada;[6] others may well have joined their Therapeutae brethren in northern Egypt or gone to the Jewish settlement at Leontopolis; some may well have gone east across the Dead Sea into Arabia.

There are three main supportive indicators for an Essenic presence in Arabia, which might also help confirm the validity of the Shapira texts, mentioned earlier. One comes from studies of the Koran. The second relates to the Shapira manuscript, and the third is the statement in the Christian Scriptures that Paul, immediately after his miraculous conversion at Damascus, went to Arabia and stayed for three years.[7]

According to Professor Kamal Salibi, a Lebanese Christian scholar, an early form of Christianity existed in Arabia, allied to a group known as Nasara, which he equates with the Nazarenes.[8]

Salibi maintains that there was an Israelite presence in the western Arabian province of Hejaz, and that the Christian Scriptures reflect knowledge learned from these sources. The Koran, in Sura 19:30, suggests that Jesus was in possession of a "scripture."[9]

The recent consensual movement toward authentication of the Shapira texts, as discussed in chapter 4, and their possible compilation by the Qumran Essenes opens up an intriguing possibility. The Shapira texts were said to have been found near Wadi Mujib, on the eastern side of the Dead Sea, and this location implies that an Essenic presence may have persisted in that area. Indeed, the Jewish sect that settled at Yathrib, modern Medina, is described in Sura 11 of the Koran as being in possession of the Scriptures, of intellectual ascendancy in the occult sciences and medicine, and awaiting the imminent arrival of their savior prophet.[10]

There could be no closer description of the exclusive talents and aspirations of the Qumran Essenes. It was among members of this strange Jewish group, located almost two hundred miles from Mecca, that Muhammad is said to have gained his earliest followers. Such was their influence on him that the first *qiblah* (direction faced during prayer) for Muslims was initially toward Jerusalem (subsequently the qiblah became Mecca).

The third indication that there was an Essene settlement in Arabia comes from the Christian Scriptures. After Paul's conversion in Damascus, which almost certainly occurred as a result of a therapeutic encounter with an Essene, Ananias, Paul goes into Arabia:

> Neither went I up to Jerusalem to them which were apostles before me; but I went into Arabia, and returned again unto Damascus. (Gal. 1:17)

However, yet another tradition has Paul journeying to the Eastern Desert of Egypt, to a place where there is still an ancient cave church near the Monastery of St. Paul.[11]

Apart from the examples of parallels between the Koran and the Dead Sea Scrolls already cited, does Muhammad refer to his own journeys bringing him into contact with the Wadi area near the Dead Sea? The unexpected answer is yes, and in a context that has strong Essenic overtones. Abraham's nephew Lot is associated with Sodom in the Hebrew Scriptures, a place not geographically identified but located somewhere in the Dead Sea area in the plain of Jordan. Lot finds obsessive mention in the Koran. In fact, if Lot is read in the Koran as a pseudonym for the admirable portion of the Qumran-Essene community who become followers of Jesus, there are many commonalities.[12]

A famous verse in the Koran to which Patricia Crone, coauthor of *Hagarism*,[13] calls attention provides a much stronger reference to Muhammad's acquaintance with the Dead Sea environment. It reminds the audience that they pass by the remains of Lot's people in the Dead Sea region "in the morning and the evening,"[14] perhaps also alluding to the Qumran-Essene morning and evening ritual of prayers and the association of Lot in the Old Testament to the salty region of the Dead Sea.

## Apocryphal and Pseudoepigraphic Texts

These texts are dealt with in chapter 13.

## Other Religions Views

According to approximate numbers of adherents, Christianity has been the dominant world religion for the past 1,500 years and still comes out on top. The order of religions by number of adherents is as follows:

| | |
|---|---|
| Christianity | 1.5 billion |
| Islam | 1 billion |
| Hinduism | 750 million |
| Buddhism | 300 million |
| Shintoism | 120 million |
| Taoism | 60 million |
| Confucianism | 50 million |
| Judaism | 14 million |
| Jainism | 3.5 million |
| Humanism | 2 million |
| Zoroastrianism | 20,000 |

Because all the world's main religions have within them different strands of belief, it is possible to talk only in terms of generalities when describing other religions' views of Jesus.[15]

**Hindu legend** recalls Jesus as a child and his mother, Mary, journeying to India; images of Jesus and the Madonna appear in Hindu culture. Hindus, exemplified by Gandhi, are drawn to Jesus by his compassionate and pacifist image. The idea that Jesus was the son of God, however, conflicts with the Hindu belief in many gods and its conviction that all human beings have the ability to reach God-consciousness through their own spiritual efforts.

**Buddhists** often see Buddha and Jesus as brothers who both taught that the highest form of human understanding is universal love. The disparities in fundamental beliefs, however, militate against any deeper acceptance of Christ as the son of God, which does not fit happily into Buddhist philosophy. For Buddhists, attainment of the perfect state, comparable to that of Buddha himself, is within reach of every person, whereas in Christianity no one can ever become Christ. The heavy Christian investment in the suffering and tragedy of Jesus's death on the cross also poses great difficulties for Buddhism, which sees life as a cycle of death and rebirth and Buddha's death as a serene event.

## Contemporary Historians and Writers of the Temple Period

### Romans and Greeks

The fact is that, other than the Christian Scriptures (collated up to 150 years after Jesus, and written in Greek outside the Holy Land) and the Koran (written by followers of Muhammad c. 640 C.E.), proof of the existence of Jesus from contemporary historians is thin on the ground. Despite the claims in the Gospels that his ministering attracted an enormous following, there are no records, in Greek or Roman or other contemporary writings on Judaea, that mention Jesus as a messianic leader. Historians such as Philo (20 B.C.E.–40 C.E.) and Pliny (23–79 C.E.), whose lives overlapped that of Jesus, make no mention of him. The one reference to Jesus that is frequently quoted is attributed to Flavius Josephus (37–100 C.E.), a Jewish historian who became a Roman citizen, but even Josephus's account is now discounted by most scholars as a forgery.

**TABLE 3**

**Nonbiblical references to John the Baptist and Jesus**

| Nonbiblical source | John the Baptist | Jesus |
|---|---|---|
| Flavius Josephus (37–100 CE) | Yes | Yes* |
| Philo of Alexandria (20 BCE–40 CE) | No | No |
| Pliny (23–79 CE) | No | No |
| Mishnah (c. 200 CE) | No | Probable |
| Midrash (1st–10th centuries CE) | No | Possible |
| Talmud (c. 500 CE) | No | Possible |

* See the text quotation below as to why this reference is questionable.

The quotation that appears in extant editions of Josephus is as follows: "At about this time lived Jesus. . . . He accomplished astonishing deeds. . . . He won over many Jews. . . . He was [called] Christ. When Pilate, upon the indictment brought by the principal men among us, condemned him to the cross, those who loved him from the very first did not cease to be attached to him, for on the third day he appeared to them restored to life. . . . And the tribe of the Christians, so called after him, has to this day not disappeared" (*Jewish Antiquities* 18:62–64, 116–19).

Josephus was in a privileged position to record the immediately previous events in Jerusalem and the Holy Land. His original writings have long since been lost. What exists today are redactions made later in history and referred to by church fathers such as Eusebius from the late third century C.E. onward. Josephus is generally considered to lack authenticity regarding Jesus. This passage in Josephus's *Jewish Antiquities* that refers to Jesus is thought to be a later addition partly because Josephus makes no mention of Jesus in his copious history *The Jewish War,* and the style and context of the quotation do not fit with the rest of the text. More definitively, a third-century Christian writer, Origen, who commented extensively on Josephus's works, makes no mention of Jesus or the relevant passage in his copy of Josephus. It is almost inconceivable that this founding father of the church would have ignored a reference to Jesus in Josephus had there been one.[16]

A clearer reference by Josephus comes in another section of his *Jewish Antiquities* when he is recording the death of James, whom he refers to as "the brother of Jesus," but even here Jesus is not the subject of his attention.

In the Slavonic version of Josephus's *Jewish War,* preserved in Russian and Rumanian copies, there are again references to Jesus Christ and the early Christians that do not appear in the Greek version. These are generally considered to be forgeries,[17] but there are some curious passages that may well echo an earlier truth. The Slavonic additions assert that Jesus "did not observe the Sabbath in the traditional manner."[18]

On the face of it, this seems to be a profound flouting of the Law—the Third Commandment of the Decalogue, to which the Christian Scriptures maintain Jesus always adhered, and which would not have been breached by his followers. This may echo the Gospels' recording of the Pharisees threatening to have Jesus killed for healing on the Sabbath—an action often cited as demonstrating Jesus's humanity in contrast to the rigidity of the Pharisees.

Another alternative is that Jesus's behavior reflects the Qumran-Essene ruling. He *kept* the Sabbath, but on a different day from the traditional one, *just like* the Qumran Essenes. They followed a solar calendar, which meant that the Sabbath fell on a Sunday instead of a Saturday. Sunday had a special festive, holy meaning for the Essenes—and it is this day that has become the day of rest for the entire Christian and Western world.[19]

Another quotation, confirmed in the Slavonic additions to Josephus, refers to Jesus, as a rule, being found opposite the city of Jerusalem on the Mount of Olives. This area was and still is referred to as the Essene Gate of the Old City. The inference from the Slavonic Josephus is clear. Jesus worked and healed close to the community of Essenes who congregated at this particular entry to Jerusalem. We shall reenter the Essene Gate later on.

The only other, very early, suggested reference to Jesus is found in a Syriac letter, inconclusively dated to 73 C.E., written by a Syrian stoic named Mara bar Sarapion, which mentions the killing of a "wise king."[20]

Other later, ambiguous references to Jesus as Chrestus (Christ) appear in Roman sources,[21] notably a record by Suetonius, a Roman biographer writing around 120 C.E., that the emperor Claudius expelled Jews from Rome around 50 C.E.: "Since the Jews were constantly causing disturbances at the instigation of Chrestus, he expelled them from Rome" (Suetonius, *Lives of the Caesars*).

Pliny the Younger (61–c. 120 C.E.) is reported to have written to the emperor Trajan (98–117 C.E.) about disturbances by Christians while he was serving in the provinces of Bithnia and Pontus: "It was their habit on a fixed day to assemble before daylight and recite by turns a form of words to Christ as a god; and . . . they bound themselves with an oath, not for any crime, but not to commit theft or robbery or adultery, nor to break their word, and not to deny a deposit when demanded."[22]

In the early decades of the second century C.E. we find the pagan Roman historian Tacitus (55–120 C.E.) in his *Annals* relating how Emperor Nero pushed the blame for a disastrous fire that swept Rome in 64 C.E. onto the Christians: "[They were] punished with the utmost refinements of cruelty, a class of persons hated for their vices, whom the crowd called Christians. Christus, the founder of the name, had undergone the death penalty in the reign of Tiberius, by sentence of the procurator Pontius Pilate."[23]

Somewhat later, around 177 C.E., Aulus Cornelius Celsus, a Roman physician and polemicist against Christianity, writing under the pagan emperor Marcus Aurelius, recorded in his *True Doctrine:* "First, however, I must deal with the matter of Jesus, the so-called savior, who not long ago taught new doctrines and was thought to be a son of God. . . . And while there are a few moderate, reasonable, and intelligent people who are inclined to interpret [Christianity's] beliefs allegorically, yet it thrives in its purer form among the ignorant."

Such was the antagonism toward the early Christian religion that following it was declared a crime throughout the Roman Empire between 110 and 210 C.E. These independent Roman sources, which are all anti-Christian in their thrust and therefore likely to be provoked by a real movement, are generally in agreement that there was such a person known as Jesus or Christ and that he suffered death on the instructions of Pontius Pilate sometime between 26 and 36 C.E.

## Jewish Sources for the Reality of Jesus

Oddly enough, it is in Jewish rabbinic literature that the most convincing nonbiblical/Koranic references to Jesus can be found. The irony lies in the fact that the significance of Jesus was exactly what the early Jewish polemicists were apparently trying to minimize. There are a number of references in the Jewish Mishnah (compiled c. 200 C.E.) and its supplements;

the Tosephta and alternative versions; the Baraitot; and the Talmud (compiled post–400 C.E.) that are perhaps more concrete than any in other non-Scripture sources. These references, however, are found in later material than the contemporary leading rabbis of the time, Hillel and Shammai (c. 30 B.C.E.–10 C.E.) and Gamaliel the Elder (early first century C.E.),* might have penned.[24]

In sourcing the references, I initially looked to the monumental work in German of Herman Strack and Paul Billerbeck for some of the rabbinic references.[25] The work is very ponderous, however, and I have tended to look more to a succinct and up-to-date edition by the somewhat autocratic Samuel Tobias Lachs, professor of the history of religion at Bryn Mawr College, Wales.[26]

Jewish tradition regarding a certain Joshua ben Perahyah alludes to the possibility that he was a teacher of a person named Jesus, and that he had a rebellious student perhaps also called Jesus. But Perahyah, who was thought to be head of the Sanhedrin,† was active around 120 B.C.E., which makes him too early by about a century to have been a contemporary of Jesus—unless the dates have been mixed up.[27] It is worth noting the apparent references to Jesus in Jewish traditional texts, mentioned above, in more detail, because they might well be the firmest external textual historical references to Jesus that exist.

In the Gospel of Matthew (2:13–15), Jesus's father, Joseph, is told to flee to Egypt with the newly born child to escape the wrath of Herod the Great. The two relevant rabbinic references to this possible event are as follows:

R. Eliezer [ben Hyrcanus] said to the sages: "Did not Ben Stada [i.e., Jesus] bring spells from Egypt in a cut which was on his flesh?" They said to him: "He was a fool, and they do not bring proof from a fool." (Talmud, B. Shab, 104b. T. Shab II 15)

When Yannai the king killed our Rabbis, R. Joshua b. Perahyah [and Jesus] fled to Alexandria of Egypt. One day R. Joshua intended to

---

*Hillel's son or grandson, mentioned in the Christian Scriptures as a teacher of Paul (Acts 22:3; 5:34–9).

†The Sanhedrin was an assembly of Jewish elders in existence from the second century B.C.E. to the fourth century C.E.

accept him [previously he had excommunicated him] and make a sign to him. Jesus thought that he repelled him. He went and put up a brick and worshipped it. R. Joshua said to him: "Repent!" He replied: "Thus I have received from you, that everyone who sins and causes the multitude to sin is not given the opportunity to repent." And a teacher said: "Jesus the Nazarene practiced magic, and led astray and deceived Israel." (Talmud, B. Sanh. 107b, B. Sot. 47a; TJ. Hag. 2.2 [77d]; TJ. Sanh. 6.9 [32c])

The killing of the rabbis by Yannai is probably a reference to the eight hundred pharisaic rebels put to death by crucifixion by the Hasmonean Alexander Jannaeus, high priest from 103 to 76 B.C.E.;[28] this would date the Talmudic reference to Jesus associated with Rabbi Joshua b. Perahyah far too early. As Professor Lachs puts it: "This passage has a glaring historical anachronism—Joshua b. Perahyah lived more than two generations before Jesus."[29]

Something is obviously wrong if this Talmudic reference has anything to do with the Jesus of the Christian Scriptures, but I believe there may be a very rational explanation for the apparent anachronism. It would not be the first time historical dates have been mixed up or personalities confused or conflated with others—bearing in mind that we are talking about records collated prior to the fourth century C.E. and transmitted to us today through numerous handed-down copies and versions.

In exploring how this rabbinic passage might validate knowledge of the Jesus of the early first century C.E., my attention is drawn to the similarity of Joshua's parental name, Perahyah, which is itself an Egyptian-sounding name, and the name of Akhenaten's high priest, Meryra. Could it be that knowledge of this name by the Qumran Essenes has crossed into rabbinic mythology and become associated with Jesus?

Later in the book it will be seen that Pharaoh Akhenaten's role as an enunciator of monotheism, together with the biblical Jacob and Joseph, when the Hebrews were in Egypt, had a profound effect on the Qumran Essenes. They were keenly aware of his revolutionary religious ideas and in fact counted him as the founder of their strand of Judaism. We will also see that they knew the name of Akhenaten's high priest, Meryra, and named him a leader in the final eschatological war (in their War Scroll) as

Merire or Meriri. A strong case can also be made to demonstrate the infiltration of Qumran-Essene thinking into later rabbinic mythology.

Another incredibly intriguing torchlight comes from a different rabbinic reference to Jesus in the Talmud:

> Rabbi Joshua came upon the prophet Elijah as he was standing at the entrance of Rabbi Simeon ben Yochai's cave. He asked him: "When is the Messiah coming?"
>
> The other replied: "Go and ask him yourself."
>
> "Where shall I find him?"
>
> *"Before the gates of Rome."*
>
> "By what sign shall I know him?"
>
> "He is sitting among poor people covered with wounds. The others unbind all their wounds at once, and then bind them up again. But he unbinds one at a time, and then binds it up again straightway. He tells himself: 'Perhaps I shall be needed (to appear as the Messiah)—and I must not take time and be late!'"
>
> So he went and found him and said: "Peace be with you, my master and teacher!"
>
> He answered him: "Peace be with you, son of Levi!"
>
> Then he asked him: "When are you coming, master?"
>
> He answered him: "Today!"
>
> Thereupon he returned to Elijah and said to him: "He has deceived me, he has indeed deceived me! He told me 'Today I am coming!' and he has not come."
>
> But the other said to him: "This is what he told you: 'Today—if you would Only hear his voice'" [Psalm 95:7]. (Sanhedrin; my emphasis)

It seems likely that this rabbinic passage is referring to the same rabbi Joshua b. Perahya and the same wounded Jesus. The content, and words I have put in italics, creates an entirely new chronological relativity. The mention of the messiah in the context of Rome suggests a date at least well after 63 B.C.E., the earliest date for the conquest of Judaea by the Romans.

The Simeon ben Yochai[30] (or Yohai) mentioned in line two implies a mid-second-century-C.E. date. Simeon ben Yochai was a pupil of Rabbi

Akiva, who, when pursued by the Roman authorities for his rebellious opinions, sought refuge in a cave in Galilee.

This reference pulls the possible time of Jesus even further forward in history. It is not unreasonable to assume these rabbinic witnesses refer to a Jesus who lived midway between the circa 120 B.C.E. of Rabbi Joshua b. Perahyah and the circa 120 C.E. of Rabbi ben Yochai, the preferred date for Jesus, and certainly well after 63 B.C.E.

There are other polemic references to a Yeshu ben Pentera in later Talmudic sources, which are taken as alluding to Jesus as the illegitimate son of Miriam and a Roman soldier named Pantera (or Pandera or Panthera). These stories were almost certainly generated in reaction to denigration of Jews by Christians in the second and third centuries, but they confirm an awareness in Jewish literature of someone called Jesus. The Roman name Pantera was a relatively common one; for instance, a tomb inscription found at Bingerbruck, Germany, dated to the first century C.E., reads "Tiberius Julius Abdes Panthera."[31]

One last rabbinic source, dated to the first century C.E., refers to Rabbi Ismael forbidding his nephew Eliezer to be healed of a snakebite in the name of Jesus.[32]

## The Resurrection: Jewish and Christian Versions

Modern Judaism, like most other religions, is not homogeneous, and it encompasses more than one view of Jesus. The views vary from those of extreme Orthodox Judaism—in which the existence of Jesus is not even acknowledged—to the more progressive modern view, which sees him as a learned, prophetlike figure, but not the messiah or a person endowed with divinity. Most wings of Judaism, however, are still awaiting a messiah, and the characteristics apportioned to Jesus in the Christian Scriptures might well fulfill many of those expectations.

While Christianity's view on death and the afterlife has not changed substantially since the early centuries after Jesus's death, the Jewish stance on resurrection and the soul has changed throughout the history of the Hebrews. For Christianity, the human being's original soul at birth is inherently evil, and salvation after death can be attained only through Jesus. The views of mainstream Judaism can best be considered an evolving progression of understanding, which, even today, is somewhat fluid. The earliest tradition, evident from Genesis 37:35 in the Hebrew Scriptures, sees an inconsolable Jacob grieving for the apparent death of his son Joseph: "No, I will go down mourning for my son in Sheol." Sheol is the place where dead bodies reside, and there is no concept of a soul that continues on after death.

That death is the end of everything, including any relationship with God, is reiterated in early biblical Psalms, such as 140:10, which shows there is still no indication of a belief in resurrection: "Let burning coals fall upon them: let them be cast into the fire; into deep pits, that they rise not up again."

As influences from Babylon, Persia, and Egypt percolated into theological thinking, texts written after the return from exile in Babylon reflected an acceptance of resurrection, in contradiction of earlier writings. In the biblical Book of Kings, chapter 28, for example, written down during this period, King Saul consults with the infamous witch of Endor to ascertain how he will fare in a coming battle against the Philistines. She obliges by raising the spirit of Samuel, his previous mentor, from the dead. Now there is a fully developed idea of the soul underlying the resurrected body.

One fundamental change in Jewish beliefs, which the Essenes already seemed to have adopted, related to the afterlife. In Ecclesiastes, written some eighty years before the Maccabean uprising, the Hebrew Scriptures' position that there is no afterlife is reiterated very clearly (9:5 and 9:6): "For the living know that they shall die: but the dead know not any thing, neither have they any more a reward; for the memory of them is forgotten. Also their love, and their hatred, and their envy, is now perished; neither have they any more a portion for ever in any thing that is done under the sun."

By the time of the uprising, the Book of Daniel took a very different line, perhaps as encouragement to the esprit de corps of the troops. Now an afterlife was seen as a possible reward for the righteous who die in battle (12:2). This new perspective on life after death was strongly promoted by the Essene movement; by the time of Jesus, the Sadducees of the Temple were the only major sect who clung to the old concept of death as a physical finality.

During the following intertestamental period, from around 300 B.C.E. to 100 C.E., the theology of God renewing life beyond death was further developed. For the Pharisees and the Essenes, resurrection became a real possibility. When the Temple was destroyed in 70 C.E., the pharisaic/Essenic view prevailed. As the Book of Daniel records, in the time of final judgment when the messiah comes:

> Many of those who sleep in the dust of the earth shall awake, some to everlasting life, and some to shame and everlasting contempt. (12:2)

This idea of everlasting heaven for the righteous and everlasting hell for the souls of the unrighteous is later taken up by Christianity, and references to "gates" as places of passage through hell, which appear in the Bible and the Koran, seem to be derived from the ancient Egyptian mythology of the afterlife.[33] Perhaps as a reactionary development, the concept of heaven and hell has been played down by Rabbinic Judaism. Even today the Book of Daniel is not read in synagogue services, and the concept of heaven and hell has dropped out of modern Jewish thought. For mainstream Judaism today, in sympathy with the concept of a compassionate God, the soul simply goes on. There is no view on the result of any final reckoning.

Strangely enough, as I mentioned in chapter 3 in discussing modern scholarly views of Jesus's connections to Qumran, the strongest evidence for the life and existence of Jesus comes out of Jewish literature, rather than from contemporary writers like Josephus and other Roman-Greek historians.

## Summation

All the available external circumstantial, indirect, and inferential indications, in addition to the Christian Scriptures, Koranic, and Jewish written witness, make the existence of Jesus as a real person a near certainty. When the evidence from archaeology, discussed in the next chapter, and from other revelations in subsequent chapters, is evaluated, Jesus's existence begins to look like the concrete reality.

# 6

# The Archaeological Evidence for Jesus's Life

Although, as we have seen, there is external evidence for the existence of the central characters who are said in the Christian Scriptures to have interacted with Jesus and his followers, there is virtually no available external *literary* evidence for these interactions.

The existence of places and people named in the Christian Scriptures that can be confirmed by archaeological evidence—largely inscriptional and numismatic—gives some degree of credence to the setting for the story of Jesus. However, the geographical details of Judaea, Samaria, and the Galilee, the apparent stomping grounds of Jesus and his followers, are often sketchy and even inaccurate in some instances. In fact, identification of Nazareth in Galilee as a place Jesus frequented is difficult, and it is questionable whether the village even existed in the time of Jesus.

## Nazareth

The Gospels of Matthew, Luke, and John say Jesus was born in Bethlehem, a village that certainly existed at the time of his birth. Nazareth, the town he is said to have lived in during most of his early life, is less easily identifiable. The question marks that hang over this period of Jesus's life, and the uncertainty of Nazareth as a place of prolonged residence for Jesus, may well have relevance when it comes to considering an alternative place of residence for his maturing years.

Although Nazareth is now a bustling town of some forty thousand people, neither Talmudic texts nor the Masoretic Testament (Hebrew Scriptures, or Old Testament), the Apocrypha, or Josephus can help verify the existence of the Nazareth of the Christian Scriptures.

45

Tellingly, Jesus, in the Christian Scriptures, performs many miracles, healings, and exorcisms across the Holy Land, but never performs anything in Nazareth. Josephus, onetime commander of the Galilee region, lists its towns and villages, but makes no mention of a place called Nazareth. The only possible external reference to Nazareth comes from a fragmentary ancient Hebrew inscription dated to the end of the third century C.E., found at Caesarea, on the north coast of Israel. This lists twenty-four priestly "allotments" of duty rotations (Hebrew, *mishmarot*) and the places from which they derived. The eighteenth allotment is given in Hebrew as *nzrt,* which could be read as Nazareth.[1]

Archaeological work at Nazareth in 1889, led by Father Prosper Viaud, and between 1955 and 1970, led by Father B. Bagatti, has yielded some clues about a possible early history, and excavations are said to have revealed graffiti in lower layers under the existing Church of the Incarnation. These are believed to indicate an early Judaeo-Christian presence.[2]

Examples of these graffiti, dated to the second or third century C.E., are traced in charcoal beneath Byzantine levels of the church in Nazareth and refer to Christos and Mary. Another engraving, of a figure, is said to represent John the Baptist holding a cosmic cross (a cross within a square). Elsewhere the engraved design of a boat, with a sail divided into eight squares, is said to represent the Christian *Ogdoad* interpretation of the eight fundamental elements of the world. (*Ogdoad* is a term introduced by Valentinius, a prominent second-century Gnostic, to describe eight emanations, grouped as male/female, active/passive pairs, by which Creation was effected.)

Interestingly, the Egyptian *Ogdoad* of Hermopolis, which long predated the Christian idea, comprised eight deities identified in the creation myth. In the Egyptian version, four frog gods were paired with four snake goddesses, symbolizing different aspects of chaos before creation. The pairings were Nun and Naunet (water), Amun and Amaunet (hiddenness), Heh and Hauhet (infinity), and Keke and Kauket (darkness). It was believed these deities brought into being the original primeval mound on which the egg of the sun god was placed to form the world.

Near the Church of the Incarnation lies another church, dedicated to St. Joseph, which is said to stand on the site of a Judaeo-Christian sanctuary. More recent excavations led by James Strange, of the University of

South Florida, indicate the early existence of a small village high in the hills that may have been the Nazareth of the Christian Scriptures.[3]

If there is little proof that Nazareth actually existed in Jesus's time, why is the name mentioned in the Christian Scriptures? The explanation put forward by a number of scholars as the most likely reason is that it has been confused with the term Nazirite or Nazarene (Nazorene). The Nazirites were a select Jewish group who took a vow of dedication to the Lord and followed a spiritual lifestyle. The three lifelong Nazirites mentioned in the Bible are Samson, Samuel, and John the Baptist; intriguingly, the term has been associated with the Essenes.[4]

So what is the explanation for the origins of the name Nazareth or Nazarene to be associated with Jesus? One I personally favor comes directly from Dead Sea Scrolls, Jeremiahic, and Isaiahic sources. The Hebrew word for "branch" or "shoot" is *nazir,* and the sense in which it is used in these sources is the same as the Greek appellation that is applied to Jesus, Nazwraioz (Ναζφραιοζ) and his followers, Nazwraioi (Ναζφραιοι), in the Christian Scriptures. Essentially the name could be taken as a theological message rather than a geographical origin. Jesus is the "branch or shoot of Jesse" that will proclaim God's salvation and return to Zion (Jer. 31:6).[5]

## The Archaeology of Pontius Pilate

The one character closely associated with the crucifixion of Jesus in the Christian Scriptures about whom we know quite a lot is the Roman procurator ruling at the time of Jesus, Pontius Pilate. What the Christian Scriptures say about him fits in quite well with historical references. We know from Josephus and Philo of Alexandria that he was in power during the reign of Emperor Tiberius, but it was only in 1961 that an inscription came to light that confirmed his existence—apart from a myth that he was born in Scotland![6] (See page 1 of the color insert.)

Excavating in Caesarea on the northern coast of Israel in 1961, an Italian archaeologist discovered a stone inscribed with Pilate's title, "Praefectus Ivdaeae." Coins struck during the period when Pilate was presiding as governor of Judaea confirm that he was a hard character, although none of the coins carried a representation of his face—a privilege reserved only for the emperor. Among the other Roman rulers of Judaea, Pilate appeared to be extreme in his lack of sensitivity toward the local Jewish population, and unique in using offensive emblems of the Roman *simpulum*[7] and *littus*[8] on his coins. For the local Jewish population to have to handle a coin with a symbol for divining or augury was anathema. Such activities were an abomination forbidden since the time of Moses. This understanding of Pilate's acerbic nature is supported by the writings of Josephus, who says Pilate deliberately set up effigies on golden shields with images of Caesar and mounted them on stands around Jerusalem (*Antiquities* 18:3). Philo describes Pilate as "inflexible, merciless and obstinate."[9]

## Caiaphas

The other character from the Christian Scriptures whose name is confirmed by archaeology is Caiaphas, high priest at the time of Jesus. An ornate ossuary engraved with the family name was discovered in a Jerusalem tomb during excavations in 1969–71.[10] More recently, in 1990,

*Fig. 6.1. Ossuary inscribed with the name Caiaphas.*

a limestone ossuary containing many sets of bones and dating to the first century C.E. was found in south Jerusalem. The ossuary bears the Hebrew inscription "Yehosef bar Kaiyafa"—"Joseph son of Caiaphas"—and includes the bones of an old man who might actually have been Caiaphas.[11]

One fascinating example of how Jesus continued in the consciousness of later Jewish tradition comes from a rather unlikely source.

### Magic Bowls

As well as being renowned for their prophecy, the Essenes were noted for their work as healers and exorcisers of evil spirits.[12] Jesus exhibited all these functionary characteristics, but his approach, in Christian Scriptures' terms, was quite different from that of the Essenes or the general populace. The use of magical rites, charms, and protective apparel against evil spirits was still quite common among the Jewish population. It was also a general fashion in healing to try to expel evil spirits by using magic bowls inscribed with incantations and magical formulas. Jesus did not appear to make use of any of these accessories.

© ROBERT FEATHER

*Fig. 6.2. Curse bowl from circa the fifth century C.E. that mentions the name Jesus. Courtesy S. Moussaieff.*

Curiously, a pointer to an ongoing awareness of Jesus in Jewish circles surfaced recently in a London auction room. The magic bowl inscribed with Jesus's name shows that among the Jewish population in the early centuries after Jesus's death, his appellation still carried weight.

As the bidding crept ever higher, the uninitiated in the audience at Christie's Auction House in June 1997 became increasingly aware that the lot being offered for sale was no ordinary historical relic. Finally it was knocked down to Mr. Shlomo Moussaieff at the bargain price of $5,400. The bowl measures six and a half inches in diameter and about two inches in depth and contains thirty lines of neatly written Jewish Aramaic script that spirals in a clockwise direction from the center of the bowl to the rim.

M163, as the bowl is designated, is a fifth-century C.E. "curse bowl," rarely found among Aramaic magic bowls. It is the only bowl text in Jewish-Babylonian-Aramaic ever found that makes a specific mention of Jesus. The translated text indicates that it was commissioned by two brothers, Mihlad and Baran, sons of Mirdukh, and directed against a certain Isha, son of Ifra-Hurmiz, who was thinking evil thoughts against them. The inscription, titled "This Press," requested that the brothers be given complete authority over their adversary.

At the beginning of "This Press" comes the invocation: "By the name of I-am-that-I-am God *zsvout,* and by the name of Jesus, who conquered the height and the depth by his cross, and by the name of his exalted father, and by the name of the holy spirits for ever and eternity. Amen, amen, selah. This press is true and established."[13] This appears to be a ritualized curse that can have been written only by a Jewish scribe.[14] The intriguing question is, Why was a Jewish scribe incorporating the trinitarian formula and including the name of Jesus as a party to the press?

There are indicators that the Jewish Aramaic vocabulary of the bowl makes some borrowings from Syriac Christian language, and that the "Pressers" were Persian, possibly Zoroastrians, and their opponent a Christian. It may well have been that the scribe figured that the best way to attack a Christian on behalf of his clients was to invoke the name of Jesus. The scribe's familiarity with Christian terminology and his knowledge of Jesus, however, implies an acceptance in Jewish understanding of Jesus's existence, although not necessarily a belief in his divinity.

## The Brother of Jesus Ossuary

We now come to what may well be the most exciting and telling archaeological discovery ever made in relation to Jesus's existence of (apart from what will be revealed later in this book). It is considered by some scholars to be the firmest evidence ever produced to confirm the reality of Jesus. If finally proved genuine, it would put the truth of Jesus's human existence beyond question and should put an end to the trivial pursuits of those who would have him the mere figment of someone's imagination.

As the respected American publication *Biblical Archaeology Review* put it in its November/December 2002 issue: "Historical evidence for the existence of Jesus has come to light literally written in stone."[15] The inscription engraved in Aramaic on the outside of a first-century-C.E. ossuary found in Jerusalem reads: "James, son of Joseph, brother of Jesus."

The cursive style of writing is consistent with the period 10 to 70 C.E., and Professor André Lemaire, paleographer at the Sorbonne University, Paris, has verified the authenticity of the inscription. Laboratory tests on the twenty-inch-long box by scientists at the Geological Survey of Israel initially confirmed that the rough limestone container originated from the Jerusalem area and that the oxidation patina is consistent with a dating of circa 63 C.E.

The find seemed to corroborate the Christian Scriptures' record of James, leader of the early church in Jerusalem, as the brother of Jesus and son of Joseph (see, for example, Mark 6:3; Matt. 13:55–56; Gal. 1:18–19). Although all three names were relatively common in the period, the family relationship and combination would be statistically unlikely, and there are no other examples of such a combination known from previous ossuary finds. Of some 233 ossuaries so far discovered in Israel, five mention a James, nineteen mention a Joseph, and ten mention a Jesus. Of the forty thousand or so males thought to have been living in Jerusalem in the first century C.E., and assuming each had an average of two brothers, the possibility of the same familial combination of names occurring together is one in two thousand. However, the inclusion of a sibling's name on a box containing a person's bones was in itself extremely unusual and would have occurred only if the brother was a person of great importance. (Only one other example of a brother being mentioned is known.)

This increases the odds of the Brother of Jesus Ossuary relating to the

Christian Scriptures' family to 1 in about 500,000 if it were genuine.

Unfortunately, in July 2003 Oded Golan, the owner of the ossuary, was arrested at his home in Tel Aviv on suspicion of fabricating ancient artifacts, including the Jesus ossuary. Golan, who has not been able to confirm from whom he acquired the ossuary, apparently had at his home equipment and materials for use in forging antiquities. Coupled with the Israel Antiquities Authority's final report concluding that the ossuary inscription showed definite signs of being of recent vintage, it now seemed certain it had no connection with Jesus—leaving quite a few people with a patina of egg on their faces.[16] Or did it? That was not the final word; Professor André Lemaire hit back at the IAA in an article in the November/December 2003 issue of *Biblical Archaeology Review* accusing the report's authors of gratuitous statements, misrepresenting their qualifications, scientific prejudice, not being able to spell Hebrew words, and baseless arguments. The story rumbles on.

What the evidence *does* confirm is the dramatically different form of burial practiced during the Second Temple period by the general Jewish population from that seen at Qumran—a subject we will look at in greater detail later in this book.

## Other Sources

There are, of course, other locations and associated personal names that might give tangible pointers or verification of quotations from the Christian Scriptures. A number of these will be considered in the context of their discussion.

However convincing some of the apparent hard physical evidence may appear, a word of caution is necessary in assessing the reports of certain archaeologists and historians and their commentators. This is especially pertinent in the case of those who are religiously partisan. Both Christian and Jewish interpreters have a habit of being less than objective in arriving at their conclusions; many have an agenda that predisposes them to find what they are looking for and conclude what they have already concluded, rather than what might actually be the truth. As objective as I try to be, I would hesitate to claim complete immunity from this particular ailment myself.[17]

The overall conclusion, nevertheless, from sources external to the Christian Scriptures, both literary and archaeological, is that someone who fulfilled many of the biblical claims relating to Jesus really did exist. Furthermore, whatever attributes he possessed, divine or otherwise, they inspired a devoted religious following that eventually grew into a movement whose influence swept the entire world.

Background detail regarding the emergence of the Essenes at Qumran, as contemporaries of Jesus and his disciples, should help set them in their historical context. Now we are tooled up to embark on the next encounter—philosophical influences at Qumran.

# 7

# The Qumran Community's Innermost Beliefs: Messianic Soldiers of Light

Buffeted from desert to temple and temple to desert by the sands of time, ancestors of the priestly Essenes had seen their country overrun by Nebuchadnezzar in 586 B.C.E. and the sacred place of worship desecrated. After returning from exile in Babylon, they had managed to preserve their beliefs and way of life and eventually found sanctuary in the forbidden reaches of the Dead Sea.

Now, toward the end of the first century B.C.E., their successors had witnessed the restoration of the Second Temple by Herod—only to see others, not of the true Zadokite line of high priests, usurping the role, and a golden Roman eagle perched on the rooftop.

The Second Temple was, therefore, to the Essenes a place of intense contradiction. The holy place, central in concept to their inheritance, was occupied by alien forces and governed by the whims of Herod, a lackey of Rome. The Temple's size and shape were not to their liking and, worse still, from around 31–30 B.C.E. onward, two lambs were sacrificed every day by the Temple priests for the "well-being" of the Roman emperor and the Roman Empire. This animal sacrifice was anathema to many Jewish groups and especially to the Qumran Essenes. No wonder they interpreted the earthquake of 31 B.C.E., which caused widespread destruction in the area of the Judaean desert and severe damage to their own settlement, as a portent that they were right and that their belief in an imminent apocalypse was justified.

# The Call of Destiny

Two central concepts need to be kept in mind when attempting to understand the motivations behind the beliefs and behavior of the Essenes, and, more particularly, the Qumran Essenes and their messianic hopes.

First, although they put immense store in traditional Hebrew teachings, they followed an apparently aberrational form of Judaism that yearned for and echoed the early days of Mosaic Sinai and which, I maintain, dates back even further to the ancient monotheism of Akhenaten and Jacob.

Second, if the early Jesus movement owed a powerful debt to the beliefs practiced at Qumran, which I suggest will become even more apparent from the evidence presented in this book, then it would not be surprising to find that some of Akhenaten's teachings and imagery would be transferred across and reflected in the early Jesus movement and later Christianity.

It is evident from the Dead Sea Scrolls that the Essenes of Qumran considered themselves an elite messianic group; they had retreated from the fray of the Temple and the priesthood and sought refuge in the wilderness to protect their piety. The opening verses of Isaiah, chapter 40, aptly describe their role:

> The voice of him that crieth in the wilderness, Prepare ye the way of
> the Lord, make straight in the desert a highway for our God.

For some of the Essenes, the need to retreat was part of their search for a reaffirmation of the divine covenant given to Moses on Mount Sinai, a quest for the purity and essence of Torah and Hebrew teachings. They looked upon themselves as the ancestral custodians of the "light of truth." Their fundamental beliefs and manner of practicing their special religion were essentially at odds with the rest of the Jewish community, and they followed an extreme form of ritualistic behavior and strict adherence to their interpretation of the Law.

The Dead Sea Scroll known as the Community Rule descibes the criteria by which one would become a bona fide member of the Essenic community (more fully described in chapter 19).

The Essenes' spiritual leader was known as the "right teacher"—a title identified with Moses in his final blessing to the children of Israel (Deuteronomy, chapter 33). Successive "right teachers" had the role of ensuring that the community adhered to the true interpretation of the Torah while they awaited the coming of a prophet similar to Moses and an unprecedented *two messiahs.*

This waiting was to be accompanied by immersion in the Holy Scriptures and by following an ascetic, celibate way of life. Each year a cumulative total of 120 nights was to be spent in prayer and study. Personal possessions and income were to be given to the Yahad, the community, and in turn the community looked after the individual's needs. Living and eating were communal, and garments were plain and purely functional. There are many similarities in this unselfish way of life to the modern ashrams of America and the kibbutzim of modern Israel.

Within the community, at least at the outset, there was a strong hierarchical structure. At the top sat the right teacher. Priests, aided by Levites (individuals of priestly descent), dictated the doctrine of the group. All full members could vote in an assembly on nondoctrinal matters, while general day-to-day administration was in the hands of a triumvirate of priests along with twelve helpers. Each member had a specific place in the pecking order in relation to level of learning and holiness, as determined by his peers.

Throughout the sectarian Dead Sea Scrolls that describe the feelings and activities of the Essenes, there are repeated themes and motifs that endow these works with a sense of collective purpose: of sons of light fighting sons of darkness, messianic portents, battles with evil, the fruits of righteousness. Their fundamental themes embody people who are:

> Righteous—Zaddikim
> Pious—Hassidim
> Holy—Kedushim
> Meek—Anavim
> Endowed with God's Spirit—Ruachim
> Faithful—Emunim

The first three are recognizably strongly Jewish; the latter three carry noticeable overtones that would later become strongly applied in Christianity.

It to was the transitional/post–First Temple prophets that the Essenes looked for their inspiration. They closely associated themselves with the Sons of Zadok—the select priests of the Tabernacle—using the term Zaddikim, "the righteous ones," to describe themselves. They were the holy caucus who would carry the true torch of light handed on to them through Moses.

There is a continual reference throughout their scrolls to the part played by the Tabernacle priests. It is clear that the Essenes considered themselves the keepers of the covenant and part of the direct line of priests that attended the holy shrines. This is evident in the manner in which the scrolls discuss the testament of the priestly Levi, Aaron, and Kohath. These are the "righteous seed"—Zaddikim—that the Essenes claim as their birthright:

> And God of gods for all eternity. And he will shine as a Light upon you and He will make known to you His great name and you will know Him, that He is the Eternal God and Lord of all creation, and sovereign over all things, governing them according to his will. Thus you will grant to me a good name among you, together with joy for Levi and happiness for Jacob, rejoicing for Isaac and blessing for Abraham, inasmuch as you guarded and walked in the inheritance. My sons, your fathers bequeathed to you Truth, Righteousness, Uprightness, Integrity, Purity, Holiness and the Priesthood. (Testament of Kohath 12, fragment 1)

Even after some fifteen hundred years, the text still contains recognizably Egyptian-style phrasing, and the continual allusions to light emphasize the significance of the sun and light, just as Akhenaten conceived them.

For Akhenaten, light was the ethereal expression of his vision of the Aten—his name for a unique, all-powerful, invisible God. The prime manifestations of this vision were the sun with its rays beaming down goodness, in the form of hands; and life, in the form of the Egyptian ankh—sign of life.

# 8

# Messiahs of Qumran

So who were the Qumran Essenes waiting for? The answer is contained in a number of the Dead Sea Scrolls texts that indicate they were waiting for two, and some scholars read three, messiahs. These messiahs, one priestly and one royal, are given various titles in different scrolls:

> *Priestly:* Interpreter of the Law, the Star; the Messiah of Aaron,[1] who was of princely descent
>
> *Royal:* Prince of the Congregation, the Scepter; the Messiah of Israel;[2] the Messianic Rule; Community Rule; the King Messiah[3]

In addition, they expected the return of a prophet similar to Moses. Fortunately, there are quite detailed descriptions of these messiahs in a number of the scrolls, so one would assume it should be relatively easy to identify who they were talking about. Unhappily, that is not the case, and conventional scholarship makes little attempt to utilize this information.

## A Davidic Messiah?

The idea of the kingly messiah referred to by the Essenes is inevitably taken as being someone emerging from the Davidic line of kings commencing with King David himself. The tacit assumption by most scholars is that King David was the role model for this returning royal messiah. If King David wasn't the role-model messiah, ordinary scholarship has nowhere else to go. The assumption, however, is fraught with problems. King David (who ruled in approximately 1000 B.C.E.) noticeably failed to live up to the righteous ideals demanded in Jeremiah, Ezekiel, Micah, Kings, and Chronicles.[4]

David had Uriah, an officer in his army, murdered in order to marry Uriah's wife, and brought destruction on seventy thousand Israelites for his evil doings.[5] In a parable by the prophet Nathan, David is roundly condemned for his evil acts against God and told that his descendants will suffer as a result of his murderous deeds.[6] This is hardly a worthy pattern for a future messiah. In fact, formal messianism in Jewish scripture does not appear until the time of Daniel in the second century B.C.E.,[7] so King David is even less likely to have been the role model the Qumran Essenes were thinking of.

One has to wonder, therefore, where the Qumran Essenes obtained their quite detailed descriptions and well-developed philosophy of these anticipated messiahs and messianism—which, in any event, appear to pre-date any of the royal kings of Israel. The problem of identifying the two messiahs, one kingly and one priestly, alluded to in the Hebrew Scriptures but distinctly specified in the Qumran-Essene literature, is so contentious that modern scholarship either ignores the problem or scratches around to try to find possible candidates using very weak evidence.

Nowhere does the Pentateuch or any succeeding text of the Hebrew Scriptures suggest that, when the faithful in Israel worshipped at the Tabernacle or later in the Temple at Jerusalem, they looked to the Aaronic high priest as a foreshadowing of a future messianic high priest.[8] Almost in desperation, some scholars have even suggested Zerubbabel, the rebuilder of the First Temple, or Joshua, the postexilic high priest, as contenders.[9]

The phrase "Davidic line" is, in my view, only an indicator of a longer royal line predating King David. In fact, in Qumran texts, and in most biblical texts, the messianic king is deliberately *not* referred to as Davidic.[10] Although many of the motifs in the expectation of a future king may be drawn from Israel's experience of kingship, other motifs can clearly be traced to pre–Hebrew Scriptures' kingship periods of Israel's history.[11] Indeed, how can King David be the personification of a messianic figure when the same messianic figure is seen by Isaiah and Zechariah, and by Dead Sea Scrolls texts such as 4Q285, as a "suffering servant" of God who is frustrated in his ambitions and killed for his efforts? None of these characteristics can be applied to King David. One eminent scholar, Kenneth Pomykala, like others has postulated that any reference by the Qumran sect to a messiah of Israel should be regarded categorically as non-Davidic.[12]

Why should this be, unless there was some memory of another previous line of royalty? In the same way as there is no reference to Jerusalem in the so-called New Jerusalem Scroll, there appears to be limited reference to a Davidic messiah in the sectarian Qumran-Essene scrolls. That the references to a Davidic messiah are limited, however, has not prevented most scholars from falling back on the assumption that David *was* the Essenes' role model for a future messiah, even given the fact that there are alternative explanations that have not yet been explored.

## Prince of the Congregation

Most controversial among the sectarian writings about a messiah is the apparent reference in Dead Sea Scroll 4Q285 to the "Prince of the Congregation" as being a suffering and executed messiah, who has been equated with Christ:

> [As it is written in the book of] Isaiah the Prophet, [The thickets of the forest] will be cut [down with an ax and Lebanon by a majestic one will f]all. And there shall come forth a shoot from the stump of Jesse [ . . . ] the branch of David and they will enter into judgment with [ . . . ] and the Prince of the Congregation. The Br[anch of David] will kill him [ . . . by strok]es and by wounds. And a priest [of renown (?)] will command [ . . . the s]lai[n] of the Kitti[m . . . ]. (4Q285, fragment 5)

In the opinion of Geza Vermes,[13] the reference here is not to be related to a contemporary Jesus but is a reference back to the messiah of Isaiah:[14]

> And he shall cut down the thickets of the forest with iron, and Lebanon shall fall by a mighty one. (10:34)

> And in that day there shall be a root of Jesse [the father of King David, who lived in Bethlehem], which shall stand for an ensign of the people; to it shall the Gentiles seek; and his rest shall be glorious. (11:10)

This explanation, it seems to me, deals with only half the picture; nor are many other obvious questions even broached by a great number of today's scholars, from Jean Starcky (member of the École Biblique translation team) in 1963 to Jean Duhaime (Faculté de Théologie, University of Montreal) in 1997, who have studied and written on the position.[15] Clearly the Qumran Essenes were not writing about a contemporary experience of Jesus, but were looking back to a royal messiah and a priestly messiah whose descendants would bring the word of God not just to the elite few but also to the wider community. Any full explanation of this Dead Sea Scrolls fragment and other references in the Dead Sea Scrolls to messiahs needs to explain where these ideas of messianic figures originated, and to answer the following questions:

1. Who were the royal and priestly messianic figures the Qumran Essenes and Isaiah were referring to?
2. Why were royal and priestly messianic figures alternatively referred to as "the Scepter" and "the Star"?
3. Why was the priestly messianic figure, often referred to as "Prince of the Congregation," designated a hereditary prince in his own right?
4. Why were there constant associations of the messiahs to light and the stretching out of hands for a bread offering?
5. Why did Isaiah, who lived circa 740 B.C.E., prophesy that the tasks that God would perform at the time of the reconstituted messiah would include recovery of remnants of his people from Egypt and Cush (Nubia)?
6. Why would the new messiah want to encompass a wider audience of "the people" rather than just the special few?
7. Why was the return of the messiah(s) always linked to an apocalyptic age that would herald the reestablishment of the kingdom of God, and what triggered these eschatological ideas?
8. Why had the figure of the royal messiah suffered and been killed?

As I have proposed in my previous book, *The Mystery of the Copper Scroll of Qumran*,[16] in which I make a firm connection between the Qumran Essenes and Pharaoh Akhenaten of Egypt, there is an explanation forthcoming that fulfills *all* the criteria needed to answer these questions—namely, from within the messianic characteristics of Pharaoh-King

Akhenaten and his high priest, Meryra, who was also a hereditary prince. As Joseph Fitzmyer, professor emeritus at Catholic University in Washington, notes: "It is a surprise to see a priestly figure become part of the Qumran community's messianic expectations, because there is little in the Hebrew Scriptures itself about a future 'priest.'" He finds no reasonable explanation for this phenomenon.[17]

In fact, I believe both the name of Akhenaten, preserved in the text of the Copper Scroll, and a variation on the name Meryra, Merveyre, as a title for a leader of the Qumran community, reflect this priestly connection, among many other indicators. Another clear example is indicated by the community's War Scroll: "And on the banner of Merari they shall write . . . God's offerings [and the name of the Prince of Merari]" (4QM).

If, as I deduce, the origins of monotheistic Judaism were Egyptian, and more specifically involved a blending of intellectual belief at a specific period in Egypt's history between Pharaoh Akhenaten and the biblical patriarch Jacob, through the intermediary of Joseph,* then a strain of priestly heirs—such as the Qumran Essenes—might well have preserved original knowledge and secrets of this period. They certainly kept the secret name of Akhenaten within their texts, and many allusions to Egyptian religious experience are documented in my book and by others.

That persecution of the ancestors of the Essene sect dated back to well before 1200 B.C.E. is attested to by a pseudepigraphic Psalm of Joshua appended to, and contiguous with, a description of the messiahs of the future.[18] This psalm is about the Joshua who succeeded Moses as leader of the Hebrews, circa 1200 B.C.E., before Israel had a king or a high priest, or a city, and yet this fragmentary Dead Sea Scrolls text talks in the past tense of events related to a king and to a high priest who are connected with persecutors of the sect and the destruction of a holy city—"cursèd be men who rebuild this City."[19]

## A Line of Priests

How could this be? There was as yet no king nor high priest nor city in Israel. The Book of Jubilees, which emanated from the Essenes, makes it

---

*Jacob's favorite son, and as Pharaoh's vizier, the most powerful administrator in Egypt.

quite clear that the patriarch Jacob passed his teachings on down through the line of Levi, the Levitical priests.[20] Yet these hereditary priests were not, according to the Hebrew Scriptures, appointed as priests until the time of Aaron several hundred years later. At the time of Jacob, there was no Israelite sanctuary or temple of worship, and yet the Dead Sea Scrolls repeatedly insist that priests were appointed at the time of Jacob.

The only explanation that makes sense is that there *were* hereditary priests[21] in Jacob's time, that there *was* a place of worship, and that it was almost certainly the Great Temple at Akhetaten.

## So on Whom Were the Individual Qumran Messiahs Modeled?

All the references to two messiahs can therefore, in my view, be explained as follows:

1. The original two messianic figures whose return was fervently awaited by the Essenes were King Akhenaten and the high priest of his holy temple, Meryra.
2. The royal and priestly messianic figures were alternatively referred to as "the Scepter" and "the Star" because the sign of the royal office of Pharaoh or King Akhenaten was a scepter. The invisible God worshipped by Pharaoh Akhenaten and his high priest in many inscriptional representations found at Amarna in Egypt was portrayed as "the Aten," a sun disk—the brightest symbol of light known to humankind.

    In the Cairo-Damascus document and the related Dead Sea Scrolls fragments from Cave 4 at Qumran, there is the clearest possible reference to a Star Messiah who equates to the messianic interpreter of the Law and Prince of the Congregation—a messiah who relates to the time of Jacob, whom I date as a contemporary of Akhenaten: "A star shall come out of Jacob and a scepter shall rise out of Israel."[22] This phrase also occurs in the Book of Numbers (24:17), but in the Damascus document (Cairo-Damascus version) the star, as the interpreter of the Law, is used to describe a figure who comes to Damascus. What the significance of this person's journey might be will be discussed later, but it has been suggested that when the Teacher of Righteousness fled into exile, another of his followers fled in a different direction—to Damascus.[23]

Nor could there be a more definitive confirmation, in the Cairo-Damascus texts, of the messiah's connection to Akhenaten and Egypt. The first task specified in the Cairo-Damascus documents for the Star Messiah to perform is not, as we would expect, to restore the Temple, revive the dead, cure the sick, bring peace to the world, attend to problems in Judaea, or get rid of the Romans. The first task is to attend to problems in Egypt—to destroy Seth: "And when he comes he shall smite all the children of Seth."[24] Any illusion that we are talking about anything other than an Egyptian-related Seth is destroyed by a Dead Sea Scroll relating to Ezekiel, where we find:

> And I will slay the wicked in Memphis and I will bring my sons out of Memphis and turn favorably towards their remnant. (4Q386)

Why Seth? Why Memphis? For conventional thinking, the only place to turn to is Seth of the Hebrew Scriptures, an obscure third son of Adam. This assumption is obviously absurd, and most scholars avoid confronting the issue, or conclude that the text is referring to some inexplicable supernatural force. The real target can be none other than the traditional enemy of Akhenaten's monotheism, the fearsome, most powerful Egyptian god of chaos and evil—Seth.[25] Memphis was the administrative hub during the reign of Akhenaten and a center of theology. It was there that the first temple to Aten was built; the city reverted to paganism after his death. Once again there is a preoccupation with settling old scores in Egypt, not in Israel.

3. The priestly messianic figure was designated a hereditary prince in his own right because the high priest Meryra was also a prince by birth,[26] just as he is referred to in the Dead Sea Scrolls.

Incidentally, the ritual clothing of the high priest Meryra can be seen on a *shabti* (funerary) figurine kept in the Metropolitan Museum in New York (an illustration of which appeared in *The Mystery of the Copper Scroll of Qumran*, chapter 10, note 14).

The robes and accoutrements of this figure are strikingly similar to descriptions of the robes worn by the high priest in the Temple of Jerusalem. The two objects Meryra holds are what can only be the Urim and Thummim (objects used as casting lots when decisions of state were in question). Nor can it be ignored that the shabti is made from blue serpentine (a translucent mineral containing hydrated magnesium silicates), just as the descriptions in Exodus and Leviticus, from the Hebrew Scriptures, required: "And thou shalt make the robe of the ephod all of the Blue" (Exod. 29:31). (An ephod was a ceremonial outfit worn by the high priest.)

4. The imagery of a messiah who "will extend his hands to the bread offering," described in the Messianic Rule of the Dead Sea Scrolls, is unmistakably reminiscent of the extended hands of Pharaoh Akhenaten offering bread to the Aten. This pictorial gesture appears as a dominant theme in many reliefs found at Akhenaten's holy city, Akhetaten (modern Amarna), in Egypt, as does the thematic vision of the extending hands of the Aten giving light, life, and sustenance in return.

In the Manual of Discipline (oftentimes called the Community Rule), there is a long description of a last meal before the messiah comes. This description of an Essene ritual meal attended by ten men and presided over by a messiah is in manner and style very reminiscent of the Last Supper description in the Christian Scriptures (Matthew, chapter 26; Mark, chapter 14; Luke, chapter 22; 1 Corinthians, chapter 11):

> Fo[r he shall] bless the first [portion] of the bread and the wi[ne and shall ext[end] his hand to the bread first. Afterwa[rds,] the messiah of Israel [shall exten]d his hands to the bread. [Afterwards,] all of the congregation of the community [shall ble]ss, ea[ch according to] his importance.[27]

As pointed out by Charles Robert Morgan in his book *Gate of Hope*,[28] Jesus's Last Supper bears almost no resemblance to a traditional Passover meal. There is no family environment with the mother of the household present, nor any traditional blessings; and of course only unleavened bread is allowed during Passover. The messiah of the Qumran banquet is not, in my view, Jesus, as some sensationalists would have it, but a picture of a messiah associated with the period of Akhenaten. The phrase "extend his hand to the bread first," found in the Qumran text, is a vivid iconography of the inscriptions that can be seen today at Amarna, Akhenaten's holy city. These show the rays of Aten tipped with outstretched hands receiving the bread and wine offering from the extended hand of the offerer, kept on the table in front of the altar of the Aten.

Crucially, the table before the altar in the Tabernacle of the Israelites was specified to contain twelve cakes of bread (Lev. 24:5–6), and in the so-called New Jerusalem Dead Sea Scroll the twelve loaves are to be in two rows of six, *just as they are seen on the offering table in front of the altar of the Great Temple at Akhetaten.* Examples of this procedure, where the bread is placed foremost on top of jars of wine, can be seen in the Tombs of Apy and Panehesy at Amarna.[29]

5. After the demise of Pharaoh Akhenaten, his followers dispersed to places of safety in Egypt, some probably traveling as far south as Elephantine Island (Isaiah's Cush), where a Hebrew-style temple, dating back at least to 800 B.C.E., has been discovered. Others, the ancestors of the Falasha, may well have later traveled farther south to settle at Lake Tana in Ethiopia. Here was a reason for the returning messiahs to recover the remnants of Jacob from Egypt and Ethiopia.

6. A central feature of Pharaoh Akhenaten's new monotheism was worship centered at his newly built Great Temple on the Nile at Akhetaten, which catered to and was opened up to the common people.

7. The only great catastrophe that has been cited to explain the apocalyptic outlook central to the Qumran-Essenes' philosophy and associated with the coming of the messiah(s) was the destruction of the First Temple in Jerusalem by the Babylonians in 586 B.C.E. Writing two centuries earlier, however, Isaiah was already talking in terms of an apocalyptic event, and particularly relating

it to Egypt (Isa. 19). Perhaps the catastrophic event Isaiah was writing about and the event the Qumran Essenes recalled was the destruction of another temple—the Great Temple of Akhenaten and his holy city—and Akhenaten's unnatural death.

It is also quite apparent from a number of the Dead Sea Scrolls (4MMT, Temple Scroll, the so-called New Jerusalem Scroll) that the Temples in Jerusalem, including the First Temple, were not constructed according to the Mosaic Law, as the Qumran Essenes saw it, and they would have had little interest in seeing them restored to anything other than their own design formula.

8. The circumstances of Pharaoh Akhenaten's death are not certain, but he died very suddenly, and his idolatrous priestly enemies, probably led by his own chancellor, Ay, moved rapidly to destroy his new capital city and reinstate Thebes and Memphis as the centers of an idolatrous Egyptian religion. (It is also possible that Smenkhkara, who assumed a transient pharaohship after Akhenaten, and who might also have been his brother, was the villain in the piece.) Ay, shortly after assuming control of Egypt, almost certainly had Tutankhamun, the rightful heir to the throne, murdered, along with his wife, Ankhesenpaten—Akhenaten's daughter—and then proclaimed himself pharaoh of all Egypt.

Not only do the circumstances of Akhenaten's reign fit most of the descriptions from the Hebrew Scriptures and the Dead Sea Scrolls relating to the messiah(s); many other perplexing scrolls from the collection, not least of which is the Copper Scroll, can readily be explained in terms of the same Amarna setting. (Several of these anomalous scrolls are discussed elsewhere in this book.)

## The Messiah(s) Awaited by the Rest of the Jewish Population

The generalized Jewish view of the awaited messiah can be understood in terms of the messianic age that the messiah would bring about. The End Days eschatology has essentially two elements: one of material restoration and one of a spiritual utopia.[30] The Jewish concepts differ from Christian ideas of redemption in that they involve the visible world, whereas

Christianity envisages a spiritual and personal redemption reflected in the soul.

## Restoration

The Jewish vision of restoration sees a messiah who would vanquish Israel's enemies, free its people, and rebuild the lost Temple. This urge for restoration is evident long before the destruction of the Second Temple by the Romans and can be seen in the writings of the Hebrew Scriptures seers Enoch[31] probably written in the second century B.C.E. but alluding to far earlier centuries), Amos and Hosea (c. 800 B.C.E.), Isaiah (c. 750 B.C.E.), and Habakkuk and Ezekiel (c. 600 B.C.E.).[32] It is reinforced in the writings of Ezra (c. 440 B.C.E.) and Daniel (c. 300 B.C.E.) after the destruction of the First Temple in Jerusalem, and reprised in Rabbinic Judaism, post–200 C.E., after the destruction of the Second Temple in 70 C.E.

Because the earliest prophetic yearnings for a restored Temple in the Hebrew Scriptures, seen even more clearly in the Dead Sea Scrolls, predate the destruction of the First Temple in Jerusalem in 586 B.C.E., we must assume that some earlier temple is being referred to, especially as the descriptions of the restored Temple bear little resemblance to what is known of the Jerusalem Temple. This visionary temple, seen in the sources just mentioned, can in my view be only the temple at Akhetaten in Egypt, a subject discussed in more detail in *The Mystery of the Copper Scroll of Qumran.*[33]

Even a casual look at Isaiah, chapters 2, 19, and 20, reveals that when the prophet is talking about "the last days," he is referring to purging the evil not just of Israel but primarily of Egypt. The land that has strayed, he relates, is full of silver and gold, chariots,[34] and idols. This can refer only to a country other than Canaan, notably Egypt, and his examples of restoration are of a people who walk in the light of the Lord, the House of Jacob, as it flourished in Egypt:

> Behold, the Lord rideth upon a swift cloud, and shall come into Egypt: and the idols of Egypt shall be moved at his presence, and the heart of Egypt shall melt in the midst of it. . . .
>
> In that day shall five cities speak the language of Canaan, and swear to the Lord of hosts; [almost certainly referring to Akhetaten]

one shall be called, The city of destruction. In that day shall there be an altar to the Lord [as there was in the time of Jacob in the Temple of Akhetaten] in the midst of the land of Egypt, and a pillar at the border thereof to the Lord [exactly as Akhenaten had set up at the borders of his holy city at Akhetaten, in middle Egypt] . . .

Blessed be Egypt my people, and Assyria the work of my hands, and Israel mine inheritance. (Isa. 19:1, 18–19, 25)

Isaiah is preoccupied with retributions and restorations primarily in Egypt, and Egypt is equated with Israel and Assyria. The thread of belief in the physical restoration of past glories is crystallized in the thinking of the Qumran Essenes, who define a kingly messiah and a priestly messiah—clearly reminiscent of Akhenaten and his high priest, Meryra—for whom they wait. The Qumran Essenes' vision of the Temple in their New Jerusalem and Temple Scrolls, which specifically avoids any mention of the word Jerusalem, is undoubtedly related to that of the biblical prophet Ezekiel, seeing a distantly remembered structure that is clearly identifiable with the Great Temple at Akhetaten.[35] Wrapped up in this vision of restoration comes the dream of rebuilding the holy kingdom and re-creating its holy boundaries.

## Spiritual Utopia

The messiah of the normative Jewish philosopher is a vague figure, full of ambiguity, not identifiable with any single clearly defined personality.[36] Conventionally, unlike Christian or Shiite Muslim messianism, there is no admitted memory of a real person, like Jesus or the Hidden Imam. There is, however, a historical development of the character of the Jewish messiah, or messiahs, who are awaited, and these ideas had to come from somewhere.

That the Messiah of Israel can be identified with the period of Akhenaten and his vizier, Joseph, who I maintain were contemporaries, is reflected in the duality of the messianic figure still seen in Rabbinic Judaism well into the Middle Ages. Here two messiahs are envisaged, one of the Royal House and the other of the House of Joseph.[37]

# ⌒ 9 ⌒

# The Teacher of Righteousness and Expectations of the End Days

Numerous testimonials among the Dead Sea manuscripts leave little doubt that the ancestral Essene community brought with it a deeply embedded apocalyptic outlook that traced its roots back well before the settlement at Qumran around 150 B.C.E.

Many of the resonances to previous times have already been set out in *The Mystery of the Copper Scroll of Qumran,*[1] and it is worth looking at some of them in more detail to clarify the numerous continuous references to Mosaic times, and more particularly to ancient Egypt and the Amarna period, that proliferate in the Dead Sea Scrolls. These have direct implications for how the Qumran Essenes perceived their own evolution and allow identification of a key figure in their rebirth—the Teacher of Righteousness.

What will become patently apparent, I believe, is that the Qumran Essenes not only knew precisely when Pharaoh Akhenaten lived, but dated their own history from the time of his reign. They knew also that the biblical Jacob and Joseph were intimately involved with the Aten monotheism of that epoch.

Along the extended trail of time between Akhetaten—Akhenaten's holy city—and Qumran, I believe the revitalizing force that brought about the settlement of Akhenaten's followers at Qumran was a manifesto their Teacher of Righteousness had developed during the time of his stay in Egypt. It must have comprised existing material, much of which was exclusive to his priestly line, together with his own interpretations of how a New Covenant was to be enacted.

To suggest that the Qumran Essenes were without a protracted pre-history and simply emerged out of conventionally understood Second Temple–period thinking completely fails to explain their unique form of religious beliefs. These included:

- Extreme reverence for light and ritual cleanliness
- Deep-rooted apocalypticism
- Expectation of at least two messiahs
- Continuous references to pre-exilic Egypt
- Rejection of the Jerusalem Temple and a retrospective devotion to the Tabernacle, the place of worship during the time of Moses and the Exodus
- Dualism
- Predestination
- Unique burial practices
- Adherence to a solar calendar

The list could go on. All these characteristics were quite contrary to generally accepted Jewish thinking and practice at the time of the supposed splitting away from the Second Temple fraternity.

## The Teacher of Righteousness

Looking first at the Teacher of Righteousness, the man who the Dead Sea Scrolls aver led the Qumran Essenes into the desert wilderness of Judaea and charged them with a renewed religious spirit, the unanswered question is, Who was he?

Historians are completely at odds with each other as to his true identity. Most see him as some anonymous unknown priest of the Hasmonean period. Many more-conscientious historians admit we just don't know who he was. Whoever he was, we do know, from quite detailed descriptions in the Dead Sea Scrolls, that he must have been a person of considerable standing, charismatic, highly learned, someone who inspired people—in fact, a major priestly figure of his time. Given these attributes, it is even stranger that scholars are so equivocal as to his identity. Such a person could hardly be invisible to history.

The view that the Essenes originated out of a devout group of Second Temple–period Jews, known as the Hassidim (or Hasidim), has long been held by some scholars (for example, Frank Moore Cross, as early as 1961 and again in 1995, and Hartmut Stegemann in 1971[2]). We know little of the Hassidim's beliefs, except that they were strong supporters of Judas Maccabee—which might explain the disenchantment of the Essenes when Jonathan Maccabee was appointed high priest in 152 B.C.E. (if the Essenes are to be equated with the Hassidim). Other scholars such as M. Hengel, in 1974, and John Collins[3] see the Hassidim in an enlarged role, attributing to them the apocalyptic writings of Enoch and Daniel. They are, to these scholars, the "chosen righteous" and "lambs" of the Enochic texts and the "children of Jubilees" of Daniel.

Yet other scholars, in what is known as the Grøningen school, which evolved in the 1990s and was led by Garcia Martinez and A. van der Woude, see the Essenes as quite distinct from the Hassidim, emerging before the Maccabean revolt. Professor Geza Vermes has similarly distanced the Qumran Essenes from the Hassidim. It is a view that most scholars now accept as correct, and one I basically go along with, although of course I maintain the roots of Essenism go much deeper. The aforementioned scholars base part of their reasoning on a passage in the Damascus document that declares:[4]

> He [God] left a remnant to Israel and did not deliver it up to be destroyed. And in the age of wrath, three hundred and ninety years after he had given them into the hand of King Nebuchadnezzar of Babylon, He visited them and He caused a plant root to spring from Israel and Aaron to inherit His land and to prosper on the good things of His earth. And they perceived their iniquity and recognized that they were guilty men, yet for twenty years they were like blind men groping the way.

It is worth looking closely at this quite specific chronology that the Qumran Essenes spell out, because I believe it is of critical significance in the development of the case I have put forward relating the Essenes to Egypt and Akhenaten and the date of the appearance of the Teacher of Righteousness.

The reference to Israel in the Damascus document as having been conquered by King Nebuchadnezzar of Babylon can only refer to the period of the destruction of the First Temple in 586 B.C.E. Three hundred and ninety years after, we are told, in "the age of wrath," the Seleucid rulers of Syria took control of Judaea and commenced a rule of disruptive Hellenization. This would, accordingly, be dated to 196 B.C.E.: 586 − 390 = 196 B.C.E. (See table 4 on page 74 for an overview of the rulers of the region at this time.)

The Damascus document is spot on. The Greek successors of Alexander the Great began their rule of Judaea in 197 B.C.E. The "plant root" is in disarray as to how to deal with the new threat, and twenty years of groping like blind men pass until the Teacher of Righteousness takes command. It is now 177 B.C.E.[5]

So from this quite specific information, can we not deduce who the Teacher of Righteousness was? For many scholars the information is too good to be true, so they choose to ignore it. They are quite happy to accept the twenty years of groping like blind men, but the figure of 390 "cannot be used for precise calculation. It was a round number of prophecy put to Essene use"![6]

In my view there can be no doubt, from other evidence and from this precise chronology given to us by the Qumran Essenes, that the Teacher of Righteousness was Onias IV, known as Jason, the last of a Zadokite line of high priests. We know from other external sources, both Roman and Greek, that Onias IV took office in 176 B.C.E.[7] Again, the Damascus document gets the date exactly right.

Three years later, Onias IV was expelled from office by the "Wicked Priest," who can be none other than Menelaus, who as the new high priest profaned and plundered the Temple.[8] Onias IV and his retinue fled to Egypt, and there he did something quite remarkable. He got permission from Ptolemy VI, in 170 B.C.E., to build a temple at Leontopolis, near Heliopolis[9] (not to be confused with another place called Leontopolis, located farther north in the Delta and now known as Tell el-Muqdam). Onias IV was obviously a powerful persuader and wealthy enough to build a magnificent temple at the center of a settlement near Heliopolis, now known as Tell el-Yahudiya (Mound of the Jews). Building a temple in competition with the Temple at Jerusalem was in itself a surprising thing

**TABLE 4**

**Rulers of Judaea, Samaria, Galilee, and Idumaea, 540–63 BCE**

| BCE | Dynasty | High Priest | Ruler/King | Power |
|---|---|---|---|---|
| 540 | | | | Persians |
| 320 | | | | |
| | Oniads | | | Ptolemaic Greeks (based in Egypt) |
| | | Onias ll | | |
| 198 | | | | |
| | | Onias lll | Antiochus lll | Seleucid Greeks (based in Syria) |
| 187 | | | Seleucus IV | |
| 175 | | Onias IV (Jason/Joshua) | Antiochus lV Epiphanes | |
| 172 | Tobiads | Menelaus* | (Lysias)† | |
| 166 | | | Antiochus V | |
| 163 | | Alcimus | Demetrius l Soter | Maccabean uprisings |
| 159 | | Death of Alcimus | | |
| | | Office vacant | | |
| 152 | | | | |
| | Maccabees | Jonathan Maccabee | Alexander Balas | |
| 145 | | | Antiochus Vl | Jewish rule |
| 143 | | Simon Maccabee | Demetrius ll–Jonathan Maccabee | |
| 135 | | | | |
| 134 | | | Antiochus Vll Sidetes | Seleucids |
| | Hasmoneans | Hyrcanus l | Hyrcanus l | Jewish rule |
| 104 | | Aristobulus l | Aristobulus l | |
| 103 | | Alexander Jannaeus | Alexander Jannaeus | |
| 76 | | Hyrcanus ll | Queen Alexandra | |
| 67 | | | Hyrcanus ll | |
| | | Aristobulus ll | Aristobulus ll | |
| | | Hyrcanus ll (reinstated) | | |
| 63 | | | | Romans |

*From a priestly family, not high priestly, known as Bilga.

†After the death of Antiochus IV, Lysias acted as regent for Antiochus V.

to do, and contrary to Deuteronomic Law. There were hardly any other legitimate buildings of worship at that time, although a number of pre–Temple period synagogues have recently been discovered.[10]

Onias IV did something else that requires explanation. He replaced the menorah (seven-branched lamp stand), specified in biblical texts as an essential holy piece of furniture for the Temple, with a single huge golden orb.[11] Why should he do that? Was the golden orb his attempt at representing the spherical golden sun of the Aten? There seems to be no other sensible answer, nor to my knowledge has anyone ever given any reasonable explanation.

There are other curious links from Leontopolis to Qumran. Solomon H. Steckholl, an archaeologist/journalist we shall meet again in the cemetery of Qumran, excavated extensively at Qumran in the late 1960s. He unearthed a strange stone cube in the ruins of Qumran that was very similar to one found at Leontopolis.[12] He also noted a common practice of burying animal bones in jars: "This practice of burying animal bones was carried out, a unique practice, to say the least, and significant, surely, by its use at the same period by Jewish Communities at both Leontopolis and Qumran, a circumstance which appears not merely one of sheer coincidence."[13]

All these unique associations between Leontopolis and Qumran, knowledge of which has come from historical sources and from the statements found in the Qumran texts, tend to confirm that Onias IV, or his followers, had a presence at both locations, and that he was indeed the Teacher of Righteousness (see table 5 on pages 76–77).

## The Different Strands

The difficulty of the three main conflicting views on the origins of the Essenes, mentioned earlier in this chapter, is readily resolved if these origins are seen as coming from two distinctive priestly strands. There was, I maintain, a continuing legacy of Akhenaten-inspired separatist priestly followers who traced their lineage and knowledge back beyond the Exodus.

Now, with the positive identification of the ex–high priest Onias IV as the Essenes' Teacher of Righteousness, we have the insertion of the George Brooke factor. Professor Brooke posited in my previous book, *The Mystery of the Copper Scroll of Qumran,* that the knowledge the Essenes absorbed about ancient Egypt, and particularly about some of the secrets the Qumran Essenes undoubtedly possessed, may have been derived from an interaction between Onias IV and residual knowledge in Egypt about Akhenaten.

As the Teacher of Righteousness, Onias IV could have reinforced his knowledge and learned more of the secrets of Akhenaten at Heliopolis

## TABLE 5

## Figures proposed for the Teacher of Righteousness and their attributes

| | Ezekiel | Onias IV | Unknown priest | | | Hyrcanus II | Jesus | John the Baptist | James, brother of Jesus |
|---|---|---|---|---|---|---|---|---|---|
| Date of emergence | 6th c. BCE | 172 BCE | c. 160 BCE | 150 BCE | 100 BCE | 67 BCE | c. 30 CE | c. 30 CE | c. 33 CE |
| High priest | X | √ | X | X | X | √ | X | X | X |
| Zadokite lineage | X | √ | ? | ? | ? | X | X | X | X |
| Charismatic leader | √ | √ | ? | ? | ? | ? | √ | √ | √ |
| Group of followers | √ | √ | ? | ? | ? | ? | √ | √ | √ |
| Flees into exile | √ | √ | ? | ? | X | √ | X | X | X |
| Suitable candidate for Wicked Priest | X | √ | √ | √ | √ | √ | √ | √ | √ |
| Connection to Egypt | X | √ | ? | ? | X | X | X | X | X |
| Proposer Eisenman[o] | Ben-Zion, Wacholder[a] | Feather[b] | Murphy, O'Connor[c], Charlesworth[d] | Milik[e], Vermes[f], Cross[g], Schiffman[h], de Vaux[i], Riesner[j] | Wise[k] | Doudna[l] | Teicher[m] | Thiering[n] | |

a. *The Dead Sea Scrolls Fifty Years After Their Discovery* (International Congress, Jerusalem, July 20–25, 1997).

b. Robert Feather, *The Mystery of the Copper Scroll of Qumran* (Inner Traditions, 2003).

c. J. Murphy O'Connor, "Paul and Qumran, Studies in New Testament Exegesis." Chicago: Priory Press, 1968.

d. James H. Charlesworth, ed., *Jesus and the Dead Sea Scrolls* (Doubleday, 1992). Charlesworth notes that J. Carmignac equates the Teacher of Righteousness with Judas the Essene ("Qui était le docteur de Justice?," *Revue de Qumran* 10, 1980).

e. J. T. Milik, *Ten Years of Discovery in the Wilderness of Judaea* (SCM, 1959). In his analysis of the Habakkuk commentary scroll from Qumran, Milik notes that the Hebrew term *masal* could not refer to a Jewish king, and therefore "The Wicked Priest must be a predecessor of Aristobulus I" (104–3 BCE).

f. Geza Vermes, *The Complete Dead Sea Scrolls in English* (Allen Lane/Penguin, 1997). Professor Vermes uses as one of his arguments the fact that his choice of the Teacher of Righteousness was opposed to Onias IV because he did not follow him to Egypt. If my contention is correct, he would have been following himself! The interactive contemporary opponent of the Teacher of Righteousness is suggested as Jonathan, son of Mattathias, the high priest from 152 to 142 BCE (notably by Vermes and J. T. Milik); Jonathan's brother Simon, who led the country between 142 and 135 BCE; and Alexander Jannaeus, king of Judaea from 102 to 76 BCE. One of the objections to the more favored theory of Vermes and Milik is that it would imply that the Teacher of

Righteousness was the high priest from 159 to 152 BCE, whereas the evidence from 4QMMT, a composition considered to be by the Teacher of Righteousness, testifies that a significant part of Judaea was not following either the author or the addressee of this composition 4QMMT. (See John Kampen and Moshe J. Bernstein, *Reading 4QMMT: New Perspective on Qumran Law and History,* Society of Biblical Literature Symposium Series, Scholars Press, 1996, especially *4QMMT and the History of the Hasmonean Period,* by Hanan Eshel, Bar-Ilan University, Ramat Gan, Israel).

g. Frank Moore Cross, *The Ancient Library of Qumran* (Anchor Books, 1961; Sheffield Academic, 1995). Cross sees the Teacher of Righteousness as being an anonymous Zadokite priest with Hassidic sympathies. He dismisses the 390 years after 586 BCE as the date for his arrival as spelled out in the Damascus documents, apparently because it was a round number!

h. L. H. Schiffman, *Reclaiming the Dead Sea Scrolls* (Doubleday, 1995).

i. Roland de Vaux, *Archaeology and the Dead Sea Scrolls* (Oxford, 1973).

J. Rainer Riesner, *Jesus, the Primitive Community, and the Essene Quarter of Jerusalem;* James H. Charlesworth, ed., *Jesus and the Dead Sea Scrolls* (Doubleday, 1992).

k. Michael O. Wise, "Dating the Teacher of Righteousness and the Floruit of His Movement," *Journal of Biblical Literature* 122(1), 2003. Michael Wise doubts that the Essenes knew with any accuracy how long before the arrival of the Teacher of Righteousness the Temple was destroyed, or even when the Persian rule ended, whereas from their own writings and Maccabees I, written in the same period of the Essenes, it is clear they knew precisely the length of the reign of Alexander the Great and a close timing for the end of Persian rule.

l. Greg Doudna, *Orion* 17, November 2001, www.mail-archive.com/orion.

m. J. Teicher, "The Dead Sea Scrolls," *Journal of Jewish Studies,* 1957.

n. Barbara Thiering, *Jesus the Man: A New Interpretation from the Dead Sea Scrolls* (Doubleday, 1992).

o. Robert Eisenman, *The Dead Sea Scrolls and the First Christians* (Element, 1996).

itself, the center of religious learning in Egypt and at one time a place where Atenism flourished. I have previously suggested that a submerged belief in Akhenaten's monotheism persisted here, as well as at Elephantine Island.[14] Or Onias's knowledge could have come through contact with the Therapeutae, a sect closely related to the Essenes that was based near Alexandria and in the Valley of Natrun, in the Delta region of Egypt. In this respect the influence of an Egyptian line of Onias priests related to the Boethians cannot be ignored.[15]

On his return to Judaea, the Teacher of Righteousness was therefore armed with a new depth of understanding to add to the store of secret knowledge available to him through the line of separatist priests. He then began the task of bringing his adherents back to the ancient traditions of the Mosaic Law and directing them toward a place where they could practice and develop the religious path he advocated.

If I am correct in identifying Onias IV as the Teacher of Righteousness, the reverse side of the coin implies that his contemporary was Menelaus, the Wicked Priest who ousted him and took his place as high priest. If, therefore, the information we have from the scrolls about the Wicked

Priest fits with the historical information, we would have a virtually watertight case for concluding they are one and the same person. There are three highly cohesive references in the Dead Sea Scrolls to the Wicked Priest and his relationship to the Teacher of Righteousness that fit the situation of Onias IV precisely and confirm that Onias IV must have been the Teacher of Righteousness and that the Wicked Priest must have been Menelaus, his contemporary. The sectarian text of Habakkuk declares that the Wicked Priest:[16]

- Originally aspired to a "trustworthy name," but abused his position
- Pursued the Teacher of Righteousness "in his place of exile" at a time when he was occupied with a religious ceremony
- Met a horrible demise at the hand of his enemies (in a manner of almost justified schadenfreude for his transgressions against the Teacher of Righteousness)

Josephus records that Menelaus assumed the role of high priest after deposing Onias IV, and then proceeded to abuse his position. If Menelaus was indeed the Wicked Priest, what more previous "trustworthy name" could he have held than that of high priest?

Pursuing the Teacher of Righteousness "in his place of exile" implies that the Wicked Priest went to an establishment outside Judaea. The Teacher of Righteousness's abode in Egypt was certainly outside his homeland, and he must have been worshipping in the temple he built at Leontopolis when confronted and attacked by the Wicked Priest and his retinue. If Onias IV and his followers were preoccupied with a religious festival (probably the Day of Atonement) and were caught unawares, why was Menelaus not observing the same festival?

The Qumran Essenes' corroborated practice of observing festivals at times different from those followed at the Temple in Jerusalem explains the discrepancy. Onias IV, as the precursor and founder of the Qumran-Essene movement, was following a solar calendar, quite different from that of normative Judaism, and a holy festival date for him would have had no significance for Menelaus, who would have been free to travel and seek out his enemy. This action attests again to Onias IV being the founder of the nonconformist Qumran-Essene movement.

The third fact we learn from the Dead Sea Scrolls is that the Wicked Priest died an unnatural death. Menelaus was, according to historical record, murdered.[17] Everything fits. The dates, characteristics, and movements of the two main contenders, Onias IV and Menelaus, as spelled out in Dead Sea Scrolls texts, conform to external historical records. There are, of course, arguments both direct and indirect against Onias IV being the Teacher of Righteousness, but they as yet do not take into account the larger picture I have painted for the *pro* case.

## Direct Arguments against Onias IV

The direct problem cited by scholars relates to part of the description of Onias IV in 1 and 2 Maccabees[18] and in Josephus as being a Hellenizing high priest. These descriptions, especially in 1 Maccabees, portray Jason, as he was known (or more correctly Joshua, as his Hebrew name is recorded), as promoting Greek influences and therefore possibly betraying his ancient ancestry.

Hellenizing influences in themselves do not, however, conflict with the possibility of Jason being the Teacher of Righteousness. On the contrary, they reinforce the idea. It may well be that this description of the Teacher of Righteousness by the authors of the Maccabean books merely reflected the infatuation of a great thinker who would inevitably have been attracted to Greek ideas, particularly Pythagorean ones.

There are indeed some similarities between the behavior advocated by this movement[19] and that of the Essene community that was later to settle at Qumran under the guidance of the Teacher of Righteousness. In fact, it is quite apparent that Jason obtained some of his ideas from these Greek sources. Like the community of mystics founded by Pythagoras, the community at Qumran attached great importance to common meals, sharing of material and intellectual property, a scientific approach to religious-related healing, strict community rules (including binding their adherents with strange oaths), ritual purity, moral asceticism, and a belief in immortality and the reincarnation of the soul.

The Books of Maccabees were undoubtedly written with a strong pro-Hasmonean slant, and when Onias IV became an enemy of their movement, fleeing to Egypt and the protection of a feared Ptolemaic king, his role in the office of high priest inevitably came under attack. His building a competitor temple at Leontopolis in Egypt added to the need for his denigration: "To keep you from the false worship of Onias IV's Temple at Leontopolis" (2 Macc. 1:1–10).

Not surprisingly, if, as I deduce, Onias IV was the Teacher of Righteousness, the Essenes would have had little regard for the hostile content of the Books of Maccabees, and no copies of them were found at Qumran—although examples of texts from virtually every other book of the Hebrew Scriptures and apocrypha were present. Not one single fragment of the Books of Maccabees has been found at Qumran; the Essenes would hardly want to keep in their possession books that were critical of their founder. As far as I am aware, no one has previously put forward this explanation for the rather surprising omission in the Qumran-Essene collection.[20]

Later, even Josephus discounted the Maccabean version of Onias IV's behavior. (The books were subsequently excluded from the Hebrew canon, although they do appear in the Catholic canon.[21])

## Indirect Arguments against Onias IV

For many scholars, Onias IV is not the favored choice for the Teacher of Righteousness, and he has few supporters.

When the indirect arguments, which relate to the alternative figures suggested for the Teacher of Righteousness, are examined in detail, it becomes apparent that Onias IV is the most likely—if not the only—candidate. A convenient way of looking at the alternative possibilities is to list the known attributes of the Teacher of Righteousness, as indicated in the Dead Sea Scrolls, against the historical figures that have been suggested for his identification.

The idea that the Teacher of Righteousness was some anonymous person insignificant to history just does not hold water. Professor Charlesworth, of Princeton University, refers to him as "a brilliant, highly educated and dedicated Jewish priest of the most prestigious lineage,"[22] but admits he does not know his identity. For Helmut Stegemann, professor of Christian Scriptures studies at the University of Göttingen, Germany, the Teacher of Righteousness was "perhaps once an officiating high priest." Even in the Dead Sea Scrolls' Thanksgiving Hymn, whose composition is generally ascribed to the Teacher of Righteousness, we find the author perceiving himself as the rejected high priest (a work that, by the way, is replete with allusions to the river Nile).[23]

The characteristic of the Teacher of Righteousness as a onetime high priest is also suggested by his Hebrew sobriquet in the Dead Sea Scrolls—Mare Hazeddek, a traditional title applied only to the Temple high priest.

As previously mentioned, one of the most telling arguments that the high priest Onias IV was the Teacher of Righteousness involves his fleeing his homeland. None of the other candidates, except Ezekiel, fits this shoe, and Ezekiel's feet are too big on other grounds. The requirement for the Teacher of Righteousness to flee his homeland is deduced from the Psalms of Thanksgiving found at Qumran, and more precisely a psalm known as D. This is written in the first person singular and is attributed to the Teacher of Righteousness himself:[24]

> For [I] was an object of scorn to them and they did not esteem me when Thou wast strengthened in me! For I was driven from my country, as the bird from the nest.

Later in the same hymn, where the author castigates his enemies, there is yet another allusion to Egypt:

> But as for them, they are the wretched, and they form thoughts of Møth-Belial, and they seek thee with a double heart.[25]

Møth here must surely be the Egyptian vulture goddess, Muth, who terrorizes the people of the earth, set in phraseology that is typically ancient Egyptian.[26] Add to the conclusion of this analysis the date spelled out in the Damascus document for the death of the Teacher of Righteousness as 110 B.C.E., and it becomes a racing certainty that the high priest Onias IV was the Teacher of Righteousness.

# ~ 10 ~

# Ethereal Melchizedek— and Kabbalah

Just as the Teacher of Righteousness was a key figure to the Qumran Essenes, so was another figure who is likewise shrouded in mystery, Melchizedek. He is another star in the cast of actors performing opposite the Qumran messiahs who has always presented an insurmountable problem for theologians. This prima donna is often referred to as a human/divine figure, but despite intense study, he has not been identified.[1] Our reasons for investigating this character, as well as the Teacher of Righteousness in the previous chapter, will become abundantly clear when we come to examine the role of Jesus and the early Jesus movement.

The information we have about Melchizedek from the Hebrew Scriptures, and from numerous Dead Sea Scrolls references,[2] is so detailed that it is curious he remains such a mystery. Those who wrote about him certainly had an image in mind of some biblical/historical character closely related to God.

For the Qumran Essenes, the messiah embodied this as yet unidentified figure of Melchizedek—the priest of God Most High (11Q Melch., Song of the Sabbath Sacrifice).

And even though Jesus's line of descent is claimed through the Davidic kings, he is also seen as Jesus the heavenly high priest. In fact, Jesus subsumes into his person all three types of messiahs awaited by the Qumran Essenes—one kingly, one priestly, and one prophet like Moses—as well as the mantle of Melchizedek.

While the name Melchizedek appears early in the Hebrew Scriptures (Gen. 14:18–20) as a king whom Abram (Abraham) encounters, for the Qumran community he is recast as a human/divine figure who will lead the "sons of light" in the final eschatological battle and act in a priestly manner to expiate the sins of his followers. The expiation that Melchizedek, the divine mediator, is to bring about is related to the Day of Atonement.

To identify the Melchizedek of Qumran, we need to look at the attributes associated with this figure in the biblical and Qumran texts to see whether it becomes clear to whom they refer. Melchizedek is variously described as:

1. An angel identified with the divine name; an "angel of the Lord"[3]
2. A human figure as "Son of God"
3. A human form who sits on a divine throne
4. A human figure who is mystically elevated to a divine status through seven heavens, having alternative names of Michael, Metatron, Adoil, Eremiel, Wazir, "the son of man"
5. A visionary figure seen by Moses as sitting on a divine throne
6. An angelic human who carries within him "the name of God"
7. Being associated with a dazzling, glorious heavenly chariot (Hebrew, Merkabah)
8. Leading the "sons of light" in the final eschatological battle against the forces of evil, and in doing so bringing expiation for the sins of humanity and a Day of Atonement

Melchizedek as a Hebrew title means "king priest" or "righteous king." It carries the sense of one person who combines the roles of king and high priest, but no one in conventional scholarship has been able to explain the origins of this mysterious being, despite intense speculation.

If we go through the above-listed attributes of Melchizedek, it can readily be seen how they relate to Egypt and, more specifically, to the Amarna period (circa 1349–1332 B.C.E.). These roles are precisely embodied in King Akhenaten in conjunction with his high priest, Meryra. Together they comfortably fulfill all the characteristics of the "angel of the Lord." Melchizedek then is surely the memory of a combined kingly/priestly union of King Akhenaten and his high priest, Meryra:

1–3. Akhenaten, in the tradition of the pharaohs, was the earthly representative of the High God. As such he at times became indistinguishable from the High God, and even for students of Egyptology it is not always clear who was being worshipped by the people. Akhenaten perceived himself as God's representative on earth, and although he was a "son of man," he had a special privilege of also being the "Son of God." His eventual place was to be beside God on a throne.

4. Seven heavenly stages are a characteristic representation in ancient Egyptian mythology of the route to eternal heaven. Understanding the choice of all these names that seem to derive from Melchizedek is not easy, however, and I have no full explanation. There could be an association between the rabbinic name Metatron and Aton. The name of God as Adon, the Lord, can readily be equated to Aton, and there may be a linkage to the name Adoil or Ado-El, as it could be pronounced.[4] Wazir might be equatable with the Egyptian name for the vizier, the right-hand man of Pharaoh, who, I maintain, was Joseph at the time of Akhenaten. Additionally, a number of names found in the Merkabah literature adopt the suffix *–on*.[5]

5. To describe the visionary figure that Moses sees, in *Ezekiel the Tragedian*,[6] Barnard College Professor of Religion Alan F. Segal analyzes a descriptive word having the double sense of "a venerable man" and "a man of light." What better way to speak of Akhenaten, a man of greatness whose symbol of God was light? For the royal figure that Moses sees to be a king of Israel, however, does not make any sense, because even the first king of Israel, King Saul, came long after Moses. The Nag Hammadi text *Ezekiel the Tragedian* must have been referring to a throned figure who preceded Moses, and that could only be a king of Egypt. The Nag Hammadi text goes on to speak of the throned figure handing Moses a scepter and placing a diadem on his head—both prime motifs of Egyptian kings. That the central figures of Judaism and Christianity, Moses and Jesus, could take on this mantle of equivalence to the "angel of the Lord" is apparently seen by the authors of these texts as essential for both the Hebrews and followers of Jesus.

6. The hieroglyph cartouche of the name Akhenaten contains within it the hieroglyph for the name of God, Aten—a semicircle over a

rippling line over an open circle preceded (or followed) by a feath-erlike symbol.[7] The modern reading of Amenhotep IV—the enthronement name the pharaoh had before he changed it to Akhenaten—did not carry the name of a god, but when he changed it it did carry within it the name of God—Akhen*Aten.*

7. The great similarity between the description of the heavenly char-iot in Dead Sea Scrolls that were apparently unique to the Essenes and those actually found in the tomb of Tutankhamun and in reliefs at Amarna cannot be ignored (see chapters 36 and 38). The pictorial representation at Amarna of Pharaoh Akhenaten riding his heavenly chariot is particularly colorful and dramatic and is unique to Amarna. No early royal chariots have ever been found in Israel, yet chariot (Merkabah) experience features strongly in Jewish and Christian mystic tradition.[8]

8. That the adjectival Hebrew word for "atonement" *(atonali)* has within it the root sound *aton,* an alternative pronunciation of Aten, can be no coincidence, nor perhaps now even a surprise. That the English word also carries the same root sound is more surprising. At Akhetaten, the time of atonement was the day when Akhenaten's return, as the divine mediator, would celebrate the name of God, whom he called Aton. In Exodus 23 the angel of the Lord embodies and carries the name of God as the Tetragram-maton (four-letter representation of the name of God).

As if to verify the contention that Melchizedek incorporated the con-cept of Akhenaten's high priest, Meryra, new light on the Christian Scriptures' Epistle to the Hebrews has been shed by the fragmentary first-century-B.C.E. document found in Cave 11 at Qumran, known as the Heavenly Prince Melchizedek (11Q Melch.). The description in Hebrews depicting Christ as the "Son of God" and "without beginning of days or end of life," as "priest according to the order of Melchizedek," now makes sense as reflecting the same image of Melchizedek portrayed by the sectarian Dead Sea Scroll.

This interpretative understanding was taken still further in discussion at a recent international conference on the Dead Sea Scrolls at the Uni-versity of St. Andrews in Scotland. A paper by Margaret Barker published in the *Scottish Journal of Theology*[9] maintains that Jesus knew of and understood Melchizedek; that he may have patterned his life on the Qumranic conception of Melchizedek; and that his earliest followers built on that understanding. In Epistle to the Hebrews, Jesus is "a priest forever, according to the order of Melchizedek" (5:6).

That this is the same high priestly figure of the Qumran Essenes is underlined by a further reference to him as the superior priest. Suggestions that this priest is Aaron, or a Zadok of his lineage, is excluded by the insistence that Jesus, like Melchizedek, is in the Greek wording *agenealogetos*, "without a genealogy." As Professor Joseph Fitzmyer, of the Catholic University of America, points out, "Every priestly family was supposed to be able to trace its lineage from Levi via Aaron and Zadok. Aaron's lineage itself was known from Exodus 6:16–19, but Melchizedek's lineage was unknown."[10]

Analysis of the Melchizedek that Jesus of the Christian Scriptures was to emulate, however, shows that this attribution, as explained by Deborah W. Rooke, of King's College, London, was "not merely of *high* priesthood but of *royal* priesthood."[11] The relationship is spelled out in Hebrews, but although the royal association is assumed to be to King David, scholars are at a loss to explain why there is no specific Davidic categorization for this royal element.[12]

David is not referred to by name in Hebrews. Instead, the king specifically mentioned is the king of Salem, who is related to the patriarchal period of Abraham, long predating the Israelite kings, and a royal figure who had nothing to do with King David.

Once again, there is no Israelite king that conventional scholarship can turn to, and the issue is stuck in the mire of preconceptions. Indeed, it is made crystal clear that the Melchizedek Jesus aspires to emulate is the king of Salem of Genesis:

> And Melchizedek king of Salem brought forth bread and wine: and he was the priest of the most high God. (14:18)

A number of scholars have noted that the Melchizedek of Hebrews can definitely be linked to the Melchizedek in the Qumran scrolls (11Q Melch.), and this character, as discussed above, is certainly not Davidic.[13]

Even if a royal association were tied only to the Genesis descriptions and not also to the Qumranic descriptions, we would have to ask why an apparently pagan king, the king of Salem, should be singled out as a prototype for a divine personage. Not only is he seemingly a pagan king; he is not even a Hebrew![14]

The answer, I suggest, lies partly in the Amarna letters, where Jerusalem is singled out by Akhenaten as his holy city forever.[15] The appellation of King Melchizedek can then clearly be seen as a sacral name combining the royal aspect of King Akhenaten and his high priest, Meryra. The problem of why Abraham and Jesus should want to associate themselves with an apparently pagan figure is thus entirely explained by the fact that Akhenaten and Meryra were not pagan but, together with Jacob and Joseph, the first true monotheists. Thus Abraham acknowledges Melchizedek's God El Elyon (God Most High) as his own God in their encounter in Genesis (14:18–24).

For this high priestly figure to have no ancestors can only mean that he was the first of his class. Once again, the literal evidence points strongly in the direction of Meryra, the first high priest of Akhenaten's new monotheism, who was nevertheless a hereditary Egyptian prince.

As will become dramatically apparent in the explosive archaeological evidence to be disclosed later on, this assumption, certainly in its latter perception, was almost certainly correct.

## Tannaitic and Rabbinic Tradition on Melchizedek

We have already seen some of the Qumranic and biblical references to the figure represented by the name Melchizedek—a figure that no one has been able to identify positively—even though there are numerous pretty precise details in the texts defining his characteristics. It is also already quite apparent that these characteristics are a very good fit with the attributes of Akhenaten, conflated with the qualifications of his high priest, Meryra.

When we come to the post-Qumran period, when the Essenes have been scattered in all directions by the Romans, their upheaval evinces even more hidden details about the persona of Melchizedek. The Tannaitic period followed after the destruction of the Second Temple and lasted about three hundred years, when the rabbis were formulating the content of the Old Testament and the Talmud. In her study *The Secret Doctrine of the Kabbalah,* Leonora Leet, a classics scholar from Yale University, looks at the post–Second Temple period and concludes that a priestly strain of influence emanating from the residual Essenes of Qumran had a profound effect on the formulation of the Talmud and that the secretive elements of this strain also emerged in the form of Kabbalah.[16] She traces this hidden knowledge to a common origin, as with aspects of Pythagorean geometry, to very ancient Egyptian sources. I believe she is basically correct in her deductions and that a central theme of the "divine son" who is also the "son of man" is an inherent part of this mystical teaching.

## Kabbalah

Appropriately, while we are on the subject, it is worthwhile taking a look at the links of Kabbalah to Egypt. These relate only partly to the Egyptian Amarna period. The pagan-derived elements are confirmed by the very alliteration of the word itself—a suggestion I am not aware that anyone

**Ka**                **Ba**                **Akh**

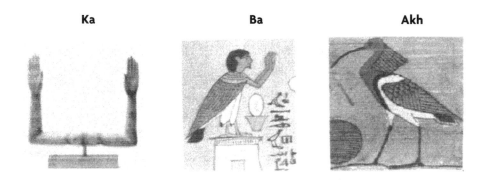

*Fig. 10.1. Hieroglyph signs representing Ka, Ba, and Akh.*

Left: Ka. Hieroglyph sign of two upstretched arms in the form of a square U; independent creative life force coming into existence at the time of a person's birth. It survived after death and needed sustenance.

Middle: Ba. Hieroglyph sign of a stork (or ram), sometimes depicted as a bird; the nonphysical attributes, or personality, that made a human unique.

Right: Akh. Hieroglyph sign of the crested ibis; the form in which the blessed dead inhabited the underworld after the successful union of the Ka and Ba, which then endured for eternity.[17]

has made before. The word can be split into the three elements* of spirituality the ancient Egyptians saw in human beings:

Resurrection was thought to be achieved after a period of three days, the deceased being having negotiated the seven halls and ten gates, each guarded by watchers. One day of the year the gates at Karnak align with the sun. On the day of the person's rebirth, the spirit goes up the channel in the burial chamber toward the north star. There the Ba and Ka join together and become the Akh.

In the Old Kingdom period, 2690 to 2180 B.C.E., the deceased was thought to continue in the afterlife as a star, and the period of seventy days of preparation of the body is probably connected to the phases of the dog star, Sirius, and the importance given to the Sothic Cycle (the length of time taken for Sirius to align exactly to its previous position in the sky; approximately one year in duration). Later the idea of an afterlife was associated with a place described as the Field of Reeds.

The connection to Egyptian ideas of death in Jewish culture can be seen from the many Hebrew words related to death or mourning that utilize the prefix sound *ka* and sometimes incorporate the root sounds of *ba* and *ah*. For example, the mourners' prayer is the Kaddish, to bury is *kaba,* a grave or tomb is *keber,* a gravedigger is a *kaberon,* while the verb "to ascend" has the sound *alah.*

When we look at the chronological development of what became known as Kabbalah, it is evident that in its initial formulation it was concerned mainly with the secret side of the Torah and specifically with the "the works of the chariot" (Hebrew, *ma'aseh merkabah*). After that it became overlaid and underlaid with mysticism until it was eventually codified in a text called the Zohar[18] in thirteenth-century-C.E. Spain.[19] The images of a heavenly chariot and a heavenly throne were also powerful iconographies for the Qumran Essenes, strongly expressed in their writings, and a number of writers have made the connection between Kabbalah and the Essenes. I have set out elsewhere (see chapter 38) an explanation of what I believe was the source of these basic Essenic ideas.

---

*The ancient Egyptians believed that an individual person was made up of five distinct parts: the physical body, Ba, Ka, the name, and the shadow *(shwt),* or sun's shade, which gave protection. All these elements needed to be sustained and protected to ensure enjoyment of the afterlife.

Comparison of the textual descriptions of the Essenes with wall-relief scenes combined with inscriptions from Amarna showing Akhenaten riding his dazzling heavenly chariot, the royal throne bathed in the glow of life, and sustenance descending to the chariot from the Aten above can leave little doubt that these were the source of their inspirations and the aspirations that they engendered.

From an examination of what the Zohar teaches about Kabbalah in relation to life after death, it becomes absolutely clear that the basic ideology is modeled on ancient Egyptian mythology. For the Zohar, after death the three separate parts of the soul experience very similar roles to those of the ancient pharaohs. The *nefesh* (vital soul) of Kabbalah tarries with the decaying body and hovers, like a bird, above the body until the Judgment of the Grave (Hebrew, *din ha-kever*). The *ruah* (spirit) desires the pleasures of the Garden of Eden and vests itself in a garment as a semblance of the body it used to abide in; on Sabbath, new moon, and festival days, it ascends to the Supernal Sphere and then goes back to the Garden. The *neshamah* (innermost soul, or supersoul) ascends to the place from which she emanated, and it is on her account that the Light is lit. Never thereafter does she descend to the earth.

Until such time as the neshamah is joined with the throne, the ruah is unable to be crowned in the lower Garden, and nefesh cannot rest easily. But these find rest when neshamah ascends. If, for some reason, neshamah is prevented from ascending, then when ruah comes to the gate of Eden it finds it closed and cannot enter. It wanders about, lost, while nefesh also flits about from place to place in the world, sees the decaying body, and mourns for it.

So both ruah and nefesh undergo suffering until neshamah is enabled to reach her proper place above. Then each of the first two becomes attached to its rightful place, because all three are then one, composing a unity, embraced in a mystical bond.[20] All the elements of the progress of the Ka-Ba-Akh spirits in ancient Egypt are found in this Kabbalistic version:

KA = nefesh
BA = ruah
AKH = neshamah

When the neshamah successfully ascends, then the Light is lit—equating to the earlier Egyptian belief that the soul becomes a light, or star, in the heavenly sky. In the later Egyptian version, the soul finds everlasting peace in the Garden of Reeds after negotiating the various gates barring access, and when all three components are united. In the Zohar version of events, the gate can be accessed only by the ruah, after the three components are combined into a unity, which then lives forever peacefully in the Garden of Eden.

The name of the mystical ideology of Kabbalah clearly spells out the three sounds of the ancient Egyptian pagan ideology associated with the spiritual side of death—*ka ba l'akh*—where the Hebrew prefix *l'-*, meaning "to," conveys the sense of the Ka and the Ba leading to the Akh.

It is also quite apparent that the fundamental tenets of Kabbalah are a mixture derived from authentic monotheism remembered from the Amarna period sandwiched between cullings from polytheistic mythology that existed in ancient Egypt before and after this period, and further cobbled together with esoteric Gnosticism and Hellenistic influences. In this respect, Kabbalah is a mixture of ideas based largely on Egyptian and Jewish mythology.

If it has any value, in my view, it is only for its insights into the period when monotheism was being enunciated, as it exemplifies the development of ideas associated with that period. It may also serve as encouragement for the individual to seek inner spirituality. This is not to say that there are not sincere devotees of the subject who take it quite seriously and seem to get a lot of benefit out of it.

## Rabbinic Judaism after the Essenes

The extreme devotion of the Essenes to the study of Torah (texts that were to become the Hebrew Bible and apocrypha), to which their own writings as well as those of Philo, Pliny, and Josephus testify, highlights a basic misunderstanding in modern teaching in relation to Rabbinic Judaism. Traditionally Rabbinic Judaism is seen as emanating mainly from Pharisaic Judaism, but this is almost certainly a mistaken assumption. This conclusion is discussed in the notes to this chapter.[21]

## So Who Was Melchizedek?

Returning to the attempt to identify the figure on whom Melchizedek was really based, a look forward to the rabbinic period after the dispersion of the members of the Essene-Qumran sect offers new insight.

The term *son of man* is seen in Ezekiel, Enoch, and Daniel, and also appears in post-Qumran rabbinic writings, where some of the hidden secrets of Qumran come more sharply into focus—almost certainly because they were now no longer in the protective environment of the closed community at Qumran. The ideas of the priestly Essenes are nevertheless highly developed and potent, ideally structured for a religious environment that did not have a central temple. To the Essenes, the previous Jerusalem institution was abhorrent in the extreme anyway, and they had learned to live without access to it.

With the attribution of the title and mantle of Melchizedek to Jesus by early Christianity, rabbinic writers of the early second century C.E. adopted the substitute name Metatron to maintain their distinctive understanding of this mystical figure. What additional characteristics does Metatron have that throw more light on his identity? As has previously been noted, the name Metatron in itself has a curious symbiosis with the title of Aten or Aton. The other characteristics we learn about from rabbinic writings are:

1. The Son, synonymous with Metatron, is associated with the Ancient of Days, a white-haired man who also sits on the throne with him (Dan. 7:9–18). The added problem for commentators is that there was only one throne for both of them to sit on.
2. Both Metatron and the Ancient of Days are associated with a bejeweled throne and a burnished bright chariot.
3. Metatron bears "a crown of glory with raiment of majesty in everlasting light."[22]
4. There is an association to Metatron with the Merkabah chariot.[23]
5. Metatron is also referred to as the Youth, or Prince, who sits on a throne with the Ancient of Days.
6. Metatron is associated with an earthly high priest.
7. The Youth, or Cosmic Child, is described in Hebrew as Arikh Anpin, "Long Face."
8. The Youth has androgynous (both male and female) features.[24]

All these characteristics of Metatron (*né* Melchizedek) fit precisely, and in many instances uniquely, the circumstances of Akhenaten and his reign. Consider these examples:

1. Many Egyptologists argue that Akhenaten ruled in a co-regency with his elderly father, both sitting on the same throne.[25]
2. Both Akhenaten and his father, Amenhotep III, enjoyed the use of a bejeweled throne and burnished bright royal chariots.
3. There is a clear allusion to royalty associated with the light of the sun—the emanation of Aten.
4. Akhenaten is depicted in tomb reliefs as riding a heavenly chariot.
5. Akhenaten came to the throne at a relatively young age under the umbrella of his aging father, whom he soon outshone. He was, of course, a prince in his own right.
6. Akhenaten at times seems to have assumed some of the role of high priest as well as that of monarch. His high priest, Meryra, was second in importance only to him, but may have taken precedence in some religious rituals. He, too, was a prince by birth.
7. Akhenaten is portrayed in a number of reconstructed statues and on wall reliefs as having unusually elongated facial features. This "Long Face" characterization is an innovative defining feature of Amarna-period art and is not seen in any other period of Egyptian history. Akhenaten's elongated features are unique among pharaonic representations.
8. Akhenaten is shown in a very few statues as having androgynous characteristics, with normal male facial features but rounded breasts and no masculine genitalia. He undoubtedly was capable of procreation, as he had at least six daughters; these representations must have been intended to convey the dual male and female elements he believed were embodied in his conception of God. Again, androgynous representations are not seen for any other pharaohs.[26]

In the last two of these examples, knowledge of the likeness of Akhenaten would not have been available, except as secret knowledge, for at least a thousand years after his demise. Within thirty or forty years of his death, his capital city, Akhetaten, was razed to the ground, and all known representations of him throughout Egypt were destroyed. Material and imagery of Akhenaten started coming to light only when excavations at Amarna began in the late nineteenth century C.E. It has to be assumed that there was a traditional memory or recording of his likeness kept in the secret archives of his Hebrew followers.

The extensive number of congruencies between Melchizedek and his derivative names and Akhenaten and his high priest, Meryra, are, I suggest, far too many to constitute mere coincidences—apart from the fact that no one has any plausible explanation of who the mysterious Melchizedek really was.

If conjecture fires a rifle at a target and hits the bull's-eye the first time, it could be put down to chance—a freak breeze, a faulty gunsight. If the shooter goes on to hit the target repeatedly from dozens of directions and distances, and even in foggy conditions, one has to concede eventually that conjecture is truth.

# ⤚ 11 ⤙

## Apocalypse Soon

There are a number of sectarian works found at Qumran, as well as biblical works from the Hebrew and Christian Scriptures, that deal with visions of the future. The sectarian works include the New Jerusalem Scroll, Temple Scroll, War Scroll, Book of Jubilees, Book of Enoch, Testament of Levi (sometimes known as the Testament of the Twelve Patriots), and commentaries on the Books of Hosea, Nahum, and Habakkuk. The latter three can conveniently be referred to as the Late Chronology Texts, as opposed to Early Chronology Texts. The biblical works include the Books of Isaiah and Daniel and the Revelation of St. John the Divine.

Revelation is the last book of the Christian Scriptures. Like the others mentioned above, it includes a visionary treatise on the past and future history of a holy group. It is seen by many scholars as coming from the "same circles as these [apocryphal texts, particularly Enoch and the Testament of Levi], and its dependence on them is now even more apparent when the Dead Sea Scrolls are seen as the missing link."[1]

In the words of Håkan Ulfgard, of Linköping University, Sweden: "The author of the Book of Revelation himself may have been part of the same hermeneutical and theological/ideological tradition as that represented in the Qumran writings."[2] If this assumption is correct, it underscores even more strongly the contention that some of the writers of the Christian Scriptures were at least well versed in the Qumran-Essene texts, and were likely to have been adherents of that group.

Interestingly, most of the apocalyptic texts found at Qumran—and there are many—are written in Aramaic, a language not used by the Essenes in their own sectarian writings.[3] Remarkably, it is precisely these non-Qumranic Aramaic apocalyptic texts that were also more fully transmitted to us by Christian scribes, namely the Book of Enoch and the Book of Jubilees,[4] preserved by the Ethiopic Church; and the Testament of Levi, preserved through Greek transmission. These specific transmissions are not, I believe, accidental, but reflect an ongoing thread of Qumran-Essene scribal activity by the early followers of Jesus. The transmission could perhaps be explained away by the presence of these Aramaic texts in the general Hebrew literature, but it would be difficult to explain the exact replication and the impact of this apocalyptic obsession on both communities, particularly as they contain a form of dualism and communal discipline unique to Qumran in the context of Second Temple Judaism.

The use of Aramaic asserts an attachment to ancient times, at least back to the First Temple period, and it has been suggested by scholars such as Devorah Dimant, of the University of Haifa, Israel, that the solar calendar and the dualistic and astrological stances of these texts can be explained by a Babylonian/Iranian connection.[5] More work for Occam's razor!

Why go to two sources when one will rationalize these anomalies much more convincingly? The special interest of the Qumran community represented by these teachings lies in the Essenes' self-image as custodians of the true ancient wisdom, transmitted through the patriarchs and revealed to Moses on Mount Sinai. In other words, the antecedent of it dated back to the time of ancient Egypt, before 1200 B.C.E. and long before Babylon, when a solar calendar, dualism, predestination, astrology, jubilees, and Levitical priests would fit much more comfortably into the then existing cultural and religious background.

## Key Dates for the Community

One of the noticeable common denominators in these Aramaic manuscripts, which form part of the Early Chronology Texts, is their reference to time periods for which the Book of Enoch and the Testament of Levi, both composed in the Hellenistic era of the third century B.C.E., appear to be using blocks of 490 years as a measure of key events in the past and future. The choice seems to be based on a seventy-week periodicity measured as years rather than weeks. Thus, the Testament of Levi talks of the appointment of a high priest in the time of Jacob, with successive priests appointed over periods of 490 years.

The appointment of a high priest in the time of Jacob, well before the building of the First Temple in Jerusalem, is, of course, an impossibility for conventional biblical scholarship. The significance of this dilemma was initially brought home to me while discussing aspects of my book, *The Mystery of the Copper Scroll of Qumran,* with Esther Eshel of Bar-Ilan University, Ramat Gan, Israel. She was then working on an analysis of the Testament of Levi, and the repeated insistence of the texts on the appointment of priests several hundred years before there was an established Temple had been a puzzle.[6]

In considering the idea that Jacob might have been contemporary with an earlier temple—that of the Egyptian king Akhenaten—she suggested that the associations in the Testament of Levi might well be an important support to my theory.

On the same theme, Jozef Milik, during one of our discussions in his Paris flat, also pointed out that in the Testament of Levi, which he judged one of the most important of all the Dead Sea Scrolls, Egyptian names are present. It is, in fact, in reference to the Levites that the Hebrew Scriptures mention most of those who bear Egyptian names.

## A Certain Event

The Book of Enoch also speaks of "blocks" of years measuring history from creation, with great events occurring at the end of each block of 490 years, in a similar manner to that seen in the Testament of Levi. The blocks begin with creation and move successively forward. At the end of the seventh block, the most important event is said to have occurred—the establishment of the Plant of Righteousness—presumably referring to the original reason for the establishment of the Qumran-Essene community. After the arrival of the Plant, the text relates that there would be only three more blocks of 490 years before the End Days arrived.[7]

As the philosophy of messianism evolved, the End Days were not just understood as the restoration of what had been lost, but were also envisaged as ushering in a reign of harmony and order and a paradise never before attained.

**TABLE 6**

**Scheme of apocalyptic events embedded in Enoch, Daniel, Testament of Levi, Jubilees, and Revelation in 490-year blocks**

| Event | Lapsed Years | Equivalent BCE Date |
|---|---|---|
| 1. Creation | 0 | 4780 |
| 2. Enoch | 490 | 4290 |
| 3. Noah and the Flood | 980 | 3800 |
| 4. Abraham? | 1470 | 3310 |
| 5. ? | 1960 | 2820 |
| 6. ? | 2450 | 2330 |
| 7. Abraham | 2940 | 1840 |
| 8. Eternal Plant of Righteousness | 3430 Akhenaten | 1350 |
| 9. Solomon's Temple | 3920 | 860 |
|  |  | 586 Solomon's temple destroyed |
| 10. End Days | 4410 | 370 |
|  |  | 177 Teacher of Righteousness* |
|  |  | 150 Essenes at Qumran |
|  |  | 110 Teacher of Righteousness dies |
|  |  | 70 Apocalypse† |
|  |  | 0 CE |
| Apocalypse | 4900 | 120 |

*Three hundred and ninety years after the destruction of the First Temple, the Plant of Righteousness (Teacher of Righteousness) comes, according to the Damascus document.

†Expected end, according to Daniel.

The sect distinguished at least four periods in its understanding of the final eschatology:[8]

1. The past, before the sect's establishment
2. Its own historical present and preoccupation with clearing the Way in the Wilderness
3. The approaching period of war to be fought by the forces of light against the forces of darkness
4. The ultimate future of full eschatological peace

At the time of the death of the Teacher of Righteousness, thought to be circa 110 B.C.E., the Essenes had calculated from the works of Daniel and Isaiah that the End Days would come in 70 B.C.E.—forty years after his demise—equating to a biblical time block related to the length of time the Hebrews were wandering in the wilderness.[9] When 70 B.C.E. came and went, some recalculations were needed, as evidenced by the Essenes' Commentary on the Book of Habakkuk, composed about 50 B.C.E. A further review of the Book of Daniel indicated that the beginning of the period of Final Judgment might now come in 70 C.E., but from reviewing works of the prophets Hosea, Nahum, and Habakkuk, a new, open-ended date, depending on the length of Roman rule, was determined. What that date was is not clear from the Dead Sea Scrolls fragments that deal with the subject, but it appears to be post–70 C.E.

The next indication of the Qumran-Essenes' thinking on this post–70 C.E. date comes from the Book of Revelation. Composed sometime in the first or second century C.E., the content of Revelation is a mixture of early Christian theology intertwined with material identified from the Essenes' sectarian Chronology Texts and a visionary taste of the apocalyptic End Days.[10] Revelation does not mention the crucifixion of Jesus. Understanding its true meaning is a challenging task, as analogy and imagery are the fabric of its composition, but built into it is the revised date the Qumran Essenes must have finally established as that for the end of time, or perhaps had established much earlier in their history.

Interestingly, the views of Paul on the timing of the End Days are peculiarly congruent with those of the Qumran Essenes. This is perhaps not such a surprise if my conjecture is accurate that Paul's mysterious three years' absence in Arabia was time actually spent with an Essenic community. He first believed that the end of the world would come around 70 C.E., but later modified his view, just as the Qumran Essenes did (2 Thessalonians, chapter 2; Rom. 12–13).[11]

According to Dr. Barbara Thiering, a lecturer at the University of Sydney, interpretation of the time scale set out in Revelation shows that the expected eschaton (final restoration) would come in 120 C.E.[12] The significance of this date is indeed testified to by a dramatic series of events that occurred among the Jewish communities scattered within the Roman Empire. An unexpected widespread, and apparently orchestrated, uprising of Jews in the Diaspora and in their homeland is recorded in 115 C.E., during the reign of Emperor Trajan.[13] This seems to support the contention that some outside knowledge was the driving force that encouraged an attempt to throw off the Roman yoke in anticipation that the messiah would return in 120 C.E.[14]

One way or another, interpretation of these Chronology Texts has proved a nightmare for scholars and a fertile hunting ground for all manner of weird theorists to play around with possibilities and numbers—666, the number of the beast, and the four horsemen of the apocalypse mentioned in Revelation being just two of the numbers that have caught the imagination of the public. Even Isaac Newton, among many others, spent an inordinate amount of time trying to analyze numerical aspects of the Book of Revelation.

Much more sense of the written matter can be made, however, when it is viewed through a pair of Egyptian glasses.

At the end of the seventh block, the most important event in human history took place, according to the Essenes' own accounts. Working back from the final days, for which both the Essenes and the early Christians (as the Book of Revelation indicates) were preparing themselves, we now have an interesting interpretation of when this most important event must have taken place. The final days were to occur at the end of the tenth block of time, and this was expected to come around 120 C.E., as Barbara Thiering and other scholars suggest. The end of the seventh block of time units of 490 years must therefore have occurred 1,470 years before the End Days, as follows:

$$490 \times 3 = 1470$$
$$1470 - 120 \text{ (C.E.)} = 1350 \text{ (B.C.E.)}$$

So in 1350 B.C.E., 1,470 years before the End Days, the most important event in the religious history of the Qumran Essenes is said to have occurred. If I seem to be belaboring the point somewhat, it is because it is of such significance.

We know the dates of the early Egyptian pharaohs with a fair amount of precision;[15] 1350 B.C.E. is the *exact* date of the enthronement of Akhenaten as pharaoh. He *was* the Plant of Righteousness, confirmed in the Chronology Texts. His distant successor, the Teacher of Righteousness, was the leader who took his community to Qumran.[16] There can be no doubt that the Plant of Righteousness was the founder of the separatist Essene movement, and not some other biblical character or event, because the Teacher of Righteousness was referred to as the Shoot or Branch of the Plant of Righteousness.

The exactness of the Qumran-Essene knowledge of a date when the most significant event in their history occurred being so close to the lifetime of King Akhenaten can hardly be a coincidence. The Hebrews had not yet entered Canaan; they were still in Egypt at this time. The associations that have already been made to the city of Akhetaten and its ruler King Akhenaten now weight the historical evidence heavily in favor of the overall contention that the Qumran Essenes had a direct connection back to the Amarna period.

Now, with some degree of confidence that we understand the origins of the Qumran-Essene settlement, we can proceed to consider what was really going on in this remote corner of the Judaean wilderness.

# ⌒ 12 ⌐

# A Community of Essenes— or Something Else?

Qumran has long been a place of controversy and intense discussion—at international conferences and seminars and in learned publications. No one is certain of the origins of the strange, reclusive sect that wrote and possessed what are now known as the Dead Sea Scrolls. Nor is there agreement as to the degree of influence it had on early Christianity, or its relationship to John the Baptist and Jesus.

Such is the intensity of feelings about the real purpose of the buildings that now stand in ruins at Qumran that it is not uncommon to see professors shouting at each other across conference rooms as they defend their respective pet theories. Numerous respected scholars have their own individual theories about what was going on at Qumran. There is a consensus on many issues, but there are also large areas where there are just no accepted answers. Perhaps part of the reason is that there are basic misunderstandings with regard to the origins of the community. As Magen Broshi, of the Israel Museum, likes to put it: "There are at least ten different theories about the origins and function of Qumran. By definition, nine of them are wrong."

## Who Were the Qumran Essenes?

The people who wrote the Dead Sea Scrolls and lived at Qumran are generally thought of as including a group known by the Greek name *Essianoi*, Essenes, who had separated themselves from the Second Temple priesthood and retreated to the silence of the wilderness to study, pray, and develop their own version of the Hebrew texts and the Hebrew religion.

As a community of devout monastic-style Jews, led by a Teacher of Righteousness, they settled at Qumran, on the northwestern edge of the Dead Sea, around 150 B.C.E. and lived there until just before the destruction by the Romans of the Second Temple in Jerusalem in 70 C.E. They wrote and possessed a collection of texts known as the Dead Sea Scrolls, which include the earliest versions of what were to become the Hebrew Scriptures, commentaries, and previously unknown biblical material, as well as their own sectarian writings describing the community's activities and its beliefs.

Among the sect's own writings, the Copper Scroll stands out as a uniquely important document that has been the subject of intense study by international scholars, although there is virtually no consensus on any of the main aspects of the scroll—its translation, origins, meaning, or the treasures it refers to.

These treasures comprise millions of dollars' worth of gold, silver, ritual clothing, jewelry, and other scrolls. The Copper Scroll was discovered in 1952 in one of the caves near Qumran, yet despite detailed descriptions of some sixty-five different locations and intense searching by archaeologists in likely areas of Israel, nothing had been located over a period of nearly fifty years.

One of the main ongoing arguments has centered on where these treasures came from, as their derivation from the Temple at Jerusalem has so many problematic aspects. Nor is it understood how the Essenes might have known or possessed such treasures (see table 7, page 104).

In my own study of the Copper Scroll, set out in *The Mystery of the Copper Scroll of Qumran,* I claim to have located a number of the items of treasure by applying the location descriptions to Amarna, in Egypt, the site of Pharaoh Akhenaten's holy city and Great Temple.

In deciphering the ancient form of Hebrew writing in the Copper Scroll, I believe I have not only solved the longstanding riddle of the meaning of its contents and located some of the treasures it lists, but also made a number of connections that relate the Qumran Essenes to a different temple from that at Jerusalem, and a much earlier time and place in Egypt—notably to the period of the Hebrews' early sojourn in Egypt and to the ancient city of Akhetaten, which lay south of Qumran. Akhetaten, now known as Amarna, had been founded as a city built on virgin land by

**TABLE 7**

**Main theories on the origins and reality of the treasures described in the Copper Scroll**

| Treasures belonged to the Essenes | Treasures came from the Jerusalem Temple | Treasures were imaginary |
|---|---|---|
| K. G. Kuhn[a] | J. Allegro[a] | J. Milik[a,b] |
| A. Dupont-Sommer[a] | C. Roth[a] | R. de Vaux[a] |
| É. Puech[a] | G. R. Driver[a] | M. Baillet[a] |
| S. Goranson[a] | F. M. Cross[a] | G. L. Harding[j] |
| B. Pixner[a] | E. Laperrousaz[a,d,j] | H. de Contenson[h] |
| R. Feather[c] | B. Lurie[a,d,j] | |
| | M. R. Lehmann[a,d,j] | |
| | K. G. Kuhn[a,e] | |
| | N. Golb[a] | |
| | G. Vermes[f] | |
| | P. Muchowski[a] | |
| | D. Wilmot[j] | |
| | M. O. Wise[a] | |
| | K. McCarter[j] | |
| | J. Lefkovits[j] | |
| | A. Wolters[j] | |
| | G. J. Brooke[g] | |
| | P. R. Davies[g] | |
| | P. R. Callaway[g] | |
| | H. Stegemann[i] | |
| | I. Knohl[a] | |
| | J. Mowinckel[a] | |

a. *Copper Scroll Studies*, G. J. Brooke and P. R. Davies, eds., Sheffield Academic Press, 2002.

b. Has modified his position to possibility of treasures being real in the light of the probability that a reading of smaller weight units than the biblical talent are justified. Now believes the Copper Scroll was definitely part of the Dead Sea Scrolls caucus (contrary to the view he is said to hold as stated by Piotr Muchowski (a) and others). Recorded interview, Robert Feather, January 17, 1999.

c. *The Mystery of the Copper Scroll of Qumran*, Inner Traditions, 2003.

d. Believes treasure postdated Temple destruction and intended for its rebuilding.

e. Changed his position after the scroll was opened.

f. *The Complete Dead Sea Scrolls in English*, Allen Lane, 1997. Geza Vermes sees difficulties with both theories.

g. *The Complete World of the Dead Sea Scrolls*, P. R. Davies, G. J. Brooke, P. R. Callaway, Thames & Hudson, 2002.

h. Recorded interview, Robert Feather, January 16, 1999.

i. *The Library of Qumran*, Brill Academic Publishers, 1998. Hartmut Stegemann does not think the Copper Scroll originated from Qumran.

j. Al Wolters, *The Copper Scroll: Overview, Text and Translation*, Sheffield Academic Press, 1996.

a pharaoh many scholars have described as the first monotheist. This pharaoh, Akhenaten, developed—in conjunction, I believe, with his contemporary Hebrew patriarchs, Jacob and Joseph—a new form of religion in Egypt that evolved into what was later known as Judaism and, more particularly, the unusual form of Judaism practiced by the Essenes at Qumran.

For a long period, between 1947 and 1991, the group of scholars who controlled the translation work and publication of the Dead Sea Scrolls remained often secretive and always intensely possessive of access to the original scroll fragments; the reasons for their behavior are discussed later in this book. But the situation changed dramatically in the early 1990s, when American scholars finally gained free access, for the rest of the academic community, to photographs of the original scroll materials.[1]

The volume of literature relating to the Essenes, Qumran, Second Temple Judaism, and early Christianity had previously been growing at a goodly rate, but with the breaking of the Dead Sea Scrolls embargo, largely through the valiant efforts of the American crusaders, the literary floodgates burst open. Much of the flow was inspired by the Dead Sea Scrolls texts, but other historical documents added their pressure to the impetus. A constant thrust behind the new deluge was the suspicion that new material and reinterpretations of contemporarily related texts might throw new light on the origins of Jesus and early Christianity.

How these recent texts clarify the possibility of such connections and advance the search for a clearer understanding of the revelations of Jozef Milik is the subject of the next chapter.

# ⌐ 13 ⌐

# Manuscripts of Contention

*When books are burned bodies are not far behind.*
HEINRICH HEINE, GERMAN POET/ESSAYIST, 1797–1856

For over two thousand years, people have been trying to locate the real Jesus—for reasons of religious, historical, dramatic, artistic, or simply intellectual curiosity. Thousands of works of literature and art have poured from furnaces of creativity, seeking the truth embedded in the nativity and crucifixion stories. So what has happened during the last part of the twentieth century to justify a renewed flood of such works?

Three main motivators have catalyzed this increased interest—apart from the calendrical effect of the anniversary of Jesus's supposed date of birth and reinterpretation of existing material. They are the discovery and subsequent ongoing translations of the Dead Sea Scrolls and two other extant early Christian documents, the Rylands Fragment and the Nag Hammadi Papyri Codex.

Table 8 on pages 108–109 provides a summary of the earliest biblical texts in their approximate order of writing. The table is intended to help clarify how the Rylands Fragment and the Nag Hammadi Papyri Codex fit into the overall picture of early biblically related texts.

One thing that is immediately striking from the contents of table 8 is that, apart from the first two items and last item, all were discovered in Egypt or relate directly to Egypt. It is also apparent that even the first two items have strong associations with Egypt. Considering that mainstream Christianity is generally thought to have developed outside Egypt, this somewhat surprising phenomenon is of some significance and will be looked at in more detail later on.

In addition to this summary of the earliest biblical texts, I have provided in table 9 (pages 112–113) a synopsis of some of the main personalities in the Christian Scriptures who will be discussed in this book and the significant events related to them so readers can see how these people fit into the greater historical picture of their time.

## The Contentiously Significant Texts

The most contentious and significant of these early documents listed in table 8, in terms of generating public literary interest and comment, are, in chronology of discovery:

- The so-called John Rylands Fragment of the Gospel of John, found in Egypt in the 1920s, dated to circa 125 C.E.
- The Nag Hammadi Gospel of Thomas, found in Egypt in 1945,[1] whose origins date to the early 4th century C.E.
- The Dead Sea Scrolls, found near the Dead Sea between 1947 and 1956, dated from 380 B.C.E. to circa 30 C.E.

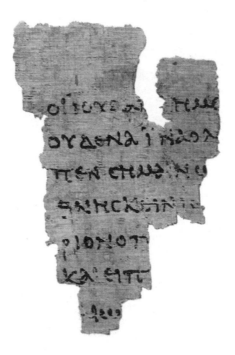

*Fig. 13.1. The John Rylands Fragment.*

**TABLE 8**

**Earliest biblical texts and their dating in approximate order of writing**

| Text | Approximate date of written text | Approximate date of discovery |
|---|---|---|
| **Hinnom Amulets**—silver strips engraved with a version of the Priestly Blessing from Numbers 6:24–26. Found in a burial chamber in the Hinnom Valley, Jerusalem. Now in the Israel Museum, Jerusalem. | 7th century BCE | 1979 |
| **Dead Sea Scrolls**—huge collection of biblical, apocryphal, pseudepigraphic, and sectarian texts found at Qumran. Written on parchment, papyrus, ceramics, and copper, in Hebrew, Aramaic, and Greek. Many preserved in the Shrine of the Book Museum and Rockefeller Museum, Jerusalem.[a] | 380 BCE–c. 30 CE | Recovered 1947–67 |
| **Rylands Fragment**—oldest example of Christian Scripture text; it contains six verses in Greek of John 18. Housed in the John Rylands Library, University of Manchester, England. Thought to come from the site of Oxyrhynchus.[b] | 125 CE | 1920s |
| **Nash Papyrus**—fragment containing 24 broken lines in square-form Hebrew of the Ten Commandments and the beginning of the Shema prayer from Deuteronomy 6:1, similar to versions seen in phylacteries found at Qumran.[b] | c. 150 BCE | Beginning of 1900 |
| **Egerton Papyrus**—apocryphal versions of the healing of a leper, as found in Mark, Matthew, and Luke; and a story of Jesus being stoned, as found in John. Now in the British Museum.[b] | 150 CE | pre-1935 |
| **Oxyrhynchus Papyri**—found at Oxyrhynchus, near modern El Bahnasa, near the Faiyum area of central Egypt. They include fragments attributed to the noncanonical Gospel of Thomas, including previously unknown sayings of Jesus.[b] | 200 CE | 1896 |
| **Bodmer Papyri Codex**—of Gospels of Luke and John in Greek. Kept at Cologny-Geneva.[c] | 200 CE | 1950s |
| **Washington Codex**—almost complete versions of the Gospels of Matthew, John, Luke, and Mark. Written in Greek. Kept in the Freer Gallery, part of the Smithsonian complex in Washington, D.C.[b] | 3rd century CE | 1906 |
| **Chester Beatty Papyri Codex**—of the Christian Scripture Gospels, half of Acts, a third of Revelation, and many of Paul's letters. Now in Dublin, Michigan, and Princeton Universities and Austrian National Library, Vienna.[b] | 2nd–4th centuries CE | 1931 |
| **Nag Hammadi Papyri Codex**—of apocryphal writings, including Apocalypse of Paul, Peter's Letter to Philip, Apocalypse of Peter, Secret Book of James, Gospel of Thomas. Written in Egyptian Coptic using Greek letters. Kept at the Institute for Antiquity and Christianity, Claremont, California.[b] | early 4th century CE | 1945 |

| Text | Approximate date of written text | Approximate date of discovery |
| --- | --- | --- |
| Sinaiticus Codex—oldest known copy manuscript in Greek uncials (capital letters), on vellum, of the Christian and Hebrew Scriptures. It contains an almost complete recension of the Christian Scriptures and the Hebrew Septuagint (previously translated from Hebrew into Greek c. 230 BCE), and some apocryphal works. Most of the modern translations of the New Testament are based on its text. Now in the British Museum.[c,d] | mid-4th century CE | 1844 |
| Vaticanus Codex—composed in Greek, contains parts of the Hebrew and Christian Scriptures up to Hebrews 9:13. Housed in the Vatican, Rome.[c.] | 4th century CE | c. 1450 CE |
| Alexandrinus Codex—Near-complete Greek version of the Christian Scriptures. Housed in the British Museum.[c] | early 5th century CE | c. 1620 CE |
| Genizah Collection—mainly Jewish documents found in a synagogue in Cairo.[b] | 17th–19th centuries CE | c. 1896 |
| Vulgate Revised—translation into Latin of the Greek text of the Christian Scriptures made by Jerome, secretary to Pope Damascus. Became the standard version for the Roman Catholic Church. | 384 CE | 716 CE |

a. Other texts, also sometimes referred to as Dead Sea Scrolls, include those found at Wadi Murabba'at (scroll of the Minor Prophets dated to 100 CE, correspondence relating to the revolt of 132–5 CE led by Simon Bar Kochba), Nahal Hever (Psalms 15 and 16, correspondence relating to the revolt of 132–5 CE led by Simon Bar Kochba), and Masada (scroll of Psalms 81–85, a 1st-century-BCE copy of Ben Sira, etc.) near the Dead Sea.

b. Found in Egypt.

c. Related to texts found at Alexandria, Egypt.

d. A small section of the Codex Sinaiticus, discovered in 1975, remains in the Monastery of St. Catherine, where the rest of the codex, now in the British Museum, was discovered (a few folios are in Leipzig).

In addition to these, the Genizah collection, first brought to light in 1897 by two itinerant Scottish ladies in an ancient synagogue in Cairo, came back into prominence when it was realized that some of the manuscripts were very similar to those found among the Dead Sea Scrolls.[2]

## The John Rylands Fragment

The significance of the John Rylands Fragment was that it seemed to contradict a previously held view of the nineteenth-century German school of biblical historians: that the Gospel of John was written much later than the so-called Synoptic Gospels (Matthew, Mark, and Luke). For a copy of

John, in Greek, to be in use in Egypt around 125 C.E. implied that the original version was set down at least ten years prior to that date, and therefore that John was written much earlier than had previously been thought. It had also been considered that John was composed at Ephesus. In light of conjectures to be presented later on, however, and when examining the role of a branch of the Qumran Essenes and their associates, the Therapeutae, in relation to early Christian outposts, it is not inconceivable that John was actually originally written in Egypt.

The language in John, previously considered to be of Greek origin, can now be seen to be actually very similar in phraseology to the Dead Sea Scrolls' internal writings. As Ian Wilson points out in his book *Jesus: The Evidence*,[4] "The John Gospel prologue speaks of a conflict between light and darkness. The whole gospel is replete with phrases such as 'the spirit of truth,' 'the light of life,' 'walking in the darkness,' 'children of light,' and 'eternal life.'" For example, we find:

| **John 1:2–3** | **Dead Sea Scroll**<br>**Manual of Discipline 11:11** |
|---|---|
| All things were made by Him; and without Him was not anything made that was made. | All things come to pass by His knowledge; He establishes all things by His design and without Him nothing is done. |

Previous to the finding of the Dead Sea Scrolls, the Gospel of John was considered to be strongly Hellenized, presenting Jesus as being relatively un-Jewish. For this reason it was thought to be a later Gospel than Mark or Matthew. Paula Fredriksen, William Goodwin Aurelio Professor at Boston University, who is not a great believer in very direct connections between the Dead Sea Scrolls and early Christian writings, nevertheless notes that this entire view had to change with the discovery of the Dead Sea Scrolls. John was talking the same language as the Qumran Children of Light in their struggle with the Children of Darkness. Its writing had to be pushed back to a much earlier date, and its associations were now seen to be strongly Jewish, albeit from a form of Judaism that was itself distinct from that of the surrounding community. The closeness of some of John's quotations to Dead Sea Scrolls sectarian works written in Aramaic would also begin to explain why John's Gospel, known to us today only in Greek, carries the strongest indications that it was originally written in Aramaic.[5]

## Gnosticism and the Nag Hammadi Texts

The Nag Hammadi finds were the second most potent stimulus for the increase in writings on the interpretation of the Christian Scriptures. There were other, earlier Christian Scriptures text discoveries, as listed in table 8, but what these documents did was indicate that the so-called mystery gnostic religion of secret teachings and inner spirituality was, in fact, inherent in the early Christian movement. The idea that Christian rites and ceremonies were buttressed by mysterious doctrines has been resisted by Christian theologians from the very earliest times right up to today. The theologians' main anxiety was to preserve the uniqueness of Christianity and distance the Christian Scriptures from gnostic mysticism.

The Nag Hammadi texts were discovered in 1945, about one hundred miles south of Amarna, Egypt, near a monastery founded by St. Pachomius, from where they are thought to have originated. Written, or copied, by members of a Gnostic sect over two centuries after the time of Jesus,[6] they comprised 1,153 papyrus pages bound as thirteen leather-covered codices* and contained fifty-two separate tractates. They were copies in Sahidic Coptic written by Egyptian fourth-century-C.E. scribes who were translating from the Greek works that are thought to have largely origi-nated within living memory of the time of Jesus.

This latter conjecture was borne out by earlier written fragments found at Oxyrhynchus (see table 8, pages 107–8); some citations in these texts are also considered to be quotations from Jesus:

These are the [secret] words [which] the living Jesus [sp]oke, an[d Judas, who is] called Thomas, [wrote down]. And he said, [whoever finds the interpret]ion of the[se] sayings will not taste [death]. Said Jesus: "If you do not fast to the world, you will not find the kingdom of God; and if you do not make the sabbath a sabbath, you will not see the Father."[7]

---

*The earliest bound books are known as *codices* (singular *codex*).

**TABLE 9**

**Significant dates relating to personalities in the Christian Scriptures and the recording of events related to them[a]**

| Date | Event |
| --- | --- |
| 7 | John the Baptist born |
| 5 | Jesus born |
| **BCE** | |

| **CE** | |
| --- | --- |
| 15 | Paul born at Tarsus |
| 26 | John the Baptist dies |
| 28 | Jesus dies |
| 40 | Q gospel of Jesus written in Aramaic by Jesus-Essenes? |
| *50* | Earliest sayings of Jesus recorded in Nag Hammadi and Oxyrhynchus texts |
| 50–60ity | Paul's early letters (Colossians and Ephesians) written in Greek (no mention of virgin birth or divinity of Jesus, or clear mention of bodily resurrection)[b] |
| 62 | James, brother of Jesus (not James the disciple), killed; His uncle, Cleopas, becomes leader of Jerusalem Jesusites |
| 64 | Paul dies |
| 67 | Peter executed[c] |
| 68 | Qumran destroyed by Romans; Essenes disperse. Last possible date for writing of the **Dead Sea Scrolls** |
| 70 | Second Temple sacked |
| *75* | Part of John's Gospel written in Greek (no mention of virgin birth or divinity of Jesus); appears copied from earlier Q document written in Aramaic |
| *90* | Mark's Gospel written in Greek[d] (no mention of virgin birth) |
| *110* | Matthew's Gospel written in Greek (follows 90% of Mark and draws on Q)[d]; Pharisees start evicting Jesus's followers from synagogues; reaction against restrictions by broadening of Gospels to encompass Gentiles and description of Jesus as having a miraculous virgin birth and being divine |
| *125* | Rylands Fragment with part of John's Gospel |
| *130* | Later Pauline letters written in Greek |
| | Luke's Gospel (follows doctrine of Matthew and draws on Q)[e] |
| 145–150 | **Egerton Papyrus—parts of Mark, Matthew, Luke, and John**[e] |
| 200 | **Bodmer Papyri with parts of Luke and John; Oxyrhynchus Papyri with parts of Thomas** |
| 300 | **Washington Codex—Mark, Matthew, Luke, and John** |
| 320 | **Nag Hammadi texts—Paul's letter to Philip, apocryphal writings** |
| | **Chester Beatty Codex—parts of Gospels, Acts, Paul's letters, Revelation** |
| 350 | Codex Sinaiticus—almost complete Hebrew and Christian Scriptures |
| *400* | Jerome's (Eusebius) Latin Vulgate |
| 900 | **Arabic translation by Saadyah Gaon** |
| 1395 | English translation by Purvey |

| Date | Event |
|------|-------|
| 1456 | First printed version, in Latin, by Gutenberg, Germany |
| 1611 | King James Version |

Dates set in **bold italic** refer to approximate date of composition of corresponding work. Words in **bold** relate to extant texts.

a. The dates given are based on analysis of a consensus cross-section of authorities, some of whom differ considerably in their conclusions, in which their name is mentioned. They include data from Ian Wilson (*The Bible Is History*, Weidenfeld and Nicolson, 1999); Russell Shorto (*Gospel Truth*, Hodder and Stoughton, 1997); Karen Armstrong (*The First Christian*, Pan Books, 1983); Professor B. L. Mack (*The Lost Gospel*, Element, 1993). Some of the reasoning for the order of events is also given in parentheses.[3]

b. Christ rising from the dead appears to be part of the "first fruits" of End Days resurrection (1 Cor. 15:20), quite consistent with Jewish eschatology. Shorto gives 45 CE and Armstrong 50 CE for the writing of Paul.

c. Peter, leader of the disciples of Jesus.

d. The Gospels of Mark and Matthew are believed to have first been mentioned by Bishop Papias of Phrygia (Hierapolis) c. 150 CE. Shorto gives c. 65 CE, Armstrong 70 CE for the writing of Mark; and 90 CE and 80–90 CE, respectively, for Matthew.

e. The Gospels of Luke and John are believed to have first been mentioned by Bishop Irenaeus of Lyon c. 180 CE. Armstrong gives a date of 90 CE for the writing of Luke.

When the Nag Hammadi texts were discovered, they were initially perceived by the church as threatening the conventional understandings about Jesus, and in an almost *devant-vu* of the way the Dead Sea Scrolls were to be received, public access to them was not permitted; nothing of their content was published for nearly thirty-two years.[8] Indeed, in 1961, Professor Hans Jonas made a complaint very similar to the "academic scandal" protest Professor Geza Vermes was to voice about the Dead Sea Scrolls two decades later. "The gnostic find from Nag Hammadi," wrote Jonas, "has been beset from the beginning to this day by a persistent curse of political roadblocks, litigations, and, most of all, scholarly jealousies and 'firstmanship'—the last factor has grown by now into a veritable *chronique scandaleuse* of contemporary academia."[9] The Nag Hammadi texts were, as far as we know, initially all purchased by the Cairo Coptic Museum. Very early on in their history, the Swiss psychoanalyst C. G. Jung became interested in the texts, seeing in them echoes of his own research into the inner meaning of Being and the human spirit interacting with the collective unconscious. Because of academic obstinacy and religious intransigence, it was not until November 15, 1953, that a portion of the Nag Hammadi texts came out of Egypt and were presented to Jung in honor of his eightieth birthday by the Jung Institute of Zurich. The rest had to wait a further twenty-five years before publication. Eventually, in 1966, a team of international scholars began serious translation, with final text publication in 1977 and a photographic edition in 1980.[10]

Following initial studies, the Nag Hammadi texts were thought to derive from the Gnostic Valentinus school, which flourished from around 135 to 155 C.E. in northern Egypt, and whose ideas were brought to Rome by Valentinus about 140 C.E. Valentinus was a particularly potent adversary of Christian orthodoxy, as he claimed to have received initiation into secret doctrines through Theudas, a disciple of Paul.[11] Some scholars, however, such as Professor Helmut Koester of Harvard University and Stevan L. Davies,[12] suggest that the sayings in the Gospel of Thomas, although compiled around 140 C.E., may include material that predates the Christian Scriptures and may have actually been written down between 50 and 100 C.E.[13]

What the Nag Hammadi texts and the subsequent reactions against the kind of gnosticism they propounded show is that the early church, far from being the unified body it had previously been thought to be, was deeply split from the very beginning. Many followers of Jesus were not in agreement on the facts of his life, the meaning of his teachings, or what form the church should take. The Gnostics did not accept the bodily resurrection of Jesus but believed in a spiritual one. To this extent, even the Christian Scriptures themselves are ambiguous. Luke (24:13–32) and Mark (16:12) both relate that Jesus appeared after his crucifixion "in another form." Even Paul (1 Cor. 15:50) describes the resurrection as "a mystery": the transformation from physical to spiritual existence. It is not difficult to see why the early church, and indeed the church to this day, has set its face against the teachings of the Gnostics.

From the Nag Hammadi Gospel of Philip and Gospel of Thomas, in which Jesus appears to have a twin brother,[14] we learn that some Gnostic Christians centered in Egypt denied that Jesus had returned in the flesh and appointed Peter his successor; that many Gnostics challenged priestly authority and believed instead in the presence of the divine within the human being; and that the way to salvation was through self-knowledge. We also learn of Gnostic groups who believed in a God who was both Father and Mother, and that men and women were spiritual equals.[15] In addition, the Gnostic texts elevate Mary Magdalene to the status of Apostle

of Apostles and appear to cast her as the most important of the disciples—
a role for the Magdalene the Cathars of southern France seemed to reac-
quire in the Middle Ages. This emancipated view led the Gnostic church,
centered in Alexandria, Egypt, to develop along a fluid, more open, indi-
vidualistic congregational structure, in contrast to the solidifying rigidity of
a male-dominated hierarchy emerging in Roman Christianity. Initially, in
Gnostic movements, women had status equal to that of men.

Permitting women to take part in the Gnostic celebration of the
Eucharist was perhaps the last straw, provoking the church father
Tertullian to rage against the entire movement: "These heretical women,
how audacious they are! They have no modesty; they are bold enough to
teach, to engage in argument, to enact exorcisms, to undertake cures, and,
it may be seen, even to baptise!"[16] Not surprisingly, the Eastern Orthodox
Church chose to try to suppress Gnostic texts, and the Gnostics were condemned as heretics as early as the first century C.E.[17]

However, not only were many of the apparent verbatim sayings of
Jesus recorded in the Gospel of Thomas gnostic in their nature, but many
also made quite clear references to the imagery of Akhenaten, as do many
of the Dead Sea Scrolls. Any doubt about the devotional attitude of the
earliest followers of Jesus toward Akhenaten and Nefertiti will be dis-
pelled by startling and visually conclusive revelations that will be presented in a later chapter.

One of the most pertinent sayings from the Gospel of Thomas presents the imagery of Jesus in luminous terms combined with the concept of
the bestowing of life on all things. This almost certainly harks back to
Akhenaten's concept of God's light extending goodness to everything, in
the form of extended hands and ankh signs. The ankh signs were Egyptian
symbols for life, depicted as a long cross with a circle around the intersection of the horizontal and vertical lines.

> Jesus said, "It is I who am the light which is above them all. It is I
> who am the all. From me did the all come forth, and unto me did the
> all extend." (Gospel of Thomas, saying 77a)[18]

In due course we shall see many more examples in early Christian
texts that relate Jesus back to the Egyptian period of Amarna and its

preoccupations with the same light, chariot, throne, and other imagery.

Before going more deeply into the relationship between the Nag Hammadi texts and the third group of documents (the Dead Sea Scrolls) that spurred such interest in early Christianity, it will be useful to become better acquainted with the background events surrounding the culture and climate in which these documents came into being.

## The Entrenchment

Within 170 years of Jesus's death, the widespread organization of Christianity was governed by a hierarchy of bishops, priests, and deacons. Initially the movement was split into three factions. James, brother of Jesus, became leader of the Jerusalem group;[19] Peter led the eastern church centered on Antioch, Ephesus, and Rome; and the Gnostic faction developed in northern Egypt around Alexandria.

The very early institution of Christian belief in Alexandria is borne out by our knowledge of Mark the Evangelist, traditionally considered the author of the Gospel of Mark. A revered missionary and patron saint in Egypt, he was probably martyred at Alexandria around 63 C.E., only some thirty years after Jesus's crucifixion, for preaching against adoration of the Apis bulls at Memphis. Nevertheless, as the Roman Empire, now the dominant force in the Mediterranean area, took an increasing interest in Christianity, Emperor Hadrian remarked in a letter from Egypt written around 134 C.E. that he had seen "those who call themselves bishops of Christ devoting themselves to Serapis" (an Egyptian cult deity[20]).

By the end of the second century C.E., these ancient cults were on the wane, and Christianity began making widespread conversions. This so alarmed the Romans that they mounted a series of persecutions in which some 144,000 Egyptian Christians are said to have been killed. So deep was the traumatic effect of these events on the psyche of the persecuted populace that the Egyptian Coptic Christian Church marked the date of 284 C.E. as the beginning of their calendar—the regnal year of Emperor Diocletian, a tyrant credited with the worst excesses.

Bitter rivalries trundled on into the third century C.E. as the Roman school, dominated by the thinking of early church fathers like Irenaeus (subsequently bishop of Lyons), Tertullian, Hippolytus, and Clement of

Alexandria, became locked in mental and spiritual combat with the philosophical Gnostic teachings promoted by Valentinus and Marcus, as well
as by Simon Magus, a first-century Samaritan said to be the successor to
John the Baptist. Finally, in 324 C.E., the adoption of Rome's form of
Christianity under Emperor Constantine as the official approved religion
heralded the beginning of a physical rooting out of Gnosticism. Rome
essentially adopted Paul's version of the Christian message, which credited
Peter with being the first true apostle—the first validated witness to the
resurrection of Jesus. The bishop of Rome, now endowed with the keys to
the entire Roman Empire, became the guardian of orthodoxy, which was
to prevail down through the ages to the present pope. By 387 C.E., fanat-
ical monks, spurred on by Patriarch Cyril of Alexandria, had attacked and
destroyed the last of Egypt's pagan temples, probably including that of
Ptah at Memphis.[21]

The Great Library at Alexandria was burned to the ground, schools of
philosophy closed, and gnosticism went underground.[22]

# ⌐ 14 ↝

# Gnosticism at Qumran and the Dead Sea Scrolls

As the Nag Hammadi texts seem to confirm, the early Jesus movement did have considerable gnostic content, and it is intriguing to find similar echoes in the Qumran community. The early followers of Jesus looked to gnosticism and the inner mysteries of religion for enlightenment and the route to salvation. The Nag Hammadi tractates, such as the secret words of Jesus in the Gospels of Thomas and Philip, undoubtedly demonstrate that there was a strain of early Christianity that relied heavily on gnosticism and a profession of the knowledge of secrets.

These apocryphal writings, particularly the Gospel of Thomas, contain sayings attributable to Jesus and as such have many gnostic allusions, which are clearly discernible in the Qumran-Essene sectarian writings relating to the static community at Qumran. These allusions include an aversion to sex and marriage, mystical visions of an early creation story, veneration of light, and care of the soul in preference to the body. These characteristics are again also very apparent in the Egyptian Therapeutae, a healer sect closely associated with the Qumran Essenes.[1]

The Gospel of Thomas also shows a closer identification than any of the four Gospels of the Christian Scriptures with the as-yet-undiscovered "Quelle" Gospel, from which both Matthew and Luke are thought to have drawn. In a sense, this underlines the legitimacy of the Nag Hammadi texts, through the similarity of some of their basic contents to canonical Christian documents.

## So What Is Quelle?

Quelle (German for "source"), or Q for short, is rather like a Deep Throat behind the Gospels of the Christian Scriptures. Most scholars believe there was such a source or sources, but no one has yet been able to tie it or them down precisely; it is the quark[2] of biblical studies. As long ago as the 1970s, people such as Athanasius Polag, Walter Schmithals, and John Kloppenborg[3] identified successive strata of Q that appeared to relate to different chronological periods, from the oldest memories of the Hebrew Scriptures through to the writings of the Qumran Essenes. These various studies, which were initiated in the nineteenth century,[4] were very effectively summarized by Burton L. Mack in 1993[5] and Edward Meadors in mid-1999. From a Christological viewpoint, they show that much of the Q material relates to the messianic aspects of Jesus's mission.[6]

Another intriguing finding demonstrates very precisely a central thesis of this book and my previous work, *The Mystery of the Copper Scroll of Qumran:*[7] that Hebrew messianism has its roots in a time *before* the arrival of the kings of Israel and *well before* the eschatological happenings of the First Temple's demise and scattering of the people.

Q analysis demonstrates that the terms *son of man, Son of God,* and *the coming one,* as messianic names applied to Jesus, are traceable back to Enoch and Samuel, writing about a period *before* the anointing of any king of Israel. Similarly, the coming of an eschatological time in which the dispersed of Judah would be reinstated by a messianic figure or figures is evidenced in Isaiah and in the early Psalms of Solomon, before the people were dispersed:

> In that day shall there be an altar to the Lord in the midst of the land
> of Egypt, and a pillar at the border thereof to the Lord. (Isa. 20:18)

The only sensible conclusion is that the messianic deliverer was a royal figure who existed before King David or King Solomon, and that the simultaneous loss of this figure and his temple and dispersion of his people occurred well before the loss of the First Jerusalem Temple and dispersal of the Hebrews. This conclusion was also arrived at in chapter 8 from a different direction, which examined the identity of the messiahs of Qumran.

Knowledge of the role of the Son of God is implicit in these sources from the Hebrew Scriptures,[8] but it is the secret knowledge of the Qumran Essenes, who knew the exact identity of the kingly messiah, that allowed them to write more specifically about this royal figure and to tell us that there was also a priestly messiah who was a prince by birth.[9]

This is especially clearly demonstrated in the various Books of Enoch, in which there are numerous citations that do not seem to apply to any royal figure in Israel but fit very comfortably in the Amarna period. For example, 2 Enoch talks of being anointed with oil that carries within it the power of "the greatest light" and "the rays of the sun" (22:6–10), the latter phrase being an unambiguous reference to the rays of the sun that are always seen in association with the Aten symbol.[10]

## Back to Nag Hammadi Mysticism

The "mystery" element of the Gospel of Thomas found among the Nag Hammadi texts is exemplified in the following sayings:

> Whosoever drinks from my mouth shall come to resemble me and I myself will become he, and the hidden things shall be revealed to such a one. (108)

> He who knows the all but fails to have self-knowledge lacks everything. (67)

A number of scholars, such as Theodor Gaster and Stephen Hoeller, have recognized the atmosphere of mysticism that undoubtedly permeated Qumran-Essene thinking.[11] Theodor Gaster describes the Dead Sea Scrolls as essentially "mystical documents" and likens their testimony to that of the Nag Hammadi collection. Stephen Hoeller, associate professor of comparative religions at the College of Oriental Studies, Los Angeles, is more determined in his associations. He writes: "It is in the relationship of the Essene messiah to the Christian Jesus, and beyond him to the Gnostic Christ, that the link may be discovered which joins the Dead Sea Scrolls of Essene origin with the collection of Gnostic gospels found in Nag Hammadi."[12]

One clear example of this ancient mystical connection comes from another Nag Hammadi passage, which features the role of Seth—a figure of puzzlement for commentators and one we met in a previous chapter:

> And a flood shall come as a prefiguration for the end of the age against the world. On account of this race [the race of Seth] the conflagrations will come upon the earth. . . . And grace cometh through the agency of the prophets and the watchmen who come from the living race. Plagues and famines also are visited upon all because [of the enmity of the Demiurge]. All these things will come to pass on account of this great, imperishable race. (Gospel of the Egyptians, Nag Hammadi texts)

Seth is also mentioned in the Dead Sea Scrolls as a being whom the coming messiah will destroy in the time of the eschaton (a period of final reckoning for the world). This shared view of the nature of Seth confirms another commonality between the Qumran Essenes and the early Christians.[13] For Nag Hammadi theological students this figure of Seth is a conundrum, often seen as a force for good but usually one of evil. For Professor Stephen Hoeller, for example, the race of Seth—emanating from the third son of Adam—is seen as a favorable force of light.[14]

I believe this view is a complete misreading of the sense of the text in the Gospel of the Egyptians. This race of Seth is not just constantly subjected to the effects of the Demiurge (the Demiurge is the devil or a promoter of evil and anti-good), as he suggests; it *is* the Demiurge. Even the title given to the Nag Hammadi text, Treatise of the Great Seth, belies the conventional explanation that the Seth being referred to is the third son of Adam—a very minor character who receives hardly a mention in the Bible. The figure is, in my view, a manifestation of the ancient Egyptian great god of evil, Seth, who constantly reappears through the generations of Egypt in different forms, but always as a force for evil. The Great Seth, who will bring conflagration to the earth, is Egyptian, and should in no way be confused with an unimportant biblical character about whom we know nothing except his and his father's name and his age.[15]

The element of secret knowledge in the Nag Hammadi texts is seen again in a sacramental passage of ecstatic initiation in the Gospel of the

Egyptians. Jesus is shown to be more powerful than this force who "sees the light," obviously having been in darkness, and succumbs to the light of Jesus, but only after prolonged exclamations of a weird incantation:

> *O Iesseus-Mazareus-Iessdedekeus!* *
> *Ieoeuooa!*
> *In very truth . . .*
> *O living water!*
> *O child of the child!*
> *O name of all glories!*
> *O eternal being! . . .*
> *O being which beholds the aeons*
> *In very truth!*
> *AEEEEEIIIIYYYYYYOOOOOOOO*

The idea of Jesus existing in a nonhuman form is a persistent theme of the Nag Hammadi texts. It is seen in one of the most famous gnostic texts, the Acts of John. This is one of the few texts that was already known, from fragmentary finds elsewhere,[16] before the Nag Hammadi discovery in 1945. In one section, John and James encounter Jesus, but he appears to be a spiritual being who has adapted himself to human perception:

> Sometimes when I meant to touch him I encountered a material, solid body; but at other times again when I felt him, his substance was immaterial and incorporeal . . . as if it did not exist at all. (Acts of John 93, Christian Scriptures' Apocrypha II)

Orthodox Christianity rejects this idea, and insists Jesus was, in his life on earth, human. Pope Leo the Great, circa 450 c.e., condemned writings such as the Acts of John as "a hotbed of manifold perversity" that should not only be forbidden, "but entirely destroyed and burned with fire." The injunction was not enough to deter the heretics, who continued to copy and hide the work, prompting the Second Nicene Council of the church, held

---

*A mystical name for Jesus, which perhaps makes an allusion to Machaerus (the place where John the Baptist was killed).

in 787 C.E., to repeat the prohibition: "No one is to copy [this book]; not only so, but we consider that it deserves to be consigned to the fire."

The justification for this ferocious attitude is to some extent unfounded. There were groups of Christian Gnostics who denied the reality of Jesus's mortal suffering on the cross,[17] but there were others who insisted that Jesus suffered and died a physical death.[18] Ironically, if the interpretation of these so-called heretical texts sees Seth as a spiritual force rather than the human form of Adam's third son, the bitterness engendered by these gnostic texts becomes unfounded. The texts then simply become allegorical stories related to ancient Egyptian mythology about the spiritual side of Jesus battling the evil spirit Seth. They can quite easily be accommodated within the orthodox framework of Jesus having human form.

The current absurd interpretation of Seth as the human third son of Adam is completely undermined by the view the Qumran Essenes held on the origins of evil and "the children of Seth" (Dead Sea Scroll 4Q417). In his masterly analysis, John Collins, professor of the Hebrew Scriptures and postbiblical Judaism at Yale, shows that the idea of Seth as an "evil inclination" is derived from "a myth of cosmic conflict"—that is, a story that relates to legendary spiritual forces, rather than a human being.[19]

However, in making an allusion to Zoroastrian influence as the source of this dualistic approach to good and evil, and ascribing the cosmic story to the Zoroastrian book of Avesta, Collins fails to make the prior connection. This type of mythology is almost certainly the basis for the good and evil spirits in humankind averred by the Qumran Essenes, but the Avesta story is merely a paraphrase of the much earlier Egyptian myth of the two Egyptian god brothers Osiris and Seth. When this latter source is examined in more detail, especially in the light of the connections I make to Egypt for the Qumran Essenes, the difficulties in demonstrating a Zoroastrian influence fall away.[20] "We cannot at present trace the channels through which Zoroastrian dualism was actually transmitted," says Professor Collins.[21] In any event, this appears to be yet another Occam's razor situation. The name Seth is unambiguously mentioned as the force of evil, so why ignore it and look for contrived sources?

In the references to Seth in the Dead Sea Scrolls, to Jesus and Seth in the Nag Hammadi texts, and to Seth in Numbers 24:17 in the Hebrew Scriptures, the implications are quite clear. Seth is being related to the

Egyptian god of evil—Seth, the Demiurge of Christianity—while Jesus is the mystical figure of light and good who fights and overcomes darkness and evil.

In a postscript to the Gospel of the Egyptians, the great Seth confirms himself as the author of the work and claims he has had it hidden on a high mountain so that the sun never rises upon it—that is, so that it was in and came out of darkness.

I conclude that the Seth of the Gnostic early Christians is the same as that of the Qumran Essenes and must be the same Seth that appears throughout the history of ancient Egypt.

To put a final nail in this particular coffin, the notion of a powerfully evil Seth as the third son of Adam is untenable not only on logistic grounds, but in Christian terms it is heresy. Chapter 3 of the Gospel of Luke lists Jesus's family tree all the way back to Adam, the son of God. His second most ancient ancestor was Seth.

The gnostic elements of the Dead Sea Scrolls that are peculiar to the Qumran-Essene sect refer continually to the mysteries behind the mere written word and action. In these references there is a clear parallel to early apocryphal Christianity; and there is yet another link to its authors, or to very early adherents of those who were, it becomes apparent, the forerunners of Christianity.

## Reservations

Certain reservations with respect to these observations need to be considered, but they do not negate the specific conclusion of the above paragraphs.

Great care has to be taken in the use and understanding of nonspecific terms like *gnosticism*, which has meant different things to different people at different times in history. In the sense of mystical, spiritual, hidden knowledge, gnosticism predated the Qumran-Essene period and almost certainly stretches back in its origins to ancient Egypt and other pagan cultic cultures. Even in the formulation of gnosticism evident among the Qumran Essenes, it is possible to detect at least two varieties of its meaning.

The gnosticism of the early church, predominantly manifested in its Egyptian branches and closely related to the experience of the Qumran Essenes, was one of mysteries—secret knowledge and inner understanding—

available only to the community; it also involved a dualism of good and evil.[22]

The other form of gnosticism, abroad in the outer population of Judaism, was known about and recorded in the Qumran writings but was not necessarily endorsed by them. This schema incorporated the ideas of trinities, demons, angels, a realm beyond of supreme incorruptibility, magic incantations, and celestial mysteries. These, like most of the other Gnostic ideas, initiated from within the Egyptian religions and then were strongly influenced by Greek philosophical and pantheonic ideas.

For the Qumran Essenes, many of the Egyptian Gnostic ideas that dominated outside the period of Akhenaten's monotheism were anathema. They survived, nevertheless, into Gnostic Christianity and remained within mainstream Judaism. When Emperor Constantine backed a more clearly defined form of official Christianity in the fourth century C.E.[23] and imposed it on the entirety of the Roman Empire, he also outlawed Gnostic Christianity and its adherents. The Great Library at Alexandria was burned and the School of Philosophy closed; Gnosticism went underground, only to erupt through the centuries in Kabbalah for a section of Jewish philosophy,[24] as alchemy in the Middle Ages in Europe, and in the mystic religions of the East.

Squeezed out beyond the borders of the Holy Roman Empire, it was taken up by the prophet Mani, as Manichaeanism in Persia, evolving into the Manichaean movement in the third century C.E., and appeared in the concept of Parabrahman, or "the beyond," of the Hindus and the Ade Buddha of Buddhism, emerging again in Europe of the thirteenth century C.E. under the Cathars of Languedoc, France, and the Knights Templar. (I will come back to the possible significance of this last link when we look at the life of John the Baptist.)

We have now taken a brief look at how some of the critical early Jesus texts relate to Dead Sea Scrolls material. Next on the menu is how Jesus, his followers, and his precursor—John the Baptist—might relate to the Dead Sea Scrolls and Qumran. First, though, what do we actually know about Jesus in historical terms, as opposed to what is preserved in the Christian Scriptures?

# ― 15 ―

# Quotations from the Christian Scriptures Derived from the Dead Sea Scrolls

Early Christian writers frequently cited passages from the Hebrew Scriptures, but also from nonbiblical apocryphal Jewish literature, which subsequently went missing. As a result, works like 1 Enoch and Jubilees were preserved only through versions transmitted in Christian communities. The scrolls from Qumran changed the situation dramatically and demonstrated not only that many of these apocryphal works existed long before the Christian Scriptures, but also that in many instances quotations from the versions in the ownership of the Qumran Essenes conformed more closely to quotations in the Christian Scriptures and early Christian writings than those from any other versions.

Examples of correlations between early Christian writings, both canonical and noncanonical, and the Dead Sea Scrolls have continued to increase as more material, mainly from Cave 4, has been made available. I quote some of the more recent revelations: a prophetic passage written by Clement of Rome, who lived in the first century C.E., which appears to be a direct quotation from Pseudo-Ezekiel:

> And I will rise you up out of your graves (1 Clem. 50:4)

> And I will raise you up fro[m] your [graves] (4Q385)[1]

Jesus heals a paralytic in Capernaum and forgives his sins:

> Except ye see signs and wonders, ye shall not believe. (John 4:46–54)

126

This parallels the Prayer of Nabonidus, the last king of Babylon, who was cured by a Jewish exorcist and who then came to believe in the Most High God (Dead Sea Scroll 4Q242).

The Gospels of Luke and Matthew quote phrases paralleled in a Dead Sea Scrolls fragment known as the Messianic Apocalypse (4Q521), which will be considered in greater depth, together with two other hugely controversial fragments, in the next chapter:

> . . . How that the blind see, the lame walk, the lepers are cleansed, the deaf hear, the dead are raised, to the poor the gospel is preached. (Luke 7:22)

> He who liberates the captives, restores the sight to the blind, straightens the b[ent]. For He will heal the wounded, and revive the dead and bring good news to the poor. (4Q521)[2]

Although Isaiah says, "The blind shall see, the deaf hear, and the lame be cured; and the Spirit of the Lord God is upon him and he brings good tidings to the poor and liberty to the captives" (35:5; 61:1), there is no mention of lepers being cleansed or the dead being raised. The conclusion, as posited by the biblical scholar J. J. Collins, is that "it is quite possible that the author of the Sayings source knew 4Q521."[3] Hershel Shanks, the American writer/editor, comes to a similar finding.[4]

Incidentally, the claim that 4Q521, linked to the so-called Pierced Messiah fragment, demonstrates that the Qumran Essenes were talking about a contemporary Jesus is negated by an even earlier reference, Psalm 22.[5] Here we find the opening words and later verses clearly echoed in the Christian Scriptures:

> My God, my God, why hast thou forsaken me? . . .

> They pierced my hands and my feet . . .

> And cast lots upon my clothes . . .

The authors of the Christian Scriptures were simply drawing on older sources to describe Jesus's crucifixion.

There are numerous other instances where early Christian authors appear to have quoted sources that are known only from Qumran literature. In addition, there are many examples where combinations of previous biblical material is drawn on, indicating that the two groups, the early Christians and the Qumran Essenes, undoubtedly had a very similar mindset when it came to choosing biblical quotations.

Professor George Brooke, of Manchester University, points to a number of these "mind-set" examples where not only are the same original sources exploited, but the material is sometimes used in the same order as well.[6] He also argues, however, that the overlap between the Qumran scrolls and the Christian Scriptures in such areas as legal, narrative, admonitory, poetic, liturgical, and prophetic is less than many suppose. He argues that there are often as many differences between Qumran texts and the Christian Scriptures as similarities, and that the diversity in eschatologically oriented first-century Judaistic writings was a common source from which both Qumran and the early Christian writers drew inspiration.

Nevertheless, the sources of these examples were not previously known in apocryphal or pseudepigraphic references. The striking repetitions of phrases unique to the Qumran Essenes in relation to, for example, dualism of good and evil, manifested in their texts as "the sons of light" and "the sons of darkness," and also seen in numerous Christian Scriptures quotations,[7] cannot be escaped or put down to the use of global quotations:

But are you not in darkness, brethren . . . or you are all sons of light and some of the day. (Thess. 5:4–5)

What fellowship has light with darkness? What accord has Christ with Belial? (2 Cor. 6:14–15)

Let us then cast off the works of darkness and put on the armor of light. (Rom. 13:12)

I am the light of the world; he who follows me will not walk in darkness. (John 8:12)

> Jesus said to them . . . he who walks in the darkness does not know where he goes. While you have the light, believe in the light, that you may become sons of light. (John 12:35–36)

The Qumran Essenes specifically referred to themselves as the "sons of light." There can be no clearer statement from the Christian Scriptures that Jesus counted himself among the same "sons of light."

When the Qumran Essenes spoke of evil, they often stylized it in the form of Belial, who catches the unwary in his three nets and casts them down to fire and damnation.[8] As Professor Robert Eisenman notes, this Belial-style language "reverberates through the whole of the New Testament (the Christian Scriptures)." His numerous books on the subject of Qumran and Jesus[9] make a formidable case for the direct influence of the Qumran Essenes on the Christian Scriptures. Because of these parallels, Professor Eisenman concludes that James and the Teacher of Righteousness—the leader of the Qumran Essenes—were one and the same.

This is a conclusion that I do not go along with. To identify James the brother of Jesus as the Teacher of Righteousness of the community, as well as the leader of the early Jerusalem church, creates all sorts of chronological problems. It completely ignores the evidence of carbon-14 dating, numismatics, and paleography—areas Professor Eisenman steers well clear of—and requires the record of the Teacher of Righteousness to have been written sometime between 60 C.E., the date of the death of James, and 68 C.E., the date of the demolition of Qumran by the Romans. It also ignores the overwhelming evidence that the Teacher of Righteousness almost certainly led his group to Qumran sometime around 150 B.C.E. The professor's tortuous tissue of a case needs to be cut with Occam's razor. The simplest explanation is often the correct one. The describers of James were merely drawing on descriptions of the Teacher of Righteousness.

Tracing the quotations in the Christian Scriptures to their assumed original Qumran-Essene and Hebrew Scriptures sources is the flavor of the decade and preoccupies hundreds if not thousands of scholars around the world. I believe that in many instances they are traveling only halfway back down the road of authenticity. Despite the fact that large chunks of the Hebrew Scriptures have been shown to have been based on much earlier Egyptian texts—the Wisdom Books, Psalms, the Succession Narratives in the Books of Samuel and 1 and 2 Kings, and the repeated Egyptology seen in the Dead Sea Scrolls[10]—little attempt has been made to investigate these texts in the light of these blazing neon signs. Taken en masse, the evidence of a connection back to ancient Egypt and to the times of Akhenaten for the Qumran Essenes is overwhelming.

Where did the Qumran Essenes get their ideas from? Where did the Hebrew Scriptures get their ideas from? We have only to look at the Book of the Dead and other ancient Egyptian theology to see that reviving the dead was a long-held belief. We find it, for example, in this noncanonical saying attributed to Jesus:

Nothing is buried which will not be raised up.[11]

The phrase is found inscribed on a mummy bandage from an Oxyrhynchus fish, sacred to the goddesses Hathor, Isis, and Mut, of which there is an example in the British Museum.

Although early Christian writers could in theory have obtained some of their information from versions of text in general circulation, it seems likely that much of the Qumran-Essenes' literature from which they were quoting was available only to the Qumran-Essene membership. The significance of these correlations is that the early Christians must have had access to sectarian texts with limited circulation and had a much closer relationship with the Qumran Essenes than has previously been acknowledged.

# ⌒ 16 ⌒

# Messianic Apocalypse, Son of God, and Pierced Messiah

A mong the relatively recent translated material from Cave 4 at Qumran, texts referring to a messiah, or messiahs, have proved the most controversial.

Some half a dozen of the Qumran-Essene texts, developed exclusively for the Essenes' own use, often duplicated in numbers of copies, refer directly or indirectly to an eschatological age when several messiahs will appear on earth and herald the dawn of a new godly era.

The main references appear in a number of the scrolls, including the Messianic Rule, the Cairo-Damascus, and the Rule of War.

- 1 Q Rule Community [the Community Rule scroll that was found in Cave 1] refers to two messiahs and a messianic prophet who would be able to remake the Law.
- 1QSb, known as Blessings and dated to 100 B.C.E., includes several benedictions to be given by the community's leader during the messianic age as he addresses the high priest messiah and the princely messiah of the congregation.[1]
- The Rule of War contains the notorious fragment 4Q521, the so-called Messianic Apocalypse fragment, dated to the beginning of the first century B.C.E. It describes in poetic terms an anointed figure as well as healing and bodily resurrection that will accompany the arrival of the kingdom of God. This last scroll is the only one of the Dead Sea Scrolls to talk of resurrection, combined with the themes of healing the blind and wounded, making the bent right, freeing captives, ministering to the poor, and the arrival of God's

kingdom. It is remarkably similar to themes in Luke chapters 4 through 7:[2]

> And in that same hour he cured many of their infirmities and plagues, and of evil spirits; and unto many that were blind he gave sight. (Luke 7:21)

> Go your way and tell John [the Baptist] what things you have seen and heard; how that the blind see, the lame walk, the lepers are cleansed, the deaf hear, the dead are raised, to the poor the gospel is preached. (Luke 7:22)

## Resurrection

That the Christian idea of messiahship draws on Essene ideas can also be seen in the parallels between ideas on resurrection, for example, in the Messianic Apocalypse Scroll mentioned above.

Belief by the Essenes in bodily resurrection is attested to by the early Christian writer Hippolytus: "The doctrine of the Resurrection has also derived support among them [the Essenes], for they acknowledge both that the flesh will rise again, and that it will be immortal, in the same manner as the soul is already imperishable. They maintain that, when the soul has been separated from the body, it is now borne into one place, which is well ventilated and full of light, and there it rests until judgment."[3]

Here Hippolytus demonstrates what earlier writers on the Essenes—Philo, Dion, and Josephus—have avoided, a clear statement of the Essenes' views on resurrection. His mature Christian orthodoxy acknowledges an explicit kindred spirituality shared by Christians and Essenes in the main areas of Jewish teaching.

For Hershel Shanks, the American author and editor of the *Biblical Archaeology Review* and *Bible Revue,* the life of Jesus is prefigured in the Dead Sea Scrolls.[4] He maintains that the idea of distinct priestly and kingly messiahs "no longer holds," on the basis that a text, 4Q521, published in his 1992 *Review,* reveals a single eschatological messiah with attributes of the Christian Messiah. This viewpoint seems difficult to sustain in light of the repeated descriptions in a number of Dead Sea Scrolls manuscripts that describe the separate roles of the two and possibly three messiahs that were awaited by the Qumran Essenes. Perhaps the text appears to talk about one messiah because it just happens to be talking, on this particular occasion, about only one of the several messiahs included among the "holy ones" working in conjunction with the Lord. The particular passage in question reads as follows:

> [The hea]vens and the earth will listen to His Messiah, and none therein will stray from the commandments of the holy ones. . . . For the Lord will consider the pious and call the righteous by name. Over the poor His spirit will hover and will renew the faithful with His power. . . . He . . . liberates the captives, restores sight to the blind, straightens the b[ent]. . . . The Lord will accomplish glorious things which have never been. . . . He will heal the wounded, and revive the dead and bring good news to the poor.[5]

The passage is very similar to Matthew 11:4–5 and Luke 7:22–23; like the Qumran text, it seems to be derived from Psalm 146 and Isaiah 35:5–6 and 61:1. Professor James Tabor, of the University of North Carolina, and Professor Michael Wise, of the University of Chicago, are more dogmatic about the connectivity:

> We now have an unambiguous statement that "raising the dead" was one of the key expectations of the Messianic age in this community. . . . Isaiah 61:1 says nothing about this Anointed One "raising the dead." Indeed, in the entire Hebrew Bible there is nothing about a messiah figure raising the dead. Yet, when we turn to the Q Source, which Luke and Matthew quote, regarding the "signs of the Messiah," we find the two phrases linked; "the dead are raised up, the poor have glad tidings preached to them," *precisely as we have in our Qumran text.* . . . It is also significant that this section of the Q Source is dealing with traditions shared between the community of John the Baptist and that of the early followers of Jesus.[6] (my emphasis)

What scholars like Professors Tabor and Wise maintain differentiates the Qumran text and the Gospel versions from sources in the Hebrew

Scriptures mentioned above is the inclusion of a reference to reviving the dead in conjunction with the messiah. Thus, from Ezekiel 37, we do have mention of the reviving of the dead at the end of time, but only as part of the final restitution of Israel. Recent work by Benjamin Wright, of Lehigh University, in Pennsylvania, concludes that even Ezekiel is being quoted by the Christian Scriptures in a form peculiar to Qumran. Comparing the Valley of the Dry Bones passage from Ezekiel 37 with the Christian Scriptures' Apocalypse of Peter 4:7–9, he says there is convincing evidence that the latter quotation came from a specifically sectarian version of Ezekiel, known as Second Ezekiel, and that the community expected resurrection of the righteous who have been faithful to the law.[7]

The overall conclusion from the above analysis is that scholars who had presumed the Dead Sea Scrolls were describing a contemporary Christ got it wrong. Their attempts to utilize the Pierced Messiah text were almost certainly led astray by a desire to bolster a preconceived case.

Yet another hotly debated fragment has added to the furor.

## The Son of God Fragment

Professor George Brooke is fond of pointing out that one must be very cautious in accepting any particular viewpoint on Dead Sea Scrolls scholarship. Everyone brings to the house of interpretation his own preconceived set of baggage, and I am sure I am no exception. Some are so entrenched in their own academic or religious cathedrals, however, that they simply cannot admit alternative views. They and their reputations are already irrevocably committed. Other more enlightened scholars, such as Professor Brooke himself, Professor Lawrence Schiffman, and Jozef Milik, are prepared to consider the interpretations of others with an open mind and change their stance if convinced. Few pieces of Dead Sea Scrolls material better exemplify Professor Brooke's "baggage" dictum than the so-called Son of God fragment. Even Jozef Milik was nervous about its contents, as the history of its consideration shows in the notes to this chapter.[8]

Of all the controversial material found at Qumran, the so-called Son of God fragment (4Q246) stands out as one of the most illuminating. This tiny piece of leather found in Cave 4, with its ancient Aramaic writing, talks in apocalyptic terms of a prince and a fallen ruler. It is worth quot-

ing in full to appreciate its significance. Note that square brackets [ ] indicate interpolations; parentheses ( ) indicate alternative translations:

> [The spirit of God] dwelt on him, he fell down before the throne.
>
> O [K]ing, wrath is coming to the world (you are angry for ever),
> and your years . . . is your vision and all of its coming to this world . . .
> great [signs] a tribulation will come upon the land . . . a great mas-
> sacre in the provinces . . . a prince of nations . . . the King of Assyria
> and [E]gypt . . . he will be great on earth . . . will make and all will
> serve . . . he will be called (he will call himself) [gr]and . . . and by his
> name he will be designated (designate) himself.
>
> The Son of God he will be proclaimed (proclaim himself), and the
> Son of the Most High they will call him. But like the sparks (meteors)
> of the vision, so will be their kingdom. They will reign for only a few
> years on earth, and they will trample all.
>
> People will trample people, and one province another province
> until the people of God will arise and all will rest from the sword.
>
> Their kingdom will be an eternal kingdom, and their paths will
> be righteous. They will jud[ge] the earth justly, and all will make
> peace. The sword will cease from the earth, and all the provinces will
> pay homage to them. The Great God will be their helper. He Himself
> will wage war for them. He will give peoples into their hands, and all
> of them He will cast before them. Their dominion will be an eternal
> dominion, and all the boundaries of . . .

One can only imagine the confusion these three short columns have
caused among biblical scholars. The phrases *Son of God* and *Son of the
Most High* occur in Luke 1:32–35 and seem to indicate reference to Jesus
the Messiah. The puzzles in 4Q246 are: Who is the dethroned ruler? What
is the civil war being described? Who is the new king who appoints himself Son of the Most High? Which provinces will pay homage to those who
vanquish the new king and reinstate peace? Why are Assyria and Egypt
mentioned? Is there a reference to Jesus?

Add to this the fact that the various translated versions differ in wording—the one quoted here being that of Professor Emeritus Geza
Vermes[9]—and it can easily be seen that the complications multiply. The

general thrust of the story, however, is readily discernible from the quoted version and is similar in other translations.

Explanations of the identity of the antihero in the text range from the Syrian tyrant Antiochus IV, to Emperor Augustus,[10] to the Seleucid ruler Alexander Balas.[11] Some, such as F. Garcia Martinez, have argued for an apocalyptic interpretation, with the Son of God being the Prince of Light, or a future Davidic messiah.[12] The array of explanations is extremely varied, but none fits more than a few of the circumstances of the passage. In fact, they amount to no more than speculation. John J. Collins of Yale is one of the few scholars to begin to take up the challenge thrown down by Professor Schiffman to look farther afield than the dusts of Judaea for explanations of difficult Dead Sea Scrolls texts.[13]

In my view, there is only one scenario in the history of the Hebrews that fits this specification. It is when Joseph, Jacob, and their Hebrew families are at the court of the monotheistic Egyptian king Akhenaten and the king is killed, together with his high priest, Meryra, who is also a hereditary prince. Simultaneously, Akhenaten's Great Temple and his holy city are destroyed. His followers and the Hebrews are dispersed as civil war breaks out.

Place the Qumran Essenes in the historical context of the events surrounding Akhenaten's death, a factor that I postulate in this and my previous book, and every perplexing phrase in 4Q246 becomes explicable through their knowledge of these events. By tracing the priestly strain of Qumran Essenes right back to the monotheistic pharaoh King Akhenaten—whom they viewed, I contend, as their vision of God's representative on earth, their Melchizedek—we find the circumstances that surrounded his life fit every essential detail of 4Q246. In addition, anyone who has even a cursory knowledge of the ancient Egyptian texts of the Amarna period (c. 1350 B.C.E.) will recognize the style of phraseology used in the Son of God fragment.

King Akhenaten's reign in his newly established holy city of Akhetaten, some 250 miles north of Thebes and 155 miles south of Memphis (Cairo), came to an abrupt end when he was almost certainly killed, probably by Ay, his trusted aide, who later usurped the throne of Egypt. Akhenaten may well have been struck down before his own throne. (If, instead, the figure before the throne is viewed as a seer, as some interpreters envisage—"wrath is coming to the world"—what better seer at the king's court could there be than Joseph?) Civil war then broke out throughout Egypt, and Akhenaten's followers were massacred throughout the provinces, or *nomes,* of Egypt.

In the words of Nicholas Weeks, director of the Amarna Royal Tombs Project, "The situation rapidly deteriorated into mayhem and widespread religious persecution."[14] There was a brief intermediate pharaoh, Smenkhkara, and then Tutankhamun succeeded to the throne, but he was too young to govern. Ay was effectively in control of Egypt, and he almost certainly also killed Tutankhamun and appointed himself king. This self-elevation of a nonroyal was virtually unknown in Egypt, as the direct family descendant invariably became ruler. The terms *Son of God* and *Son of the Most High* are typically Egyptian of the period, viz. Melchizedek (the king-priest), and appear in many ancient Egyptian texts. The phrases allude to the pharaoh's direct equation with the highest god, Amun, supported by Khons, Ra, and all the other lesser gods. Akhenaten's holy city of Akhetaten was destroyed within twenty or thirty years of Ay assuming power and reestablishing Thebes as the capital of Egypt. In doing so he appropriated the traditional pharaonic title of Son of God.

The text of 4Q246 then moves to a vision of the future, anticipating the "people of God," the followers of Akhenaten, regaining power by sweeping away and "trampling" the followers of the treacherous Ay. When they succeed, "their dominion will be an eternal dominion, and all the boundaries of . . . "

Akhenaten's newly built, virgin holy city was demarked by fifteen boundary stelae, some up to twenty-six feet high, carved out of natural rock features. The area inside these boundary markers was considered to be holy, outside was not, and to be buried outside the holy city was a disaster.

The dream of Akhenaten's followers would inevitably have been that the people of God would eventually triumph and that he would one day be restored to power with the "provinces again paying tribute" to him. His holy city would likewise be restored.

Reference to Assyria and Egypt in 4Q246 as being under the hegemony of the antihero king can only be a reference to an Egyptian king. Egypt was the only power ever to be exclusively referred to as the controller of both these regions. The only time in ancient history when any country controlled both Egypt and Assyria was pre–1200 B.C.E., and that controlling country was Egypt itself. At the time, the people of Mesopotamia were being referred to as an Assyrian empire and as vassals of Egypt. Subsequent to the eighth century B.C.E., the region was controlled by the Babylonians, and then successively by the Persians, Greeks, and Romans. Their empires were vast but were never spoken of as being controlled by a king exclusively controlling Egypt and Assyria.

The idea suggested by some scholars, that the reference might be to the "broadly speaking" domination of the Romans of Assyria and Egypt, just doesn't fit. The northern region of Asia was no longer called Assyria and had not been since pre-Babylonian times, and Rome dominated most of the countries bordering the Mediterranean. There would be no sensible reason to single out Egypt and Assyria as part of the king's, or more precisely emperor's, empire.

All the conventional explanations of 4Q246 are forced, but put on a very ancient pair of Egyptian glasses and read the passage again. All the elements of Akhenaten's story are there, a story known fairly accurately from historical records: a king (Akhenaten) who faces disaster and possible treachery—"a tribulation will come upon the land"—and is almost certainly slain, betrayed and killed by a close friend (Ay), and becomes a messianic figure for his people of God. Civil war breaks out "throughout the provinces [*nomes*]" of the country; the traitor appoints himself king (pharaoh) of Egypt and Assyria and proclaims himself the new "Son of the Most High" incarnate on earth, as all previous pharaohs were accustomed to do; he is the anti-Christ; the people of God dream of their redeemer, a kingly messiah (Akhenaten), returning and taking revenge on the peoples of the anti-Christ; "the people of God" restore "all the boundaries" of Akhenaten's Holy City.

All the surrounding flavor of other related Dead Sea Scrolls texts, and the phrases that keep cropping up in them, fits this interpretation of 4Q246. This was the messiah the Qumran Essenes were waiting for, *a king who carried a scepter*[15]—the emblem of kingship in Egypt. The second *priestly messiah, the Prince of the Congregation,*[16] was accompanied by his high priest, Meryra[17]—who was by birth a hereditary prince of Egypt, while the priestly leader of the Qumran community was called Mervyre.[18] Light[19] was the overriding motif of Aten, Akhenaten's One God, with the "hands"[20] of life, bounty, food, and goodness radiating outward from a central winged sun image—an image that continued to appear in Egypt after Akhenaten and keeps popping up in excavations across ancient Canaan, modern Israel. We even find two of the Akhenaten motifs combined in the Essenic phrases "by the hands of the Prince of Lights" and "Prince of Light"[21] seen in other Dead Sea Scrolls material.

The Dead Sea War Scroll is even more specific. It unequivocally names Akhenaten's high priest, Meryra, as a leader in the final battle of the "sons of light" against the "sons of darkness":

> On the standard of *Merari* they shall write the votive offering of God, . . .
>     And the Prince of Light Thou hast appointed from ancient times.
> (my emphasis)

An external contemporary of the Qumran Essenes, Flavius Josephus, who recorded a number of descriptions that identify the sect, even gives an oblique indication that he also knew of the name Aten as that of God. In Book 2 of his *Antiquities of the Jews,* he refers to the caution of discovering the four-letter name of God.

## Pierced Messiah

Read in conjunction with the highly controversial Dead Sea War Scroll and the so-called Pierced Messiah fragments found in Cave 4 (4Q285)[22] "(As it is written in the book of) Isaiah the Prophet (the thickets of the forest) will be cut [down]," the thread of the story is continuous. The phrases found in these fragments, as previously discussed, can clearly be identified with Egypt and Akhenaten.

The future dream of the people of God, now in the hands of the Qumran Essenes, speaks of God shining his face toward his people and giving them life and bounteous fruit and food in plenty (4Q285, fragment 1). Rays of light with hands giving life and food are the defining symbols of Akhenaten's vision of his One God, Aten.

The Kittim that are to be slain by the forces of light cannot be the Romans, as some scholars suggest, because the fragments (4 and 5 of 4Q285) clearly incorporate themes already taken up by Isaiah and Ezekiel long before the time of the Romans. *Kittim* is, in fact, a word also used by the ancient Egyptians when referring to their enemies.[23]

Some scholars suggest that the messiah being referred to in these controversial fragments is related to references to King David in the Book of Isaiah. King David cannot possibly be this kingly messiah, however, because these passages talk about a slain king. King David died peacefully at a ripe old age.

The identity of a messiah who embodies the titles Son of God and Son of Man is also readily equated to Akhenaten from numerous hieroglyph descriptions of him. Stela 324, in the British Museum, is a good example. Here the cartouches show the double nature of the king as divine son and earthly regent. This is a recurring laudation of the two natures of the Father-God, along with the divine human son, characterizing the pharaoh as Son of God.[24]

Considering that the three hugely controversial fragments discussed above almost certainly espouse one theme—a slain religious leader and his high priest—the overall conclusion is that the Qumran community was writing about messiahs in the far distant history of its movement, none of whom was Jesus, but that the original characteristics of Jesus might have fulfilled many of its expectations. It would not therefore be surprising to find that a strand of the Qumran-Essene community would become followers of Jesus as a messianic figure, and might have spread his message to other Essenes outside Qumran.

# — 17 —

## Paul's Smoking Gun

The one man who never met Jesus, and yet who did more than any other early Christian to spread the word and fashion the embryonic new religion, was Saul, from Tarsus, a Hellenized city of Asia Minor.[1] The Christian Scriptures refer to him as Saul, later known as Paul, and he is reputed to have studied under Rabbi R. Gamaliel the Elder, in Jerusalem, as we learn in Acts:

> I am verily a man which am a Jew, born in Tarsus, a city in Cilicia, yet brought up in this city at the feet of Gamaliel, and taught according to the perfect manner of the law of the fathers, and was zealous towards God, as ye all are this day. . . .
>
> And it came to pass, that, as I made my journey, and was come nigh unto Damascus about noon, suddenly there shone from the heaven a great light round me.
>
> And I fell unto the ground, and heard a voice saying unto me, Saul, Saul, why persecutest thou me?
>
> And I answered, Who art thou, Lord? And he said unto me, I am Jesus of Nazareth, whom thou persecutest. (22:3, 6–8)

From being an apparent persecutor of the Christians, Saul became their greatest proponent. According to the Christian Scriptures, after experiencing a divine revelation of Jesus, he withdrew into Arabia to contemplate his dramatic role reversal and adopted the new name, Paul. Following a period of retreat, he began preaching and effectively laying the foundations of a Christian doctrine that could encompass non-Jews, and eventually have a profound effect on world civilization. The influences of Greek philosophy, Hebrew testaments, and—most significant, as

141

will become increasingly apparent—the doctrines of the Essenes are evident in his writings.

Three years after his revelation, the Christian Scriptures record, Paul went down to Jerusalem and met the disciples Peter and James—the latter being the brother of Jesus—and there Paul must have begun to enunciate a campaign of proselytization. The opening up of Christianity to Gentiles that Paul advocated inevitably created a rift with those Jews who wanted it to remain within the community of Torah—the Jerusalem Jesus movement. Progressively, Paul's view of emancipation won the day, although communities of the so-called Judaizers or Nazarenes survived well into the fourth century C.E.

Paul's missionary efforts continued, achieving success in Syria, Cyprus, Asia Minor, Macedonia, and Greece, where, in 51 C.E., he established a Christian community at Corinth, and later another at Ephesus.

In the late 60s C.E., Jewish uprisings, championed by the Zealots, led to a severe reaction from the Romans and the capture of Jerusalem by Titus and the sacking of the Temple. By then the baptism of a Roman centurion, Cornelius, and other prominent Romans in Palaestina had taken the message back to Rome, and it was not long before a groundswell began in the Roman environment. Rome, the center of the ancient world's most powerful empire, like a great crouching eagle, had its talons gouged deep into every country circumscribing and within the Mediterranean Sea—stretching from Morocco to Egypt in northern Africa, through Syria, Iraq, Turkey, Greece, France, and Spain, and on across Europe into Britain. One might almost postulate that if Rome had not conquered Israel, Christianity would not have spread much beyond the Middle East. (God moves in mysterious ways!)

There were now three primary strains of a pubescent new religion:

1. The Essenic/early Jesus movement awaiting a kingly warrior messiah (rooted in Essenism, Gnosticism, and Judaism)
2. Pauline-Gentile Christianity (rooted in Paul's Hellenistic spiritual doctrine of resurrection and divine salvation in another world)
3. Nazorean (Essenic)-Mandaean Johanism (rooted in John the Baptist)

Two centuries have passed. Essenic Judaism has become closely associated with Christianity in the minds of the rabbinate. It can no longer be mentioned in any rabbinic texts. Nor do the Christian Scriptures clearly refer to Essenism (although the Essenes are mentioned under various pseudonyms in the Christian Scriptures). The element of Essenism, which never committed itself to Jesus and still waited for at least two messiahs, weakens in its patience and in disillusionment turns increasingly toward Gnosticism and the mystery side of its beliefs—soon to be persecuted and pilloried by a Roman Empire converted to Pauline Christianity. Why the early faith in Jesus, a Jew, should start to turn outward to a wider non-Jewish audience is interesting to contemplate.

It was probably at quite an early stage in the evolution of Christianity that Peter's stance, like that of Paul, moved toward trying to promulgate Jesus's view of Judaism to a wider Gentile world, a motivation exemplified by the vision that Peter had while standing before the house of Simon the Tanner in Jaffa (just south of modern Tel Aviv). Apparently seeing unclean (non-kosher) food coming down from the skies, he interpreted this as a sign of the future direction Christianity should follow, spreading the grace of God to non-Jews as well as Jews.

## The Washington Freer Gospels: Spreading the Gospel and Satan

A curious addition to the New Testament can be seen in the Freer Gallery, Washington, which houses one of the oldest extant manuscripts of the Gospels, dating to the third century C.E. (the Washington Freer Codex addition). It gives a possible motivation for Peter's, and later Paul's, stance on the need to spread the word of Jesus beyond Judaism.[2] While there is reference in Matthew 12 and Luke 2, in the authorized version of the Christian Scriptures, to judging and enlightening the Gentiles, it is only in the later-composed Epistles of Paul (Eph. 3:8; 2 Tim. 1:11) that teaching to a wider audience is advocated.[3] In fact, in Matthew 10:5–6, Jesus unambiguously tells his disciples:

> Do not go into the way of the Gentiles, and do not enter a city of the Samaritans. But go rather to the lost sheep of the house of Israel.

It is quite striking that whereas the Hebrew Scriptures rarely mention Satan and say nothing about a conspiracy of Satan or demons in league with human beings against the divine governance of the world, when we come to the Dead Sea Scrolls and the Christian Scriptures, Satan is developed as a formidable antagonist of God. As the Washington Freer Codex addition and passages in John 8 confirm, it is now a full-scale battle of the Qumran Essene–style forces of good against the forces of evil.[4] (See page 3 of the color insert.)

## The Essenes in the Writings of Paul

If there were a close connection between early Christianity and Qumran, it would likely manifest itself more strongly in the earliest writings of the Christian Scriptures. As the writings of Paul are generally accepted as being the earliest testimonies to Jesus, composed perhaps between 50 and 60 C.E., it is among these works that we would expect the closest correlations. (Strangely, Paul seems to know little about Jesus's life before the Last Supper, nor were the stories about Jesus's tomb apparently known to him.) It is worth looking at three examples of distinctive words or phrases that Paul uses verbatim or paraphrases to convey certain ideas not seen in the Old Testament, in addition to those already mentioned, which are exclusive to the Qumran texts.

- *The righteousness of God* (Rom. 1:17; 3:5, 21–2; 10:3). Never found in the Hebrew Scriptures but used verbatim in sectarian texts of the Dead Sea Scrolls.[5]
- *Justification by grace through faith* (Rom. 3:23). Whereas in Mosaic Law righteousness could be achieved simply by observing its commandments, Paul uses the phrase in relation to sin in the sense of God bestowing it on humanity through Jesus's death and resurrection. This sense of divine bestowal, absent in the Hebrew Scriptures, appears in sectarian Dead Sea Scrolls and has been interpreted as a transitional concept[6] between Mosaic teaching and that of Paul.

  A recently translated fragment from Cave 4, however, makes the transition in quoting the Maskil (community teacher) as saying,

"No man is righteous before God," implying that the Law is not enough to attain a state of righteousness or grace. Dr. Timothy Lim, of the University of Edinburgh, sees this Qumran text as being closer to Paul's writings than any previous quotation.[7]

However, it has been pointed out that Isaiah 64:6 has this same intimation that simply observing the law is not good enough in the eyes of God. "All our righteousness are as filthy rags."

- *The works of the Law in pursuit of righteousness* (Romans 3:28; Galatians 2:16; Washington Freer Codex, Mark 16:16, etc.). Similar sentiments are not found in the Hebrew Scriptures or rabbinic literature, but *are* found in uniquely sectarian texts from Qumran.[8]

Paul also demonstrates that he had absorbed a deep sense of the dualist struggle between the powers of light and darkness, but this was not a mainstream Judaistic concept. No Jewish sect apart from the Qumran Essenes held similar views.

Many of the original conclusions about Paul were tempered in the 1960s, when something less than a third of the available Dead Sea Scrolls texts had been published. As more and more material filtered out, culminating in the exposure in the 1990s of highly pertinent details from the sectarian texts, it became increasingly obvious that not only did Pauline and Johannine testimony draw heavily on Qumranic experience, but so did the early teachings and practices of Jesus sustain their impetus from Essenic knowledge.

Even the least convinced conservative commentators acknowledge that parallels between Paul's writing and the Qumran literature often make it possible to understand difficult passages in the Christian Scriptures. Many other scholars, such as W. F. Albright and R. E. Brown, have noted the frequent parallels between the Dead Sea Scrolls texts and both the Synoptic Gospels—particularly John—and Paul. For David Flusser, "The same moral dualism [as in the Qumran texts] appears throughout the Christian Scriptures but is expressed more emphatically in John's and Paul's writings. Moreover, Essene thought stands out prominently in the Epistles to the Ephesians and Colossians which suggests that their origin was pseudo-Pauline and that they did not derive from the Pauline school of thought."[9]

The designations of Jesus as Christ, or the Messiah, appear to have been superimposed at a later date when the Gospels came to be written. No one can dispute that these witnesses, with the information that they had, genuinely believed Jesus was the divine offspring of God. But as Frank Moore Cross, one of the original translation team, now a professor at Chicago University, observed, the Qumran material "will trouble the person who has been led by the clergy or by Christian polemics to believe that . . . the titles Jesus held as the Christ or Messiah were unanticipated in Jewish messianic apocalyptism. In short, I think anyone who has accepted claims of the discontinuity between Christianity and Judaism uncritically, may be shocked and may have to rethink his faith."[10]

## The Revelatory Conversion of Paul

The journey of Saul of Tarsus to Damascus, as described in Acts 9, has always presented difficulties for biblical commentators.[11] Ostensibly he was sent there to detain Nazoreans. The problem is that the Book of Acts makes no mention of a Nazorean community in Syria, nor does it seem likely that a Jesus-inspired community could have been established so far north of Jerusalem within such a short period after his death.

The religious affiliation of the community at Damascus was up and running well before the arrival of Christianity, and it was not defined in terms of Jesus. The community member, Ananias of Damascus, who restores the sight of Saul is described in a manner that, on analysis, makes him almost certainly a healer-Essene. His reference to "thy Saints at Jerusalem" in Acts 9:13 is a clear identification with the Essenes, who called themselves Saints, among other titles. Ananias is depicted, in Acts 9 and 22, as:

> a devout man according to the Law, with a gift of healing, who tells Saul he has been chosen to see and hear the Just One, and urges him to wash away his sins by baptism.

From the Dead Sea Damascus document, it is also apparent that the Just One is not Jesus, but none other than the Qumran-Essenes' Teacher of Righteousness,[12] who, it is believed, came to Damascus and affirmed the New Covenant as prophesied by Jeremiah.

The account in Acts 9 of Saul's baptism by Ananias is in itself rather puzzling. One would have expected Paul, in his later writings, to have mentioned the baptisms of John the Baptist in relation to this event, and to John's ministry. Paul is strangely silent, however, about John the Baptist.

From the later writings of Paul and their unquestionable closeness to the Qumran-Essene ways of thinking, he must have made contact with the community quite early in his theological journey. In fact, it may well have been at Damascus that Paul received his first initiation into the Essene philosophy of Judaism and learned that a section of the Qumran Essenes were followers of Jesus. References to Paul in the Christian Scriptures and a number of other factors make it almost certain that Paul's conversion came through the ministering of the Essenes:

- Reference to "the Saints"—a term the Essenes used to describe themselves.
- Reference to "the Just One"—a title that appears in the Dead Sea Scrolls Damascus document in relation to the Essenes' Teacher of Righteousness.
- Reference to baptism—an Essene characteristic.
- Reference to healing—an Essene characteristic.
- It would have been too soon after Jesus's death for a Christian community to have existed at Damascus, a place the Dead Sea Scrolls refer to as the location of one of the Essenes' settlements.

Acts goes on to relate how, after his conversion on the road to Damascus, Paul (previously Saul) stays in another Nazorean community in the Nabataean country of Arabia (Gal. 1:16–19). Nabataean epigrammatic examples are readily detectable in some of the Dead Sea Scrolls, and it seems likely that these arrived through an Essene branch community in Nabataea.[13] It is possibly here that Paul also picked up the Mandaean influences that appear in his doctrines of the Heavenly Messiah and Second Adam.

The above analysis and its inevitable conclusions are now being accepted by an increasing number of scholars, contrary to previous thinking. Christianity has conventionally been seen as having been derived from a background of the dominant Jewish movement of Paul's time, that of Pharisaism. This is, however, a very simplified picture and quite ignores other influences. Christianity, as Professor Frank Moore Cross points out, "was not a child of a single parent";[14] it is shot through with an apocalyptic vision that is characteristically Essenian, a vision picked up by early Christianity as a certain heir to a tradition that is, in many respects, unique to the Essenes. Professor Cross goes on to cite example after example of how Paul and the Christian Scriptures mirror the often unique sayings and teachings of the Essene community: "Contrary to the tendency of Christian Scriptures' theologians to assume that the 'eschatological existence' of the early Church, that is, its community life lived in anticipation of the Kingdom of God, together with forms shaped by this life, was a uniquely Christian phenomenon, we must now affirm that in the Essene communities we discover antecedents of Christian forms and concepts."

That Paul was fundamentally influenced by the philosophy, election/ predestination to the calling of God, holiness/sanctification, light/dark contrasts, wrath/salvation dualism, and eschatological/apocalyptic similarities of the Qumran Essenes is evident from his writings in the Christian Scriptures. His pro-celibacy stand, rejection of the material world, and sense of physical isolation are also consistent with the views of the Qumran Essenes. In the words of Karl Donfried, of the Hebrew University, Jerusalem: "A number of key points in 1 Thessalonians, his earliest letter, reveal striking similarities to the thought of the Community reflected in fundamental documents of the Dead Sea Scrolls occur both conceptually and linguistically. . . . At critical points it is, both positively and negatively, the influence of yahad (the Community), rather than Pharisaic–rabbinic tradition that is determinative in shaping Paul's pre-Christian Judaism."[15]

One can see that Paul is drawing on the same sense of understanding of individual concepts, words, and phrases that were in many instances unique to the Qumran community. For example, "truth" in the sense of revelation was first used by Paul in a letter written at Ephesus,[16] and this meaning for the word *truth* was commonly employed by the Qumran Essenes.

Not everyone is yet convinced that Paul's writings were heavily dependent on Essene texts, particularly those commentators on the conservative wing of scholarship. But with the eventual publication in 1994, after prolonged delays, of a Qumran letter (known as 4QMMT) purportedly composed by the Teacher of Righteousness, the founder of the Qumran community, the matter was resolved for most nonpartisan observers.[17]

## The Forensic Evidence

Martin Abegg, codirector of the Dead Sea Scrolls Institute at Trinity Western University, British Columbia, has gone further than most in claiming that Paul knew of and employed the kind of dualistic ideology and legal diktats espoused by the Qumranites: "4QMMT, however, provides 'the smoking gun' for which students have been searching for generations."[18]

As previously noted, if there is to be a clear connection made between the Christian Scriptures and the Qumran material, it seems likely that this connection would be most apparent in the earliest Christian witnesses, namely in the testimony of Paul.[19] This indeed appears to be the case. The writings of Paul, whose letters are thought to predate the setting down of the Gospels, are now seen by most academics as being strongly influenced by Qumran thinking. His earliest letter, 1 Thessalonians, has striking similarities to Qumran literature both conceptually and linguistically. Despite the fact that Paul spoke and wrote in Greek and the Christian Scriptures say he was a Jewish Pharisee,[20] what Martin Abegg dubs the "smoking gun" has finally shot down any lingering doubts concerning Paul's true affiliations.

The unique commonalities between the evolutionary religious beliefs and behavior patterns of the select Qumran Essenes and those of the early Christians and today's Christianity make a close association irresistible.

# — 18 —

# Beyond Paul

When it comes to the works of the Christian Scriptures composed after Paul, the elements related to Essene writings are again too numerous to reflect anything but considerable common interests. In some cases the detailed knowledge of purely sectarian texts and ritual can be explained only by some original intimate contact with the Qumran community. Many of these commonalities are listed in table 10, and a number of the more significant ones are expanded on in detail.

**TABLE 10**

**Ideas and theology exclusively promoted by the Qumran Essenes; they appear in the Christian Scriptures or Christian practice and are not apparent in other Jewish sources**

- Belial as a personalized incarnation of the powers of evil
- The temple as a metaphor for community
- Dualism in terms of light (good) and darkness (evil)
- Equating righteousness with the sun[1]
- The demand to keep separate from the way of darkness and to walk in the light
- Courts of justice at Qumran and Corinth following the same novel judicial system
- A conviction of humankind's hopeless sinfulness
- A humble teacher of justification through grace (recognized by Paul as Christ)
- Knowledge of mysteries (creational and eschatological) of God is revealed only to the absolutely righteous
- The terms *wisdom, knowledge,* and *understanding* used in the same sense
- Three cardinal sins of fornication, impurity, greed (which leads to idolatry)
- Foolishness and silliness as punishable offenses
- An imperative for mutual fraternal correction—that is, the urgent need to make people aware they are sinning and bring them back to the light of goodness
- The Qumran community and the Christian Church as the "chosen ones"
- Liturgical times of prayer, vigils, quarter-tense (days of fasting and abstinence) coming to the church from Qumran
- Tendencies toward monasticism and male chauvinism

There are so many examples in which Jesus's own characteristics and teaching are parallel to and often congruent with those of the community but are not reflected in the normative Jewish experience of his time that it becomes irresistible—if the accounts in the Christian Scriptures of Jesus's words and views are genuine and not those of later redactors—to assume he was once a member of the Qumran Essenes. I give but a few telling examples.

- Significantly, light (Hebrew, *nehira*) is a symbol of the messiah[2] and is one of the names used for Jesus. The uninitiated were people who sat in darkness (Matt. 4:12–17). For the Qumran Essenes, the "sons of darkness" were those who would be destroyed on the day of judgment while the "sons of light" would be saved.[3]
- In calling Jesus "the Righteous One" (Hebrew, *zadek*), a direct parallel is made between him and the Teacher of Righteousness of the Dead Sea Scrolls, who led the Qumran-Essene community.[4]

  In Matthew 5:22 Jesus says: "Whoever insults his brother shall be liable to the council" (Greek, *to Sunedrio*). It can hardly be that he is suggesting the guilty party be called before the Sanhedrin, or Jewish High Court, because the offense would not have been actionable there. But it would have been an offense within the confines of the Qumran-Essene community, where an accused would have been called before the community's council.[5]
- Jesus and his followers are said not to have kept the national fast days connected with the destruction of the First Temple (Matt. 9:14–17; Mark 2:18–22; Luke 5:33–39). Why should this be, when Jesus had asserted that he always followed the letter of Jewish Law and tradition? But the Qumran Essenes followed a different calendar and would have observed the festivals on different days.
- In a letter to the Roman emperor Trajan, Pliny the Younger mentions that the Christians "met on a certain day before it was light, and sang an antiphonal chant to Christ, as to a god." The letter was written when Pliny was governor of Bithynia, in Asia Minor, around 112 C.E. Singing a dawn hymn was a Qumran-Essene custom described in one of their scrolls.[6]

## Lord and Son of God

One of the more contentious areas of so-called parallels involves the titles given in the Christian Scriptures to Jesus. The Greek word Kyrios that appears as a stand-alone name for Jesus was for a long time thought to be unique to the Christian Scriptures. The eminent German scholar Rudolf Bultman's view ruled the roost right up until the latter part of the twentieth century: "At the very outset the unmodified expression 'the Lord' is unthinkable in Jewish usage. 'Lord' used of God is always given some modifier; we read: 'the lord of heaven and earth,' 'our Lord,' and similar expressions."[7] The wholesale acceptance in scholarly circles of this perspective was forced to change with the discovery in Cave 11 of a fragmentary Aramaic text relating to the Book of Job, and others concerning Enoch and Psalms. Here God is referred to in a stand-alone form as "Lord." Significantly, the Hebrew word that appears in Psalm 151 for Lord is Adon—a sound I have already suggested corresponds to Aten, the name Akhenaten gave to God; and another Hebrew word for "the Lord," Marya, is highly reminiscent of the name of Akhenaten's high priest, Meryra.[8]

Yet another title for Jesus evidenced in the Dead Sea Scrolls is "Son of God." Again, earlier scholars asserted that this was an original Christological title referring to the Messiah that was not found in contemporary Jewish writings.[9] Subsequently, the entire acceptance in scholarly circles of this notion had to change with the finding in Cave 4 of another Aramaic fragment (4Q246) in which the phrase was utilized (see chapter 7).

### Sons of Light and Sons of Darkness

The Christian Scriptures refer to "sons of light" and "sons of disobedience" or "sons of perdition" in the dualistic sense of dividing humanity into two groups, one good and one evil.[10] This division is never found in the Hebrew Scriptures but finds full expression in the sectarian Qumran literature.[11] There can be little doubt that early Christians identified themselves with the Essene community when they called themselves "sons of light," the same term that was used as a self-description at Qumran.

**TABLE 11**

**Comparison of unique commonalities in beliefs and practices between the Qumran Essenes and early and modern Christianity, not apparent in early mainstream Judaism**

| | Qumran Essenes | Early Christians | Modern Christianity |
|---|---|---|---|
| **Beliefs** | | | |
| Messiah(s) | Imminent return of two earthly messiahs—one priestly, one princely (one prophet like Moses) | Imminent return of Jesus, who subsumes the role of royal and high priestly messiahs | Jesus expected when conditions favorable |
| Immortality | Believed in | Believed in | Believed in |
| Apocalyptic expectations | Imminent final war between good (led by messiah) and evil; Kingdom of God reestablished | Imminent final war between good (led by Jesus) and evil; Kingdom of God reestablished | Final war between good (led by Jesus) and evil; Kingdom of God reestablished |
| Dualism | Belief in good and evil | Belief in good and evil | Belief in good and evil |
| Original Sin | From birth | From birth | From birth |
| Predestination | Believed in | Believed in | Believed in |
| New Covenant | Vision of their movement | Vision of their movement | Ongoing |
| Inner holiness | Heightened self-view | Heightened self-view | Apparent in Gnostic church |
| Prophetic role of leader | Affirmed its continuity | Affirmed its continuity | Affirmed its continuity |
| Quotations | Unique to Dead Sea Scrolls | Many repeated in Christian Scriptures | In Christian Scriptures |
| Interpretation of Hebrew Scriptures[a] | Quotations from Hebrew Scriptures in terms of 1st-century-CE experience | Quotations from Hebrew Scriptures in terms of 1st-century-CE experience | |
| Common vocabulary | For words like *congregation, overseer* in sectarian texts (e.g., 1QS) | *Majority, overseer* in Gospel texts (e.g., Corinthians, Timothy, Philippians) | |
| Favorite books of Hebrew Scriptures | Psalms, Deuteronomy, Isaiah | Psalms, Deuteronomy, Isaiah | Psalms, Deuteronomy, Isaiah |
| Focus on individuals | Founder of the sect—the Teacher of Righteousness; Melchizedek—priest of God Most High | Jesus as high priest of heaven and of the order of Melchizedek | Jesus, Mary, Joseph |
| Concept of the Holy Spirit | Developed by Essenes | Used frequently in Christian Scriptures[b] | Ongoing |

|  | Qumran Essenes | Early Christians | Modern Christianity |
|---|---|---|---|
| **Practices** | | | |
| Temple practices | Rejected | Rejected[c] | Rejected |
| Attitude to enemies | Hate them | Hate them | Love them |
| Animal sacrifices | Opposed | Opposed | Opposed |
| Baptism | For purification and repentance of sin; element of Holy Spirit | For purification and repentance of sin; element of Holy Spirit | For purification and repentance of sin; element of Holy Spirit |
| Celibacy | Advocated and practiced | Advocated and practiced | Only for Catholic priests and select orders |
| Divorce | Condemned | Condemned | Opposed |
| Community organization leadership structure | 12 judges under leader, 3 with special prerogatives[d] | 12 disciples under Jesus, 3 with special prerogatives[e] | Roman Catholic—1 pope, 109 cardinals[f]; Church of England—1 archbishop, Synod of Bishops |
| Leader's title | Overseer (*episcopus* in Greek) | *Episcopus* | Bishop |
| Legal structures | Community courts, penitential judicial system[g] | Community courts, penitential judicial system | Ecclesiastical courts |
| Property | Communal ownership | Communal; shared with the poor | Capitalist structure; charitable |
| Healing | Practiced | Practiced | Through faith |
| Ritual meals | Communal, breaking of bread, drinking of wine[h] | Communal, breaking of bread, drinking of wine | Sacrament of communion, Eucharist |
| Literary style | For example, in the Qumran Messianic anthology[i] | Similar to Christian Testimonia[i] | Similar, modernized |
| Ritual prayers | Prayers at sunrise | Prayers at daybreak | Prayers at sunrise only for the devout |
| Praying | In direction of rising sun; unusual emphasis on prayer | In direction of rising sun; unusual emphasis on prayer | In direction of rising sun |
| Buried writings | In earthen vessels | In earthen vessels (Cor. 4:7) | Obsolete practice |
| Calendar | Solar | Solar[j] | Gregorian |

a. Habakkuk 2:4, for example, is cited in the sectarian text 1QpHab and in Galatians 3, to demonstrate similar underlying assumptions.

b. F. F. Bruce, *Holy Spirit in the Qumran Texts* (Leeds University Oriental Society, 1969); M. Delcor, *L'Esprit Saint*, Supplement au Dictionnaire de la Bible.

c. It has been argued (for example, by Eyal Regev, *Temple Righteousness in Qumran and Early Christianity: Tracing the Social Differences Between the Two Movements*, Text, Thought, and Practice in Qumran and Early Christianity, The Orion Center, Jerusalem, 11–13 January, 2004) that Jesus, Peter, and Paul (according to Acts) visited the Temple many times. Acts was written much later than Paul's letters and the Gospels, however, which makes it very clear that the Temple is considered corrupted. See Jesus condemning the moneychangers (Matt. 21:12; Mark 11:15; Luke 19:45; John 2:14) and declaring the Temple would be physically destroyed and replaced with a spiritual Temple (John 2:19), just as Acts implies.

d. Twelve chief priests, 4Q164.

e. The three pillars of early Jesusism were James, brother of Jesus; Simon Peter; and John.

f. At the start of the year 2000, there were 109 voting cardinals and 33 cardinals over the age of eighty who are nonvoting. In 1965 the Catholic Church instituted the Synod of Bishops, made up of representatives from bishops around the world, which has consultative powers.

g. Paul and Qumran. 2 Corinthians 13:1–2, parallels Qumran in relation to the number of witnesses required in testimony to a crime for a conviction and punishment. (Lawrence H. Shiffman, "The Qumran Law of Testimony," *Revue de Qumran* 32, 1975.)

h. Mathias Delcor, "Repas cultuels Esseniens et Therapeutes, Thiases et Haburoth," *Revue de Qumran* 23, 1968. L'Abbé Delcor, professor of Old Testament and Semitic languages, faculty of theology, Toulouse, France, concluded, "There is hardly any doubt that the banquets of the Therapeutae, like those of the Essenes, were partaken in relation to a sacred function."

i. According to Professor Geza Vermes (*The Complete Dead Sea Scrolls in English*, Allen Lane/Penguin, 1997), Christian Testimonia messianic proof texts echo the Qumran-Essene Messianic Anthology (4Q175 ), an early first-century-BCE Testimonia.

j. A. Jaubert, *La Date de la Cène* (Sorbonne, Paris, 1957). Madame Jaubert, a prominent French scholar, also argues that the discrepancies between John and the Synoptic Gospels over which day the Last Supper took place is due to the use of different calendars. According to her, Jesus would have celebrated the Essene solar calendar rather than the traditional lunar calendar interpreted by the Synoptics. The Slavonic version of Josephus's *Jewish Wars* confirms that Jesus "did not observe the Sabbath in the traditional manner" (G. A. Williamson, *Josephus: The Jewish War*, Penguin Books, 1959). It is also striking that the priestly solar calendar influenced Christian groups of the second and third centuries as well as the Montanists of Asia Minor (A. Strobel, "Ursprung und Geschichtedes Frühchristilichen Osterkalenders," *Texte und Untersuchungen* 121, 1977).

---

Table 11 gives only an outline of the main commonalities between early Christianity and the Essenes. Many of them are succinctly set out and referenced by Professor James Charlesworth in his article "The Dead Sea Scrolls and the Historical Jesus,"[12] although, despite admitting a "vast amount of commonality between Jesus and the Essenes," he does not seem prepared to accept the demonstrated conclusion of his own evidence.

For scholars with conservative views on the subject, the numerous examples in table 11 are frequently referred to as parallelisms, implying that they do not start together and never meet, and are therefore somewhat discountable. The term *parallelmania* has been coined to imply that those who present too many examples are subject to some kind of obsessional dysfunction. If this were the case, the majority of Dead Sea Scrolls–biblical scholars could be labeled dysfunctional.

This misused geometric description is in itself a pejorative way of referring to many of the commonalities. They are not parallel pictures, but are often examples of congruencies—positions that coincide exactly when superimposed: that is, which initially come from the same point source.

Undoubtedly other influences, Jewish and Hellenistic, had an impact on early Christianity, but many of the Essenic congruencies are unique, and in many instances they are so completely against the Jewish norm—baptism for repentance, predestination, dualism, solar calendars, and so forth—that a direct connection cannot be dismissed. In fact, when the congruencies are viewed together, they make an overwhelming case for such a relationship between the Qumran Essenes and early Christians, even apart from other vectors—such as geographical locations, attitudes, behavioral patterns, and external manifestations—that lead to the same conclusion, and which are discussed elsewhere in this book.

## Examples of Nonmainstream Beliefs

Two significant doctrines that Jesus preached are sometimes cited as not being within mainstream traditional Jewish teaching: the ideas of "turning the other cheek" rather than an "eye for an eye" and the eschatological urgency of preparing for the end of the world and the coming of the kingdom of God.

> Ye have heard that it hath been said, An eye for an eye, and a tooth for a tooth: But I say unto you, That ye resist not evil: but whosoever shall smite thee on thy right cheek, turn to him the other also. (Matt. 5:38–39)

The first doctrine appears to be in conflict with Jesus's support for observance of existing Jewish Law, but not when it is considered in terms of relations between individuals rather than crimes dealt with by the courts. In this sense it is an extension of the traditional Law, which advocates seeking harmony between people on a personal level.

Both doctrines are, in fact, particular to the teachings of the Essenes, especially the idea of an imminent end to an unsatisfactory world. The Community Rule has an even clearer connection to the philosophy of Jesus in its inclusion of the idea of "turning the other cheek," previously unknown in the Hebrew Scriptures, but which is expressed by both Matthew (5:39) and Luke (6:29).[13]

The relevance of the Qumran Essenes' writings in this respect can also be seen in the moral stance of a number of the Gospel authors. There is, for example, a clearly discernible interplay between the attitude of the Dead Sea Scrolls and Matthew's version of the Sermon on the Mount in relation to murder, vengeance, divorce, and adultery (Matt. 4–7).

For Professor Yigael Yadin, Jesus's injunction to "love your enemies" in Matthew 5:44 is a deliberate attack on the Essenes' uniquely held view, expressed in their Community Rule, to "hate everyone whom God has rejected." In singling out the Essenes' stance, Jesus not only identifies his awareness of and probable closeness to their teachings, but also gives a clue to the divergence of views that subsequently separated him from their ranks.[14]

Matthew's "wilderness of Judaea" as the place of ministry for John the Baptist is a similar interpretation to that in the Dead Sea Scrolls' Community Rule.

### Divorce

Jesus taught that there should be no divorce (Mark 10:2–9; Matt. 19:6), as did the Essenes. This was not the stance of any other Jewish group at the time. The Essene requirement, set out in its Temple Scroll (11QTemple 57), initially applied to "the King"; by inference, others were supposed to follow this example. Where the Essenes obtained their quite revolutionary views on divorce is not explained by conventional scholarship. The real source, I believe, has to be sought from much earlier times.

The Temple Scroll, or 11QT, as it is professionally known, is the longest of the Dead Sea Scrolls manuscripts and in some ways the most puzzling. Recovered in 1967 from Bethlehem, where it had been hidden under an Arab trader's bed,[15] it now resides in the Shrine of the Book in Jerusalem.

One of the more perplexing narratives in the Temple Scroll is the author's assertion that the Lord revealed to Jacob at Bethel, as he did to the Levi (confirmed in another Dead Sea Scroll, the Testament of Levi), that the Levites would be the priests in the temple of the Lord. There is no such mention in the Bible, where the Levi are not appointed as priests until the time of the Tabernacle and Moses. This identification of Levitical priests prior to their appointment by Moses implies a history for the Temple Scroll dating back to the time of the patriarchs Joseph and Jacob, and inevitably their contemporary Pharaoh Akhenaten.

The dating and interpretation of the scroll is an ongoing controversial issue. According to Lawrence Schiffman, of New York University, the scroll's date hinges on the meaning of a section in it known in Hebrew as Torah Ha-Melech—"Law of the King." Much of the sense of this section can be seen to come from sources in the Hebrew Scriptures, but regulations relating to the queen, provision of a round-the-clock royal bodyguard, the king's army council, conscription in the case of war, and division of booty are not found in the Bible. The stipulation regarding the queen in fact goes against the Bible in requiring the king to stay with her all the days of her life; in the Bible it is entirely permissible for the wife to be "sent away."[16]

The question of where the author of the Temple Scroll got his information has always been a conundrum. If the king he was referring to was Akhenaten, however, we know he remained, for a pharaoh, unusually faithful to his wife, Nefertiti, and that he was constantly attended by bodyguards. Assuming a background of Akhetaten, and that the requirements of the Law of the King related to an idealized renewal in Israel, many of the anomalies of the Temple Scroll fall away and reasonable explanations are forthcoming. For example, the phrase "He should not return the people to Egypt for war," which appears in the Temple Scroll, makes little sense for any candidate kings of Judaea or Israel unless there was some locus in Egypt. The king's army council is aptly described in Cyril Aldred's insightful *Akhenaten, King of Egypt:*[17] the army commanders "formed a council of management around the king, like henchmen around their warlord"—in almost a paraphrase of the description in the Temple Scroll.

> "All those selected, which he selects, shall be men of truth, venerating God, enemies of bribery, skilled men in war, and they shall always be with him day and night. . . . He will have twelve princes of his people with him and twelve priests and twelve levites who shall sit next to him for judgement and for the law. He shall not divert his heart from them or do anything in all his councils without relying on them."[18] No decisions on going to war were made without their consultation.

More-detailed explanations for the reasoning behind all the examples given in table 11 are spread through the book as they become germane to the discussion.

## Contraindications: The Main Apparent Incongruities

Lest I be accused of selectively picking only those teachings of Jesus that are seen in Qumran-Essene practice, there are a few more examples where his behavior patterns and attitudes do not appear to fit in with Dead Sea Scrolls sectarian writings.

What Jesus and the Gospel authors did not garner from the Essenes were the later-to-be-propounded ideals of God in human form, original sin, and redemption through Christ. The preaching of Jesus often took the form of stories and parables as he sought to convey his message in simple terms to the ordinary, untutored people with whom he mixed without prejudice. While the Christian Scriptures maintain that Jesus came to preach only to the Jewish community, there was an implication that he wanted to spread the message of God to a wider audience, who did not need to be Jewish.

The message was one of brotherly love, rejecting violence as a way of ridding the country of the occupying Roman forces but promising a hope for the future with God's kingdom at hand. For many, a message that offered escape from suffering and poverty under the yoke of their oppressors must have been attractive. There are other examples of apparently dichotomous behavior on Jesus's part as well.[19]

The main contrasts between the teachings of Jesus, as indicated in the Christian Scriptures, and of the Essenes, as observed in their writings and the evidence of primary historians Josephus, Pliny, and Hippolytus, are:

- The Sabbath
- Ritual cleanliness
- Tolerance of others: sinners, the physically disadvantaged, and those in frowned-on professions
- Circumcision
- Spreading the message of God and the impending apocalypse to a wider audience

These differences are invariably related to a realization on the part of John the Baptist and Jesus that the message of the Scriptures, as it was perceived at Qumran, should be available to *ordinary people* in the Jewish community. This realization manifested itself, in most instances, as a deliberate reaction by Jesus and the Baptist to the unique Essene doctrine of Qumran.[20] It is this almost obsessive preoccupation with either following or taking issue with Essenic views that, in my view, ties Jesus even more closely to an original membership in the Qumran community.[21] An overriding reservation must also be kept in mind. All the differences cited are deduced from the Christian Scriptures, written many years after Jesus's death, and may not accurately reflect his or John the Baptist's actual teachings.

One could almost draw a straight-line graph showing the increase in disrespect for Halacha (Jewish Law), the Temple, and the Jews by the pubescent Christian religion and its increase in lip service to the Romans, against the progressive chronological writings of the Christian Scriptures.

**Distancing of the early Jesus movement from its Jewish roots in early Christian writings**

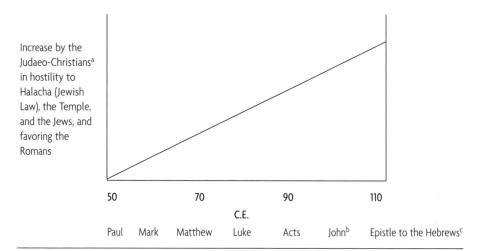

a. Graduating from the earliest followers of Jesus through to Pauline Christians.

b. Although John is often dated in its writing to after the other Gospels, it contains elements that may well predate the writing of Mark and even Paul.

c. The Epistle to the Hebrews in the Christian Scriptures, probably written in Alexandria in the last years of the first century CE, continues to repudiate the Temple but takes a much more favorable line toward Judaism. This latter stance is almost certainly because its intention is to confirm the position of Jesus as outranking any previous biblical figure. He is equated with all three of the messianic aspects of the Qumran doctrine—the prophetic, kingly, and high priestly—and compared to Melchizedek with the purpose of showing Jesus as superior.

## Summation

Having established so many connections between the philosophy of the early Christians and that of the Qumran Essenes, we can now look at whether either John the Baptist or Jesus was ever a member of the community.

If the theory that the early Jesus movement and the Qumran-Essene community were closely linked is sound, it would allow us to make predictions about textual, historical, and archaeological extrapolations from the theory. One such prediction is that the two founding architects of early Christianity, John the Baptist and Jesus, if they knew the texts of Qumran, must have been intimately involved with the Qumran Essenes and members of the community at one period in their lives. As we shall see later, there is strong physical evidence that this is indeed the case.

A closer look at whether John the Baptist, or even Jesus, was a member of the Qumran-Essene community will therefore put the theory under scrutiny.

# ⌐ 19 ⌐

# The Missing Years

## *Argumentum ad ignorantiam:*
## Conclusions from Lack of Evidence

Between descriptions of the birth of Jesus and the beginning of his ministry, the Christian Scriptures give sparse detail of his formative years. The brief mention there is comes from Luke 2:41–52, where we are told he came up, "according to custom," to Jerusalem at the age of twelve. Jesus then stayed on in Jerusalem to converse with, and confound, the learned men of the Temple.

The tradition of a boy going up to Jerusalem "according to custom" at twelve years of age is in itself rather strange, as the normal "Son of the Commandment" (Bar Mitzvah) ceremony, or coming of age for a Jewish child, occurs when the child is thirteen.* An explanation may be that the earlier age involved a biblical linking to the beginning of the prophet Samuel's ministering period, which commenced during his twelfth year.

What happened after this event and up to the time of the beginning of Jesus' ministry is not clear from the Gospels,[1] which say nothing about the eighteen intervening years.

As I proceeded on my quest, I was increasingly coming around to the view that during the "lost years," Jesus had been a member of the Qumran-Essene community from a very early age. Why would the Christian Scriptures be silent about a period spanning more than half of Jesus's critically formative adult life? The heading at the beginning of this

---

*There are circumstances in Jewish custom in which a child does not need to rely on his mother's administration and may therefore be called on to serve the Law at an earlier age.

chapter alludes to what is known as an argument "from ignorance"—that is, deducing something on the basis of a lack of evidence for it; such an argument is usually considered fallacious. But in this instance the absence of information in the Gospels becomes evidence in itself. It also fits in well with what is known about the educational requirements of Jewish children from an early age in antiquity. The best source of this information is the Talmud, a formulation second in authority only to the Hebrew Scriptures.

In the Talmud[2] we learn that it was the custom, before the time of Joshua Ben Gamla, for youths in Judaea to be enrolled in school at sixteen or seventeen. The record of this custom is entirely consistent with the account in Luke. Prior to circa 63 C.E., when Joshua Ben Gamla was high priest in Jerusalem, Jesus would not have been required to attend school until he was sixteen or seventeen, and there would have been no hindrance for him to travel to Jerusalem with his parents at the age of twelve.

Passover was a national holiday, one of the pilgrim Festivals, when every Jew was supposed to go up to Jerusalem, and this requirement is remembered to this day by Jews celebrating Passover in their homes with the exclamation at the end of the service of 'Next year in Jerusalem!' It would also, therefore, seem likely that when Jesus reached the age of sixteen or seventeen, his parents were required by law to place him into a recognized school. And from the knowledge that Jesus and the Christian Scriptures subsequently exhibited, it seems certain that they opted for the intense learning center of Qumran.

Our information on the requirements for recruitment to the community comes largely from three sources: the Dead Sea Scrolls; Josephus, Philo, and Pliny; and a recently found ostracon, or pottery fragment.

For continuity of the story, we need to have a brief look at all three sources.

## The Dead Sea Scrolls

The Qumran Dead Sea Scroll called the Community Rule (also known as the Manual of Discipline), sets out the requirement for a ten-year period of study, after which, at the age of twenty, students had to undergo a public examination before their peers to verify their integrity and their understanding of the Law. A year of probation followed, and then the student was again examined. If he passed this test, he served a further year of probation before a proposal for full membership in the Brotherhood was put to the vote. If accepted, he was required to swear an oath of loyalty. The minimum age to hold office in the Brotherhood was twenty-five, and the "fourth degree of holiness" (referred to by Josephus) could not be reached before the age of thirty. (It is interesting to note the similarity in the use of the terms *brotherhood, degree,* and *master* to those used in the Masonic movement. This is discussed more extensively in *The Mystery of the Copper Scroll of Qumran.*[3])

The most likely scenario is, therefore, that Jesus "graduated" at the age of thirty and then chose to become an "urban Essene," taking his own path with his own cadre of followers. Basing himself in Capernaum on the Sea of Galilee, he set forth with several close disciples to preach the basic message of the Essenes and Torah, enriched by his own divine revelation.

### Josephus, Philo, and Pliny

Recruitment to the community appears to have taken place at any age, but the preferable age for an apprentice was when he was quite young. Philo and Pliny report that adults were taken in for qualification, but Josephus says boys were also admitted for training.[4]

### Recently Found Ostracon

The excitement was almost palpable as people crowded around pictures of an ostracon,[5] or inscribed pottery fragment, trying to get a better view. The subject of the Copper Scroll, which had drawn delegates to an international conference in Manchester, England, in 1996, was for the moment forgotten. This was the star turn of the day. Esther Eshel, of Bar-Ilan University, was showing what appeared to be the first-ever archaeological proof that the inhabitants of Qumran considered themselves a community—a Yahad.

The ostracon contains a legal text in Hebrew, apparently recording the surrender to the community by a new recruit of his personal property. The procedure is entirely consistent with that prescribed in the Manual of Discipline, and as such represents the first solid outside evidence that conventional scholarship is correct in its assessment of activities at Qumran.

That the Gospels and historical external evidence tell us almost nothing of Jesus's formative years is not surprising if those years were spent at

Qumran. If I am correct, he was closeted away in a desert environment from an early age and excluded from outside contact with his parents and four brothers,* and this is indeed borne out by the Gospels and the Nag Hammadi texts:

> And on the third day there was a marriage in Cana of Galilee. . . . And when they wanted wine, the mother of Jesus saith unto him, They have no wine. Jesus saith unto her, Woman, what have I to do with thee? (John 2:1–4)

> Jesus said: "Whoever does not hate father and mother cannot be a follower of me, and whoever does not hate brothers and sisters . . . will not be worthy of me." (Nag Hammadi Gospel of Thomas)

A relatively recently discovered apocryphal text narrates that as Jesus was being crucified, there was an acknowledgment by Jesus that his forced separation from family was for a higher reason:

> There is no man that hath left house, or parents, or brethren, or wife, or children, for the kingdom of God's sake, who shall not receive manifold more in this present time. (Luke 18:28–30)

So the biblical evidence at least supports the contention that Jesus was out of public circulation during his early years, right up to his thirtieth year, when the Gospels tell us he began his ministry—a long period for one so radical and precocious in learning. The minimum age given in the Rule of the Congregation for when a novice could attain his full accreditation, thirty years, is exactly the same age as the Gospels state for the reappearance of Jesus into the outside world. By the time Jesus reached this age, he would have been fully immersed in the teachings of the Qumran Essenes, and their protocols would have been engraved on his conscious and subconscious mind. This is a potent piece of correlation, which does not appear to have been connected to Jesus before.

It is not surprising, therefore, that so many of the echoes of the

---

*James, Joses, Juda (Jude), Simon (Mark 6:3).

Qumran Essenes can be detected in the later transcribed words and recordings of Jesus's acts. If the view that John the Baptist was also at one time or another a regular visitor to, or even for some period a resident member at, Qumran, it is reasonable to assume that his rebellious nature may have inspired Jesus to reassert his own radicalism. What is more natural than on reaching his majority at the age of thirty, Jesus should strike out on his own, leave the community, and seek out John the Baptist for reassurance and communion?

## What Islam Thinks of Jesus's Lost Years

The holy texts of the Muslims also support the contention that Jesus was out of circulation for a major part of his life. For Muslims, Isa (Jesus) was a prophet and servant of Allah (God), but he was not the son of Allah. The Koran records that Isa was born of the virgin Maryam (Mary) and that his birth was a miracle at Allah's command (19:17–21). He is said to have commenced his prophecy at the age of thirty and preached for three years (19:29–34). He was not crucified, but rather taken up by Allah (4:157–158).

Muslims do not believe in the coming of a messiah to redeem the world as such, but instead that the hour will come when Allah will raise those in graves (22:5–7).

## Graduation Day

If the deductions made from the Gospel stories are correct, as soon as his graduation was attained, at the minimum-allowed age of thirty, Jesus left the community and started on his own ministry. It is only from thirty onward that the activities of Jesus begin to be recorded again in the Christian Scriptures. Jesus seeks out John the Baptist, perhaps meeting him at Qasr al-Yahud,* by the Jordan, and their friendship is renewed.

John the Baptist still preached a fierce form of spiritual emancipation, but Jesus went further in developing a spiritual and physical emancipation from the brutish Roman regime that polluted the Temple and Jewish reli-

---

*On the western bank of the Jordan, near the Dead Sea, traditionally believed to be a site where John the Baptist carried out baptisms. Jordanians believe the site was at Wadi al-Kharrar, on the eastern bank of the Jordan.

gious life and burdened the people with taxes. Pontius Pilate, the harshest protagonist Imperial Rome had ever placed over the Israelites, was a prime target for Jesus's parabolic barbs.

Resistance, spearheaded by the Zealots (freedom fighters), morally and perhaps physically supported by the mobile Essenes and the Nazoreans, brought the general populace flocking to hear the message of Jesus. In their eyes he would have become the personified messiah of the prophets Isaiah and Daniel of the Hebrew Scriptures, who would free the people from the yoke of Rome.

Jesus's close attendants were not only his spiritual disciples; they were also his bodyguards. Some of the group were clearly armed, as the naming of Simon called Zelotes, and Judas Iscariot—the dagger carrier—indicate (Luke 6:15–16).

Jesus told the disciples:

[H]e that hath no sword, let him sell his garment, and buy one. (Luke 22:36)

As has, I believe, already been demonstrated, and will become even more apparent later in our narrative, Jesus was strongly influenced by the Essene movement, which had a gentle side but also an aggressive wing, just as the early Christian movement did. Paolo Pasolini's memorable film portrayal of Christ in *The Gospel According to St. Matthew*[6] as a powerful, outspoken character is a more plausible representation than his usual depiction as mild and meek.

We know that the Essenes mentioned by Flavius Josephus (Jewish historian, 37–100 C.E.), Philo (Alexandrian philosopher, 20 B.C.E.–40 C.E.), and Pliny the Elder (23–79 C.E.) were almost certainly the brotherhood of reclusive Jews described in the Dead Sea Scrolls found near Qumran. Conventional reference to the Essenes as reclusives is, however, somewhat misleading in that although their locations were often remote from populated centers and some of the members rarely left their abode, others took on a proselytising role and traveled around preaching and recruiting. Josephus talks of Essenes who did *not* inhabit the desert, as do the Zadokite documents found in Cairo and at Qumran. Nor were the Essenes particular advocates of passivity. There are passages in their texts where they liken themselves to Roman Velites (armed soldiers), as fighters in the "War of the Sons of Light against the Sons of Darkness."

The mixed messages of passiveness and potential for violence have caused confusion to some analysts of the Essene sect, but if the movement is considered as having not one single philosophy but rather a basic duality of branches, the existence of specific separate motives becomes clearer. Those of the Essenes who wished to remain in relatively studious seclusion were essentially passive; those who chose the urban or missionary life, like John the Baptist, were made of sterner material and were well prepared to fight and die for their beliefs.

This diversity also helps explain the duality of Jesus's teachings and behavior: showing mildness and charity in the extreme, and yet being ready to stand up to the cruelty and persecution visited on the populace by the Romans and to mix freely and associate with the Zealots.

In his *Wars of the Jews* (Book 2, chapter 8) Josephus says of the Essenes:

> And as for death, it will be for their glory, they esteem it better than living always; and indeed our war with the Romans gave abundant evidence what great souls they had in their trials, wherein, although they were tortured and distorted, burned and torn to pieces, and went through all kinds of instruments and torment, that they might be forced either to blaspheme their lawgiver, or to eat what was forbidden them, yet they could not be made to do either of them . . . but they smiled in their very pains, . . . and resigned their souls with great alacrity . . .

While Philo described the Essenes as pacifists living on the northwest shores of the Dead Sea, Josephus, who was supreme military commander for the Jews of the Galilean area at the beginning of their revolt against the Romans in 66 C.E., and therefore able to speak with some authority, tells us that the commander of the Jaffa and Lydda area was none other than "John the Essene."

Another episode indicating the activist nature of some Essenes comes in a final act of the Jewish revolt, played out at Masada, a mountain fortress located a few miles west of the Dead Sea and some five miles south of Qumran. In 66 C.E., the Roman garrison at Masada was overrun by Zealots led by Eleazar ben Yair, and it remained in their hands until a last fateful stand in 73 C.E. Starved of food and supplies and near collapse, the 960 mainly Zealot defenders committed suicide rather than face Roman capture.

One of the most remarkable finds related to this tragic episode, made during excavations at Masada, were some Dead Sea Scrolls fragments identical with those found in the caves at Qumran. Identified as Essene documents, they were almost certainly brought to Masada by Essenes who took their place side by side with the Zealots in defense of their country and their beliefs (see chapter 25). The idea that Jesus's disciples, like himself, were drawn from the working classes is quite inconsistent with their apparent literacy. In Judaea at the time, 95 percent of the population would have been unable to read or write. For Jesus's disciples to be knowledgeable about the holy texts, and his brother James to become head of the Jerusalem church, they would all have had to come from a learned group, such as the Sadducees, the Pharisees—or the Essenes. When James, Jesus's brother, who was thought to be leader of the early Jesus church in Jerusalem, was put to death, Josephus records in his *Antiquities* that "those of the inhabitants of the city who were considered the most fair-minded and who were strict in observance of the law were offended at this." They agitated against the action of High Priest Ananus in having James stoned to death, and it is most likely that these offended ones were the prime movers who subsequently got Ananus removed from office.

The most likely group to take offense at the death of James would, of course, have been his followers. In referring to the offendees, Josephus uses the same phrasing as he employs elsewhere to describe the Essenes: as those who were "strict in observance of the law." Yet again there is an implication that James, an early follower of Jesus, was strongly identified with the Essenes, which further links Jesus to the Essenes.

According to the Christian Scriptures, after three years of preaching and healing, at the age of thirty-three, Jesus brought his small group of followers to Jerusalem to celebrate a festival, the springtime Festival of Tabernacles, or Passover. As discussed in chapter 26, the details of the events described indicate that they may have actually taken place during the autumn festival of Succoth. We know from the earliest Gospels that there were Zealots among his followers, and as his support grew in Jerusalem, the established authorities must have become apprehensive.

It is true that many scholars, from Father Roland de Vaux and

Lankester Harding in the 1950s, to Father Émile Puech and Professor Geza Vermes in the 1990s,[7] do not accept that Jesus was an Essene. A highly perceptive modernist scholar, Dr. Jonathan Campbell, of Oxford and Bristol Universities in England, noted in his 1998 book *Dead Sea Scrolls: The Complete Story*,[8] "The above outline makes it highly unlikely that Jesus was an Essene." Dr. Campbell's conclusion is arrived at after a very cursory review of Jesus's life, and he then goes on to make at least six important links between the Qumran community and early Christianity. He acknowledges a most notable link in the Essene Community Rule (1QS) as "a common note of repentance against the background of eschatological urgency," but then concludes, "With this kind of general parallel, however, the similarities end," despite the fact that his book is replete with specific examples of linkages. One page later Dr. Campbell concedes Jesus might well have been an Essene prior to commencing his ministry.

While I do not go along with theories that the Essenes actually mention Jesus in their Dead Sea Scrolls, I believe that many scholars make two fundamental mistakes when comparing the message of Jesus and his followers with that of the Essenes:

1. Insufficient weight is given to the continually accumulating synchronicity between the two communities, not just in their messages, but also in similarities of practices, community/hierarchic structure, and geographical community allegiances. Each community had personalities like John the Baptist, Jesus's mentor, and James the brother of Jesus, who were both generally acknowledged to have had joint membership in the two communities at some period in their lives.

2. Comparisons between an understanding of a static Essene philosophy and a static concept of established Christianity do not take account of Jesus's dynamically evolving vision, which, in the earliest records of the Jesus movement (through Paul and Mark), can be equated most closely with the Essenes.

There is a third fundamental reason why I think Jesus was attached directly to the Essenes, and we are about to enter that ground in self-evident force.

# ~ 20 ~

# Jesus, The Essenes, and The Gospels of The Christian Scriptures

In the light of modern scholarship and the research described earlier in this book, my view of the most likely scenario of events encompassing the life of Jesus and the subsequent maturation of messianic expectation goes as follows:

John the Baptist was a member of the Qumran-Essene community. It is unlikely that he rose up the hierarchy to become its leader, but he was a revered and respected, if at times rebellious, adherent. He may not have completed his full training period through to the age of thirty, leaving early to become a mobile Essene traveling the countryside while preaching his own brand of salvation, baptizing, and visiting outlying Essene communities.[1] Nevertheless, he returned from time to time to Qumran, especially at the annual gathering of members at High Holy Day festivals, and was always a welcome prodigal son.

Jesus had been placed in the community as a sixteen- or seventeen-year-old recruit, perhaps even younger, and proceeded to overlay a precocious knowledge of his Hebrew ancestry with years of diligent, intense study of ancient texts and the exclusive works of the Qumran Essenes, with their archaic inheritance and Egyptian perspective. Each year of study, discussion, and interaction with the fundamentals of Israel's heritage culminated with a compulsory period of twenty-five days of total isolation in the desert wilderness of Judaea. It was here that Jesus must have begun to formulate his own philosophy of belief, heavily influenced by the Hebrew Scriptures, sectarian literature, and the freethinkers of the community, such as John the Baptist.

In such a close environment, it would be inevitable that like-minded novitiates would gravitate toward each other, particularly related contemporaries of a similar age group. Jesus and John the Baptist were reputedly born very near to each other and, more significant, to Qumran. There was also a family connection, as their respective mothers, Mary and Elizabeth, were apparently cousins.

It seems certain, as we learn from Josephus, that John the Baptist, who was not much older than Jesus, was a forthright and eloquent exponent of his ideas. Jesus, a radical at heart, would have been attracted to this picturesque, fierce-featured, freethinking, physically powerful character. Neither of them could be easily contained within the constraints of a closed community—least of all the Baptist, who perhaps left before completing his internship.

When Jesus came out before Israel, he too must have joined the Baptist's circle of disciples and would have been baptized by him. This is, if nothing else, indicative evidence that Jesus followed the same path, a path prepared by John the Baptist, and also spent his intervening years at Qumran. Their closeness is confirmed by the disciples that the Christian Scriptures say Jesus gathered around him after the demise of the Baptist. At least two of them, Andrew and Peter, are said to have been previous disciples of John the Baptist.

Within the Qumran community there was a strong hierarchical structure. At the top sat a "right teacher." All members could vote in an assembly on nondoctrinal matters. General day-to-day administration was in the hands of a triumvirate of priests, along with twelve helpers. These priests, aided by Levites, administered the doctrine of the group. There was a pecking order according to level of learning and holiness, as determined by their peers.

While there is no evidence that Jesus rose within the Essenes to become the "right teacher," there is evidence from Hegesippus, a late-second-century Christian historian, that James, described in the Christian Scriptures as one of Jesus's disciples, was the Essenes' "true teacher of the Law." The Christian Scriptures' Letter of James has been shown to have strong affiliations with the fourth section of the Dead Sea Community Rule (1QS), and it seems he was well acquainted with Essene terminology and made frequent use of it.[2]

Another strong indication that Jesus had been a member of the

Qumran Essenes comes in Mark 1:21–27, when the Gospel writer and disciple describes Jesus's first public appearance in the synagogue at Capernaum[3] on the Sabbath:

> They were astounded at his doctrine; for he taught them as one that had authority, and not as the scribes.

While the term Essene does not appear in the Christian or Hebrew Scriptures, or even in the writings of the people called by this name by Roman and Greek historians, they can be identified in the Christian Scriptures by a variety of names that they called themselves in their own writings. Some of these designations are sons of the light, pious ones, eunuchs (in the sense of celibate), false prophets, poor in spirit, Herodians, saints, and scribes.[4]

All these phrases are to be found in the Christian Scriptures, and in most instances they are terms associated exclusively with the Essenes, which do not appear in the Hebrew Scriptures or Jewish literature.[5] For example, the Essenes' self-designation "sons of the light" and parallel terms appear in both Paul and John (12:36).

As the elite of scholarly Judaism, the Essenes are identified by the pseudonyms used in the Christian Scriptures as a group quite distinct from the Pharisees or Sadducees. In this respect there is no other group, apart from the Essenes, that the Christian Scriptures can be referring to, as a number of scholars conclude.[6] We see, for example in Luke 5:21, that for the Christian Scriptures the scribes and the Pharisees are distinct groups: "And the scribes and the Pharisees began to reason . . . "

The reaction to Jesus's teaching at Capernaum can only be interpreted as astonishment that, having been taught by the scribes—the Essenes—Jesus nevertheless has developed his own authority and appears no longer dependent on them.

I believe Mark 1:21–27 is one of the most telling passages in demonstrating Jesus's original membership in the Essene community. Another equally persuasive phrase in the Gospel of Matthew seems to confirm the Christian Scriptures' awareness of the Essenes:

> Blessed are the meek: for they shall inherit the earth. (5:6)

Who were "the meek"? The question has long troubled historians and theologians. This characterization, sometimes translated as "poor in spirit," is not found in any other Jewish writings, but it does appear in the Qumran Essenes' War Scroll[7] and is also referred to in the Messianic Apocalypse fragment (4Q521).

For there to be a clear connection between the Christian Scriptures and the Qumran textual material, it seems it would need to be more apparent in the earliest Christian witnesses—namely, in the testimony of Paul—than in the later Gospels. This is indeed the case, as we have seen in previous chapters. The early writings of Paul, whose letters are thought to predate the setting down of the Gospels, are, in the view of a number of eminent scholars, strongly influenced by Qumran thinking. In his earliest letter, 1 Thessalonians, perhaps written from Corinth circa 50 C.E., it is the influence of the Qumran community, rather than the Pharisaic-rabbinic tradition, that determines the shaping of Paul's Judaism.

Conventional scholarly commentators assign varying degrees of different overlays on the teachings of Jesus—Hellenism, Gnosticism, Hebrew Scriptures' tradition, and Essenism. However, many scholars and historians do not even mention Essenism or consider it significant. This is strange in light of the overwhelming documentation that points strongly in the direction of a connection.

My own view is therefore somewhat different, as set out at the beginning of this chapter. While I do not go along with any of the "lemming" theorists who claim that the Qumran Essenes wrote about a contemporary Jesus, I believe both Jesus and John the Baptist, and some of Jesus's followers, were initially members of and had a long-term association with the devout religious community that lived at Qumran in Judaea.

The reason many of the writings of the Qumran Essenes appear to prefigure details in the life, teachings, and death of Jesus is that this association enabled the authors of the Christian Scriptures to draw on the writings of the community and incorporate them into the holy texts.

This type of procedure is evident throughout the Bible, as well as in later rabbinic and church writings, where there are numerous examples of earlier texts being drawn on to validate and give authority to later teachings and personalities.

All the allusions in the Dead Sea Scrolls that are mistakenly attributed to personalities of the Christian Scriptures are references to other messianic figures that were expected by the Essenes to return or appear for the first time at the coming of the apocalyptic era—an era the Qumran Essenes awaited with eager anticipation. They were writing about this era sometime between 150 B.C.E. and 68 C.E. but drawing on much more ancient texts and memories dating back perhaps a thousand years and more.

In many ways the Jesus of the Christian Scriptures would have fulfilled their anticipations—particularly his apocalyptic vision and heralding of the End Days[8]—but in a number of vital aspects, the Jesus described by the apostle Paul would not have been a messiah the Qumran Essenes would have recognized.

## Apocalyptic Outlook

The idea of End Days and apocalypticism seems to have first developed in the Books of Enoch and Daniel in the late third and early second centuries B.C.E. For the Qumran Essenes, however, the end was not only nigh; it was already happening, and they were the privileged few who would enjoy its rewards.[9] In this respect, the Teacher of Righteousness preached an eschatological message similar to that of Jesus, and in the manner of chapter 61 of the Book of Isaiah.

Four potent aspects of apocalypticism exhibited by the Qumran Essenes and early Christianity testify further to their common roots:

1. In how they frame their vision of the world, both Christianity and Essenism show evidence of a mutual understanding of apocalypticism that is far stronger than anything in the Hebrew Bible.
2. Both the Qumran Essenes and the early Christians believed that angelic and demonic forces shaped human destiny. They considered history to be in its final stages, with God's intervention and judgment close at hand.
3. Both movements were animated by the hope of life beyond death. That both groups could formulate their views in distinctively original apocalyptic imagery is further testimony to their common background.

4. Both the early church and the Qumran community believed they were living in the End Days. It was only when resurrection became a dominant theme in Christianity, along with the veneration of Jesus as the Christ, that their viewpoints diverged.

This apocalyptic development in the Zadokite faction of Israelites is most evident from a Scroll of Instruction (4QInstruction)—a scroll of considerable importance to the community, as seven copies were found in Caves 1 and 4. It illustrates an earlier stratum of wise proverbial advice on living and behavior, supplemented by a later post–second century B.C.E. stratum on Enochian apocalyptic end-of-time revelations and divine mysteries at last revealed to the select few. Guidance for the select "eternal planting" of God did not come from Torah, but it was believed to come from knowledge of these mysteries.[10]

The Dead Sea Scrolls contain no mention of the name Jesus, nor do the descriptions of the messiahs the Qumran Essenes were awaiting incorporate the vitally distinctive Pauline characteristics of Christ's arrival by virgin birth and divine Son of God status within a trinitarian deity, or Christ's dying on the cross for the sins of the people.

That Jesus and John the Baptist were part of the Qumran-Essene community is, I believe, from the evidence already cited, a strong possibility—and as we shall soon see from tangible evidence, more than a near certainty. Nevertheless, it can be only after Jesus left the community and began his ministry that, regardless of any proven connection to Qumran, he developed the charisma and appeal that would later energize Paul and subsequent authors of the Gospels to picture him as the inspirational Messiah who was slain and resurrected.

Substantiation of John and Jesus's linkage to Qumran is the subject of the next chapter.

# ⌒ 21 ⌒

# John the Baptist
# Strides into View

According to the Christian Scriptures, Jesus first encountered John the Baptist on the banks of the Jordan River, where he was baptized by John. As we have already stated, it may be of some significance that tradition recalls that the place where Jesus is thought to have been baptized is no more than three miles from Qumran, and the site of his Temptation on the Mount is only some seven miles north of Qumran.[1] In fact, most of the geographical activities of both Jesus and John the Baptist—their birthplaces, areas of ministry, baptizing, and deaths—are centered on Qumran.

Although there are no certain confirmations of Jesus in historical witnesses of the period, as we have seen in chapter 5, Flavius Josephus does refer to John the Baptist and to his apparently original form of baptism as a once-and-for-all cleansing of sins. Josephus also talks about the backlash against Herod Antipater for having John the Baptist put to death, confirming the essential details of the Christian Scriptures' version of his execution.

I quote the Josephus passage in full because it has great relevance to the attempt to verify what Jozef Milik revealed to me in the quiet confines of his Parisian flat:

> But to some of the Jews the destruction of Herod's army seemed to be divine vengeance, and certainly a just vengeance, for his treatment of John, surnamed the Baptist. For Herod had put him to death, though he was a good man and had exhorted the Jews to lead righteous lives, to practice justice toward their fellows and piety towards God, and in so doing to join in baptism. In his view this was a necessary preliminary if baptism was to be acceptable to God. They must not

177

employ it to gain pardon for whatever sins they had committed, but as a consecration of the body, implying that the soul was already thoroughly cleansed by right behaviour. When others, too, joined the crowds about him, because they were aroused to the highest degree by his sermons, Herod became alarmed. Eloquence that had so great an effect on mankind might lead to some form of sedition, for it looked as if they would be guided by John in every thing they did. Herod decided therefore that it would be much better to strike first and be rid of him before his work led to an uprising, than to wait for an upheaval, get involved in a difficult situation and see his mistake. Though John, because of Herod's suspicions, was brought in chains to Machaerus, the stronghold that we have previously mentioned, and there put to death, yet the verdict of the Jews was that the destruction visited upon Herod's army was a vindication of John, since God saw fit to inflict such a blow on Herod. (*Antiquities* 18.5.2)

The passage is generally accepted as authentic, a contention supported by the fact that Josephus does not associate John with Jesus, nor does Origen, a third-century Christian writer, in his *Contra Celsum* 1.48.[2]

The key attributes of John the Baptist that Josephus recalls are his powerful oratory to turn the minds of the people and his characterization of baptism. When the phrasing of the description of John the Baptist's role in preparing the way for Jesus in the Gospel of Mark is compared to a quotation in the Dead Sea Scrolls, John's words are so close it seems impossible not to conclude that the Gospel author, or John the Baptist himself, had intimate knowledge of the Qumran Essenes' writings.

The voice of one crying in the wilderness,
Prepare ye the way of the Lord
Make his path straight. (Mark 1:3)

. . . go into the wilderness to prepare the way of the Lord. (The Community Rule 1QS)

There are several analogous references to the "way" in the Hebrew Scriptures (Isa. 40:3, Genesis, Psalms), but the content of this important phrase to Christianity is nowhere as significantly expressed in the Hebrew Scriptures as it is at Qumran. The Christian Scriptures' concentration on this phrase, in stressing the anticipation of Jesus's arrival, is emphasized in the Qumran-Essene Isaiah Scroll, where the phrase is actually physically highlighted within the scroll from the rest of the text.[3]

When the main behavioral and belief characteristics of John the Baptist that do not conform to those of the general Jewish population, as in table 12, are compared with those exhibited by the Qumran Essenes, it becomes readily apparent that John and the Qumran Essenes had many commonalities.

**TABLE 12**

**Attitudes and practices advocated by John the Baptist and his attributes not evident in normative Judaism compared to those of the Qumran Essenes**

| Attributes | John the Baptist | Qumran Essenes |
| --- | --- | --- |
| Pharisees and Sadducees | Despised them | Despised them |
| Religiosity | Deeply religious | Deeply religious |
| Eschatological outlook | Expected a new messianic age | Expected a new messianic age |
| Sexuality | Celibate | Celibate[a] |
| Priestly background | Priestly father | Priestly community |
| Baptism[b] | Of repentance, purification from sin, initiation into a new covenant | Of repentance, initiation into a new covenant |
| Ownership of property | Communal, sharing with the poor | Communal[c] |
| Incest | Uncle–niece marriage condemned | Uncle–niece marriage forbidden |
| Temple | Abhorred | Ignored |
| Lifestyle | Abstemious | Abstemious |
| Area of activity | Judaean wilderness | Judaean wilderness |
| Gift of prophecy | Strongly exhibited | Strongly exhibited |

a. In Essene communities where women were allowed, marriage was encouraged, but only as a route to procreation.

b. Baptism is discussed in more detail in chapter 23.

c. Communities outside Qumran appear to have had certain ownership rights.

Some of the parameters listed in the left-hand column of table 12 are expanded on in the chapter notes.[4] They are ownership of property, incest, the unacceptable Temple, the abstemious lifestyle, and the gift of prophecy.

The possibility that John the Baptist had an association with the Qumran Essenes is, for most scholars, much stronger than they would allow for Jesus. A reflection of this view is seen in the audiovisual presentation that is shown to tourists visiting the site of Qumran today. It clearly depicts John the Baptist as being, at one period in his life, a member of the Qumran community. Magen Broshi, of the Israel Museum, a consultant on the video production and a preeminent expert on the subject, is not alone in his view of John the Baptist's close association with the Qumran Essenes.

As previously mentioned, a similarly close association between Jesus and the Qumran Essenes has nevertheless generally been resisted, particularly by Christian theologians. The more emerging information from the Dead Sea Scrolls is examined and existing ancient texts reevaluated, however, the more apparent it becomes that the hotbed of spiritual industry bubbling away at Qumran on the northwestern edge of the Dead Sea was a cauldron from which were cast many templates for early Christian ideas.

It is a matter of debate whether the early prevarications of the predominantly Christian scholars involved in publishing translations of the Dead Sea Scrolls were due to a fear that if too much sensitive material came out too quickly, it could damage Christianity. Joseph Fitzmyer, professor emeritus at the Catholic University in Washington, D.C., complains, "It is regrettable that New Testament (Christian Scriptures) interpreters had to wait more than forty years for the publication of [the Qumran Beatitudes]."[5] When the embargo was finally broken in 1990–91 (largely by Americans led by Professor Robert Eisenman, of California State University, and Professor Ben Zion Wacholder, of the Hebrew Union College, Cincinnati), newly translated texts showed that it was increasingly likely that Jesus, like John the Baptist, had an association with Qumran.

Even before these events, the discovery in 1945 in Egypt of a previously unknown Gospel of Thomas among the Nag Hammadi codices, containing what appeared to be verbatim sayings of Jesus, indicated a gnostic or hidden-knowledge aspect to early Christianity. This style of gnosticism is readily recognizable in sectarian writings from the Qumran community, a form of belief that the church has long striven to suppress (see chapter 13). Indeed, there are those who claim that John the Baptist was never a member of the Essene community, much less Jesus, but they tend to be from a staunchly religious background.

Professor J. Van der Ploeg, of the University of Nijmegen in the Netherlands, an ordained member of the Dominican Church, who was closely associated with the École Biblique's work at Qumran in the early days, has noted: "Undoubtedly, the Baptist reminds us in many ways of the views, the way of life and the practices of the Essenes. But to call him an Essene, and to assert that he grew up at Qumran, is going beyond the evidence."[6]

The position of the early caucus in the 1960s and the line it would seek to defend is unambiguously spelled out by Father Pierre Benoit, editor in chief of the Dead Sea Scrolls translation team from 1971 to 1987, in a multiauthor publication, *Paul and Qumran:*[7]

> Even supposing that John the Baptist did depend on the Essenes, Christianity would owe nothing on that score. It is only apropos of Jesus that the question becomes crucial. Yet here the dependence is still less likely. In the measure that direct influence of Qumran on the Christian Scriptures appears to be established, it does not necessarily follow that this influence was exercised at the very beginning, so that Christianity would derive from Essenism as from its source. This influence could rather have been exercised at a later stage, and would have assisted the new movement only to express and organise itself, but would in no sense have created it. . . . The contacts with Qumran came less from through John the Baptist and Jesus, than through Paul, John and even the faithful of the second generation.

However, even the drawers of the Benoit line had to concede that in Paul's letters to the Corinthians and the Ephesians, mystery theology, and fundamental teachings in Mark and Matthew—the earliest witnesses to Jesus—there are exclusive congruencies with Qumran. As Father Jerome Murphy-O'Connor was forced to admit in 1960, "As [Ephesians] shows, Paul was definitely in contact with someone who knew Essenian teaching thoroughly. Timothy belonged to the same circle."[8] Perhaps the strongest, most direct reference by Paul to Qumran comes in his second letter to the Corinthians, chapter 4, where he discusses the glory of light and "hidden things." We know that the Qumran Essenes had the extremely unusual practice of storing their holy texts in earthenware jars and hiding them in caves near Qumran. Paul declares:

> But we have this treasure in earthen vessels, that the excellency of the power may be of God, and not of us. (2 Cor. 4:7)

A sample of the parallels discussed is shown in table 10 in chapter 18.

At this point, we need to look a bit more closely at the origins of the Qumran Essenes and the strangeness of their form of Judaism to see how it might have impinged on the consciousness of John the Baptist, Jesus, and others of their followers.

# ～ 22 ～

# Was John The Baptist a Member of The Qumran Community?

The possibility that John the Baptist had an association with the Qumran Essenes is for most modern and many early scholars much stronger than they would allow for Jesus. The enigmatic last verse of Luke regarding John living in the desert, as pointed out by l'Abbé René Laurentin,[1] a French authority of the Church Council, makes little sense unless it is saying that John the Baptist was, from his childhood, a member of the Qumran community:

The verse becomes clear, asserts l'abbé, when the testimony of Flavius Josephus is considered, when he says of the Qumran community it was their custom to adopt "children from others, at an age when their spirit is still malleable enough to easily accept instruction" (*Jewish Wars* 2). John Allegro, a member of the original Dead Sea Scrolls translation team, has also pointed out that the Baptist's parents were elderly, and when his father died, he may have been adopted by the community.[2] Both W. H. Brownlee and L. Mowry,[3] two early Dead Sea Scrolls scholars, agreed that John the Baptist probably spent his childhood in the wilderness. If he was not enrolled as a member of the Qumran-Essene community, it is difficult to envisage what he was doing as a child wandering around in the wilderness of Judaea. The only logical deduction, from all the evidence, is that he spent at least part of his early life at Qumran.

If Jesus and John the Baptist *were* members of the Qumran community, as I have maintained, their teachings, practices, and beliefs were inevitably strongly influenced by those of the community, as were later Christian

183

**TABLE 13**

**Analysis of scholarly opinion on John the Baptist's membership in the Qumran-Essene community[4]**

| Member at some period in his life | In contact and influenced but not a member | Little contact or influence |
| --- | --- | --- |
| (Josephus)* | Jean Danielou | H. Rowley |
| R. Eisler | Jack Finnegan | Frank Cross |
| Otto Betz | Daniel Schwartz | Pierre Benoit |
| Jean Steinmann | Raymond Brown | Cyrus Gordon |
| Yigael Yadin | R. Harrison | Edmund Sutcliffe |
| John Allegro | Charles Scobie | John Pryke |
| Barbara Thiering | John Robinson | Joan Taylor |
| Charles Fritsch | Oscar Cullmann | James Charlesworth |
| Millar Burrows | Robert Webb | Carsten Thiede |
| David Flusser | William Brownlee | Ian McDonald |
| Kurt Schubert | George Brooke | |
| Michael Grant | Lucretta Mowry | |
| Joseph Fitzmyer | James VanderKam | |
| Magen Broshi | The Jesus Seminar | |
| Jozef Milik[†] | | |
| Geza Vermes | | |
| Robert Feather | | |

*The extensive descriptions of John the Baptist by Flavius Josephus in *Jewish Antiquities* have been taken by some scholars, such as H. Lichtenberger,[5] as a portrayal of John as an Essene.

[†] Jozef Milik's opinion will be discussed in a later chapter.

writers, but both John and Jesus had developed their own unique interpretation of their ancient Hebrew heritage and that of the Qumran Essenes. Their emphasis was on spreading the message of the Essenes to a much wider audience, helping the disenfranchised, poor, and handicapped, and preparing urgently for the coming of the kingdom of God.

The coterie of followers that remained behind at Qumran and in Jerusalem itself later split into two basic groups: those who considered Jesus a son of man, led by James, the brother of Jesus; and those who considered him divine, the awaited Messiah.

That Jesus was divine from birth, performed miraculous healings and

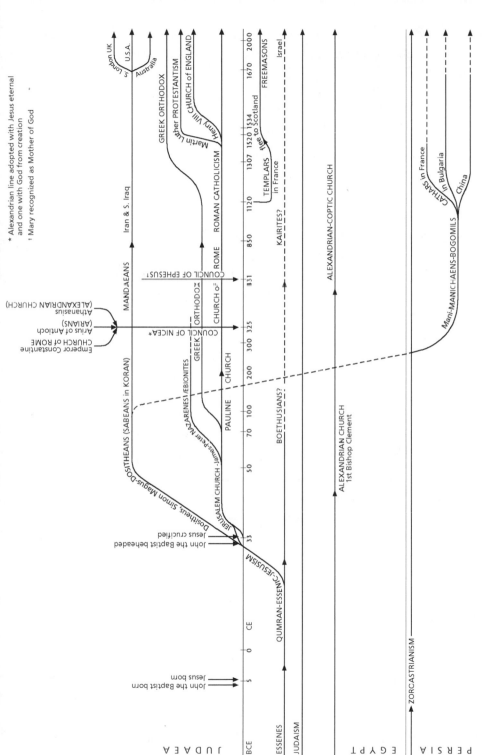

Fig. 22.1. Flow chart showing evolution of the Christian Church, the Essenes, and associated religious movements.

© ROBERT FEATHER

acts, was the Son of God, and experienced a spiritual resurrection after his death are not challenged by this stance on his upbringing. These are entirely a matter of personal belief.

## The Split

Yet another scholar, Bargil Pixner, of the Hebrew University in Jerusalem, has identified a split that occurred between the Essenes (who may have later become known as the Ebionites, or Boethusians) and the followers of Jesus, led by the family of Jesus. For there to be a split, the two groups must previously have been unified.[6]

We may never know the fundamental reasons for the split that took John the Baptist and Jesus away from the bosom of the community. We can surmise that John the Baptist's abrasive, outspoken nature, described by both Josephus and the Gospels, would not have allowed him to rest peaceably within the Qumran community. John the Baptist's and Jesus's broadening of the message that the Qumran Essenes espoused to encompass ordinary people, the poor and crippled, and more specifically women may have been a root cause for the parting of the ways. While the Essene movement allowed marriage under strict conditions, the Qumran community, and probably the community of the Essene Gate in Jerusalem, was made up entirely of men; women did not participate in their religious ceremonies.

Equality of the sexes, which one would have expected to be a feature of Essene philosophy in light of the complete equality in worship that appeared to exist between Pharaoh Akhenaten and Queen Nefertiti, might seem to pose a problem for the theories relating Qumran to Akhetaten. The equality that existed between the royal couple, however, has become known to us only through inscriptions and reliefs showing the pharaoh and his wife worshipping on what appear to be equal terms. It may not have been evident to the Essenes of Qumran from the handed-down textual material.

Even had they been aware of the emancipated nature of this earliest monotheism, there is another factor that might have fostered the Qumran Essenes' chauvinistic tendencies. The development of exclusively male communities almost certainly related to the eschatological anticipation of the coming of the kingdom of God and the requirements of the ancient texts in this respect. The members of the priestly sect were the "soldiers of light" mustering in preparation for the holy war to come, and the scriptural texts demanded a "purity of their camps"—what Professor Frank Moore Cross calls "an eschatological asceticism."[7] Sexual relations and marriage disqualified one for holy war.

This, of course, raises a question. Why should the early Jesus movement have exhibited such a strongly favorable and contrasting attitude toward the status of women? That it did is evidenced by the number of women Jesus surrounded himself with, by the equal religious role women were allowed to play in Gnostic Egyptian early Christianity (see chapter 13), and by Paul's earliest conception of women being at least his equals and even his religious superiors:

Salute Andronicus and Junia, my kinsmen, and my fellow prisoners, who are of note among the apostles, who also were in Christ before me. (Romans 16:7)

Although the term used is *kinsmen,* in *The Gnostic Gospels* Elaine Pagels, professor at Barnard College, Columbia University, takes those Paul salutes to be women, among a long list of women he is greeting. According to Pagels: "Paul discusses this, saying 'In Christ . . . there is neither male nor female' [Galatians 3:28], and endorses the work of women he recognizes as deacons and fellow workers; he even greets one, apparently, as an outstanding apostle, senior to himself in the movement."[8] (This favorable view of women was altered in later centuries as the church moved to eradicate Gnosticism and portray Paul as antiwoman.)

The answer to the question comes partly from Josephus and from within Dead Sea Scrolls material itself and partly from an increased awareness of the origins of the Hebrew beliefs that came from Egypt.

Josephus states that Essene women were trained, like the men, for three years, presumably before initiation[9] into one of the branch communities. The Dead Sea Scrolls talk of a "daughter of truth" and also allude to the examination of women concerning their intelligence and understanding.

The awareness of women's rights must have increasingly impinged on the consciousness of the Qumran community from the time of the Teacher of Righteousness, who I maintain was Onias IV. As a refugee high priest of the Temple of Jerusalem, he fled to Egypt, where he and his followers would have learned more of the Therapeutae and their practice of forming separate male and female communities of equal status.[10] Had any of the Qumran Essenes actually visited the ruins of Akhenaten's holy city, they would have seen evidence of the equality of worship practiced by the pharaoh and his queen and realized that a more inclusive recognition of women in the Qumran philosophy was desirable. Perhaps John the Baptist and Jesus came to this very conclusion, and it became a main reason for their dissension.

Hang on a minute! you say. Where does the idea that early Christians or Essenes visited Akhenaten's holy city come from? Is there any evidence at all that anyone connected with the Qumran Essenes and their period, or followers of Jesus, ever visited Akhetaten? The incredible answer, as we shall see later, is a resounding, definite yes.

There were, therefore, ample reasons, in the earliest memories of the Essenes' ancestors, to have viewed women as being entitled to participate at the very heart of their religious activities, and an increasing awareness of this requirement must have emerged, particularly in Jesus's time.

## John's Death and Demotion

The Gospels of both Matthew (14:3–12) and Mark (6:17–19) differ from Josephus's version of the detainment and death of John the Baptist. They maintain that he was arrested by Herod because he had criticized Herod for marrying Herodias, his brother Philip's wife. Both Gospel versions also state that Herodias's daughter enticed Herod to have John the Baptist beheaded and his head brought out on a platter.

This was a very weird request indeed and an unprecedented form of execution, virtually unknown in Jewish literature.[11] However, the significance of this evidence from the Christian Scriptures is highly pertinent to the story that I unfold and the information that Jozef Milik related to me.

### Subordinating John the Baptist

Once Jesus was recognized as the Son of God, everyone else in the Gospels, especially John the Baptist, had to become subordinate. The idea of John the Baptist baptizing Jesus to remove his sins presented a real embarrassment to the first- and second-century-C.E. Testament writers. Why should Jesus exhibit any sins that needed washing away? Why should someone immerse him in cleansing waters, when he was to become the supreme spiritual immerser?

The process of downgrading John the Baptist can be seen to progress through the Gospels of Mark, Matthew, and the latter parts of John as the Baptist becomes a prophet heralding the way for Jesus, rather than a leader with disciples in his own right. The process culminates in the second-century-C.E. Gospel of the Nazareans in which when Jesus's mother and brothers urge him to come and be baptized by John he replies, "How have I sinned, that I would need to be baptized by him?" (Incidentally, the progressive intensity of this downgrading of John the Baptist gives a good indication of the order in which the Gospels were written. In this respect, Luke, in some ways, seems to project a truer account of the Baptist's life.[12])

As we go through the commonality of attitudes and attributes listed in table 14, it becomes clear that while some of them could be applied to other Jewish groups of the period, most of them were peculiar to the Qumran Essenes and John the Baptist, and in this regard they further confirm his at least temporary membership in the community.

## Summation

The Gospels of Mark, Matthew, Luke, and John agree that John the Baptist lived in the desert and preached a baptism of repentance for the forgiveness of sins, anticipated an imminent eschatological event, and saw himself as preparing the way for a messiah—just as the Qumran Essenes saw themselves preparing for a divine coming. All four Gospels and the rule book of the Essenes,[13] the Community Rule, draw on Isaiah 40:3 to explain their presence in the desert—in the case of John, to prepare the way for Jesus; for the Qumran Essenes, for the study of the Law and a pathway for God—but the common use of the very same passage from Isaiah can be no mere coincidence.

For about a third of the scholars studying the subject, there is sufficient evidence to conclude that John the Baptist was a member of the Qumran-Essene community at some period in his life. Another third are equivocal on the issue, while the remainder do not see much connection.

These variations in opinion from today's Christian thinkers has been ably summarized by Professor Lawrence Schiffman of New York, who notes that liberal Christians tend to see the Qumran community as a prototype of Christianity, whereas conservative Christians tend to look for and emphasize the differences between the Jewish sect and the early church.[14]

This summation is not surprising, in that most of the leading scholars in the Dead Sea Scrolls field are biblical scholars, and most of those are concerned with Christian Scriptures studies, biblical criticism, and the philology of the subject. The picture needs expansion, however. Opinions on the Dead Sea Scrolls environment from Jewish thinkers, adopting a Jewish perspective, have been thin on the ground. Matters have subsequently improved, but apart from a few enlightened scholars, Orthodox Jews will not even look at the Dead Sea Scrolls; and even the progressive, Reform, and Conservative strands tend to marginalize such study. For Muslim scholars, there has been virtually no serious contemplation of the subject, although, as indicated in other parts of this book, some very fruitful and pertinent associations to Islam can be made. From a nonreligious, broader historical viewpoint, little, unfortunately, has been added to the entrenched scholarship, despite the availability of a caucus of original, unedited biblical material that predates any previous material by almost a thousand years.

# ~ 23 ~

# John's Trademark: Ritual Immersion

As baptism was the central raison d'être of the activities of John, among others, its enactment warrants closer examination.

One of the characterizing features claimed for early Christianity was its form of baptism with water blessed by the first practitioner of this rite, John the Baptist. Baptism was used symbolically to enroll and bless a convert into the new religion, and the ceremony has been perpetuated over the centuries. As an initiation into Christianity, it has become endowed with a unique spiritual significance, and in some modern churches, particularly in America, there has been a trend back to the original form of full-body immersion.[1] Ritual immersion is also part of traditional and current Orthodox Jewish practice—for example, for a woman as a prelude to marriage—although the procedure is quite different from the Christian idea of sprinkling holy water on new converts or an infant.

The sources of information available for comparing the kind of aqueous baptism performed by John the Baptist, as described in the Christian Scriptures and by Josephus,[2] are quite limited. They come from rabbinic literature, the Hebrew Scriptures, Josephus himself, and Qumran. In addition, there is archaeological evidence of ritual washing baths from the pre–70 C.E. period.

At Qumran, cleansing by entry into ritual water seems to have been practiced before meals and it is suggested that this procedure was quite different from the baptism performed by John the Baptist; therefore, John's form of baptism had no connection to Qumran-Essene practices. As stated, this conclusion is correct, but it is also evident from Josephus that there were other types of baptism, including purification by immersion in special water for an initiate who had completed his first year of probation. Should a senior member be touched by a less pure junior member, he would bathe to regain his cleanliness. There was also a baptism of repentance.

The form of baptism by John the Baptist is described as one of:

- Repentance
- A cleansing of sins by prior confession and adoption of righteousness
- Full bodily immersion
- In running water; in the river Jordan
- Initiation into a new way of life
- A one-time event, but also a prelude to a final spiritual baptism by Jesus

## Ritual Cleansing and Immersion

### Rabbinic Literature

The use of rabbinic literature to discern normative Judaistic practice pre–70 C.E. requires a certain caution. Formalization of this type of literature did not commence much before 135 C.E., so reading what it describes back into the Second Temple period must be done with extreme reservation. When I refer to "normative" Judaism, I mean specifically that generally being espoused in the period 150 B.C.E. to 68 C.E.—the period during which the Essenes were settled at Qumran.

For the conversion of a Gentile to a Jewish proselyte, rabbinic literature describes a need for circumcision, an immersion, and the offering of a sacrifice in the Temple. Whether immersion was required in Second Temple times has been the subject of fierce debate. Protagonists such as Joachim Jeremias assert an early date for proselyte immersion,[3] whereas Robert L. Webb concludes that there is no clear evidence in Jewish literature for such immersions prior to 70 C.E.

### Hebrew Scriptures

The forms of ablution advocated in the Hebrew Scriptures show that washing or sprinkling was used for a number of purposes: ritually to cleanse objects such as furnishings and clothing that had come into contact with unclean things;[4] to cleanse people to make them holy or after contact with a corpse; to wash the hands and feet of priests in the bronze laver of the Tabernacle or Temple before they approached the altar.[5] The objective of these ritual washings was invariably self-administered purification, but there are some examples in which ablution language is used metaphorically to refer to self-cleansing or cleansing by God from a sin—for example, in Psalm 51, Isaiah, and Ezekiel.[6]

In some instances, when a contagious disease was seen as particularly severe, there was a requirement for bathing in running water, and the river Jordan was seen as especially effective.[7] There are, however, also references to a cleansing baptism by fire as being superior to that of water in Isaiah[8] and in Talmudic literature.[9]

Almost certainly this latter example of baptism by fire being superior to water represents a stance taken by normative Judaism around 300 C.E. in reaction to a prevalence of cleansing baptism by water, and interestingly it refers to a rabbi Abbahu rejecting water as a means of removing sin while responding to questioning by a "certain sectarian" (Hebrew, *min*), who might well represent a sectarian group such as the Qumran Essenes.

There are ancient public and private ritual washing structures across Israel similar in design to some of those found at Qumran. There are, however, also ritual bathing areas at Qumran that were unique in their design. (See page 1 of the color insert.)

### Josephus

Josephus describes a need for cleansing from leprosy, after sexual intercourse, and after nocturnal emission.[10] He mentions his own experience in following an ascetic named Bannus, who probably lived in the lower part of the Jordan valley, who practiced bathing morning and evening and prior to meals. This practice was similar to that of the Essenes, and it has been suggested that Bannus may represent a class of Essene.[11] Josephus also mentions the need for a proselyte to be circumcised, but he makes no mention of an accompanying immersion.

### Qumran

As previously stated, Josephus tells us that the Essenes practiced at least three forms of bathing: one to cleanse themselves from the accidental contamination of oil on their bodies after defecating and, for senior members, after being touched by a junior member; another designed for purification before eating and prayer; and a third that was reserved for a member of the novitiate after serving one year of probation, who then "partakes in the cleaner water for purity."[12]

Whatever the formula of the bathing, Josephus says that it was different enough from that performed in the Temple to exclude the Essenes from entry.[13]

The final form of bathing noted by Josephus was that for the Essene group, presumably the one at Damascus, among whom marriage was permitted. Here both men and women bathed, and both were covered in a brief garment.[14]

Perhaps the most significant description of ritual bathing comes from the Qumran Essenes' own literature, which in general confirms Josephus's commentaries. The Testament of Levi, an Aramaic text from Cave 4 dated to around 100 B.C.E., calls for washing as a cleansing from sin as well as a commitment to God. Uniquely the washing must take place in running water, that is, in a river, unlike the requirement articulated in the Hebrew Scriptures in which running water is reserved for serious physical ailments.[15]

This latter type of ritual immersion seems to be the closest to that adopted by John the Baptist, a conclusion also reached by a world expert on the subject. One of the most penetrating studies of John the Baptist was recently published by Robert L. Webb, of the University of Sheffield in England. He concluded, in light of the Qumran Testament of Levi, that "an actual immersion is performed in running water to symbolise cleansing from sin and conversion to God. This text is particularly significant, for it clearly antedates John's baptismal practice."[16]

From the Qumran Community Rule (1QS) it is apparent that a novice who fulfilled the first year of his membership and demonstrated his atonement from sin was welcomed into the fold with a ritual immersion. In the sense that all outsiders to the community, Gentiles and Jews alike, were "sons of darkness" in a state of sin, the immersion was equivalent to becoming a proselyte.

While archaeology at Qumran has identified some ten cisterns for possible use in ritual washing, a few must have been used for the other various ritual washing rites.[17] The Community Rule also talks of a requirement for immersion "in seas or rivers."[18] The river Jordan is only a little more than six miles from Qumran, so it was reasonably accessible for special immersions, but it is also possible that use was made of the nearest running-water source at Ain Feshka, some two miles to the south.

This mandatory rite of passage imposed on candidates entering into the covenant of the community had a requisite four elements:

1. Atonement for iniquities, in order to look on "the light of life"
2. To accept the Holy Spirit of the community in truth
3. To attain a spirit of uprightness and humility
4. Humility of the soul toward all the precepts of a new Covenant with God by consecration with cleansing waters

Not only are all the main elements of John the Baptist's form of immersion present in the induction immersion at Qumran, but there is also an indication of a movement toward a feature of baptism added by Jesus—a baptism into the Holy Spirit.

There are also similarities with elements cited in the Hebrew Scriptures, but in the words of Robert L. Webb, "The community was distinctive in its belief that the uncleanness caused by sin required an immersion, and that immersion had to be coupled with repentance (or similar spiritual dispositions) in order for the immersion to be efficacious."[19]

To summarize, it can now be seen, as set out in table 14 (see page 196), that John the Baptist's form of baptism contained elements that are not described in the Hebrew Scriptures or in rabbinic literature, but all these elements were known and practiced at Qumran.

The table shows that there are clear distinctions between the form of baptism practiced by John the Baptist and that of the contemporary Jewish milieu.

When it comes to comparison with practice at Qumran, particularly that related to the initiation ceremony for "freshmen," it is only in the last two features of immersion practice that the distinctions are apparent. After baptism by John the Baptist, most of the participants are said to have returned to their homes,[21] while only a few remained to become followers of the Baptist. At Qumran, the initiation immersion ceremony required the initiate to remain as an inhabitant of the community. This ceremony clearly did not include any anticipation of a final baptism by

**TABLE 14**

**Comparison of ritual-washing characteristics performed by John the Baptist, the Qumran Essenes, and in the contemporary Jewish milieu**

| Type of Ritual Washing | John the Baptist | Qumran Essenes | Contemporary Jewish Milieu |
|---|---|---|---|
| Bodily cleansing | √ | √ | √ |
| Confession of sins | √ | √ | Limited element |
| Atonement for sins | √ | √ | Limited elements |
| Initiation rite into a new Covenant | √ | √ | X |
| Spiritual initiation | √ | √ | X |
| Frequency | √* | √ | Frequently |
| With water | √ | √ | √ (oil, blood, and fire) |
| In running water | √ | √ | For severe ailments |
| In the river Jordan | √ | √ (or Ain Feshka) | √ (and elsewhere) |
| Full body immersion | √ | √ | √ (and sprinkling) |
| Only for Jews | √ | √ | √ |
| Administered by another | √ | √ | X |
| Entry into a community | X (some followers) | √ | X |
| In anticipation of final spiritual baptism by Jesus | √ | X | X |

*It is not completely clear from the Christian Scriptures whether John the Baptist baptized people more than once. The only specific reference is in Mark 1: 9–11, which implies Jesus was baptized only once by John. However, Joseph Fitzmyer interprets the Scriptures as saying John administered his baptism to any Jew, "and as often as one would come to him."[20]

Jesus—although it could be argued that neither did John the Baptist's in its original form (as previously noted, there is much evidence that the later Gospels downgraded the role of the Baptist and made him secondary to Christ). Nevertheless, as a commitment to the spirituality of the community and its unique understanding of Torah, the "sophomore" would be taking on an understanding that the kingdom to come would be heralded by the arrival of two messiahs.

The last seven attitudes/attributes listed in the above table as being common to John the Baptist and the Qumran Essenes are all challenged by Joan E. Taylor, of the University of Waikato, in New Zealand, and Visiting Lecturer and Research Associate in Women's Studies in Religion (New Testament) at Harvard Divinity School, a specialist writer who lectures in religious studies at the University of Waikato.[22]

In terms of scholarly consensus on whether John's baptism was unique, derivative of Jewish practice, or entirely dependent on it, there is none. The discussion is ongoing. Whether later revelations in this book will contribute to a more certain view remains to be seen.

Having attempted to present all the relevant evidence, I leave the reader to make his or her own judgment on these matters. However, all the evidence indicates that the form of baptism performed by John the Baptist was much closer to Essene practice than any other previously known Jewish custom. According to the Christian Scriptures, John the Baptist's ceremonial baptism seemed to require complete bodily immersion and was performed as a once-and-for-all act of repentance for sin, initiating the subject into a new faith. It was, however, to be followed by a final baptism into the Holy Spirit, to be performed by Jesus, for whom John the Baptist's version was a "preparing of the way." For the Qumran Essenes it was only he who:

> bows his soul to the law of God, has his flesh purified by the sprinkling of the purifying waters, and is sanctified in the water of purity. . . . By the spirit of holiness . . . a man is cleansed from all his sins. (The Community Rule 1QS)

## Why Baptism?

While some early scholars like H. H. Rowley[23] do not see any borrowing from Qumran baptismal rites, others, like John Heron,[24] demonstrate that both styles of baptism demanded the notion of repentance.

Part of the argument against a borrowing from Essenic baptism is that the immersion rite performed by John the Baptist was a one-off event, or at least preparation for a unique future baptism by Jesus, and involved cleansing a person of sin by acceptance of an outward acknowledgment of repentance. From the Qumran literature it is apparent that ritual cleansing took place on numerous occasions, particularly before meals, and at Qumran in static water. However, the Community Rule (3:4–9) also implied an initiation baptism conditional on a moral cleansing and repentance as a prerequisite of this initial ceremony as well as subsequent lustrations.

Although baptisms at Qumran could have used only static water, unlike John's baptisms, William Brownlee translates a section from the

Qumran Community Rule as requiring rippling water, implying that some forms of baptism might have taken place elsewhere, in a stream or river:

> So that he may purify himself with water for impurity and sanctify himself with rippling water.[25]

If this was the case, the most likely locations, as previously noted, would have been at the freshwater spring of Ain Feshka, some two miles from Qumran, and in the Jordan River.

It is also argued that baptism was open to Gentile as well as Jew, whereas at Qumran only the children of Israel were eligible. There can be no question that baptism, as described in the Synoptic Gospels, became available to non-Jews sometime in the first century C.E., but there is no evidence, from the Christian Scriptures or elsewhere, that John the Baptist extended his baptismal rite to Gentiles. It has to be borne in mind that the Christian Scriptures' record reflected a later view of pre–33 C.E. activities.

If the contention that John the Baptist was indeed at one time a member of the Qumran Essenes is correct, he would have been fully aware of the ritual washing that preceded many events within the cycle of the community's life. The ten *mikvaot,* or ritual pools, excavated at Qumran testify to the importance of this procedure, as do the texts of the Community Rule and other scrolls.[26]

## Origins

Finally, we must ask the obvious question about the origins of baptism. How did it commence as a religious ritual? The required presence of water in the Tabernacle of Moses indicates the importance of water from a very early time in Hebrew history. That it was also used in religious rites across the Middle East prior to this time is also apparent from various pictorial sources. Its use for baptism as an initiation rite, however, appears to have originated in Egypt. In the induction baptism of Queen Hatshepsut, for instance, water was poured over the new pharaoh, who is surrounded by a circle of ankh crosses. This ceremonial scene, dated to circa 1476 B.C.E., can still be seen on the temple walls at Karnak.

The importance of sacred pools in ancient Egyptian temple culture is evident from many site examples across Egypt, and it is not too difficult to see how this religious format of sacred pools might have evolved into the ritual baths seen in the Great Temple of Akhenaten. In *The Mystery of the Copper Scroll of Qumran* I drew attention to the similarity in number and design of these ritual baths at Qumran to those at the Great Temple of Amarna as yet one more example of the connections that can be made between the Amarna period and the Qumran-Essene period. It would not be surprising, therefore, to find that John the Baptist adapted this *mikvah* style of ritual cleansing into a spiritual induction by anointing with holy water.

The question remains, Why would John the Baptist take to sprinkling heads with holy water? Did he also get this idea from the Qumran Essenes? Purification rituals described in fragments from Cave 4 indicate water as being used to cleanse and atone:

> [And on completin]g [his] seven days of puri[fication] . . . and he shall wash his clothes with w[ater and cleanse his body] and he shall put on his garments and shall bless ag[ain] . . . the God of Isra[e]l. (4Q512)

The explanation for John the Baptist's extension of this ritual, I believe, lies in the same thread that connects religious practices of Akhenaten to those of the Qumran Essenes, as can be seen on page 10 of the color insert. Here, in a relief discovered at Amarna dating to circa 1350 B.C.E., one of Akhenaten's princesses is seen being blessed as purifying water is poured over her head from a jar held in the hand of a projecting ray from the Aten.

The arguments against John the Baptist being a member of the Qumran Essenes at one period of his life invariably compare the lifestyle he must have led after leaving the community with the lifestyle in the community. This is a chronologically invalid comparison. When the overall similarities of his attitudes and beliefs are compared with those of the Qumran Essenes, there can be no doubt that he was heavily influenced by the Qumran community, and his knowledge of their ways can be satisfactorily explained only by a previous membership.

Only further external proof can confirm this probability, and that some kind of extraordinary evidence might be forthcoming would seem unlikely on the face of it two thousand years after the events.

# ~ 24 ~

# John's Ministry

A ccording to the Gospel of Luke, John the Baptist would have started his ministry at about the age of thirty. This evidence ties in with Josephus's timing for the death of John the Baptist and can be deduced from the following passage from the Christian Scriptures:

> In the fifteenth year of the reign of Tiberius Caesar, Pontius Pilate being governor of Judaea, and Herod being the tetrarch of Galilee, and his brother Philip, tetrarch of the region of Ituraea and Trachonitis, and Lysanias tetrarch of Abilene in the high-priesthood of Annas and Caiaphas, the word of God came to John the son of Zechariah in the wilderness. (Luke 3:1–2)

The significance of this dating means that John the Baptist would have come out into public view at the exact age specified in the Community Rule (Manual of Discipline) for graduation from the Qumran-Essene community. This timing, surely, can be no coincidence in itself, and is even more intriguing when we find Jesus commenced his ministry at the same age of thirty. The location for the enactment of John's ministry was, according to Mark, Matthew, and Luke,[1] in the wilderness and near the river Jordan.

Leonard Badia, of St. John's University, New York, who has made a special study of John the Baptist,[2] concludes, "John's baptismal ministry was almost certainly close to the fords of the Jordan near Jericho, which is less than ten miles from Qumran." He also notes, "Both John's baptism and the Qumranian 'baptism' seem to be identical in their view of Repentance."

# Summary of Evidence Connecting John the Baptist to the Qumran-Essene Community

- He was born at Ein Kerem (Ain Karim), some twenty miles from Qumran.
- He spent his early life in the wilderness of Judaea, where Qumran was located.
- His father was a priest, a preferred qualification for enrollment at Qumran.
- Little is known of his early life, except that it was spent in the wilderness—a term the Qumran Essenes applied to their own environment.
- He commenced his ministry at thirty, the age for graduation at Qumran.
- He had many religious commitments in common with the Qumran Essenes (see table 12, page 179). He conducted his baptisms within ten miles of Qumran.
- His baptism was identical to that of the Qumran Essenes in relation to repentance.

Many of the key features of John the Baptist's life relate him in spiritual, religious, and practical terms to Qumran. It is now worth looking in more detail at the four geographical commonalities set out immediately above, as they complete the homogeneous picture that links John the Baptist to the Qumran Essenes.

# 25

# Geographical Juxtapositions of Christian and Essene Settlements

O ne of the strongest physical indicators that seem to confirm that John the Baptist and Jesus were actively involved with the Essene communities comes from geographic congruencies.

The settlement at Qumran was finally destroyed by the Romans in 68 C.E., but other Diaspora Essene settlements had already been established in and outside Judaea. It is, I believe, no coincidence that a number of these locations are also known from the Christian Scriptures and historical sources to have been in exactly the same places where the earliest Christian settlements were founded, notably:

- At the Essene Gate by the city of Jerusalem wall, identified by Flavius Josephus as a traditional gathering place of the Essenes and by later commentators as a Christian area of Jerusalem
- In Damascus, where the Christian Scriptures record that Paul met Ananias, an Essene-like character, to whom the Essenes refer in their Damascus document
- In the Valley of Natrun, in Egypt, where there was a settlement of Therapeutae,[1] a sect closely associated with the Essenes, where there is still today a Christian monastery that is thought to date back to the time of Jesus
- At Ephesus, in Asia Minor (modern Turkey), where Paul spent two years of his mission and wrote his letters to the Corinthians and Philippians[2]
- At Cochaba, in Batanaea (modern Jordan), where Christian

Nazoraioi (a term used to describe Christians in Muslim countries), Jewish Christians, and Ebionites (a group linked to the Essenes[3]) were associated.[4]

That so many widespread communities—in fact, all the key main centers of early Christianity—could have become so well established within, in some instances, five years of Jesus's death is quite improbable. It would mean their antecedents were there long prior to the crucifixion and recognition of Jesus's uniqueness. It was as if Christianity hit the ground running before the starting gun had gone off or the first spear had been thrown.

## The Essene Gate: Jerusalem

Historians Philo, Pliny the Elder, Josephus, and Dion, whose lives overlapped the period when the Essenes were living at Qumran, all mention the Essenes and a connection to Jerusalem. Hippolytus, a second- to third-century Roman Christian writer, also appears to have had access to sources that mentioned the Essenes.[5] We know from the Dead Sea Scrolls text known as the Damascus document that the only other place in the Holy Land, apart from Qumran, where celibate male priests of the Essene group lived was in Jerusalem:

> No man shall sleep with a woman in the City of the Sanctuary.
> (Cairo-Damascus document 12:1)

Jesus, according to the Christian Scriptures, was a lifelong celibate. This predilection would have been very unusual among the general Jewish population, and for a rabbi even more so. The biblical injunction to "go forth and multiply" was taken seriously by devout Jews then as today.

The detailed location of the Essene Gate in the wall surrounding the city of ancient Jerusalem is described quite precisely by Josephus.[6] Of the west wall of the city, he writes, "It descended past the place called Betsoa to the Gate of the Essenes." Josephus thus places the Gate of the Essenes midway between what are today called the Zion Gate, to the south, and the Jaffa Gate, to the north (see figure 25.1). In all probability, an Essene community lived inside the city walls close to this gate. The Hebrew name Betsoa is thought to refer to a lavatory, from the Hebrew words *beth*, meaning house, and *tzoa,* meaning excrement. This suggestion[7] fits in well with our knowledge of the Essenes' strict purity laws, which would have required them to defecate outside the city walls. Correctness for this location of the Essenes' latrines is also supported by a passage in the Dead Sea Temple Scroll that reads:

> And you shall make them a place for a hand, outside the city, to which they shall go out, to the northwest of the city, [where they shall make] roofed buildings with pits within them, into which the excrement will descend [so that] it will [not] be visible at any distance from the city, three thousand cubits.[8]

This evidence is reinforced by recent excavations adjacent to the Essene Gate, which have revealed a number of ritual cleaning baths, very similar in design to those at Qumran.[9]

Today the area immediately adjacent to where the Essene Gate would have been is an Armenian-Christian quarter; by tradition, it has been there since early Christian times. The Armenians claim to have had the oldest continuous Christian presence in Jerusalem. Bargil Pixner, a respected long-term archaeologist of the Jerusalem area, has concluded that the exact location of the Essene Quarter in Jerusalem was later occupied by "Jewish Christians" who were shunned by other Christians as heretics because they refused to accept the doctrinal decision of the Council of Nicaea (325 C.E.).[10]

If Pixner's assessment is correct, these early "Jewish Christians," as he calls them, were almost certainly intimately related to and involved with the Essenes, and as such would have held gnostic-Essenic views on Christianity. Not surprisingly, they would have been branded as heretics by the Eastern Christian Church.

The overall conclusion must be that a strictly devout, celibate, predominantly male Essene community lived in Jerusalem in the exact location that was later in history to become known as a place where early Christians lived, and where their descendants live to this day. From the close proximity of holy Christian sites to the Essene Gate, it is not unreasonable to deduce that the earliest followers of Jesus also lived there. That these early followers of Jesus could indeed have been members of the Jerusalem Essenes is also suggested from other evidence just cited and elsewhere in this book.

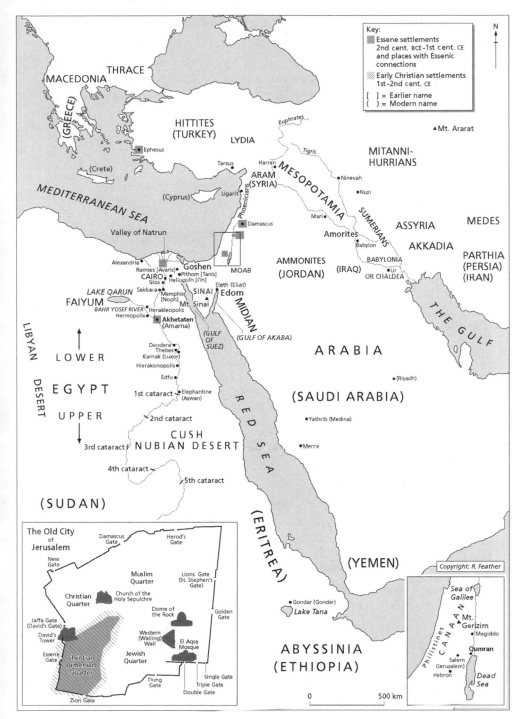

Fig. 25.1. *Map of the Middle East in the time of Jesus, showing supposed location of the Essene Gate and including sites of current interest.*

Even Roland de Vaux, head of the staunchly conservative École Biblique, who died in 1971, in an unguarded moment is reported to have said, "After the destruction of A.D. 68, many of them [the Qumran-Essene community] must have been brought into the Church."[11]

The Book of Acts indicates quite forcibly that a sizable number of the senior priestly members of the Essenes joined, or became, some of the earliest followers of Jesus:

> And the word of God increased: and the number of the disciples multiplied in Jerusalem greatly; and a great company of the priests were obedient to the faith. (6:7)

This can hardly be a reference to priests of the Temple, the Sadducees, as they did not believe in resurrection and were fiercely opposed to Christians. Nor could it be Pharisaic priests, as they were very thin on the ground. It can only be referring to priestly members of the Essene community, which archaeology, the Dead Sea Scrolls, and the contemporary historian Josephus tell us was situated right next to, if not concomitant with, the early Christian community.

Of course, not all Essenes were priests. Only the highly literate, senior members were of that status. After they became followers of Jesus, in the words of Professor Carsten Thiede (professor of Christian Scriptures history in Basel, Switzerland), "It is inconceivable that the messianic, eschatologically-minded followers of the teacher Jesus would have left his words and deeds to the literary endeavours of later communities a generation or two after their own time."[12] Thiede has a drum to beat in this conclusion. Following up the work of Jose O'Callaghan, Thiede has long contended that two scroll fragments found in Cave 7 (7Q4 and 7Q5) contain original Christian texts and shed light on a number of aspects of how the Christian Scriptures might have related to the works of the Qumran Essenes. Professor Émile Puech, however, insists that O'Callaghan and Thiede are not sufficiently expert in the Qumran texts; the fragments they believe are from Mark and Timothy are, according to Puech, very like other Dead Sea texts from Enoch.[13]

One thing Professor Puech does go along with, however, is the possibility that some Qumran Essenes could have been drawn to the newly formed Christian sect after the destruction of their habitat in 68 C.E. Some ended their lives with the defenders of Masada. Others, he says, could potentially have been drawn to reconstitute their faith by becoming brothers of the first Jewish-Christians.[14]

## Damascus

The texts found in the caves at Qumran and in the Genizah (synagogue storage place) in Old Cairo are collectively known as the Cairo-Damascus documents. From these and other Dead Sea Scrolls material it has been concluded by most scholars that the Essenes had established a settlement at Damascus long before the coming of Jesus.

## Valley of Natrun

Although traditionally the Therapeutae were thought to have lived near Alexandria in the vicinity of Lake Mareotis, a strong case can be made that they also had a presence elsewhere in the Delta region of Egypt, at Wadi Natrun.

Located in a depression just west of the Nile, near Kom Abu Billu, Wadi Natrun[15] was the traditional site where natrun,* one of the main ingredients of the materials used for mummification, was mined. The Wadi, or valley, is rich in salts and carbonates of sodium and consists of a flat area of land surrounded by ten lakes. Today you can see the extensive mining pits where extraction is still taking place. Driving thirty to forty miles southwest from the ancient digging sites, you reach a small settlement and the Monastery of John the Short. Graham Simmans, coauthor of *Rex Deus*,[16] who has explored extensively in this area, believes that at one time a sizable population of Christians lived at the settlement, augmented by Christian pilgrims who trekked hundreds of miles to visit the site. He has located what he thinks are the remains of up to two hundred buildings dating back to Coptic times in the early centuries C.E.

The area of the Valley of Natrun is also traditionally thought to be where the Therapeutae, an ascetic Jewish group closely related to the

---

*Natrun (or natron) consists of sodium carbonate and sodium bicarbonate.

Essenes, lived during the centuries spanning the zero millennium. Philo of Alexandria spoke of the Therapeutae as "the Essenes of Egypt" and described the many beliefs they held in common with the Essenes,[17] including the following of a similar solar calendar. The Therapeutae were known as religious healers who used herbs and plants for medicinal treatments and followed hidden teachings. According to Graham Simmans, a resident expert at Rennes-le-Château in the south of France, the monks at the Monastery of John the Short still refer to themselves as healers.

The monks today believe that the site was the place where the family of Jesus fled from Judaea during the persecutions of Herod the Great (Matt. 2). Simmans says there is a wider local tradition that Wadi Natrun is the site where Jesus and his family stayed when they came to Egypt.[18] A Christian presence, confirmed by archaeology, dating back to at least the fourth century C.E. testifies to the religious significance of Wadi Natrun. Today there are four active monasteries in the area,[19] and at nearby Deir al-Surian there is a Church of the Virgin dating back to at least the seventh century C.E.[20]

Apart from their close religious outlook, a curious physical link can be made between the Essenes and the Therapeutae of Egypt.[21] As Hartmut Stegemann, professor of Christian Scriptures studies at the University of Göttingen, points out, a main craft activity at Qumran and its companion settlement at Ain Feshka was the production of leather and scrolls.[22] Elsewhere in Judaea, scrolls were made using tannin, obtained from the bark of certain trees.

But the Qumran Essenes knew from another source an alternative technique for manufacturing leather, which was unlike anything employed anywhere else in Judaea. This technique avoided the terrible stench associated with leather production using tannin and animal feces and provided a superior product. The key to their new process was the use of calcium carbonate as an alternative. Chemical analysis of residues in the tannery basins at Ain Feshka has shown them to consist mainly of calcium carbonates, with no trace of tannin. No doubt the calcium carbonate would have been obtained from the Dead Sea. Production of leather for scroll-base material must have begun shortly after the time of the Essenes' settlement at Qumran, circa 150 B.C.E. Their close spiritual and religious association with the Therapeutae, however, makes it almost certain that the technology of their novel production technique came from Egypt and from the Therapeutae, who were settled in the Valley of Natrun, where calcium carbonate was readily available.

Carbon dating of the base leather material from samples of the Dead Sea Scrolls shows many were from much earlier than 150 B.C.E., with some dating to before 300 B.C.E. (see table 15). The inevitable conclusion is that the Qumran Essenes not only shared some of the specialist knowledge of leather production with the Therapeutae, but also either obtained base scroll material from their Egyptian colleagues as early as 350 B.C.E. or had a stock of older material when they settled at Qumran to keep them going until their own production line came onstream.

**TABLE 15**

**Carbon and paleographic dating for a number of Dead Sea Scrolls**

| Dead Sea Scroll | Carbon dating | Paleographic dating |
| --- | --- | --- |
| Testament of Kohath (Qahat) (4Q542) | 388–353 BCE | 100–75 BCE |
| Reworked Pentateuch (4Q158) | 339–324 BCE | 125–100 BCE |
| Isaiah (1QIs^a,b) | 335–327 BCE | 125–100 BCE |
| | 202–107 BCE | |
| Testament of Levi (4Q537–41) | 191–155 BCE | 2nd–1st century BCE |
| | 146–120 BCE | |
| Book of Samuel (4Q160) | 192–63 BCE | 100–75 BCE |
| Temple Scroll (11QT) | 97 BCE–1 CE | 1st century BCE–1st century CE |
| Genesis Apocryphon (1Q20) | 73 BCE–14 CE | 1st century BCE–1st century CE |
| Thanksgiving Hymns (1QH, 1Q36, 4Q427–32) | 21 BCE–61 CE | 50 BCE–70 CE |

# Ephesus

Not only was the Christian settlement at Ephesus contiguous with an already existing Qumran-Essene settlement, but also the design of the cathedral at Ephesus, which eventually became the central place of Christian worship, was based on a Qumran design. As Barbara Thiering points out in her book *Jesus of the Apocalypse*,[23] this building was later rededicated as a Christian monastery using the building plan from the Temple Scroll, a purely sectarian document, adapted to Christian usage, and the room of worship in the monastery was to form a model for all future churches.

Thiering has not been the only person to suggest that the architecture of early church worship was based on a Qumran design. Roland de Vaux, head of the École Biblique, in one of his reflective moments, wrote that the "circle of stones"[24] in the Qumran cemetery area "was a forerunner of the ambo of the Byzantine churches."[25]

The implication of this analysis is quite fascinating. If it is correct, and the evidence is strongly indicative that it is, the early Christian places of worship were based on the design of the worship area at Qumran, and these became the templates for future church designs. The design link for Christian churches does not, however, commence with Qumran. As I describe in my previous book, *The Mystery of the Copper Scroll of Qumran*,[26] Qumran itself was patterned on a much earlier building—the Great Temple at Akhetaten in Egypt. Although on a much smaller scale, the outer walls of the Qumran buildings are in exact alignment with the perimeter walls of the Great Temple. The number of ritual cleansing vessels, ten in all, was the same in each building, and there was a unique four-section bath in the Great Temple at Akhetaten and at Qumran. Church design would therefore seem to have had a much more ancient ancestry than has hitherto been acknowledged.

## The Galilee

If geographical factors support my contention that Jesus and John the Baptist emanated from Qumran, the traditional view that Jesus was a Galilean and came from Nazareth in Galilee is called into question. The difficulty of demonstrating that there even was such a place as Nazareth at the time of Jesus, as discussed earlier, also argues against the traditional view.

Even more telling in some ways than the geographical coincidence of early Christian establishments with Essene settlements is the lack of Christian establishments in Galilee—the one region where one would expect a glut. Historians such as Joan Taylor and H. Kasting[27] minimize the possibility of the Judaea wilderness as a stomping ground for Jesus, ostensibly to distance him from Qumran and place his ministry predominantly in Galilee. Yet direct information on the existence of early Christianity or any churches in Galilee is virtually nonexistent.[28] Even the Gospels, as Professor Sean Freyne, of the University College of Dublin, notes in his monumental study on the province of Galilee, are surprisingly silent about Galilee. Luke and Acts have evangelists going to Samaria, Gaza, Lydda, Joppa, Caesarea, and Judaea—anywhere but Galilee.

Professor Freyne puts the situation in Galilee in the early centuries C.E. in a nutshell: "It is surprising that we have not met more definite traces of this movement [Jesus's missions] in our other sources, where Galilee is for the most part a memory from the past, and we meet the occasional isolated *min** still functioning on the fringes of Judaism, but with no apparent Christian Community there."

The obvious questions remain: Why are so many places in Galilee named in the Christian Scriptures, and why do both Matthew and Mark assert that Jesus commenced his ministry in the Galilee? There are no clear answers. It must be assumed that Jesus (and the twelve apostles and seventy evangelists) did indeed spend periods preaching in the Galilee, in addition to Judaea and the area around Qumran, as there was a greater population there. Perhaps Jesus concentrated on that area initially because John the Baptist was already more active in Judaea.

Nevertheless, the readings of the first two Gospels are ambiguous on the point, whereas Luke is fairly clear in his positioning of Judaea as being more significant to Jesus. When it comes to the Gospel of John, Galilee is certainly of importance to Jesus, but John reiterates no fewer than five times that Jesus came from Judaea into Galilee when he was received at Cana.[29] The Christian Scriptures readings are, in fact, entirely consistent with, and more indicative of, Jesus coming out of Judaea, having spent his early life in study there, and coming into Galilee at a later date.

Geza Vermes, emeritus professor at Oxford University, while considering Jesus a "child of the Galilean countryside," finds it quite remarkable that there is no mention whatever in the Gospels of any of the larger Galilean towns. Jesus is never seen in Sepphoris, a large and important Galilean city only four miles from Nazareth, or any other regional center. Nor is there any reference in the Synoptic Gospels to Tiberias, a lakeside town built by Herod Antipas (governor of Galilee and Perea) in 18 C.E.,†

---

*Rabbinic Hebrew term for Jewish-Christians, or those who did not follow Jewish Law (Halachah).

†Tiberias, a newly built Hellenistic capital of the region, replaced Sepphoris around 18 to 20 C.E.

which was at the heart of Jesus's supposed ministerial area. Despite these anomalies, Professor Vermes, on rather thin evidence, associates Jesus with the charismatics, or Hassidim, who may have inhabited the area. In particular he singles out Hanina ben Dosa, a minor figure in Jewish history who apparently went about healing and exorcising, as a possible exemplar for Jesus.[30]

Jesus's traveling equipment is yet another vector that argues strongly against the theory that he was not a renegade Essene but rather an itinerant religious philosopher traveling around Judaea and Galilee, as Professor Vermes suggests and as is generally assumed (see table 16).

**TABLE 16**

**Comparison of traveling gear for Jesus, the Essenes, and itinerants**

| Rules for equipment in Jesus tradition | Essene rules for traveling | Typical characteristics of itinerant Jewish radical preacher-philosophers |
|---|---|---|
| Sandals | Worn-out sandals | Often barefoot |
| Staff | Staff only for self-defense | Staff as a weapon |
| No bag for provisions | No bag | Invariably a bag for provisions |
| One coat | Worn-out clothes | Cloak folded twice |

Based on descriptions in the Gospel of Mark and Josephus.

## Summation

It is now possible to establish a base position in relation to Qumran, Christianity, and the key people of the Christian Scriptures that is consistent with what many respected scholars assert.

- John the Baptist was at some stage in his life a member of the Qumran-Essene community.
- Jesus had a close association with John the Baptist, may have had some association with the community, and certainly would have had knowledge of it.
- Early Christianity was rooted firmly in Judaism.
- Early Christianity and the early Christian Scriptures had many exclusive features of commonality with the teachings, beliefs, and practices of the Qumran community.

The texts of the Dead Sea Scrolls may prefigure someone identifiable with Jesus, but they do not mention Jesus per se. Although there are similarities between the messianic expectations of the community and the role fulfilled by Jesus, the Qumran Essenes did not conceive of a messiah, in the Christian sense, who was the divine Son of God, born of a virgin, or of spiritual resurrection before the End of Time. From the analysis now presented, and in light of scholarship emerging from study of the Dead Sea Scrolls, this base position can, I believe, be moved on to a much firmer understanding, and the balance of probability is strongly indicative that:

- John the Baptist was a member of the Qumran community and kept in close contact with the community in his role as a mobile Essene.
- Jesus was almost certainly a member of the Qumran-Essene community at some period of his life, commencing his ministry after his graduation at the age of thirty.
- The earliest Christian communities were closely associated, in a spiritual and geographical sense, with the existing locations of Essene communities.
- The authors of the Christian Scriptures drew heavily on the Dead Sea Scrolls texts, beliefs, practices, and community structure of the Qumran Essenes.

As a chess-playing friend of mine, Robert Matthews, of the Royal Automobile Club in London, puts it, rather prosaically: "I know why the Qumran Essenes disappeared so suddenly from history—most of them became Christians!"

Conservative and fundamentalist Christian theologians have traditionally viewed many of the Dead Sea Scrolls as the enemy, fearing they could compromise the originality of Jesus and the Christian Scriptures story. Perhaps the scrolls should be looked at in an entirely different way; in fact, they could be the truest friend of Christianity. Apart from the Christian Scriptures and Josephus, there are no near-contemporary witnesses to the lives of Jesus, John the Baptist, and the disciples. Even the earliest of the books of the Christian Scriptures were allegedly written at least forty years after the deaths of Jesus and John the Baptist, and the earliest authenticated versions we have of these testimonies are dated to at least two hundred years after the events.

The Dead Sea Scrolls that anticipate some of the information in the Christian Scriptures, the teachings of Jesus, and the life of John the Baptist are the only original contemporary writings we have covering the period of their lives—and they are written in their own ethnic language. They are the greatest supporters of the validity of the Christian Scriptures, and even if 90 percent of the Christian Scriptures could be shown to have been derived from Dead Sea Scrolls sources, the core values of Christianity would not be affected. On the contrary, the existence of Jesus and John the Baptist would, for the first time, be buttressed by verifiable fact.

On the basis of these proposed firmer realities, the moment is now ripe for them to be tested on the ground at Qumran, to ascertain whether there is any evidence to support them.

We can now proceed to see how the dramatic revelation Jozef Milik imparted to me on that drizzly October day in Paris and the logistics of Qumran and its structural environment relate to the probable scenario of events surrounding the life of Jesus and his trailblazer, John the Baptist.

# — 26 —

# Trial and Crucifixion

An interesting consequence of analyzing stories of the Christian Scriptures in light of Jewish tradition obtaining at the time of Jesus involves the events of Jesus's last days. This analysis has particular relevance to the contention that Jesus and his followers danced to the rhythm of the same exclusive calendar that orchestrated the lives of the Qumran Essenes.

It is even more pertinent in setting the scene for the denouement of the book and the revelation of Jozef Milik.

## The Last Supper

Christian Scriptures place the Last Supper that Jesus celebrated in Jerusalem before his arrest and crucifixion at the time of Passover—the traditional Jewish festival commemorating the Exodus from Egypt. It was usual for all Jewish males to come to Jerusalem at each of the pilgrim festivals: Passover (Pesach), Pentecost (Shavuoth), and Tabernacles (Succoth). In many respects the description of this Last Supper, from Matthew 26, seems to conform to the traditional Passover seder, or evening supper, where wine is served, psalms of praise are recited, and the meal is enlivened by theological discussion. That the meal was held at night, within the walls of Jerusalem, would also have conformed to Jewish convention of the time.

As Jacqueline Tabick, senior rabbi at North West Surrey Synagogue, has pointed out,[1] in the Gospel of John, chapters 18 and 19, the judgment of Jesus is said to have taken place on the eve of Passover, which would mean a previous night's repast would not have been a Passover meal. Nor are bitter herbs and the eating of lamb mentioned—traditional requirements of the Passover supper.[2] In trying to assess whether the Last Supper took place at Passover or later in the year, it will be useful to refer to table 17 for background on the dates of Jewish and Christian festivals.

**TABLE 17**

**Holy Day festivals—Jewish and Christian equivalents**

| Jewish month[a] | Jewish festival | Christian festival | Secular date |
|---|---|---|---|
| Adar 14th (Feb–March) | Lots (Purim), 1 day | | |
| Nisan 15th (March–April) | Passover (Pesach), 7 days | Easter | March–April |
| Sivan 6th (May–June) | Pentecost or Weeks[b] (Shavuoth), 1 day | Pentecost | May–June |
| Tishri 1st (Sept–Oct) | New Year (Rosh Hashanah), 1 or 2 days | | |
| 10th | Day of Atonement (Yom Kippur), 1 day | | |
| 15th | Tabernacles (Succoth),[c] 7 days | | |
| 22nd | Termination (Shemini Atzeret), on 8th day | | |
| 22nd | Giving of the Torah (Simchat Torah), on 8th day | | |
| Kislev 25th (Nov–Dec) | Dedication (Hanukkah), 8 days | [Thanksgiving][d] | 4th Thursday in November |
| Teveth | | Christmas | Dec. 25 |

Based on Progressive/Reform Judaism practice. Festivals underlined are pilgrim festivals.

a. As the Jewish calendar is lunar–solar based, festival dates vary from year to year, although always falling in the appropriate season. The Essenes celebrated the Jewish festivals, except for Purim and Hanukkah, but they followed a solar calendar, so their festivals always fell on a fixed day, with Passover and the New Year always falling on a Wednesday. They also celebrated three new, unknown festivals of wine, oil, and wood.

b. Festival of Wheat Harvest.

c. Harvest Festival, including processing of the Lulav.

d. Celebrated in America; originally a harvest festival.

In the earliest representation of the Last Supper, seen on a wall fresco in the Catacomb of Priscilla just outside Rome, there is no sign of the traditional Passover foods apart from wine, but bread—which is proscribed during Passover—*is* shown on the table.

Later evidence from the Didache, a Christian work thought to date back to the first century C.E., makes no mention at all of the Passover meal.[3] The dating of Passover in the Jewish calendar coincides with the first full moon after the spring equinox, which places it on the fifteenth of the Jewish month of Nisan. Easter, the comparable Christian spring festival, is fixed on a Sunday after this date in March or April.

Rabbi Tabick suggests that, in addition to the evidence against Jesus's crucifixion having taken place at Passover, there are other pointers. The eating of the Last Supper in the upper room of the house[4] and the mention of palms being waved and laid at the feet of Jesus as he entered Jerusalem[5] indicate the festival in question was actually Succoth. For this autumn festival, it is customary to this day to build a temporary leafy shelter in an open space—which, in a crowded city, could have been on a roof or in an upper room—and to eat meals there. It is also customary to wave a bound swath of palm *(lulav)*, willow, and myrtle leaves at home or in synagogue as part of the festival service. An autumn setting also ties in with the biblical mention, shortly before the death of Jesus, of fig trees bearing their fruit.[6]

Madame A. Jaubert, a prominent French scholar, also argues that the discrepancies between John and the Synoptic Gospels over which day the Last Supper took place is due to the use of different calendars. According to her, Jesus would have celebrated the Essene solar calendar rather than the traditional lunar calendar interpreted by the Synoptics.[7]

Considering the many other indications of Jesus's affiliation to the Essene community, her basic contention is almost certainly correct.

## Waving of the Lulav

Interestingly, in the Temple Scroll of the Essenes, the waving of the lulav sheaf is elevated to a major ritual. As this is not a requirement in the Pentateuch, what could the biblical source have been for this radical departure from normative Judaism? In his study of the Temple Scroll,[8] Yigael Yadin concludes that the scroll's author seems to make use of injunctions in Leviticus (23:15–16) and Exodus (34:22) to describe three previously unknown festivals—of new barley, wine, and oil—in addition to the biblical festival of First Fruits (wheat), Shavuot, or Pentecost. Could these have had their origins in earlier Egyptian times? Succoth, as one of the three pilgrim festivals, predated the festivals of Rosh Hashanah (Festival of the New Year) and Yom Kippur (Day of Atonement) and was almost certainly the main festival (or the "Ha Hag") prior to the introduction of these two festivals. Yadin goes on to identify an additional festival of six days' duration, which he concludes was yet *another* new festival—of wood.

So what were the festivals being observed at Akhetaten?

As far as we can tell, the festivals celebrated by Pharaoh Akhenaten were related to new crops, organized around the spring and autumn harvest products, and would have paralleled those described in the Temple Scroll. So is there any other evidence to tie in the four festivals mentioned in the Temple Scroll, three of which—wine, oil, and wood—are completely unknown? In addition, the Temple Scroll elevates the Festival of Waving of the Sheaf (grain for bread) to the status of a major festival. The answer, I believe, is spelled out precisely in Psalm 104 of the Hebrew Scriptures.

Psalm 104 has long been noted by numerous scholars[9] as being remarkably similar to, and almost certainly based on, the Great Hymn of Akhenaten found carved on the tomb wall of Ay at Amarna, which dates back to circa 1350 B.C.E. In referring to the fruits that come forth out of the earth, we find a sequence of products exactly matching the festivals of wine, oil, wheat, and wood:

> That he may bring forth food out of the earth: and *wine* that maketh glad the heart of man, and *oil* to make his face to shine, and *bread* which strengtheneth man's heart. The *trees* of the Lord are full of sap. (Psalm 104:14–16; my emphasis)

Even more intriguing is the indication that the ceremony of waving the lulav, the most important of the First Fruits Festivals for the Essenes, which is observed to this day during Succoth by Jews around the world, is almost identical to a ceremony seen in the Great Temple of Akhetaten and must therefore have originated in Egypt of the fourteenth century B.C.E., long before the existence of a Temple at Jerusalem. The image on page 10 of this book's color insert shows courtiers in a ceremony waving a palm frond in the Great Temple at Akhetaten.[10] The clinching evidence is the four binding rings wrapped around the long palm. These palm-leaf wrappings are not part of the palm, but are added in exactly the same manner as on palm fronds used today.

If there can be any lingering doubt that some of the festival ceremonies enacted in synagogues to this day are rooted in ceremonies that were introduced at the time of Jacob and Joseph in the Great Temple of Akhetaten, a visit to the Museum of Luxor will dispel that doubt. Engraved on a long wall composed of reconstructed talatat (building blocks) showing scenes in and around the Great Temple of Akhetaten is the figure of a priest parading a covered, decorated scroll, with the Tree of Life (Hebrew, Etz Chaim), central binding pole and disk ends, in precisely the same manner as the Torah scroll is carried around synagogues to this day. (See page 10 of the color insert.) There are thousands of examples across Egypt, carved on temple and tomb walls, of papyrus scrolls being carried or *in situ*, but there are no other examples of a scroll matching that paraded in the Great Temple at Akhetaten.

Close examination of the scroll cover shows that it might actually be incised, perhaps even on copper, with decorations of pomegranates (Hebrew, *ribonim*)—a traditional Hebrew emblem for fertility—and a decoration on the robe of the High Priest (Exodus 28:33). The two cartouches on the cover appear to carry emblems related to the Aten.

I believe this kind of revelation does not devalue the authenticity of modern Judaism or of the Hebrew Scriptures. On the contrary, it verifies the ultimate antiquity of its traditions and the reality of its central characters, like Jacob and Joseph. In effect, it confirms that many of the stories of the Hebrew Scriptures are not, as some detracting minimalists claim, based on fiction and myth, but instead on hard, engraved fact.

Returning to the subject of the timing of Jesus's crucifixion, a rather powerful piece of evidence comes from a relatively recent finding. Sometime in the fourth century C.E., Byzantine Gentile Christians took possession of what had been a Judeo-Christian sanctuary on Mount Zion, Jerusalem. Records of the consecration of the most holy of the sites on Mount Zion, the Church of the Apostles, must have been handed down through the Byzantine Eastern churches. In 1984 a Belgian scholar, Michel van Esbroeck, made public a remarkable document. Discovered shortly before in a Georgian monastery in Russia, it relates a statement by Bishop John of Bolnisi that the Feast of Anastasis, in commemoration of the resurrection of Jesus Christ, took place on September 13:

> And the 15th of the same month was the dedication of the Holy and Glorious Zion, which is the mother of all churches, that had been founded by the Apostles, which Emperor Theodosius the Great* has

---

*Reigned 379–395 C.E.

built, enlarged, and glorified, and in which the Holy Spirit had come down on the holy day of Pentecost.[11]

This evidence implies that the resurrection, which according to the Christian Scriptures took place three days after Jesus's crucifixion, occurred in autumn. Succoth, the Jewish harvest festival, takes place fifty days *after* Passover.

The highlight of the Essene year was an event that members would not have boycotted. It was the custom for all members to return to "headquarters" for an annual gathering. According to Dead Sea Scrolls sectarian texts 1QS and 4QDe, this event took place during the Autumn Feast of Tabernacles (Succoth). It therefore seems likely, if Jesus was at one time a member of the Essene community, that he would have paid a visit to Qumran, with the intention of then moving on to Jerusalem, a seven- or eight-mile walk across the Judaean desert, for the Last Supper.

That Jesus might have been partaking of the Last Supper in an Essene establishment is strongly indicated by a passage in the Christian Scriptures. In the Gospel of Luke, Jesus's disciples Peter and John ask him where they are to prepare the meal, and Jesus enigmatically replies:

> Behold, when ye are entered into the city, there shall a man meet you, bearing a pitcher of water: follow him into the house where he entereth in. And ye shall say unto the goodman of the house, The Master saith unto thee, Where is the guest chamber, where I shall eat the Passover with my disciples? And he shall show you a large upper room furnished: there make ready. (Luke 22:8–13)

Jesus obviously knows of a place his disciples were not aware of, where he would be made welcome and housed.[12] Josephus confirms the open-house policy of the Essenes toward one another.[13] The only community in Jerusalem likely to maintain an everyday guesthouse for its members would have been the Essenes.[14] No doubt the disciples entered the city via the Essene Gate, where many Essenes would be walking about. Jesus's description of a man carrying water would appear to be completely inadequate to clearly identify anyone among the throng who frequented the walled city of Jerusalem.

In the Essene quarter, however, it would have enabled instant recognition of a fellow Essene. In other parts of the city anyone carrying water would have been a woman or a slave. Here, in this predominantly male Essene community area, slaves were not kept and female Essenes were excluded. Consequently, a male carrying water would almost surely be an Essene. Jesus had no need to be more specific in his description.

**TABLE 18**

**Summary of evidence for Jesus's Last Supper being at Passover (Easter) or Succoth (Tabernacles) from the Christian Scriptures (CS) and other sources**

| Passover | Succoth |
|---|---|
| • Mentioned in CS | • Coincides with time of annual gathering of Essenes at Qumran, near Jerusalem |
| • Mention in CS of eating bread, forbidden at Passover | • Mention in CS of palm leaves, usually associated with autumn festival |
| • No mention in CS as a traditional family meal or with wife and children | • Mention in CS of figs, which would be ripe in August until late September |
| • No mention in CS of bitter herbs, Pascal lamb, and other traditional Passover foods | • CS says Supper takes place in upper room, traditional place for Succoth meal |
|  | • Byzantine texts of John of Balnisi state autumn for time of Last Supper |

Items in *italic* indicate arguments against Passover and for Succoth.

The evidence for Succoth and against Passover as the time of the Last Supper appears overwhelmingly in favor of Succoth being the correct period.

My view of the most likely scenario is that Jesus and his followers returned to Qumran for the annual Succoth gathering and then walked the eight or so miles to Jerusalem. They entered the city via the Essene Gate amid an abundance of palm leaves brought to build the Succoth Festival shelters. This, then, was the preamble to the enactment of the Last (Succoth) Supper and the betrayal of Jesus.

This controversial chronological view does not necessarily contradict the traditional Christian commemoration of Jesus's trial and crucifixion at Easter (Passover). It is quite possible that he was arrested during Succoth and held in prison until Easter, when there would have been enormous crowds in Jerusalem and a show of Roman authority would have had maximum effect. The relevance of the Succoth date to our story, however, is that it reinforces the argument that Jesus and his followers were dancing to a different festival rhythm than the rest of the Jewish population of the time, although one that seemed to be synchronous with that followed by the Essenes.

## The Trial of Jesus

Whether the Sanhedrin (Jewish high court, which met in the Hall of Hewn Stone in the Temple) or the Romans took initial action against Jesus is unclear from the Gospels. There are a number of biblical references on the proceedings of the trial that pose questions about its occurrence. Traditionally, Jewish trials were never held at night and never on feast days; capital offenses would always require a second hearing; and a meeting of the priests would normally have taken place in the Temple.

Versions of Jesus's trial in the Christian Scriptures conflict with these traditional understandings. While the Sanhedrin had the authority to try Jesus for blasphemy, it did not have the authority to execute him. That power remained with Pontius Pilate, the Roman procurator at the time, who, as we have already noted, was an extreme and cruel authoritarian.

The Christian Scriptures relate that the Sanhedrin took Jesus into custody by force after he was betrayed by one of his disciples:

> And immediately, while he yet spake, cometh Judas, one of the twelve, and with him a great multitude with swords and staves, from the chief priests, and the scribes, and the elders. And he that betrayed him had given them a token, saying, Whomsoever I shall kiss, that same is he; take him, and lead him away safely. (Mark 14:44)

The need for a "multitude" of armed men seems to imply that Jesus was not just a threat to religious thinking but also a threat to the stability of Roman military rule. It may well have been that the support Jesus amassed had become more than simply an irritation to the Romans and that it was tantamount to an insurrection of disobedience and violence. The Gospel goes on to relate how Jesus was delivered by the council to Pontius Pilate, who found him guilty of claiming to be the king of the Jews. He was taken out and crucified at Golgotha.

## After Jesus's Crucifixion

The messianic leader is gone, but heathen Rome still body-presses the Jews to the canvas of Judaea. Hope is not abandoned, because those of the Essenes who construe Jesus as the kingly warrior-messiah of their texts talk of his physical resurrection, as do Isaiah, Daniel, and Ezekiel. James, the brother of Jesus (and possibly leader of the Essene community, or, as described by Hegesippus,[15] a lifelong Nazirite), picks up the reins of Jesus's teachings until his judicial murder in 62 C.E.[16] Messianic fervor continues to foment until it erupts in the First Jewish Revolt of 66 C.E. Revolutionary bacteria contaminate the land, obliging Rome to send the mighty Vespasian to sanitize the festering wound of rebellion. Qumran is destroyed in 68 C.E., the Second Temple in 70 C.E.[17]

Now, not only has the Messiah failed to return to save his people, but also Jerusalem is in ruins; the country has been decimated and its inhabitants scattered. Not surprisingly, many of the adherents of an imminent physical warrior-savior messiah are disillusioned and turn to the Pauline version of Jesus as a spiritual Messiah who offers salvation in a life to come.

The Christian Scriptures record that after Jesus's death, his tomb was found empty, and the Gospels describe various versions of his resurrection and appearances to his disciples and followers. Despair at his death began to turn to ecstatic expectancy, and the disciples set about spreading the word of his miraculous life.

# ⌐ 27 ↝

# A Return Visit to Paris

It was at this stage in my research, in October 1999, that I went again to visit Jozef Milik to present him with a copy of *The Copper Scroll Decoded,* which had recently been published by HarperCollins. Monsieur Milik had been extremely helpful in giving advice and encouragement in its preparation. He had also introduced me to his friend Henri de Contenson, the French archaeologist with whom he had worked in the 1950s and who had actually discovered the Copper Scroll, one of the Dead Sea Scrolls, near Qumran.

In chapter 1, I related that Jozef Milik had left the Catholic priesthood to get married. I also intimated that my conversations with him had led me to believe that there were other, more profound reasons, related to his study of the Dead Sea Scrolls, behind his decision to leave the priesthood.

He has not been the only person heavily involved in Dead Sea Scrolls studies to rethink his or her religious convictions. Others include John Allegro, a onetime probationary Methodist priest;[1] Karen Armstrong, previously a nun;[2] John Dominic Crossan,[3] who was ordained in 1957 and resigned from the priesthood in 1968; and Geza Vermes, previously a Catholic priest. Professor emeritus of Jewish studies at Oxford University, Geza Vermes probably has the greatest overarching understanding of any scholar of the entire Dead Sea Scrolls corpus. His book, *The Complete Dead Sea Scrolls in English,*[4] is the standard work of reference for all scholars working in the field.

I do not cite the foregoing examples as any criticism of fundamental beliefs in Christianity. There are many more students of the Dead Sea Scrolls who have remained steadfast in their religious convictions. Other students of the Bible, such as the controversial writer Ian Wilson, have converted to Roman Catholicism.

There are, however, a number of revelations and implications in the Dead Sea Scrolls and Gnostic texts that make it difficult to reconcile certain accepted episodes in the Gospels, and it is self-evident that many aspects of the Christian Scriptures stem from Essene teachings. Any objective study must inevitably come to the conclusion that the teachings of Jesus bear striking resemblances to those of the custodians of the Dead Sea Scrolls. For example, Jesus was aggressively against the teachings of the Pharisees, traditional Jewish law, and the institution of the Temple.[5] Many other congruencies have been discussed earlier.

## The Revelation

We are back in the dimly lit room of Jozef Milik's flat, with its worn carpet and gloomy shelves full of books and manuscripts—the inner sanctum of a lapsed Catholic priest. It is October 5, 1999, and the Parisian evening is beginning to wrap itself around the edges of light. Darkness creeps into the room, but the mind of my companion is as bright and sharp as ever.

We have been talking about his current work, which he is preparing for publication sometime in the vague future. He has already completed two hundred pages of a study on reconstructions of ancient inscriptions, the locations of which range from Lebanon through Syria and down to southern Arabia. The study will include a detailed treatise on an Aramaic-Nabataean-Greek inscription relating to ancient gods, found on a second-century-B.C.E. temple in southern Syria.

Two hours into our conversation, Jozef Milik quietly and almost casually speaks of a certain event in the cemetery of Qumran, by the shores of the Dead Sea. We are discussing the seasons of excavation work that he and Henri de Contenson had conducted during the early 1950s, as we skirt about the details of the burial site. I mention that Henri de Contenson recalls the excavation of bones from the cemeteries and Monsieur Milik suddenly interjects:

"I too excavated a corpse, without a head. It was clear from the presence of brown dust that it must have been in a wooden coffin. Yes, there were arms and the skeleton, but no skull . . . "

I am intensely curious, not immediately recognizing the significance of what he is saying.

"Was it buried close to the Khirbet Qumran ruins?"

"No!" he replies. "It was some two kilometers distant."

"Why would the corpse have no head? Who could it have been?"

"John the Baptist, no doubt," comes the rapid response.

It is one of those nerve-tingling moments. My mind reels with the impact of what he is saying.

"So was he the leader of the community, heir to the Teacher of Righteousness?"

A rat-a-tat-tat of negatives flies back at me.

"No, no, no, no, no! He was not the leader, but almost certainly one with the Essenes."

"You say you believe that the body had been buried in a wooden box. All the reports I have read indicate that most of the bodies were buried naked in shallow pits. Why would they have buried this person in a coffin? If he wasn't the leader of the community, why was he so special as to warrant a different type of burial?"

"It is obvious. He did not die there. His body was brought there in the coffin. He was someone to them, but his burial was different because he died somewhere else."

"Where would that have been?"

A thin smile spreads across his pallid face. "Machaerus. It is not far away."

I probed, as barrister-like and yet as benignly as I could, but no further details of interest were vouchsafed, and I became aware that there was an area of resistant sensitivity that Jozef Milik would not allow me to enter. There was more information that he was not prepared, at that time, to mention. He had given me sufficient clues; the rest I had to find out for myself. In a later video recording, he repeated his recollections of excavations in the cemetery at Qumran and then went on to divulge more details—the information I had previously sensed he wasn't ready to discuss.[6]

If what Jozef Milik suggested was true, the whole course of our understanding of the role of John the Baptist in the Christian Scriptures would be altered, and his burial place would become one of the most important religious holy sites in the world.

When I checked again with Henri de Contenson, he could not recall much of the detail of the events that had occurred some forty years earlier.

Was it possible that Monsieur Milik had mixed up his facts, or even made them up? Why had this information not been previously reported? Did anyone else know of his discovery?

During my conversations with Monsieur Milik, some lasting as long as three hours, he had never shown any signs of mental tiredness; his mind and memory were always sharp and precise. There was no reason for him to make up such a story. I believe he entrusted the information to me because it was something he no longer wanted to keep secret.

That some of Jozef Milik's original colleagues may also have been aware of the find is quite likely, but they may well have considered it best to keep it quiet to avoid the controversy it would have provoked. At that time, they were already heavily embroiled in defending against claims being made by other scholars—like John Allegro, André Dupont-Sommer, and Edmund Wilson—that Jesus himself had been presaged in some of the Dead Sea Scrolls. A revelation that John the Baptist might have been buried at Qumran would have completely undermined their case.

Later, the full force of what Jozef Milik had told me sank in. The conclusions that I had previously arrived at in my research, notably that there was a strong connection between John the Baptist and Qumran, all seemed to confirm the validity of Jozef Milik's claim. Further insights with regard to Jozef Milik's beliefs were later shared with me by his wife, Yolanta, a respected scholar in her own right. (Please see appendix 3 for Yolanta Milik's commentary.)

The historical evidence that John the Baptist was beheaded by Herod (at Machaerus) is confirmed by Flavius Josephus and reiterated in the Gospels of the Christian Scriptures:

> He went and beheaded him in the prison, brought his head on a platter. . . .
>    When his disciples heard about it, they came and took his body, and laid it in a tomb. (Mark 6:27–29)

> His disciples, having consigned the headless body [of John the Baptist] to the grave, went and told Jesus all that had occurred. (Matt. 14:3–12)

In the time of John the Baptist, the site of the Herodian fortress of Machaerus would have been a little more than nine miles southeast of Qumran, in the province of Peraea, on the opposite side of the Dead Sea from Qumran. Everything fit.

There is, indeed, another apparent myth that lends credence to the story. If John the Baptist's body was important, so also was his head, and one can imagine that it too would have been carefully preserved. There is fairly reliable evidence, from Guillaume d'Arbley of France among others, that in the fourteenth century C.E., the Knights Templar, an order of soldiers that came into existence after the First Crusade of 1099 C.E., possessed and revered what legend decreed had been a bearded head.[7]

This head was known as the Baphomet. For these self-appointed Poor Knights of Christ, the head of St. John the Baptist would have been an object of devotion, and his feast was to be celebrated by command of the Templar Rule of Order.

There were therefore two main areas of interest that demanded investigation in relation to the revelations of Jozef Milik: first, the headless skeleton of what he referred to as the remains of John the Baptist; and second, what profound findings in the Dead Sea Scrolls, if any, had influenced the thinking of Jozef Milik?

Many people, from as far back as Emperor Constantine in the fourth century C.E. and the Knights Templar in the twelfth century C.E. to modern scholars, have searched for and theorized over the location of the final resting places of Jesus and John the Baptist. No one is certain where their bodies were finally buried, and the Christian Scriptures are, in fact, our only direct source of information on these matters.

## John the Baptist's Final Resting Place: Previous Theories

Traditional stories allude to the body of John the Baptist having been removed from Machaerus by his followers and buried in one of two places: at East Anatolia (modern Sebastiye, Turkey) or in Samaria in Israel at a place called Sebaste, in a tomb in the Cathedral of St. John the Baptist. This latter contention is rejected by most modern scholars on the grounds that the connection results from a confusion of Herod Antipas with his famous father, Herod the Great, who built a fortress at Sebaste after being granted the city by Octavian in 30 B.C.E. The tomb itself is a Roman one dating from the second to third century C.E. and therefore cannot possibly be the tomb where John the Baptist found his final rest.[8] (The tomb was apparently pillaged by pagans in the fourth century C.E.)

What we are told in the Christian Scriptures is that John's disciples took his body and laid it in a tomb (Matt. 6:29), a statement indicating that the location of the tomb of John the Baptist was known at the time the Gospels were written.[9] Apart from these two indicators referring to a tomb and knowledge of the tomb's whereabouts, there are no plausible suggestions for the location of John the Baptist's corporeal remains.

I decided to undertake an urgent mission to confirm or refute the dramatic revelation vouchsafed to me by Joseph Milik during our conversation; and with all the other pointers that followed from this astonishing announcement, I began to consider which other of John the Baptist's contemporaries might be buried at Qumran.

# — 28 —

# The Search Begins

The time has come, as the walrus said, to move into the final theater of our drama. Our stage is the now desolate site that stretches some fifty-five yards from the outer limits of the settlement ruins at Qumran near the shores of the Dead Sea.

Qumran is located on a relatively flat plain running along the western shores of the Dead Sea and backed by steep hills. One aspect that had puzzled me for some time about the Qumran site was the lack of detailed archaeological reports on the ruins and nearby cemetery. What is known is that the Qumran ruins themselves comprise a complex of buildings dating back some 2,100 years.* About fifty-five yards east of the ruins, on an undulating site covering an area of about one hectare (approximately two acres), lies a cemetery that looks out over distant views of the Dead Sea. In the surrounding vicinity are other burial sites.

There are approximately 1,180 graves in the Qumran cemetery,[1] and, although in some sections they are laid out in discernible rows, all the graves are described in the existing and limited literature as being unidentified. Virtually all the graves that have been excavated in the main cemetery contained bodies of males, with the presence of a very few females and infants in a secondary cemetery. (See page 12 of the color insert.)

Of the limited number of burial excavations that have been done, all showed that the bodies of the dead had been buried naked and placed in shallow, trenchlike graves, with the head turned carefully to the south. Occasionally an inkwell had been placed beside the body, perhaps to indicate that the deceased had been an exceptional scribe of the community. Otherwise, no worldly possessions whatsoever were buried with the bodies.

---

*Some remains at Qumran are dated to an earlier, eighth-century-B.C.E. period of occupation of the site.

Most of the graves at Qumran are oriented north–south, whereas Jerusalem and the Holy Temple were located to the west. The deliberate turning of virtually every corpse's head toward the south is one more puzzle that scholars have been unable to explain, just as the strange form of burial, quite different from any usual procedure in the Holy Land, has no conventional explanation.

Considering the atypical nature of these burials, very few archaeologists or historians have seemed capable of posing the simplest of questions:

- Why was the cemetery at Qumran so different from conventional burial places?
- Why were virtually all the graves oriented north–south?
- Why were the bodies invariably buried naked?
- Why were there almost no artifacts, jewelry, or worldly goods buried with the incumbents?

The answers have not been forthcoming from studies that have concentrated on analyzing the minutiae while ignoring the fundamentals. No one seems to have faced up to these anomalies.

In my previous book, *The Mystery of the Copper Scroll of Qumran*,[2] I set out a plausible explanation for the unusual orientation and form of burial at Qumran. This explanation is based on the large amount of evidence that links the Qumran Essenes to a much earlier time and place in Egypt—notably to the period of the Hebrews' sojourn in Egypt, and to the ancient city of Akhetaten, which lay south of Qumran.

The simplicity of these burials at Qumran, quite unlike anything seen in the usual burial practices of Judaea in the Second Temple period, could also be explained by a connection to this specific period of ancient Egyptian history when the pharaoh Akhenaten ruled Egypt. In addition to instituting a pure form of monotheism, Akhenaten had also swept away the previous Egyptian custom of including gifts, protective charms, and material treasures along with the corpse, and inaugurated a simple form of burial without any worldly goods.

The specificity of a connection to this period is reinforced by the fact that, immediately after the death of Akhenaten, burial practices in Egypt reverted to the old ways of including huge amounts of ritual materials in the tombs of the deceased.

## Final Scenes

What somber scenes of bereavement must have been played out on this brown, pebble-strewn landscape at Qumran, scenarios repeated some 1,177 times as a procession of white linen–garbed figures filed out from their sanctuary, snaking their way through the graveyard to gather around a newly dug mound of sand and stone.

Slowly the stiffening body would be laid on the ground, the white covering shroud gently unwound, and the body placed in a shallow, trench-like grave. Stooping forms were starkly outlined against the blood-red shadows cast by the dying sun and stretching toward the darkening blue sea of salt rippling nearby. The wail of Hebrew chanting, initiated by the leader of the congregation, would echo eerily out over the field of death:

> *For without Thee no way is perfect,*
> *and without Thy will nothing is done.*
> *It is Thou who has taught all knowledge*
> *and all things come to pass by Thy will.*
> *There is none beside Thee to dispute Thy counsel*
> *or to understand all Thy holy design,*
> *or to contemplate the depth of Thy mysteries*
> *and the power of Thy might.*
> *Who can endure Thy glory,*
> *and what is the son of man*
> *in the midst of Thy wonderful deeds?*
> *What shall one born of woman*
> *be accounted before Thee?*
> *Kneaded from dust,*
> *his abode is the nourishment of worms.*
> *He is but a shape, but molded clay,*
> *and inclines towards dust.*
>
> COMMUNITY RULE, 1QS XI, 17–22

## What Was Really Going On at Qumran?

Before considering the excavations that have already taken place in the Qumran cemetery and its surrounding district, it is necessary to dispense with some of the sometimes quite absurd claims as to the function of Qumran and its closely associated cemeteries. Verification of the real purpose of the original settlement at Qumran is fundamental to a proper assessment of Jozef Milik's startling revelation.

A great majority of scholars and academics are convinced that Qumran was a place where the so-called Essenes wrote the Dead Sea Scrolls, which include material describing their activities and beliefs. A small but reputable and highly vociferous minority are stuck in their own mire of disagreement, so we need to examine the legitimacy of the consensus view.

Many scholars have recognized the extreme importance of the unusual burial practices at Qumran in confirming the nature of the beliefs of the Qumran Essenes. I quote, for example, a journal article by Ferdinand Röhrhirsch, published in 1996,[3] wherein the author uses the nature of the burials at Qumran to test various theories about the original complex of buildings at Qumran. In this work, Röhrhirsch examines three theories in detail:

1. The original complex of buildings was a villa
2. It was a Jewish fortress
3. It was a religious settlement

The first of the two minority theories is suggested by Jean-Baptiste Humbert and Alain Chambon,[4] authors of a report in French (based on the original work of Roland de Vaux) on the archaeology of Qumran. The second theory is advocated by the controversial American professor Norman Golb,[5] and the third is the generally accepted theory of most scholars, such as Roland de Vaux, Jozef Milik, Frank Moore Cross, Professor Geza Vermes, and Professor George Brooke.

Ferdinand Röhrhirsch, in his study of Qumran, applies the form of burials at Qumran (among other factors) as a sort of litmus test to these theories and draws several conclusions.

If it was a villa, there would be no connection between the villa and the grave sites. Pottery found at the settlement ruins, for example, would be different from that associated with the graves. It isn't; therefore, the villa theory is false.

If it was a military fortress, the graves would indicate normative

Jewish burial rites. The graves and form of burial are unique to the location; therefore, the theory is false. And to quote Joseph Zias (previously curator at the Rockefeller Museum, Jerusalem), "The site [Qumran], however, on the basis of the cemetery, is unique and all attempts (being argued again by those individuals whom have never studied PA [Palestine]) to argue that it was a military cemetery etc. are simply wrong. The cemetery defines the site and the clues to its correct assessment lie there, not at Ein Gedi or elsewhere."[6]

If the graves were associated with a religious settlement, they would reflect the uniquely distinctive beliefs of the incumbents. They do; therefore, the theory is true.

One could apply the "graves test" to many other alternative Qumran theories such as that it was a trading post,[7] a winter villa,[8] or a health spa.[9] All fail the test.

## The Scriptorium Question and Other Anomalies

While on this topic, we might look at another piece of evidence cited by Professor Norman Golb, of the University of Chicago, and by Hershel Shanks, the editor of *Biblical Archaeology Review* and *Bible Review,* a partial supporter of Professor Golb. Where Professor Golb believes Qumran was a fortress, Hershel Shanks, on balance, believes it was a religious settlement, but neither of them believes the Dead Sea Scrolls were produced there.

Their argument hinges on the existence, or nonexistence, of a scriptorium (writing room) at Qumran and whether the tablelike structures that were found at Qumran were used for writing. Other researchers, notably Professors Robert Donceel and Pauline Donceel-Voûte, at Louvain Catholic Seminary in Belgium, whose work on the Qumran Essenes we will discuss a little later in this book, believe the structures referred to as writing tables were actually benches, rather like the Roman tricliniums that were used for reclining while eating.

Father Roland de Vaux and various other scholars have maintained that a proportion of the Dead Sea Scrolls must have been composed and written at Qumran and that the benchlike structures found in one of the larger rooms were, in fact, writing tables. The finding of two inkwells in the nearby debris seems to support this idea.

In his book *The Mystery and Meaning of the Dead Sea Scrolls,*[10] published in 1998, Hershel Shanks illustrates his (and Professor Golb's) argument that the scrolls were *not* produced at Qumran with a photograph of the benchlike structures as they appear in the Rockefeller Museum, Jerusalem, and then a visualization of how a scribe would have had to sit in what he calls "an impossibly awkward position" to use the items as writing desks. (Hershel Shanks also doubts that writing tables existed in the first century B.C.E.)

However, figure 28.1 shows an example of the use of a structure of similar height as a worktable in the workshop of Iuty, an Egyptian sculptor, dated to the fourteenth century B.C.E. The table even bears a remarkable similarity to the structures found at Qumran. (Iuty was the chief sculptor of Queen Tiy, the mother of Akhenaten.)

The figure is seen sitting at one of the low tables with his knees bent in an almost identical posture to that postulated by Hershel Shanks as "an impossibly awkward position."

Examples of tables can also be seen in numerous Egyptian reliefs dating back to 1,200 years before the time of the Qumran Essenes. Obviously, the graphic evidence effectively refutes Shanks's argument.

Professor Golb's other main contention is that bones found in the

*Fig. 28.1. A relief from the tomb of Huya at Amarna showing Iuty at his worktable during the Amarna period (c. 1350 B.C.E.). The low-level desk is similar to those found at Qumran. Courtesy Egypt Exploration Society.*

cemetery at Qumran showed evidence of battle trauma in the form of signs of burning and fracture (among 10 percent of the skeletons). This evidence has been dismissed as unreliable by other scholars, such as Magen Broshi, of the Israel Museum (a leading Qumran archaeologist and adviser on the Qumran Museum's audiovisual presentation), and Joseph Zias, the curator of archaeology and anthropology for the Israel Antiquities Authority from 1972 to 1997, who looked after Dead Sea Scrolls artifacts at the Rockefeller Museum in Jerusalem. As Magen Broshi has pointed out, the suggestion that the inhabitants of Qumran were killed while fighting the Romans would indicate the need for a mass grave, which is not the case, and the site could never have sustained 1,200 individuals at one period.

Joseph Zias adds that anyone familiar with osteoarchaeology would realize that material left in the ground for over two thousand years inevitably suffers from taphonic (seismic) changes resulting in bone breakage.[11] Cemeteries with military personnel also generally exhibit skeletons with injuries that are predominantly on the left side of the body, as a result of soldiers attempting to ward off blows from right-handed attackers. None of this type of evidence was seen at Qumran. Reports of burned bones are also considered suspect, as they appear to have come from a somewhat sensationalist journalist excavator at Qumran, Solomon H. Steckholl, who was subsequently ordered off the site by the Israel Department of Antiquities in 1967.

The philosopher Philo, writing about the Essenes, confirms their peaceful nature:

> Some Essaeans work in the fields, and others practice crafts contributing to peace. . . . In vain would one look among them for makers of arrows, or javelins, or swords, or helmets, or armor, or shields; in short, for makers of arms, or military machines, or any instrument of war, or even of peaceful objects which might be turned to evil purpose.[12]

No weapons of any kind have ever been located at Qumran for the period when the Essenes were in occupation.

A final nail in the coffin refuting Golb's contention that the Qumran Essenes were not a religious community came in the form of hard archaeological evidence in 1996.

Two ostraca (inscribed pottery fragments) were found on the east side of the Qumran plateau in 1996 by amateur excavators led by Professor James F. Strange, of the University of South Florida. The larger ostracon had fifteen fragmentary lines and seems to be a contract transferring a certain Honi of Jericho's possessions to the Yahad community at Qumran *as part of his initiation oath.*

Also, interestingly, there may be a connection between this term Yahad (the name the Essenes appear to have applied to their community) and a book of the Mandaean-Nazarenes (a baptizing sect still in existence today in the area of the Euphrates River, who especially revered John the Baptist). One of the books of the Mandaeans is known as Sidra d'Yaha (Book of John the Baptist), and it has been shown to have links to the Dead Sea Scroll Genesis Apocryphon, written in Aramaic.[13] (See chapter 19, note 5, for more detail).

For the detractors of the conventional perceptions of Qumran, such as Professor Golb, this small piece of ceramic material was a knife at the throat of his reputation, cutting into his pet theory that the Qumran Essenes did not exist as a religious community. He vented his exasperation at the international conference held in Jerusalem in 1997 that marked the fiftieth anniversary of the finding of the first of the Dead Sea Scrolls. His accusing finger pointed first at Adolfo Roitman, curator of the Israel Museum, for assuming in his exhibition displays and publicity that the Dead Sea Scrolls were written at Qumran. Then he turned his fire on Esther Eshel, a world expert in epigraphy, for reading into the text the words *la-Yahad*, "to the Commune," which he could not see. Ben Zion Wacholder, a renowned professor at Cincinnati University, and the vast majority of the massed delegates agreed with Eshel's reading.

© ROBERT FEATHER

*Fig. 28.2. Professor Norman Golb at the 1997 Jerusalem Conference makes a point on the validity of Qumran as a religious center.*

# ⌒ 29 ⌒

# Fields of Death and Silence

*The hand of the Lord was upon me, and carried me out
in the spirit of the Lord, and set me down in the midst
of the valley which was full of bones, and caused me to
pass by them round about: and, behold, there were very
many in the open valley; and, lo, they were very dry.*

EZEKIEL 37:1–2[1]

Armed with information gleaned from the latest publications and
my own conversations with various sources, in April 2000 I was
ready to investigate Qumran for myself. At the time, I was not
aware that the Sabbath Haftorah* section of Ezekiel chapter 37, which
was due to be read in synagogue for that week, was prophetically appropriate
to my activities.

Palm Sunday fell on April 16, and the previous Friday I found myself
wandering among the ruins of Qumran. Having experienced the scenically
spectacular trans-Judaean desert from an open truck on my previous visit,
I decided on a bit more comfort this time. I arrived early that Friday
morning, having traveled the twenty-three or so winding miles from
Jerusalem by taxi. Seventy shekels poorer, I walked through the new complex
of facilities that had sprung up in one year, replacing the previous
one-man drinks kiosk. Now there was a multimedia audiovisual presentation,
a small museum, and large gift store/bookshop. (The multiscreen
presentation will not please the likes of Professor Golb, because it
unequivocally portrays the Qumran Essenes as authors of the Dead Sea
Scrolls, and John the Baptist as a onetime member of the community.)

---

*Portion of the Hebrew Scriptures, other than the Five Books of Moses, read in synagogue
after the main reading.

By 8:30 A.M., parties of tourists were already being conducted around the central ruins of Qumran before their subsequent coach trip to the hot springs of Ein Gedi and the fortress of Masada. By midday the heat had become oppressive, and the site was emptied of echoing noise, the drone of official guide monologues, and the babble of camera-clicking tourists. I turned in the direction of the Dead Sea and walked apprehensively some forty yards from the ruins toward the blue-and-white signpost marking the beginning of the cemetery. The Dead Sea, now in the far distance, has been retreating from Qumran over the centuries, mainly through evaporation, but at the time of the Essenes it would have been no more than a couple of hundred yards from their buildings.

Reaching the western edge of the cemetery, I sat and gazed at the expanse of irregular piles of whitish gray loose stones and the occasional open scars on the terrain where graves had previously been excavated.

The large flat open area of the cemetery immediately fronting the ruins gave way to short, fairly steep slopes, down to a lower section, which then divided into three main roughly equal-sized promontories stretching gently eastward and upward toward the Dead Sea. The graves, often no more than a few yards apart, were aligned in fairly recognizable rows, although there were areas where they appeared to be randomly located.

According to every description I had read, all the dead were buried in unmarked graves.[2] Yet here was a graveyard containing the mortal remains of a tight-knit group who lived and worked at Qumran over a period of perhaps 250 years, a group of people so meticulous and precise in their habits that they tidied up every single scrap of their written work at the end of each working day and placed the parchment carefully in nearby caves for safety.

Over the years, many of the community's leaders, or Mervekyre, members of their council of twelve, senior scribes, even perhaps their founding Teacher of Righteousness himself, had been buried alongside new recruits ranked well down on the list of the strictly followed, hierarchical pecking order. Given that they were so careful and meticulous with their written work, would it not follow that they would have been just as careful about knowing who was buried where in their cemetery?

As stated previously, virtually all the graves in the main cemetery are oriented north to south,[3] apart from a few that are east to west. There had to be some reason for this variation. Perhaps half an hour passed as I sat enthralled by the scene, and then it suddenly dawned on me. There was a pattern to the layout of the graves. *They were not unmarked!*

Wherever graves had been excavated, sparse vegetation had grown up in and around the grave area. There was virtually no vegetation on or near the unexcavated graves, and every single grave was marked by one dark brown stone, very occasionally two, in stark contrast to the uniformity of the other, whitish gray stones. Where graves had been excavated, the original stone pile and excavated material from the grave itself had been clumped together beside the opened grave and any record of the position of the marker stone had been lost by the carelessness of the excavator.

The dark stones vary in size from large pebbles to relatively small boulders, but invariably they had been deliberately placed at the top center of the pile. I believe that this is but one of the strategic patterns that overlay the cemetery at Qumran. The larger the brown marker stone, the more important the individual buried beneath it. The *location* of the graves also followed a pattern, with the larger marker stones often being found on graves with the best views from the higher points of the gently sloping promontories. These sites with the best vistas and unrestricted views of the Dead Sea had perhaps been reserved for more senior members of the community.

On closer examination of a dozen or so of the marker stones, it became apparent that there was at one time some kind of scratched inscription on some of them. Such is the weathering and inherent cracking of the stones that it was difficult to discern anything definitively, although on one of the darker stones a capital *P* was clearly noticeable, and there was an *X* on another.

How was it that a pattern of identification had not been noticed before? It is, I believe, a classic example of what I call the Great Man Syndrome. In fields like history and archaeology, when information is presented in a learned journal, it is vetted by referees, but once printed it usually becomes gospel for others to repeat. If a Great Man makes a statement in a lecture, respected journal, or book, it invariably becomes sacrosanct. However, in the fields of science and medicine, while presentations go through a similar process of vetting by the authors' peers, after appearing in print they are subjected to rigorous reexamination and repetitions of the exact experimental procedures before they begin to be accepted by the discipline's community.

In this instance, the Great Man, Father Roland de Vaux, head of the École Biblique, had said that the graves were unmarked, and that's how everyone subsequently has thought of and referred to them. Small wonder so many houses of history are built on rickety foundations with so many sloping floors!

## Passing By and Around

Some ways away from the site I discovered another small but similarly patterned cemetery. As I wandered carefully among the piles of apparently irregularly laid marking stones covering each grave site, my attention was drawn to a group of three excavated graves. Significantly, one of the graves had a feature I found nowhere else in the cemetery. A long straight palm frond had been laid, almost certainly with some precision, midway along the length of the open, dug-out grave. Judging by its state of preservation, the palm leaf had not been in place for a long period, perhaps a week at most, and I surmised that it may well have been laid in anticipation of Palm Sunday (which fell two days after my expedition). No other grave in the cemetery carried such an emblem. (See page 13 of the color insert.)

During a subsequent meeting with Jozef Milik, in November 2000, he again confirmed his recollection of excavating a headless skeleton at Qumran. When I asked him to indicate the place on a site map, he indicated the position of the grave as being that of the one adorned by the palm frond—almost the exact location that I had deduced as being the final resting place of John the Baptist![1]

Unfortunately, Milik's health had deteriorated since I had last seen him, the year before. He complained of tiredness in his legs and was having regular massage of his stomach. Nevertheless, his mind appeared unaffected and retentive and he was very up-to-date on current research as it pertained to the scrolls at Qumran. On being told that Esther Eshel, of Bar-Ilan University, Jerusalem, was currently working on the Testament of Levi Scroll, Monsieur Milik said he knew of her work and considered her one of the better of the younger crop of Dead Sea Scroll scholars; he mentioned, in passing, that he hoped she would be able to correct the anomalies. He then said something quite enigmatic, but would not elaborate further: "There are some things that I would not mind were not corrected for fifty or a hundred years after my death."

This cryptic statement of his completely puzzled me. *What, indeed, was going on at Qumran?*

# 30

# The Excavations at Qumran

In an attempt to uncover the mysteries and secrets buried at Qumran, we need to take a moment to review the excavations that have over time been done there.

In the earliest explorations, only one of the graves was excavated, by the French explorer Charles Clermont-Ganneau in 1873, and little detail is known of his findings apart from an indication that the excavated grave was 52.5 yards from the buildings. (As well as excavating at Qumran, Charles Clermont-Ganneau was instrumental in bringing most of the Moabite Stone to the Louvre Museum in Paris.)

Forty-three more graves were excavated between 1947 and 1956 by Father Roland de Vaux, director of the École Biblique seminary in East Jerusalem, together with his colleagues Father Jozef Milik and Henri de Contenson, each leading a team of ten Bedouin helpers. A preliminary report giving a general description of the archaeological finds and site layout was presented to the Royal Academy in London in 1959, but since that time no detailed analysis has been published. The reason for the delayed release of information has not been explained. (I discuss this in greater detail in the following chapter.)

*Fig. 30.1. Charles Clermont-Ganneau, the first excavator of the cemeteries at Qumran. Courtesy Palestine Exploration Fund.*

One unfortunate aspect of the excavations conducted by Father Roland de Vaux and his colleagues, and indeed by all the other early excavators of the main cemetery at Qumran, is that no one, apart from Henri de Contenson, was a specialist expert in this field of work. Indeed, some were amateurs. As a consequence, stones from excavated graves were piled randomly around, and apparently no record was made of their original positions, or of the position a marker stone might have occupied.

Valuable information was lost forever, and application of incorrect techniques made later analysis uncertain. In the words of Hugh Miller, an expert on forensic medicine, in discussing the exhumation of multiple burials and particularly of fragile ancient bone material: "You really need to know a lot about bones to be able to excavate a skeleton successfully under these conditions."[1] Today, a detailed, state-of-the-art map would be made of all bones and artifacts before any removal. An infrared theodolite would be used to establish three-dimensional fixed reference points of the skeleton, numerous photographs would be taken, and supervision would be overseen by an expert in osteology.

Between April 1966 and 1967 (the last year in which the area remained in Jordanian hands and was thus open to excavation), Solomon H. Steckholl, a journalist/scholar, excavated in the main part of the cemetery. (When the area of Qumran came under Israeli control after the War of 1967, no further deliberate excavations of cemeteries were permitted, for religious reasons.) One of the graves Steckholl investigated at this time was similar to those excavated by de Vaux and his colleagues and contained the remains of a sixty-five-year-old man. Stones were found positioned near the head and thorax of the skeleton.[2]

Later in 1966 and in March of 1967, Steckholl excavated eight more graves, which apparently contained five men, two women—one of whom had been buried with a two-year-old child—and a small girl. Anthropological studies showed that one of the individuals had probably been a scribe, one a horse rider, one someone who walked barefoot, and one a laborer who carried heavy weights on his shoulders. In 2001, further remains were *accidentally* recovered; and these are discussed in more detail later on in the book. Full details of Steckholl's work have not been made available to date.

As discussed, the first major seasons of excavation work in the Qumran cemetery and surrounding region were undertaken in the period 1947–56 by Father Roland de Vaux, head of the École Biblique, with the help of his colleagues Father Jozef Milik; Gerald Lankester Harding, from the Jordanian Department of Antiquities; and French archaeologist Henri de Contenson.

Of the forty-three graves excavated by de Vaux and his team between 1947 and 1956, twenty-eight were excavated from the main cemetery[3] (see table 19).

Outline findings were presented to the public by Father Roland de Vaux at the Schweich Lectures of the British Academy in 1959.[4] The pattern of burials described was similar in each instance, with a rectangular cavity, oriented from north to south, dug through the gravelly surface into the firmer marl to a depth of four to six and a half feet. At the bottom of the cavity, a separate chamber had been cut sideways into the sandy earth, almost always under the eastern wall of the cavity. The body had then been placed in this side chamber, stretched out on its back, the head turned to the south (except for a very few cases where the orientation was east–west), and the hands folded on the pelvis or stretched alongside the body. The chamber was closed off by mud bricks or flat stones, and the gaps were filled in with earth. In two instances, two bodies had been placed alongside each other in the same side chamber.

De Vaux also reported one instance of "re-inhumation," or reburial (Grave No. 24). In another case, the incomplete remains of two bodies were found in one grave (Grave No. 16). All the male bodies were found to have been buried naked, without any accompanying adornments or objects. Only among the graves said to contain females (who had also been buried naked) were a few beads and earrings recovered.

A slightly different form of burial was found at the extremity of the cemetery where a group of three tombs, marked by a circle of stones, was excavated. At the bottom of one trench the remains of a wooden coffin were found under a covering of mud bricks. The body here had been laid in the dorsal position. Another grave, also on the edge of the cemetery, consisted of a broader and shallower rectangular trench. The skeleton was found lying on its back, head to the south, with the left hand on the pelvis and the right hand on the chest.[5]

On the east of the cemetery plateau, in an area with graves that were not as regularly spaced, de Vaux recorded two other trenches where the remains of brown dust testified, he thought, to the use of wooden coffins.[6]

**TABLE 19**

## Excavations in the cemeteries at Qumran between 1873 and 2001

| Excavation | C. Clermont-Ganneau, 1873[a] | R. de Vaux's team between 1947 and 1956[b] | S. H. Steckholl between 1966 and 1967[c] | M. Broshi and H. Eshel, 2001[d] |
|---|---|---|---|---|
| Main cemetery (1,177 graves) West section | 1 grave | 28 graves in western section (2 skeletons in nos. 16 & 24; secondary burials in no. 24; 3 females) | 10 graves (4 females, inc. 25-year-old mother with 2-year-old child in no. 42) | |
| Easterly running promontories | | 6 graves in southern promontory; 1 (no. 11) in central promontory; 0 northern promontory; (secondary burials in graves nos. 11 & 37; 5 females; 2 skeletons in no. 35; 1 female child in 36) | | 2 graves (1 male, 2 females) |
| Northern cemetery | | 2 graves (nos. 9 & 10) | | |
| Farther north cemetery | | 2 graves (1 female) | | |
| Secondary southern cemetery (30 graves) | | 4 graves (1 female, 3 male children, 1 unclassified child) | | |
| Total of graves excavated | 1 | 43 | 10 | 2 |
| **Classification of skeletons** | | | | |
| Male | | 34 | 6 | 1 |
| Female | | 11?[e] | 4 | 2 |
| Child | | 5 | 1 | |
| Unclassified | 1 | 1 | | |

a. The first known excavations of graves at Qumran were performed by Captain C. R. Condor, Captain H. H. Kitchner, and Charles Clermont-Ganneau, on November 29, 1873. The findings of Clermont-Ganneau, a French diplomat/archaeologist attached to the consulate in Jerusalem, were published in 1896 (C. Clermont-Ganneau, *Archaeological Researches in Palestine*, Palestine Exploration Fund, 1896), where he described the excavation of a grave 1CG. One interesting feature Clermont-Ganneau noted was the presence of small rectangular areas marked by stones smaller than those found on the grave sites. These he attributed to a ritual custom, subsequently recorded in the Mishna, where mourners would stop at predetermined "halting places" to recite prayers for the dead prior to interment.

b. R. De Vaux, *Archaeology and the Dead Sea Scrolls* (Oxford University Press, 1973).

c. S. H. Steckholl, "Preliminary Excavations Report—The Qumran Cemetery," *Revue de Qumran* 23 and 25, 1967, 68.

d. Magen Broshi, of the Israel Antiquities Museum; Professor Hanan Eshel, of Bar-Ilan University; and Richard Freund, of the University of Hartford, 2000–2001. They identified dozens of new graves from GPR and visual assessment. See "New Data on the Cemetery East of Khirbet Qumran," *Dead Sea Discoveries* 9, no 2.

e. Five of the skeletons identified as female in the main cemetery are doubtful.

All the skeletons were considered to be male, apart from one female skeleton found in an abnormal grave situated apart from the more regularly aligned rows of graves. By contrast, in the extensions of the cemetery to the east of the hillocks, four of the six skeletons examined were considered by de Vaux to be female, and one of a child.

There have been suggestions that similar shallow coffinless, tombless interments can be found on the Jordanian side of the Dead Sea and elsewhere in Israel,[7] but there is nothing like the cemetery at Qumran that dates back to its same period. If there are similar graves to be found in the Middle East, the only ones I have been able to locate are those at Abydos, in ancient Egypt. In this southernmost part of Egypt, near Elephantine Island, is a mixed cemetery with examples of burials from across the spectrum of Egyptian history. Here the shallow grave types are similar to those found at Naqada, Diospolis Parva, and El Amrah,[8] but they also bear some remarkable similarities to the Qumran cemetery burials.

In these examples of Egyptian burials, the graves are shallow and rectangular or oval in shape, penetrating through the surface sand into soft underlying sandstone. Each grave has a ledge along one side of the cutting. The ledge is generally on the west side, rarely on the east, and only one grave has been found with the ledge at the grave's north end. Orientation of the graves was invariably with the long axis parallel to the direction of the Nile at this point in its course. The bodies almost always lay on the left side, with the head turned toward the south, though in a few rare cases the head had been turned toward the north. In some instances, the bodies were wrapped in loose mats; in others, they had been buried naked. The shallow-type graves date from pre-pharaonic times to the seventeenth century B.C.E. or, for poorer classes, to later periods.

Table 19 summarizes the excavations that have taken place at Qumran between 1873 and 2001. It is based mainly on publications by Roland de Vaux[9] and Hanan Eshel[10] of Bar-Ilan University, Jerusalem, and the latest International Conference on the Qumran Cemetery held at Brown University, Rhode Island, in November 2002.

## Recent Excavations

Magen Broshi, of the Israel Antiquities Museum; Professor Hanan Eshel, Bar-Ilan University; and Richard Freund, University of Hartford, took part in a survey of the Qumran cemeteries in 2000–2001 that was funded mainly by the Americans John and Carol Merrill as a joint project among the University of Hartford, Bar-Ilan University, and California State University. Using Ground Penetrating Radar (GPR) and other techniques, they discovered the bones of two females near one of the east-facing promontories. One of the skeletons had no toes.

Another full skeleton of a five-foot, four-and-a-half-inch-tall male was found buried under the remains of a small tower structure nearby with a jar, dated to the first century C.E., on its chest.

The skeleton was oriented east–west and designated, in the latest numbering system, T1000. Carbon-14 dating has indicated a Roman period date for this skeleton.

*Time* magazine reported that the expedition leader, Richard Freund, believed the bones to be those of the Teacher of Righteousness[11] (a sentiment echoed by Professor Robert Eisenman, who was an official on the project). The *Time* magazine article also established that many scholars believe that the Teacher of Righteousness and John and the Baptist were the same person, leading some to believe that the bones in question could actually be those of John the Baptist.

To set the record straight, at a Brown University conference in November 2002, the topic of which was "The Site of the Dead Sea Scrolls: Archaeological Interpretations and Debates," Professor Freund made a statesmanlike apology for any possible misinterpretation of the information put out in relation to the finds when he acknowledged that it was generally accepted that the male remains could *not* have been those of John the Baptist for various reasons, including the fact that a head was present.

The excavating team had also discovered the strange remains of a metal coffin (samples of which were sent to me for testing), but there was no associated bone material. This zinc material measured approximately twenty-three by sixteen inches and contained about 98.5 percent zinc, 0.5 percent lead, and traces of iron, copper, and chlorine. In my view, this material could not have been used as a coffin, as it would not have been able to support the weight of a body, but it could have been used to *line* the inner area of a coffin.

This latest burial find was made in an area that was, in all probability, the one mentioned by Roland de Vaux in his original notes as "a circle of stones." Some speculative links can be made when the geography of the Broshi-Eshel-Freund finds of 2001 are assessed. One clarion call comes from the practice of the Ethiopian Falasha, who I have previously suggested were, like the Qumran Essenes, also heirs to an Egyptian monotheistic source, through a connection to the Elephantine pseudo-Jewish settlement.[12]

A Falasha burial ceremony involves a processional pilgrimage in which members of the community carry stones up a hill as an act of contrition and, while reciting prayers, place them in a circle around an assembly of priests. Three times during the day, handfuls of seed are placed on the stones to commemmorate the dead and for birds to eat. When the community members return down the hill to their place of worship, more prayers are said over bread and beer.[13]

This practice establishes another speculative link between the Broshi-Eshel-Freund finds and the remarks of one of the earliest workers at Qumran, John Allegro. The male skeletal remains, the full skeleton we are discussing, were found during the 2001 expedition in an area surrounded by a low wall of rocks that the excavation team refers to as a "mourning enclosure."

This mourning enclosure is situated at the top of a hill rising toward the Dead Sea. In a letter written in 1957 to Frank Moore Cross, John Allegro refers to the possible burial of the Teacher of Righteousness in the Qumran cemetery. He makes the point that one of the Dead Sea Scrolls (3Q) talks of the "grave of the Just" (Hebrew, *keber zedek*) and the "garden of the Just" (Hebrew, *ginah zedek*), and that the former has a garden around it (see appendix 1). (The term "Teacher of Righteousness" is translated from the Hebrew Moreh Zedek, which appears in the Dead Sea Scrolls.)

In light of the new findings, was John Allegro correct, all those years ago, in suggesting that the Teacher of Righteousness actually *had* been buried at Qumran? Are the bones that the Broshi-Eshel-Freund expedition found really those of the Teacher of Righteousness? It seems a possibility, although the east–west orientation of the skeleton militates against this, as I consider the anomalous orientation indicates a person with contrary views to the central brotherhood, or not yet fully accepted into the community.

Future DNA and forensic tests may give a better indication of the date of the male bone remains.

# ⌐ 31 ⌐

# Years of Silence

ifty years after Father Roland de Vaux's work, a detailed report on his original notes is still awaited. Perhaps this is largely because the main effort of the external scholars has been directed at trying to prise out the 40 or so percent of Dead Sea Scroll material that, up until 1991, was not available to them. The cemetery issue remains deadly silent.

In the 1980s, however, after pressure from other academics, copies of the original excavation notes were entrusted to Professors Robert Donceel and his wife Pauline at the Louvain Catholic Seminary in Belgium, with a view to their analysis of those excavation notes being published in the official *Discoveries in the Judaean Desert* series.

The work of the Donceels was to have included the study and categorization of the complete inventory of de Vaux's findings from the cemetery at Qumran. The arrangement was projected as a cooperation between learned institutions (albeit Catholic institutions) to deal with the material. The documents that the Donceels were to consider dealt with the objects recovered from Qumran and the structures of the environment in which the objects had been found, as well as notes, drawings, plans, and inventories made during the course of the excavations.

In November 1988, the Donceels were given a number of items of glassware for study and restoration, utilizing the facilities of L'Institut Royal du Patrimoine Artistique in Brussels. The items mainly comprised what were thought to be balsam and perfume containers.

One of the other most important groups of materials to be analyzed by the Donceels was to be that of the coins found at Qumran. These artifacts, by virtue of the dates that can invariably be assigned to their minting, are extremely useful in confirming chronologies of archaeological sites. The coins were originally listed in de Vaux's preliminary notes as totaling 1,231 bronze or silver coins or fragments of coins.[1]

Pauline Donceel reported, however, that despite intense efforts, she and her husband were able to account for only less than 30 percent of the coins. The others seem to have disappeared from their known locations in Jordan, Jerusalem, and the United States. More than 70 percent of this most valuable parcel of historical evidence had apparently gone missing!

To add insult to injury, not only had a significant amount of the evidence vanished, but the École Biblique team then apparently decided that the findings of the Donceels should not be published. No doubt frustrated by this, the husband-and-wife team eventually presented a paper on the subject to the Academy of Sciences in New York. The paper was subsequently published in the annals of the academy in 1994, and another version appeared in a French archaeological journal in the same year. Even though they have managed to publish *some* of their findings, they are reported to have said that they may never complete the publication of their studies.[2]

A current view of the state of the information given in de Vaux's original notes was given to me in conversation with Madame Donceel in February 2000.[3] In essence, Professor Pauline Donceel does "not believe the people at Qumran wrote the scrolls and the scrolls do not relate to the people there. . . . They were simply librarians. . . . They were concerned in looking after their gardens and producing perfumes, balsam and so on." She was quite scathing about the quality of archaeological work that had been carried out by Father Roland de Vaux and was also critical of the present editorial team, which does not want to admit an alternative viewpoint on the archaeology of Qumran.

Other scholars, however, are of the opinion that the findings of the Donceels are not convincing and that their analysis, particularly in relation to the *function* of the Qumran community, is incorrect. The Donceels claim that Qumran was not the habitat of an isolated religious community, but a place of retreat for wealthy inhabitants from Jerusalem who built a *villa rustica* to escape the rigors of winter.

The Donceels' unorthodox view, it is maintained, is part of the reason that continuation of their work on the Qumran material no longer received official backing and is why they were not allowed to publish their findings in the official *Discoveries in the Judaean Desert (DJD)* series of publications, which is under the control of the Dead Sea Scrolls translation team. Without access to the *DJD* series, the Donceels are now able to publish only parts of their findings in a variety of journals, and their publication of the analysis of material related to the bones found at Qumran will not appear, if ever, for another few years, possibly in an edition of the *Revue Archaeologie de Louvain*.

In any event, the fundamental question remains: Why did the École Biblique team commission the analysis from the Donceels, and then refuse to publish it?

One can only imagine that this wariness (like the wariness initially exhibited by the early Catholic researchers on the scrolls) has to do with the possible undermining of the uniqueness of Jesus's teachings, or with something that will radically change the public's perception of the Qumran community. A threat to the church's interpretation of the formative years of Christianity could also be envisaged if some of the bones at Qumran turned out to be those of St. John the Baptist or of some of the disciples.

Since the time of the Convocation of Nicaea in 325 C.E., when the early Pauline Christian Church became the official church backed by the power of the Roman Empire, its Gnostic- and Essene-related branches were seen as heretical elements, and their members became persona non grata. Throughout the ages, wherever these movements have surfaced in the form of Mandaeanism, or the Knights Templar in the twelfth century C.E., or the Cathars in the twelfth and thirteenth centuries C.E., or more recently in Freemasonry, the official church has moved quickly to suppress or marginalize such movements.

Nor is orthodox Judaism immune to this variety of phobia. The evidence of the Dead Sea Scrolls, in calling into question the exactness of the canonical Masoretic version of the Hebrew Scriptures, is perceived as a real threat. Discussion of the subject is therefore invariably marginalized or avoided by Orthodox Jewry as well.

The discovery and proof that John the Baptist, or associates of Jesus, was buried at Qumran and therefore closely associated with the Essene movement would inevitably open up this thorny subject yet again. Therefore, the suppression of the evidence, by official or unofficial parties, would not be a surprise.

## The Despair of Hershel Shanks

Coins were not the only materials that had apparently gone missing from Qumran. The bones of all the fifty-five bodies recovered from the cemetery at Qumran were not accounted for as well. It would not be the first time that important artifacts had disappeared from institutional collections; however, to lose the remains of so many bodies seems somewhat careless, to say the least. By an act of legerdemain, someone had spirited away some of the most important material found in Israel.

Hershel Shanks (editor of *Biblical Archaeology Review* and *Bible Review*), in his book *The Mystery and Meaning of the Dead Sea Scrolls*, which was published in 1998, was moved to write about the situation, "Unfortunately the bones excavated at Qumran in the 1950s are nowhere to be found and may never be found."[4]

As my own research continued, it became clear that we possibly had another Eva Peron–type[5] saga on our hands—only this time, fifty-five times as ridiculously macabre. For something of this nature to have happened in relation to one of the most important archaeological sites in the world would be inexcusable, to put it mildly.

There could only be a few sensible explanations for this sorry state of affairs:

- The remains have been purloined and have ended up in someone's private collection.
- They have accidentally or deliberately been thrown away.
- Bureaucratic incompetence has led to their being mislaid.
- Due to ulterior motives, they are being kept from public scrutiny.
- Information on their whereabouts is not common knowledge and details will eventually be released, albeit nearly fifty years after their original excavation.

The fourth and fifth explanations seem to be closest to a combination of the truth.

# 32

## MISSING BONES

### The Questions Mount, So I Go to the Mount

As my inquiries continued, I felt increasingly like Hercule Poirot* re-creating a crime. Questions to scholars in the field of Dead Sea Scrolls research had drawn a blank, but one person's name kept coming up as a likely fount of knowledge. It was Joseph Zias, who, as previously stated, was the curator of archaeology and anthropology for the Israel Antiquities Authority from 1972 to 1997; he had looked after Dead Sea Scrolls artifacts at the Rockefeller Museum in Jerusalem. If anyone should have been in the know, it was he.[1]

Joe Zias spent more than a year researching the contents of the cemetery at Qumran, and he came to quite different conclusions from the German team on the cemetery study. Like the Professors Donceel of Belgium, he does not believe that the burials at Qumran are all specific to the Qumran community. According to him, "Aside from one woman on the margins, the men are Second Temple and the women and children on the margins are of recent origin; the Bedouin reused the cemetery."[2]

In conjunction with Mark Spiegelman, who is both a surgeon and an archaeologist, Zias was due to present a paper at the November 22, 1999, meeting of the Society of Biblical Literature in Boston. The proposed presentation related to his hypothesis that some of the graves contained the bodies of Muslims, which would explain partly the north–south orientation of remains as being aligned toward Mecca. At the presentation, however, the paper was modified, due to uncertainty over some of the information available for his research.

---

*Hercule Poirot is a fictional Belgian detective who appears in more than thirty books written by Agatha Christie.

In early 2000, however, the prestigious journal *Dead Sea Discoveries* published an article by Zias, which contained the following in a footnote: "I also wish to thank the anonymous colleagues who alerted me to the fact that additional human remains from Qumran, despite years of vigorous denial, were being stored in the École Biblique. This is unfortunate for Qumran scholars, particularly since earlier publications were incomplete due to the omission of this material. As I was finally able to briefly view this material, I have included the findings in this study."

While Joseph Zias's report on his brief examination of the remains at the École Biblique[3] does not include mention of a headless skeleton, he maintains that some of this material, excavated in 1953 and allegedly lost (including a set labeled Q18 and hereinafter referred to as such), was housed in the École Biblique. (He also believes that the remains of these bones, Q18, were *originally* at the École Biblique before being transferred to the Rockefeller Museum, Jerusalem.)

In my understanding, partial remains of two additional skeletons, which may be from Qumran but are unlabeled, are still at the Rockefeller Museum. Some other of the remains excavated by de Vaux are now reportedly in Paris,[4] and the original material examined by Professor Henri V. Vallois in the late 1940s and early 1950s is said to be still in storage at the Musée de l'Homme, Paris.[5] Dr. D. Olav Röhrer-Ertl, of Ludwig-Maximilans-Universität, Munich, confirmed that some of the Qumran bone remains are housed in Paris and at the École Biblique.[6] Short of issuing a writ of *habeus corpus,* scholars may never get to examine this material.

Given all this, there seemed little else for me to do but go to the source—the École Biblique, and the Rockefeller Museum in Jerusalem, located just outside the ancient city walls that encircle the Temple Mount.

As I walked up the dusty Nablus Road from the direction of the walled ramparts of Jerusalem's Old City and passed the Tomb of the Rock, I reflected on the journey that the original members of the scrolls' translation team had made each day between the two centers on their way to and from their lunch break.

None of the original team now remains at the École; its current senior resident Dead Sea Scrolls scholar is Father Émile Puech. He was kind enough to talk to me before rushing off to give a lecture prior to his imminent departure for an extensive visit to Italy. "We have nothing from the Qumran cemetery here at the École," he informed me. He was able to guide me, however, to a recent publication on the subject and a location in Germany where I might find some answers to my questions.

The paper he had referred me to, from Munich University, was from a very recent (June 1999) issue of *Revue de Qumran*.[7] Back at the Rockefeller Museum Library, I was able to study this fortuitously timed article and at last discover that some of the bones from the cemetery had been analyzed and described in some detail. Most of the bone fragment remains from Qumran described therein were apparently being housed in the Kurth Collection at the Jura Museum, in Eichstätt, Germany. The paper appeared to answer many of the mysteries surrounding the long-awaited details of the Qumran cemetery. Although there were some crucial omissions, I now had much of the detailed analytical information that I had been seeking, and I prepared to head back to Qumran.

The riddle of the lost bones was partly solved by this timely *Revue de Qumran* publication, and the whereabouts of many of the bones was again confirmed during a subsequent conversation with Magen Broshi, of the Israel Museum. He understood that most of the excavated grave remains had been taken to Munich, but he informed me that one skeleton was still in the Rockefeller Museum and two were, he believed, still in the Centre National de la Recherche Scientifique (CNRS) in Paris.

Although the availability of the long withheld information seemed to answer many of my outstanding questions, a key question remained: *Why had*

Fig. 32.1. *Émile Puech in the École Biblique, East Jerusalem, 2000.*

*these three skeletons been separated from the main collection? And why were there two remaining in France?* Even as recently as June 2000, one of the original 1952–1953 excavators at Qumran, Henri de Contenson, Honorarie de CNRS (which was the most likely place in France that the bones would be stored), informed me that they were not at the CNRS. He had also been told that the Qumran bones were being submitted for physical anthropology, by the Donceels, in Belgium.[8] The Donceels deny that the bones are with them and suggested "asking the Israelis."

When I questioned Dr. D. Olav Röhrer-Ertl, a coauthor of the seminal *Revue de Qumran* article, he again confirmed that the Kurth Collection in Germany held "bone fragments and some more or less complete skeletons from the Main (Number Q) and the South Gravefield (Number QS) from Khirbet Qumran." Samples for further testing had also been sent to an Anglo-Israeli team coordinated by Joseph Zias in Jerusalem.

In the confusion of these conflicting reports, my mind kept coming back to the phrase that appears in a letter that John Allegro (an early Dead Sea Scrolls scholar) wrote to a colleague, Frank Moore Cross, back in 1956.[9] The recipient is now a professor at Harvard, but was then the only fellow member of the original translation team that John Allegro could count on to be sympathetic to his seemingly radical views. Discussing

*Fig. 32.2. Henri de Contenson and his wife in Paris*

messianic aspects of the sectarian scrolls, Allegro wrote: "But surely you've guessed by now, why all this secrecy before the excavations?"

Frank Moore Cross remained an advocate of some of John Allegro's theories after his death. Commenting on the Qumran texts, he observed that they would "trouble the person who has been led by the clergy or by Christian polemics to believe that . . . the titles Jesus held as the Christ or Messiah were unanticipated in Jewish messianic Apocalypticism."[10]

Again, any strongly established link between John the Baptist (such as finding the grave of John the Baptist at Qumran) and the Essene community might be considered anathema by the Christian Church of today, as the teachings of the Essene community, though having much in common with the teachings of Jesus, are deemed, in part, to be a view that diverges from that offered by the Gospels. Thus, while the truth might set the church free, it would also necessitate a complete revision of its established history.

# — 33 —

# The Bones of John the Baptist

From subsequently published material, from details that have become available to this author, and from unpublished material, as stated earlier, it is apparent that *most* of the original bone remains from the Qumran cemetery were removed to Germany and France, but the contents of one grave in particular were held back in Jerusalem, and their whereabouts today are not known. It cannot be a coincidence that this body, of the fifty-five graves excavated, was the one that, according to the original reports, was associated with brown dust residue—evidence of its having been buried in a wooden coffin. It is also the only one of two graves where there is no confirmation that the skeleton included a cranium, whereas in every other instance where information relating to bone remains is recorded, there is mention of a head originally being present.

This particular grave is also the same grave identified by me, in my exploration of the cemetery, as being that of John the Baptist. Most significant, it is located in the position marked by Jozef Milik on a map of the remote cemetery as the place where he recalled he had excavated a headless corpse, which *he* also believed was the mortal remains of John the Baptist. This evidence alone is far stronger than for any other claimed burial place of John the Baptist.

## Was John the Baptist Really Buried at Qumran?

The circumstantial, indirect, and direct evidence is so overwhelming that I believe the answer to this question has to be answered in the affirmative. At the risk of being repetitive, the essential elements of the evidence are as follows:

1. The testimony of the Christian Scriptures, and of Flavius Josephus, that John the Baptist was beheaded—an extremely unusual form of execution at the time—not far from Qumran.

2. The view of a good proportion of international scholars that John the Baptist, at one period in his life, belonged to the community of the Qumran Essenes. In addition, the evidence previously cited in this book seems to confirm this probability. It would, therefore, be entirely possible that John the Baptist was buried at Qumran because of his role as a previous member.

3. Analysis of the literature, and of unpublished material, including Jozef Milik's revelation that he excavated a grave at Qumran containing a headless skeleton, which he considered might be that of John the Baptist; and Joseph Zias's confirmation that one particular skeleton had been singled out and held back from examination—a skeleton whose skull is not referred to in the literature, unlike detailed results for bones from almost every other grave.

4. Location of the grave containing the held-back bone material as that identified by Jozef Milik, and its being marked by a single palm frond—not seen on any other grave in the cemeteries at Qumran.

5. Ongoing stories and legends that the head of John the Baptist was preserved beyond his death.

6. Procrastination of those in possession of the detailed reports of the 1950s excavations in the Qumran cemetery, to allow publication of the information or access to bone remains, until the late 1990s, and then only as a result of peer pressure. Even now, the whereabouts of but a percentage of the material is known, and a final report has not been published. Analytical results for the material from the grave identified as that of John the Baptist have also not been published, unlike detailed results for bones from other graves.

7. Denial by the École Biblique in East Jerusalem, right up to 1999, that *any* bone material was being concealed from examination by scholars, but at the same time, verification from other sources that some material had been held back.

All but the last item of this summary of evidence has been discussed earlier. The last item therefore requires further explanation. While I am not a great conspiracy theorist, it is difficult to understand why *any* bone material found at Qumran and the nearby burial area should be kept hidden from general scholarship, unless it had some interpretative significance that might be thought to prove embarrassing in some way. Nevertheless, I had for some time felt that something was being kept back and that it might be being held at one or another of the following places, listed here in order of likelihood as locations for the missing material:

- École Biblique, East Jerusalem (a Catholic Dominican establishment)
- The Rockefeller Archaeological Museum, Jerusalem (set up with Catholic funding)
- The Musée de l'Homme, Paris
- The Department of Anthropology and Religion, Sorbonne, Paris (which has links to the École Biblique); Father Émile Puech obtained his doctorate in the history of religions at this department in 1992
- Centre National de la Recherche Scientifique (CNRS), Paris (director Father Émile Puech has been the head of research at CNRS since 1983 and a professor at the École Biblique)
- Katholischen Universität, Eichstätt, Germany (a Catholic college and the location of the Kurth Collection)
- Holy Cross College, University of Notre Dame, Indiana (has close links to the École Biblique)

Perhaps it is of some significance that all the institutions listed above have links to the École Biblique, but this may just be the result of networking by like-minded acquaintants.

Most of the 1,180-odd graves that can be counted in the four sections of cemeteries at Qumran are in the main eastern cemetery, where Jozef Milik

© ROBERT FEATHER

*Fig. 33.1. Dr. D. Olav Röhrer-Ertl and Dr. Susan Sheridan at the Brown University Conference in 2002.*

indicated the possible location of John the Baptist's skeleton. As you walk eastward some fifty-five yards from the boundary of the Qumran ruins, you see stretched before you a vast array of closely arranged stone heaps laid out in three sections separated by wider pathways. This neatness of layout contrasts dramatically with the higgledy-piggledy geography of other Jewish cemeteries of the period, again pointing up how different the Qumran cemeteries and form of burial were from anything found elsewhere in the Holy Land.[1]

As stated earlier, excavations of forty-three of these graves, between 1949 and 1957 while the site was under the control of Jordanian authorities, revealed that of those oriented north–south, where the gender has been confirmed by recent studies, only *male* skeletons were found in the main cemetery (see table 19).* All the other recently examined bones in graves oriented east–west were found to be female. Several female and child remains were found in the secondary cemeteries. As the de Vaux excavations were conducted on a random basis, it is statistically 99.99 percent certain that only males were buried in the main cemetery.

While I do not propose to go too deeply into the difficulties the presence of female bones has presented for the monastic theorists on Qumran, I will outline my views on the matter.

The fact that the female remains were found only in a secondary cemetery seems to indicate that females played a secondary role in the life of the community. Their presence does not, on balance, contradict the avowed position of the Qumran Essenes toward women as related in their sectarian texts. The apparently conflicting messages in their texts regarding the role of women in the Essene movement can readily be explained in terms of the existence of two wings of the Essene movement with differing lifestyles—one abstemious, celibate, secretive, and rigidly tied to a fixed location like Qumran; the other more gregarious, matrimonial, proclamatory, and mobile.

---

*Joseph Zias, in his study of the Kurth Collection remains, concludes that the bones in Q22, originally identified by Professor Kurth as masculine but listed as female in the 1999 study by Röhrer Ertl and colleagues, are in fact masculine, largely because of the recorded height of the body. He also says the bones in Q37 are masculine, although Professor Kurth originally identified them as feminine.

**TABLE 20**

**Analysis of excavations in the cemeteries of Qumran from 1873 to 2002**

| Grave no. | Skeleton details | Sex | Age | Oriented | Remarks |
|---|---|---|---|---|---|
| **1873 Clermont–Ganneau excavation** | | | | | |
| CG1 | — | — | — | N–S | Grave some 48 m from buildings |
| **1949 R. de Vaux excavations** | | | | | |
| Q01 | — | — | — | N–S | |
| Q02 | — | — | — | N–S | |
| **1951 R. De Vaux excavations, examined by Prof. H.-V. Vallois, Paris (1950s); reexamined by Dr. S. Sheridan, Univ. Notre Dame, USA, (1999–2000)** | | | | | |
| Q03 | Skull part, pelvis | — | — | N–S | Dr. Sheridan says male |
| Q04 | Cranium, pelvis | — | — | E–W | Dr. Sheridan says male |
| Q05 | Cranium, pelvis | — | — | N–S | Dr. Sheridan says male |
| Q06 | Cranium | — | — | N–S | Dr. Sheridan says male |
| Q07 | Cranium, pelvis | F? | — | N–S | Dr. Sheridan? male. J. Zias maintains height indicates male |
| Q08 | — | — | — | N–S | Dr. Sheridan says male |
| Q09 | Cranium, pelvis | — | — | N–S | |
| Q10 | Cranium, pelvis | — | — | N–S | Dr. Sheridan says male |
| Q11 | Cranium | — | — | N–S | Reburial. Dr. Sheridan says male |
| **1953 R. de Vaux excavations, examined by Prof. G. Kurth (1950s, cataloged 1990–1) in Munich; reexamined by Dr. S. Sheridan (1999–2000)** | | | | | |
| Q12 | Whole skeleton | M | c. 30 | N–S | Dr. Sheridan says male |
| Q13 | Whole skeleton | M | — | N–S | Dr. Sheridan says male |
| Q14 | Whole skeleton | — | — | N–S | |
| Q15 | Whole skeleton | M | c. 16 | N–S | Dr. Sheridan says male |
| Q16–1 | Whole skeleton | M | c. 30 | N–S | Dr. Sheridan says male |
| Q16–2 | Whole skeleton | M | 30–40 | N–S | Dr. Sheridan says male |
| Q17 | Paraffin wax model | — | — | N–S | Wooden coffin debris, 15 Roman-period iron nails |
| Q18 | Paraffin wax model | M | c. 30 | N–S | Dr. Sheridan says male; wooden (cypress) coffin debris; 30 Roman-period iron nails |
| Q19 | Cranium, pelvis | M | c. 30–40 | N–S | Dr. Sheridan says male |
| **1956 R. de Vaux excavations, examined by Prof. G. Kurth (1950s, cataloged 1990–1), in Munich; reexamined by O. Röhrer-Ertl, F. Röhrhirsch, D. Hahn in Eichstätt (1998)** | | | | | |
| Q20 | Whole skeleton | M | c. 30–35 | N–S | |

| Grave no. | Skeleton details | Sex | Age | Oriented | Remarks |
|---|---|---|---|---|---|
| Q21 | Whole skeleton | M | c. 35 | N–S | Eichstätt team says 50–59 |
| Q22 | Whole skeleton | M? | c. 30–35 | N–S | Eichstätt team says female, J. Zias says male |
| Q23 | Whole skeleton | M | c. 50 | N–S | Eichstätt team says 30–39 |
| Q24–1 | Whole skeleton | M | c. 25 | N–S | Reburial; Eichstätt team says 30–39 |
| Q24–2 | Whole skeleton | M? | c. 18–20 | N–S | Reburial; Eichstätt team says female c. 20–21 |
| Q25 | Whole skeleton | M | c. 50 | N–S | |
| Q26 | Whole skeleton | M | c. 35–40 | N–S | Eichstätt team says 30–39 |
| Q27 | Whole skeleton | M | c. 30 | N–S | |
| Q28 | Whole skeleton | M | c. 22–23 | N–S | |
| Q29 | Whole skeleton | M | c. 40 | N–S | |
| Q30 | Whole skeleton | M | c. 30–35 | N–S | |
| Q31 | Whole skeleton | M | c. 25–30 | N–S | Eichstätt team says 40–49 |
| Q32 | Whole skeleton | F | c. 30–35 | E–W | Eichstätt team says 25–30; 19 beads, 2 earrings, bronze ring |
| Q33 | Whole skeleton | F | c. 30 | E–W | Earrings |
| Q34 | Whole skeleton | F? | c. 25 | E–W | J. Zias says male |
| Q35–1 | Whole skeleton | F | c. 30–40 | E–W | |
| Q35–2 | Partial skeletal remains | — | — | E–W | |
| Q36 | Whole skeleton | — | c. 6 | E–W | Infant and child? |
| Q37 | Whole skeleton | F? | c. 30–40 | N–S | Reburial; J. Zias says male |

### 1966–67 Dr. S. Steckholl excavations

| Grave no. | Skeleton details | Sex | Age | Oriented | Remarks |
|---|---|---|---|---|---|
| Q38–1 | Whole skeleton | M | c. 70 | N–S | |
| Q39–1 | Whole skeleton | M | c. 65 | N–S | |
| Q39–2 | Partial skeletal remains | — | c. 40 | N–S | Two individuals? |
| Q40 | Whole skeleton | M | c. 40 | N–S | |
| Q41 | Whole skeleton | M | c. 22 | N–S | |
| Q42–1 | Whole skeleton | F | c. 25 | N–S | |
| Q42–2 | Partial skeletal remains | — | c. 2 | N–S | |
| Q43 | Whole skeleton | F | 14–16 | N–S | |
| Q44 | Whole skeleton | F | c. 23 | N–S | |
| Q45 | Whole skeleton | M | c. 65 | N–S | |
| Q46 | Whole skeleton | M | 25–26 | E–W | |
| Q47 | Whole skeleton | F | 45–50 | N–S | |

### 1955 R. de Vaux excavations, farther North Cemetery, examined by Prof. G. Kurth

| Grave no. | Skeleton details | Sex | Age | Oriented | Remarks |
|---|---|---|---|---|---|
| QNo1(A) | Whole skeleton | F | c. 30–35 | N–S | |
| QNo2(B) | Whole skeleton | M | c. 50 | N–S | |

| Grave no. | Skeleton details | Sex | Age | Oriented | Remarks |
|---|---|---|---|---|---|
| 1956 R. de Vaux excavations, Southern Cemetery, examined by Prof. G. Kurth (1950s, cataloged 1990–1), in Munich; reexamined by O. Röhrer-Ertl, F. Röhrhirsch, D. Hahn in Eichstätt (1998) | | | | | |
| QSo1 | Whole skeleton | F | c. 30–40 | E–W | Thirty beads, two earrings |
| QSo2 | Whole skeleton | — | c. 6 | N–S | Eichstätt team says male |
| QSo3–1 | Whole skeleton | — | 7–8 | E–W | Eichstätt team says male |
| QSo3–2 | Partial skeletal remains | — | — | E–W | Eichstätt team says child 7–9 |
| QSo4 | Whole skeleton | — | 8–10 | E–W | Eichstätt team says male |
| 2001 M. Broshi and H. Eshel excavations, Main Cemetery, Central Promontory | | | | | |
| T1000 | Skeleton with cranium | M | c. 40–50? | E–W | Skeleton dated to Roman period; 2nd Temple period cooking pot at foot and jar on chest |
| T1000.1 | Partial remains | F | 25–35 | — | Carbon-dated to 2nd Temple period |
| T1000.2 | Partial remains | F | c. 50 | — | Carbon-dated to 2nd Temple period |

An interesting theory as to why women and children were buried at Qumran comes from Dr. Jonathan G. Campbell, of Bristol University, England, in his book *Dead Sea Scrolls: The Complete Story.*[2] He suggests that the bones of women and children were found in the main cemetery and secondary cemetery because some would have died during the annual assembly convened by the "Guardian of all the camps," or the leader of the Essenes, who would have been the Maskil or Mervekre at Qumran. This assembly was an event designed to renew the movement's Covenant with God. According to a Dead Sea Deuteronomic scroll (4QDe), the gathering took place in the "third month" of each year, probably at Tabernacles (Succoth) in autumn.

This annual gathering may well have been the motive that brought Jesus—as a past member of the Qumran community—to Qumran, some seven and a half miles from Jerusalem, in the period immediately before his arrest and crucifixion. The sequence of events would tie in well with the theory put forward by Rabbi Jacqueline Tabick (see chapter 26) that Jesus's Last Supper took place at Succoth rather than at Easter.

If we step back from the detail and take a look at the overall picture of excavations that have taken place at Qumran from the late 1940s up to the latest explorations in 2001–2, particularly in relation to the cemeteries, a number of factors stand out.

Here was an exclusively Jewish settlement, with predominantly male Jews buried in its main cemetery, and yet:

- From the very first serious archaeological excavations of the cemetery in the early 1950s, all the excavations have been supervised by non-Jews, right up until the latest excavations of 2001–2.
- All the associated analytical studies of the remains excavated from the cemeteries have been undertaken primarily by Catholic researchers at Catholic-denominated institutions, and all the burial remains appear to have been kept at one or another of these institutions from the early 1950s to the present day, despite the fact that both Jews and non-Catholics have been involved in research work from the earliest days and *intimately* involved since 1967.
- Critical bone remains appear to have been separated out from the bulk of the collections and are not accessible for examination.

To recapitulate, according to Joseph Zias and other sources,[3] the contents of graves excavated by de Vaux's team between 1947 and 1956 were transferred to Paris for study by Professor Henri Vallois at the Sorbonne and, subsequently, the CNRS. Material from one grave, Q18, was held back and taken to Jerusalem, probably transferred to the École Biblique and later to the Rockefeller Museum. But no one, at this point in my quest, seemed to know the contents' exact whereabouts.

The remaining material was studied by Professor Gottfried Kurth in 1953 and 1956 and transferred to Eichstätt, Germany.[4]

The seminal *Revue de Qumran* article that Father Émile Puech had kindly referred me to, which had helped to answer some of my outstanding questions and clarify my thinking, also contained a site map of the cemetery. This site map had indicated a grave, marked Q17, that was close to, if not the same as, the position of the excavated grave site that contained a single long, straight palm frond placed in a north–south direction in the middle of a shallow depression.[5]

The report in *Revue de Qumran,* published some forty years after the events of the excavations, confirms the evidence of burial in a wooden coffin in the western section of the cemetery, as does information from a private report given to the author by Joseph Zias, curator of the Rockefeller Museum 1972–1997.[6] This was also the only grave where the bones were singled out and initially retained in Jerusalem. To summarize the evidence:

- Jozef Milik recalls excavating a headless body buried in a wooden coffin, in a group of three graves, in the early 1950s. He believes it to be that of John the Baptist.
- Roland de Vaux and Jan Van der Ploeg published articles in the late 1950s confirming the presence of a wooden coffin in the cemetery area identified by Jozef Milik.
- O. Röhrer-Ertl and colleagues published an article in June 1999 in *Revue de Qumran* referring to a grave near where remains of a wooden coffin were found as Q18. According to this article, Q18 and another adjacent grave are the only graves of fifty-five excavated where there was no confirmation of a head being found.

  The bones from Q18 are the only remains reported to have been separated out, back in the 1950s, and kept in Jerusalem. Roland de Vaux, in his field notes, mentions that these body remains and the remains of an attendant coffin were specially preserved in paraffin.[7] Wood fragments from this area of the graveyard were also referred to by Joan Taylor in 1999.[8]

  There can be no question that the remains from the grave referred to as Q18 were singled out for special treatment from the time of their first discovery.

Some of the Kurth Collection material held at the Jura Museum, Eichstätt (near Munich), was sent to ZTH Zürich Laboratories for dating, but accurate readings were not possible because of contamination and lack of sufficient collagen (connective tissue protein) in uncontaminated bone material. The collagen was almost certainly broken down as a result of the high salt concentration in the cemetery area, varying from 0.25 to 1.4 percent sodium and 0.66 to 2.61 percent chloride, and total mineral content of the earth ranging from 4.11 to 7.06 percent.[9]

## The Unanswered Questions

Where were the remains of Q18 at this point? Were they still in Jerusalem? How were the contents of Q18 described in the comprehensive review article by Röhrer-Ertl, Röhrhirsch, and Hahn, published in *Revue de Qumran*? If Q18 was recorded as having a cranium, then clearly it could not be that of John the Baptist, nor the body described by Jozef Milik.

To answer the last question first, in every instance where information on the bone remains of all fifty-nine bodies (from the fifty-five graves) excavated at Qumran is given in the *Revue de Qumran* article, it is given as either "whole skeleton," or "head," and/or "pelvis." Again, as articulated in the *Revue de Qumran* article, in only two instances is the presence of the head not mentioned, and that is for graves Q18 and Q17.

In association with these graves, and these graves only, was the presence of dust reported, and this is taken to prove the presence of a coffin or coffins. Both are graves from which the bones had gone missing, and the only remains available to the German team were solid-wax models. There is no information recorded for Q17, but the contents of Q18, at the time of its excavation, were described as "those of a male approximately 30 years of age." (See page 15 of the color insert.)

With the information from Joseph Zias that the bones of Q18 were the only ones held back in Jerusalem when the rest were sent to Paris, and the information from the Kurth Collection analysis that only Q18 and Q17 were not available for analysis and therefore there was no confirmation that a head was present, it seemed that Q18 must have been kept back because it was indeed the bones of John the Baptist.

And yet, despite this conclusion, matters were to take one final, weird, contradictory, and astonishing twist.

While the remains of twenty-two graves in the Kurth Collection were being analyzed in Germany, Dr. Susan Guise Sheridan, associate professor of biological anthropology at the University of Notre Dame in Indiana, who had close associations to the École Biblique in East Jerusalem, was entrusted with analysis of the material that had been sent to France and finally surfaced after nearly fifty years in hiding.

Her summary report on the remains of eighteen graves that had been sent to France reveals that the skeletal bones Q18 were originally held back in Jerusalem, were preserved in paraffin wax, and had been on display in the Rockefeller Museum for decades. Strangely enough, no one, from Father Émile Puech, head of the École Biblique, to Hershel Shanks, editor of the all-seeing American magazine *Biblical Archaeology Review,* and even Joseph Zias, curator at the Rockefeller Museum for twenty-five years, was aware of their existence—let alone their exhibition.

Graveside photos taken in the mid-1950s of the remains labeled Q18, compared to those received at Notre Dame in 1999, are said to confirm that the bones, indicating a male of thirty to thirty-five years of age, came from the same grave, although it is difficult to see the head, and the bone lengths appear somewhat different. Unlike the report in the *Revue de Qumran* article, which stated that the two skeletons in question did not have heads, Dr. Sheridan confirms that Q18 *did* have a cranium, so it cannot be that of John the Baptist after all.

So what of Q17, located beside Q18 and the only other remains for which the Kurth Collection had only a wax impression and therefore could not confirm the presence or absence of a cranium? Graveside photographs confirm that this skeleton, assessed as a male adult, of all those available for examination or described in the records, definitely did not have a head. Adjacent to Q18 in the Qumran cemetery, Q17 was in the same location described by Jozef Milik as the place where he excavated a headless body.

*So where are the bones of Q17?*

According to Dr. Sheridan, the bone material presented for examination was, in most instances, carefully bagged and labeled. When the box that should have contained the remains of grave Q17 was opened, it was empty apart from some nails and pieces of wood. The bones were missing, and no one seems to know where they are now!

The strong evidence that John the Baptist was a member of the Qumran Essenes and the secrecy surrounding the bone contents of Q17 mean that they are, I believe, almost certainly those of John the Baptist. With all the other pointers that follow from this astonishing conclusion, I began to consider which other of John the Baptist's contemporaries might be buried at Qumran.

..S TIBERIEVM
...[PO]NTIVS PILATVS
[PRA]ECTVS IVDA[EA]E
The Tiberium
Pontius Pilate
Prefect of Judaea
[consecrated]

Latin inscription
found at Caesarea,
in 1961, carved with
the name Pilate.

Four-section mikvah,
or ritual bathing
pool, at Qumran.
© Robert Feather

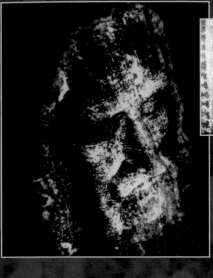

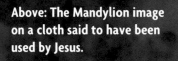

**Above:** The Mandylion image on a cloth said to have been used by Jesus.

**Left:** Face on the Turin Shroud thought to be that of **Jesus.** Courtesy of *Hera Magazine*

**Right:** Painting of St. Veronica's veil, perhaps of the Turin Shroud, from a 15th-century wood panel in the Barber Institute, Birmingham, England.

**Below:** Rennes-le-Château wall fresco containing strange symbolism and thought to show Jesus preaching on the Mount of Beatitude. © Barry Weitz

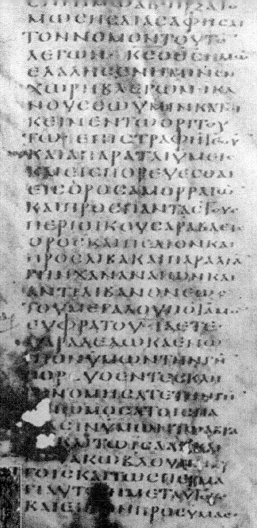

**Above: An example of a page from Mark 14, dated to the 4th century** CE**.**

**Left: Portrait of St. Luke (left) and St. Mark on wood panels from the Four Freer Gallery Gospels, Washington, D.C.**

© Robert Feather

# Mediterranean Sea

Alexandria

Marioot Lake

Damietta

Manzala Lake

Sakha

Samanoud

Meniet Samanoud

Tel Basta

Zagazig

Wadi El-Natroun

El Baramose Monastery

El-Sorian Monastery

Abu Makar Monastery

Anba Beshoy Monastery

Belbeis

Mostorod

Ain Shams
Matariyah - Zeitoun
Zeweila Alley - El E:

Babylon-Old Cair

Badrashain (Memphis)

Maadi

Bahnassa

Beni Mazar

Altar, said to be the oldest in history, at the monastery of Al-Moharraq

Western Desert

Samalout

Monastery of Virgin M (Gabal El-Tair)

Al-Ashmounein

Mallawy

Dairout

Qoussia

Akhetaten (Amarna)

Meir

Monastery of Al-Moharraq Gabal Qussqam

Assiut

Gabal Dronka

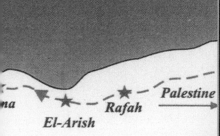

**The Garden Tomb, a traditional site of Jesus's burial.**

Traditional site where Jesus and his family spent the longest period of their stay in Egypt, not far from the area of Akhenaten's Holy City.

This stretch of the Nile has the greatest concentration of Christian holy sites in Egypt, and there was a very early place of worship within Akhetaten, and even evidence that Jesus might have been taken to the city.

**The Church of the Holy Sepulchre, Jerusalem, the earliest traditional site of Jesus's burial.**

**Above: Rays of the Aten extending hands to receive offerings of bread in the Great Temple. From a tomb relief at Amarna.** © Robert Feather

**Left: Scene in Panehesy's tomb at Amarna showing Akhenaten riding his royal chariot. Footholds have been carved out so that pilgrims could reach up and place prayers in niches in the relief.** © Robert Feather

Close-up of Jesus (with yellow halo) in the arms of Nefertiti, perhaps the earliest ever representation of Jesus as an infant.

Figures of Nefertiti and Akhenaten adorned with the early Christian sign of the Alpha and the Omega in Panehesy's tomb, Amarna. The faint figure, probably of Jesus, with a yellow halo can be seen in the arms of Nefertiti (see close-up inset at left). Beneath the scene are three apparently important figures, perhaps bearing gifts. The font to the left shows a bird, or possibly an angel, in the apse of the structure.

© Robert Feather

Above: Baptism at Amarna. A hand from the Aten (upper left) holds a jug and pours holy water over a royal princess. Courtesy of the Norbert Schimmel Collection

Left: Scroll paraded by a priest in a temple scene led by Pharaoh Akhenaten. Luxor Museum, Egypt.
© Robert Feather

Opposite page: Hieroglyph relief of the Great Hymn in the tomb of Ay, Amarna, showing a figure on a cross at the center.

Below: Waving of notched palm fronds in the Temple of Akhenaten (Amarna), probably during a harvest festival—remarkably similar to the waving of the Lulav in synagogues of today at Succoth. Courtesy of the Norbert Schimmel Collection

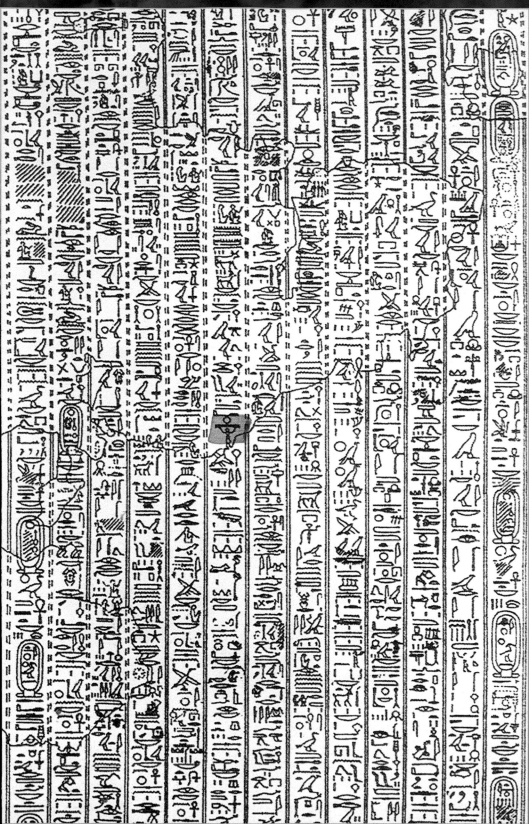

White shells that appear to have been used to decorate some of the graves at Qumran.

© Robert Feather

בית קברות
مقبرة
CEMETERY

**Above:** Palm leaf laid carefully in a north–south direction on the supposed grave of John the Baptist.

© Robert Feather

**Left:** View of the cemetery at Qumran, looking toward the Dead Sea.

© Robert Feather

**Front view of the Stone of Thorns, near Qumran.** © Robert Feather

**Rear view of the Stone of Thorns gravestone, marked with a cross.** © Robert Feather

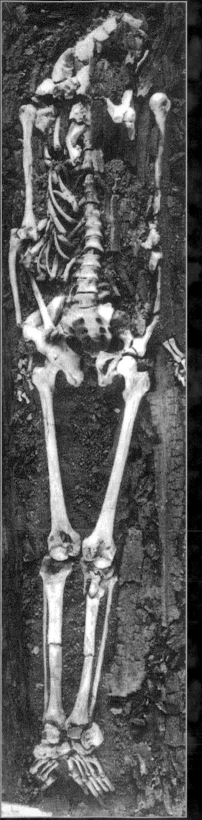

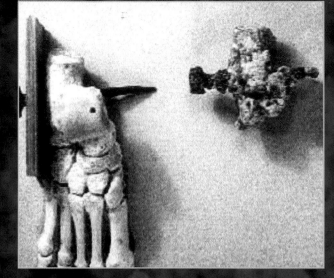

**Above: Heel of crucified remains thought to belong to Yehochanan, found at Givat Hamivtar, Jerusalem, in 1968 and dated to the first century CE.**
Courtesy of Joseph Zias, Century One Foundation

**Left: Skeleton from grave Q18, which was separated out from other bone remains and held back in Jerusalem.**
Courtesy of Fribourg University Press

**Above: Bones excavated from Q17 in the early 1950s, which have now gone missing.** Courtesy of Fribourg University Press

**Father Jozef Milik with K. I. Shahin (Kando) and his brother, dealers who acquired some of the earliest of the Dead Sea Scrolls.**
Courtesy of the Estate of John M. Allegro

**John Allegro (center) in the early 1950s with King Hussein of Jordan and Dr. Awni Dajani, Director of Antiquities, at the Palace of Amman.**
Courtesy of the Estate of John M. Allegro

**Jozef Milik and the author in Paris, April 2001.**
© Robert Feather

# ⤳ 34 ⤵

# The Stone of Thorns

Bearing in mind the close links between John the Baptist and Jesus, I continued my exploration of the cemetery looking for anything unusual. Much of the literary evidence that applies to John the Baptist in his relationship with the Qumran Essenes applies also to Jesus. In fact, there is other evidence from the Christian Scriptures that Jesus might even be a strong contender to have been a longer-term member of the Essene community.

As stated previously, the Christian Scriptures are silent about Jesus's life from the age of twelve until adulthood, but relate that he commenced his ministry at the age of thirty. This is the age spelled out in the Community Rule for a graduate to complete his studies and become a full member of the community. The Qumran Essenes were known to recruit apprentice members from a very young age, and this may well be an explanation for Jesus's missing years.[1]

Like John the Baptist, Jesus, according to the Christian Scriptures, was born not far from Qumran, and for most of his life was geographically centered in the area of the northwest shores of the Dead Sea. John the Baptist is reputed to have baptized Jesus in the river Jordan, some three miles from Qumran. Jesus's Temptation is thought to have taken place only a little more than four miles from Qumran.

My prolonged observation of the landscape of the area between the ruins of Qumran and the coastal road to the east indicated a number of significant common factors for the main cemetery:

- A single dark brown stone marking each grave, varying from pebble size to approximately football size, some of which appear to have been inscribed

269

- A correlation between the size of the marker stone and the desirability of the location of the grave in terms of its view of the Dead Sea

I made a further observation: There are small white snail shells around certain graves that are oriented east–west and are grouped on the southern spur.

## White Shells

A number of graves in close proximity located within the central spur near the slope closest to the Qumran ruins are surrounded by small white shells. It seems impossible that the creatures that once inhabited these shells feasted recently on bodily remains, or that they could have stayed *in situ* for nearly two thousand years. There is no doubt that the Dead Sea was considerably closer to the cemetery in ancient times, perhaps a matter of tens of yards away, and might conceivably have flooded parts of the cemetery at some time in the past. However, no living creature can survive in the Dead Sea, so they cannot be the remnants of seashells. (See page 12 of the color insert.)

As yet I am not sure of the reason for this phenomenon, nor of its significance, if any. Could it be that they have been deliberately placed in relatively recent times around graves that have some commonality?

The next pattern of groupings is, I believe, of much greater significance.

## East–West Orientations

Table 20 illustrates the frequency and gender occupancy of graves dug in a north–south or east–west orientation. The presence of female skeletal material in the main cemetery was anathema to Roland de Vaux and Jozef Milik, leaders of the original École Biblique team studying Qumran. For them, the Dead Sea Scrolls painted a picture, also described by Pliny and Josephus, of a male-only, celibate community dedicated solely to the pursuit of biblical learning and spiritual devotion to God, rather like their own Dominican monastic existence.

The fact that the remains in one of the graves (Q07) excavated in the earliest years were initially identified as being female, while all the others were male, was not particularly welcome news for the Jerusalem cadre.

Subsequently, another five graves, excavated in 1956, were identified as containing female bones (Q32–34, Q35-I, Q37), making matters even worse for their theories.

It may well be, however, that the original team's instincts were more correct than people have allowed. As can be gleaned from the accompanying table 20, a close analysis tends to validate the instincts of the original team in that of the aforementioned graves, those with a distinctly east–west orientation probably contain female bones, while those graves with a north–south orientation most likely contain the bones of men.

As I explored the vicinity of the cemetery, I considered the possibility that if the grave site of John the Baptist had been marked by a palm sign, perhaps another place nearby, of significance to him, might show some indication of further remembrance. Wadi al-Kharrar was one of the traditional locations of John's baptisms and was only three miles north of Qumran.

The tranquilizing heat of a midafternoon sun poured down as I continued on my carefully woven path. Having gone no more than halfway to my planned destination, I was drawn cautiously but inexorably onward, humming to myself the melody of a song by Barbra Streisand, "On Holy Ground." As I approached an unusual feature on the bleak profile of the landscape, I stopped, and a strange feeling of apprehension came over me. A small, squat pile of rocks, about four feet high, stood guardian over what appeared to be a group of graves similar to those in the cemetery at Qumran.[2]

My gaze moved on, just beyond and to the right, and alighted on a stone pile with particularly large beige-white boulders, generally oriented in an east–west direction. A feeling of trepidation came over me as I noted the profuse outgrowth of a thorny, pyracantha-type bush growing from directly under and around what appeared to be a marker stone. Something was quite strange about this grave. I warily circled the burial area; then my steps came to a sudden, rigid halt. The marker stone, the size of a man's head, carried the indistinct but clearly discernible carving of a man's face with deep-set eyes, a wide forehead, and a strong, straight nose. The thorny bush that grew from beneath the stone formed a near perfect halo of thorns around the head when viewed from behind. (See page 14 of the color insert.)

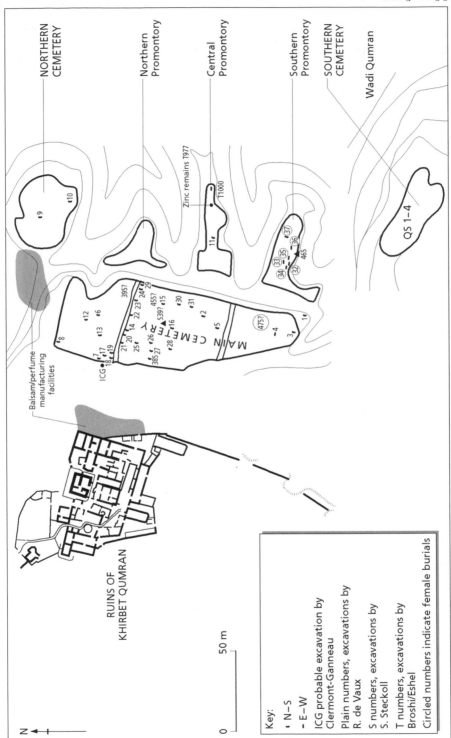

*Fig. 34.1. Map of Qumran showing positions of excavated caves in the cemeteries.*

They dressed him up in purple, twisted some thorns into a crown and put it on him. And they began saluting him, "Hail king of the Jews!" (Mark 15:16–19)

As I stared transfixed at the face for at least twenty minutes, a cyclone of thoughts raced around in my mind. Increasingly, I became convinced that this was a likeness of Jesus and that his mortal remains lay beneath this irregular pile of gravestones. All my previous research had shown that the presence of Jesus at Qumran was a strong possibility. Subsequent research, after the discovery, strengthened this possibility.

## Reflections

Was this really a carving of the face of Jesus? Were his remains buried beneath this image? Could this not just be the burial place of an important Essene who had had his image carved on his marker stone?

There can be no definitive answer to these questions unless the grave is excavated. The present evidence is admittedly circumstantial, but there are numerous factors that, when collated, point powerfully toward the dramatic conclusion that Jesus possibly was buried at this spot near Qumran. The physical evidence is there to see in the powerful face carved on the Stone of Thorns. There is a considerable amount of artistic and literary material that tends to corroborate that the image may be that of Jesus.

Although I did not notice it at the time of my explorations, a subsequent study of photographs showed something else quite startling. On the back of the Stone of Thorns there is an emblem of the cross.[3]

Why, on this particular grave, had the marker stone been deliberately positioned in an east–west direction, just as most of the graves in this remote area were? For many Qumran Essenes, Jesus's interpretation of their beliefs must have been hard to tolerate. In the words of the Christian Scriptures, he is said to have associated with publicans and sinners, practiced a relaxed observance of the Sabbath, and taught that all the secrets (so dear to "the Saints"[4]) were to be revealed. Nevertheless, he had come out of the bosom of their Nazirite fold.

What better way for the unconvinced Qumran Essenes to indicate that he had been one of them, but had "turned in a different direction," than to bury him, and his followers, lying east to west rather than facing south, like almost every other grave in the main cemetery? If this contention is correct—and there must be a reason for the change of burial direction—it could mean that all those buried in the small number of graves that are oriented east to west in the main cemetery were buried in this manner because they were also followers of Jesus.

On the basis that Jesus was once a member of the Qumran-Essene community, for which a very strong case can be made, his subsequent divergence of religious views would inevitably have estranged him from many of its members, but his membership and burial rights would not have lapsed—allowing him a final resting place away from the central area of the main cemetery, surrounded by some of his followers. East–west burial of females in the main sector of the cemetery seems to indicate their nonconformist membership of the Qumran-Essene community and would fit in well with the possibility suggested above.

The presence of female graves is consistent with biblical stories that women were part of Jesus's inner entourage. The Christian Scriptures make it quite clear that Jesus mixed with women during his period of ministry. For example, the evidently unmarried sisters of Lazarus, Mary and Martha, who lived in Bethany, often had Jesus as a guest (Matt. 22:6; Mark 14:3; John 11:1–3; Luke 10:38).

Perhaps other followers—Mary Magdalene, Joanna, Mary, mother of Jesus, and Salome—lie close to Jesus. Perhaps so does Joseph, the father of Jesus. That many of the women mentioned in the Christian Scriptures who were associated with Jesus were also from the Essene community has been proposed by a number of scholars.[5]

The possibility of Mary Magdalene and other women of the Christian Scriptures being buried near Jesus gives part of the reason for the antipathy of some modern theologians toward Mary, continuing a medieval tradition. Perhaps this is also part of the long-standing resistance of the church toward the gnostic associations demonstrated in the Qumran-Essene creed and in other early centers of gnosis and female emancipation. Jane Schaberg, professor of religious studies and women's studies at the University of Detroit–Mercy,[6] together with Virginia Woolf, identifies multiple layers of strategies of suppression of the memory of Mary

Magdalene and a diminishment in much contemporary scholarship of the women of the cross and tomb.

One thing is certain: The grave where the Stone of Thorns was discovered is not only marked by one of the largest stones in this remote burial place, but it also commands a privileged view of the Dead Sea, indicating that someone considered its occupant of great importance.

Could this carved face have withstood the vicissitudes of Dead Sea weather for nearly two thousand years and still be an accurate representation of its original creation? The air at Qumran has a certain salty balm about it, but the atmosphere is essentially free from any artificial pollution. There is no industry within miles of the site. Storms and winds can ravage the region, but they are violent and short-lived. Rain, which potentially could cause the most surface damage, is in some years nonexistent, and when it does fall, its accumulation is generally less than two inches per year.

Would a carved skull be placed on a grave site? The Dead Sea Scrolls make it clear that to walk over a grave is an act of defilement, and therefore human graveyards are identified with the sign of a skull to deter this occurrence.[7]

A passage in the Gospel of Mark (15:22), in fact, connects the death of Jesus to Golgotha, "the Place of the Skull," as do the Gospels of Luke and John, but there was no contemporary tradition that such a place was a site of public executions. There are today several sites where the body of Jesus was thought to have been entombed. One of these is the Church of the Holy Sepulchre at the end of the Via Dolorosa in Old Jerusalem. The square behind the church is thought to mark the place where Jesus was crucified—the Calvarium, or Golgotha.

The other main competing site is in the Garden Tomb, ironically right next to the École Biblique.[8] There one can see a hill shaped like a skull and evidence of a two-room Herodian tomb.[9] These sites where Jesus is, by tradition, thought to have found his final resting place are considered in more detail in a subsequent chapter.

In his relatively recent work *Jesus the Jew,* Professor Geza Vermes deduces that the apparently weakest biblical evidence, as presented in the Gospels, is likely to be the most reliable, as in later Gospel versions the detail is bolstered to make the evidence appear stronger. Thus he notes that Mark may present the earliest account of the resurrection, as in the Gospel of Mark the resurrection is testified to by three women who learned of it from a white-robed youth. The later Gospels of Matthew and Luke bolster the evidence by describing a greater number of witnesses to the resurrection. Strangely, the fourth Gospel, that of John, generally considered to be the earliest version of events, presents a tradition that the body of Jesus was taken from its original place and interred somewhere else by people unconnected with Jesus's party.[10]

As discussed earlier in this book, I, like a number of others, consider that parts of the Gospel of John may well be somewhat earlier than any of the other Gospels. If this is the case, then its recollections could be more reliable than the other Gospels on this particular point, and they fit in well with the possibility that Jesus's body was taken to Qumran for burial. This could have been accomplished by members of the Qumran-Essene faction who supported his beliefs but were still resident near the Qumran headquarters, or perhaps—and more likely because of the probable location of Jesus's crucifixion at Jerusalem—it could have been accomplished by Essenes from within the Essene Gate community of Jerusalem.

# 35

# Facial Likenesses

I puzzled over why others had not seen the likeness on the Stone of Thorns before and how it had come to be carved in the first place, but there were no simple answers. Perhaps part of the explanation is that the facial appearance on the stone can be noticed only from a very narrow angle of observance among the encompassing thorny vegetation.[1] The tomb location is also in one of the remotest parts of a burial site, some distance from Khirbet Qumran and difficult to access without some physical effort, and certainly not on the itinerary of the casual tourist visiting Qumran. The archaeologists have long since moved on to other pastures, having assumed that earlier workers in the 1950s had fully covered the ground. One thing is evidenced by the effects of weathering: The carving was made a very long time ago and is not a recent work.

Although the face carved on the rock seemed initially to be in a configuration reminiscent of many early Renaissance paintings of the face of Jesus—as portrayed, for example, in Piero della Francesca's *The Baptism*, or Duccio's *Christ Heals the Blind*—it also bears remarkable resemblance to much earlier representations. Some of the earliest portraits of Jesus appear on the walls of the catacombs of Priscilla and Domitilla near Rome. Dating back to the second century C.E., these deep burial chambers contain the oldest known representations of Mary, mother of Jesus. On one of the walls there is a scene showing Jesus partaking of the Last Supper together with his disciples, in a likeness not dissimilar to that seen on the marker stone at Qumran.

The oldest claimed representation of Christ is on a Vatican relic known as the Mandylion, or Mandelion.[2] (See page 2 of the color insert.) Comparison of the image seen on this face towel, said by church legend to carry the facial impression of Jesus and to date back to his time, also shows an uncanny likeness to the face carved on the Stone of Thorns of Qumran. Another solid claimant to being the earliest depiction of Jesus appears on a mosaic with *Christ as Helios,* now in the Mausoleum of the Julii, Grotte Viticane, St. Peter's, Vatican City. This is dated to the second century C.E.

Is there any other evidence that Jesus might have been buried near the Dead Sea, rather than in Jerusalem as the Christian Scriptures maintain? Apart from all the evidence previously cited that connects Jesus to Qumran, there is one other physical piece of evidence, relating to events subsequent to the Crucifixion, that might be relevant.

## The Shroud

While there would be enough wood from relics claimed to be part of the original cross of Jesus's crucifixion scattered around the world to constitute a small copse, one notorious mystery warrants consideration in relation to the image of Jesus—the Shroud of Turin.[3] Although carbon-14 dating and weave patterns of the base fabric, among other tests, now seem to have confirmed that the shroud dates from the fourteenth century C.E. and therefore cannot possibly be the burial cloth of Jesus, one piece of evidence is puzzling. In 1973, Professor Max Frei, a leading Swiss forensic scientist, in cooperation with Professor Gilbert Raes, of the University of Ghent, Belgium, examined pollen particles from the shroud. Among forty-eight different examples, mostly originating from France and northern Italy, seven proved to be from halophilic (salt-loving) plants usually found in the Dead Sea area.[4]

The most compelling evidence comes, however, from the similarity in features exhibited by the Stone of Thorns' face and that of the face on the Turin Shroud. If it is a forgery, the similarity in likenesses is uncanny.

Apart from the results of carbon-14 dating in three independent laboratories (Zürich, Oxford, and Tucson), recent work by Orit Shamir, of the Israel Antiquities Authority, seems to ratify the conclusion that the shroud must be of later provenance than the first century C.E. She has shown that the three-on-one fabric weave of the linen material used for the shroud is far more complicated than any known example of weaving from the first century C.E. This conclusion was further verified by the discovery of a wool shroud in a tomb in the Hinnom Valley near Jerusalem in 1999. It is the only known example of a shroud found in the Judaean hills, away from the dry desert areas of Judaea, and has been firmly dated to the first century C.E. Samples of hair and bone found associated with the material indicate its original use as a shroud that exhibits the simple, plain single-weave pattern of the period.[5]

If the Turin Shroud adds anything to the question of the likeness of facial features seen on the Stone of Thorns, even though it is undoubtedly not contemporary with Jesus, it is that the image it carries is consistent with other very early representations of the face of Jesus. The features of the face seen on the Turin Shroud, and some other artifacts, may perhaps replicate a genuine visual recollection of Jesus, and in so doing bear a marked resemblance to the face seen on the Stone of Thorns—in the shape of the head, length of face, broadness of forehead, and shape of the eyes. The Turin Shroud therefore gives some credence to the possibility that eye-witness memories of the Stone of Thorns remained in conscious visual and/or oral awareness because it is a carving of the real face of Jesus.

## A French Connection?

While considering the type of burial Jesus might have been subjected to, there is another bizarre tradition relating to a small mountain village named Rennes-le-Château in the south of France that is worth a detour to examine. There is no intention to go into detail on the myriad of theories that surround the town's picturesque Catholic church, with all its anachronism, that sits in the middle of the village. A more detailed outline is given in the notes.[6]

Suffice it to say that there have been persistent stories that this center of Cathar and Knights Templar country has some connection to biblical treasure and to a knowledge of Jesus's crucifixion. There are certainly mysteries that have not been solved concerning both its renegade priest, Bérenger Saunière, who, at one point, suddenly became immensely rich, and the weird embellishments that adorn the mountaintop church. On entry, one immediately sees something not normally encountered in a church—a warning in Latin over the entrance that says: "This is a terrible place."

Inside the church are some very odd, vividly colored symbolistic paintings and statues and one huge wall fresco that may have some direct relevance to Jesus's burial. Generally labeled as showing the Mount of Beatitude, from where Jesus gave his Sermon on the Mount,[7] it is, I believe, wrongly ascribed. The so-called Mount is more like a small mound and is very reminiscent of the geographical feature seen near the Stone of Thorns grave in the vicinity of Qumran. The fresco showing the mound with a covering of garlanded roses seems to imply a burial place with Jesus rising after death and emerging, in all his finery, from the grave.

The model of a crucifixion, at the bottom of the picture, and a shrouded body lying in a shallow grave add to the impression that this is a *recollected* scene relating to the death and resurrection of Jesus. The three men, four women, three children, and one infant depicted in the fresco hardly constitute a multitude listening to a sermon. (See page 2 of the color insert.) Perhaps the mound depicted in the fresco in the church of Rennes-le-Château is, in fact, the geographical feature seen near the Stone of Thorns grave in the vicinity of Qumran and was wrongly assumed to have been the site of the Sermon on the Mount.

One other feature of the church at Rennes-le-Château is worth mentioning before moving on. Throughout the imagery of the church, John the Baptist is given precedence over Jesus, and there are several examples where a skull is jarringly juxtaposed with one of Jesus's followers. Is this some kind of cryptic indication that the head of John the Baptist lies hidden within the purview of the church?

Since 1965, the sign that greets the visitor who completes the steep, long winding climb to Rennes and enters the village reads "Fouilles interdites"—"Excavations are forbidden." The sign does not deter the locals, however; if you stand in the middle of the village late at night, you can often hear the faint clinking and tapping of tools biting into rock and soil as the search for hidden treasures continues unabated. No doubt in due course the entire village will collapse into underground passages and shafts.

In 2002, it was reported that a team of Americans had located, without excavating but by using sensitive electronic equipment, a crypt beneath the church. As well, a box measuring thirty-eight by forty-one inches had been found about thirteen feet beneath the Tour Magdala. This tower had been built by Father Saunière on the western edge of the ramparts of

Rennes-le-Château. Professor Robert Eisenman, of California State University, led a subsequent excavation project.

Such was the apparent interest in what this mysterious box might contain that it was reported that the Vatican intended to send three representatives to observe the work. These reports have turned out to be so much hot air. In the summer of 2003, with TV cameras standing by to record the unearthing, the mysterious black box was revealed to be nothing more than a dense block of stone.[8] If the initial speculations had had some substance, the Catholic Church would, no doubt, have had more than a passing interest in what might lie concealed at Rennes-le-Château, especially if it reflected on anything related to Jesus.

One last observation about this most mysterious place. In 1885, at the age of thirty-three, François-Bérenger Saunière was appointed curé of the impoverished church of Sainte-Madelaine, which stands at the top of the main village street, where once the Visigoths had built a mighty fortified palace.

Parts of the original church have survived on the same site from Visigoth times of the sixth century C.E., and when Saunière commenced renovation work, he is said to have found four parchment manuscripts dating to the Visigoth period hidden beneath a slab that formed part of the altar.

From that time onward, Saunière exhibited wealth far beyond the resources of his modest stipend. He is known to have spent vast amounts of money refurbishing the church, its surroundings, and the amenities of the village. He entertained lavishly, inviting influential guests from Paris and other parts of France, and struck up a long-lasting romantic relationship with one of the world's most beautiful and famous opera singers, Ema Calvé. What treasures—Templar or Visigoth—or historical relics Saunière uncovered have never been confirmed, but to date more than three hundred books have been written speculating on the riddle of his newfound wealth and the secrets of Rennes-le-Château.

It is the slab under which Saunière is said to have made one of his discoveries that is of immediate interest. A carving on the underside, in a style of the sixth or seventh century C.E., shows an arched, cryptlike room with two mounted figures. The figure on the left is very indistinct, but the figure on the right seems to be holding a staff, and by its head is an object that has been described as a disk or sphere of some kind, and which looks very much like a solar disk. Why this characterizing emblem of Akhenaten should appear in this unlikely place is a mystery.[9]

## Final Proof?

There were other confirmatory features related to the grave that I had identified as possibly containing the mortal remains of Jesus that became apparent when I was able to study the published and private documentation relating to the cemetery—particularly that coming from Joseph Zias, curator of archaeology and anthropology for the Israel Antiquities Authority from 1972 to 1997.

The one action that could determine conclusively whether the bones of Jesus lie under the Stone of Thorns grave would be to excavate it and carry out a series of scientific tests. This will not happen as long as Israel and Orthodox Jewish rulings apply. A Jewish cemetery is sacred ground that cannot be excavated. After the Palestinian peace settlement, the area of Qumran could remain within the borders of Israel, so there would be no prospect of any exhumations. It is not completely clear where the final borderline will be drawn, however, or who will have control of the area.[10]

## Was Jesus Really Buried Near Qumran?

The tangible evidence for the burial place of Jesus is in some ways less conclusive than that for John the Baptist. The grave pinpointed as possibly being that of Jesus has not been excavated. The visual and circumstantial evidence is striking, however, and a large proportion of scholars who have studied the theological position believe Jesus was at least in contact or influenced by the Qumran community, so it has to be a possibility.

# ～ 36 ～

# ALTERNATIVE BURIAL
# SITES FOR JESUS

Many people, from as far back as Emperor Constantine in the fourth century C.E. and the Knights Templar in the twelfth century C.E., to modern scholars, have searched for and theorized about the final resting places of Jesus and John the Baptist. No one is certain where their bodies were finally buried, and the Christian Scriptures are, in fact, our only direct source of information on these matters.

The suggestion that Jesus might have been buried near Qumran, even if it is correct, does not contradict the assertion of the Christian Scriptures that Jesus was first laid to rest in the tomb belonging to Joseph of Arimathaea (Matt. 27:57–60; Luke 23:51; John 19:38); nor would it in any way compromise the Gospels' claim that Jesus was resurrected from the dead and seen in a human/spiritual form by his disciples and followers.

## Jesus's Final Resting Place: Previous Theories

Traditionally, Jesus is thought to have been buried at the site of the Church of the Holy Sepulchre or in the Garden Tomb in Jerusalem, but there is nothing more than legend to support either of these suppositions. These are the two main rival theories.[1]

### Church of the Holy Sepulchre, Jerusalem

The Church of the Holy Sepulchre in Jerusalem is the traditional site of Jesus's crucifixion and burial around 33 C.E. (See page 5 of the color insert.) A hundred years after these events, the site was covered by a Roman temple dedicated to the goddess Aphrodite. In 325 C.E., Emperor Constantine's mother, Helena, who had embraced Christianity, went searching for the grave of Jesus. She had the temple demolished and found a cavelike tomb cut in the face of the underlying quarry. A small stone enclosure was created around the cave and a basilica built on top of it. The building was successively destroyed and renovated up until the time of the Crusaders in 1099 C.E.; they built a church on the site, which remains largely in its original form today.

A recent examination of the tomb area by Professor Martin Biddle, of Oxford University, has shown, as have all previous investigations, that nothing of the original tomb remains, and there is no evidence that any kind of human remains have ever been found there.

Control and administration of the Church of the Holy Sepulchre is divided among six different Christian denominations who jealously guard their rights of occupation. The position was set out in a document agreed upon in 1757, which defines ownership of every single item in the church. One of the most comical incidents relating to these divisions must be the one that was reported in August 2002, when fights broke out over control of the church's roof. The fracas involved Ethiopian Orthodox monks and monks from the Coptic Egyptian church.

Other fights have taken place over the centuries, but this was one of the most vigorous. The pugilistics were provoked by a Coptic monk who normally sits on a chair on the roof to assert his church's rights. He decided to move the chair out of the sun on a particularly hot day. The Ethiopians, who over the centuries have been ousted from the main church and have now built African-style huts on the roof to act as their monastery, took umbrage and challenged his right to move the chair.

After several days of rising tensions and taunts, the Coptic monk was eventually punched by, of all indignities, a woman. Calling for reinforcements, the monk was soon joined on the roof by colleagues who proceeded to do battle with the Ethiopian church monks, using fists, stones, and iron bars. Israeli police were called in and order was eventually restored. Four Coptic monks and seven Ethiopian monks, one unconscious, were subsequently taken to hospital for treatment.[2]

### The Garden Tomb, Jerusalem

First identified by General Gordon (of Khartoum) in 1883 as the tomb of Christ, the Garden Tomb is cut into a quarry and approached through a garden. There is no tradition to support the claim that this is the final resting place of Jesus, although the area had been identified with Golgotha ("Place of the Skull") since the nineteenth century, when a knoll in the rough shape of a skull and two caves that look like eyes led observers to the belief. The Garden Tomb, however, is part of a system of Iron Age (eighth to seventh century B.C.E.) tombs and therefore fails to fulfill the Christian Scriptures' explicit requirement that Jesus's body be placed in a tomb "wherein was never man yet laid" (John 19:41). As previously noted, the Garden Tomb is adjacent to the École Biblique on Nablus Road, not far from the walls of the Old City of Jerusalem. (See page 5 of the color insert.)

Although few theologians are prepared to concede that Jesus was actually an Essene, and most historians have not been convinced of a derivative relationship, many are beginning to moderate their position in the light of current scholarship, coming mainly from the Dead Sea Scrolls. When I posed the question to Jozef Milik as to whether Jesus was a member of the Qumran-Essene community, there was a long pause before his enigmatic answer: "No, I think he is an itinerant predicator [preacher]. He was not a monk. They were a predicator . . . nor was he a Zealot."

The question of whether Jesus might have been a member of the Qumran Essenes cannot be answered easily on the basis of what any particular religious grouping might have believed. The reason for Jozef Milik's extended silence before answering the question put to him, as Professor George Brooke points out, may well have been that there was no clear-cut set of beliefs for any of the many interpretations of Judaism that existed in Second Temple times. A kaleidoscope of differing viewpoints held by different factions were blurred at the edges where beliefs held in common overlapped.

I rather like to think of the situation in terms of each group being defined by its own special mix of beliefs, as well as its own uniquely held beliefs.

When the circumstantial, indirect, and perhaps stronger direct evidence is taken into account, the possibility of Jesus being buried at Qumran becomes that much greater on the basis of the following:

1. The small proportion of international scholars who take the view that Jesus, at one period in his life, belonged to the community of

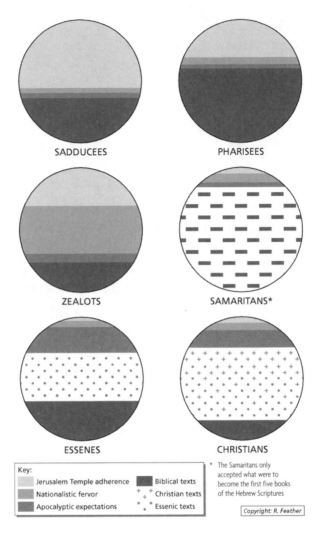

*Fig. 36.1. Analysis of Second Temple–period religious groupings in the Holy Land.*

Qumran Essenes. It would be quite possible from their point of view that he could have been buried at Qumran because of his role as a previous member.

2. My own analysis of the literature and unpublished material, including John Allegro's letters (see appendixes 1 and 2); communications from Joseph Zias; and the enigmatic reaction of Jozef Milik on being shown a picture of the Stone of Thorns grave.

**TABLE 21**

**Analysis of scholarly opinion regarding Jesus's membership in the Qumran-Essene community[3]**

| Member at some period in his life | In contact and influenced but not a member | Little contact or influence |
|---|---|---|
| A. Dupont-Sommer | R. Eisler | H. Rowley |
|  | Jean Danielou | Frank Cross |
|  | Jack Finnegan | Pierre Benoit |
|  | Daniel Schwartz | Cyrus Gordon |
|  | Raymond Brown | Edmund Sutcliffe |
| John Allegro | R. Harrison | Carsten Thiede |
| Barbara Thiering | Charles Scobie | Joan Taylor |
| Laurence Gardner | John Robinson | James Charelsworth |
|  | Oscar Cullmann | Jonathan Campbell |
|  | Robert Webb | Geza Vermes |
|  | William Brownlee |  |
|  | George Brooke |  |
| Bargil Pixner | Lucretta Mowry |  |
| Jozef Milik | Otto Betz |  |
| Robert Feather | James VanderKam |  |
|  | The Jesus Seminar |  |
|  | Yigael Yadin |  |
|  | Charles Fritsch |  |
|  | Millar Burrows |  |
|  | David Flusser |  |
|  | Kurt Schubert |  |
|  | Joseph Fitzmyer |  |
|  | Magen Broshi |  |

3. The strong probability that John the Baptist, a close compatriot of Jesus, was buried at or near Qumran, and that Jesus would have merited the same privilege of burial.

4. The peripheral location of the possible grave of Jesus, with the largest marker stone of any grave. It is aligned approximately in an east–west direction, whereas virtually every other grave in the main cemetery is aligned north–south. The relative size of the marker stone and its orientation are consistent with acknowledging his

importance, and with the possibility that Jesus was at one period in his life a member, but that his teachings did not conform to those of the Qumran community.[4]

5. The marker stone carved in the discernible shape of a face, with a cross marked on the back of the stone, surrounded by a thornbush.
6. A stone shrine of sorts that has been erected near the possible site of Jesus's burial subsequent to the original excavations.
7. The possible grave of Jesus, surrounded by graves oriented east–west.

According to Laurence Gardner, Chevalier Labhràn de Saint Germain, the Dead Sea Scrolls make it clear that "human graves were identified with the sign of a skull."[5] Walking over the dead was, and still is, considered an act of defilement, so the marking of a grave with a skull carving would not be a surprise. Even the Christian Scriptures talk about Jesus being laid to rest in a place associated with a skull "which is called in the Hebrew Golgotha" (John 19:17, 41; Matt. 27:33; Mark 15:22; Luke 23:33 names the place of crucifixion as Calvary).

Both Laurence Gardner and the Australian biblical scholar Dr. Barbara Thiering[6] conclude that Qumran was the place where Jesus was buried, but more incredibly the Christian Scriptures' Book of Revelation is more specific. It spells out in no uncertain terms that Jesus was buried at a place associated with Qumran:

> And their dead bodies shall lie in the street of the great city, which spiritually is called *Sodom and Egypt, where also our Lord was crucified.* And they of the people and kindreds and tongues and nations shall see their dead bodies three days and an half, and shall not suffer their dead bodies to be put in graves. (Rev. 11:8–9; my emphasis)

There is no satisfactory conventional explanation of this passage. Suffice it to say the key words Sodom and Egypt are taken by translators to be cryptic analogs for places anywhere but those indicated by the actual words themselves—a device often used by scholars to get around words that do not support a preconceived position.

The Gospels record the crucifixion as being enacted at a loosely defined location somewhere not far from Jerusalem. The site of Jesus's temporary entombment is said to be in a nearby sepulchre, but that was perhaps not the final resting place, as Jesus's body disappears after three days. The Gospel versions appear to be leaving open the possibility that the last resting place of the mortal remains of Jesus was somewhere else.

Most of the Christian Scriptures maintain that Jesus was buried quite near the place of his crucifixion, somewhere outside Jerusalem, but the passage in Revelation is saying that Jesus was crucified at a place other than Jerusalem. Jerusalem is certainly not known by the name Egypt or Sodom, but Qumran *has* been associated with the location of Sodom by the Dead Sea, and the name Egypt was used as a designation for Qumran by the Therapeutae, an Egyptian sect closely related to the Essenes.

The Book of Revelation also talks about two prophets who are killed by the Gentile multitude in a great city with a temple where a reed is used for measurement. A possible interpretation of this passage as referring to Akhetaten, apart from its reverberations to the place of Jesus's burial, is discussed in the notes to this chapter.[7]

## Ultimate Proof?

Signs of crucifixion, the presence of iron nails, damage to the skeleton, carbon dating, forensic examination determining age at death, and other signs such as spear-inflicted rib-cage damage to the left side and contents placed within the grave could be definitive in determining that the body placed under the Stone of Thorns was that of Jesus.

The lack of examples of this form of Roman punishment is extremely surprising in the light of our knowledge that thousands of people were subjected to crucifixion during the first centuries B.C.E. and C.E. in and around Jerusalem.

One plausible explanation is that crucifixion was employed by the Romans not only as a punishment but also as a deterrent to insurrection. To achieve the greatest possible deterrent effect, it was therefore common practice to leave the crucified body on its cross as a warning to others for as long as possible—in fact, until carrion birds, wild animals, and insects had consumed virtually everything. Then again, as it is forbidden by Jewish law to deliberately excavate a cemetery, there may well be many crucified bodily remains still lying undisturbed in their burial places.

Despite the thousands of crucifixions that are known to have been carried out by the Romans, the only skeleton showing signs of crucifixion that is known from the Roman-Judaean period was discovered accidentally in June 1968 at Givat Hamivtar, in northeast Jerusalem, near the Nablus Road. Coincidentally, the site is close to the École Biblique.[8] This first-century-C.E. tomb was found among four tombs carved as small rooms into an outcropping of soft limestone rock.[9] Each tomb has an antechamber and a burial chamber containing deep-cut niches large enough to accommodate a body. (It was customary to first allow the bodies to decompose and then to place them in family ossuaries.)

Fifteen ossuaries were found at Givat Hamivtar containing the bones of eleven males, twelve females, and twelve children. Of these, one mother and infant had died at childbirth; three children aged between six months and eight years had died of starvation; and five people had died violent deaths: a male and female by burning; a female from a macelike blow to the head; a child of about three years old by an arrow wound; and a male of about twenty-four years of age and five feet, five inches in height by crucifixion. The latter's name, inscribed on the ossuary, which also contained an incomplete adult and his four-year-old son, was "Yehochanan the son of Hgqwl."

Studies by members of the Israel Department of Antiquities and of the Hebrew University Hadassah Medical School, Jerusalem, concluded that Yehochanan had been crucified by having his arms tied to the bar of a cross and his legs placed on either side of a vertical beam with separate nails securing his heel bone to the wood on each side. A small olive-wood spacer had been placed between the heel bone and nail head to prevent the foot from being torn loose from the nail, and this was found still attached to the heel bone in the ossuary. (See page 15 of the color insert.)

Whether the leg bones of the victim were broken is not entirely clear. According to Dr. Nicu Haas, of Hadassah Medical School, the legs were brutally smashed,[10] but Joseph Zias has contradicted many of Dr. Haas's findings and suggests postmortem breaks may have occurred through the taphanomic process (effects of geological movement) over the period of two thousand years.[11]

Dr. Haas had very little time to study the bone remains before they were reinterred; the much more intensive study of 1985 by Joseph Zias and others would appear to be more reliable in its findings. The relevance of whether the bones were broken relates to the Christian Scriptures' requirement that the bones of Jesus not be broken at his death:

> But when they came to Jesus and found that he was already dead, they did not break his legs. (John 19:33)

This complies with Psalm 34:20, said by Christian sources to apply prophetically to Jesus: "He keeps all his bones, not one of them is broken."

## "The Tomb Is Empty"

If the whereabouts of the headless bones of John the Baptist are known and I am correct in the assumption that Jesus was buried near Qumran, there are a number of indications that others, particularly in the Catholic Church, are also aware of this truth. It would be very strange indeed if the headless corpse that Jozef Milik uncovered was not known to others in his circle. The skeleton would have been brought back to the École Biblique or possibly taken directly to the Rockefeller Museum, but either way quite a few people would have been aware of its existence. Yet no one, apart from Monsieur Milik, is prepared to recall the discovery as relating to John the Baptist, and it has never been reported in the literature. One possibility, of course, is that those of his colleagues at the École Biblique who knew of the discovery decided not to reveal it to the outside world, and none of them is now still alive.

We can understand the reasons for this discovery not being spoken about, but it is hard to imagine that others on the excavation team at Qumran, or at the École Biblique, did not later become aware of what subsequently was kept secret. Henri de Contenson has said that he did not recall the incident of the finding of a headless skeleton, but he admits he was not present at Qumran on all the campaigns Jozef Milik might have been involved in.

There is a strange passage that appears in an apocryphal text known as the Pseudo-Clementine Recognitions, written at the end of the second century C.E., that might indicate that someone very close to Jesus could have been aware of his burial place not far from Jericho. During a period of persecution, James, the brother of Jesus, is said to have retreated to Jericho with several thousand followers, but James and some of these followers then risk going "outside Jericho to visit the graves of some fellow brethren which miraculously 'whitened of them themselves every year.'"

Was this place Qumran, a distance of a little more than six miles from Jericho? Was this "whitening" a clue that salts in the occasional fallout of briny deposits from the Dead Sea were the cause?

We are now reaching the end of our journey, and, although the incredible revelations of Jozef Milik have been confirmed by a volume of physical and circumstantial evidence, they have led on to stark visual evidence that Jesus himself was also buried near Qumran.

I would like to claim to be the first to have made this latter discovery, but the indications were there to see; and if Jozef Milik knew about John the Baptist, he must also have had an inkling about his Master. If Jozef Milik had an inkling, so must others: people such as Father Roland de Vaux, perhaps also Father Émile Puech, Father James Murphy O'Connor—all of the École Biblique in Jerusalem—Professor H. Vallois, of the Department of Anthropology and Religion at the Sorbonne; Dr. Ferdinand Röhrhirsch, of Catholic University, Eichstätt; Dr. Susan Sheridan, of Holy Cross College, University of Notre Dame—all at Catholic institutions, all party to intimate, exclusive knowledge about the remains found in the cemetery of Qumran.

Now we enter the realms of speculation.

If so many of these senior Catholic figures knew the greatest secret of Qumran, would one of them have not felt obliged to vouchsafe it to the ear of His Holiness the Pope himself?

## Summation

Analysis of current thinking shows that a majority of scholars consider Jesus to have been influenced by and to have had some contact with the Qumran Essenes at some period in his life. A relative few believe he was actually a member of the Qumran community. In view of the wealth of evidence that has already been presented connecting Jesus and John the Baptist to Qumran, together with the further evidence that is to come, and the fact that one of the books of the Christian Scriptures implies that the denouement of Jesus's life took place near Qumran, there would seem to be a real possibility that he was interred near Qumran.

# 37

## Closing the Circle

*Bring me my bow of burning gold!*
*Bring me my arrows of desire!*
*Bring me my spear! O clouds unfold!*
*Bring me my chariot of fire!*
WILLIAM BLAKE, "MILTON"

Many of the earliest Christian settlements, as highlighted in chapter 25, were established in exactly the same places as those where Essene settlements already existed. This factor is almost conclusive proof, on its own, of an intimate relationship between early followers of Jesus and the Essenes. If my theories on the origins of monotheism are holistically correct, and the Qumran Essenes had a special interest in Pharaoh Akhenaten, one would predict that the earliest supporters of Jesus would also have had such an interest.

There is one other place, therefore, that we might expect to find an Essene or Christian presence, and that is Akhetaten, modern-day Amarna, Egypt. It has often been put to me that surely, in light of my claims, there would be some indication of an Essenic presence in Amarna or a physical attempt by an Essenic element to return to the holy city of Akhenaten. If, as I maintain, the Copper Scroll of the Qumran Essenes mentions Akhenaten, and other sectarian texts demonstrate a knowledge of the geographical layout of Akhetaten and its Great Temple, there ought to be some other evidence linking Akhenaten's holy city to the Essenes. The suggestion in this book, that a small select strand of the Qumran Essenes became followers of Jesus, implies that this group would also have had some continuing allegiance to Akhetaten.

More than a thousand years after Akhenaten, in the time of Jesus, few people, except those with secret knowledge, would have even known about Akhenaten's existence, let alone the location of his holy city. I believe I have already demonstrated that the Essenes had that secret knowledge and expressed it in coded format in some of their writings. Were it possible to show that early Christians deliberately sought out the place where Akhenaten had built his holy city, in a remote part of Egypt long since forgotten to ordinary memory, there would be a remarkable confirmation of the case I have made. As it turns out, the truth is even more astounding than I could ever have imagined.

Until recently, it has not been easy to show a direct, continuous physical link extending back from the time that the Essenes settled at Qumran (around 150 B.C.E.) to the Egyptian New Kingdom eighteenth-dynasty period of Akhenaten circa 1350 B.C.E.—a jump of over a thousand years. Nevertheless, I believe I have established, in *The Mystery of the Copper Scroll of Qumran,* a substantive case for the Essenes as heirs to a priestly line that went back to the First Temple in Jerusalem, to be linked through the remaining four-hundred-year gap via Moses and Joseph, to the Egypt of Akhenaten. Table 22 summarizes how that lineage might have been maintained after the dispersal of the Jacob/Joseph Hebrews and followers of Akhenaten to the main locations of On and Yeb after Akhenaten's death. Recent archaeological studies at Amarna have revealed startling new evidence that strongly supports my claims.

Some of the earliest detailed archaeological work at Amarna was documented by Norman de Garis Davies in an Egypt Exploration Fund publication of 1905.[1] More recently, Gwil Owen, faculty photographer in the Faculty of Archaeology and Anthropology at the University of Cambridge, and field workers at Amarna have reexamined earlier surveys of the tombs at Amarna. Some of their findings were published in the autumn 2000 edition of *Egyptian Archaeology,*[2] a journal of the Egypt Exploration Society, London.

While considering what will be discussed in this chapter, please bear in mind that early Christian churches and other places of worship were invariably established at sites significant to the new religion. As well, traditionally it has been customary to insert written prayers and entreaties in niches in holy places, such as in the Wailing Wall at the site of the Temple in Jerusalem, as the Pope did on his last visit.[3]

Table 22 on page 296 shows how the descendants of a separate line of priests, originally appointed at the time of Akhenaten, could have maintained their cohesion down to Qumran times. During the period of the Exodus they were pro-Moses and anti the Aaronide priests and settled around Shiloh on entry into Canaan. When King Solomon came to the throne they were out of office and were banished to Anathoth, only to come back into prominence through Ezekiel and at the time of Onias IV.

The finding that one of the larger tombs located in the steep northern hills of Amarna was used as a place of worship by early Christians, from at least as early as the second or third century and probably earlier, is, to say the least, extremely surprising. These early followers of Jesus must have sought out what was then an obscure site, distant from water and extremely difficult to access. On this steep, hilly location, they chose to settle near the tomb of Panehesy, who had been one of Akhenaten's highest-ranking supporters, and worship in what was effectively a cave. That this kind of existence and worship in a cave might not have been novel to them is suggested, in another context, at Qumran (a discussion on cave worship follows in chapter 38).

Whereas other imagery in the tomb, dating to the time of Akhenaten, was plastered over, the evidence indubitably shows that these early Christians must have worshipped in front of a relief of Akhenaten, dating back to 1350 B.C.E., and that they carved steps to climb up on the wall of the tomb and placed prayers in niches on the wall bearing Akhenaten's figure. They also marked the figure of Nefertiti, Akhenaten's wife, with the sign of the cross and an Alpha and Omega in red paint (see pages 8–9 of the color insert).

Perhaps even more remarkable is the vaguely discernible figure of a small infant with a golden halo around its head that appears to be held in the arms of Nefertiti. Nicholas Montserrat labels the image as that of a saint,[4] but the relative head sizes and the positioning of the figure, as if being held in Nefertiti's arms, seem to rule out this possibility. In the view of Samir Anis, director of Egyptian Antiquities for sites south of El Minyah, this image was the figure of the infant Jesus. If this is the case, the representation would almost certainly be one of the earliest ever of Jesus.

To the left of the figures of Nefertiti and what appears to be the infant Jesus, beneath a curved roof structure, is a deep baptismal well dug out by

**TABLE 22**

**Timeline showing priestly lineage from Akhetaten to Qumran**

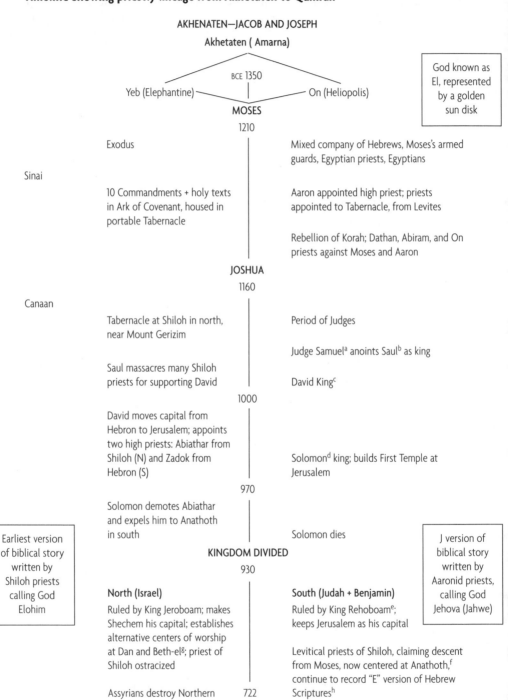

AKHENATEN—JACOB AND JOSEPH

Akhetaten ( Amarna)

BCE 1350

Yeb (Elephantine) — On (Heliopolis)

| | God known as El, represented by a golden sun disk |

**MOSES**

1210

| Exodus | Mixed company of Hebrews, Moses's armed guards, Egyptian priests, Egyptians |

Sinai

| 10 Commandments + holy texts in Ark of Covenant, housed in portable Tabernacle | Aaron appointed high priest; priests appointed to Tabernacle, from Levites |

| | Rebellion of Korah; Dathan, Abiram, and On priests against Moses and Aaron |

**JOSHUA**

1160

Canaan

| Tabernacle at Shiloh in north, near Mount Gerizim | Period of Judges |

| | Judge Samuel[a] anoints Saul[b] as king |

| Saul massacres many Shiloh priests for supporting David | David King[c] |

1000

| David moves capital from Hebron to Jerusalem; appoints two high priests: Abiathar from Shiloh (N) and Zadok from Hebron (S) | Solomon[d] king; builds First Temple at Jerusalem |

970

| Solomon demotes Abiathar and expels him to Anathoth in south | Solomon dies |

| Earliest version of biblical story written by Shiloh priests calling God Elohim | | J version of biblical story written by Aaronid priests, calling God Jehova (Jahwe) |

**KINGDOM DIVIDED**

930

**North (Israel)**

Ruled by King Jeroboam; makes Shechem his capital; establishes alternative centers of worship at Dan and Beth-el[g]; priest of Shiloh ostracized

**South (Judah + Benjamin)**

Ruled by King Rehoboam[e]; keeps Jerusalem as his capital

Levitical priests of Shiloh, claiming descent from Moses, now centered at Anathoth,[f] continue to record "E" version of Hebrew Scriptures[h]

Assyrians destroy Northern Kingdom; exile 10 tribes of Israel northward    722

| | |
|---|---|
| 700 | King Hezekiah, reformer with Atenist links[i], Aaronid priests control Temple at Jerusalem, maintain J version of Hebrew Scriptures |
| 680 | E and J versions combined; P version[j] written to enhance Aaron's role within J and E versions |
| 630 | King Josiah, reformer with Atenist links[k] |
| 622 | Book of Deuteronomy, D version, revealed, written by E priests at Anathoth, directed by Jeremiah[l] |
| 587 | Babylonians conquer Southern Kingdom, destroy First Temple at Jerusalem, exile bulk of Israelites and elite, including Ezekiel, to Babylon; Jeremiah flees to Egypt |
| 538 | Persians conquer Babylonians; allow exiles to return to rebuild Temple at Jerusalem, now under control of Aaronid priests |
| | Ezra, an Aaronid priest, and Nehemiah return from Babylon with a complete version of the Five Books of Moses |
| 320 | Greek Ptolomaic rule from Egypt, initiated by Alexander the Great |
| 198 | Greek Seleucid rule from Syria |
| 175 | Onias IV, an E sympathizer, becomes high priest of Second Temple in Jerusalem |
| 172 | Onias IV ousted by Menelaus, the wicked priest, and flees to Egypt, where he builds a temple at Leontopolis and installs a huge golden orb |
| 167 | Maccabean revolt ousts Greek Seleucids, restores Jewish state |
| | Onias IV returns from Egypt |
| 150 | Onias IV, the Teacher of Righteousness, leads separatist E priests to Qumran |

a. Samuel was a prophet, priest, and judge from Shiloh, and a descendant of Korah.

b. Saul came from the tribe of Benjamin.

c. After Saul's death, at the hands of the Philistines, the kingdom was temporarily divided with the south ruled by Ishbaal, Saul's son, and the north by David. When Ishbaal was assassinated, David, from the tribe of Judah, became king and reunited the Kingdom.

d. Before David died, two of his sons contested for the throne. Adonijah was supported by the high priest Abiathar and the priests of Shiloh, and Solomon, David's son by Bathsheba, was supported by the high priest Zadok and the priests of Hebron. King David chose Solomon to succeed him and then King Solomon had Adonijah killed, and banished Abiathar to Anathoth in the south. Dead Sea Scroll 4Q245 clearly confirms the method of transmission of a written testimony (or testimonies) of instruction, originating long before Moses, which was passed down through Kohath (son of Levi and grandfather of Moses) to Uzziel (grandson of Levi) and then to Abiathar.

e. Rehoboam was Solomon's son.

f. A village near Jerusalem.

g. Jeroboam used golden calves as alternative iconography to golden cherubs in the Jerusalem Temple.

h. The E version in the Hebrew Scriptures refers to God as Elohim (up to the time of the appearance of Moses, after which the title Jahwe is used); the J version in the Hebrew Scriptures refers to God as Jahwe. The P version flows through all of the first four Books of Moses. The D version appears to be independent.

Significantly, as Richard Elliot Friedman (*Who Wrote the Bible,* HarperSanFrancisco, 1987) points out, "The overall picture of the E stories is that they are a consistent group, with a definite perspective and set of interests, and that they are profoundly tied to their author's world." The E groups concentrate on Moses and the Tabernacle, from which one can deduce they where closely associated with guarding its contents, and they are not at all interested in the Temple, just as the Qumran Essenes denigrate the Temple and talk mainly in terms of the Tabernacle.

i. See Robert Feather, *The Mystery of the Copper Scroll of Qumran* (Inner Traditions, 2003), chapter 20.

j. According to Richard Elliott Friedman (*Who Wrote the Bible,* HarperSanFrancisco, 1987), $P_1$ was written in the time of King Hezekiah (c. 700 BCE) and $P_2$ in Second Temple times.

k. A recently found bulla (seal impression), dated to the seventh century BCE records Natan-melech as a high official of King Josiah. He is equated with the Natan-melech of 2 Kings 23:11, referred to as a "eunuch" and chamberlain to King Josiah. His name could indicate an allegiance to Atenism—n'ATAN—and the term *eunuch,* as a member of an elite group, is identical to one of the terms used by the Qumran Essenes to refer to themselves. See P. Kyle McCarter Jr., "Biblical Detective Work Identifies the Eunuch," *Biblical Archaeology Review* 28, no. 2, 2002.

l. Probably set down by a Shilonite scribe, Baruch.

---

the early worshippers. On the ceiling of this baptistry can still be seen the faded painting of a winged bird, strikingly similar to that seen in the catacombs of Priscilla near Rome, which have been dated to the early part of the second century C.E.

When it is realized that very early Christians, and possibly Essenes, prayed in front of a scene of King Akhenaten riding on his royal chariot at his holy city of Akhetaten in Egypt, it is not surprising that heavenly chariot imagery, and King Akhenaten himself, was a powerful part of their historical memory.

Again, reiterating the association of Akhenaten's heavenly chariot and the stunning effect it must have had on the earliest Christians who journeyed to Akhenaten's ruined city, recent excavations at the monastery of Kom el-Nana—part of the Amarna City site, as reported by the Egypt Exploration Society—demonstrate this influence. Excavations in 2000 and 2002 at the monastery have now been supplemented by a tray-by-tray analysis of the wall plaster in the church of the monastery, overseen by Gillian Pyke of Birmingham University, England.

The subject of the decoration is a line of male figures, almost certainly apostles, wearing gold, pale red, and green cloaks. Flanking what may be the figure of the Virgin Mary, one figure appears to be that of St. Peter, while the names of Andrew, John, and James are positively identified from associated inscriptions. Another figure, above the group, robed in white and riding a chariot, is believed to be that of Jesus. A similar motif is seen in the church of Bawit, a few miles from Kom el-Nana.[5]

The site of the monastery at Kom el-Nana is a little more than two miles from the Great Temple, well within the southern concession of the central city of Akhetaten. The similarities between the inscriptions on the walls of the monastery and those on the walls of tombs of Akhenaten's officials in the northern hills confirm an intentional connection of these early Christians to Akhenaten.[6] This is a connection that we have already seen through the worship of very early followers of Jesus in the very tombs themselves. However, another highly significant element in the relationship can be seen in the positioning of the monastery.

As has been previously noted, religious buildings in ancient times were not built just anywhere, without reference to surrounding features or orientation. The Christian monastery at Kom el-Nana is no exception. It was placed exactly midway between Akhenaten's Great Temple and the stele "N" (one of fifteen stelae that demarked the boundaries of the holy city of Akhetaten). Not only that, just as the orientation of the main prayer hall at Qumran was aligned almost exactly with the main outer walls of the Great Temple, all the main walls of the Kom el-Nana monastery were built in exact alignment with those of the Great Temple at Akhetaten!

The obvious question is, Why would the earliest followers of Jesus decide to build a house of worship at Kom el-Nana in the first place? The answer comes from the findings of Barry Kemp, an archaeologist who has been in charge of excavations at Amarna on behalf of the Egypt Exploration Society since 1985. Together with Michael Mallinson, he has undertaken a study of the geometric alignments of buildings and structures at Amarna.[7] They note that the site now known as Kom el-Nana was originally a holy place of worship for Queen Nefertiti.

The location of a Christian place of worship at Kom el-Nana was not an accident, a chance, or coincidence; it was an action of deliberate, purposeful intent. It clearly confirms that the earliest followers of Jesus revered the memory of Akhenaten and his wife, Nefertiti, and wanted to associate Jesus with them. This unimpeachable finding necessitates a complete revision of the understanding of the origins of Christianity, and

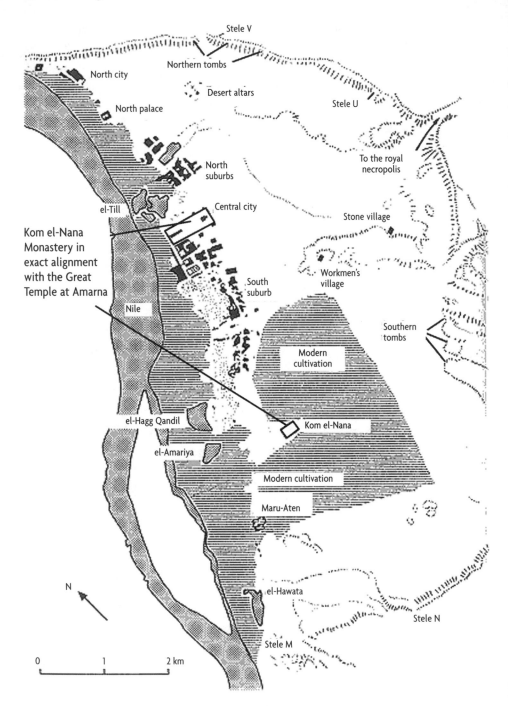

Stele V

Northern tombs

North city

Desert altars

North palace

Stele U

North suburbs

To the royal necropolis

el-Till

Central city

Stone village

Kom el-Nana Monastery in exact alignment with the Great Temple at Amarna

South suburb

Workmen's village

Nile

Southern tombs

Modern cultivation

el-Hagg Qandil

Kom el-Nana

el-Amariya

Modern cultivation

Maru-Aten

N

el-Hawata

Stele N

0    1    2 km

Stele M

*Fig. 37.1. Map showing the location of the monastery at Kom el-Nana, Amarna, and its alignment with the Great Temple.*

means that the Akhenaten-Nefertiti-Jacob-Joseph axis was the basic formulation for the beginnings of Christianity, as well as for Judaism, and Amarna was the cradle of both religions.

I have previously suggested in my book *The Mystery of the Copper Scroll of Qumran*[8] that the northern hill tombs are mentioned in the Copper Scroll as a place where other scrolls might have been hidden, and that Panehesy's tomb might well have been that of the biblical Joseph. This would indeed add even more significance to the choice of this particular tomb as a place of worship.

We can imagine the awe of these itinerant Jesus Essenes when they first entered the cavernous tomb of Panehesy. There on the wall, in even brighter colors than survive today, lit by the flickering light of their oil lamps, they would have seen a huge, glorious frieze of a royal figure wearing a crown and driving a chariot led by two magnificent, prancing, plume-bedecked white horses. Above this royal figure's head, the hands of God stretch forth to endow plenty and blessing on His disciple, and immediately above Akhenaten's head is the sign of the cross in the form of an ankh.

More than any other pharaoh, Akhenaten had raised the sign of the ankh, the symbol of life, to the highest plane of importance. This sign would become the earliest insignia of Jesus's followers. What more convincing imagery could there be than the scene that must have confronted those first pilgrims, a scene that we can still see to this day? The heavenly golden chariot pulled by white horses had been written about in the Hebrew Scriptures and the Dead Sea Scrolls.

Here was the messianic figure that the distant memories of Ezekiel and Elisha[9] described, and the same chariot that the Qumran Essenes themselves wrote about in their own unique texts. This chariot image and its associated royal figure foreshadow the allusions to them in the Book of Revelation—which perhaps had not yet been written (it is thought to have been composed in the second century C.E.). Elsewhere in the tomb of Panehesy, these early Jesus Essenes would have seen scenes of Akhenaten and Nefertiti worshipping in the finely decorated Great Temple of Akhetaten: the king riding his royal chariot while aiming his bow; a legendary winged bird; the sun disk of the Aten and its extended rays tipped by the ankh sign, giving life; and the outstretched hand giving sustenance. All these images were to be become burned into the psyche of Christianity forever and would be reproduced in literature, prayer, art, and design throughout the history of the church.

Here is the place where Jesus, as Melchizedek, is seen riding the chariot of Akhenaten flanked by his followers. Here is the place where the Holy Family of Mary and Joseph might have stood at the shrine held sacred to Akhenaten's One God.

Venturing into another nearby tomb, prepared for Akhenaten's chief administrator, Ay, these early pilgrims would have seen even more wonders, such as an inscribed wall beside the entrance to the tomb that records a hymn believed to have been composed by Akhenaten himself. It is paraphrased in Psalm 104 of the Bible and was the most dominant form of homage seen at Amarna.[10] While the pilgrims would not have been able to read the hieroglyphs, the pictograms, dominated by images of birds and ankh crosses, would have left lasting impressions on them. One image might well have made them step back and utter a gasp of astonishment. Almost at the center of the massive wall relief is the figure of a man pictured as if being crucified on a cross. (See page 11 of the color insert.)

Underlying the effect of these experiences, the importance of Egypt to early Christianity is testified to by the large number of churches and monasteries that developed along the Nile and in more remote parts of the country. To this day, there is a large Coptic presence in the area. In fact, the earliest presence of followers of Jesus in Egypt is attested to by the claim of Mark, sometime between 50 and 58 C.E., no more than twenty-five or so years after Jesus's crucifixion, that he was the first bishop of Alexandria.[11]

If Amarna was as important to the early followers of Jesus as the evidence here presented insists, then it will come as no surprise to learn that Panehesy's tomb was later extended into a more sophisticated church and the tomb itself enlarged. Nevertheless, the original reliefs of Nefertiti and Akhenaten were not erased, and the scene of Akhenaten driving his heavenly chariot is still recognizable today. It was most likely even more visually intact to the early followers of Jesus when they first saw it some two thousand years ago.

## Hebrew Writing at Akhetaten

From the evidence cited above, there can be little doubt that a very early presence of early followers of Jesus at Akhetaten is certain, and this link can be explained only by a link to the Essenes. The finding of actual hard, written evidence of a Hebrew presence, or evidence of the Essenes themselves, would be quite astounding. Surely, you are saying, there cannot be such evidence. If such evidence did exist, it would reinforce the demand for a radical change in our understanding of early Hebrew history. Well, prepare for a radical change in our understanding of early Hebrew history!

While there are numerous examples of hieroglyphic and hieratic writing from the Amarna period—and correspondence with Canaan in the Amarna letters[12] show a knowledge of Akkadian, Assyrian, Hurrian, and Hittite—there has been no previous manifestation of a Hebrew presence in a fourteenth-century-B.C.E. Akhetaten setting, apart from those I have previously demonstrated. The earliest credible reference to Israelites in Egypt comes in the time of Pharaoh Merneptah, circa 1200 B.C.E.

In February 1980, Geoffrey Thorndike Martin, Edwards Professor of Egyptology at the University of London, was reexamining the site of the tombs prepared for Akhenaten and Nefertiti at Akhetaten. On the floor of Room F in the Royal Tomb at Amarna, he came across some sherd debris bearing inscriptions. One of the sherds appeared to be from the shoulder of a cream-slipped amphora used as a wine container, with a hieratic docket written in black ink. The docket reads:

[Year] 17, sweet wine [of the estate (?) x of] the western river, the chief of the basin [N].[13]

The writing on the sherd also carries an ancient version of early script-form Semitic Hebrew with some letters consistent with pre–tenth-century-B.C.E. shapes, but others readily recognizable as direct antecedents of later Hebrew script writing. For an interpretation of the lettering, I consulted a number of Hebrew scholars, including Robert D. Leonard, past president of the Israel Numismatic Society in Illinois, who confirmed that the sherd contained early paleo-Hebrew writing. No one was certain of its meaning, although it was suggested that the words might mean "my soul" or "my spirit" (see figure 37.2).

Another scholar, Carol Brauner, of the Leo Baeck Education Centre, Haifa, Israel, reads the larger inscription as "RINHADHU" or "RONICHADHU" with a root term relating to "unity" or "a community." Alternatively the first letter might be a G (Hebrew, *gimmel*), as seen in tenth-century-B.C.E. inscriptions, rather than an *R* (Hebrew, *resh*).

On examining the inscriptions, I was immediately struck by two elements. The numbering system was the same as that seen in the Copper Scroll of Qumran, with exactly the same symbols used for single units, tens, and twenties, a precise system not found in any other Hebrew documents in Israeli history except those from Qumran. The Hebrew lettering reminded me, in style and shape, of lettering that appears on the shoulder of large ceramic jars found at Qumran that were almost certainly used for

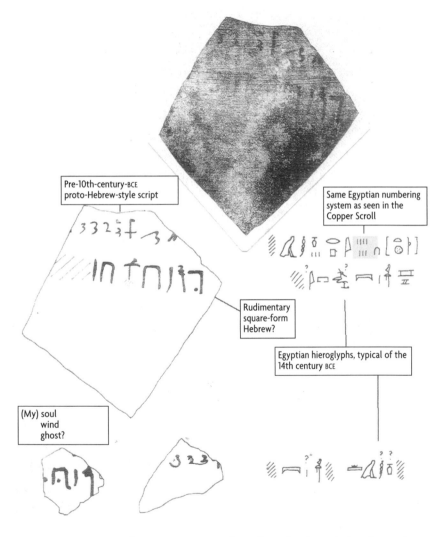

Fig. 37.2. *Ancient Hebrew inscription found in the Royal Tombs at Amarna.*

© ROBERT FEATHER, BASED ON AN ILLUSTRATION IN *THE ROYAL TOMB AT AMARNA*

(EGYPT EXPLORATION SOCIETY, 1989)

storing wine and other liquids rather than scrolls. Later research showed that one of the "Grandes jarres de la Periode 1b," illustrated in *L'Archeologie et les Manuscrits de la Mer Morte* by Roland de Vaux,[14] bears an uncanny resemblance to the inscription seen on the Room F sherd from the Royal Tomb at Amarna—even down to the lettering and its order.

The incredible evidence set forth in this chapter completes the circle: Akhenaten—Joseph/Jacob—Moses—Zadokite priests—Ezekiel—Qumran Essenes—early Christians—Akhenaten.

# ~ 38 ~

# The Holy Family in Egypt

If early followers of Jesus, and almost certainly those most closely associated with the Qumran Essenes, sought out Akhenaten's holy place in Egypt, is it possible that Jesus, who I maintain was at one time a member of the Qumran Essenes (in his childhood and also in his adult life), might have visited Akhetaten? With his knowledge of early Essenic history, there would have been a strong pull to do so. There are, indeed, several quite independent indicators that this actually occurred:

- The Christian Scriptures state that the Holy Family fled with Jesus to Egypt when he was a child (Matt. 2:13–15).
- Jewish tradition records that Ben Stada, a polemical name given to Jesus, was in Egypt in his adult life: "But is it not [the case that] Ben Stada [i.e., Jesus] brought magic spells from Egypt in the scratches on his flesh? They said to him, 'He was a fool and you cannot base laws on [that action of] fools.' Was he then the son of Stada? Surely he was the son of Pandira? Rabbi Hisda (a third-century Babylonian) said . . . " (traditions of Rabbi Eliezer, B. Sanh. 107b); "And a Rabbi has said, Jesus the Nazarene practiced magic and led Israel astray" (Babylonian Sanhedrin 107b/43a).
- The Nag Hammadi Codices (see chapter 13), alleged to be verbatim sayings of Jesus, were, like almost every other early text of the Christian Scriptures, found in Egypt. They show a Gnostic tendency closely identifiable with the outlook of the Qumran Essenes and their related movement of the Therapeutae in Egypt.
- In the Nag Hammadi text known as Gospel of the Egyptians, there is a pointed interest in Egypt and a clash of forces of light and darkness, in this instance exemplified by the Egyptian god of evil, Seth.

# Burial Practices at Qumran, Egypt, and Early Christian Settlements

Marked as this last example is, there is one further finding that also makes the link from Egypt, through the Essenes, and on into early Christianity. During his exploration of the Qumran cemetery in April 1966, Solomon H. Steckholl excavated a grave that, he noted, bore remarkable similarities to burials in the Minor Cemetery at Giza, Egypt. It was cut in the form of a shaft grave, with a recess at the bottom on the eastern face for the body. The space under the head of the corpse had been carefully marked for positioning, and an air pocket protected by bricks had been created to avoid any possibility of soil falling onto the dead body.[1]

This same form of burial, quite unknown in other parts of Judaea, was also recorded by Charles Clermont-Ganneau when describing one of the tombs in a cemetery in Wadi Yasul, near Jerusalem, an important early Christian burial site. His comment is extremely pertinent to the evidence indicating a Qumran-Essene early Christian connection: "The curious thing about it is that the place for the head and shoulders of the corpse is distinctly marked."[2]

The logical conclusions are that the Essenes were practicing a form of burial at Qumran that harked back over a thousand years to distant Egypt and that the early Christians had such a close association with the Qumran Essenes that they too adopted this strange and unique form of burial.

If a religious group emerges with apparently new teachings and beliefs, but shows marked similarities in basic beliefs, religious practices, social outlook, sexual mores, hierarchical structure, style of writing and phraseology, and choice of proof texts, and, in addition, lives at or adjacent to that existing group and copies its unique burial practices, it is not unreasonable to conclude that the new group emerged from, and was part of, that preexisting group.

# The Holy Family's Journey to Egypt

Another hugely telling piece of evidence asserts the validity of what retired professor Harold Ellens calls "the hermeneutical circle" connecting the Qumran Essenes and Jesus to the Egypt of Akhenaten.

Both the Christian Scriptures and historical tradition maintain that Jesus and his parents, Mary and Joseph, fled to Egypt from Judaea around 4 to 7 B.C.E. to escape the tyrannical threats of Herod the Great (Matt. 2:13–20).

As Robert Bauval notes in his book *Secret Chamber*,[3] the flight to Egypt and the appearance at Jesus's nativity of a star and the Magi are recorded only in the Gospel of Matthew, which many scholars believe may well have been composed in Alexandria, Egypt. This might help explain the story of the star of Bethlehem signaling the birth of Jesus, through the fascination the Egyptians had with Sirius as a star symbolizing the birth of a significant being.

If one had to predict where the family of Jesus might have stopped en route in their journey through Egypt, on the basis of the proposed connections I claim existed between the Qumran Essenes and Akhenaten, and between the Qumran Essenes and the earliest followers of Jesus, the following four destinations would have been hot favorites in their itinerary:

- Lake Mereotis (Marioot), near Alexandria, traditional location of the Therapeutae, close Egyptian associates of the Essenes
- Valley of Natrun, traditional location of the Therapeutae
- Leontopolis, near Heliopolis (Cairo), site of the temple founded by Onias IV, who, I maintain, was the Essenes' Teacher of Righteousness
- Amarna, site of Akhenaten's holy city

In horse-racing parlance, my shortest odds would be on Amarna, and the combination odds of all four of these highly significant Essenic-connected places featuring as important locations in the Holy Family's journey would be about ten thousand to one.

Take a look at the figure map on page 4 of the color insert in this book. It shows the route, strongly entrenched in Egyptian legend and tradition, of the Holy Family in Egypt. All four locations are included in the journey and are considered the most important of the numerous monastic centers that have grown up in Egypt.[4] So which of these locations is believed to be the most important?

The words of Pope Shenouda III, guardian of the national traditions of the Coptic Church in Egypt, give us the answer: "Now it was time for the Holy Family to set out for what is, arguably, the most meaningful destination of all in the land of Egypt, the place where there would be 'an altar to the Lord in the midst of the land of Egypt'—Gabal [Mount] Qussqam."[5] (See page 4 of the color insert.)

Nestled in the foothills of this mountain lies the monastery of Al-Moharraq, on the site where the Holy Family were reputed to have lived for six months, their longest stay at any one place in their four-year travels through Egypt. It was the culmination of their journey, and to this day the area surrounding the monastery is redolent of the Coptic Christian ethos, so much so that it is named the Second Bethlehem.[6] Why should this place have become so important to the Coptic Christians? At first glance, it appears to be in the middle of nowhere.

At the turn of the millennium, the vast site of Amarna would have been as bleak and desolate as it is today. The only pockets of habitation would have been small settlements on the west bank of the Nile, near the village of Qussqam. The monastery of Al-Moharraq lies directly opposite Amarna, at what was then one of the closest habitable places to Amarna. Whatever you believe about the legends surrounding the journey of the Holy Family in Egypt, there is almost always a kernel of truth that kindles a legend. That kindling has resulted in a surfeit of historical Christian places of worship in the vicinity of the Nile, some often in quite remote locations, which makes it difficult to justify the charge that they were invented to attract tourists.[7]

The preponderance of these witnesses to an earlier legend is concentrated around Amarna, the site of Akhenaten's ancient capital. The grain of truth, if there is one, behind the legends in this region indicates that the main destination of the Holy Family was the Amarna area. *Something* must have sparked the tradition, and the raft of other evidence that points to Amarna as a site of special interest to the Qumran Essenes and, by association, to the earliest followers of Jesus underlines the essential truth of this assertion.

## Cave Worship Theory

The traditional places of worship in the ancient Middle East, and particularly in Israel, were invariably associated with temples and with altars built on high places or in the open countryside.

The extraordinary finding that what appear to have been very early Christians worshipping in what was effectively a tomb-cave carved out of a hillside at Amarna adds an even more unusual aspect. One could argue that the worshippers were fleeing from persecution and simply sought refuge in a remote place for safety. They appear to have stayed for a long period, however, in a most inconvenient location, far from water and food sources.

It is worth quoting the description of the Christian cave dwellers of Akhetaten given by one of the earliest explorers of Amarna, Norman de Garis Davies, to get a flavor of what was going on in this remote part of Egypt:

> All this is clear proof that this hill-side was for some time the abode of a population numbering several hundreds. Security seems to have been a matter of consideration, for some of the little colonies are built like birds' nests on ledges of rock at the summit of the cliff, in spite of great inconvenience and danger. Even at the very end of the range, an hour's walk from the river, I found a large cave reached by a stairway cut in the rock, which staples for pendant lamps and the remains of coarse pottery showed plainly to have been the lonely home of some anchorite or refugee. . . . So sundered from the life of Egypt were these mountain dwellers that the use of mud bricks is limited to some buildings outside Tomb 6 [Panehesy's], which was then their place of worship. . . . Although I have not found a single Coptic graffito in these houses, I do not doubt that the builders were Copts.

Burials on the summit of the cliff around the area comprised round cairns built of the globular boulders that strew the hill, highly reminiscent of those at Qumran.

Describing the inner chamber of Panehesy's Tomb, Norman de Garis Davies continues:

> The apse seems to have been designed with a view to baptismal

immersion, for a font five-feet deep occupies nearly the whole space. Two rough steps would enable a person to scramble from the edge into the inner room through a narrow aperture that has been cut in the back wall.

The apse having been made, it was impossible to leave the pagan sculptures close by it in naked assertiveness. Yet the earliest worshippers seem to have thought it enough to daub the sacred cross, and an Alpha and Omega in red paint, over the figure of the Queen.[8] (See pages 8–9 of the color insert.)

One has to wonder if these early Christians had not, in fact, been led to the city of Akhetaten by Jesus himself—following Qumran Essenes who were already there. Although the main place of worship at Qumran was in the central building complex, where most of the daily activities took place, a precedent does seem to have been set at Qumran for cave worship.

In support of the so-called Worship-Cave Theory, there is evidence that a dissenting splinter group of Qumran Essenes existed that lived in caves farther afield from Qumran.[9] These caves (numbers 1, 2, 3, and 11), up to two miles distant from Qumran, were found to contain oil lamps and phylacteries (Hebrew, *tefillin*).[10]

This theory is still not proved, but in light of the incredible archaeological proof found in Panehesy's cavelike tomb at Amarna, the possibility that these dissidents were among the Qumran Essenes who became the earliest followers of or sympathizers with Jesus and took to worshipping in caves near Qumran may be of great significance.

So how early on in the history of Christianity did the followers of Jesus first gaze on these symbols in the ruins of Akhenaten's capital city? These symbols included the Aten sun disk; a king seated on a heavenly throne or riding a divine chariot, sometimes holding a bow and arrow; and a radiantly beautiful mother-figure queen, on whose image the Christians painted the ankh-cross sign and the Alpha and Omega. That all these iconic images had a profound effect on the psyche of those who gazed upon them is beyond question. These images are repeatedly referred to in verbal and physical imagery and in Christian literature, and we can get some idea of their impact and chronological provenance from biblical literature and artistic formulations.

## Verbal Imagery

Verbal descriptions of all the symbols seen in the tombs of Amarna are a central repetitive theme in the writings of the Christian Scriptures. Here are but a few examples:

### Sun

And [Jesus] was transfigured before them, and his face shone like the sun, and his clothes became as white as the light. (Matt. 17:2)

. . . by which the rising sun will come to us from heaven . . . (Luke 1:78)

And his countenance was as the sun shineth in his strength. (Rev. 1:16)

### Divine King Thrones

To him that overcometh will I grant to sit with me in my throne, even as I also overcame, and am set down with my Father in his throne. (Rev. 3:21)

### Divine Queen

A woman clothed with the sun, and the moon under her feet, and upon her head a crown of twelve stars. (Rev. 12:1)

### Cross

Far be it from me [Paul] to glory except in the cross of our Lord Jesus Christ. (Gal. 6:14)

### Alpha and Omega

I am Alpha and Omega, the beginning and the ending, saith the Lord. (Rev. 1:8)

## Physical Artifact Imagery

If the sun, as a divine designation, features strongly in the verbal imagery of Jesus's followers, manifestations of it in primitive Christian art forms are just as recognizable. Examples of the sun disk are also seen down through the history of the Israelites, in some instances positioned above the heads of the subjects.[11]

In the earliest Christian paintings, the sun disk sits in intimate contact with the subjects as a glowing golden sphere surrounding their heads. In some examples, such as Maestro Delle Vele's *Flight into Egypt,* which is in the church of St. Franceso Assis, in Umbria, Italy, Jesus and his family are seen with the disk around their heads incorporating Aten-like sun's rays within the design.

Perhaps even more remarkable is the eleventh-century crucifix painting *Betrayal of Jesus* in the Academia, Florence. Here Jesus is seen being kissed by his betrayer, Judas. Jesus's head is framed by a sun disk, and immediately above him the rear wall carries a relief that is almost certainly a memory of the Egyptian cartouche that appears immediately above the head of Akhenaten in the tomb of Panehesy. Not only is the shape and design similar to the Akhenaten cartouche, but it appears to incorporate some of the Egyptian hieroglyph shapes as well.

A more subtle connection to the Akhenaten period is seen in the occasional representation of the halo around the head of Jesus, a halo that incorporates sunspots. An example of this can be seen in the Bible Moralisée, dated 1235–1245 (Laborde facsimile 1911–27, British Library). In other instances, the halo exhibits part of the cross, especially in the case of members of the Holy Family; but as Maurice Cotterell puzzles over in his *Tutankhamun Prophecies,*[12] it is remarkable to find sunspot loops in the halo of Jesus. What could be the reason for this strange symbolism? Examination of the occurrence of this coincidence could yield the answer, apart from the obvious echoes of Amarna.

The Sothic cycle is an astronomical periodicity that reconciles the solar year of 365$\frac{1}{4}$ days against the 365-day annual helical rising of the star Sirius. It was well known in ancient times and is used to chronicle the history of Egypt. Once in every 1,460 years (365 ÷ 0.25), the rising of Sirius coincides with the rising of the sun on New Year's Day. Previous occurrences of this synchronicity were witnessed in 1599 C.E., in 139 C.E., and in 1321 B.C.E. The latter minimum appearance of sunspots occurred at a date very close to the Amarna period of Akhenaten. Perhaps the symbolism reflected in the Bible Moralisée was a deliberate attempt to indicate a temporal link between Jesus and the period of Akhenaten's reign.

Another feature of early Christian art was the inclusion of a dovelike bird. The earliest versions of this creature can be seen in the catacombs of Priscilla, near Rome. Of course, divine birds feature in pre-Christian Hebrew imagery, and that may have been a motivation for their usage, but it does not explain their employment in the Hebrew Scriptures in the first place or why it should be associated with Christian scenes.

A possible common interest in Akhenaten's vision gives a better explanation. In the earlier cartouches showing the name Aton or Aten, a single bird immediately adjacent to an ankh cross can be seen, and the dovelike bird is adorned with a sun disk. A good example of this vision, deeply etched on the Christian memory, can be seen in an eleventh-century-C.E. Greek Orthodox mosaic showing the Day of Pentecost, where Jesus's disciples are baptized by tongues of fire. Central to the scene is a dovelike bird with a golden sun disk around its head.[13]

There is no reasonable explanation for this early iconography, unless the artists were perpetuating a desire for early followers of Jesus to be intimately associated with a divine solar image that had all the characteristics of the Aten. When the question of why the golden halo appears so frequently in Christian art is posed to theologians or art historians, there is no cohesive answer, although one notable scholar, Giovanni Filoramo, writing about the Nag Hammadi codex, states: "If you read this slowly and carefully, with an open mind you will see that it is the SUN that Jesus is describing, which is the ancient Aten/Sun from the past ages of Egypt."[14]

Numerous other exemplars exist, particularly in early Egyptian icons and Italian paintings, and even though these were executed hundreds of years after Jesus, the power of handed-down oral detail should not be underestimated, and must have derived from these sources. Individual items of this imagery are, of course, found in other ancient representations, but none in the kind of combinations that appear at Amarna.

### Sign of the Cross

What the earliest actual form of the cross looked like, and how early in Christian history it became a symbol of reverence, is a matter of hot debate. To quote three currently expressed views of its existence in the first three centuries C.E.: "In the first three centuries of the Christian era the

Cross had been a symbol of minor importance" (Jan Wilhelm Drijvers[15]); "[The cross was] almost unknown as a Christian emblem" (Michael Grant[16]); "There is no known depiction of the Crucifixion until after the time of Constantine the Great" (Cyril Pocknee[17]).

These views are demolished by the evidence of Professor Carsten Peter Thiede, of Basel University in Switzerland, and by the evidence I have advanced that the earliest followers of Jesus, in the second and possibly first centuries C.E., worshipped in front of a wall relief in the tomb of Panehesy that was replete with signs of the ankh cross. They would almost certainly have also seen the simple cross that formed the centerpiece of a wall relief in the nearby tomb of Ay.

In their recent book *The Quest for the True Cross*,[18] Carsten Thiede and Matthew D'Ancona cite a number of examples where the cross was clearly in use long before Emperor Constantine's time. At Herculaneum (near Pompeii) a simple cross was found in a house, marked on the wall of an upper room. Elsewhere in the ruins of the same desolated town, the so-called SATOR palindrome, a palindromic raster that incorporates a simple cross, can be seen:[19]

R O **T** A S

O P **E** R A

**T E N E T**

A R **E** P O

S A **T** O R

As Herculaneum was destroyed by a volcanic eruption in 79 C.E., both these inscriptions must predate that event.

More recently, archaeological excavations at Bethsaida,* Israel,[20] have unearthed a piece of pottery marked with a Greek cross† with a circle in the center. This appears to have been subsequently modified to form

---

*Bethsaida was located on the opposite side of the Galilee and is said to have been the birthplace of St. Peter.

†A Greek cross has equidistant arms, whereas the Roman cross has a horizontal arm intersecting the vertical arm at a distance one third of the way down the vertical arm.

a Roman cross. The context of the find dates the pottery to between 100 B.C.E. and 70 C.E. Father Bargil Pixner, an Israeli archaeologist, found a similar cross marked on a basalt stone near Bethsaida, and made the piquant comment that the cross "was originally meant to symbolize the sun as a cross-like symbol of Christ."[21]

So what was the form of the cross initially used by the earliest followers of Jesus? To quote Professor Carsten Thiede: "There is strong prima-facie evidence to suggest that the simple, unadorned image of the Cross was in use as a mainstream Christian symbol long before Constantine's long reign. The two signs used were the Egyptian 'ankh' and the 'Chi-Rho.' "[22]

That the *chi-rho* utilized the first two letters of the Greek word for Christ, Khristos, is accepted as a highly plausible explanation for its use, but why the ankh sign?[23] No one has yet given a sensible reason for the adoption of this usage.

As noted earlier, central to the sight the first pilgrims saw when they entered the tomb of Panehesy would have been a vision of a huge heavenly king in glowing, golden, sunlit glory, riding a dazzling chariot drawn by two white horses. Directly above the king's crowned head, in the center of the wall-relief cartouche, was the sign of the ankh—a cross with a circle at the top.

For the Egyptians and Akhenaten, the ankh was the symbol of life— "the breath of life." The design, being one of the very earliest motifs seen in Egypt, was derived from a vertical line—representing the Nile—with a circle at its top, which represented the Delta region, the horizontal line intersecting the vertical line designating where the first capital city of Inebhedj (Memphis) stood on the Nile. For the early followers of Jesus, the ankh incorporated the sign of a cross on which Jesus had died and a circular shape they took to be the sun. It became their earliest symbol of worship and one of mutual recognition: the ankh cross incorporating the sun.[24]

# ~ 39 ~

# The Qumran Essenes' Presence at Amarna

If early Christian literature reflected the imagery of Panehesy's tomb, how much more powerful must have been the Qumran Essenes' memory of their ancestors' presence at Amarna?

Ezekiel's visions in the first and tenth chapters of his book in the Hebrew Scriptures already intertwined winged creatures, chariots, and a heavenly throne glowing with light.[1] The Qumran-Essenes' texts have a much clearer view of the scene and describe it in words that demonstrate the memory of an eyewitness account—words one might well use today for the incredible pictorial representations of Akhenaten's chariot and the Great Temple structure and chambers that can still be seen in the tombs of Amarna. A series of Qumran texts, Songs for the Sabbath Sacrifice, specifically describes and praises "wall images and movements of chariot throne" and is but one of many examples of references to these scenes recalled in the Qumran scrolls. One would be hard pressed to find an Israelite setting for these notions:

> The Cherubim praise the vision of the Throne-Chariot above the celestial sphere, and they extol the [radiance] of the fiery firmament beneath the throne of His glory. And the holy Angels come and go between the whirling wheels, like a fiery vision of most holy spirits; and around them stream rivulets of molten fire, like incandescent bronze, a radiance of many brilliant colors, of exquisite hues gloriously mingled. The Spirits of the living God move in constant accord with the glory of the Wonderful Chariot. The whispered voice of blessing accompanies the roar of their advance, and they praise the

Holy One on their way of return. . . . The vestibules by which they enter, the spirits of the most holy inner Temple . . . is engraved on the vestibules by which the King enters, luminous spiritual figures. . . . Among the spirits of splendor there are works of [art of] marvelous colors . . . glorious innermost Temple chambers, the structure of [the most ho]ly [sanctuary] in the innermost chambers of the King. (Dead Sea Scroll fragment 4Q405)

There can be little doubt that the king being referred to in this passage is not an Israelite king. There are no biblical descriptions that match these temple chambers. Nor can there be any doubt that the description of the heavenly chariot matches the reality of a Pharaonic state chariot of the period of Akhenaten, as, for example, described by Cyril Aldred in his book *Akhenaten, King of Egypt:* "The decorative panels are made of heavy gold foil worked in a repoussé technique, backed with gesso and

*Fig. 39.1. Akhenaten's successor, Tutankhaten (who later changed his name to Tutankhamun), riding his royal chariot with bow and arrow in hand.*

linen, with scenes of the chastising of foreign foes by the king as a sphinx. The gold is enhanced with bosses and borders inlaid with colored glass, faience and similar ornamentation, to produce a gorgeous and dazzling appearance."[2]

The Book of Revelation of the Christian Scriptures takes up the theme:

I am Alpha and Omega, the first and the last. . . . And I saw, and behold a white horse: and he that sat on him had a bow; and a crown was given unto him; and he went forth conquering, and to conquer. (1:10; 6:2)[3]

## Jewish Memories of Chariots

One of the most striking features of excavations in Israel has been the prolific findings of mosaic decorations in ancient synagogues. Of these, the floor in a synagogue at Sepphoris, in the Galilee, is one of the most beautiful and extensively preserved, but it has posed a number of intractable problems for commentators. Dated to the fifth century C.E., it was discovered almost accidentally in 1993, and its central piece is a huge astronomical picture. The director of the dig, Zeev Weiss, of the Hebrew University, Israel, wrote of the dig: "As surprising as it may seem to find a zodiac in a synagogue, it is even more shocking to find a depiction of the sun god, Helios, riding in his chariot drawn by four horses (the *quadriga*). But the fact is that both the zodiac and the Helios with his *quadriga* have been found in several ancient synagogues—at Hammat-Tiberias, Beit Alpha, Na'aran and Ussfiyeh, among others. . . . The Sepphoris mosaic represents him only with a sun disk and chariot."[4]

After struggling for an explanation, Weiss eventually leaves it to the reader to decide.

The simple explanation is that in this and other examples there is a clear allusion to Egypt and the sun disk of the Aten. That the person riding the chariot is Akhenaten, not Helios, is clearly indicated by the design of the chariot depicted; it and other associated symbolisms are typical of the period one thousand years earlier.

## The Heavenly World

While looking at the heavenly chariot, it is timely to make some comparison between the language of the Qumran Essenes and Jewish and Christian mysticism in relation to the heavenly world in general. In the Qumran-Essene texts, there is a vision of angels and a certain Melchizedek, a heavenly being who appears to be both a priestly and a heavenly warrior, and who will exact vengeance on behalf of God. He has been identified as both the Angel Michael and the Angel of Light.[5] There has been much supposition as to where this imagery came from. A Zoroastrian connection is cited for the introduction of ideas on angels, and this may well be the source, although one is tempted to look yet again to ancient Egypt, where there were similar cherubic and seraphic mystical guardians of the heavens. Much more work needs to be done in this area.

One aspect that does ring a bell, however, is the seven heavenly sanctuaries of the world to come mentioned in the Dead Sea Scrolls, again from the Songs of Sabbath Sacrifice. In this heavenly environment, there is also a notion of seven archangels. One has only to look at the ancient Egyptian concept of seven forms of Osiris waiting in the underworld for the dead to transfer through the different compartments, or gates, into a new life to see the related allusions. This Osiris symbolism is expanded in the Egyptian Book of Caverns, which describes a heavenly journey through successive caves between sunset and sunrise. Here, however, there are now seven mythical genii of the High God in attendance.[6]

Osiris is lord of the past night, and the journey of the dead was often depicted as a being overseen by a boat with three Watchers, almost certainly one of the subjects of the Book of Enoch, where they are seen as keeping lookout against the appearance of the evil Seth. This late New Kingdom–period theater recorded in the ancient Egyptian Book of Gates involves a night journey of the sun and closely reflects the ideas of the time just after the collapse of the Akhenaten period.[7]

## The Heavenly Throne

One particular Dead Sea Scrolls fragment (4Q491) found in Cave 4, very near the Qumran ruins, talks of a human taking a place "among the gods." This exalted individual is also an exceptional teacher. Several other Qumran and biblical texts promote heavenly enthronement as a reward for the pious in the afterlife.[8]

Countless attempts have been made to find someone to fit the role—Enoch, Moses, Aaron, King David, the Teacher of Righteousness—but the glass slipper never fits comfortably. As John J. Collins, professor of Hebrew Bible and postbiblical Judaism at Chicago University, concludes, "The implied authorship remains enigmatic."[9]

There is, however, one long, slender 4Q186 perfect foot that fits the glass slipper. The phrase "beloved of the King"[10] is so typical of an oft-repeated epitaph of Egyptian pharaohs that it gives the game away. This enigmatic figure whose feet are described in the Dead Sea Scroll fragment 4Q186 is never openly named, but he appears in a Greek formulation in the Copper Scroll as ΚεΝΧΑΓΗΝΘε*—King Akhenaten, as the supreme teacher of his new religious philosophy, who rides a heavenly chariot, and even boasts that his exalted position brings him into close proximity to God himself.[11]

Can there be any doubt that Matthew, at the very beginning of the Christian Scriptures, makes a special effort to establish Jesus's Egyptian credentials?

> When he arose, he took the young child and his mother by night, and departed into Egypt: and was there until the death of Herod: that it might be fulfilled which was spoken of the Lord by the prophet, saying, Out of Egypt have I called my son. (Matt. 2:14–15)

The question is: Why did Matthew feel such a strong need to tie Jesus to Egypt? It is my contention that both of the messiahs awaited by the Qumran Essenes originated in Egypt, and therefore it is no surprise to find that the new Messiah, Jesus of the Christian Scriptures, was also to be associated with Egypt. These two messiahs were, I maintain, King Akhenaten and his high priest, Meryra.

It could be argued, as the Dead Sea Scrolls seem to indicate, that a possible third "Egyptian" messiah was awaited by the Essenes, and that this

---

*The Greek letters Χ, Γ, and Θ have the English sounds of *kh*, *g*, and *th*, respectively.

"prophet like Moses," who clearly came out of Egypt, was the Egyptian antecedent to whom Matthew was alluding.

The prophets Isaiah, Jeremiah, Ezekiel, Daniel, Hosea, Joel, and Zechariah, however, whose words were to be fulfilled, refer to a restoration out of Egypt that is linked to the time of Joseph or the distant future End Days. Joseph lived much earlier than Moses, and, of course, I equate Joseph with the dates of Pharaoh Akhenaten and his high priest, Meryra.

# ~ 40 ~

# Conclusions and Significance of the Discoveries

I f my findings at Qumran are correct, this is the first time that the burial places of John the Baptist and Jesus have been identified with any degree of certainty. The earthly burial grounds of Jesus have previously been posited as being at the site of the Church of the Holy Sepulchre and alternatively at the Garden Tomb, both locations in Jerusalem.

In the research I would present another possibility—a burial of Jesus near Qumran. The significance of the new discoveries, if correct, is potentially of immense and profound importance to Christianity, as well as to Judaism and Islam. These discoveries will necessitate a revision of the understanding of how the Christian Scriptures came to be written and the nature of their roots. Nevertheless, none of these suggested possible locations matters in terms of the "risen Christ" and the central interest for Christians of His spiritual reality.

The consequences of Jesus's afterlife not involving a bodily resurrection have been the subject of an ongoing and fierce debate since the foundation of the Jesus Seminar in 1985 by Robert Funk, a Guggenheim Fellow and professor at the University of Montana. Initially comprising seventy-four senior members, the Jesus Seminar is made up primarily of Americans, including John Dominic Crossan, a professor at DePaul University, Chicago; Marcus Borg, a professor at Oregon State University; Lane McGaughy, a professor at Willamette University, Salem, Oregon; Episcopal Bishop John Shelby Spong, of Newark, New Jersey; and Barbara Thiering, of Sydney University. Many of these scholars maintain that a bodily resurrection of Jesus did not occur and tend to take the view that a spiritual resurrection and a gnostic understanding of Jesus's message are the path to true Christianity.[1]

Many other Christian scholars and clerics around the world have adopted this type of stance, but many more traditionalists hold firm to the belief that Jesus had a corporeal resurrection, including N. T. Wright, dean of Lichfield Cathedral, England, and former professor of theology at Oxford University; Professor William Farmer, a professor at Southern Methodist University; Craig Blomberg, of the Christian Research Institute; and J. P. Moreland and Mike Wilkins, in their book *Jesus Under Fire*. The traditionalists also tend to reject any possibility of Jesus being a member of the Qumran Essenes.

One prominent member of the Jesus Seminar, John Dominic Crossan, sets out a theological position that would protect the integrity of the church were the remains of Jesus ever to be discovered. In his book *Birth of Christianity* he declares, "Bodily resurrection has nothing to do with a resuscitated body coming out of its tomb."[2]

Ironically, if the hard-line Christian theologians were more amenable to the idea of Jesus being a member of the Qumran Essenes, the potential net gains could be of enormous value to Christianity. Even for the more liberal forces, historical speculation could become historical fact.[3]

The opinion of mainstream modern research with regard to the reality of Jesus and how it has shifted over the decades can be briefly summarized as follows:

- In the 1930s: "I do indeed think that we can know almost nothing concerning the life and personality of Jesus, since the early Christian sources show no interest in either, are moreover fragmentary and often legendary; and other sources about Jesus do not exist" (Rudolf Bultman).[4]
- In the 1950s: "Dissatisfaction with this position engenders renewed research for the historical Jesus" (Ernst Käsemann).[5]
- In the 1980s: "The dominant view today seems to be that we can know pretty well what Jesus was out to accomplish, that we can know a lot about what he said, and that those two things make sense within the world of first-century Judaism.
    1. Jesus was baptized by John the Baptist.

2. Jesus was a Galilean who preached and healed.
3. Jesus had a following of disciples and spoke of there being twelve.
4. Jesus confined his activity to Israel.
5. Jesus engaged in a controversy about the temple.
6. Jesus was crucified outside Jerusalem by the Roman authorities" (E. P. Sanders[6]).

These latest conclusions are based on internal readings of the Christian Scriptures and a study of the sociohistorical setting of Jesus's lifetime. The external evidence, independent of the Christian Scriptures, for any of these conclusions is admittedly thin, and even the contemporary historical record of Jesus's very existence is virtually nil. The conclusions do not assume any membership of John the Baptist or Jesus in the community of Qumran, and yet Professor E. P. Sanders calls these "almost indisputable facts."

If Jesus and John the Baptist were onetime members of the Qumran Essenes, however, as I maintain, and the first five conclusions of Professor Sanders become linked to a real historical background, his "almost . . . facts" become virtual certainties. There is now a known heritage of factors unique to Qumran—baptism, healing, a council of twelve, extreme apocalyptic concern for Israel, antagonism toward the Temple—to support Professor Sanders's conclusions. If Jesus was buried at Qumran, less than ten miles from Jerusalem, even the crucifixion of Jesus comes into the frame. Placing Jesus as a member of the Qumran-Essene community, or even as a previous member who was perceived as no longer adhering to its strict formula, provides, for the first time, a coherent and rational explanation for the reactions to many of Jesus's actions and statements—for example, why the Temple authorities in Jerusalem abruptly came down so heavily on Jesus.

There is no historical evidence for the assertion in the Christian Scriptures that Jesus, as the apparent leader of a new movement, presented any threat to their authority. At Jesus's trial (Matt. 27:23; Mark 15:14; Luke 23:13; John 18:38), he was not found guilty of any misdemeanor against the Temple or its teachings, except for the charge of blasphemy, which in itself presented no danger to the Sadducean Temple authorities.

Place Jesus as a member of the Qumran Essenes, however, and the context and background of mutual hostility makes him an altogether different kind of challenge for the Temple hierarchy. For the Sadducees, the Essenes' religious philosophy had long been a serious threat to their privileged position of controlling Temple finances and influence on the Jewish populace. A fragmentary letter from the Qumran community found among the Dead Sea Scrolls (4QMMT), believed to have been written by the Teacher of Righteousness himself, castigates the Temple authorities for their misdemeanors.

Many of the challenges espoused by the Essenes struck at the very heart of old-fashioned Judaism and found a sympathetic ear among the hard-pressed majority suffering under the yoke of the Roman occupation:

- The righteousness of the poor
- The value of spirituality as opposed to material things
- The possibility of resurrection
- The expectation of an imminent apocalyptic era when all wrongs would be righted
- A messiah, or messiahs, who would oust the Romans and shepherd in the apocalyptic age

That Jesus reviled the Temple, just as the Essenes did, can be seen in his attitude to it and from the attitude of one of his close followers, Stephen. Attested to have died circa 40 C.E., Stephen sets out his views on the Temple in Acts chapters 6 and 7. Here there is a specific repudiation, not only of the Herodian Second Temple, but also of Solomon's Temple. It seems that the early followers of Jesus held exactly the same view as did the Qumran Essenes on the legitimacy of these temples—a view unlike that of any other contemporary religious movement. Even more telling, both groups avowed that the Tabernacle of the Wilderness was the only place ordained by God.[7]

Now it can be seen that the arrival of Jesus on the streets of Jerusalem, preaching a potent form of all these new Essenian ideas, combined with his own divine message, presented a real threat to the Sadducees and the Temple authorities, headed by their supreme court, the Sanhedrin. These authorities had already witnessed, and perhaps been instrumental in, the death of John the Baptist and the removal of one thorn in their side. Now they wanted the downfall of an even more potent advocate of the new ideas. If Jesus was a member of the Qumran Essenes who had struck out on his own after graduation, as I suggest and as the evidence forcefully indicates, the reasons for his trial and crucifixion as described in the Christian Scriptures suddenly take on a new, realistic background.

This may well be the reason why the Temple authorities drew the Roman authorities' attention to an upstart who was known as the King of the Jews, not that the Roman prefect Pontius Pilate would have been unaware of Jesus's rebellious activities (as portrayed in the Christian Scriptures). Anyone known as the King of the Jews would have been a direct affront to the emperor and to Roman rule. Previous governors of Judaea had already crucified at least four claimant messiahs before Jesus, and more would later be dealt with in the same merciless manner. John the Baptist had been put to death by Herod Antipas, a Roman collaborator, and there is no reason to imagine that Rome would not have applied the same harsh punishment to Jesus—a punishment exacted many times in other parts of the empire wherever a leader arose to challenge the emperor's authority—regardless of the demands of a clique of Temple priests.

Why the Christian Scriptures should cast the Jewish rabble in such a poor light is not hard to discern. Paul, a cosmopolitan freethinker who moved freely around Rome's empire, would have been keen to present the story of Jesus's death as the responsibility primarily of the hierarchical Jews, because he wanted to expand the message of Jesus to the Gentile world and mainly to the Romans.

## Monumental Gains for Christianity

The Stone of Thorns may well confirm that Jesus was guided and nurtured within a devoutly special form of Judaism—a community of Essenes with roots firmly in the traditional Testaments of Moses.

Does this recognition undermine the uniqueness of the origins of Jesus's teachings and really pose a threat to Christianity? The simple answer is no. An acceptance of this common heritage, in fact, adds beauty to the unique aspects of Jesus. In the view of an enlightened Christian like Father Joseph Fitzmyer, a mature Christian should accept these commonalities but remain secure in a faith that holds that Christ had divine attributes as the Son of God, and that he came back from the dead to remind the world that his message lived beyond the grave.

Placing Jesus in the historical context of Qumran has another benefit. Resetting him in an authentic monotheistic community of beliefs and ideas obliterates the attempts that have been made to coat Jesus artificially in Hellenism and the Syrio-Greek-Roman-Egyptian cults of Adonis, Tammus, Mithras, Dionysus, Isis, Osiris, and so on. Jesus is not an amalgam of mythical stories, as some storytellers have suggested. His message and teachings are mainstream monotheism, underpinned by the traditions of a devout sect that strove, more than any other group of its time, to bring back its religion to its essential roots.

The gnostic elements of the Qumran Essenes, their hidden teachings and inner spirituality, should hold no fears for Christianity as it long predated the kind of gnosticism that the church was later to do battle with when ethereal philosophizing came to question whether Jesus was a real person.

Far from undermining the Christian bastion of belief in Jesus, Jesus's earlier membership in the Qumran Essenes reinforces the reality of his teachings and sets him in a historical context that is based on verifiable fact. It also helps clarify many ambiguous passages in the Christian Scriptures (as many Christian scholars already acknowledge) and explains where the inspiration for much of his teaching may have come from. It in no way compromises the many aspects of what Jesus taught or the Christian belief in his virgin birth, divinity, and resurrection after death, which are, in the end, a matter of faith.

## Gains for Judaism and Islam

If there are gains for Christianity in a recognition that Jesus was closely associated with a Jewish sect, there are also potential gains for Judaism and Islam.

For Muslims, Jesus is a rabbi and prophet, heir to a long line of Jewish teachers, but he is not a god or Son of God. The corroborative evidence here advanced for the existence of a real Jesus adds to the justification of Islam's view of Jesus.

Jews would no doubt view Jesus in a similar manner were it not for Paul's interpretation of Jesus as Jesus Christ. It was mainly as a reaction to Paul's Jesus as Son of God, and the subsequent denigration of Judaism in the light of this revelation, that motivated Judaism to reject Jesus in his entirety.

Enlightened Christians, following the lead of the Catholic Church under Pope John Paul II, have today admitted and apologized for this denigration, which in its extreme manifestation helped bring about the horrors of the Holocaust.

Pope Paul's moving visit to Israel in the spring of 2000 was an endorsement of the Vatican's *Nostra Aetate* declaration of 1965 and recognition of the State of Israel in 1993. The church condemned anti-Semitism, renounced the Christian mission to the Jews, and confirmed the justness of God's continued Covenant with the Jewish People.[8]

To mix some metaphors, the mountain has moved toward reconciliation with Judaism. Judaism needs to move closer toward the mountain. The mechanism to build a bridge between Judaism and Christianity and the rest of the world was encapsulated by Solomon Shechter, an early-twentieth-century Jewish scholar,[9] when he explained that the idea that God chose the Jews as His special people does not mean to the exclusion of other nations of the world. The rabbinic understanding of the idea that the Jews were a "chosen people" is that God gave His unconditional love first to the Jewish people, but that this love was from then on available to everyone in the world to find by many different routes.

Unto me every knee shall bow, every tongue shall swear devotion.
(Isaiah 45:23)

Judaism and Islam have nothing to fear from an enlightened view of Jesus, and much to revere.

The first part of this book set out evidence that points to a close association between Jesus and John the Baptist and the Essene community living at Qumran during the early part of the first century C.E. Collectively, the evidence is overwhelming that John the Baptist was buried at Qumran. If this is true, then it adds to the tangible physical and circumstantial indications that Jesus, his closest contemporary, was also buried near Qumran.

There is more than just a pile of inanimate stones and timeless scenery in the silent wilderness ruins and cemeteries at Qumran. There is something that cannot be defined, something that asks a question more eloquently than I ever can. Is this a place of mystery and true holiness? I can only answer, Go there, and see and feel the inspirational atmosphere for yourself.

Is this, then, the burial place of Jesus? All the indications seem to confirm the possibility, but there is, as yet, no absolute proof. All I can do is present the powerful literal and visual evidence. All I know is that Jesus's teachings shine a crystal-clear beam of coherent light back through the ages to the unconditional love of God professed by Jacob and Joseph, Akhenaten and Nefertiti. It is a light that shines forward to the pure distillation of those same ideals enshrined by Muhammad, leading one to believe that Judaism, Christianity, and Islam may well be the one true Holy Trinity.

# — Appendix 1 —

## 1956 Letter from the Jerusalem Team and Allegro's Response

Letter from the Jerusalem Team published in
*The Times* (of London), March 16, 1956

Dear Sir,

It has come to our attention that considerable controversy is being caused in certain broadcasts* of Mr. John Allegro, of the University of Manchester, concerning the Dead Sea Scrolls. We refer particularly to such statements as imply that in these scrolls a close connection is to be found between a supposed crucifixion of the "teacher of righteousness" of the Essene sect and the Crucifixion and the Resurrection of Jesus Christ. The announced opinions of Mr. Allegro might seem to have special weight, since he is one of the group of scholars engaged in editing yet unpublished writings from Qumran.

In view of the broad repercussions of his statements, and the fact that the materials on which they are based are not yet available to the public, we, his colleagues, feel obliged to make the following statement. There are no unpublished texts at the disposal of Mr. Allegro other than those of which the originals are at present in the Palestine Archaeological Museum where we are working. Upon the appearance in the press of citations from Mr. Allegro's broadcasts we have received all the pertinent materials, published and unpublished. We are unable to see in the texts the "findings" of Mr. Allegro.

We find no crucifixion of the "Teacher," no deposition from the cross, and no "broken body of their Master" to be stood guard over until

---

*The contents of the BBC broadcast were picked up, and given considerable publicity, by the *New York Times*.

Judgement Day. Therefore there is no "well-defined Essenic pattern into which Jesus of Nazareth fits," as Mr. Allegro is alleged in one report to have said. It is our conviction that either he has misread the texts or he has built up a chain of conjectures which the materials do not support.

Yours faithfully,
Roland de Vaux, O.P., J. T. Milik, P. W. Skehan, Jean Starcky, and John Strugnell
Palestine Archaeological Museum, P.O.B. 40, Jerusalem

## Response by John Allegro published in
## *The Times* (of London), March 20, 1956

Sir,
My attention has been drawn to a letter appearing in your columns of March 16 written by my colleagues of the "Dead Sea Scrolls team" in Jerusalem. It appears that they take exception to my reconstruction of the history of the Qumran sect and the death of its founder, the so-called "Teacher of Righteousness," on the grounds that I have misread or misconstrued the evidence.

It should be appreciated by your readers, in the first place, that any such reconstruction must, of necessity, be based largely on inference, since nothing in the nature of a history book or "Gospel" of the New Testament type has been or is likely to be forthcoming from Qumran. We shall not, therefore, expect to find Hebrew texts giving intimate details of the lives of Qumran personalities. We do have certain vague references in biblical commentaries from the sect's library that have to be interpreted as best we can.

We know, for instance, that the teacher was persecuted by a certain "wicked priest," in the "house of his exile," presumed to be Qumran. It was long ago suggested that this persecutor could be identified with Alexander Jannaeus, the Jewish priest-king of the second and first century B.C., and this view has steadily gained ground among scholars. From Josephus we learn that Jannaeus practised the cruel punishment of crucifixion, and, indeed, on one occasion had 800 Pharisaic rebels executed in this way in Jerusalem, following an unsuccessful revolt.[1] From this alone it would have been a not unreasonable inference that the teacher suffered the same fate, since he, too, had rebelled against the

Jerusalem priesthood. But now, as my colleagues are well aware, a newly discovered biblical commentary from Qumran not only offers some support for the Jannaeus dating by certain historical allusions, but mentions this practice of crucifixion, or, as it says, "hanging men up alive."

Since the Qumran commentators do not refer to events unless they have some special importance for themselves or their times, we can reasonably assume that this form of execution had some particular relevance for their own history, although the commentary mentions their master. My publication of the column concerned has been unfortunately delayed for a number of reasons outside my control, but should be available to scholars in the summer number of the Journal of Biblical Literature. Yet, important as this reference is, the theory remains no more than inference, claiming only probability, and I have myself never gone further than this in advancing it.

Years ago it was suggested by scholars that the teacher was expected to rise again as priestly Messiah. Allusions gleaned from a number of unpublished fragments from the fourth cave seem to support this idea, and an article now in the course of preparation will lay most of the new messianic material before scholars in the next few months. But it must be appreciated again that we have no detailed theological treatise from Qumran comparable, for instance, with the Pauline letters, and we can only work by inference. Yet, if indeed the covenanters did expect the resurrection of their teacher, as I am convinced they did, then they must have buried him with particular care, and, if he had been crucified, taken his body down from the stake, instead of leaving it to moulder there, as was the custom with this form of execution. Perhaps we shall learn more of this matter of the burial anon.

I presume the real core of my colleagues' objections is in the inferences that have been drawn by others by a comparison of the hypothetical reconstruction of events with similar occurrences recorded in the Christian gospels. I, too, deplore such wide sweeping generalizations about the historicity of the person of Jesus or the validity of the Church's claim from such points of details. It is true that in my last talk I referred back to my reconstruction of events as a bridge to the following discussion of the importance of these scrolls from the point of view of Christian origins. However, the remainder of my talk made it quite clear that any further identification of the two masters was out of the question, since the one was a priest, expected to come again as a priestly Messiah, and the other was a layman, whose followers claimed for him the office of Davidic Messiah.

In the phraseology of the New Testament in this connection we find many points of resemblance to Qumran literature, since the sect also were looking for the coming of a Davidic Messiah who would arise with the priest in the last days. It is in this sense that Jesus "fits into a well-defined messianic (not 'Essenic,' as I was wrongly quoted—the question of whether this sect were Essenes is still open) pattern."

There is nothing particularly new or striking in the idea. As far as I am aware, it has never been doubted that the messianic ideas and phraseology of the New Testament are taken over from Jewish sources. The importance of the scrolls is that for the first time we have contemporary documents bearing witness of those ideas over the most crucial years before the Church's birth. The vast difference between the Greek Church's divine Saviour of the world and the Davidic Prince of Qumran is obvious enough, and is best described by theologians of the standing of my Jerusalem colleagues.

No one has been more surprised at the reception of these "popular" talks in certain quarters than myself, since I was not aware that I was saying anything particularly new or which could not have been inferred by anyone else on the published evidence. It is true that unpublished material in my care made me more willing to accept certain suggestions made previously by other scholars on what have appeared to me to be insufficient grounds. Professor Dupont-Sommer, for instance, went far beyond my position several years ago, and I would still not follow his views entirely now. Nevertheless, his acute perception of the importance of these scrolls for the study of Christian origins from the very beginning is to be applauded.

As to the question of whether I have misread my texts or not, the question can best be decided by the consensus of scholarly opinion when these texts have been published, but, in fact, it hardly affects the general inferences which I have drawn and which appear to be the subject of your correspondents' letter.

Yours truly,
John M. Allegro
12, St. Ives Crescent
Brooklands, Sale, Cheshire

# Appendix 2

## 1956 Letter from John Allegro to Frank Moore Cross

**Letter to Frank Moore Cross dated March 6, 1956**

12, St. Ives Crescent
Brooklands, Sale, Cheshire

Dear Frank,

I received your letter before I had stuck down the flap of the envelope containing pNahum,* and was very glad to have it. At least, it was friendly, and that, believe me, is something at the moment, and a good deal more than I have been receiving from de Vaux and Harding, as you will have gathered from my covering letter.

No, there is nothing on the messianic angle in 3Q, and I was not using that fabulous document in making my talks. But I am very annoyed that Skehan should have apparently been shown its contents, when you haven't. Why don't you write to de Vaux or Harding and demand to be told what is in it: you've certainly as much right to know as Skehan, in fact, a hell of a sight more. But surely you've guessed by now, why all this secrecy before the excavations.

I know, of course of your view about the Teacher, an eschatological figure. But it won't do you know. I'll be interested to know what you think when you've read the pNah† article. And unless you are disassociating the *dwrs htwrh* from the Teacher (Florilegium), how can you explain his coming "with the *smh* David"?—in "the last days." I fully agree about their regarding themselves as living in the Last days in one

---

*Variant name for scroll fragment 4QphNahum (Dead Sea Scrolls)
†Variant name for scroll fragment 4QphNahum (Dead Sea Scrolls)

sense, their "forty years" was the last straight, so to speak, but there was a period which they call the Last Days, or the End of Time, etc., which was quite definitely, like Time of Trial, in the future. It is clear that "the Last Priest will stretch forth his hand against Ephraim." And presumably you don't deny that the Teacher lived and died in the past.

Was he crucified? How the hell do I know? But I think it highly probable, which is all I said. If the Wicked P. was Jannaeus, we know from Josephus (and 4Q, if the Lion of Wrath is the same person) that he crucified people. I think it more probable that the Teacher was practising sacrifice at Qumran, was thus regarding himself as High Priest, and was thus a political as well as religious rebel, and therefore deserving of this punishment in the eyes of Jannaeus. Strugnell believes also that they practised sacrifice, from a document he has; you are inclined that way, and when I tell you that 3Q has a reference to a *byt sm* . . . (for your eyes and ears alone, for God's sake). But where was it? Not at Qumran, I think, but in the Buqeia somewhere. I am becoming convinced that Qumran was only part of the works, and not the most important part either. So I do think it highly probable that the T. was crucified, and if we are to believe 1QpHab, "in the house of his exile." (Beside, 3Q speaks of the *qbr sdwk* [grave of a righteous person] and the *gnt sdwk* [garden of the righteous person], and the former has a cloister round it.)*

I am awfully pleased about Harvard. Not only because this Christianity business is played out (!), but because you can work more on research, and without the ties of denominational calls.

I am interested in your record of the activities of my senior colleague. He told me the other day that his correspondence had been doubled on account of my broadcasts (with foreign scholars; it aroused only normal healthy interest here—because they had heard the whole thing, and not just what some news-hungry journalist cared to report). But this was long after the event, and although willing to answer all these letters, and generally discredit me, he never once asked to see the script (since he heard none of the talks) nor asked me to tell him what it was all about. He had a letter from de Vaux who had told him how sad he was, and this Rowley has been spreading round the world, also. So all in all he's had a good time. Incidentally he's been at work in the University too, I gather. Well, I hope my book sells well, because its proceeds will probably have to keep us alive while I learn how to sweep roads.

---

*Bracketed phrases are translations by Robert Feather

I wanted to get out to Jer. this Spring, as I told you. but no money was forthcoming from here for the fare, the application being insufficiently backed, of course. In fact I was told by the gent. referred to above, that as an Assistant Lecturer I had no right to think about such things. I might even so have raised the money by draining the dregs of the family resources again, but such is the hostility of our "friends" in Jordan at the moment, I hardly think it would be fun. Furthermore, the international situation just now, with the removal of Glubb, is mighty touchy, and I think I prefer to remain here in safety. I frankly am wondering whether either of us are likely to see our fragments again. Anyway, I fully intend having a bumper publication year with anything of interest, so whatever happens, I shall have got the interesting and important stuff out.

I am very pleased about your new car, and the more so that my startling revelations (!) have helped bring it about. But I, too, am losing my health. In fact, I'm as near a nervous breakdown as I have ever been. But I'm easing up a bit now, and with the despatch of the next article shall feel freer. I am avoiding public lectures as much as possible, for they are not worth it even financially in this country. But the BBC have done me well, and since I began the first of the series on the Scrolls in January, I've been performing practically every week. Today I am going to a conference on a TV show we are supposed to be putting on next Monday. Did you hear that damp squib of a trans-Atlantic discussion which Yadin and I here in Manchester did with a character called Bonnell and another Aginsky or the like in New York. They were supposed to wade into me, but the clots knew next to nothing about it. Still, it was fun.

That Times thing was lousy, and I did not say "Essenic pattern." I said "messianic"! And that awful photograph.

Whether I shall be coming out in the Summer, I don't know. Even if the international situation allows of it, I'm not sure whether I want to. I've not recovered from the last one yet, which, though producing the book, really took it out of my [sic] physically. But, my golly, I'd like to see your ugly mug again, and if I don't make it, you really have got to stop off this time and see us.

My love to Betty Anne and the bairns, and best wishes to yourself,

John

# Appendix 3

## Yolanta Zaluska Milik's Commentary

The idea that the earliest followers of Jesus were at Qumran is not an alien concept to Jozef Milik. Since our marriage in 1968 he has been a source of support for me in my work on early religious manuscripts and art, and I in turn have been privy to some of his innermost thoughts, although he is a deeply personal individual not prone to revealing his ideas, and he keeps much to himself.

One of the things that still puzzles Jozef and which he would like to have more time to study is the question, in his own words, "How did they [the Essenes] come to Qumran? No one has an explanation." As he never makes notes about his thoughts on this and other profound matters, the ideas are all in his head. He adds: "You have absolutely no example of a monastery in the Jewish milieu. The nearest example you can find is the Therapeutae, in Egypt, but that does not explain the establishment of a *priestly* group at Qumran." Jozef does not believe the explanation is that they split off from the Temple. "No, they had nothing to do with the Temple," he says. "We just do not know where they came from."

When we discuss certain of the subjects that are pertinent to the contents of this book it is apparent that Jozef's private thoughts are not unsympathetic to the possibility that John the Baptist was a member of the Qumran community. As the son of a priest, the Baptist would be expected to have been associated with and to have been part of the Temple environment, but this apparently was not the case. If he *was* at Qumran he must have been against his father, Zachariah, and that is consistent with what we know about the Baptist.

For these and other reasons Jozef concludes that John the Baptist must have been a member of the Yahad at Qumran, but that he established a group for himself within the community. Jesus of Nazareth was certainly influenced by John the Baptist, and as such was also a member of the community. It is regarding the outcome of their association at Qumran that Jozef's thoughts are most interesting. He does not think that Jesus simply left the Qumran community, but that he was excluded.*

---

Yolanta Zaluska Milik is an authority on early religious manuscripts and art and is currently working on Gospels and *évangelaires* (evangelical texts or manuscripts) preserved in France, including the Évangile of Saint Marc d'Épinal and the *évangelaire* in the Friry Museum of Remiremont.

Her previous books include:

*L'Enluminure et le scriptorium de Cîteaux au XIIe siècle* (Cîteaux, 1989).

*Manuscrits enluminés de Dijon* (Éditions CNRS, 1991).

*Manuscrits enluminés d'origine italienne* (Paris National Library, 1980–84).

*Manuscrits enluminés de la péninsule ibérique* (Paris National Library, 1983).

---

*Other scholars have also suggested that a split occurred in the community at Qumran. At the Dead Sea Scrolls—Fifty Years After Their Discovery International Congress, Jerusalem, July 20–25, 1997, Timothy Lim, of Edinburgh University, presented a paper that considered a description by Hippolytus in his *Refutation of All Heresies* that the Essenes splintered into four parties.

# ⌐ NOTES ⌐

## Chapter 1: Conversations with Monsieur Jozef Milik

1. Hershel Shanks, *The Mystery and Meaning of the Dead Sea Scrolls* (Random House, 1998).

## Chapter 2: A Historical Canter through the Intertestamental Years (320 B.C.E. to 132 C.E.)

1. If the Christian Scriptures are taken as the guide to the date of Jesus's birth, and there is no other historical information, then the statement in the Gospel of Matthew that he was born during the reign of King Herod implies a date before 4 B.C.E., the known date of Herod's death. Michael Molnar, of Rutgers University, has suggested that the biblical "star of Bethlehem" that heralded the birth of Jesus could have been determined by astrologers of the period from predictable celestial occultations (eclipses). He notes that on April 17, 6 B.C.E., the moon eclipsed Jupiter in Aries, and that this occurrence fits well with the biblical descriptions. Rather than by observation at the time, Molnar believes it would have been possible to calculate in advance the date for the birth of Jesus (Marcus Chown, "Invisible Star of Bethlehem," *New Scientist,* December 23–30, 1995). To astrologers, the occultation of Jupiter by the moon was said to signify the appearance of a great king, regardless of what it looked like in the sky. The Magi weren't traveling in the direction of a very bright star; they were traveling in the direction of the location of the astronomical phenomenon in the zodiac. The earliest external account of the date of Jesus's birth comes from Clement of Alexandria, but he gives it as being in May. Later, Pope Julius I (337–352 C.E.) designated December 25 as the true date.

2. Flavius Josephus, *Jewish Wars*; *Jewish Antiquities.*

3. Hugh Schonfield, *The Passover Plot* (Element, 1993).

## Chapter 3: Scribblers, Squabblers, and Scholars

1. André Dupont-Sommer (translated from the French by A. Margaret Rowley), *The Dead Sea Scrolls: A Preliminary Survey* (Oxford/Blackwell, 1952). Professor Dupont-Sommer was also director at the École des Hauts Études; the French edition of his book was published in 1950.

2. Edmund Wilson, *The Scrolls from the Dead Sea* (W. H. Allen, 1955; Fontana, 1957).

3. BBC Radio broadcasts made in 1956.

4. John Marco Allegro, *The Sacred Mushroom and the Cross* (Bantam, 1971).

5. John M. Allegro, *The Dead Sea Scrolls and the Christian Myth* (Westbridge, 1979).

6. Robert Eisenman, *James the Brother of Jesus: The Key to Unlocking the Secrets of Early Christianity and the Dead Sea Scrolls* (Penguin, 1997).

7. Robert Eisenman and Michael Wise, *The Dead Sea Scrolls Uncovered* (Penguin, 1992).

8. Michael Baigent and Richard Leigh, *The Dead Sea Scrolls Deception* (Jonathan Cape, 1991). Much of Baigent and Leigh's thesis is commendable. In their follow-up on the work of Robert Eisenman in exposing the delays in publication of Dead Sea Scrolls material, however, their ideas on the status of Qumran and the Essenes are extremely tenuous. Their assertion that Pliny the Elder's description of Engedi, an Essene community by the Dead Sea, was unlikely to have referred to Qumran takes no account of the possibility that Pliny was referring to the situation before the destruction of Jerusalem, and that Engedi just happened to be destroyed before Qumran. Nor do they consider the numerous solid correlations between the descriptions of Pliny, Josephus, and Philo and what we know about the Qumran community from the sectarian Dead Sea Scrolls, even though there are some inevitable discrepancies. Even more telling is their complete failure to suggest any alternative theory of what these contemporary historians were talking about, if it was not an Essene-style community at Qumran. One cannot denigrate an existing theory without coming up with something more plausible. Many of Baigent and Leigh's problems with the Essenes involve their inability to distinguish between the static and mobile strands of the movement. Their six main points of contradiction between the accounts of Philo, Josephus, and Pliny concerning a community of Essenes living by the Dead Sea are:

*The three historians claim the Essenes were mainly celibate, but remains of women and children were found in the cemetery at Qumran, and the Rule of the Congregation refers to marriage and the raising of children.* These apparent discrepancies are explained by the existence of at least two strands of the Essene movement, one static and one mobile. Members of the mobile groups were encouraged to marry and procreate, whereas the static groups remained celibate. Each year members of the movement convened at Qumran for a religious reunion, and at that time some of the followers who had died could have been buried at Qumran.

*None of the classical writers mentions that the Essenes used a solar calendar, whereas the conventional Judaic calendar would have been lunar.* The Judaic calendar today is lunar-based, but in the first century C.E. a combination of solar and lunar calendars was in use (see, for example, Adolfo Roitman, *A Day at Qumran: The Dead Sea Sect and Its Scrolls* [Jerusalem: The Israel Museum, 1997]). A solar calendar is well attested to in early Psalms and might not have seemed remarkable to contemporary historians. An argument *in absentia* is in itself rather weak, and there are many other aspects of the Qumran community that are not mentioned in external sources.

*According to Philo, the Essenes did not practice animal sacrifice, whereas the Temple Scroll gives precise instructions for sacrifices.* Most scholars agree that the Temple Scroll dates from a much earlier period than the sectarians. It describes activities in a temple setting, rather than at Qumran, and the Essenes had moved on in their understanding of what God wanted in the way of sacrifice. If they envisaged sacrifice, it was only to be in the context of a temple, with a design quite different from that of the one in Jerusalem.

*The classical writers refer to Essenes as a major subdivision of Judaism, but there is no mention of the name Essene in the Dead Sea Scrolls.* Why should there be? One of the classical writers was using a Greek word to describe what he thought were the activities of the community.

*Herod the Great, according to Josephus, admired the Essenes, but the Qumran Essenes were militantly against non-Judaic authority. Qumran was abandoned because of persecution by Herod.* It is quite possible that Herod had an intellectual admiration for one strand of the Essene movement, but not necessarily that at Qumran. In any case, he was an intemperate, vacillating person prone to loving his relatives and others one day and murdering them the next. Even if he was referring to Qumran, why should the admiration be mutual? The Essenes abandoned Qumran because of an earthquake, not because of Herod.

*The classical writers maintain the Essenes were pacifists, but the ruins at Qumran contain a military-style defensive tower, and their texts describe warlike attitudes. Their texts indicate that they were more like Zealots.* The modest tower at Qumran shows no signs of fortification, nor does any other part of the ruins at Qumran. No weapons or military effects of any kind have ever been found at Qumran dating to the period of occupation by the Qumran Essenes. Their bellicose texts refer to a future eschatological time when the forces of light would overcome the forces of darkness. Their unique form of burial, as Ferdinand Röhrhirsch points out (see note 4, chapter 28), excludes any Zealot occupation.

9. Michael Baigent, Richard Leigh, and Henry Lincoln, *Holy Blood, Holy Grail* (Dell, 1982).

10. Barbara Thiering, *Jesus the Man: A New Interpretation from the Dead Sea Scrolls* (Corgi, 1992). Barbara Thiering was a lecturer at the University of Sydney's School of Divinity for twenty-two years.

11. Barbara Thiering, *The Book That Jesus Wrote: John's Gospel* (Transworld Publishers, 1998).

12. Laurence Gardner, *Bloodline of the Holy Grail* (Element, 1996).

13. Solomon Zeitlin, *Who Crucified Jesus?* (New York: Bloch, 1964). Joseph Klausner, *From Jesus to Paul* (Macmillan, 1922). His main point was that Jesus's ethics were Jewish ethics.

14. A translation by James H. Charlesworth was included in *Medicine, Miracle and Magic in New Testament Times*, edited by Howard Clark Kee (Cambridge University Press, 1986), but omitted from the 1988 edition.

15. John Allegro, *The Dead Sea Scrolls and the Christian Myth* (Westbridge Books, 1979). This translation by John Allegro included the names of Hyrcanus Yannai and Zachariel Yannai, and the apparent author of the text, Omriel.

16. Lecture given by Professor Torleif Elgvin, University College London, October 26, 1998.

17. G. A. Wells, *The Historical Evidence for Jesus* (Prometheus, 1982).

18. Albert Schweitzer, *The Quest for the Historical Jesus: A Critical Study of Its Progress from Reimarus to Wrede* (A and C Black, 1910).

19. Timothy Freke and Peter Gandy, *The Jesus Mysteries* (HarperCollins, 1999).

20. Ahmed Osman, *Jesus in the House of the Pharaohs* (Bear & Company, 2004);

*Christianity: An Ancient Egyptian Religion* (Bear & Company, 2005). Ahmed Osman equates many of the key biblical characters with real individuals in the Egyptian eighteenth dynasty, and sees, for example, Jesus as Pharaoh Tutankhamun. I am inclined to agree with many of the associations he makes, although not the personifications. His analysis of features of royal Egyptian characters and the parallels he sees in the leaders of the Hebrew and Christian Scriptures underlines many of the connections I also make back to the Amarna period.

21. Earl Doherty, *The Jesus Puzzle: Did Christianity Begin with a Mythical Christ?* (Canadian Humanist Publications, 1999).

22. Alvar Ellegard, *Jesus: One Hundred Years Before Christ* (Overlook, 1999).

23. *The Virgin Mary*, BBC1 TV documentary, December 22, 2002.

24. Eliette Abécassis, *The Qumran Mystery* (Phoenix, 1999).

25. Alfred Edersheim, *The Life and Times of Jesus the Messiah* (W. B. Erdmans, 1959); Hugh Schonfield, *The Passover Plot* (Bernard Geiss, 1965); Hugh Schonfield, *The Jew of Tarsas* (Macdonald, 1946); Pinchas Lapide, *The Resurrection of Jesus* (Augsburg Publishing House, 1983); David Flusser, *Jesus* (Hebrew University Jerusalem, Magnes Press, 1997); Martin Buber, *Two Types of Faith: A Study of the Interpretation of Judaism and Christianity* (Harper & Row, 1965).

26. Matthew Black, *The Scrolls and Christian Origins* (Thomas Nelson, 1961).

27. Hugh Schonfield, *The Passover Plot* (Element, 1993); *Those Incredible Christians* (Element, 1985); *The Essene Odyssey* (Element, 1984); *The Authentic New Testament* (Dennis Dobson, 1956); *Jesus: A Biography* (Banner, 1948). One of Schonfield's main contentions is that Jesus was a member of a Nazorean sect and planned his own demise in collusion with the owner of the garden where his body was to be placed. The plot involved Jesus being drugged on the cross and a gardener removing his body from the garden tomb to another place where he could recover. Jesus regained consciousness temporarily but then died and was buried in an unmarked grave. The gardener, relaying the news that Jesus survived crucifixion, is mistaken by the followers for Jesus himself. It appears that Schonfield's Nazoreans fulfill most of the characteristics of the Essenes, and in distinguishing the two groups he seems not to have made this connection. For example, he refers to James, the brother of Jesus, as a Nazorean, whereas many scholars now consider that James was an Essene. Schonfield also finds difficulty in explaining why, when Saul (Paul) goes to Damascus to arrest Nazoreans, what he calls a Nazorean community is already well established there, while the Nazorean community of followers of Jesus in Jerusalem had only recently come into existence. However, when it is considered that an Essene community was well established in Damascus before the time of Jesus, it becomes clear that the community Saul visited must have been essentially Essenic.

28. In a lecture at the Spiro Institute, London, on March 15, 2000, Maccoby spoke for over two hours on the origins of Christianity without once mentioning the Essenes.

29. Matthew Black, *The Scrolls and Christian Origins* (Thomas Nelson, 1961).

30. John Dominic Crossan, *Jesus: A Revolutionary Biography* (HarperSanFrancisco, 1995). In describing the contents of Cave 4 as amounting to "hundreds of

thousands of fragments," Professor Crossan seems unaware that the total number of fragments from Cave 4 is about fifteen thousand and from all the Qumran caves no more than ninety thousand. He says that the Temple Scroll concerns "detailed plans for Jerusalem's purified Temple," but in fact the scroll never mentions Jerusalem, and the temple it describes could never have been accommodated on the Temple Mount.

31. Douglas Lockhart, *Jesus the Heretic* (Element, 1997). Lockhart refers to the documentary *The Dead Sea Scrolls*, Compass ABC Television Australia, 1995, Roger Bolton Productions and BBC North in association with the Israeli Broadcasting Authority, 1994.

32. Joseph Klausner, *Jesus of Nazareth* (Macmillan, 1925).

33. Heinrich Graetz, *History of the Jews* (Jewish Publication Society of America, 1946).

34. The Cairo-Damascus documents of the Essenes contain regulations specific to the eating of locusts and honey. Although insects are generally not considered kosher foods acceptable to the strict Jewish dietary laws, locusts are specifically singled out as being acceptable to eat (Lev. 11:20–23).

35. Yigael Yadin, *The Temple Scroll* (Weidenfeld and Nicolson, 1985). In between his academic career Yigael Yadin, the son of Professor E. L. Sukenik of Jerusalem University, became chief of operations in Israel's War of Independence, 1948–49, and later a deputy prime minister of Israel before returning to academia and archaeology. He became a world-renowned authority on biblical archaeology and Dead Sea Scrolls research.

36. Otto Betz, "Was John the Baptist an Essene?" *Biblical Revue* (December 1990); Jean Steinmann, *Saint John the Baptist and the Desert Tradition* (Harper and Brothers, 1958).

37. Jerome Murphy-O'Connor, ed., *Paul and Qumran: Studies in New Testament Exegesis* (Chapman, 1968).

## Chapter 4: Perceived Dangers for the Church

1. It was only in 1991, when Strugnell was forced to resign as editor in chief of the Dead Sea Scrolls translation team after making an anti-Semitic remark, that the first Jew, Emanuel Tov, was appointed editor in chief.

2. Jerome Murphy-O'Connor, ed., *Paul and Qumran: Studies in New Testament Exegesis* (Chapman, 1968).

3. Michael Baigent and Richard Leigh, *The Dead Sea Scrolls Deception* (Jonathan Cape, 1991).

4. Robert Eisenman, *The Dead Sea Scrolls and the First Christians* (Element, 1996).

5. Norman Golb, *Who Wrote the Dead Sea Scrolls? The Search for the Secret of Qumran* (Scribner, 1995).

6. Hershel Shanks, *The Mystery and Meaning of the Dead Sea Scrolls* (Random House, 1998).

7. Eventually some eighty-five thousand separate items of text, ranging from tiny fragments to nearly complete scrolls, were to be retrieved from eleven caves in the hills overlooking Qumran. There are rumors of additional hidden material that

still remains in the control of the Vatican or other private collections. Quite recently *The Jerusalem Report* (October 11, 1999) carried an article about a lost Dead Sea Scroll, nicknamed the Angel Scroll, that allegedly contains material pertinent to early Christianity. It has apparently been in the possession of a Benedictine monastery. Apparently about six and a half feet long, containing about one thousand lines of text, it purports to describe the author's mystical journey around the heavens under the guidance of an angel named Pnimea. The scroll is said to be dedicated to "Yeshua son of Pediya the priest . . . the holy one . . . from . . . Ein Eglatin which is on Mount Makur." In other mystical-celestial journeys the author is shown the secrets of the universe and how to forecast events from the movement of the sun and stars, how to predict the future, and how to cure diseases. The scroll transcript has apparently been studied by Stephen Pfann, a respected Dead Sea Scrolls scholar and one of the fifty-five editors on the official translation team, who says it is a serious literary work but that its veracity must be defined as "hovering between rumour and plausibility."

I find the tone of the information made available unconvincing in terms of the scroll's authenticity. The scroll was apparently tracked down in the mid-1970s and acquired from an antiquities dealer in Amman by monks from a Dominican monastery located on the Austria-Germany border. The scroll was apparently discovered by Bedouins in a jar in a cave on the western slopes of mountains that descend to Wadi al-Mojab (Nahal Arnon, in Hebrew). The fact that no photographs have been made available, the story that the scroll was offered to the Israelis, who declined to make a purchase, and the idea that German monks would be running around the Middle East looking for lost scrolls or would pay huge sums for texts in Hebrew square Assyrian all make the scroll's genuineness somewhat doubtful. Moreover, the suggestion that a German-born member of the Benedictine monastery, Father Gustave Mateus, when he died in 1996 willed details of the scroll to a German-born Israeli sounds more like a John le Carre novel than reality, especially since a leading Dead Sea Scrolls scholar based in Israel, Bargil Pixner, who is also a Benedictine monk, has no knowledge of a Father Gustave Mateus. The entire aroma of secrecy surrounding the scroll would seem to be unjustified if it were genuine.

8. Robert Feather, recorded conversation with Mrs. Joan Allegro, March 1, 2000, on the Isle of Man. John Allegro appears initially to have had a firm faith in Christianity but slowly became disenchanted and eventually believed Jesus was no more than a myth. Born on February 17, 1923, Allegro was commissioned as a naval officer and stationed in Glasgow toward the end of the Second World War. The local Methodist church minister who was chaplain to the navy encouraged navy personnel to attend his church, and it was there that John met his future wife. When his ship, which was being fitted out at Greenock, was ready, he sailed to Hong Kong as secretary to the admiral. He had kept in contact with Joan from his home in Carshalton, Surrey. When the Japanese war ended, Allegro, inspired by the minister in Glasgow, offered himself to the ministry. He was accepted and sent as a probationer minister to a small country church near Edinburgh. There he started studying Hebrew and Greek on his own initiative, and the following year he was sent to Hartley Victoria College in Manchester, a Methodist training college, and then transferred to Manchester University to

study for a degree. He was, according to his wife, already beginning to question the beliefs of Christianity—a questioning that would later turn to criticism and then hostility, culminating in a claim "that the myth of Jesus of Nazareth as recorded in the Gospels was just one of a number of Redeemer mythologies" (*The Dead Sea Scrolls and the Christian Myth*, Westbridge, 1979). As a probationer minister, he was not allowed to marry for seven years. He decided to leave the church and married Joan in 1948. While his wife worked as an accountant, John Allegro completed his degree and then, becoming more and more interested in the roots of language, studied for an M.A. on the interpretation of the Baalim Chronicles. A year later he went to Oxford University to work with Geoffrey Driver on Hebrew dialects and obtained his M.A. Joan remained at their house in Manchester, having given birth to their first daughter, Judith. A few months later, in 1953, Dr. Driver was asked by the École Biblique in Jerusalem to send someone to help with the editing of the early Dead Sea Scrolls fragments, and he recommended his brightest pupil. By this time John Allegro had given up all interest in the church. His secondment was financed by the Levershulme Trust, and after a year's work in Jerusalem a post came up at Manchester University as assistant lecturer in the theology department under Professor H. H. Rowley.

In the meantime, the Copper Scroll had been discovered on March 20, 1952, near Qumran, but had not yet been deciphered. John Allegro thought he could find someone at Manchester who could open the heavily oxidized metal scroll. He first approached the metallurgy department at Manchester, but they were reluctant to get involved and didn't think they could help. After trying several other sources, he met Dr. B. V. Bowden (later Lord Bowden), principal at the College of Technology in Manchester (now UMIST), who was more helpful and enlisted the services of Professor H. Wright Baker. As part of the search for a suitable organization to undertake the work of opening the Copper Scroll, an approach had been made, as early as May 1952, through Professor W. H. Albright of Johns Hopkins in Maryland, to Professor Rutherford J. Gettens at the Freer Gallery of Art, Washington, D.C. Some small fragments of the Copper Scroll were sent to America, but the project was considered extremely difficult to undertake, and before a suitable procedure could be developed, the scroll was on its way to Manchester. Some splinters from the Copper Scroll had been examined microscopically and others sent for spectrographic analysis to Charles Milton at the U.S. Department of Interior Geological Survey in Washington, D.C. A few of the original splinters of the Copper Scroll are still in the possession of the Freer Gallery of Art.

The American institutions concerned, not surprisingly, felt somewhat thwarted, especially as a similar abortive outcome had occurred previously with the so-called Lamech Scroll (Genesis Apochryphon), which had been offered to the Fogg Art Museum at Harvard for unraveling. That scroll had been taken out of America through the efforts of Yigael Yadin in 1954. Having written his first Penguin book on the Dead Sea Scrolls (*The Dead Sea Scrolls: A Reappraisal*, 1966), John Allegro became rather more high profile than his superior at Manchester University, who resented Allegro's new status as well as the fact that his university had not been entrusted with the Copper Scroll, even though it had initially been offered to it. This was the beginning of the hostility that John Allegro would encounter from many quarters over the coming years.

9. John Marco Allegro, *The Treasure of the Copper Scroll* (Routledge and Kegan Paul, 1960). He says that the Copper Scroll was discovered on March 29, 1952, in Cave 3 in the hills above Qumran by the French archaeologist Henri de Contenson.

10. John M. Allegro, *The End of the Road* (Dial, 1971).

11. Paper presented by John Allegro on April 19, 1985, at an international symposium at the University of Michigan, Ann Arbor, on Jesus and the Gospels, entitled "Jesus in History and Myth."

12. John Marco Allegro, *The Shapira Affair* (W. H. Allen, 1965).

13. Wherever the name of God appears in the text, it is nearly always in the form of Elohim, whereas the alternative, Jehovah (or Yahweh), predominates in the normative Masoretic text. The wording of the Ten Commandments varies considerably in the Shapira texts. For a complete translation, see John Marco Allegro, *The Shapira Affair* (W. H. Allen, 1965); Herman Guthe, *Fragments einer Lederhandschrift, enthaltend Moses's Letzte an die Kinder Israel* (Leipzig, 1883).

14. The Moabite Stone was found in 1868 by a German pastor, F. A. Klein, some twelve miles east of the Dead Sea at Dibo, near the Arnon River. It was subsequently broken up by Bedouins disenchanted with the prevarications of potential purchasers, but many of the fragments were hunted down by the French diplomat-explorer Charles Clermont-Ganneau and an English archaeologist, Captain Charles Warren. Eventually, in 1873–74, most of the fragments were donated to the Louvre Museum in Paris, where the Moabite Stone was reconstructed. The stone recorded an apparently successful uprising by the king of Moab against the Israelites in the ninth century B.C.E., a story confirmed in 2 Kings 3. The stone appears to prove the truth of the Old Testament story when it mentions the kingdom of Moab, its king, Mesha, its god, Chemosh, and its main city of Dibon. The chronology of the Moabite Stone, however, varies from the Bible version of events in naming King Omri as the Israelite ruler who oppressed the Moabites; the biblical account places the revolt after the death of Ahab, Omri's son.

15. Among the scholars who doubted the authenticity of the Shapira texts were Dr. Konstatine Schlottmann, professor of Old Testament at the University of Halle, Germany; Dr. Christian Ginsberg, an English expert on biblical texts working on behalf of the British Museum; Professor A. Neubauer, reader in rabbinical literature, Oxford University; and the French diplomat-explorer Charles Clermont-Ganneau.

16. Bernard Quaritch Ltd. was established in 1847 and currently has premises at 5-8 Lower John Street, Golden Square, London W1. In its catalog of 1887, it offered the fifteen Shapira fragments for sale at twenty-five pounds. They were apparently acquired by the chancellor of the University of Sydney, and it is believed they were destroyed when his library burned to the ground in 1899 (Brad Sabin Hill, "Ephraim Deinard on the Shapira Affair," *The Book Collector,* A Special Number to Commemorate the 150th Anniversary of Bernard Quaritch Ltd., 1997; see also A. D. Crown, "The Fate of the Shapira Scroll," *Revue de Qumran* 8, 1970).

17. For example, John Allegro was convinced the Shapira strips were genuine, as were

Mehanem Mansoor ("The Case of the Shapira's Dead Sea (Deuteronomy) Scroll 1883," *Transactions of the Wisconsin Academy of Sciences, Arts and Letters* 47, 1959) and H. G. Jefferson ("The Shapira Manuscript and the Qumran Scrolls," *Revue de Qumran* 23, 1968), who compared the manuscript with Qumran-Essene texts and concluded, "The evidence from palaeography does not seem to prove the Shapira a forgery." Dr. J. L. Teicher, of Cambridge University, wrote in *The Times* of London (March 22, 1957), "The Shapira manuscripts were genuine and . . . their contents are most fittingly described as representing the Book of Deuteronomy which was re-drafted for liturgical and catechetic purposes in the Jewish-Christian Church."

## Chapter 5: Was Jesus a Real Person? The Literary and Other Sources

1. Burton L. Mack, *The Christian Myth: Origins, Logic, and Legacy* (Continuum, 2001); Marcus J. Borg, *Jesus in Contemporary Scholarship* (Trinity, 1994); John Dominic Crossan, The *Historical Jesus: The Life of a Mediterranean Jewish Peasant* (HarperSanFranciso, 1991); James M. Robinson, "A New Quest of the Historical Jesus," in *Studies in Biblical Theology* 25, SCM Press, 1959); Bart D. Ehrman, *Jesus, Apocalyptic Prophet of the New Millennium* (Oxford University Press, 1999); John P. Meier, *A Marginal Jew: Rethinking the Historical Jesus* (Doubleday, 1991–2001); Geza Vermes, *Jesus in His Jewish Context* (Fortress, 2003); J. Harold Ellens, *Jesus as the Son of Man: The Literary Character* (Institute for Antiquity and Christianity, Claremont Graduate University, Occasional Papers No. 45, 2003).

2. Chaim Rabin, "Islam and the Qumran Sect," in *Qumran Studies,* Scripta Judaica 2 (Oxford University Press, 1957).

3. N. J. Dawood, trans., *The Koran* (Penguin, 1990).

4. G. R. Hawting, *The Idea of Idolatry and the Emergence of Islam* (Cambridge University Press, 2000); Ibn Warraq, ed., *The Quest for the Historical Muhammad* (Prometheus, 2000).

5. Tradition has it that Muhammad acquired his knowledge of Jews and Christians in Mecca from his wife's cousin Waraqa ibn Naufal.

6. A number of scroll fragments found at Masada are considered to have originated at Qumran, such as Songs of Sabbath, Wisdom of ben-Sira (Ecclesiasticus), Book of Jubilees, Joshua Apocryphon (see Yigael Yadin, *Masada: Herod's Fortress and the Zealots' Last Stand,* Weidenfeld and Nicolson, 1966); Shemaryahu Talmon, "Fragments of a Joshua Apocryphon," *Journal of Jewish Studies,* vol. 47, no. 1., 1996.

7. Galatians 1:17–18.

8. Kamal Salibi, *Conspiracy in Jerusalem: The Hidden Origins of Jesus* (I. B. Tauris, 1988).

9. Sura 19:30, "He spake: Lo! I am the slave of Allah. He hath given me the Scripture and hath appointed me a Prophet."

10. Mohammed Marmaduke Pickthall, *The Meaning of the Glorious Qur'an: An Explanatory Translation,* rev. and ed. by Arafat K. El-Ashi (Amana, 1996).

11. "Digging Diary 2000—St. Paul's Monastery (Eastern Desert)." *The Journal of Egyptian Archaeology* (Egypt Exploration Society, Spring 2001).

12. Lot, mentioned in Genesis 13 and 19, was a nephew of Abraham. After they left Egypt to return to Canaan, it was mutually decided that they would take their families in different directions to find adequate feeding ground for their large flocks of animals. Significantly, Lot chose the land to the east in the plain of Jordan. He lived in the city of Sodom but was advised by two angels to leave the place, as God was about to destroy it along with the city of Gomorrah. As he and his family fled, Lot was warned not to let any of his family look back on the destruction being rained down on the two evil cities. Unfortunately his wife disobeyed the instruction and was turned into a pillar of salt. Lot, his daughters, and his remaining family later settled in the mountain region near the city of Zoar and incestuously gave rise to the tribes of Moab and Amon. The Quran relates: "And unto Lot we gave judgement and knowledge, and we delivered him from the community that did abominations" (Sura 21:74).

13. Patricia Crone and Michael Cook, *Hagarism: The Making of the Islamic World* (Cambridge University Press, 1977).

14. Patricia Crone, "An Uncertain Start," *Times Literary Supplement,* January 26, 2001.

15. Gordon Heald, "Now Here's the Good News," *The Tablet,* April 14, 2001. A recent survey of British attitudes toward belief in Jesus, reported by Heald, showed that 60 percent of Britons believe Jesus died by crucifixion. This figure rose to 80 percent among Catholics, and was 65 percent among Church of England members and Protestants. Sixty-seven percent of the population believe Jesus lived on this earth; this figure rose to 81 percent among Catholics and 72 percent among Church of England members and Protestants. Comparable views of the resurrection showed that 48 percent of the population believe Jesus rose from the dead three days after his crucifixion. This percentage rose to 73 percent among Catholics, but it was only 57 percent among Church of England members and Protestants.

16. Geza Vermes, "The Jesus Notice of Josephus Re-Examined," *Journal of Jewish Studies* 38 (1987). Professor Vermes, of the Oriental Institute at the University of Oxford, quoting from Josephus, *Testimonium Flavianum: Jewish Antiquities* 18, concludes that Josephus described Jesus as a "wise man" and "performer of paradoxical deeds." Origen, in *Contra Celsium,* explicitly asserts that Josephus did not believe Jesus was the Messiah.

17. S. Zeitlin, *Josephus on Jesus with Particular Reference to the Slavonic Josephus and the Hebrew Josippon* (Dropsie College, Philadelphia, 1931); J. M. Creed, "The Divinity of Jesus Christ" (Collins, 1964).

18. *Josephus: The Jewish Wars,* translation by G. A. Williamson (Penguin, 1959).

19. Yadin Roman and Adolfo Roitman, "Scroll Work," *Eretz* (July–August 1997).

20. Gerd Theissen and Annette Merz, *The Historical Jesus* (SCM, 1998).

21. The Roman/Samaritan historian Thallus is thought to have mentioned Jesus's crucifixion in his history of the world, written as early as the first century C.E. His original work has been lost, but the chronographer Julius Africanus (c. 170–240 C.E.) was believed to have quoted Thallus's description of "darkness as an eclipse" occurring at the time of Jesus's crucifixion.

22. R. Freudenberger, *Das Verhalten der Romischen Behorden gegen de Christen im 2. Jahrhundert dargestellt am Brief des Plinius an Trajan und den reskripten Trajans und Hadrians* (C. H. Beck, 1967).

23. The event is echoed by Jean Malaplate, a modern French poet, in his poem "Rome Burns . . . Oceans of Flames": Rome brûle . . . Océan de flamme inespéré! / Vrai poème que rêve un Virgile en délire! / Du toit de son palais, l'empereur inspiré / Y mêle artistement les accords de sa lyre" (*Petite Chronique du feu,* Éditions des Moires, 1995).

24. Samuel Sandmel, *A Jewish Understanding of the New Testament* (Society for the Promotion of Christian Knowledge, 1977).

25. Herman Strack and Paul Billerbeck, *Kommentar zum Neuen Testament aus Talmud und Midrash* (Munich, 1922–26).

26. Samuel Tobias Lachs, *A Rabbinic Commentary on the New Testament* (KTAV, 1987).

27. Hyam Maccoby, *Early Rabbinic Writings* (Cambridge University Press, 1988).

28. Alexander Jannaeus officiated as high priest and, according to Josephus, was despised by the people. The Pharisees plotted to call on the help of the Seleucid king Demetrius III around 88 B.C.E. The attempted coup failed, and Jannaeus had eight hundred Pharisees crucified. This act is alluded to in Dead Sea Scroll 4QpNah 1, which mentions Demetrius, king of Greece, and the passage is interpreted as referring to "the furious young lion (Jannaeus)" who exacts revenge on those who seek smooth things (interpreters of the law) and hangs men alive (see Allegro's letter in appendix 2).

29. Samuel Tobias Lachs, *A Rabbinic Commentary on the New Testament* (KTAV, 1987).

30. The Zohar—a formalization of Kabbalah (see chapter 10)—is attributed to Simeon ben Yochai. He is said to have hidden in a cave at Meron, Galilee, for thirteen years.

31. Ian Wilson, *Jesus: The Evidence* (Weidenfeld and Nicolson, 1984).

32. Tosefta Hullin II, 22 (Mishnah supplement).

33. The sun's journey through the evil darkness of the night is marked by its passage through twelve gates until it emerges in the heaven of light in the morning. Similarly, in the afterlife a person has to know the secret passwords that allow traverse through the ten gates of the underworld to the heaven that awaits on the other side. See, for example, Alfred Wiedermann, *Religion of the Ancient Egyptians* (H. Grevel, 1897); Siegfried Morenz, *Egyptian Religion* (Cornell University Press, 1994); E. A. Wallis Budge, *The Book of the Dead* (Gramercy, 1960) and *Egyptian Religion* (Gramercy, 1995); and Ian Shaw and Paul Nicholson, *British Museum Dictionary of Ancient Egypt* (British Museum Press, 1995).

    Examples from the Bible that appear to be drawing on the analogy of "gates" in relation to heaven and hell are as follows: "And the gates of hell shall not prevail against it" (Matt. 16:18); "But He hath not given me over unto death. Open to me the gates of righteousness" (Ps. 118); "And the gates of it shall not be shut at all by day: for there shall be no night there" (Rev. 21:25).

## Chapter 6: The Archaeological Evidence for Jesus's Life

1. M. Avi-Yonah, "A List of Priestly Courses from Caesarea," *Israel Exploration Journal* 12 (1962). It seems likely that references to Nazareans, rather than being related to a place called Nazareth, which did not appear to exist at the time of Jesus, are to the Hebrew word *nozrim*, meaning "guardians of the Covenant." This plural word is derived from the Hebrew *nazr habrit* and is related to the people who lived at Qumran at the time of Jesus, the Essenes. On the basis that Jesus might have been a member of the Qumran-Essene settlement, Dr. Gershon Harris, of Sheffield, England, has put forward an interesting theory that, as "keepers of the Covenant," *nozrei habrit* or *nozrim* in Hebrew suggests that the name Nazareth might have been a derivation of this term ("Out of Place," *Jewish Chronicle,* January 5, 1996).

2. Gaalyah Cornfield, ed., *The Historical Jesus: A Scholarly View of the Man and His World* (Macmillan, 1982).

3. Russell Shorto, *Gospel Truth* (Hodder and Stoughton, 1997).

4. The vows taken by Nazirites are recorded in Numbers 6:1–21. They require abstinence from wine, allowing the hair to grow uncut, and avoiding pollution of the body. It has been suggested that these characteristics were evident among the Essenes, who considered themselves in the same category, and it seems that the name Nazarene might have been synonymous with the Essenes. (www.askwhy.co.uk. Search "Nazarene" to access the relevant article by Dr. M. D. Magee.)

5. Håkan Ulfgard, "The Branch in the Last Days: Observations on the New Covenant Before and After the Messiah," in *The Dead Sea Scrolls in Their Historical Context,* ed. by Timothy H. Lim (T & T Clark International, 2000); and Eugene C. Ulrich, in "The Qumran Biblical Scrolls: The Scriptures of Late Second Temple Judaism" presented at the same conference: "The Dead Sea Scrolls in their Historical Context," Faculty of Divinity, the University of Edinburgh, May 5–6, 1998. Ulrich's presentation gave more evidence that the Nazorean appellation applied to Jesus had nothing to do with Nazareth. He observed that although the Gospel of Matthew 1–2 drew on what became the Hebrew Bible for four out of five structured vignettes about the birth of Jesus, one quotation, "He shall be called a Nazorean," did not come from the Hebrew Scriptures. The author suggests that the source of the term was *nazir,* which appears in Dead Sea Scroll 4QSama.

6. As a child Pontius Pilate is said to have played under a yew tree that stands in the churchyard at Fortingall, Perthshire, Scotland. The tree, thought to be over eight thousand years old, is one of the oldest in Europe. Legend has it that Pilate's father, a Roman envoy, was visiting a local king on behalf of Caesar Augustus around 10 B.C.E. and became embroiled with a local lass who subsequently gave birth to Pilate (*The Independent,* February 24, 2000). However, there is no record of the Romans entering Scotland that early in history.

7. The *simpulum* was a type of ladle with a high handle used to make libations during sacrifices by the Roman priesthood.

8. The *littus,* also known as an augur's wand, was used by a Roman cult in divination ceremonies. Interpretation of the will of the Roman gods required specialized

training, and colleges of augury were established to study and to teach pupils how to determine the portents of phenomena such as "lightning flashes, flights of birds, positions of clouds and stars, the rush of the winds, the whir of the insects, and even a cat's crossing of one's path." Before he became prefect of Judaea, Pilate was a committed augur, and his involvement in these practices might have brought him favor in the sight of Emperor Tiberius, who was an ardent believer in augury.

9. Philo, *Legatio ad Gaium* 301–2.

10. Z. Greenhut, "The Caiaphas Tomb in North Talpiot," in *Ancient Jerusalem Revealed* (Israel Exploration Society, 1994); N. Avigad, "Excavations in the Jewish Quarter of the Old City, 1969–71," in *Jerusalem Revealed* (Biblical Archeology Society, 1976).

11. Ian Wilson, *The Bible Is History* (Weidenfeld and Nicolson, 1999). Unfortunately, in my view Wilson gets wrong most of his dates for the chronology of biblical events, and as a result many of his conclusions are suspect. For example, he places Rameses in the 1600–1500 B.C.E. period, whereas that pharaoh clearly ruled some three centuries later.

12. Flavius Josephus records a method of exorcism demonstrated to the emperor Vespasian (*Jewish Antiquities* 8:46–48) in which a person was dispossessed of an evil spirit by Eleazar. The demon's departure was apparently proved by the upsetting of a nearby water container. Sectarian writings of the Qumran Essenes (11QApoc Psalms, 4Q510, 4Q511) testify to their knowledge of exorcism rituals.

13. Dan Levene, " ' . . . and by the name of Jesus . . . ': An Unpublished Magic Bowl in Jewish Aramaic," *Jewish Studies Quarterly* (1999).

14. Shaul Shaked, "Jesus in the Magic Bowls: Apropos Dan Levene's ' . . . and by the name of Jesus . . . ,' " *Jewish Studies Quarterly* (1999).

15. André Lemaire, "Burial Box of James the Brother of Jesus," *Biblical Archaeology Review* (Nov.–Dec. 2002). The November 5, 2002, edition of the Israeli newspaper *Ha'aretz* reported that the ossuary was in the possession of an Israeli, Oded Golan, and was apparently purchased some fifteen years previously from a Jerusalem dealer, but the significance of the inscription was not realized until recently. The same fate seems to have dogged a series of ossuaries found in 1980 in a tomb at East Talpiot, Jerusalem, and now in the possession of the Israel Antiquities Authority. They were inscribed with the names Jesus son of Joseph, Mary, Joseph, and Jude, but were not brought to public attention until the screening of a BBC documentary, *The Body in Question*, on April 7, 1996. The ossuaries contained no bones, and the general conclusion has been that the names were quite common for the period and therefore not necessarily related to the family of Jesus Christ.

16. BBC News, June 18, 2003. See also *Ha'aretz*, July 23, 2003. Members of the Israel Antiquities Authority's final report on the James ossuary who were vehemently attacked by Professor André Lemaire included Professor Amos Kloner, Dr. Tal Ilan, Professor Ronny Reich, Dr. Esther Eshel, Dr. Elisabetta Boaretto, Dr. Orna Cohen, Dr. Avner Ayalon, and Professor Yuval Goren. According to Randall Price, Joseph Zias, formerly curator of the Rockefeller Museum in East Jerusalem, saw the James ossuary in a Jerusalem antiquities shop in the 1990s, and it did not have the brother of Jesus addition. Randall Price, "Is the James Ossuary Genuine? Yes, and No!" *World of the Bible*, vol. 6, 2003–2004.

17. A classic example is that of Rabbi Nelson Glueck, an American who, just before the Second World War, announced that he had located King Solomon's "vast copper refinery" at Tell el-Kheleifeh (midway between Eilat and Aqabah). He claimed to have found Solomonic pottery, large quantities of copper slag, casting molds, and a green-stained structure he interpreted as a smelting furnace. Rabbi Glueck's findings were accepted and widely quoted for another twenty years, until his former assistant, Beno Rothenberg, of Tel Aviv University, revealed that the smelting furnace was nothing more than an ancient burned-out granary store. There never had been any copper remains or verifiable Solomonic pots. See Werner Keller, *The Bible as History* (Bantam, 1982); and Ian Wilson, *The Bible Is History* (Weidenfeld and Nicolson, 1999).

## Chapter 8: Messiahs of Qumran

1. Cairo-Damascus and Community Rule documents of the Dead Sea Scrolls, and the Cairo Genizah collection. According to Richard Elliott Friedman in his *Who Wrote the Bible?* (HarperSanFranciso, 1989), there was a very clear distinction between the family of Moses (priests in the north of Israel) and the family of Aaron (Zadokite priests based at Hebron in the south).

2. Cairo-Damascus, Community Rule, and Messianic Rule documents of the Dead Sea Scrolls. See, for example, translations in Geza Vermes, *The Complete Dead Sea Scrolls in English* (Allen Lane/Penguin, 1997).

3. The Dead Sea Scroll of Blessing (1QSb) has a long description of a kingly messiah who is fierce and can kill the sinner.

4. Jeremiah 22; Ezekiel 34; Micah 3; 1 and 2 Chronicles; 1 and 2 Kings.

5. 1 Chronicles 21:14–17; 2 Samuel 11.

6. 2 Samuel 12. Intriguingly, Nathan's condemnation of David recounts that the Lord will deal with him publicly, "before all Israel, and before the sun." Appending the latter witness to the Lord's judgment against King David makes little sense unless "the sun" has some profound value. I argue elsewhere that, although there may well have been aberrational pagan worship of the sun in Israel, authentic references to it by such God-fearing Jews as King Hezekiah and King Josiah are almost certainly Egyptian-inspired imagery related to Akhenaten's vision of God, alluded to in the form of a sun disk. In 1 Samuel 19:12–14, there is further evidence that David was not an ideal character to perceive as a messiah. In the section where he is being pursued by King Saul, who seeks to kill him, his wife, Michal, helps him escape and then wraps the household idol in a goatskin cloth.

7. Joseph A. Fitzmyer, *The Dead Sea Scrolls and Christian Origins* (Eerdmans, 2000).

8. Daniel I. Block, "My Servant David: Ancient Israel's Vision of the Messiah," in *Israel's Messiah in the Bible and the Dead Sea Scrolls,* by Richard S. Hess and M. Daniel Carroll (Baker Academic, 2003). In a chapter in the same work, "If He Looks Like a Prophet and Talks Like a Prophet Then He Must Be . . . ," J. Daniel Hays finds it difficult to substantiate the idea that Moses or even David could be the messianic figure behind Isaiah's suffering servant. In "The Imagery of the Substitute King Ritual in Isaiah's Fourth Servant Song," *Journal of Biblical*

*Literature* 122 (4), 2003, John H. Walton has no doubt that the suffering-servant messianic figure has royal connotations.

9. Robert L. Webb, "John the Baptizer and Prophet: A Socio-Historical Study," *Journal for the Study of the New Testament*, suppl. series 62 (Sheffield Academic, 1991). Interestingly, in the Masoretic text of Zechariah 6:12–13, the prophet is told to make "crowns" and set them on the head of Joshua, the high priest. This can only be an allusion to a practice unique to Egypt, in which enthronement involved two crowns representing the "Two Lands" of Upper and Lower Egypt. See also Frank Moore Cross, *The Ancient Library of Qumran* (Sheffield Academic, 1995).

10. For example, in Ezekiel 34, 37, and 40–48, the prophet carefully avoids naming David as the restored lineage of a new order. Also, as Professor Ben Zion Wacholder of Hebrew University, Cincinnati, points out in "Ezekiel and Ezekielianism as Progenitors of Essenianism" (*The Dead Sea Scrolls, Forty Years of Research*, editors Devorah Dimant, Uriel Rappaport, and Yan Yitshak Ben-Tsevi, Brill Academic Publishers, 1992), Ezekiel carefully avoids mentioning Jerusalem as the place where a reconstituted Temple will be built at the time of the coming of the messiah, but refers to it, as other sources have picked up on, as a place in which "the Lord is there."

11. Robert L. Webb, "John the Baptizer and Prophet: A Socio-Historical Study," *Journal for the Study of the New Testament*, suppl. series 62 (Sheffield Academic, 1991).

12. K. Pomykala, *The Davidic Dynasty Tradition in Early Judaism* (Scholars Press, 1995). See also Richard S. Hess and M. Daniel Carroll, *Israel's Messiah in the Bible and in the Dead Sea Scrolls* (Baker Academic, 2003).

13. Geza Vermes, *The Complete Dead Sea Scrolls in English* (Allen Lane/Penguin, 1997). It should be noted that Isaiah 10 and 11 do not specifically mention King David, and the Hebrew text in the scroll mentions a "branch of David" and not King David himself.

14. According to Professor Hartmut Stegemann, head of the Göttingen Qumran Research Center at the University of Göttingen, lecturing at University College London on November 23, 1998, the Qumran Essenes awaited figures from the Hebrew Scriptures who would be anointed through God's holy spirit. Stegemann sees Psalms 17 and 18 as the only pre–Dead Sea Scrolls references to a "future messiah—a royal messiah." The priestly messiah who will atone for sins, he says, has nothing to do with Jesus; the function was the traditional role of the high priest.

15. Lawrence Schiffman, "Messianic Figures and Ideas in the Qumran Scrolls," in *The Messiahs: Developments in Earliest Judaism and Christianity* (Fortress, 1992); Garcia Martinez, "Messianische Erwartungen in den Qumranschriften," *Journal of Biblical Theology* (1993); J. VanderKam, *Messianism in the Scrolls: The Community of the Renewed Covenant* (Notre Dame University, 1994); E. Puech, *Messianism, Resurrection, and Eschatology at Qumran and in the New Testament* (Notre Dame University, 1994); W. M. Schniedewind, "King and Priest in the Book of Chronicles and the Duality of Qumran Messianism," *Journal for the Study of Judaism* 45 (1994); J. J. Collins, *The Sceptre and the Star: The Messiahs of the*

*Dead Sea Scrolls and Other Ancient Jewish Literature* (Doubleday, 1995); Jean Duhaime, "Recent Studies on Messianism in the Dead Sea Scrolls," paper presented at Dead Sea Scrolls Fifty Years After Their Discovery, International Congress, Jerusalem, July 20–25, 1997.

16. Robert Feather, *The Mystery of the Copper Scroll of Qumran* (Inner Traditions, 2003).

17. Although it has been argued that there are messianic portents of a royal figure in earlier parts of the Hebrew Scriptures, they are not crystallized until the time of the Qumran Essenes and their writings. There is no messianism before 500 B.C.E., and any reference to Moshiah (Messiah) is applied to a historical figure, never to expected or eschatological figures (John Collins, *The Sceptre and the Star: The Messiahs of the Dead Sea Scrolls and Other Ancient Literature*, Doubleday, 1995). Modern Jewish scholars, like H. L. Ginsberg and David Flusser (*Encyclopaedia Judaica*, Keter, 1971), see Jewish messianism as emerging only in the Roman Second Temple period. See also Joseph A. Fitzmyer, *The Dead Sea Scrolls and Christian Origins* (Eerdmans, 2000).

18. Geza Vermes, *The Complete Dead Sea Scrolls in English* (Allen Lane/Penguin, 1997).

19. Jozef T. Milik, *Ten Years of Discovery in the Wilderness of Judaea* (SCM, 1959). Father Milik noted that, in 4QTestimonia (Florilegium), three biblical passages relating to the future messiahs are immediately followed by a section from the Psalms of Joshua that alludes to past events connected with the persecutors of the Hebrews: "When Josh[ua] fini[sh]ed off[ering prai]se in [his] thanksgivings, [he said]: c[ursed be m]an who rebui[l]ds [this cit]y!' (4Q175). The essence of these connected texts is that the original exemplars for the three messiahs predated the Exodus, as the pseudepigraphical Psalms of Joshua allude to past events connected with persecutors of the sect.

20. John M. Allegro, *The Dead Sea Scrolls and the Christian Myth* (Westbridge, 1979).

21. In *The Mystery of the Copper Scroll of Qumran* I point out that recent DNA analysis of members of the Cohanim (Jews thought to have descended from the priestly Levitic class, who through the ages have traditionally intermarried only with other Cohanim) shows that they carry distinctively marked hereditary chromosomes. These markers differentiate them from other Jews, but it appears that the biological event that caused the distinctive chromosome marker occurred at least twenty-nine thousand years ago! Other Web sites give a figure of 11,375 years ago for the differentiating event: www.familytreedna.com/nature97385.html and www.bsu.edu/classes/fears/relst251/dna.html. In other words, the line of priestly Cohanim existed aeons before they were apparently separated out for appointment as priests in the time even of Jacob, let alone Moses (K. Skorecki, S. Selig, S. Blazer, et al., "Y Chromosomes of Jewish Priests," *Nature* 385 (January 2, 1997)).

22. Geza Vermes, *The Complete Dead Sea Scrolls in English* (Allen Lane/Penguin, 1997). It has been suggested—for example, by Charles Fritsch (see note 23 below)—that "the Star" refers to the leader who took the Qumran community off to Damascus when they came under threat from King Herod the Great, only to return after his death in 4 B.C.E.

23. Charles Fritsch, *The Qumran Community: Its History and Scrolls* (Macmillan, 1956).

24. Geza Vermes, *The Complete Dead Sea Scrolls in English* (Allen Lane/Penguin, 1997).

25. This reference to Seth is, I believe, to the same Seth who appears in the Nag Hammadi texts, significantly in a codex known as the Gospel of the Egyptians (see chapter 14). It is surely not a reference to Adam's third son, briefly mentioned in the Hebrew Scriptures, or to the "Sons of Sheth" mentioned in Numbers 24:17, who have been identified with a nomadic tribe living to the north of Canaan, which unconvincing conventional explanations propose.

26. Norman de Garis Davies, *The Rock Tombs of El-Amarna*. The Tomb of Meryra (The Egypt Exploration Fund, 1903).

27. Lawrence Schiffman, *The Eschatological Community of the Dead Sea Scrolls: A Study of the Rule of the Congregation* (Scholars Press, 1989).

28. Charles Robert Morgan, *The Gate of Hope* (Pinnacle, 1987).

29. Norman de Garis Davies, *The Rock Tombs of El-Amarna*, Part 4 (Egypt Exploration Fund, 1906).

30. Gershom Scholem, *The Messianic Idea in Judaism* (Schocken, 1995).

31. The majority of the recognizable fragments of 1 Enoch were found in Cave 4, written mostly on leather in Aramaic. The complete text of 1 Enoch is available only in the Ethiopic Ge'ez version.

32. It is worth noting that the works of these prophets appear to have been of considerable importance to the Qumran Essenes, with Enoch and Habakkuk being of special interest. Possibly they were seen as direct messengers of the earlier Egyptian period who included descriptions of the Amarna period in their writings. Enoch and Habakkuk are especially strong in their writings relating to heavenly thrones, chariots, and Atenist imagery. 1 Enoch has the oldest known example of throne mysticism. Examples from Enoch are given elsewhere in the book, but a noteworthy reference comes from Habakkuk 3:1–19. Here, in a passage that appears to describe God's future vengeance on the people of Cush, Midian, Neharim, and Yam, there is unambiguous Amarna-period iconography. The translation is taken from the Hebrew Tanakh, published by The Jewish Publications Society, 1985. In the King James version of the Bible, the translation of the Hebrew names Neharim and Yam is given as the single noun "rivers." The quotation continues: "His majesty covers the skies, his splendour fills the earth: It is a brilliant light which gives off rays on every side—and therein His glory is enveloped." "Gives off rays on every side" seems to describe the rays of Aten, which radiate in every direction—a depiction seen only in the Atenist period.

    Noticeably, the people of Yam who are to be targeted for vengeance have nothing to do with the contemporary setting of Habakkuk's time in the late seventh century B.C.E., or with Israel, or with its neighborhood enemies, for that matter (nor do any of the other targeted peoples). Yam is the ancient name for Nubia, an area stretching from Aswan to Khartoum in the south of Egypt. The name was in use up until around 1300 B.C.E., shortly after the time of Pharaoh Akhenaten, but then it was gradually replaced by the name Cush, which had come into use about 1650 B.C.E. As we know from archaeology, Akhenaten built a city and temple at Sesebi, in middle Yam, and may have been appointed a prince of Kush by his father Amenhotep III, and later designated himself Lion of Cush. It is not inconceivable that Habakkuk's recording of recriminations to be enacted against this region of upper Egypt might reflect a distant memory of Pharaoh Akhenaten being ambushed and murdered while on a visit to his southern capital city. This might explain his sudden disappearance from the pages of history and Habakkuk's attitude toward the peoples of Cush. Even the nature of Akhenaten's death might be indicated by the form of revenge to be extracted: "You will smash the roof of the villain's house, raze it from foundation to top. You will crack his skull with your bludgeon; blown away shall be his warriors, whose delight is to crush me suddenly, to devour a poor man in an ambush" (1QpHabakkuk).

33. Robert Feather, *The Mystery of the Copper Scroll of Qumran* (Inner Traditions, 2003).

34. Remains of pre–First Temple–period chariots have never been found in Israel, whereas numerous examples from the post-Hyksos period in Egypt (c. 1550 B.C.E.) have been discovered. A number are on exhibit in the Cairo Museum. Only one hoard of pre-coinage (any metal used in trade before the first coins or marked metal came into use, around 620 B.C.E.) has ever been found in Israel, at Gezer, and that comprised a small ingot and an electrum coil (see Robert D. Leonard, Jr., "A Numismatic Illustration of the Bible," *World Coins*, December 1987).

35. Although most commentators cannot conceive of the descriptions of these temple buildings as being anything other than utopian, they are curious about the mundane mention of latrines, the specific dimensions, their vast size, and what appear to be remembered details of their construction. As I argue in *The Mystery of the Copper Scroll of Qumran*, these memories are not imaginary; they are vague recollections of the Great Temple at Akhetaten. Ezekiel 47, for example, gives the distance of the temple from a "Great River"; it is exactly the distance of the present ruins of Akhenaten's temple from the Nile—which, according to geologists, has not altered significantly over the intervening period. Enoch 26:3 also mentions a river running eastward of the temple. Other studies on the Dead Sea Temple Scroll and New Jerusalem Scroll—neither of which ever actually mentions Jerusalem (nor does Ezekiel, in the context of the temple he is describing, while references in Deuteronomy 12:5 studiously avoid mentioning Jerusalem)—make it clear that the writers of these scrolls knew the layout and design of the city of Akhetaten and its buildings. See, for example, Jeorg Frey, "The New Jerusalem Text from the Qumran Library in Context," paper presented at Dead Sea Scrolls Fifty Years After Their Discovery, International Congress, Jerusalem, July 20–25, 1997; Shlomo Margalit, "Aelia Capitolina," *Judaica* 45 (March 1989); Michael Chyutin, "The New Jerusalem Scroll from Qumran: A Comprehensive Reconstruction," *Journal for the Study of the Pseudepigrapha*, suppl. 25 (Sheffield Academic, 1997); Jacob Licht, "An Ideal Town Plan from Qumran: The Description of the New Jerusalem," *Israel Exploration Journal* 29 (no. 1, 1979). Another Dead Sea Scroll, 1QH6, shows God as a builder of both a holy city and a temple existing in the present (Otto Betz, "Jesus and the Temple Scroll," in James H. Charlesworth, ed., *Jesus and the Dead Sea Scrolls*, Doubleday, 1992).

36. According to tractate Sanhedrin in the Babylonian Talmud, the messiah was expected to come in 239 C.E., just four thousand years after the beginning of creation according to the Jewish calendar. As he did not arrive, he is still expected, to be heralded by Elijah. Belief in the coming of the messiah has been a cornerstone of traditional Judaism and was the twelfth of thirteen principles of faith enunciated by the great medieval Jewish philosopher Moses Maimonides (1135–1204). In his *Guide to the Perplexed,* Maimonides foresaw the messiah bringing the exiles back to Israel, the rebuilding of the Temple, the resurrection of the righteous dead, and the universal recognition and worship of God. One branch of contemporary Judaism, as represented by the Lubavitch, has many followers who believe the messiah has already arrived on earth in the form of their late leader Rebbe Menachem Schneerson, who died in June 1994 in America. Some of Schneerson's followers fully expected him to return seven years after his death to redeem the world. Others were more patient, and this has caused divisions in the movement. There are certain parallels in this modern scenario to the events subsequent to the death of Jesus as well as to an event in Jewish Hassidic history. In the Middle Ages, the Magid of Mezeritch, a disciple of the Ba'al Shem Tov, the founder of Hassidism, died without leaving a successor. The divisions that this uncertainty engendered caused his followers to spread far and wide, laying the seeds of future dynasties.

37. Siegmund Hurwitz, *Die Gestalt des sterbenden Messias* (Zürich, 1958). See also Mark L. Winer, *Messianic Ideas Among the Rabbis of the First Two Tannaitic Generations,* master's thesis, Hebrew Union College (New York, 1970). Rabbi Winer cites early rabbinic Tannaitic literature (70–135 C.E.) in which the messiah is referred to as Ben David ("house of David") and Melech Maschiach ("kingly messiah" or "anointed king"), indicating there were, perhaps, two concepts of the messiah.

## Chapter 9: The Teacher of Righteousness and Expectations of the End Days

1. Robert Feather, *The Mystery of the Copper Scroll of Qumran* (Inner Traditions, 2003).

2. Frank Moore Cross, *The Ancient Library of Qumran* (Anchor, 1961; Sheffield Academic, 1995); Hartmut Stegemann, *The Library of Qumran* (Eerdmans/Brill, 1998).

3. John. J. Collins, *Apocalypticism in the Dead Sea Scrolls* (Routledge, 1997). Martin Hengel, *Property and Riches in the Early Church: Aspects of a Social History of Early Christianity* (SCM, 1974).

4. Ibid.

5. Professor Devorah Dimant, of Haifa University, Israel, takes the period of 390 years given in the Damascus document as dating from the beginning of Nebuchadnezzar's reign, and therefore places the emergence of the Essenes to nearer 200 B.C.E., even though the Dead Sea Scroll clearly talks about the destruction of the Second Temple as the significant date for the start of the 390-year period. Having made this assumption, she then finds that a commonly held view that the

Teacher of Righteousness was associated with Jonathan the Maccabee—the so-called Wicked Priest—becomes quite untenable. She cannot assert anyone as the Teacher of Righteousness that fits her chronology, however, and leaves the matter as "still an uncharted land waiting to be exploited" (lecture to the Institute of Jewish Studies, University College London, December 4, 2002).

6. H. H. Rowley, *The Zadokite Fragments and the Dead Sea Scrolls* (Oxford University Press, 1952); Frank Moore Cross, *The Ancient Library of Qumran* (Anchor, 1961; Sheffield Academic, 1995).

7. Emil Schürer, Geza Vermes, and Fergus Millas, eds., *The History of the Jewish People in the Age of Jesus Christ (175 BC–AD 135)* (T & T Clark, 1973). That the Qumran Essenes could have had a reasonably accurate knowledge of previous chronology is attested to by their writings and by the knowledge in contempory Jewish circles. For example, in 1 Maccabees, written around the first century B.C.E., it is clear the authors, who were antagonistic to the Qumran Essenes, knew the exact length of the reign of Alexander the Great and dated Antiochus IV Epiphanes (who started his rule in the Holy Land in 175 B.C.E.) as coming into office 137 years after the Persians were ousted by the Greeks. Ptolemy, the Greek ruler of Egypt, annexed the Holy Land and drove out the Persians in 312 B.C.E—the exact period of years recorded in 1 Maccabees. See P. R. Davies, G. J. Brooke, and P. R. Callaway, *The Complete World of the Dead Sea Scrolls* (Thames and Hudson, 2002).

8. Ibid.

9. Tel el-Yehoudiah (according to Josephus, Leontopolis was in the nome of Heliopolis) was first described by travelers in the early part of the nineteenth century, and subsequently excavations were undertaken by E. Brugsch Bey, and more extensive work was done by Edouard Naville and F. Griffith commencing in 1887 (*Mound of the Jew and the City of Onias*, Kegan Paul, Trench, Trübner, 1890). It lies some fourteen miles north of where Heliopolis (where modern Cairo now stands) is thought to have been located. Remains from the Middle Kingdom period and from the periods of Seti I, Ramses II and III, and Merneptah found at the site include a representation of the huge Temple of On. This shows a double flight of steps leading to the sanctuary level. The steps are guarded by sphinxes and two great pylons flanking the double gate of the sanctuary, and these are fronted by tall masts or flagstaffs. Only one main god, Tum Harmakhis, seems to have been worshipped at the site, which is located north of the supposed location of the Temple of On (Heliopolis). A later-period necropolis, about one mile from the main site, contained *fours à cercueils*–style burials similar to those found in Jewish cemeteries with tombs inscribed in Greek and Hebrew. The adjoining Jewish settlement is identified as that founded by Onias IV, as described by Josephus. It included a large temple with a tower sixty cubits (ninety-eight feet) high. The inner furnishings were apparently patterned on those in the Jerusalem Temple, except that the candelabra (menorah) was replaced by a golden lamp or orb hanging on a golden chain. The Jewish temple at Leontopolis survived for some 340 years and was eventually closed and destroyed on the instructions of the Roman emperor Vespasian, who knew the settlement as Scence Veteranorum ("Old Establishment") after the destruction of the Second Temple in Jerusalem,

probably to prevent it from being used as a rallying point for further revolts.

10. Until recently it was thought that synagogue-style worship did not exist before the destruction of the Second Temple in Jerusalem in 70 C.E. In the 1960s, however, an open synagogue area on top of Masada was identified as having been built before 70 C.E. In the same period, another synagogue was excavated at Herodian, near Hebron, in Israel. More recently, in the 1990s archaeologists from Hebrew University uncovered a synagogue dating to circa 100 B.C.E. beneath the ruins of a palace built by King Herod near Jericho. The synagogue, together with the remainder of a Hasmonean winter palace complex, was destroyed in the earthquake of 31 B.C.E. (which also damaged the buildings at Qumran). The excavations have revealed a *genizah* niche cut into a wall like that at the Ben Ezra Synagogue in Cairo, probably for the storage of holy texts; a *mikvah* (ritual bath); and a room for ceremonial meals. The synagogue at Jericho is now the oldest known example in Israel, predating by some thirty years the Gamla synagogue, discovered in the Golan Heights (J. Hunting, "Archaeology Near Jericho," *The Vineyard*, David Press, March 2001). Michael Grant, however, claims that the earliest form of synagogue worship for which there is evidence comes from Schedia, some fourteen miles from Alexandria, dating to circa 225 B.C.E. (Michael Grant, *The Jews in the Roman World*, Weidenfeld and Nicolson, 1973).

11. Flavius Josephus, *Jewish Wars* 7 (for example, H. St. J. Thakeray, *Josephus, The Jewish War*, Heineman, 1957; William Whiston and Paul L. Maier, *The New Complete Works of Josephus*, Kreel, 1999).

12. S. H. Steckholl, "The Qumran Sect in Relation to the Temple of Leontopolis," *Revue de Qumran* 1967, vol. 6, no. 21 (see also 1969, vol. 7, no. 25).

13. S. H. Steckholl, "Marginal Notes on the Qumran Excavations," *Revue de Qumran* 25 (1969).

14. Robert Feather, *The Mystery of the Copper Scroll of Qumran* (Inner Traditions, 2003). In a presentation at Harvard Divinity School in April 1996, Professor F. M. Cross suggested that Simon the son of Boethus, Herod the Great's father-in-law, was the descendant of the priestly house that served in the Onias Temple near Leontopolis. Simon originated from Alexandria, in Egypt. This family line of priests, calling themselves Boethians, continued after the demise of Qumran and could well be the link back, from a separate ancient priestly line of true heirs, to the old high priesthood through to Onias IV. Simon's predecessor, Jesus the son of Phiabi, carries an Egyptian name that was found on a Jewish inscription at Tell el-Yehudia, near Leontopolis. Having a close relative who was part of the Egyptian priestly line that founded the Qumran-Essene establishment would help explain Herod's favorable attitude toward the Essenes, as recorded in Josephus's writings. It would also neatly confirm why Onias IV would have had the historical priestly credentials and learning, as the Teacher of Righteousness, to lead a separatist community into the wilderness of Judaea to Qumran. See Israel Knohl, "New Light on the Copper Scroll and 4QMMT," in *Copper Scroll Studies*, ed. by G. J. Brooke and P. R. Davies (Sheffield Academic, 2002).

15. Ibid.

16. See Dead Sea Scroll 1QpHab, and also 4QpPsa.

17. Josephus records that Menelaus was executed by Antiochus around 163 B.C.E.:

"Accordingly, the king sent Menelaus to Bervoe in Syria, and there had him put to death" (*Jewish Antiquities* 12).

18. 1 Maccabees is thought to have been written in Hebrew around 120 B.C.E. and 2 Maccabees around 160 B.C.E. The books are not included in the version of the Hebrew Scriptures used by Jews and Protestants, but the first two of the four known books of the Maccabees are part of the Catholic canon.

19. Pythagoras (580–500 B.C.E.) was, in the words of the philosopher Bertrand Russell, "intellectually one of the most important men that ever lived" (*A History of Western Philosophy,* Allen and Unwin, 1946). He founded a mystic group in the Greek colony of Croton in southern Italy. Josephus, in fact, equates the Essenes to Pythagoreans (*Jewish Antiquities* 15.371). The degrees of sympathy to Greek thought and culture in the Jewish communities fell roughly into three categories: traditionalists, exemplified by Joshua ben Sira, author of the Wisdom of ben Sira (Ecclesiasticus), who rejected any Greek assimilations; moderates, who admired the philosophical works of Greek thinkers such as Pythagoras, Socrates, Plato, and Aristotle; and extreme Greek sympathizers, exemplified by those who underwent operations to reverse the visible signs of circumcision so they could participate naked in the Greek gymnasium built by Antiochus IV (175–163 B.C.E.). Tuvia Fogel, president of the literary agency Caduceo S.R.L., Milan, has pointed out that there is a tradition that Pythagoras actually met Ezekiel when they were both exiled in Babylonia, and that the influences may have been mutually beneficial. Bearing in mind Professor Ben Zion Wacholder's assertion that Ezekiel was the first Essene, this possible meeting becomes even more pertinent and credible.

20. Christopher Knight and Robert Lomas, in their book *The Second Messiah* (Barnes and Noble, 2000), suggest that the Anglican King James version of the Bible drops the two Books of Maccabees because they were anti-Nasorean, implying there was a link from the Essenes to the Nasoreans through James, the brother of Jesus, that Jacobite interests did not want criticized. This idea ties in with their thesis that Freemasonry can trace its ancestry back through the Jacobite king James VI of Scotland and the influence of remnants of Templar crusader knights who fled to Scotland in the fourteenth century, bringing with them Nasorean knowledge and who were thus pro-Essenic. In *The Jews in the Roman World* (Weidenfeld and Nicolson, 1973), Michael Grant suggests that one of the reasons why Judas Maccabeus, for all his heroic triumphs in recovering the Temple at Jerusalem (165–64 B.C.E.), is never mentioned in the Mishnah (oral laws forming part of the Talmud) is that he got in bed with the Romans in his attempts to resist Seleucid influences.

21. The reason for exclusion of the books of Maccabees from the Hebrew Scriptures may well be yet another indication that Essenic thinking dominated early rabbinic thinking. One of the prime characteristics of the Jewish Hassidim ("devout ones"), who have been linked to the early ancestry of the Essenes, was their apparent ability to perform miracles. One such exponent, living at the time of Jesus, was a certain Honi, referred to by Josephus as Onias the Righteous and also as Onias in the Mishnah (tractate Taanith 3.9). The implication seems to be that his abilities were being compared to an Onias, perhaps Onias IV, who also had miracle-performing talents.

22. James H. Charlesworth, "Jesus as 'Son' and the Righteous Teacher as 'Gardener,' " in *Jesus and the Dead Sea Scrolls*, ed. by James H. Charlesworth (Doubleday, 1992).

23. Ibid.

24. André Dupont-Sommer, *The Dead Sea Scrolls: A Preliminary Survey*, trans. by A. Margaret Rowley (Oxford/Blackwell, 1952).

25. Classified as Psalm D by A. Dupont-Sommer, and as Hymn 12 of the Thanksgiving Hymns in Geza Vermes, *The Complete Dead Sea Scrolls in English* (Allen Lane/Penguin, 1997). Vermes translates Møth-Belial as "devilish schemes," however.

26. Ian Shaw and Paul Nicholson, *British Museum Dictionary of Ancient Egypt* (British Museum Press, 1995).

## Chapter 10: Ethereal Melchizedek—and Kabbalah

1. Hartmut Stegemann, professor of New Testament studies at the University of Göttingen, Germany, has even suggested that Melchizedek is the fourth awaited anti-messiah.

2. Descriptions of Melchizedek appear in the Bible in Genesis 14:18–24, where he meets and blesses Abraham; Hebrews 5–8, where Jesus is likened to him; Psalm 110; and in 11QMelch, 4QShirShabb, 1QM of the Dead Sea Scrolls.

3. Alan F. Segal, "The Risen Christ and the Angelic Mediator Figures in Light of Qumran," in *Jesus and the Dead Sea Scrolls*, ed. by James H. Charlesworth (Doubleday, 1992).

4. Robert Feather, *The Mystery of the Copper Scroll of Qumran* (Inner Traditions, 2003).

5. Gershom Scholem, *Kabbalah* (Penguin, 1978).

6. See Psalm 82; also Alan F. Segal, "The Risen Christ and the Angelic Mediator Figures in Light of Qumran," mentioned in a contribution in *Jesus and the Dead Sea Scrolls*, ed. by James H. Charlesworth (Doubleday, 1992). In the Book of Tobit, Raphael appears as an angel who helps Tobit. The book has been included in the Christian canon from Greek, Latin, and Syriac versions, but it has long been recognized that a Semitic version lay behind these. (According to Jerome, there was an Aramaic version, but neither Tobit nor the Book of Judith was available in Hebrew.) However, the ancient story of Ahiqar, alluded to in Tobit, was found among the Elephantine papyri in 1907, written in Aramaic, and sections of Tobit in Aramaic and Hebrew have come to light at Qumran. Although the story appears to be set in Assyria, it clearly draws on Egyptian words and folklore. Raguel, one of the names for Moses's father-in-law, appears in the story, and there are themes based on the classic Egyptian "Tale of Two Brothers," and the so-called tractate of Khons (see Joseph A. Fitzmyer, *The Dead Sea Scrolls and Christian Origins*, Eerdmans, 2000). Khons was one of the Theban triad of gods, whose mother was Mut and father Amun. He is usually seen as a moon god and is depicted as a youth. Perhaps even more significant is the amplification of the role of a figure named Ahiqar. The Qumran text puts him as chief cupbearer, keeper of the signet rings, treasury accountant, and second only to the king, Esarhaddon, whose name con-

tains the syllable –*adon.* These titles are exact in phrasing and are almost certainly borrowed from Egyptian epithets for the highest-ranked courtiers, in this instance the courtier I have previously identified as the biblical Joseph (see Robert Feather, *The Mystery of the Copper Scroll of Qumran,* Inner Traditions, 2003).

7. Two of the same featherlike symbols commence the hieroglyph word for Israel seen in the stela of Pharaoh Merneptah, dated to c. 1210 B.C.E. This is the first known representation of the name of Israel, in the sense of its being the name of a people rather than a place-name. Here the double *yy* sound of the two symbols, meaning God, almost certainly explains the use of the double-Yod as an abbreviation of the name of God that appears in Hebrew (Messod Sabbah and Roger Sabbah, *Les Secrets de l'Exode,* Jean-Cyrille Godefroy, 2000).

8. It is not surprising that Merkabah, or "heavenly chariot," mysticism was strongly condemned by later rabbis, who proscribed discussion on the subject (m.Hag 2.1). The subject led straight back to the heavenly chariot of Pharaoh Akhenaten, Egypt, and a possible eclipsing of Moses. Nevertheless, the tradition of mysticism and heavenly transformation left a strong footprint in both the Hebrew and Christian Scriptures, in the latter particularly through the Christian Scriptures' continuing concentration on the subject (Rom. 8:29; 1 Cor. 15:49; 2 Cor. 3:18, 4:4; Phil. 3:21).

9. Margaret Barker, "The Time Is Fulfilled: Jesus and the Jubilee," *Scottish Journal of Theology,* vol. 53, no. 22, 2000. Melchizedek also appears in Psalm 110 and in the Epistle to the Hebrews. In extrabiblical texts, Melchizedek is known from Egyptian Coptic tradition—for example, in the Epistle of Sofia, as Receiver of Light and Treasurer of Light, where he was once a man; in the Book of Jehu; and Coptic text NHX9.1, where Jesus is identified with Melchizedek. Philo of Alexandria (*Legum Allegoriarum* 3.79–82) mentions Melchizedek as a divine mediator. Another figure associated with Melchizedek, and his later alternative name of Metatron, is known as "the Youth." The Youth appears in the Cambridge University Library collection (more specifically, the Cairo Genizah Taylor Schecter collection 21.95) and in Siddur Rabbah (see James R. Davila, "Melchizedek, the 'Youth,' and Jesus: The Dead Sea Scrolls and Messianism, Christology, and Mysticism," International Conference of the Dead Sea Scrolls as Background to Postbiblical Judaism and Early Christianity, University of St. Andrews, June 26–28, 2001). The possibility that pagan Egyptian influences slipped back into Israelite imagery should also not be ignored. The characteristics of the Youth might possibly be based on the idea of Horus, who embodied divine kingship and was protector of the reigning pharaoh. As a child, Horus had the power to overcome harmful forces, and in this guise is sometimes seen sitting on the lap of his mother, Isis. He can be seen in a *cippus,* a protective amulet or stela, from 750 B.C.E. onward, or on votive statuettes in Egypt. In some stories Horus himself becomes king of all Egypt after a prolonged struggle over control of the "two lands" with his bitter rival, Seth. In another possible example, a cultic ceremony is described in Qumran scrolls 4Q510 and 4Q511, the details of which are not understood (see James R. Davila, "The Dead Sea Scrolls and Merkavah Mysticism," in *The Dead Sea Scrolls in Their Historical Context,* ed. by Timothy H. Lim; T & T Clark, 2000). The fragmentary references to the ritual being one of exorcism accompanied by music and singing, and "on the eighth day I will

open my [mouth]," have all the basic formulae for the Egyptian ceremony of "opening of the mouth," whereby royal succession was legitimized and the predecessor's body was brought back to life and transformed into a vessel for the Ka (life-giving force, perhaps equivalent to the modern concept of the soul) of the deceased. See Ian Shaw and Paul Nicholson, *British Museum Dictionary of Ancient Egypt* (BCA, 1995).

10. Joseph A. Fitzmyer, *Responses to 101 Questions on the Dead Sea Scrolls* (Paulist Press, 1992).

11. D. W. Rooke, "Jesus as Royal Priest: Reflections of the Interpretation of the Melchizedek Tradition in Heb. 7," *Biblica* 81 (2000).

12. Florentino Garcia Martinez and Julio Barrera Trebolle, *The People of the Dead Sea Scrolls—Their Writings, Beliefs and Practices,* translated by Wilfred Watson, Leiden, 1995. Florentino Garcia Martinez, *The Dead Sea Scrolls Translated,* E. J. Brill, 1996.

13. Y. Yadin, "A Note on Melchizedek and Qumran," *Israel Exploration Journal* 15 (1965); M de Jonge and A. S. van der Woude, "11Q Melchizedek and the New Testament," *New Testament Studies* 12 (1966); J. A. Fitzmyer, "Further Light on Melchizedek from Qumran Cave 11," *Journal of Biblical Studies* 86 (1967).

14. In the Epistle to the Hebrews 7:6 ("But he [King Salem] whose descent is *not* counted of them [i.e., who did not come out of the loins of Abraham and was not a Hebrew] received tithes of Abraham, and blessed him"), just as Abraham has to be seen to be associated with the divine figure of Melchizedek (retrospectively in terms of the authors of the Hebrew Scriptures and futuristically in terms of the chronology of Abraham in relation to King Akhenaten and his high priest, Meryra), so Jesus has also to be associated with the kingly priestly figure. That the high priest of the Great Temple at Akhetaten was the prototype for later Israelite high priests can be seen from a *shabti* (small figurine) in the Metropolitan Museum of Art, New York. The descriptions of the robes of the Israelite high priests (Lev. 8:8; Ezra 2:63; Neh. 7:65; Exod. 28:7–8, 29:32) closely match the color and design of the robes seen on the Meryra shabti. As William L. Lane, "Hebrews 1–8," (WBC 47A, Dallas 1991) rightly points out, even though Melchizedek united the dual honors of royalty and priesthood, he was unlike the Hebrew kings. This article can also be found in *Jesus as Royal Priest: Reflections on the Interpretation of the Melchizedek Tradition* in Heb. 7, by D. W. Rooke, in *Biblica* 81, 2000.

15. The Amarna letters are collections of some four hundred cuneiform tablets comprising records of correspondence between the Egyptian court and vassal states, composed in the mid-fourteenth century B.C.E. They were discovered at Amarna in 1887. In Amarna letter EA 287, the governor, Abdi-Heba (also translated as Abdi-Khepa), is writing to Pharaoh Akhenaten, setting out his fears for the safety of the city: "As the king has placed his name in Jerusalem forever, he cannot abandon it—the land of Jerusalem" (*The Amarna Letters,* ed. and trans. William L. Moran, Johns Hopkins University Press, Baltimore and London, 1992). As far as I am aware, this is the first-ever mention of Jerusalem in written texts. Confirmation that the king of Salem, of Genesis, is a holy king comes from Joshua 10:3, where the king is referred to as Adoni-Zedek, relating him to God, as Aton, and high priest.

16. Leonora Leet, *The Secret Doctrine of the Kabbalah* (Inner Traditions, 1999), gives numerous examples of Egyptian traditions taken up into Kabbalah. Graham Phillips, *The Moses Legacy* (Pan, 2002), notes that the Sabean Stone, an inscribed block measuring approximately nineteen by eight by eight inches found in the Valley of Edom near Wadi Musa (Moses's Wadi) and close to Jebel Madhbah—a mountain said by the author to be one possible site where the Ten Commandments were handed down to Moses—carries the design of a six-branched tree with a serpent wrapped around the trunk. It is almost identical to later depictions of the Kabbalistic Tree of Life. The Sabean Stone was discovered in 1982 and is dated to around the time of Jesus, as its inscription mentions King Aretas IV, who is known from other sources to have reigned from 8 B.C.E. to 40 C.E. Above the inscription is the carving of a dish shape beneath what can only be a sun disk.

17. After the death of a pharaoh or other important person, the body was taken to a receiving temple for thirty days of mummification, preparation, and mourning. This temple was offset at a distance from the pyramid or final burial structure. After thirty days the body was moved up a causeway to a mortuary temple, located directly opposite the pyramid or place of final burial, where the body lay for a further forty days. Here the dead were judged before Osiris and forty-two judges, as illustrated in chapter 125 of the Book of the Dead. Anubis then led the deceased into the judgment chamber, where the heart (considered to be the organ responsible for thought, wisdom, emotion, and memory, and, therefore, unlike all the other organs, not permanently removed from the body in the mummification process) was weighed by Anubis, on a balance, against a feather—the sign of justice and truth. (In his study of a passage from the Hebrew Scriptures, "An Often Overlooked Alphabetic Acrostic in Proverbs 24:1–22," *Revue Biblique,* 2000, Victor Avigdor Hurowitz, Department of Bible and Ancient Near East Studies, Ben Gurion University of the Negev, Beersheva, Israel, concludes, "The middle line of the composition (v 12b) has a textual and iconographic parallel in the Egyptian *Book of the Dead,* the balance of the composition reflecting the weighing of hearts in the beam balance by Toth.")

    The feather was the symbol of *maat*—pure truth, justice, order, and harmony. If the heart was found to be as light as the feather, the heart could be returned to the deceased, who could then proceed to the next stage of attaining the afterlife. The result of the weighing was recorded by Thoth, the god of writing and knowledge (depicted as a baboon or later as an ibis-headed man), and the candidate was then led on by Horus to meet Osiris, his father. The deceased was identified with the god Osiris as he or she underwent a transformation into Osiris and achieved resurrection, just as Osiris did after being killed by his evil brother, Seth, and avenged by the efforts of his wife, Isis, and their son, Horus.

18. The Zohar was largely developd within a Jewish community living around Toledo, in Spain, in the thirteenth century C.E. It was written down by Moses b. Shem Tov de León in Guadalajara, Spain, between 1280 and 1286 C.E. The earliest extant manuscripts of the Zohar are in Cambridge, England, and are dated to the last third of the fourteenth century C.E.

19. In his classical history of the evolution of Kabbalah (*Kabbalah,* Penguin, 1978), Gershom Scholem ascribes the first appearance of apocalyptic literature to either

the Pharisees or the Essenes of Qumran and is left with numerous unanswered questions on the origins of Kabbalah. With hindsight it is easy to be critical, but had Scholem had access to all the Dead Sea Scrolls material now available, no doubt he would have written a rather different book. After the expulsion of the Jews from Spain in 1492, the movement spread throughout the Diaspora while continuing to be embellished and expanded, and it took root in centers such as Safed in the Holy Land; Venice, in Italy; Salonika, in Turkey; and Fez, in Morocco. Throughout the Middle Ages, Kabbalah continued to develop a spectrum of forms, culminating in Westernized versions that have caught the imagination of people seeking a deeper spiritual understanding, such as Barbra Streisand, Madonna, Richard Gere, Winona Ryder, Sir Elton John, Sir Mick Jagger, Britney Spears, Demi Moore, Jeff Goldblum, Naomi Campbell, and Elizabeth Taylor.

20. Willis Barnstone, ed., *The Other Bible* (Harper & Row, 1984). Diagrammatic symbolism and reading significances into words through positioning and numerology (*gematria,* a procedure of assigning numbers to Hebrew letters) became a central part of Kabbalistic studies. Parallels to Egyptian mythology can be traced in many areas of Kabbalah. One example is the concept of Da'at, or knowledge, present in the divine process through a series of ten Sefirot symbolizing the evolution of primeval man, often shown in the form of a Tree of Emanation, Life, or Knowledge. The Egyptian concept of *dat* was of a place where the formation of the living out of the dead and the past occurred—the source of new life, but also a dangerous place where demons of the underworld lurked (see, for example, R. T. Rundle Clark, *Myth and Symbol in Ancient Egypt,* Thames and Hudson, 1978).

21. Rabbinic Judaism involved the development of the Mishnah and Talmud as supplementary law, regulation, and commentary on how Judaism could be sustained in an environment devoid of Temple-centered worship, which is thought to have developed from Pharisaic teaching. When the Second Temple no longer existed, the disenfranchised Sadducees were considered to have played little part in the evolution of so-called Rabbinic Judaism in the early part of the millennium. Although there were undoubtedly men of learning among the Pharisees, the movement was made up of predominantly the laity. Major Jewish scholars, like Hillel, Shammai, and Gamaliel, must have had an influence on the pre-Tannaitic period when the Hebrew Scriptures were in the process of being solidified, but they were not present during the final stages. Hillel was a first-century-B.C.E. Jewish scholar, born in Babylon, who became president of the Sanhedrin and founder of the school known as the House of Hillel. His main rival was Shammai, who founded the House of Shammai, and who may have been a Pharisee. Gamaliel the Elder, early first century C.E., was the most important of a line of Palestinian rabbis. He was a grandson of Hillel and also became a president of the Sanhedrin in Jerusalem. He is mentioned in the Christian Scriptures as a teacher of Paul (Acts 22:3). Both Hillel and Shammai lived in the first century B.C.E., and Gamaliel in the early first century C.E. We know very little about the original teachings of the Pharisees except by implication, and we have nothing of their first-century-C.E. writings. We do, however, know that the knowledge and depth of hermeneutic expertise (hermeneutics involves the study of the meaning and interpretation of, in this context, biblical Scriptures) was paramount among the Essenes at the time

of the development of Rabbinic Judaism. Their nucleus was made up of devoutly learned Zadokite Kohanim priests, who dated their lineage back at least to the time of the First Temple. From 1947 onward, with the discovery of the Dead Sea Scrolls, we have learned a huge amount about the religious sophistication of the Essenes. Their texts show clear pre-Mishnaic form and conceptualization, and it is they who must have been the prime movers in the new structure of Judaism that needed to be developed after the Roman destruction of the Second Temple.

The main preoccupation of the Essenes, particularly at Qumran, was study and prayer related to their personalized form of religion, and they were almost certainly more biblically knowledgeable than any other group in Judaea at the time of the destruction of the Second Temple. From what we now know of the Essenes' doctrines and depth of understanding, and because they had already developed a highly sophisticated philosophy of religious worship independent of the Temple long before its destruction in 70 C.E., it is almost certain that Essenic Judaism formed the main basis for Rabbinic Judaism. (See Hartmut Stegemann, *The Library of Qumran,* Eerdmans/Brill, 1998; and Günter Stemberger, *Jewish Contemporaries of Jesus: Pharisees, Sadducees, Essenes,* Fortress Press, 1995).

This is not the place to enter into the detail of how the Essenic viewpoint can be seen to have dominated rabbinic thinking, a subject that warrants a book in its own right. The Eighth Orion International Symposium, held in January 2003 at the Hebrew University of Jerusalem, focused on the subject, concluding that there was substantive agreement between Qumran and early rabbinic *halakha* (religious law), and that sectarian thinking had a far more powerful influence on Pharisaic thinking than has previously been acknowledged. A few examples will suffice:

- Return to and preservation of the authentic Hebrew language was a sacred task of the Essenes, unlike the surrounding Jewish community, which used Aramaic in everyday speech and writing. The Qumran Essenes' reference to, and usage of, paleo-Hebrew (dating back to 1000 B.C.E.) and style of contemporary Hebrew writing can clearly be seen to be pre-Mishnaic, in a form taken up by Rabbinic Judaism.

- Later Judaism, of Talmudic times, talks of the Messiah as the Anointed One— a king who will appear in the cataclysmic End Days. Although the Hebrew Scriptures talk of the End Days, they do not combine this event with an anointed messiah, which was a purely Essenic understanding.

- The manner for deciding what regulations and laws would govern the new situation Judaism found itself in after the destruction of the Second Temple, as envisaged today, was very similar to that already established by the Essenes at Qumran (see Dead Sea Scroll 1QS; also Stephan J. Pfann, "The Writings of Esoteric Script from Qumran," paper presented at Dead Sea Scrolls Fifty Years After Their Discovery, International Congress, Jerusalem, July 20–25, 1997, www.hum.huji.ac.il. Here decisions were voted on by a council and voting members, after a period of intense consideration of the holy books, discussion, and reference to previous decisions. Once agreed to, a decision took on divine authority. Subsequently, the collection of *mishpatim* (laws, regulations) was recopied and organized topically. (The Mishnah tractate Abot, chapter 1, gives a fragmentary account of the succession of Pharisaic authorities. Were the Pharisees the main authors of Rabbinic Judaism, one might expect a more detailed record. In addition, tractate Abot refers to the first sages not as Pharisees, but as an anonymous body called "the men of the Great Council," who were regarded as existing around 350 B.C.E. If this assembly was the Temple Sanhedrin, it would almost certainly have been named as such, so the logical conclusion is that this anonymous council was a forerunner of the type of council established by the Essenes at Qumran, and that the sages of that council were proto-Essenes.) The Essenes already had an established format for synagogue-style worship, which did not depend on the existence of the Temple. Their ritual of worship three times each day, using *tefillin* (phylacteries), became the accepted periodicy of daily prayer in Rabbinic Judaism.

Apart from the many positive correspondences that can be drawn between worship practice by the Essenes and post–Second Temple synagogue worship, there are differences that, where documented, are equally telling. Although many of the worship features adopted by the Qumran Essenes appear to have been based on Temple worship and their own theology, the singing of hymns or psalms seems not to have been the worship custom at Qumran. Neither Josephus nor Philo refers to any singing or chants by the Essenes. However, Philo, in his *De vita contemplativa,* is very specific about the singing of hymns by the Therapeutae. The lack of singing in Essene worship may explain the same lack in early Rabbinic Judaism–period worship. Psalm singing did not enter into synagogue liturgy until rather late in its development (see Eileen M. Schuller, "The Use and Function of Psalms from Qumran: Revisiting the Question," paper presented at Liturgical Perspectives: Prayer and Poetry in Light of the Dead Sea Scrolls, Orion Symposium, Hebrew University of Jerusalem, January 19–23, 2000, http://orion.huji.ac.il.

It is generally assumed that after the war with Rome, a Pharisaic group led by Johanan ben Zakkai set up a center of learning at Jabneh (Javneh) on the coast near modern Tel Aviv, and there began the formalization of the Hebrew Scriptures, the Mishnah, and the Talmud. Many scholars doubt the existence of a rabbinic school at Jabneh, however, and the so-called Pharisees, who are thought to have formed the caucus of putative Rabbinic Judaism and were known to be a separate group, had many characteristics of the Essenes. The Essenes, also referred to as Hassidim ("Saints"), were extremely devout charismatic wonder workers and healers; in my view, they almost certainly came from the Qumran or Jerusalem centers of Essenism. (André Dupont-Sommer, professor at the Sorbonne, noted in his *Dead Sea Scrolls: A Preliminary Survey*, Oxford/Blackwell, 1952, that the word Hassidim is derived from the Hebrew word *hasidh,* meaning "pious," the equivalent of the Aramaic *hese.* "I am persuaded," he asserts, "that Essenes and Hasidim are in fact identical."

Even Johanan ben Zakkai himself may have been an Essene leader. He was regarded as adept in the mysticism of the Heavenly Chariot—the Ma'aseh Merkabah, a particular specialty of the Qumran Essenes. Their texts, known as The Songs for the Holocaust of the Sabbath (see Geza Vermes, The *Complete Dead Sea Scrolls in English,* Allen Lane/Penguin, 1997), are replete with descriptions of the heavenly chariot and a temple of worship, which have clear intimations of Egyptian-style temple worship. (Although he has subsequently softened the firmness of his view, in 1982 Professor Lawrence Schiffman, of New York

University, was moved to say, "It is possible to conclude that *merkavah* mysticism had its origin at Qumran or in related sectarian circles") L. H. Schiffman, "Merkavah Speculation at Qumran: The 4Q Serek Shirot 'Olat ha-Shabbat' in *Mystics, Philosophers and Politicians: Essays in Jewish Intellectual History in Honor of Alexander Altmann*, eds., J. Reinharz, D. Swetschinski, and K. P. Bland (Duke University Press, 1982). It is perhaps for this reason that later versions of the Mishnah prohibit reading in synagogue of Chariot texts as prophetic readings, or even private discussion without the supervision of a sage (Hyam Maccoby, *Early Rabbinic Writings,* Cambridge University Press, 1988). The discovery by early Jesus-Essenes of a wall engraving at Amarna of Akhenaten riding on a chariot may also be at the root of this rabbinic aversion to heavenly chariots, despite the fact that the imagery was given to them from the stories in the Hebrew Scriptures of Elijah and Ezekiel, as described in chapter 38. Knowing from their Essene contingent that the heavenly chariot was once occupied by an Egyptian pharaoh would have raised serious inhibitions. Yet another concept, which developed post–Hebrew Scriptures, is that of Shekinah, the presence of the spirit of God. Although this idea appears in the Christian Scriptures, it is absent from the Hebrew Scriptures. The only source for it is the Dead Sea Scrolls and Qumran. According to Professor J. Charlesworth, the concept was developed by the Qumran Essenes as a foil against the Temple hierarchy and to allow the possibility of the Holy Spirit existing outside the Temple, even in a desert environment (J. H. Charlesworth, ed., *Jesus and the Dead Sea Scrolls,* Doubleday, 1993). Two different views appear in the Qumran writings concerning their idealized temple. Earlier works such as the War Scroll, Temple Scroll, Jubilees, and Testament of the Twelve Patriarchs refer to what appears to be a real temple, whereas later works such as Rule of the Community, Rule of the Congregation, the Thanksgiving Hymns, Cairo-Damascus Documents, and Florilegium talk of a spiritualization of the temple in the form of worship.

This explanation fits with the existing belief in God dwelling in the inner sanctum of the Temple, in the Holy of Holies, but it does not explain the Qumran Essenes' apparently original visualization of Shekinah as a kind of light reflected from God, which had no separate existence. Although God could not directly contact humankind, this light of Shekinah, in the form of rays, could endow grace, tenderness, and bounty on humanity, as a sort of poetic intermediary. One could hardly have a more apt description of Akhenaten's visualized intermediary between God and his people in the form of the Aten: a blinding-bright solar reflection of God's loving nature, with rays radiating bounteousness, goodness, and sustenance as well as life itself.

Johanan ben Zakkai's possible provenance as an Essene is further indicated by his paradoxical behavior toward the Qumran-Essene concept of End Days and an eschatological messiah. Initially he was opposed to such speculation, but on his deathbed, around 82 C.E., he relented and confessed to a belief in an ultimate messiah, whom he identified as none other than King Hezekiah of Judah. The connections that have already been made for King Hezekiah, in my last book, as a radical reformer who nevertheless employed the symbols of the Aten in his royal insignia demonstrate that ben Zakkai's fundamental beliefs were consistent with a continuum of adherence to the Akhenaten-Jacob-Joseph form of monotheism

(Michael Grant, *The Jews in the Roman World,* Weidenfeld and Nicolson, 1973).

Another indicator comes from the exclusion of all the books of the Maccabees from the Hebrew Scriptures. In the words of David Hyatt, a British Jewish religious educator, "It's odd the Books of the Maccabees, which recount the story of Chanukah, never became part of the Bible" (*Purim from a Yiddish Angle,* West London Synagogue, 2001). Odd indeed, as Hanukkah is one of the major festivals of Judaism, celebrating a historic event, and yet there is no mention of it in the Hebrew Scriptures. Of the six books of the Maccabees, the first four are included only in the Apocrypha (Jewish texts additional to the thirty-nine books of the Hebrew Scriptures), and the last two are left in theological limbo.

The conventional explanation is that God is not the major force described in 1 Maccabees in the recapture of the Second Temple by the Maccabean fighters. This oversight is somewhat rectified in 2 Maccabees, but apparently not enough to justify inclusion in the Hebrew Scriptures by the rabbinic authorities of the first and second centuries C.E. The explanation is somewhat weak, as Purim, a sister festival to Hanukkah (linked, for example, in the Birkat HaMatzon blessings after meals said only during Purim and Hanukkah), does have its own record in the Hebrew Scriptures, the Book of Esther—a book that does not mention God at all.

A more plausible explanation is that the antagonism expressed in 1 and 2 Maccabees toward Onias IV, who, as I have argued earlier, was the Essenes' Teacher of Righteousness, had two effects. First, not even a fragment of any of the six books of Maccabees have ever been found at Qumran. Second, if Essenism was a major influence in early Rabbinic Judaism, as I maintain, it would not be surprising to find that any work derogatory of their Teacher of Righteousness would be excluded from the Hebrew canon at this formative stage, as was the case.

Another interesting convergence comes in the exclusive burial practices of Qumran and those advocated in Rabbinic Judaism. The Qumran community maintained a strict code of conduct toward purity in relation to the dead and burial. In the Qumran Damascus document (12) we read: "And all wood and stones and dust which are defiled by the uncleanness of a dead human being shall be reckoned like them for conveying defilement: according to their uncleanness shall he that touches them become unclean. And every utensil, nail or peg in the wall that are with the dead person in the house shall become unclean in the same manner as any working tool." Compare this with Mishnah, Ohalot 1.2–4: "If vessels touch a corpse and a man touches the vessels, and then vessels touch this man, they all contract seven day uncleanness. . . . If a tent peg was stuck into the tent, the tent, the peg, the man that touches the peg, and the vessels that touch the man contract seven day uncleanness."

In November 1873 Charles Clermont-Ganneau, an explorer/archaeologist, noted the presence in the Qumran cemetery of small rectangular areas marked by stones smaller than those found on the grave sites at Qumran. These he attributed to a ritual custom recorded in the Mishnah, in which mourners would stop at seven predetermined "halting places" to recite prayers for the dead prior to interment (Mishnah, Megillah 4.3, Mishnah, Ketubot 2.10, and Mishnah, Baba Bathra 6.7). See S. H. Steckholl, "Excavation Report in the Qumran Cemetery," *Revue de Qumran* 23 (1968).

A final example of how Qumran thinking influenced later Talmud writing relates to astrology. It is generally believed that astrology did not surface in Judaism before the fourth or fifth century C.E. The finding in Cave 4 at Qumran, of an Astrology Scroll (4Q186), demonstrates that secrets of the Qumran Essenes that were kept within Rabbinic Judaism can have come only through a direct input of Essenic knowledge. Scroll 4Q186 was written in a most cryptic mode, mixing proto-Hebrew, Greek, and cryptic symbols, so that even within the Qumran-Essene community it was accessible only to the priestly leaders. Yet analysis of Talmudic literature shows that this secret Qumran literature was being drawn upon. In Talmud, Babli, Shabat 30b–31a, written post–500 C.E., a story is related concerning questions posed to the Jewish sage Hillel, who lived around 60 B.C.E. to 10 C.E. Manfred Lehman ("New Light on Astrology in Qumran and the Talmud," *Revue de Qumran* 32, 1975), concludes that the characteristics of body parts, such as head, eyes, and feet, are said to be influenced by the stars, according to 4Q186, and the same characteristics (dimensions and appearance) of these specific parts are also the subject of the questions posed to Hillel. He is asked three questions about the characteristics of heads, eyes, and feet of various peoples. These questions were previously thought to have been meaningless, posed simply to test Hillel's patience. Scroll 4Q186 demonstrates that the questions were far from meaningless. They follow a precise formula related to astrology as set out in 4Q186, and Hillel's responses are designed to teach the lesson that astrology was in conflict with his belief in free will and was therefore to be avoided.

For John J. Collins, professor of Hebrew Bible and postbiblical Judaism at the University of Chicago, the Dead Sea Scrolls represent "a form of Judaism before the great codification of rabbinic religion in the Mishnah and Talmud. In recent years there has been a growing appreciation of the common interests shared by the Dead Sea sect and the rabbis on issues of purity and halakah" (*Apocalypticism in the Dead Sea Scrolls*, Routledge, 1997).

Although the position taken by the Essenes is often at variance with later rabbinic rulings, the fact that they were addressing similar issues indicates that both parties were reading from the same basic script.

22. Manual of Discipline (otherwise known as Rule of the Community), trans. by Millar Burrows, *The Dead Sea Scrolls* (Viking Press, 1956).

23. Midrash: Shiur Kamah.

24. Leonora Leet, *The Secret Doctrine of the Kabbalah* (Inner Traditions, 1999).

25. John Pendlebury, *Tell el-Amarna* (L. Dickson & Thompson Ltd, 1935); Herbert W. Fairman, "Once Again the So-called Coffin of Akhenaten," *Journal of Egyptian Archaeology* (1961); Cyril Aldred, *Akhenaten, King of Egypt* (Thames and Hudson, 1988); Nicholas Reeves, *Akhenaten* (Thames and Hudson, 2001).

26. Indications of Egyptian pharaohs exhibiting androgynous features are rare, apart from Queen Hatshetsup, who later in her reign adopted male appurtenances, largely to hide the fact that she was a woman.

## Chapter 11: Apocalypse Soon

1. Barbara Thiering, *Jesus of the Apocalypse* (Corgi, 1997).

2. Håkan Ulfgard, "The Branch in the Last Days: Observations on the New

Covenant Before and After the Messiah," in *The Dead Sea Scrolls in Their Historical Context,* ed. by Timothy H. Lim (T & T Clark, 2000).

3. These scrolls are all written in Aramaic and include the Book of Enoch (4Q201–2, 4Q204–9), the Document of Levi (4Q213–4), the New Jerusalem scroll (1Q32, 2Q24, 4Q554–5, 5Q15, 11Q18), Pseudo-Daniel (4Q243–5), and the Prayer of Nabonidus (4Q242).

4. It has been argued that the Book of Jubilees was the central text in the Qumran collection (Charlotte Hempel, "The Place of the Book of Jubilees at Qumran and Beyond," in *The Dead Sea Scrolls in Their Historical Context,* ed. by Timothy H. Lim, T & T Clark, 2000), and that it was set within a framework dominated by the period of the patriarchs and a rich literary tradition attached to the figure of Moses. Professor Ben Zion Wacholder, of Hebrew Union College in Cincinnati, has gone so far as to label Jubilees "the Super Canon" (B. Z. Wacholder, "Jubilees as the Super Canon: Torah Admonition Versus Torah Commandment—Legal Texts and Legal Issues," in *Proceedings of the Second Meeting of the International Organisation for Qumran Studies,* Cambridge, 1995 (Brill, 1997). In light of the connections I have proposed between early Christianity and Qumran, it would not, therefore, be surprising to find that Jubilees is not found in the Hebrew Scriptures but plays a strong role in Christian liturgy. It was handed on by later Christian communities and retained as Pseudepigrapha, and in an Ethiopic version. M. E. Stone has even suggested that "the channel of transmission is the dominant criterion for inclusion of a writing in the Pseudepigrapha" ("The Dead Sea Scrolls and the Pseudepigrapha," *Dead Sea Discoveries* 3, 1996).

5. Devorah Dimant, "The Scrolls and the Study of Early Judaism," in *The Dead Sea Scrolls at Fifty: Proceedings of the 1997 Society of Biblical Literature, Qumran Section Meetings* (Scholars Press, 1999); Devorah Dimant, "The History of the Dead Sea Scrolls Ascetic Community: What Is New," paper presented at the Institute of Jewish Studies, University College London, December 4, 2002. Professor Dimant's views of the origins of the solar calendar used at Qumran are refuted by evidence from the Dead Sea Scrolls. The Jubilees scroll, for example, asserts that the 364-day year had been recorded in the "heavenly tablets" going back to the time of Moses. This conclusion was initially arrived at by A. Jaubert, of the Sorbonne. (A. Jaubert, *La Date de al Cene,* Sorbonne, Paris, 1957.) It was also noted by Professor Ben Zion Wacholder, of the Hebrew Union College, Cincinnati, it has been accepted by many scholars ("IV Kongress der International for Qumran Studies," Basel, August 5–7, 2001). In a detailed study published as the *Calendars in the Dead Sea Scrolls* (Routledge, 1998), Professor James VanderKam of the University of Notre Dame assesses the latest available translated material from Qumran and comes to the conclusion that the scrolls determinedly assign the use of the solar calendar to a very early, pre-Babylonian-influence period, dating back to at least the time of King David.

6. Aramaic fragments of the Testament of Levi found at Qumran refer to the coming "reign of the sword" and "anointing of Levi," and making him "greater than anyone." He is then dressed in priestly clothing by Jacob and invested as the highest priest. See James R. Davila, "The Dead Sea Scrolls and Merkavah Mysticism," in *The Dead Sea Scrolls in Their Historical Context,* ed. by Timothy H. Lim (T &

T Clark, 2000). Another clear example of the understanding the Qumran Essenes had of the earliest role of priests comes from 4Q213–214. Here Levi is talking about his father, Jacob, as he goes about tithing (giving a tenth of all he owned) to God, while Levi is for the first time at the head of a procession of priests and Joseph teaches Torah (from holy scrolls). The setting is a place with an altar, presumably a temple, which is being used to make offerings to God. All these functions are testified to by wall reliefs and archaeological finds at Amarna, and yet the period must be nearly several hundred years before Moses appoints any priests and four hundred years before there is a Temple in Jerusalem. Views of a line of Egyptian priests, unusually interspersed with a foreign-looking priest—whom I identify as a Hebrew from his headgear and garb—can still be seen at Amarna, as can the parading of what appears to be a Sefer Torah–style scroll. Offering jars, labeled as tithes, have also been found at Amarna.

7. Barbara Thiering, *Jesus of the Apocalypse* (Corgi, 1996); the Book of Daniel, the Testament of Levi. Dead Sea Scroll 4QEnoch (4Q212) correlates with the First Book of Enoch chapters 91 and 93: "(At its close) the chosen ones will be selected as witnesses of the justice from the Plant of Everlasting Justice [the Plant of Righteousness]; they will be given wisdom and knowledge sevenfold. They shall uproot the foundations of violence and the work of deceit in it in order to carry out (justice). After this, the eighth week will come, . . . And after (that, the tenth week. In its seventh part) there will be an eternal judgement and the moment of the great judgement (and he will carry out revenge in the midst of the holy ones) . . ."

8. Jacob Licht, "Time and Eschatology in Apocalyptic Literature and in Qumran," *Journal of Jewish Studies* vol. 16, nos. 3 and 4 (1965); J. Carmignac, "La Notion d'eschatologie dans la Bible et à Qumran," *Revue de Qumran* (December 1969).

9. Émile Puech arrives at a figure of 72 B.C.E. (*Madrid Qumran Congress: Proceedings of the International Congress on the Dead Sea Scrolls, Madrid 18–21 March, 1991*, ed. by Julio Trebolle Barrera and Luis Vegas Montaner, Brill, 1992), ("Dead Sea Discoveries 3, Developments on the Dead Sea Scrolls"), as does Hartmut Stegemann (*Die Essayer, Qumran, Jonah's deer Tougher undo Jesus*, Herder, 1993) and A. Steeled ("Texts from Qumran," *Reif de Qumran* 16, 1993). A figure of 60 B.C.E. is arrived at by Professor John Collins, of Chicago University, in *Apocalypticism in the Dead Sea Scrolls* (Routledge, 1997).

10. The Book of Revelation took a contrary stand to the then evolving Christian ideal of finding a personal salvation for the coming End Days through Christ and replaced it with the description of a social apocalypse to which everyone would be victim. Mainly for this reason, it was strongly resisted as a candidate for inclusion in the Christian Scriptures. Because it was considered to have been written by St. John the Divine, the "Beloved of Jesus," however, it was finally included. Modern research assigns its composition to a disgruntled early Christian who lived on Patmos, a small rocky island off the coast of Asia Minor. He appears to have inserted elements related to a symbolic vision obtained from a first-century-C.E. Jewish work known as the Oracle of Hystaspes (Cana Werman, "A Messiah in Heaven? A Re-evaluation of Jewish and Christian Apocalyptic Traditions," paper presented at Text, Thought, and Practice in Qumran and Early Christianity, International Symposium, Hebrew University of Jerusalem, January 11–13, 2004).

11. Michael Grant, *The Jews in the Roman World* (Weidenfeld and Nicolson, 1973).

12. Barbara Thiering, *Jesus of the Apocalypse* (Corgi, 1997).

13. The Roman historian Dio Cassius records that no sooner had Emperor Trajan committed Roman troops to a campaign against the Parthians in Mesopotamia than a general call throughout the eastern Mediterranean summoned the Jews to rise up in an attempt to reassert their independence. Revolts flared up in Cyrene, Cyprus, Egypt, and Mesopotamia, and in the Jewish homeland, commencing in 115 C.E. and only finally being suppressed in 117 C.E., after Hadrian took his seat on the throne of Rome. See also Michael Grant, *The Jews in the Roman World*, Weidenfeld and Nicolson, 1973).

14. M. Cary and H. H. Scullard, *A History of Rome* (Macmillan, 1975); J. Allegro, *The Chosen People* (Hodder and Stoughton, 1971).

15. Various publications give different dates for the end of Akhenaten's reign; I have taken the date as an average figure given by five authoritative Egyptologists as listed in *The Sceptre of Egypt: A Background for the Study of Ancient Egyptian Antiquities in the Metropolitan Museum of Art*, by William C. Hayes (Metropolitan Museum of Art, 1990). See also Robert Feather, "Egyptian-Pharaoh-Ruler Chronology and Probable Scheme of Dates for the Hebrew Patriarchs," in *The Mystery of the Copper Scroll of Qumran* (Inner Traditions, 2003).

16. Even if Barbara Thiering's calculations detailed in her book *Jesus of the Apocalypse* (Corgi, 1997) are wrong—and I must admit some reservations about her reasoning—the date of 70 C.E. deduced from the texts by a number of other eminent scholars as the revised date for the Eschaton would come almost exactly 1,470 years after the birth, as opposed to the death, of Akhenaten. Either way, the dates are so close to the time of Akhenaten as to be hardly coincidental.

## Chapter 12: A Community of Essenes—or Something Else?

1. Hershel Shanks, *The Mystery and Meaning of the Dead Sea Scrolls* (Vintage, 1998).

## Chapter 13: Manuscripts of Contention

1. See, for example, James Robinson, *The Nag Hammadi Library* (Brill, 1977), and Gerd Theissen and Annette Merz, *The Historical Jesus* (SCM, 1998). The Nag Hammadi codices were written in Coptic and are thought to be copies of an earlier Greek work incorporating traditions dating to around 50 C.E. They contain a collection of sayings attributed to Jesus but no mention of the crucifixion or the resurrection.

2. The so-called Genizah texts were first brought to public attention by Agnes Lewis and Margaret Gibson, and the bulk of them were brought back to England by Dr. Solomon Schechter, of Cambridge University, in whose library they now reside. They include two versions of the Dead Sea Scrolls Damascus documents and other texts similar to those found at Qumran, among manuscripts dated in their writing from between 600 C.E. and the nineteenth century C.E. (see Robert Feather, *The Mystery of the Copper Scroll of Qumran* (Inner Traditions, 2003).

3. Other sources include *The Oxford Companion to the Bible,* ed. by Bruce M. Metzger and Michael D. Coogan (Oxford University Press, 1993), and *The New Jerome Biblical Commentary,* ed. by Raymond E. Brown, Joseph A. Fitzmyer, and Roland E. Murphy (Cassell, 1996).

4. Ian Wilson, *Jesus: The Evidence* (Weidenfeld and Nicolson, 1985); Paula Fredriksen, *Jesus of Nazareth, King of the Jews* (Macmillan, 1999).

5. Ibid.

6. The Nag Hammadi texts were found in a three-foot-tall red earthenware jar at a place called Nag Hammadi near the Nile in Upper Egypt. They were hidden in a cave near the base of a mountain range with more than 150 caves called Jabal al-Tarif. Apparently the papyrus texts, bound in leather, were found by a local Bedouin, Muhammad Ali al-Samman. He broke the jar and took its contents to his home at Al-Qasr. His mother burned some of the pages, but the rest subsequently came onto the black market and was acquired by the Coptic Museum, Cairo. The finding of the Nag Hammadi codices in a clay jar is in itself perhaps of some significance. This form of secretion was one advocated by the Qumran Essenes, and, of course, was also how they hid the Dead Sea Scrolls collection.

7. Scroll fragment POxy654, 1–5 in the Bodleian Library, Oxford, England; scroll fragment Poxy1, 4–11 in the British Museum, London.

8. Hans Jonas, *Journal of Religion,* volume 41, 1961.

9. Ibid.

10. J. M. Robinson, ed., *The Nag Hammadi Library* (HarperSanFrancisco, 1990). The translation team was led by Professor James M. Robinson, Institute for Antiquity and Christianity, Claremont Graduate School, California.

11. Clemens Alexandrinus, Stromata 7.7.

12. Stevan L. Davies, "The Christology and Protology of the Gospel of Thomas," *Journal of Biblical Literature* 111 (Winter 1992); www.misericordia.edu/users/davies/thomas/jblprot.htm. Other scholars, like Glenn Miller (www.christian-thinktank.com), maintain that the majority of sayings in the Gospel of Thomas are derivative of the canonical four Gospels and therefore cannot predate them, although some of the gnostic-related previously unknown sayings may be of an earlier origin.

13. Helmut Koester, "Introduction to the Gospel of Thomas," in J. M. Robinson, ed., *The Nag Hammadi Library* (HarperSanFrancisco, 1990).

14. It is interesting that in Thomas's full name, Didymus Jude Thomas, Didymus—from the Greek *didumos,* meaning "twin"—implies he was a twin. The question is, If this was the case, who was he twinned with? It is possible he was one of the twin babies seen in the statues in the Church of Rennes-le-Château, France, which show Mary and Joseph, Jesus's parents, each holding one of what appear to be twin infants.

15. Elaine Pagels, *The Gnostic Gospels* (Random House, 1979). Professor Pagels received her doctorate from Harvard University in 1970; she has taught at Barnard College, Columbia University, and has participated in editing several of the Nag Hammadi translations.

16. Douglas Lockhart, *Jesus the Heretic* (Element, 1997).

17. Helmut Koester, "Introduction to the Gospel of Thomas," in J. M. Robinson, ed., *The Nag Hammadi Library* (HarperSanFrancisco, 1990).

18. *The Gospel of Thomas*, trans. by Thomas O. Lambdin (Brill, 1989).

19. Up to 135 C.E., the Judaeo-Christian church of Jerusalem appointed only bishops of Jewish descent. The community persisted until the fifth century C.E.

20. Serapis was a new deity, introduced into Egypt during the reign of Ptolemy I (died 284 C.E.), that combined the names and attributes of two ancient gods—Osiris and Apis—and also the Hellenistic characteristics of Zeus, Asklepios, and Dionysus. Thus Serapis was a god of the underworld and fertility as well as a healer of humankind. Ptolemy built a huge temple, known as the Serapeum, at Alexandria for the god, but worship by the Egyptians was never enthusiastic.

21. Max Rodenbeck, *Cairo: The City Victorious* (Picador, 1998).

22. In 1974, President Richard Nixon visited Alexandria and asked about the location of the ancient Great Library. This casual inquiry led to the construction of the Bibliotheca Alexandrina complex, a $240 million project, which houses the world's largest reading room and a projected eight million books (the Library of Congress, Washington, D.C., has some eighteen million books). See http://portal.unesco.org/ci/en/ev.php-URL_ID=4539&URL_DO=DO_TOPIC&URL_SECTION=201.html.

## Chapter 14: Gnosticism at Qumran and the Dead Sea Scrolls

1. The Therapeutae were thought to have lived in the vicinity of Lake Mareotis, near Alexandria, at the time of the Qumran Essenes and on into the first centuries of the Common Era, a period in Egypt when overlapping religious activity swirled around mixtures of Hellenistic Judaism, gnosticism, paganism, magic, and Christianity. Practices of the Therapeutae are described by the first-century historian Philo in his *De vita contemplativa*. His descriptions imply he believed the Therapeutae followed the beliefs of the Hebrew Scriptures and that some accepted an early form of Christianity, thus forming a continuous succession of ascetics connecting Jesus to the prophets of the Hebrew Scriptures. Both sexes of the Therapeutae community were said to pray together, but they were separated by a barrier, perhaps the first examples of a partition (Hebrew, *mehitsa*) that is still utilized in Orthodox Jewish places of prayer and synagogues, as well as in Islamic mosques, to separate men and women. In a similar manner to the Qumran Essenes, the Therapeutae also rose early to worship at sunrise with ritual hymns.

2. The quark is a postulated component of nuclear particle physics.

3. Athanasius Polag, *Die Christologie der Logienquelle* (Neukirchener Verlag, 1977); Walter Schmithals, *Einleitung in die drie ersten Evangelien* (De Gruyter, 1985); John Kloppenborg, "Literary Convention, Self-Evidence and the Social History of the Q People," *Semeia* 55 (1992).

4. In the early eighteenth century a German professor, Hermann Samuel Reimarus, of Hamburg University, wrote that Jesus was a failed revolutionary, and that his disciples removed his body from its tomb to create a story about his resurrection (*On the Aims of Jesus and His Disciples: Fragments*, SCM, 1971). His ideas instigated a movement, centered in Germany, that questioned the authorship of the

Christian Scriptures and concluded that none of the Gospels was written by eye-witnesses to Jesus. The Gospel of Mark was considered to predate that of Matthew and Luke, and because of its inaccuracy in describing geographical locations associated with Jesus, it was determined that all three of the so-called Synoptic Gospels (Matthew, Mark, and Luke) were composed outside the Holy Land, and at much later times than that of Jesus. The Gospel of John, which follows a much looser chronological thread in the life of Jesus, was considered a separate Gospel from the other three and a later version. The three Synoptic Gospels were thought to be related, both Matthew and Luke drawing on the earlier Mark for content; but an unknown text, labeled Q (from the German word *quelle,* meaning "source"), was also identified as a basis for detail contained in Matthew and Luke. In *The Synoptic Problem: A Critical Analysis* (Mercer University Press, 1976), W. R. Farmer argues that Mark's Gospel is dependent on Matthew and Luke.

In modern scholarship, most of these theories are accepted as being basically correct, except that the Gospels are now thought to have drawn on original Aramaic versions, which were subsequently translated into Greek. Ironically, the Gospel of John, believed by early German Bible critics to be a later Greek composition, may well be closer to the authentic Aramaic in which Jesus would have conversed. The consensus is that Jesus was bilingual, speaking sometimes in Aramaic and sometimes in Hebrew but also having familiarity with Greek (Pinchas Lapide, "Insights from Qumran into the Languages of Jesus," *Revue de Qumran* 32, 1975). In fact, the language used in John, originally thought to be in a Hellenistic style, is remarkable similar to the style found in some of the Qumran-Essenes' Dead Sea Scrolls literature. The Q original source that the Germans were seeking—like the missing "mass neutrino," which might resolve the greatest riddle of particle physics—could well turn out to be coincidentally correct (meaning that there was an as yet undiscovered autograph text on which the Gospels drew and, by coincidence, it will have close connections to Qumran literature) with Qumran being the source of much of the language used in the Christian Scriptures.

5. Burton L. Mack, *The Lost Gospel: The Book of Q and Christian Origins* (Element, 1993). Professor Mack, of the Claremont School of Theology, California, sees the early sayings of Jesus, visualized in Q, as being corrupted in the Christian Scriptures and jumps to the extraordinary conclusion that the Christological elements of the Christian Scriptures are therefore based on myths. He avoids any consideration of the Essenes or of Qumran.

6. Edward P. Meadors, "The 'Messianic' Implications of the Q Material," *Journal of Biblical Literature* (Summer 1999).

7. Robert Feather, *The Mystery of the Copper Scroll of Qumran* (Inner Traditions, 2003).

8. Job 1:6; Psalms 2:12; Isaiah 9:6; Daniel 3:25. See also chapter 16 on the so-called Son of God scroll, 4Q246.

9. For example, the Floreligium (4Q174) Dead Sea Scroll talks of an eschatological prophecy concerning the building of a perfect temple and the coming of two messiahs. See also Messiahs of Qumran (chapter 8 of this book).

10. Perhaps a more pertinent reference to Amarna occurs in 1 Enoch 14:18–20, in which a holy vision helps him understand "everything": "And I saw a lofty throne, and its appearance was like ice; and its wheels were like the shining sun; and its guardians were cherubim; and from beneath the throne issued streams of flaming fire. And I was unable to see. And the Great Glory sat upon it; his raiment was like the appearance of the sun and whiter than much snow." The allusions to cherubim, the sun, and a lofty thronelike chariot can clearly be associated with the imagery on the tomb walls of Amarna.

11. Theodor H. Gaster, *The Dead Sea Scriptures in English Translation* (Doubleday, 1976).

12. Stephen A. Hoeller, *Jung and the Lost Gospels* (Quest, 1994).

13. The Gospel of the Egyptians is known to have been written at a very early time, as it was frequently quoted by Clement of Alexandria around 200 C.E.; a generation later, Origen records the Gospel as being rejected by the church (Gerd Theissen and Annette Merz, *The Historical Jesus*, SCM, 1998).

14. Stephen A. Hoeller, *Jung and the Lost Gospels* (Quest, 1994).

15. The name Seth appears briefly in Genesis 5:3 and Luke 3:38, where we learn only that he was the son of Adam, begat Enos at the age of 105, had further sons and daughters, and died aged 912. For a more detailed coverage of the Egyptian legend of the evil great god Seth, his brother, Osiris, and Seth's bitter rivalry with Horus, see Robert Feather, *The Mystery of the Copper Scroll of Qumran* (Inner Taditions, 2003). From the eighteenth to the nineteenth pharaonic dynasties, apart from the period of Akhenaten when his existence was discounted, Seth was the main rival to Ra as the evil god of darkness contending with the good god of light (Alfred Widemann, *Religion of the Ancient Egyptians*, H. Grevel, 1897). The biblical Seth is also the subject of Jewish tradition that considered him the first of the patriarchal heroes who "walked with God" (Michael Grant, *The Jews in the Roman World*, Weidenfeld and Nicolson, 1973), making it even less likely that the biblical figure is a force for evil.

16. Elaine Pagels, *The Gnostic Gospels* (Random House, 1979).

17. Testimony of Truth. See, for example, James Robinson, ed., *The Nag Hammadi Library* (HarperSanFrancisco, 1990).

18. Secret Book of James; Second Apocalypse of James; Apocalypse of Peter. See, for example, James Robinson, ed., *The Nag Hammadi Library* (HarperSanFrancisco, 1990).

19. John J. Collins, *Apocalypticism in the Dead Sea Scrolls* (Routledge, 1997).

20. For example, the dualistic content of one Dead Sea Scroll, in the form of a horoscope (4Q186), assigns to a person with thick, hairy fingers, thick thighs, and short thick toes eight parts in the House of Darkness and one part in the House of Light. Long, lean thighs and toes, by contrast, endow a person with six parts in the House of Light and three parts in the House of Darkness. Egyptian overtones are not hard to detect, and the image of the predominantly good person with elongated limbs may well be based on the classic depictions found at Amarna, showing Pharaoh Akhenaten with exaggeratedly long thighs, fingers, and feet.

21. John J. Collins, *Apocalypticism in the Dead Sea Scrolls* (Routledge, 1997).

22. John M. Allegro, *Physician Heal Thyself . . .* (Prometheus, 1985).

23. Called by the Roman emperor Constantine, some 250 Christian bishops (according to Eusebius) attended the Council of Nicaea (in modern Turkey) in 325 C.E. The bishops agreed that Jesus was divine, but those favoring the Alexandrian line said he existed with God before the beginning of time, whereas those following the line promulgated by Arius of Antioch claimed he had been created later and was subordinate to God. Emperor Constantine ruled in favor of the Alexandrian line and required inclusion in the creed (established by Eusebius, bishop of Caesarea) that Christ was *homousion,* "of one substance," with God.

24. Initiated in the Zohar in the second century C.E., this later form of Gnosticism was proscribed in early Rabbinic Judaism. Gnosis from the earliest Christian period has also survived in modern Iraq and Iran, where Mandaeans follow a form of Christianity that holds John the Baptist to be superior to Jesus.

## Chapter 15: Quotations from the Christian Scriptures Derived from the Dead Sea Scrolls

1. Benjamin G. Wright, "Qumran Pseudepigrapha in Early Christianity: Is 1 Clem. 50:4 a Citation of 4QPseudo-Ezekiel (4Q385)?" http://orion.mscc.huji.ac.il/symposiums/2nd/papers/Wright97.html.

2. Geza Vermes, *The Complete Dead Sea Scrolls in English* (Allen Lane/Penguin, 1997).

3. J. J. Collins, *The Sceptre and the Star: The Messiahs of the Dead Sea Scrolls and Other Ancient Jewish Literature* (Doubleday, 1995).

4. Hershel Shanks, *The Mystery and Meaning of the Dead Sea Scrolls* (Random House, 1999).

5. See also Psalm 69: "And they gave for my bread gall, and for my thirst they gave me to drink vinegary wine."

6. George Brooke, "Biblical Interpretation in the Qumran Scrolls and the New Testament," paper presented at Dead Sea Scrolls Fifty Years After Their Discovery, International Congress, Jerusalem, July 20–25, 1997. See also George Brooke, "Shared Intertextual Interpretations in the Dead Sea Scrolls and the New Testament," paper presented at Liturgical Perspectives: Prayer and Poetry in Light of the Dead Sea Scrolls, Orion Symposium, Hebrew University of Jerusalem, January 19–23, 2000, http://orion.mscc.huji.ac.il.

7. Other examples include: "For once you were in darkness, but now you are light in the Lord; walk as children of light. . . . Take no part in the unfruitful works of darkness" (Eph. 5:8–11); "In him was life, and the life was the light of men. The light shines in the darkness, and the darkness has not overcome it" (John 1:4–5); "And this is the judgment, that the light has come into the world, and men loved darkness rather than light, because their deeds were evil. For everyone who does evil hates the light" (John 3:19–20); "God is light and in Him is no darkness at all. If we say we have fellowship with Him whilst we walk in darkness, we lie . . . but if we walk in the light, as He is in the light, we have fellowship with one another" (1 John 1:5–7). Richard Bauckham, of the University of St. Andrews, Scotland, is not convinced of the special relationship seen by some between the Qumran Essenes and the Gospel of John. He argues that the most striking resemblance is in

the dualism of light and darkness in 1QS and John, but that it can be explained as a development of Jewish tradition independent of Qumran ("The Qumran Community and the Gospel of John," Dead Sea Scrolls Fifty Years After Their Discovery, International Congress, Jerusalem, July 20–25, 1997).

8. A description of the Three Nets of Belial is included in the Damascus document of the Dead Sea Scrolls.

9. Robert Eisenman, *The Dead Sea Scrolls and the First Christians* (Element, 1996); *James the Brother of Jesus* (Faber and Faber, 1997). See also Robert Eisenman, *Maccabees, Zadokites, Christians and Qumran* (Brill, 1983) and *James the Just in the Habakkuk Pesher* (Brill, 1986); and Robert Eisenman and Michael Wise, *The Dead Sea Scrolls Uncovered* (Penguin, 1993).

10. As discussed in this and my previous book, *The Mystery of the Copper Scroll of Qumran* (Inner Traditions, 2003).

11. Émile Puech, *Revue de l'histoire des religions* 147 (1955). The same idea is expressed in quotations from Matthew 10:26 and Luke 12:2, for which there are no biblical or rabbinic parallels (see Samuel Tobias Lachs, *A Rabbinic Commentary on the New Testament*, KTAV, 1987).

## Chapter 16: Messianic Apocalypse, Son of God, and Pierced Messiah

1. Geza Vermes, *The Complete Dead Sea Scrolls in English* (Allen Lane/ Penguin, 1997).

2. Ibid.

3. Hippolytus, "Refutation of All Heresies," in *The Essenes According to the Classical Sources,* ed. by G. Vermes and M. Goodman (Sheffield Academic, 1989).

4. Hershel Shanks, *The Mystery and Meaning of the Dead Sea Scrolls* (Random House, 1998).

5. Geza Vermes, *The Complete Dead Sea Scrolls in English* (Allen Lane/Penguin, 1997).

6. James Tabor and Michael Wise, "4Q521 'On Resurrection' and the Synoptic Gospel Tradition: A Preliminary Study," in *Qumran Questions,* ed. by James Charlesworth (Sheffield Academic, 1995).

7. Wright cites Richard Bauckham, who gives four reasons why the Apocalypse of Peter is taken from the Qumran text rather than directly from Ezekiel 37. His reasons are: (1) 4Q385 2.5 starts in the same sequence as the Apocalypse quotation; (2) the effect produces a formula characteristic of Ezekiel; (3) both the Apocalypse and Qumran versions use the phrase "bone to bone," which is different from the biblical text; (4) the phrase "joint to joint" in 4Q385 2.5–6 parallels the Apocalypse quotation, but has no basis in the Masoretic text. B. G. Wright, "Qumran Pseudepigrapha in Early Christianity: Is 1 Clem. 50:4 a Citation of 4QPseudo-Ezekiel (4Q385)?" http://orion.mscc.huji.ac.il/symposiums/ 2nd/papers/Wright97.html.

8. Jozef Milik was assigned publication of 4Q246, the Son of God fragment, in 1958, and although he eventually gave a lecture on it in 1972 at Harvard University, it was not published until 1996. Émile Puech, "246. 4QApocryphe de Daniel," in *Qumran Cave 4: XVII—Parabiblical Texts, Part 3,* ed. by G. Brooke et al. (Clarendon, 1996).

9. Geza Vermes, *The Complete Dead Sea Scrolls in English* (Allen Lane/Penguin, 1997).

10. Carsten Peter Thiede, *The Dead Sea Scrolls and the Jewish Origins of Christianity* (Lion, 2000).

11. Lecture by Jozef Milik at Harvard University, reported by J. A. Fitzmyer in *New Testament Studies* 20 (1973–74).

12. Jozef Milik was assigned publication of 4Q246, the Son of God fragment, in 1958, and although he eventually gave a lecture on it in 1972 at Harvard University, it was not published until 1996. Émile Puech, "246. 4QApocryphe de Daniel," in *Qumran Cave 4: XVII—Parabiblical Texts, Part 3,* ed. by G. Brooke et al. (Clarendon, 1996).

13. John J. Collins, "The Nature of Messianism in the Light of the Dead Sea Scrolls," in *The Dead Sea Scrolls in Their Historical Context,* ed. by T. Lim (T & T Clark, 2000). As professor of Old Testament at Yale University and a president of the Catholic Biblical Association, Collins lifts his eyes to the far horizons of the Mediterranean and does not ignore Egypt: "There is also evidence for the anointing of non-royal officials in Egypt and of Egyptian vassals in Syria"; "The sonship in question is generally recognized as adoptive, and does not imply the degree of divinization that we find, for example, in Egypt." See also Robert Feather, *The Mystery of the Copper Scroll of Qumran* (Inner Traditions, 2003).

14. Nicholas Weeks, *Egypt's False Prophet Akhenaten* (Thames and Hudson, 2001).

15. Scrolls 4Q252, 4Q285, 4Q161, 4QSa, and 1QSb.

16. CD (Cairo-Damascus scrolls), 1QSb.

17. 1QM (War Scroll).

18. From the Damascus document. A. Dupont-Sommer (*The Dead Sea Scrolls: A Preliminary Survey,* Blackwell, 1952) points out that the sect was led by a Mebhakker, who was over the priests. He had supreme control of administration, as well as having a spiritual role. I equate this title, in sounding and role, to the name of Meryra or Meryre, Akhenaten's high priest at Akhetaten. See also *Qumran 73,* 1999.

19. Scroll 4Q542.

20. Scroll 1QS (Rule of the Community, sometimes called the Manual of Discipline); 4Q521.

21. 1QM (War Scroll).

22. Geza Vermes, *The Complete Dead Sea Scrolls in English* (Allen Lane/Penguin, 1997).

23. See the Harris Papyrus dated to 1200 B.C.E., now in the British Museum, London.

24. Norman de Garis Davies, *The Rock Tombs of El Amarna: Part II, The Tombs of Panehesy and Meryra II* (The Egypt Exploration Fund, 1905).

## Chapter 17: Paul's Smoking Gun

1. Little if anything is known from external sources of Paul's life, apart from passages in his own letters and other works of the Christian Scriptures. He is believed to have been born in the first decade C.E. and been put to death around 67 C.E. in

Rome, under Emperor Nero. The finding of an inscription at Delphi in 1905 confirms the existence of a Roman proconsul of Achaea named Gallio; he appears to be the same person mentioned in relation to Paul in the Christian Scriptures. Acts 18:12–17 mentions Paul being brought before Gallio's tribunal on his first visit to Corinth, which would date the incident to around 50 C.E. (Arthur Paterson Lee, *The Controversial Jesus,* Guardian, 2000).

2. Henry A. Sanders, *Washington Manuscripts of the Four Gospels* (University of Michigan, 1912). The Washington Freer manuscripts comprise works from Deuteronomy and Joshua, Psalms, the Epistles of Paul, the minor prophets, and the four Gospels—Matthew, John, Luke, and Mark—bound in a codex in the so-called Western order of Gospels. The four Gospels are incomplete, notably parts of Mark and John. They were written on sheepskin and goatskin in Greek and are generally dated from the fourth century C.E., but stratification of the texts indicate some fragments could date from the time of the Roman emperor Diocletian, circa 300 C.E., who attempted to wipe out Christianity by destroying its records. The outer covers of the codex consist of wood panels bearing colored Coptic-style paintings of the four evangelists dated to the seventh century C.E.

3. Bruce M. Metzger, *Manuscripts of the Greek Bible* (Oxford University Press, 1981). Part of the additional verses to Mark were apparently known to Jerome, the fourth-century Christian scholar, who reported that they were present "in certain copies and especially in Greek codices."

4. Frederick M. Schweitzer, *The Tap-Root of Anti-Semitism: The Demonization of the Jews* (Manhattan College, New York).

5. Paul describes Zedek El (The Righteous God) in terms identical to those found in 1QM 4.6; 1QS 10.25, 11.12.

6. Joseph A. Fitzmyer, *The Dead Sea Scrolls and Christian Origins* (Eerdmans, 2000). The concept appears in the Thanksgiving Psalms (1QH 4.30–38); and in the Rule of the Community is found: "And if I stagger, God's grace is my salvation forever" (1QS 11.12). The Qumran concept of "trusting in the Teacher of Righteousness" is echoed in the Galatian letters of Paul, written about 55 C.E., where he talks of "faith in Jesus Christ." This is a departure from conventional Jewish texts, which refer to observance of the Torah rather than individual faith as the path to redemption. There are many other examples where Paul draws on Qumranic ideas: in his lists of vices and virtues, attention to the importance of the calendar, recognition of the era as the last period of evil, and the use of curses against dissidents. The phrase "works of the Law" is a favorite of Paul's. It is never found in the Hebrew Bible or rabbinic literature, but it does appear in Qumran texts (A. Fitzmyer, *The Dead Sea Scrolls and Christian Origins,* William B. Eerdmans, 2000.)

7. Timothy Lim, "Studying the Qumran Scrolls and Paul in Their Historical Context," paper presented at the International Conference of the Dead Sea Scrolls as Background to Post-Biblical Judaism and Early Christianity, University of St. Andrews, Scotland, June 26–28, 2001.

8. Scrolls 4QFlor 1–2, 4QMMT.

9. D. Flusser, "The Qumran Sectaries and Early Christianity Before Paul," in *The Historical Jesus,* ed. by Gaalyah Cornfeld (Macmillan, 1982).

10. Hershel Shanks, ed., *Frank Moore Cross: Conversations with a Bible Scholar* (Biblical Archaeology Society, 1994).

11. Theologians such as Gerd Theissen, professor of New Testament, and Annette Merz, lecturer in New Testament studies, both at the University of Heidelberg, see no mention of the Essenes in the Christian Scriptures, except possibly in the guise of Pharisees. Patently, when the Christian Scriptures refer to Pharisees, they mean Pharisees. These scholars appear to take almost no account of the huge number of parallels between early Christian and Essene teachings and practices or of the numerous pseudonyms for the Essenes in the Gospels.

12. Philip Davies, professor of Old Testament at the University of Sheffield, England, and codirector of the Manchester-Sheffield Centre for Dead Sea Scrolls Research, has proposed that the Damascus Scroll describes an Israelite exilic group that originated in the sixth century B.C.E. and that this group, as originators of the Essenes, was associated with Damascus. He argues that the Teacher of Righteousness of the Cairo-Damascus and other Dead Sea Scrolls texts broke away from the main Essene movement around 150 B.C.E. and set up an establishment at Qumran. The idea is supported by Garcia Martinez and A. S. van der Woude of Göningen University in Holland. See also Hugh J. Schonfield, *The Jew of Tarsus* (Macdonald, 1946), chapter 7, in which there is an extremely perceptive description of Paul's encounter in Damascus with those he calls the Messianists.

13. The tribe of Edom, said to have derived from Jacob's brother, Esau, was located in southern Arabia adjacent to Canaan. Its presence has been demonstrated by archaeological finds dating back to the twelfth century B.C.E., including an ivory brooch found at Teman with what appears to be an Aten sun disk carved on it. A group within Edom appears to have practiced a distinct form of Hebrewism related to that of the Qumran Essenes. Around 620 B.C.E., the reforming King Josiah attacked Edom and destroyed its high place of worship at Beth-El. Not everyone supported Josiah, and notably the prophet Habakkuk, a favorite of the Qumran Essenes, decried the destruction. This is but one clue to the existence of a religious congregation in Edom with some empathy to the Essenic strand. Shortly after Josiah's attack, Nabataean tribesmen from Arabia invaded the region and dominated the area until the time of the Greeks. They exploited a strategic position astride busy trade routes, developing a wealthy culture and building an impressive capital city at Petra on the site of the previous Edomite main city of Teman. When the Greeks conquered the entire region, in the fourth century B.C.E., they renamed the land of Edom/Nabataea and called it Idumea.

It is from the Greek historian Diodorus Siculus (first century B.C.E.) that we learn of an "Atenistic" learned congregation within the Nabataeans who treated each other like brothers, held women as equals, married partners only from within their own congregation, shunned slavery, shared their possessions, and would not consume the blood of animals: "They honour the meek and dispossessed, and value mercy, peace and forgiveness of transgressions." They appeared to believe in only one God—without any likenesses—and set up stone blocks, which they anointed with oil. Another Greek writer, Athendorus (c. 40 B.C.E.), recorded by Strabo (c. 60 B.C.E.–c. 21 C.E.), noted what appeared to be the same congregation partaking of communal meals in groups of thirteen people, with a kingly leader who mixed freely with his brethren. All these characteristics mark the Edomite congregation as following a Hebrew style of religion, but many of their unconventional beliefs and practices indicate a closer relationship with the Essenic strand of Judaea. One other connection is noted by Professor George Brooke, of Manchester University. He maintains that to understand the wording of the Copper Scroll it is necessary to consider its Hebrew, Aramaic, and Arabic language content, but also "Nabataean cognates"; so the Qumran Essenes seem to have had some knowledge of Nabataean. Could this separatist Edomite/ Nabataean congregation, related to the Qumran Essenes, have been been the one Paul studied with when he went into Arabia for the next three years of his life after visiting Damascus?

14. Frank Moore Cross, *The Ancient Library of Qumran* (Sheffield Academic, 1995).

15. Karl P. Donfried, "Paul and the Community of the Renewed Covenant: Convergence and Divergence," paper presented at Dead Sea Scrolls Fifty Years After Their Discovery, International Congress, Jerusalem, July 20–25, 1997.

16. Ephesus is a coastal city in today's western Turkey, which in the time of Paul had a large Jewish population and contained the largest temple to Diana in the Greek world.

17. E. Qimron and J. Strugnell, *Qumran Cave 4, V: Miqsat Ma-ase Ha-Torah, Discoveries in the Judaean Desert X* (Clarendon, 1994). Torleif Elgvin made this observation: "I find it strange that MMT contains no elements of Apocryphal or Sapiential elements. It does not reflect apoc and Sap of the Yahad of the period" (lecture at University College London, October 26, 1998). Geza Vermes notes that MMT and the War Scroll do not mention Zadok priests.

18. Martin Abegg, "Paul, 'Works of the Law' and MMT," *Biblical Archaeology Review* 20 (1994). Abegg, together with coauthors Peter Flint and Eugene Ulrich, has produced a monumental revised edition of the Hebrew Scriptures that takes into account variants evident from the Dead Sea Scrolls and other works (*The Dead Sea Scrolls Bible,* T & T Clark, 1999).

19. Of the Epistles of Paul, only Romans, 1 and 2 Corinthians, Galatians, Ephesians, Philippians, 1 Thessalonians, and Philemon are considered to have been written by him, post–50 C.E. The others are Colossians, 2 Thessalonians, and 1 and 2 Timothy.

20. The author of Acts of the Apostles says that Paul studied under the pharisaic rabbi Gamaliel (22:3). Rabbi Gamaliel was the grandson of Hillel (a famous Jewish teacher), who lived during the time of Jesus and was president of the Sanhedrin, the ruling Jewish religious body in Jerusalem. Paul does not mention Gamaliel but claims he himself was a circumcised Pharisee who persecuted the church before his conversion (Phil. 3:5–6).

## Chapter 18: Beyond Paul

1. Matthew 13:43. See also Robert Eisenman, *The Dead Sea Scrolls and the First Christians* (Element, 1996).

2. Samuel Tobias Lachs, *A Rabbinic Commentary on the New Testament* (KTAV, 1987).

3. The War Scroll. See, for example, Geza Vermes, *The Complete Dead Sea Scrolls in English* (Allen Lane/Penguin, 1997).

4. Samuel Tobias Lachs, *A Rabbinic Commentary on the New Testament* (KTAV, 1987).

5. Matthew 13:43. See also Robert Eisenman, *The Dead Sea Scrolls and the First Christians* (Element, 1996).

6. Celebrating Morning (4Q408). Geza Vermes, *The Complete Dead Sea Scrolls in English* (Allen Lane/Penguin, 1997).

7. Rudolf Bultman, *Theology of the New Testament* (SCM, 1952–55).

8. Scrolls 11Qtg-job 24.6–7; 4QEnb; 11QPsa; 4Q403. The term Adon occurs in Psalm 151, but it also appears in the canonical Psalm 114; see Joseph A. Fitzmyer, *The Dead Sea Scrolls and Christian Origins* (Eerdmans, 2000). It should be noted that a number of Psalms besides 150 in the Hebrew Scriptures have been identified from Qumran texts. See Robert Feather, *The Mystery of the Copper Scroll of Qumran* (Inner Traditions, 2003).

9. W. Bousset, *Kyrios Christos: A History of the Belief in Christ from the Beginnings of Christianity to Irenaeus* (Abingdon, 1970).

10. Luke 16:8; John 12:36, 17:12; 1 Thessalonians 5:5; 2 Thessalonians 2:3; Ephesians 2:2, 5:5, 5:8.

11. Scrolls 1QS 1.9–10 and 1QM 1.1.

12. James H. Charlesworth, ed., "The Dead Sea Scrolls and the Historical Jesus," from *Jesus and the Dead Sea Scrolls* (Doubleday, 1992).

13. James Charlesworth, *Jesus Within Judaism* (Doubleday, 1988). Also James VanderKam, "The Dead Sea Scrolls and Christianity," in *Understanding the Dead Sea Scrolls: A Reader from the Biblical Archaeology Review,* ed. by Hershel Shanks (Random House, 1992).

14. Yigael Yadin, *The Temple Scroll* (Weidenfeld and Nicolson, 1985); Kurt Schubert, "The Sermon on the Mount and the Qumran Texts," in *The Scrolls and the New Testament,* ed. by K. Stendahl (Crossroad Publishing Company, reprint December 1991).

15. Kando was an Arab trader who had previously acquired a number of Dead Sea Scrolls from the Bedouin in the period 1947–56. See chapter 1, note 4, of Robert Feather, *The Mystery of the Copper Scroll of Qumran* (Inner Traditions, 2003).

16. Serge Frolov, "'King's Law' of the Temple Scroll: Mishnaic Aspects," *Journal of Jewish Studies* 50 (no. 2, 1999).

17. Cyril Aldred, *Akhenaten, King of Egypt* (Thames and Hudson, 1996).

18. Temple Scroll description taken from *The Dead Sea Scrolls Translated,* by Florentino Garcia Martinez, E. J. Brill, 1996.

19. Another aspect of Jesus's behavior that on the surface seems to indicate his disenchantment with the Essenes is detected by the Rumanian scholar Dr. Constantin Danicl. He sees Jesus's derisory attitude to "false prophets" in the Sermon on the Mount (Matt. 7:15–20) as a clear reference to the Essenes. His analysis is based on the use of the same etymology for the word *prophet,* as found in the Greek of the Septuagint and Christian Scriptures, and the equivalent Hebrew of the

Hebrew Scriptures and Dead Sea Scrolls. In the latter the Essenes refer to themselves in exactly the same terms as Jesus describes them—as prophets dressed in white robes. It is known from Josephus, Philo of Alexandria, and Hippolytus that the Essenes wore white robes, and no other Jewish sect of the time can be more aptly described as *voyants,* "prophets."

Why Jesus should verbally attack the Essenes, if, as I claim, he was originally one of them, is not too difficult to explain. Once he had struck out on his own revolutionary path, the bulk of the Qumran Essenes would have had quite ambivalent feelings toward him, and he toward them. Those who continued to prophesy that the messiah was yet to come would not have been looked on with much favor by Jesus or his followers. Later Christian writers would also have been at pains to distance emerging Christianity from its Gnostic-tainted roots. Nevertheless, these attacks by Jesus were aimed specifically at Essene values and as such reflect the paramount importance Jesus must have attached to their ideas and the intimate understanding he had of them. (Constantin Daniel, "Faux Prophetes: Surnom des Esseniens dans le Sermon sur la Montagne," *Revue de Qumran,* December 1969. Dr. Daniel was scientific secretary in the department of Oriental studies, Rumanian Society of Historical and Philological Sciences, Bucharest.)

20. In fact, where there are apparent differences, Jesus seems to have a deliberate preoccupation with defining himself over and against Essenism. M. Simon, *Jewish Sects at the Time of Jesus* (Fortress Press, 1980).

21. Following are details of other contrasts between the view of Jesus and those of the Qumran Essenes involving the Sabbath, ritual cleanliness, tolerance of others, circumcision, and divinity.

- *The Sabbath.* The Sabbath day of rest was far more strictly observed by the Essenes than by those outside their movement, and some of Jesus's teachings seem to go against strict Sabbath observance. The literature of the Talmud (the comprehensive manual of Jewish observance, compiled between 200 and 500 C.E.), however, shows that observance of the Sabbath laws was less stringent in the general community than is generally believed. For example, Jesus, according to Matthew 12:11, questioned refraining from saving a sheep that falls into a pit on the Sabbath. The phrasing of his question is, as Professor James Charlesworth points out, impressive and astounding in its similarity to a passage in one of the Dead Sea Scrolls: "The link is found in a stunning way in the Damascus Document, which was revered at Qumran and probably edited by the Essenes. This direct exploitation of a sectarian quotation is so marked that it actually demonstrates a very close intimate knowledge of Qumran-Essene texts." James H. Charlesworth, "The Dead Sea Scrolls and the Historical Jesus," *Jesus and the Dead Sea Scrolls,* ed. James H. Charlesworth (Doubleday, 1992). The likelihood that Jesus and his followers, like the Essenes, did not observe the Sabbath on the same day as the general community might well be part of the explanation for their apparent disrespect for the usual convention.

- *Ritual cleanliness.* The Essenes were obsessed with formal physical cleanliness, whereas Jesus appeared deliberately to refrain from washing before eating. The most notable of these anomalies relates to ceremonial purification. In Matthew 15:1–20 and Mark 7:1–23, the disciples of Jesus are said to eat without previously washing their hands. Punctilious ritual immersion in a *mik-vah* before eating was apparently always practiced by the Qumran Essenes, a significant extension of the traditional simple washing of hands. There is a possible explanation that is entirely consistent with Jesus's enhanced teachings. Having ventured from the confines of the community into areas where ritual bathing facilities were not readily available—and to continue the agenda of not doing what the Pharisees and other Jews were doing—Jesus may have decided that if the facilities weren't available, the procedure would be abandoned. Also, in his and John the Baptist's new concept, the use of ritual water had taken on a rather different significance. It was no longer a procedure for cleansing, but a procedure of baptism for atonement. On the surface this looks like a direct contradiction of Essene practice, but in another sense it follows as a logical conclusion once it is accepted that ritual baptism has been elevated to a physical and spiritual cleansing. The continuation of ritual washing in water as practiced at Qumran and elsewhere by the Essenes would inevitably have devalued the Christian once-and-for-all baptism. Jesus did not appear to endorse many of the Essenes' ritual purity laws, although there is clearly ambiguity on the subject in the Gospels. He seems to have extended the Essene philosophy that humans would remain unclean as long as they rejected the will of God (Community Rule 3.3–6) as meaning that contact with impure physical things would not make any difference to a person's state of spiritual purity.

- *Tolerance of others.* Another clear example of a tailored reaction by Jesus to Essene practice can be seen in the Essene prohibition of the poor, maimed, unclean, and blind from entering the inner circle of the community or sharing their table of fellowship. For the very devout Pharisees, sinners were excluded from their table as well as the Temple, but the Essenes were even stricter in additionally excluding various categories of physically and mentally disadvantaged, whereas, in direct contrast, Jesus asserts that "the poor and maimed and blind and lame" will be brought in to his banquet (Luke 14:21). The phrasing used in Luke follows so precisely that of a number of the Essene sectarian documents that there can be little doubt that he knew of the Essene practice, and that the writers of Luke recorded this awareness.

- *Circumcision.* In Second Temple times (and to this day) it was a requirement that all male Jews be circumcised on the eighth day of life. Without this ritual procedure, they would not be accepted as true followers of the faith. One reason for the writers of the Christian Scriptures to argue against the need for circumcision was their commitment to recruiting Christians from the Gentile population. Another reason could have been the total ban on circumcision introduced around 117 C.E. by the Roman emperor Hadrian. The Greco-Roman cultures had long looked on bodily mutilation with disdain, and Hadrian saw the practice as yet one more barrier to an integrated culture throughout the Roman Empire. A discussion on the origins of circumcision is included in my previous book, *The Mystery of the Copper Scroll of Qumran* (Inner Traditions, 2003). Source material has also been taken from Hershel Shanks, *Understanding the Dead Sea Scrolls* (Random House, 1992).

Although some of these examples appear to show serious deviations from

Qumran practice and belief, it should be remembered that they were enunciated tens of years after Jesus's death, and it is not completely clear that they were always part of his, or his disciples', perceptions. Even if they were, the directness of the challenges demonstrates a preoccupation with and intimate knowledge of Qumran. As many scholars have pointed out, in the words of Professor James VanderKam, of Notre Dame University, "A larger number of the early Church's beliefs and practices than previously suspected were not unique to it"; the Dead Sea Scrolls have demonstrated this quite clearly. James C. VanderKam, *The Dead Sea Scrolls and Christianity, Understanding the Dead Sea Scrolls: A Reader from the Biblical Archaeology Review* (Random House, 1992). Most of the teachings of Jesus that are apparently contrary to those of the Qumran Essenes can be readily explained through one common denominator. The dissension and subsequent split between the original Jewish followers of Jesus and the followers of Paul were generated by Paul's desire to spread the word of Jesus to a Gentile audience. A prerequisite for this process was to water down strict Jewish Halachic observances so that they were acceptable to a wider Gentile population. These included, in particular, strict observance of the Sabbath, which would have required cessation of work for one day a week and prayers in a Jewish synagogue; ritual cleanliness, which was closely related to Temple procedures (Gentiles were excluded from the Temple); acceptance of the poor, crippled, diseased, prostitutes, and tax collectors—in fact, any class of Gentile in any state of health or wealth; and acceptance of the uncircumcised, which for adult Gentile men would have presented a painful barrier. There was no way Paul could have achieved his aim of spreading his belief in Jesus without changing these strict Qumranic-Jewish requirements and moving away from the early Jewish followers of Jesus. His other imperative was to make his new religious ideas acceptable to the Romans. The criticisms by mainstream Judaism of Jewish Jesusism, or the Judaeo-Christians, as they are referred to by Professor Michael Black of the Universities of Cambridge, Edinburgh, and Khartoum—one of the few scholarly historians able to straddle the two worlds of Israel and Egypt—become increasingly virulent as the theology of the Christian Scriptures developed. And as I maintain, the Jewish followers of Jesus were originally drawn from the ranks of the Qumran Essenes.

Statements in this endnote draw on material from a number of sources. Re: "Tolerance to Others": Gaalyah Cornfeld, ed., *The Historical Jesus: A Scholarly View of the Man and His World* (Macmillan, 1982); re: "Sabbath," "Ritual Cleanliness," "Tolerance to Others": James H. Charlesworth, ed., *Jesus and the Dead Sea Scrolls* (Doubleday, 1992). The relevant quotations from Matthew and the Damascus documents are: "Which man of you, if he has one sheep and it falls into a pit on the Sabbath, will not lay hold of it and lift it out?" and from the Cairo-Damascus document (11.13), "And if it [a beast] fall into a cistern or into a pit, let it not be lifted out on the Sabbath." Jesus's defense in Mark 2:23 of what appears to be breaking of Sabbath law—his followers plucking grain as they pass through a field—is based on the biblical principle that human need is above Sabbath observance (James C. VandeKam, *Calendars in the Dead Sea Scrolls: Measuring Time*, Routledge, 1998). Professor VanderKam quotes S. Talmon in concluding that the Essenes counted the Sabbath as commencing at sunrise, rather than at sunset of the previous day, as other Jews observed.

Ambiguity in the Christian Scriptures over the exact timing of the Sabbath is reflected, for example, in Acts 10, where Peter is unsure whether he can enter an unbeliever's house. See Paolo Sacchi, "Recovering Jesus's Formative Background," in *Jesus and the Dead Sea Scrolls,* ed. by James H. Charlesworth (Doubleday, 1992). Paolo Sacchi concludes, "Jesus's formative background was of an Essene type."

Other relevant material comes from the Rule of the Congregation (1QSa 2.3–10); Cairo-Damascus documents (4QCDb); the War Scroll (1QM 7.4–6); the Temple Scroll (11QT 45.12–14).

- *Divinity*. Jesus as the Christ—the divine Son of God, his spiritual resurrection, and the gift of Spirit—is a different category of divergences. These divergences may well be presaged in the writings of the Hebrew Scriptures and the Essenes, but their uniquely Christian message in the Christian Scriptures or in the beliefs of the early Jesus movement is an act of faith and cannot be challenged on the grounds of being derivative. In the Hebrew Scriptures and the Dead Sea Scrolls, it is God who will empower the raising of the dead, healing, and so on, not a future messiah.

## Chapter 19: The Missing Years

1. There is a strong tradition in India that in his teenage years, Jesus left his parents and journeyed to Southeast Asia, where he learned yogic meditation, and brought these ideas back to Judaea. "The Other Jesus," by Kenneth L. Woodward, Anne Underwood, Heather Won Tesoriero. *Newsweek,* March 27, 2000.

2. "Originally children were taught by their parents. . . . Even then if a child had parents, they would take them up to Jerusalem to learn, and if not they did not go. Then the Sages ruled that teachers be set up in each district and that youths enter school at sixteen or seventeen. This was done, but when some teenagers were disciplined they would rebel and play truant. So Joshua ben Gamla came and ruled that teachers of little children be set up in each town, and that children enter school at the age of six or seven" (Talmud, Bava Batra 21a).

3. Robert Feather, *The Mystery of The Copper Scroll of Qumran* (Inner Traditions, 2003).

4. Geza Vermes, *The Complete Dead Sea Scrolls in English* (Allen Lane/Penguin, 1997).

5. Two ostraca were found on the east side of the Qumran plateau in 1996 by amateur excavators led by Professor James F. Strange, of the University of South Florida. The larger ostracon had fifteen fragmentary lines and seems to be a contract transferring the possessions of a certain Honi of Jericho to the Yahad community at Qumran as part of his initiation oath and entry into the community. Interestingly, there may be a connection between this term Yahad, the name the Essenes appear to have applied to their community, and a book of the Mandean-Nazarenes (a baptizing sect, still in existence today in the area of the Euphrates River, who especially revered John the Baptist). One of the books of the Mandeans is known as Sidra d'Yaha ("Book of John the Baptist"), and it has been shown to have links to the Dead Sea Scrolls Genesis Apocryphon, written in Aramaic (Douglas Lockhart, *Jesus the Heretic,* Element, 1997).

6. In the 1964 film *The Gospel According to St. Matthew,* Christ is portrayed as a political revolutionary who is not averse to violence.

7. Respectively, head of the École Biblique, Jerusalem; director of antiquities under the British Mandate, subsequently retained as director by the Jordanian Antiquities Department; director, *Revue de Qumran,* at the École Biblique; professor emeritus, Oxford University.

8. Jonathan G. Campbell, *Dead Sea Scrolls: The Complete Story* (Ulysses, 1998).

## Chapter 20: Jesus, the Essenes, and the Gospels of the Christian Scriptures

1. According to James Trimm (posting to the Yahoo Groups forum on the Essenes), careful reading of the Gospels shows that John the Baptist had his own group of disciples (John 1:35), who continued as such apart from the Jesus movement even after John and Jesus had died (Acts 19:1–3). Http://groups.yahoo.com, "Modern Essene List" message 1337, May 27, 2001, subject "Yochanan and Qumran." The flavor of John chapter 1 also indicates, says Trimm, that John did not live alone in the wilderness but rather with a community of followers near Bethabara, a village only some eight miles from Qumran, and even closer to some of the caves the Qumran community members frequented.

2. T. C. Penner, *The Epistle of James and Eschatology* (Sheffield, 1996); D. J. Moo, *The Letter of James* (Wm. B. Eerdmans Publishing Company, 1985).

3. Excavations at Capernaum have revealed the remains of a fourth-century-C.E. synagogue, and work conducted by Fr. Virgilio C. Corbo and Stanislau Loffreda suggests that there was a settlement going back to the first century B.C.E. Corbo proposes that Peter's house was located near an early Judeo-Christian quarter of the town (Gaalyah Cornfield, ed., *The Historical Jesus: A Scholarly View of the Man and His World,* Macmillan, 1982).

4. See, for example, John P. Meier, "The Historical Jesus and the Historical Herodians," *Journal of Biblical Literature* (Winter 2000); Hartmut Stegemann, *The Library of Qumran* (Brill, 1998); H. H. Rowley, "The Herodians in the Gospels," *Journal of Testament Studies* 41 (1940); Constantin Daniel, "Les Herodiens du Nouveau Testament, sont-ils des Esseniens?" *Revue de Qumran* 6 (1967). The term Herodians occurs in Mark 3:6, 12:3, and 12:13 as well as in Matthew 22:16; the general consensus is that the term was synonymous with the term *scribes* used to designate the Essenes.

5. S. Talmon, following F. Grintz, suggests that rabbinic references to a group called the Boethusians as having a different calendar from the rest of the Jewish community indicates they are equatable with the Essenes (C. Rabin and Y. Yadin, eds., "The Calendar Reckoning of the Sect from the Judaean Desert," in *Aspects of the Dead Sea Scrolls, Scripta Hierosolymitana* 4, Magnes, 1958).

6. Hartmut Stegemann, *The Library of Qumran* (Eerdmans/Brill, 1998); Constantin Daniel, "Esseniens et Eunuques," *Revue de Qumran* 23 (1968); Constantin Daniel, "Faux prophètes: Surnom des Esseniens dans le Sermon sur la Montagne," *Revue de Qumran* (December 1969).

7. Michael Grant, *The Jews in the Roman World* (Weidenfeld and Nicolson, 1973). One facet of the War Scroll is its prophecy that ultimate judgment will be visited

upon the stubborn-hearted by the weak-kneed, the oppressed, and the "poor," or the downcast in spirit. It also denounces, with particular outspokenness, the fiscal oppression and exploitation of the poor in Israel. This philosophical entreaty may well be part of the explanation of why Jesus took up the cause of the poor.

8. E. P. Sanders, *Jesus and Judaism* (Fortress, 1985). For example, Mark 11:15, in which Jesus drives out the moneychangers from the Temple, is seen by Sanders as an action designed to begin the throwing over of the old order and establishment of a new, purified religious state.

9. The idea that the first fruits of the future were already to be tasted is reechoed in an early Christian document, the Epistle of Barnabas 1.7, where the concept of Da'at as one of knowledge and understanding of the past, present, and future is mirrored in Qumran material. Interestingly the concept is remarkably similar to the early Egyptian concept of Ma'at, and one must wonder if this is not where it, and the word for it, originated.

10. Torleif Elgvin, "Wisdom and Apocalypticism in the Early Second Century B.C.E.: The Evidence of 4Q Instruction," paper presented at The Dead Sea Scrolls Fifty Years After Their Discovery, International Congress, Jerusalem, July 20–25, 1997.

## Chapter 21: John the Baptist Strides into View

1. Aenon, near Salim, in Judaea, is given in the Gospel of John (3:23) as the place where John the Baptist baptized Jesus. Aenon is possibly associated with the modern-day location of Ainun, southwest of Nablus. Another traditional place is just north of the Dead Sea at Kasser el-Yehud ("fortress of the Jews"), from where Joshua led the attack against Jericho. The Christian Scriptures also refer, however, to Jesus being baptized at "Bethany beyond the Jordan" (as opposed to the other Bethany, near Jerusalem), which many historians take to mean on the eastern bank of the Jordan. Between 1996 and 1998 the Jordanian archaeologist Mohammad Waheeb excavated at Wadi al-Kharrar, about a mile east of the river, and uncovered three Christian monasteries dating to the third century C.E. He claims to have also found in the area coins and pottery dating to the first century B.C.E. and to have identified John's baptismal site near a patch of reeds that sprouted around a natural spring (Charles M. Sennott, *The Body and the Blood*, Public Affairs, 2001).

2. This nonrecognition is in itself strange, as both the Gospels of Matthew (3:13–17) and Mark (1:9–11) record John the Baptist baptizing Jesus (Samuel Tobias Lachs, *A Rabbinic Commentary on the New Testament*, KTAV, 1987).

3. James H. Charlesworth, *Jesus and the Dead Sea Scrolls* (Doubleday, 1992).

4. Some of the parameters listed in table 12, which compares the attitudes and practices advocated by John the Baptist with those of the Qumran Essenes, are expanded on as follows:

   • *Ownership of property.* On entry into the community of Qumran, the new recruit was required to contribute all his possessions into a common pool; everything the community possessed was then shared by its members. Motivation for John the Baptist's apparent copying of this practice has been attributed not to the Qumran-Essenes but to the teaching of Ezekiel (18:5–9), who requires the righteous person to give bread to the hungry. Ezekiel's injunction may well have been one of the motivations for the extreme position adopted by the Qumran Essenes, but Ezekiel is talking about *zedakha*, the act of giving charity to the poor, which was and is today an injunction binding on all Jewish people. This is rather different from the Qumran-Essene stance of sharing everything. John's position is, like that of the Essenes, one of extremes in advocating giving away virtually every personal possession.

- *Incest.* In Jewish Law, it was not considered incest for a man to marry his brother's wife. In fact, if the brother died childless, it was the brother's duty to implement a "Leverite marriage" and marry the widow (Deuteronomy 25:5–10). John the Baptist reacts to Herod Antipas marrying his brother Philip's wife, Herodias, by condemning him for considering to marry his sister-in-law: "It is not lawful for you to have the wife of your brother" (Matt. 14:3–12). There is no qualification in this statement that the wife has not obtained a valid divorce and is still an *agunot,* a woman marrying illegally because her previous husband has not granted her a *get,* or license to remarry. According to the Christian Scriptures, John's bald statement earned him his execution. Josephus's account of John the Baptist's confrontation with Herod Antipas (*Antiquities* 18.136) seems to blame Herodias because she "confounded the directives of the fathers," but if she was legitimately divorced, she was doing nothing against biblical law in remarrying. That Philip would have given way to the wants of his forceful brother can hardly be doubted. John's stance appears contrary to biblical law, yet it is exactly the same stance taken by the Qumran Essenes. For the Essenes, the marriage of an uncle to a niece was forbidden (Damascus document CD 6.17–18). This seems to be yet another example of the Qumran-Essene view of Jewish Law that is against the normative requirement; nevertheless it was followed by John the Baptist and picked up in the New Testament.

- *The unacceptable Temple.* John the Baptist's attitude to the Temple in Jerusalem is not clear from the New Testament. He certainly seemed to have a low opinion of the Temple hierarchy, the Sadducees, as well as the Pharisees: "Then went out to him all Jerusalem, and all Judaea, and all the region around about Jordan, and were baptised of him in Jordan, confessing their sins. But when he saw many of the Pharisees and Sadducees come to his baptism, he said unto them, O generation of vipers, who hath warned you to flee from the wrath to come?" (Matt. 3:5–7). There is no mention of his ever visiting the Temple, which would have been required for a devout Jew, as he was, at least three times a year. The conclusion must be that he ignored the Temple, not thinking it a suitable place for holy worship.

- *Abstemious lifestyle.* All the evidence from the Christian Scriptures and Josephus confirms that John the Baptist followed an abstemious lifestyle, living on minimal indigenous foods, without any luxuries. This attitude was mirrored by the Qumran Essenes. In considering the association, or lack of association, of John the Baptist with the Qumran Essenes, it must be borne in mind that evidence in the Christian Scriptures comes from Gospel writers who had an agenda. "Everyone in the field of biblical writing and research has an agenda," as Professor George Brooke puts it. It is only because we have substantial external commentary from Josephus on John the Baptist (albeit also with his own agenda) that we can get a fairly clear picture of the real man. There are two main scenarios that the early Gospel writers needed to address in relation to John the Baptist: to ensure that he became subordinate to Jesus Christ and to minimize his more obvious roots as a devout Jew in the context of a "new religion." Confirmation of these relative positions comes largely from the Christian Scriptures, the Dead Sea Scrolls, and commentaries by and on contemporary historians such as Flavius Josephus. Josephus is particularly forthcoming on the subject of prophecy.

- *Gift of prophecy.* Josephus is ambiguous about the prophetic talents of John the Baptist, but the Christian Scriptures specifically identify John as a prophet (Luke 3:2, 7:26; Mark 11:32). Further evidence that the Essenes were especially blessed with the gift of prophecy comes from at least two sources. Josephus speaks generally of the Essenes being able to tell the future and identifies three separate examples of Essenes exhibiting this talent between 100 B.C.E. and 6 C.E.—Judas, Menachen, and Simon, who are categorized as prophets (Flavius Josephus, *Jewish Wars* 1.78–80, 2.159; *Jewish Antiquities* 13.311, 15.373, 17.345). The Essenes themselves, in their own writings, also claim to have the gift of prophecy within their community (1QpHab). Josephus also mentions a number of other non-Essene solitary prophets and prophets who gathered large followings during the run-up to the destruction of the Second Temple.

5. Joseph A. Fitzmyer, *The Dead Sea Scrolls and Christian Origins* (Eerdmans, 2000).
6. J. Van der Ploeg, *The Excavations at Qumran* (Longmans, 1958).
7. Jerome Murphy-O'Connor, ed., *Paul and Qumran: Studies in New Testament Exegesis* (Chapman, 1968).
8. Ibid.

## Chapter 22: Was John the Baptist a Member of the Qumran Community?

1. L'abbé René Laurentin, *Petite Vie de Jean Baptiste* (Desclée de Brouwer, 1993).
2. John Allegro, *The Dead Sea Scrolls and the Origins of Christianity* (Criterion, 1967).
3. William H. Brownlee, *John the Baptist in the New Light of Ancient Scrolls* (Interpretation, 1955); Lucretta Mowry, *The Dead Sea Scrolls and the Early Church* (University of Chicago, 1962).
4. Joseph A. Fitzmyer, *The Dead Sea Scrolls and Christian Origins* (Eerdmans, 2000); H. H. Rowley, "The Baptism of John and the Qumran Sect," in *New Testament Essays: Studies in Memory of T. W. Manson* (Manchester University Press, 1959); Daniel Schwartz, *Studies in the Jewish Background of Christianity* (Mohr-Siebeck, 1992); R. Eisler, *The Messiah Jesus and John the Baptist According to Flavius Josephus' Recently Rediscovered "Capture of Jerusalem" and Other Jewish and Christian Sources* (The Dial Press, 1931); Barbara Thiering, *The Gospels and Qumran,* (Sydney Theological Explorations, 1981); Otto Betz, "Was John the Baptist an Essene?" *Biblical Revue* (December 1990); Yigael Yadin, *The Temple Scroll* (Weidenfeld and Nicolson, 1985); John Allegro, *The Dead Sea*

*Scrolls and the Origins of Christianity* (Criterion, 1967); William H. Brownlee, *John the Baptist in the New Light of Ancient Scrolls* (Interpretation, 1955); Lucretta Mowry, *The Dead Sea Scrolls and the Early Church* (University of Chicago, 1962); R. K. Harrison, *The Dead Sea Scrolls* (Harper and Row, 1961); Charles Scobie, *John the Baptist: The Scrolls and Christianity* (Talbot, 1969); John A. Robinson, "The Baptism of John and the Qumran Community," *Harvard Theological Studies* 50 (1957); Oscar Cullmann, "The Significance of the Qumran Texts for Research into the Beginnings of Christianity," *Journal of Biblical Literature* 74 (1955); Kurt Schubert, *The Dead Sea Community: Its Origin and Teachings* (Adam and Charles Black, 1959); Jean Danielou, *The Work of John the Baptist* (Helicon, 1966); Jean Steinmann, *St. John the Baptist and the Desert Tradition* (Longmans, Green, 1958); Jack Finnegan, *Light from the Ancient Past* (Princeton University Press, 1959); Raymond E. Brown, "Second Thoughts: The Dead Sea Scrolls and the New Testament," *The Expository Times* (October 1966); Charles Fritsch, *The Qumran Community* (Macmillan, 1956); Millar Burrows, *More Light on the Dead Sea Scrolls* (Viking, 1958); Pierre Benoit, *Paul and Qumran* (Priory, 1968); Frank Moore Cross, *The Ancient Library of Qumran and Modern Biblical Studies* (Doubleday, 1961); Carsten P. Thiede, *The Dead Sea Scrolls and the Jewish Origins of Christianity* (Palgrave Macmillan, 2001); Cyrus Gordon, *Adventures in the Nearest East* (Phoenix, 1957); Edmund Sutcliffe, *The Monks of Qumran* (Newman, 1960); Robert L. Webb, "John the Baptiser and Prophet: A Socio-Historical Study," *Journal for the Study of the New Testament,* suppl. series 62 (Sheffield Academic, 1991); James H. Charlesworth, ed., *Jesus and the Dead Sea Scrolls* (Doubleday, 1992); David Flusser, *Jesus* (Herder and Herder, 1969); Michel Grant, *The Jews in the Roman World* (Weidenfeld and Nicolson, 1973); James C. VanderKam, "The Dead Sea Scrolls and Christianity," in *Understanding the Dead Sea Scrolls: A Reader from the Biblical Archaeology Review* (Random House, 1992); Joan E. Taylor, *The Immerser: John the Baptist Within Second Temple Judaism* (Eerdmans, 1997); John Pryke, "John the Baptist and the Qumran Community," *Revue de Qumran* 16 (1964); Ian McDonald, "What Did You Go Out to See? John the Baptist, the Scrolls and Late Second Temple Judaism," in *The Dead Sea Scrolls in Their Historical Context,* ed. by T. Lim (T & T Clark, 2000). The Jesus Seminars, listed in the middle column of the table, are meetings of a group of biblical scholars who discuss New Testament topics and then vote to determine a majority view. Founded in 1985 in America, the conclusions of the Jesus Seminar on the issue of John the Baptist's relationship with the Essenes is purportedly summed up by John W. B. Tatum, who says the Baptist may have been a Essene at some period in his life (*John the Baptist and Jesus: A Report of the Jesus Seminar,* Polebridge, 1994). Geza Vermes, in a lecture at University College London, December 7, 1998, declared, "On balance John the Baptist was a member at Qumran" (Joan E. Taylor, *The Immerser,* Eerdmans, 1997).

5. H. Lichtenberger, "The Dead Sea Scrolls and John the Baptist: Reflections of Josephus' Account of John the Baptist," paper presented at Dead Sea Scrolls Symposium, Jerusalem, April 1988.

6. Bargil Pixner, *Das Heilige Land,* nos. 2–3, Köln, 1979. See also, "Unravelling the Copper Scroll Code: A Study on the Topography of 3Q15," *Revue de Qumran* 43

(1983). Seven fragments of the Gospel of the Ebionites have been preserved in the *Panarion* of Epiphanius of Salamis (see Gerd Theissen and Annette Merz, *The Historical Jesus,* SCM, 1998).

7. Frank Moore Cross, *The Ancient Library of Qumran* (Sheffield Academic, 1995).

8. Elaine Pagels, *The Gnostic Gospels* (Random House, 1979).

9. Flavius Josephus, *Jewish Wars* 2.161.

10. Geza Vermes, *The Complete Dead Sea Scrolls in English* (Allen Lane/Penguin, 1997).

11. According to Midrash, Memukhan told King Ahasuerus that he should have the head of the disobedient Queen Vashti brought in on a platter (Esther 1:19).

12. For the Gospel writers, the more John the Baptist could be disassociated from Judaism, or a sect of it, such as the Qumran Essenes, the more detached Jesus could also become. If John the Baptist was an avowed Jew, then Jesus was also scented with the same perfume. It is not surprising, therefore, that the Christian Scriptures are quite ambiguous, and appear to be noncommittal, as to John the Baptist's allegiances to any particular Second Temple Jewish grouping. John's main defining characteristic—the act of baptism—was not a practice of Jesus; indeed, he is said to have refrained from it (John 4:2). Nor, from the Christian Scriptures, is there any clear statement of where John gained his religious education. We know little of his background; he simply appears in the wilderness (Matt. 3). In comparing characteristic behaviors of John the Baptist and the Qumran Essenes, it should be noted that those specific to Qumran have been quoted, as indicated in the Halachic (Law) sections of the Damascus documents and Rule of the Community. It is clear, however, that the Halacha was different for Essene communities outside Qumran, where less rigid laws were applied, and these specifically Qumranic characteristics are marked with a footnote: table 12. For example, the Damascus community of Essenes was unique in allowing a form of family life—albeit extremely strict—and apparent ownership of property (Philip R. Davies, "Reflections on DJD XVIII," in *The Dead Sea Scrolls at Fifty: Proceedings of the 1997 Society of Biblical Literature, Qumran Section Meetings,* Scholars Press, 1999). Thus, celibacy was not enforced at the Damascus community, but sexual relations were strictly for procreation; the presence of priests was not so dominant; and the apparent ownership of property was attended by a demand to donate a proportion of a person's income to the poor. Sharing with the poor was a facet of John the Baptist's behavior, but Acts is more specific in stating, "Now the congregation of believers were of one heart and soul, and no one said that any of the things he possessed were his own, but they had everything in common" (Acts 4:32).

13. Community Rule 1QS 8.12–16.

14. Lawrence H. Schiffman, *Reclaiming the Dead Sea Scrolls* (Doubleday, 1995).

## Chapter 23: John's Trademark: Ritual Immersion

1. The sources in the Christian Scriptures are primarily those in Matthew 3, Mark 1, and Luke 3; and from Josephus, *Jewish Antiquities* 18, 117.

2. Joachim Jeremias, *Infant Baptism in the First Four Centuries* (SCM, 1960).

3. Robert L. Webb, *John the Baptizer and Prophet*, published by the *Journal for the Study of the New Testament* (1991).

4. Objects could include the Tabernacle tent and furnishings (Num. 19:18) and clothes and utensils that had come into contact with a person with a discharge or a menstruating woman (Lev. 15:4–12, 20:7).

5. There are a number of examples from the Hebrew Scriptures where water was used in ritual cleansing. People who had contact with a corpse were cleansed by sprinkling with the water of the Red Heifer (Num. 19:18); atonement by local elders as atonement for an unsolved murder (Deut. 21:1–9); cleansing of a leper (Lev. 14:10–32); bathing by the high priest on the Day of Atonement (Lev. 16:4, 20–24); priests washing the hands and feet before approaching the altar (Exodus 30:18–21).

6. Psalm 51; Isaiah 1:16–17; Ezekiel 36:25–26.

7. Naaman's leprosy cure in the river Jordan (2 Kings 5:9–14); Lev. 14:5–6, 50–52; Num. 19:17; Deut. 21:4).

8. Isaiah 6:6–7 (probably composed at the time of King Uzziah's death c. 740 B.C.E.): "Then one of the seraphs flew over to me with a live coal, which he had taken from the altar with a pair of tongs. He touched it to my lips and declared, 'Now that this has touched your lips, your guilt shall depart and your sin be purged away.' "

9. B. Sanh. 39a. Quoted in Samuel Tobias Lachs, *A Rabbinic Commentary on the New Testament* (KTAV, 1987).

10. Flavius Josephus, *Against Apion* 1 and 2, *Jewish Antiquities* 3 (see also Specialibus Legibus).

11. J. Thomas, *Le Mouvement Baptiste en Palestine et Syrie (150 B.C.E.–300 C.E.)* (Duculot, 1935).

12. Flavius Josephus, *Jewish Wars*.

13. Flavius Josephus, *Jewish Antiquities*.

14. Flavius Josephus, *Jewish Wars*.

15. Testament of Levi 2.3, Manuscript E. Although this fragment is not complete, it has been positively identified with an eleventh-century C.E. manuscript of the Testaments of the Twelve Patriarchs, found at the Monastery of Koutloumous on Mount Athos in Greece (see M. De Jonge, *Testament Critical Edition*, volume 17, Brill, 1975; and Robert L. Webb, "John the Baptizer and Prophet: A Socio-Historical Study," *Journal for the Study of the New Testament*, suppl. series 62, Sheffield Academic, 1991).

16. Robert L. Webb, "John the Baptizer and Prophet: A Socio-Historical Study," *Journal for the Study of the New Testament*, suppl. series 62 (Sheffield Academic, 1991).

17. Ronny Reich, "The Miqwa'ot [Immersion Baths] of Qumran," paper presented at The Dead Sea Scrolls Fifty Years After Their Discovery, International Congress, Jerusalem, July 20–25, 1997. The Cairo-Damascus documents from Qumran and Cairo also speak of immersions in rock pools.

18. Scroll 1QS 3.4–5.

19. Robert L. Webb, "John the Baptizer and Prophet: A Socio-Historical Study," *Journal for the Study of the New Testament,* supplement series 62 (Sheffield Academic Press, 1991).

20. Joseph A. Fitzmyer, *The Dead Sea Scrolls and Christian Origins* (Eerdmans, 2000).

21. C. H. H. Sobie, *John the Baptist* (SCM, 1964).

22. Joan E. Taylor, *The Immerser: John the Baptist, Within Second Temple Judaism* (Eerdmans, 1997).

23. H. H. Rowley, *The Dead Sea Scrolls and the New Testament* (Talbot, 1964).

24. J. Heron, "The Theology of Baptism," *Scottish Journal of Theology* 8 (1955).

25. William H. Brownlee, "The Dead Sea Manual of Discipline: Translation and Notes," *Bulletin of the American Schools of Oriental Research* (1951). Geza Vermes, in his translation of this passage, reads "cleansing" rather than "rippling" water (*The Complete Dead Sea Scrolls in English,* Allen Lane/Penguin, 1997).

26. Ronny Reich, "The Miqwa'ot [Immersion Baths] of Qumran," paper presented at Dead Sea Scrolls Fifty Years After Their Discovery, International Congress, Jerusalem, July 20–25, 1997. The Cairo-Damascus documents from Qumran and Cairo also speak of immersions in rock pools.

## Chapter 24: John's Ministry

1. "John appeared in the wilderness, preaching a baptism of repentance for the forgiveness of sins" (Mark 1:4); "In those days came John the Baptist, preaching in the wilderness of Judaea, Repent for the kingdom of heaven is at hand" (Matt. 3:1–2); "And he went into all the region about the Jordan, preaching a baptism of repentance for the forgiveness of sins" (Luke 3:2–3).

2. Leonard F. Badia, *The Qumran Baptism and John the Baptist's Baptism* (University Press of America, 1981).

## Chapter 25: Geographical Juxtapositions of Christian and Essene Settlements

1. The Therapeutae were said to be of Hebrew stock, and their devotions were reminiscent of the Essenes of Qumran, although more philosophical in their approach. They met only on the Sabbath and for nocturnal festivals, at which they performed musical liturgies. See Michael Grant, *The Jews in the Roman World* (Weidenfeld and Nicolson, 1973); also Eusebius Book 2.

2. Barbara Thiering, *Jesus of the Apocalypse* (Corgi, 1997).

3. J. Fitzmyer, "The Qumran Scrolls, the Ebionites, and Their Literature," *Theological Studies,* vol. 16.

4. Sean Freyne, *Galilee: From Alexander the Great to Hadrian, 323 B.C.E. to 135 C.E.* (T & T Clark, 1998).

5. Hippolytus of Rome, *The Refutation of All Heresies.*

6. Flavius Josephus, *Jewish Wars 5.*

7. "11QMiqdash 46.13–16, The Temple Scroll," edited by Yigael Yadin, *Israel Exploration Society*/Ben Zvi, vol. 1.

8. Ibid.

9. Bargil Pixner, *An Essene Quarter on Mount Zion?* (Franciscan Printing Press, 1976); "Jerusalem's Essene Gateway: Where the Community Lived in Jesus' Time," *Biblical Archaeology Review* (May/June 1997; www.centuryone.com/essene.html). In his excavations, Pixner also discovered a water channel running from inside the city from the Essene quarter to the *mikvaot* (ritual washing baths) outside the city wall. This finding fits with an Essene requirement that no non-Essene should come into contact with mikvaot water. Pixner believes there is an irrefutable link between the Essenes and early Christianity. This conclusion is also expressed in Yigael Yadin, *The Temple Scroll: The Hidden Law of the Dead Sea Sect* (Weidenfeld and Nicolson, 1985).

10. Ibid.

11. R. de Vaux, "Qumran and the Dead Sea Scrolls," *Jerusalem Star* (Spring 1966).

12. Carsten Peter Thiede, *The Dead Sea Scrolls and the Jewish Origins of Christianity* (Lion, 2000); J. O. Callaghan, "Papiros Neotestamentarios en la cueva 7 de Qumran" (*Biblica* 53, 1972). Examples of texts written in Greek from the books of Exodus and Jeremiah were also found in Cave 7. Thiede and O'Callaghan claim that small fragments of papyrus text found among the Dead Sea Scrolls are taken from part of a very early version of the Christian Scriptures. The Spaniard José O'Callaghan is an eminent papyrologist who is editor of *Studia Papyrologica* and professor of papyrology at Biblium in Rome. Carsten Peter Thiede, his main supporter, is an ordained minister of the Church of England, professor of early Christian history at the University of Basel, Switzerland, and, he claims, a world authority on first-century papyri. Both claim to be backed by a host of respected international papyrologists. The fragments, written in Greek, came from Cave 7 (hence the designations 7Q4 and 7Q5) at Qumran and were discovered around 1956. In 1972 O'Callaghan suggested that some of the fragments were from Mark's Gospel and 1 Timothy. Other scholars pointed out that Qumran had been destroyed in 68 C.E., and it would therefore have been impossible for these texts to have been in the possession of its inhabitants. Conventionally, Mark is not considered to have been penned before 70 C.E. and 1 Timothy much later. That appeared to quash the debate, but Professor Thiede would have none of it, and for the past ten years has argued that the fragments really are from the Christian Scriptures: "The Qumranites could have ordered their copies from Jerusalem . . . or [from] where they had been written and published . . . Rome." Professor Thiede's arguments that the two fragments come from Mark 6:52–53 and 1 Timothy 3:16–4:1, 3 and were copied at Qumran are convincing. But other eminent contemporary scholars, like Father Émile Puech, professor at the École Biblique, Jerusalem; a German scholar, G.-Wilhelm Nebe; Ernst A. Muro Jr., University of Central Florida; and Geza Vermes, emeritus professor at Oxford University, dismiss his claims as unproven (G.-W. Nebe, "7Q4 Möglichkeit und Grenze einer Identifikation," *Revue de Qumran* 13, 1988; Ernst A. Muro Jr., "The Greek Fragments of Enoch from Qumran Cave 7," *Revue de Qumran* 70, 1997; É. Puech, "Notes sur le fragment Grecs du Manuscrit 7Q4,"

*Revue de Qumran* 70, 1997). The significance of Professor Thiede's claims, if he is correct, would be that Mark and Timothy were written at least pre–68 C.E., much earlier than scholars usually claim.

One of Professor Thiede's strongest points is that the name mentioned in one of the Greek fragments (7Q5) for the place where the disciples land after crossing the Sea of Galilee can be read as Gennesaret, as in the Christian Scriptures, and that this form of spelling does not occur previously in the Septuagint. It does, however, he maintains, occur in precisely the same form in Mark's Gospel: " . . . understood about the loaves; their hearts were hardened. And when they had crossed over, they landed at Gennesaret and anchored there. And when they got . . . " (Mark 6:53). And according to archaeological surveys in the 1980s, says Professor Thiede, Gennesaret did not exist after 68 C.E., having been destroyed by the Romans.

My view is that, as we have seen earlier, many passages from other Dead Sea Scrolls material can be detected in the Christian Scriptures. There is no reason to single out these two particular fragments and to suggest that parts of the Christian Scriptures were written tens of years earlier than most scholarly opinion will allow. The conundrum is readily resolved if one accepts the contention that a strain of Jesus's followers existed among the Qumran Essenes. There are then three reasonable possibilities: (1) The literati best qualified to write about and be interested in Jesus were at Qumran, and in one sense Professor Thiede is correct in that 7Q4 and 7Q5 may well have been composed, rather than simply possessed, there. He would then be wrong, however, about the fragments being copies of existing proto-Christian Scriptures text; they could have been the exemplars from which the verses of the Christian Scriptures were subsequently written. (2) The fragments were simply sectarian ideas from previously known stories, written in Greek (Cave 7 contained other documents in Greek, as did Cave 4), a language the Qumran Essenes were happy to work in, as other distinctly non-Christian Scriptures documents demonstrate, which were picked up and utilized by later Gospel writers.

What worries Professor Thiede most is that eminent scholars, like Émile Puech and others, whom he refers to as "merely the proverbial dwarfs," should wage such a fierce fight against the possibility of these two fragments from Cave 7 being copies of verses from proto-Christian Scriptures. "Those who are convinced," he writes, "that there must not be and cannot have been 'Christian' texts at Qumran stoop to a polemic approach which includes a palpable misleading of non-specialist readers. One wonders why this should be necessary? . . . No harm is done to anyone's faith, nor to the historical context as such, if 7Q4 is finally accepted as I Timothy and 7Q5 as Mark." Of course Professor Thiede is correct in his analysis of the relatively modest damage his dubious conclusions might have—apart from the damage to some academic reputations and a need to revise the dates for the writing of 1 Timothy and Mark.

So we come to possibility number 3. I, like most scholars, do not consider that other Qumran texts, such as 4Q215 and 4Q251, are contemporary reports on Jesus or prefigure him. The documents from which such conjectures derive were almost certainly written before the time of Jesus, and there are ample precedents for their composition from sources related to the Hebrew Scriptures. Professor Thiede's fragments are, however, rather different. Cave 7 was discovered on

February 5, 1955, and all nineteen manuscripts found there were in Greek, all written on papyri. The only other cave where fragments written in Greek have been
found was Cave 4, and here, out of some fifteen thousand fragments representing
575 manuscripts, only six were in Greek, and of those only two were on papyrus.
It appears that the manuscripts in Cave 7 were a special cache containing rather
different material from the other ten caves of Qumran. Cave 7 was unique in
another respect; it contained a ceramic jar, made at Qumran, that had Hebrew letters inscribed on its neck. Bargil Pixner reported that a clay jar found in Cave 3
at Qumran had the Hebrew letter *tet* inscribed on its edge and shoulder
("Unravelling the Copper Scroll Code: A Study on the Topography of 3Q15,"
*Revue de Qumran* 43, 1983). Jozef Milik describes a ceramic jar found in Wadi
Qumran that had charcoal lettering indicating a volume of two *se'ab* and seven
*log*—the *se'ab* being approximately four gallons (J. Y. Milik, *Ten Years of Discovery in the Wilderness of Judaea*, SCM, 1959). The inscription, written twice,
comprises four Hebrew letters: *resh*, *vav* (Thiede calls it a *wah*), *mem*, and *aleph*.
What this inscription reads is not certain, bearing in mind that Hebrew has no
vowels; but it is suggested that it reads ROMA, implying that the manuscripts it
contained had some connection with Rome (John Fitzmyer, "A Qumran Fragment
of Mark," *America* 126, 1953) although it is possible this might be a mnemonic
for Jerusalem. To Professor Thiede's question as to why such an effort has been put
into defending any possibility of Christian-linked texts being found at Qumran, perhaps the answer is that such a confirmation leads inevitably to the real possibility
that 7Q4 and 7Q5 were not copied at Qumran, but that versions were originally
composed at Qumran or by the Essenes in Jerusalem. If there is strong evidence
that Mark and 1 Timothy were written well after the destruction of Qumran in
68 C.E., as most scholars assert, then this conclusion remains just as strong.

I will come back to this possibility later, as it has a considerable impact on
revelations that are to come later in this book, and the special role that Émile
Puech (who, far from being a dwarf in the field, is a giant of interpretation, bent
on protecting what he sees are the legitimate truths of the church) may have
played in their history. (Professor Thiede passed away on December 14, 2004.)

13. Interview with Émile Puech by Francesco Garufi, "I rotoli dei Figli della Luce"
("Scrolls of the Sons of Light"), *HERA* (May 2002).

14. Ibid.

15. The main center for the extraction of natrun in ancient Egypt was at Wadi Natrun
in the Delta region of northern Egypt. Deposits are also found at Beheira in northern Egypt and at Elkab in southern Egypt. The material accumulated on the shores
and beds of ancient lakes. It was also used for scouring utensils and in domestic
cleaning; after the Ptolemaic period (332–30 B.C.E.) it was exploited as a source of
alkali in glassmaking and in glazes. (See A. T. Sandison, vol. 22, 259–269, "The
Use of Natron in Mummification in Ancient Egypt," *Journal of Near East Studies*,
1963; A. Lucas, *Ancient Materials and Industries*, London, 1962.) The main
monastery in Wadi Natrun is that of St. Pschoi, a disciple of St. Macarius (c. 330
C.E.). It comprises five churches, the main church being that of St. Bishay, in the east-
ernmost part of the Wadi. The remains of another ancient settlement in the Valley
of Natrun were discovered in 1964. Known as the Kellia Hermitages, and thought
to be founded by St. Amun in the early Christian period, they comprise some fifteen

hundred cells in five clusters spread between Nitria and Wadi Natrun. They were abandoned in the ninth century C.E. (http://interoz.com/Egypt/alkellia.htm).

16. Marilyn Hopkins, Graham Simmans, and Tim Wallace-Murphy, *Rex Deus* (Element, 2000).

17. C. Daniel, "Faux Prophètes surnom des Esseniens dans le Sermon sur la Montagne," *Revue de Qumran* (December 1969); Philo of Alexandria, *The Contemplative Life*, 26.

18. Conversations between Robert Feather and Graham Simmans at Rennes-le-Château, September 2000.

19. The four existing monasteries at Wadi Natrum are at Deir el-Baramus, Deir al-Surian, Deir Amba Bschoi, and Deir Abu Makar (Hugh G. Evelyn-White, "The Monasteries of the Wadi 'n Natrun," *Publication of the Metropolitan Museum of Art* 2, by Arno Press, 1926.)

20. "Egyptian Archaeology," "Digging Diary 2000, Wadi Natrun," *Egypt Exploration Society* (Spring 2001).

21. A second physical correspondence demonstrates that the Qumran Essenes gave legal injunctions to at least one settlement outside Qumran, as evidenced in a fragment known as Ordinances (4Q159).

22. Hartmut Stegemann, *The Library of Qumran* (Brill, 1998).

23. Barbara Thiering, *Jesus of the Apocalypse* (Corgi, 1997). Thiering sees Ephesus as the center for the early Christians from 49 to 57 C.E. It was also an already well-established Jewish area of settlement. She says Revelation 21 shows clearly that it is describing "not the cathedral in the city at Ephesus, but a building which had been erected an hour's distance away. . . . As Revelation 11 shows, the seer, at the time of the schism of 44 C.E., had been given a measuring rod and told to build a reproduction of the Qumran vestry. At this stage, the Ephesus building whose construction he directed was a hermitage, occupied by Jewish men living like the Therapeutae. But when a later seer was given a measuring rod in Revelation 21, and sent to the same building, it was being re-dedicated as a Christian monastery. From the point of view of Christians with a more eastern orientation, the climax of the history came when the plan of the Temple Scroll was adapted to Christian usage. The room used for worship was from now on the model for all ordinary churches."

24. R. de Vaux, "Qumran and the Dead Sea Scrolls," *The Jerusalem Star* (Spring 1966); S. H. Steckholl, "Marginal Notes on the Qumran Excavations," *Revue de Qumran* (December 1969).

25. Ibid.

26. Robert Feather, *The Mystery of the Copper Scroll of Qumran* (Inner Traditions, 2003).

27. Joan E. Taylor, *The Immerser: John the Baptist Within Second Temple Judaism* (Eerdmans, 1997); H. Kasting, *Die Anfange Christlichen Mission* (Kaiser, 1969).

28. It is only after Emperor Constantine's time, in the fourth century C.E., that churches were built at Tiberias, Diocaesarea (previously Sepphoris), Capernaum, and Nazareth (Sean Freyne, *Galilee: From Alexander the Great to Hadrian, 323 B.C.E. to 135 C.E.*, T & T Clark, 1998).

29. John 4:43–47, 54.

30. Geza Vermes, *Jesus the Jew* (SCM, 2001). Vermes cites a limited number of expressions attributed to Hanina ben Dosa, which in similar forms turn up in the Gospels, and his apparent lack of interest in legal or ritual affairs or personal possessions, as indicators of a commonality with Jesus. However, ben Dosa's marital views; isolated lifestyle; disinterest in the communal meal; lifestyle of abject poverty; the assertion, in other sources, that he was rigorous in pursuit of the law and rituals (Berakhoth and Demai, Jerusalem Talmud); and the lack of any mention of him or the Hassidim in the Christian Scriptures militate against anything more than a marginal influence on Jesus.

## Chapter 26: Trial and Crucifixion

1. Jacqueline Tabick, study session at West London Synagogue, November 20, 1997.

2. The omission of any mention of lamb is all the more strange, as Christian theology assigns great symbolic importance to it. John himself, in 1:29, talks of Jesus dying on Passover as the crucified lamb "who takes away the sin of the world." The importance of lamb symbolism is apparent from the preeminence of the lamb in representations of Christ in early art forms. Prior to the second century C.E., Christ was represented only by symbolic images, such as the lamb, fish, and sacred monogram—the Alpha and Omega. The reason for this inhibition was probably inherited from Judaism, where any visual representation of God was forbidden (*Son of God*, BBC television documentary, April 1, 2001). Some of the earliest examples of Christian icons can be seen in the Victoria and Albert Museum in London, including the Alpha and Omega on a linen curtain with the Egyptian ankh sign, adapted to Coptic tradition dating to the fourth century C.E., found at Akhmin in Egypt. Another example appears on a piece of linen embroidered with a silk floral wreath showing the apostles with a global sphere around their heads.

   Some scholars, however, say the crucifixion was not depicted by early Christians and emerged only gradually as the principal image of the faith at about the end of the seventh century C.E. (Nigel Spivey, *Enduring Creation: Art, Pain and Fortitude,* Thames and Hudson, 2001). This is a view I find hard to support, and I will later present evidence that undermines the idea. Even more surprising are the statements in all four of the Gospels (Matt. 26:26; Mark 14:22; Luke 22:19; John 13:18) that, at the Passover meal, Jesus ate bread. Throughout the period of Passover, yeast bread is rigorously excluded from the household and is replaced with matzoh, which is unleavened. Bread is never eaten at the Passover meal.

3. The Didache, alternatively known as the Teaching of the Twelve Apostles, is referred to in ancient texts but only came to light in 1875 as a codex dating to 1057 C.E. It was originally composed in the late first century C.E. and describes ethical instruction and regulations on baptism, fasting, the eucharist (ritual partaking of bread and wine as a symbolic union for Christians with the body and blood of Christ), welcoming visitors into a community, and the development of the early church. The section of the Didache called "The Two Ways" seems to be a direct translation from the Dead Sea Scroll 1QS (Community Rule 3.13–4.1) and was repeated almost verbatim by the Epistle of Barnabas (see J. T. Milik, *Ten Years of Discovery in the Wilderness of Judaea,* SCM, 1959).

4. Mark 14:15; Luke 22:12.

5. John 12:12–13.

6. Matthew 24:32; Luke 21:29.

7. A. Jaubert, *La Date de la Cène* (Sorbonne University, Paris, 1957). Philo records a Passover-like meal being celebrated by the Therapeutae, a sect closely related to the Essenes, on the eve of Shavuot (Feast of Weeks) and not at Passover.

8. The Mishnaic tractate Sukkah mentions, in relation to Ezekiel 8, the practice of palm, willow, and myrtle branches being waved by pilgrims during the singing of Hallel (Psalm 118) while priests walked around the altar waving branches during the daily ceremony of water libation. The ceremony appears to have very early derivations, as it is mentioned in relation to the Feast of the Booths (Succoth) in Leviticus 23 and in the Book of Jubilees, in which the rite of branch waving is attributed to the time of Abraham (J. Glen Taylor, "Yahweh and the Sun," *Journal for the Study of the Old Testament*, suppl. series 111, Sheffield Academic, 1993). The passage from Leviticus specifies only fruit of goodly trees, palm, boughs of leafy trees, and willow, and these have been interpreted by the rabbis as comprising palm, myrtle, and willow, whereas the fruit of the citron tree, known as the *etrog,* is also held in the hand. It is this latter combination of lulav that is waved during the Succoth festival of today. The promotion of the festival of waving of the sheaf, as described in the Temple Scroll (Yigael Yadin, *The Temple Scroll,* Weidenfeld and Nicolson, 1985), to a major festival was, according to Rabbi Mark Winer, of West London Synagogue, paralleled in biblical times and reflected in the current designation of Succoth as Ha Hag, "the festival," ahead of Passover and Shavuot in importance.

9. James B. Pritchard, ed., *The Ancient Near East: An Anthology of Texts and Pictures* (Princeton University Press, 1958); Jan Assmann, *Moses the Egyptian* (Harvard University Press, 1997); Erik Hornung, *Idea into Image* (Timken, 1992); Messod Sabbah and Roger Sabbah, *Secrets of the Exodus* (HarperCollins, 2002); Robert Feather, *The Mystery of the Copper Scroll of Qumran* (Inner Traditions, 2003); *The Pharaoh's Holy Treasure,* BBC2 TV documentary, March 31, 2002.

10. There is a difference of rabbinic opinion about whether the lulav should comprise one or three types of leaf. A modern commentary states: "The Hebrew word for fronds or branches 'Kappot' is written defectively, without the letter 'vav', so that the word could also be read in the singular rather than the plural. Hence the traditional view that a single palm frond was to be held by each worshipper" (*Prayers for the Pilgrim Festivals,* Reform Synagogues of Great Britain, 1995). This seems to be confirmed by the single palm seen being waved on the inscription at Luxor.

11. Michael van Esbroeck, *Les Plus Anciens Homilaires Georgiens,* Louvain, Belgium, 1975; "Jean II de Jerusalem," *Analecta Bollandiana* 102 (1984); Bargil Pixner, "Church of the Apostles Found on Mount Zion," *Biblical Archaeological Review* (May/June, 1990).

12. A. Jaubert, *La Date de la Cène* (Sorbonne University, Paris, 1957).

13. Josephus states, in *Jewish Wars* 2, that when the Essenes traveled they entered the houses of other Essenes "whom they have never formerly seen as though they were the most intimate friends" (William Whiston, trans., Paul L. Maier, commentary, *The New Complete Works of Josephus,* Kregel, 1999).

14. J. H. Charlesworth, in his book *Jesus and the Dead Sea Scrolls* (Doubleday, 1993), has deduced that the Essenes maintained a network of "safe houses" where wandering brothers could find sanctuary.

15. Hegesippus was a second-century historian who studied the traditions of the apostolic teachings of the church in relation to gnosticism. Sections from his *Memoirs* have survived in Eusebius; they include accounts of the martyrdom of James and of the grandsons of Jude, another of Jesus's brothers.

16. According to Josephus, writing originally in Aramaic: "So he [Albinus, the new procurator of Judaea] assembled the Sanhedrin of judges, and brought before them the brother of Jesus, who was called Christ, whose name was James, and some others; and when he had formed an accusation against them as breakers of the law, he delivered them to be stoned; but as for those who seemed the most equitable of the citizens, and such as were the most uneasy at the breach of the laws, they disliked what was done" (Flavius Josephus, *Jewish Antiquities* 20).

17. The First Jewish Revolt against Rome was led by Zealots from 66 to 70 C.E. Vespasian crushed the revolt with sixty thousand troops, and by 68 C.E. the rebels were largely confined to the area of Jerusalem. His son, Titus, captured Jerusalem in 70 C.E. and sacked the Second Temple. The final remnant of 960 rebels, comprising mainly Zealots and a few Essenes, was besieged at Masada, where virtually all committed suicide rather than be captured, in 73 C.E. Two women and a few children were reported as survivors (Yigael Yadin, *Masada*, Book Club Associates, 1966). Robert L. Leonard Jr., largely from coin evidence, argues that Qumran did not fall to the Romans until 70 or even 72 C.E. ("Numismatic Evidence for the Dating of Qumran," *The Qumran Chronicle* 7, no. 3/4, 1997).

## Chapter 27: A Return Visit to Paris

1. See chapter 4 for more on John Allegro.

2. Karen Armstrong entered an English teaching order of nuns in 1962 and left the order in 1969. She continued her studies at Oxford University and subsequently taught at Bedford College and London University. She has written extensively on Christianity, including *The First Christian: St. Paul's Impact on Christianity* (Pan, 1983), the subject of a Channel Four television documentary in Great Britain.

3. John Dominic Crossan, who was eventually appointed emeritus professor of religious studies at DePaul University, spent two years at the École Biblique in Jerusalem, from 1965 to 1967, and was heavily involved in Dead Sea Scrolls studies when he resigned from the priesthood. From the numerous books he has written on Jesus and the church, it is evident that his views have shifted away from those of a conventional Catholic, but it may well be that he left the church to get married, which he did a year after his departure.

4. Born in 1924, Professor Geza Vermes grew up in Hungary in a Catholic environment, although his parents, who had converted to Christianity when he was a child, were originally Jewish. He was baptized at the age of six, and at the age of eighteen entered the priesthood. His parents were murdered during the Second World War, but he escaped. Eventually he came to Newcastle University and then Oxford University, where he concentrated on his studies of the Dead Sea Scrolls

and their relevance to Jesus and Judaism. A number of books followed on the theme of Jesus as a Jew *(Jesus the Jew, Jesus and the World of Judaism, The Religion of Jesus the Jew),* and in 1957 Geza Vermes left the priesthood to get married. Of the role of Christianity in his life, he says: "I did not leave but imperceptibly grew out of it. . . . My religion had become that of the 'still small voice' which those who listen can hear . . . the voice of an existential God, acting in and through people, who stood behind all the providential accidents of my life." In 1970, he joined the Liberal Jewish Synagogue in England. His wife, Pamela, who died in 1993, was a biblical scholar and an expert on Martin Buber.

5. Russell Shorto notes, in his *Gospel Truth* (Hodder and Stoughton, 1997), that when Jesus visited the Temple, he looked around but did not pray—nor would an Essene have prayed there.

6. Robert Feather and Martin Weitz, video recording made on May 30, 2001, in Paris.

7. Guillaume d'Arbley, preceptor of the Templar house at Soissy in Meaux, France, testified on October 22, 1307, that he had twice seen the bearded head, which was adorned with silver and wood. During the trials of the Knights Templar, one of the accusations against them, listed in the charges drawn up by the Inquisition on August 12, 1308, was: "Item, that in each province the order had idols, namely heads, of which some had three faces and some one, and others had a human skull. . . . Item, that they venerated as their savior. . . . Item, that they said that the head could save them." At one of the trials, Brother Jean Tillefer of Genay, who had been received into an Order of the Templars, testified that at his initiation "an idol representing a human face" was placed on the altar before him. It was "about the natural size of a man's head, with a very fierce looking face and beard" (www. templarhistory.com.).

However, Professor Helen Nicholson, of Cardiff University, maintains that it was the Knights Hospitaliers who revered the head of John the Baptist, not the Templars. According to her, the Templars were martyr-oriented and the Hospitaliers were people-oriented ("The Knights Templar: A New History," paper presented at the Saunière Society meeting, Conway Hall, London, October 4, 2003). Scribes as early as 500 B.C.E. are thought to have devised a code using the twenty-two letters of the Hebrew alphabet in reverse order. Baphomet could thus be read as Sophia, the Greek word meaning wisdom.

8. Joan E. Taylor, *The Immerser: John the Baptist Within Second Temple Judaism* (Eerdmans, 1997).

9. Ibid.

## Chapter 28: The Search Begins

1. Hanan Eshel, "New Data on the Cemetery East of Khirbet Qumran," *Society of Biblical Literature,* Toronto, 23–26 November 2003. There have been incomplete reports of the discovery of tombs similar to those at Qumran, notably at Beit Safafa in southwest Jerusalem (*Jewish Chronicle,* August 13, 1999; also B. Zissu, " 'Qumran Type' Graves in Jerusalem: Archaeological Evidence of an Essene Community?" *Dead Sea Discoveries* 5, 1998). P. Bar-Adon reported on the excavations of twenty graves at Ain el-Ghuweir, about nine miles south of Qumran.

One grave was aligned east–west and all the others were similar in direction to the graves at Qumran ("Another Settlement of the Judean Sect at 'En el-Ghuweir' on the Shores of the Dead Sea," *Eretz Israel,* vol. 10, 1971). K. D. Politis refers to some 3,500 second- and third-century-C.E. graves in Jordan ("Rescue Excavations in the Nabataean Cemetery at Khirbet Qazone 1996–1997," *Annual of the Department of Antiquities, Jordan,* no. 42, 1998), but these are ethnically Nabataean. None of these examples of burials is confirmed as being identical to those at Qumran.

2. Robert Feather, *The Mystery of the Copper Scroll of Qumran* (Inner Traditions, 2003).

3. Ferdinand Röhrhirsch, "Wissenschaftstheorie und Qumran: Geltungsbegründungen von Aussagen in der Biblischen Archaologie am Beispiel von Chirbet Qumaran und En Fescha," *Novum Testamentum et Orbis Antiquus,* vol. 32 (Vandenhoeck and Ruprecht, 1996).

4. J.-B. Humbert and A. Chambon cite 1,138 graves (*Fouilles de Khirbet Qumran et de Ain Feshkha,* Éditions Universitaires Fribourg, 1994), whereas the latest survey by M. Broshi, H. Eshel, and R. Freund gives a figure of 1,177. H. Eshel, M. Broshi, R. Freund, B. Shultz "New Data on the Cemetery East of Khirbet Qumran," *Dead Sea Discoveries,* vol. 9, no. 2, 2002. See also Brian M. Schultz, Bar-Ilan University, "New Data and Reflections Concerning the Qumran Cemetery," paper presented at the 2003 ASOR Annual Meeting, November 19–22. An abstract of this paper can be found on www.asor.org.

5. Norman Golb, *Who Wrote the Dead Sea Scrolls?* (Simon and Schuster, 1995). Yizhar Hirschfeld, of the Hebrew University, Jerusalem, describes Qumran as a rural manor house overseeing farming operations ("Qumran, Ein Feshka, and the Perfume Industry of Judaea During the Reign of Herod the Great," paper presented at Qumran: The Site of the Dead Sea Scrolls, Brown University, November 17–19, 2002.

6. Joseph Zias, e-mail to author, January 14, 2005.

7. Alan Crown and Lena Cansdale, "Qumran: Was It an Essene Settlement?" *Biblical Archaeology Review* (September/October 1994). See also Lena Cansdale, "The Qumran Scrolls: A 2,000 Year Old Apple of Discord," in *Ancient History: Resources for Teachers* 21, no. 2 (Macquarie University, 1991).

8. P. Donceel, "Les Ruines de Qumran réinterprées," *Archeologie* 298 (February 1994); R. Donceel and P. Donceel, "Archaeology of Qumran," *Annals of the New York Academy of Sciences* (1994). See also Hershel Shanks's reference to Robert Donceel and Pauline Donceel in *The Mystery and Meaning of the Dead Sea Scrolls* (Random House, 1998).

9. Gloria Moss, "Religion and Medicine: The Case of Qumran," *Faith and Freedom: A Journal of Progressive Religion* 146 (1998).

10. Hershel Shanks, *The Mystery and Meaning of the Dead Sea Scrolls* (Random House, 1998).

11. Joseph Zias of the Science and Antiquity group, Hebrew University, doubts the existence of coffin dust remains, apart from those associated with Tombs 17–19. Professor J. Van der Ploeg, a Christian scholar who was present in Jerusalem dur-

ing the critical years between 1947 and 1955 and was privy to the activities of the inner circle at the École Biblique, maintains, "Only one of the dead was buried in a wooden coffin" (*The Excavations at Qumran,* Louvain, 1958). Susan Sheridan reports finding pieces of wood in the otherwise empty box for Tomb 17, and says R. Donceel and P. Donceel reported cypress wood from Tomb 18 ("Scholars, Soldiers, Craftsmen, Elites? Analysis of French Collection of Human Remains from Qumran," *Dead Sea Discoveries* 9, no. 2, 2002.

12. G. Vermes and M. Goodman, *The Essenes According to the Classical Sources* (Sheffield Academic, 1989).

13. Douglas Lockhart, *Jesus the Heretic* (Element, 1997).

## Chapter 29: Fields of Death and Silence

1. Strangely enough, a fragment of Ezekiel 37, the vision of the valley of dry bones, was found in the ruins of Masada.

2. Jozef T. Milik, *Ten Years of Discovery in the Wilderness of Judaea* (SCM, 1959); Olav Röhrer-Ertl, Ferdinand Röhrhirsch, and Dietbert Hahn, "Über die Gräberfelder von Khirbet Qumran die Funde der Compagne 1956. 1. Anthropologische Datenvorlage und Erstauswertung aufgrunde der Collectio Kurth," *Revue de Qumran* 73 (June 1999).

3. The alignment of most of the graves at Qumran is in a north–south direction, and the deliberate turning of the head of each skeleton toward the south has long been a puzzle for scholars. The bodies were interred, naked, in shallow graves with the heads carefully turned to the south. There is no agreed explanation for the peculiar orientation, especially as Jerusalem and the Holy Temple were located in a westerly direction. I have previously suggested that the orientation relates to connections the Qumran Essenes had with the holy city of Akhetaten in Egypt, which lay in a southerly direction, and perhaps more pertinently with the north–south direction of the river Nile at that location. The type of burial is quite unlike anything found elsewhere in Israel, where burial generally took place in randomly arranged family tombs. The deceased was laid on a stone platform and left for a year for the body to rot; the bones were then collected and put into a ceramic casket, known as an ossuary, which was usually labeled with the occupant's details.

4. Robert Feather, recorded conversation with Jozef Milik, November 19, 2000, in Paris. In relation to the three adjacent burials it occurred to me that there might be some connection to an ancient legend (which emerged from France in the thirteenth century and is embedded in poems by Baudoin de Conde and Nicholas de Margival) as regards three living and three dead men, especially as the portrayal of their situation in a painting by Bernardo Daddi was remarkably similar to that seen at Qumran. This fourteenth-century work, originally from the Convent of San Pancrazio in Florence, can be seen in the Accademia Gallery, Florence.

## Chapter 30: The Excavations at Qumran

1. Hugh Miller, *Secrets of the Dead* (Channel 4 Books, 2000).

2. S. H. Steckholl, "Preliminary Excavation Report in the Qumran Cemetery," *Revue*

de *Qumran* 3 (1968); N. Haas, H. Nathan, "Anthropological Survey of the Human Remains from Qumran," *Revue de Qumran* 3 (1968).

3. Professor Hanan Eshel, of Bar-Ilan University, Israel, says de Vaux excavated twenty-eight graves in his review of Cansdale (review of *Qumran and the Essenes: A Re-evaluation of the Evidence* by Lena Cansdale, *The Jewish Quarterly Review,* January–April 1999).

4. Roland de Vaux, *Archaeology and the Dead Sea Scrolls* (Oxford University Press, 1973).

5. In my previous book, *The Mystery of the Copper Scroll of Qumran* (Inner Traditions, 2003), I drew attention to the similarity in arm positions between the skeleton found in Qumran, with its left hand extended down toward the pelvis and right hand placed across the chest (unlike any other skeleton found at Qumran), and a skeleton found in Tomb KV55 in the Valley of the Kings, Egypt. This latter is thought to be the remains of a royal personage dating to the time of King Akhenaten. The normal position was for the pharaoh to be laid in his coffin with hands crossed at the wrists and lying centrally on the chest.

6. Joseph E. Zias, "The Cemeteries of Qumran, Celibacy, Confusion: Laid to Rest?" Planned presentation to Society of Biblical Literature Conference, Boston, November 22, 1999. Joseph Zias, an expert in the field, has been investigating skeletal and other remains from Qumran in cooperation with surgeon/archaeologist Mark Spigelman.

7. Some fifty tombs, somewhat similar to those at Qumran, are reported to have been found at Beit Safafa in southwestern Jerusalem (Patricia Pitchon, "Digging Deep: Archaeology in Israel," *Jewish Chronicle,* August 13, 1999).

8. Edouard Naville, *The Cemeteries of Abydos, Part 1* (Egypt Exploration Fund, 1914).

9. Roland de Vaux, *Archaeology and the Dead Sea Scrolls* (Oxford University Press, 1973).

10. Hanan Eshel, review of *Qumran and the Essenes: A Re-evaluation of the Evidence* by Lena Cansdale, *Jewish Quarterly Review* (January–April 1999).

11. Matt Rees and David Van Biema, "Digging for the Baptist" Associated Press Report, *Time* magazine, August 2002.

12. Robert Feather, *The Mystery of the Copper Scroll of Qumran* (Inner Traditions, 2003).

13. Wolf Leslau, *Falasha Anthology* (Yale University Press, 1951).

## Chapter 31: Years of Silence

1. The earliest coins found at Qumran are eight late-second-century-B.C.E. Seleucid coins, dating to Antiochus III and IV, and ten coins of John Hyrcanus I, all typical of those circulating in Judaea. The latest examples are a hoard of 561 Tyrian shekels dated to 8 or 9 B.C.E. The last stage of occupation of the Qumran site, circa 68 C.E., as indicated by numismatics, is attested to by coins of Herod Archelus, Roman procurators, and Agrippa I (see, for example, Yaakov Meshorer, *Coins,* The Israel Museum, Jerusalem, 2002). Charles T. Fritsch, associate professor of Old Testament at Princeton University and an early visitor to Qumran,

gives a total of 750 coins found at Qumran in his book *The Qumran Community* (Macmillan, 1956).

2. According to Hartmut Stegemann, professor of New Testament studies, University of Göttingen, Germany, preparation of a final report on Roland de Vaux's work has been taken back in-house and is being completed by Père Jean-Baptiste Humbert, an archaeologist at the École Biblique, East Jerusalem.

3. Recorded conversation between Professor Pauline Donceel and Robert Feather, February 28, 2000.

4. Hershel Shanks, *The Mystery and Meaning of the Dead Sea Scrolls* (Random House, 1998).

5. Eva Peron was the second wife of Juan Peron, president of Argentina. When she died in 1952, her body was spirited out of Argentina and kept hidden by her supporters until the early 1970s, at some periods being carted around Europe from hotel to hotel.

## Chapter 32: Missing Bones

1. www.centuryone.org.

2. E-mail communication to the author from Joseph Zias, July 19, 2000.

3. Joseph E. Zias, "The Cemeteries of Qumran and Celibacy: Confusion Laid to Rest?" *Dead Sea Discoveries* 7, no. 2 (2000).

4. Émile Puech, "The Necropolises of Khirbet Qumran and Ain el-Ghuweir and the Essene Belief in Afterlife," *BASOR* 313 (1998).

5. Joan E. Taylor, "The Cemeteries of Khirbet Qumran and Women's Presence at the Site," *Dead Sea Discoveries* 6, no. 3 (1999). Charles Fritsch, who later became associate professor at Princeton Theological Seminary, was an early visitor to the Qumran area and reported that parts of nine skeletons were sent for examination to Professor H. Vallois in Paris.

6. Robert Feather and Dr. D. Olav Röhrer-Ertl, Munich, personal communication, June 8, 2000.

7. Olav Röhrer-Ertl, Ferdinand Röhrhirsch, and Dietbert Hahn, "Über die Gräberfelder von Khirbet Qumran die Funde der Compagne 1956. 1. Anthropologische Datenvorlage und erstauswertung Aufgrunde der Collectio Kurth," *Revue de Qumran* 73 (June 1999).

8. Personal correspondence between the author and Henri de Contenson, June 7, 2000.

9. Copy of a letter dated March 6, 1956, from John Allegro to Frank Moore Cross, shown to the author in 1999 and now in the possession of Joan Allegro (see appendix 2).

10. Emanuel Tov, "Hebrew Biblical Manuscripts," *Journal of Jewish Studies* 39 (1988). Tov is editor in chief of the Dead Sea Scrolls translation team.

## Chapter 33: The Bones of John the Baptist

1. Jewish burial at the time of Jesus usually took place in two stages. Immediately after death the body would be washed, cleansed with oil, perfumed with ointment, wrapped, and laid full length on a slab in the family tomb. The body would be

checked three days after burial to make sure the person was really dead, and then the tomb sealed for a year. When the tomb was reopened, the remaining bones would be put into an ossuary inscribed with the name of the dead person, and the ossuary placed in a niche (Hebrew, *kokh*).

2. Jonathan G. Campbell, *Dead Sea Scrolls: The Complete Story* (Ulysses, 1998).

3. Olav Röhrer-Ertl, Ferdinand Röhrhirsch, and Dietbert Hahn, "Über die Gräberfelder von Khirbet Qumran die Funde der Compagne 1956. 1. Anthropologische Datenvorlage und Erstauswertung aufgrunde der Collectio Kurth," *Revue de Qumran* 73 (June 1999).

4. The Kurth Collection is housed at the Jura Museum, Eichstätt, Germany. It comprises mostly complete skeletons from the Main Cemetery and South Cemetery of Qumran.

5. Röhrer-Ertl, Ferdinand Röhrhirsch, and Dietbert Hahn, "Über die Gräberfelder von Khirbet Qumran die Funde der Compagne 1956. 1. Anthropologische Datenvorlage und Erstauswertung aufgrunde der Collectio Kurth," *Revue de Qumran* 73 (June 1999).

6. Joseph E. Zias, *The Cemeteries of Qumran and Celibacy: Confusion Laid to Rest?* Private communication to the author, July 2000.

7. J-B. Humbert and A. Chambon, *Fouilles de Khirbet Qumran et de Ain Feshkha* (Éditions Universitaires Fribourg, 1994). De Vaux refers to "parafinage du cercueil et du corps."

8. Joan E. Taylor, "The Cemeteries of Khirbet Qumran and Women's Presence at the Site," *Dead Sea Discoveries* 6, no. 3 (1999). Taylor, of the University of Waikato, New Zealand, reported that Professors R. Donceel and P. Donceel sent a fragment of wood from de Vaux's Q18 grave to E. Gilot of the Laboratory of Inorganic, Analytical and Nuclear Chemistry, University Catholique de Louvain, but it was not possible to test satisfactorily as a result of paraffin contamination of the sample. According to Roland de Vaux, brown dust, which he attributed to the presence of wooden coffins, was found in two other trenches in the southeastern section of the cemetery. These graves, known as T32 and T33, apparently contained botanical evidence that the deceased were buried in coffins. Joseph Zias, in his private communication with the author, disputes the possibility that coffins were used for these two burials.

9. *Jericho und Qumran: Neues zum Umfeld der Bibel*, Eichstatter Studien (Friedrich Pustet, 2000).

## Chapter 34: The Stone of Thorns

1. Joseph E. Zias, "The Cemeteries of Qumran and Celibacy: Confusion Laid to Rest?" *Dead Sea Discoveries* 7, no. 2 (2000). Dental evidence from one adult male buried at Qumran shows that he died at about the age of sixteen.

2. Analysis of photos taken in the 1950s and 1960s of the cemeteries, in relevant books, publications, and photo collections, failed to reveal this structure, nor does the literature refer to the structure. It must be assumed that it was erected subsequent to that period. When I pointed it out to Jozef Milik, he thought it some kind of Bedouin shelter but did not recognize it.

3. It seems likely that this mark of the cross was made subsequent to the burial period at Qumran. The simple cross is generally not thought to have come into use as a Christian symbol until the early part of the fourth century, although discussion in chapter 37 contests this assumption. The presence of an acanthus-like spiny shrub growing from beneath the carved stone is not seen with any other marker stone in the cemetery. It may simply be there as a matter of chance, but in light of the other factors—the carved face, the positioning of the grave, and so on—it seems to be of some significance. Perhaps there is some connection to the story related at certain Freemasonry ceremonies in which a member is raised to the level of Master Mason. In the story, some of the Brethren discover the grave and body of their Master, "and to distinguish the spot, stuck a sprig of acacia at the head of the grave, then hastened to Jerusalem" (Christopher Knight and Robert Lomas, *The Hiram Key*, Arrow, 1997).

4. That the Qumran Essenes referred to themselves as "saints" is testified to in a number of their sectarian works, including 1QS: "[The Master shall teach the sai]nts to live(?) {according to the Book} (4Q255, 257) of the Community [Rul]e, that they may seek God with a whole heart and soul, and do what is right before Him" (translation from Geza Vermes, *The Complete Dead Sea Scrolls in English*, Allen Lane/Penguin, 1997).

5. Rainer Riesner quotes Professor Eugen Rucksthül of Lucerne and W. Pesch as scholars who held this view ("Jesus, the Primitive Community, and the Essene Quarter of Jerusalem," James H. Charlesworth, ed., *Jesus and the Dead Sea Scrolls*, Doubleday, 1992). According to Joseph Zias, Q37, a north–south grave containing what he judges to be a male skeleton, showed signs of secondary burial—that is, the body was removed from elsewhere and reburied. Solomon Steckholl recorded a number of young females and elderly males buried in the western part of the cemetery. His testimony is unconfirmed by modern testing, however, and is not considered very reliable.

6. Jane Schaberg, *The Resurrection of Mary Magdalene* (Continuum, 2002).

7. Laurence Gardner, *Bloodline of the Holy Grail* (Element, 1996).

8. It is, I believe, no coincidence that in 1890 the École Biblique was located by its founder, Father Marie-Joseph Lagrange, next to the Garden Tomb. Professor Gabriel Barkay, of Bar-Ilan University, Tel Aviv, and the University of Notre Dame, excavated in the grounds of the École in the early 1970s and discovered two Byzantine tomb complexes and Iron Age remains. There is also evidence that an Egyptian temple once stood in the grounds, possibly dating from the nineteenth dynasty (Gabriel Barkay, "What's an Egyptian Temple Doing in Jerusalem?" *Biblical Archaeology Review*, May/June 2000).

9. There are many other, more fantastical suggestions for the place of Jesus's tomb. One recent claim (R. Andrews and P. Shellenberger, *The Tomb of God: The Body of Jesus and the Solution to a 2,000-Year-Old Mystery*, Little, Brown, 1996), puts Jesus's tomb in the south of France, near Rennes-le-Château.

10. Geza Vermes, *Jesus the Jew* (SCM, 2001).

## Chapter 35: Facial Likenesses

1. Jospeh Zias, previously curator of archaeology at the Rockefeller Museum, Jerusalem, sometimes spent days on end over a period of two years waiting for the sunlight to finally reveal the letters of an inscription on Absalom's Tomb in Jerusalem.

2. According to Byzantine legend, when Abgar, or Angarus, a fabled king of first-century-C.E. Edessa, became ill, he sent to Jesus for help. Jesus sent him an impression of his face, via Ananias, that had been left on a towel (Greek, *man-ulion*). The gift apparently not only cured the king but also helped repel an attack on Edessa by the Persians. Not surprisingly, the Mandylion became a holy relic. By the tenth century it is known to have arrived in Constantinople, and was there until the thirteenth century. A painting showing the cloth and the face of Jesus can be seen on a triptych from the middle of the tenth century kept at the monastery of St. Katherine in Sinai. See also Bamber Gascoigne, *Christianity* (Robinson, 2003).

3. The Turin Shroud is a rectangular piece of cloth measuring approximately twelve by three feet that bears the faint yellowish brown imprint of a bearded figure. First mentioned by Robert de Clari in 1203 as having been seen during the sack of Constantinople by Christian knights during the Fourth Crusade, it apparently turned up again 150 years later in the possession of Geoffrey de Charney, over-lord of the French town of Lirey. In 1453 it was acquired by Louis, Duke of Savoy, and housed in the church of Sainte-Chapelle in his capital, Chambéry. When the duke moved his household to Turin in 1578, the shroud found its permanent lodging in the city's cathedral.

4. Franck Smyth, "Analyzing the Turin Shroud," *Mysteries of the Church—Miracles of Holy Mysticism,* ed. Peter Brookesmith, published by Orbis Publishing, London, 1984.

5. *The Mystery of the Shroud,* Channel 3 ITV, March 31, 2002. See also Shimon Gibson, W. F. Albright Institute, "In the Shadow of Mount Zion: A First-Century Burial Shroud at Akeldama in Jerusalem," paper presented at the 2003 ASOR Annual Meeting, November 19–22, 2003.

6. Another strange feature of the Rennes-le-Château Church of Sainte-Madelaine is the placement of two large statues on either side of the altar showing Jesus's parents, each holding an infant. These are noteworthy in relation to legends that have survived relating to Jesus having a twin brother. Sources for this legend include mention of a twin brother of Jesus in the Gospel of Thomas from the Nag Hammadi texts. The chronicler Julius Africanus, writing about Jesus of Nazareth, stated that "the relatives of the Lord" lived there when he recorded the genealogies of his family tree. They were, apparently, the descendants of Jude, described by Hegesippus, a Judaeo-Christian writer of the second century, as a "consanguineous brother of the Lord." It has been suggested that a twin brother of Jesus might be the explanation for the appearance of a Jesus-like figure after the crucifixion. Interestingly, a recent discovery of a page written in old French, found inserted in an eighteenth-century paroissial book (Department of Archives, Church of Rennes-le-Château), reads: ". . . us de Galilee n'est point icy" (" . . . us from Galilee is not here"). The text refers to Abbé Antoine Bigou (a predecessor of François-Bérenger Saunière, who had been

appointed curé of the village in the 1780s), and it is suggested that " . . . us" could be the last two letters of Jesus (www.rennes-le-chateau.com/anglais/bigou.htm).

7. Today the Mount of Beatitudes, traditional site of the Sermon on the Mount, is marked by the Church of the Beatitudes, which stands on a hillside near Capernaum on the Sea of Galilee. Although the Sermon on the Mount, where the Beatitudes were proclaimed, is recorded in Matthew 5–7 and Luke 6, neither Gospel gives an exact location for the sermon, and there are suggestions that it might have been farther south.

8. Conversation between Robert Feather and Tuvia Fogel, president, Il Caduceo s.r.l., Agenzia Letteraria, Milan, August 25, 2003.

9. Brian Innes, *Rennes-le-Château, Mysteries of the Church—Miracles of Holy Mysticism,* ed. Peter Brookesmith, Orbis Publishing, London, 1984.

10. What of the site of this burial in the future? As a cemetery, the burial grounds of Qumran have to be treated with respect. This remote site near Qumran is not easily accessed, but it would be a desecration to have hordes of people trampling its graves. Covering an area the size of about two soccer fields, the very emptiness of this "ground of Illyrium" endows it with a mood of spiritual tranquillity that could easily be lost with the ingress of large numbers of devotees and tourists—or worse, souvenir hunters. At the moment, hardly any of the large numbers of people who visit Qumran are guided anywhere near the cemetery. Inevitably there will be logistical problems of access that will need urgent attention. One simple solution might be to simply cordon off an area around the grave securely and to mark out a restricted path through the graveyard from the site of the Qumran buildings up to where the grave is located.

## Chapter 36: Alternative Burial Sites for Jesus

1. Many other speculative theories have been put forward through the years, including the possibility of burial locations at Rennes-le-Château in France, as well as in India and many other countries (see, for example, Barry Carter, "Re: Where did Jesus go for all those years?" www.floweroflife.com). Lynn Picknett and Clive Prince, *The Templar Revelation: Secret Guardians of the True Identity of Christ* (Touchstone, 1997). H. M. G. Ahmad of Qadian, *Jesus in India* (Islam International Publication, 1989).

   More recently Joan Bakewell, a BBC television researcher/presenter, has suggested that ossuaries (stone caskets) found in a tomb in East Talpiot, Jerusalem, and inscribed with the names Joseph, Mary, and Jesus son of Joseph, could have been those of the Holy Family (Joan Bakewell, "The Tomb That Dare Not Speak Its Name," *The Sunday Times,* March 31, 1996; *Heart of the Matter: The Body in Question,* BBC 1, Spring 1996). The likelihood of the empty ossuaries being those of the Holy Family is largely discounted by the common occurrence of these names in many other Second Temple–period burials.

2. The incident was reported in *The Daily Telegraph,* Sunday July 28, 2002.

3. André Dupont-Sommer, *The Dead Sea Scrolls: A Preliminary Survey,* A. Margaret Rowley, trans. (Oxford/Blackwell, 1952); John Allegro, *The Dead Sea Scrolls and the Origins of Christianity* (Criterion, 1967); Laurence Gardner, *Bloodline of the*

*Holy Grail* (Element, 1996); B. Thiering, *Jesus and the Riddle of the Dead Sea Scrolls: Unlocking the Secrets of His Life Story* (HarperCollins, 1992). R. Eisler, *The Messiah Jesus and John the Baptist According to Flavius Josephus' Recently Rediscovered 'Capture of Jerusalem' and Other Jewish and Christian Sources* (Methuen, 1931); Jean Danielou, *The Work of John the Baptist* (Helicon, 1966); Jack Finnegan, *Light from the Ancient Past* (Princeton University Press, 1959); Daniel Schwartz, *Studies in the Jewish Background of Christianity* (Mohr-Siebeck, 1992); R. K. Harrison, *The Dead Sea Scrolls* (Harper and Row, 1961); Charles Scobie, *John the Baptist: The Scrolls and Christianity* (Talbot, 1969); John A. Robinson, "The Baptism of John and the Qumran Community," *Harvard Theological Studies,* no. 50 (1957); Oscar Cullmann, "The Significance of the Qumran Texts for Research into the Beginnings of Christianity," *Journal of Biblical Literature* 74 (1955); Robert L. Webb, "John the Baptizer and Prophet: A Socio-Historical Study," *Journal for the Study of the New Testament,* suppl. series 62 (Sheffield Academic, 1991); William H. Brownlee, "John the Baptist in the New Light of Ancient Scrolls," *Interpretation* (1955); George Brooke, "Biblical Interpretation in the Qumran Scrolls and the New Testament," paper presented at Dead Sea Scrolls Fifty Years After Their Discovery International Congress, Jerusalem, 1997; Lucretta Mowry, *The Dead Sea Scrolls and the Early Church* (University of Chicago, 1962); Otto Betz, "Jesus and the Temple Scroll," in *Jesus and the Dead Sea Scrolls,* James H. Charlesworth, ed. (Doubleday, 1992); J. VanderKam, "The Dead Sea Scrolls and Christianity," in *Understanding the Dead Sea Scrolls: A Reader from the Biblical Archaeology Review* (Random House, 1992); Jesus Seminar, see John W. B. Tatum, *John the Baptist and Jesus: A Report of the Jesus Seminar* (Polebridge, 1994); Yigael Yadin, *The Temple Scroll* (Weidenfeld & Nicolson, 1985). Charles Fritsch, *The Qumran Community, Its History and Scrolls* (Macmillan, 1956); Millar Burrows, *More Light on the Dead Sea Scrolls* (Viking, 1958); David Flusser, *Jesus* (Magnes Press, 1997); K. Schubert, *Die Qumran-Essene: Texte der Schriftrollen und Lebensbild der Gemeinde* (UTB, 1973); Joseph A. Fitzmyer, *The Dead Sea Scrolls and Christian Origins* (Eerdmans, 2000); Magen Broshi, "The Archaeology of Qumran: A Reconsideration," in *The Dead Sea Scrolls: Forty Years of Research* (Brill, 1992); H. H. Rowley, *The Dead Sea Scrolls and the New Testament* (Talbot, 1964); Frank Moore Cross, *The Ancient Library of Qumran and Modern Biblical Studies* (Doubleday, 1961); Pierre Benoit, *Paul and Qumran* (Priory, 1968); Cyrus Gordon, *Adventures in the Nearest East* (Phoenix House, 1957); Edmund Sutcliffe, *The Monks of Qumran* (Newman, 1960); Carsten P. Thiede, *The Dead Sea Scrolls and the Jewish Origins of Christianity* (Palgrave Macmillan, 2001); Joan E. Taylor, *The Immerser* (Eerdmans, 1997); James H. Charlesworth, ed., *Jesus and the Dead Sea Scrolls* (Doubleday, 1992); Jonathan Campbell, *Dead Sea Scrolls: The Complete Story* (Ulysses, 1998); Geza Vermes, *Jesus the Jew* (SCM, 2001). One unusual witness comes from an unnamed spiritualist in channeled conversations with Joseph of Arimathea (*The Way of Love,* ed. by Peter Wheeler, The Leaders Partnership, 1996), which records that Jesus's parents were high-order Essenes. Father Bargil Pixner, a highly respected priest/archaeologist, insisted that Jesus had Essene connections and that Jesus's extended family was close to the Essenes (*The Independent,* May 17, 2002). J. Milik's position is not clear, and his remarks on the subject have been hesitant. In his early life he would have rejected the possibility, but he seems to have modified his position.

4. There are three main theories as to why women and children were buried in spatially separated areas on the fringes of the Qumran cemetery and, it appears, were buried in a deliberately aligned east–west direction. One theory, proposed by Geza Vermes (*The Complete Dead Sea Scrolls in English,* Allen Lane/Penguin, 1997) and Magen Broshi ("The Archaeology of Qumran: A Reconsideration," in *The Dead Sea Scrolls: Forty Years of Research,* Brill, 1992), is that they were members of other Essene communities who, for some reason, were brought to Qumran for burial. Another theory suggests alternating phases of celibacy and noncelibacy at Qumran (L. Bennett Elder, "The Woman Question and Female Ascetics Among Essenes," *Biblical Archaeology* 57, 1994). Yet another theory, presented by Joseph Zias, argues that the female burials were later-period Muslim interments ("The Cemeteries of Qumran and Celibacy: Confusion Laid to Rest?" *Dead Sea Discoveries* vol. 7, no. 2, 2000). Zias argues that some of the burials were later Muslim interments on the basis of beads apparently found with the female remains. The validity of his arguments has not yet been acknowledged. My own view is that the concentration of female burials in this southern section of the cemetery fits well with the coterie of women who are portrayed in the Christian Scriptures as having surrounded Jesus during his lifetime. Evidence of brown dust (Zias, "The Cemeteries of Qumran") found during the excavation of several of the female graves has been taken as indicating the original presence of coffins and therefore the likelihood that some of the female bodies were brought to Qumran from a distance.

5. Laurence Gardner, *Bloodline of the Holy Grail* (Element, 1996).

6. Barbara Thiering, *Jesus the Man* (Doubleday, 1992). In *Jesus of the Apocalypse* (Corgi, 1996), however, Thiering has Jesus surviving the cross and making his last visit to Ephesus in 70 C.E., and then presumes he is buried in or near Rome. Not content with these speculations in "The Qumran Origins of the Christian Church" (*Theological Explorations,* 1983), Thiering suggests Jesus was buried in a cave near Qumran.

7. Chapter 11 of the Book of Revelation seems to be pulling in various strands of information that are not easy to interpret. The ingredients are: someone given a measuring rod in a holy city with a temple; destruction of the city; two prophets who are slain by the devil and whose bodies lie in the streets of the great city called Sodom and Egypt; an association with Jesus and his resurrection after three days; resurrection by the power of God of the two prophets after three and a half days and their ascent into heaven; and destruction wreaked on their enemies. (In The Oracle of Hystaspes, a Jewish apocalytic work of the first century C.E., which the Book of Revelation draws on, the period between death and resurrection is three days; see Cana Werman, *A Messiah in Heaven? A re-evaluation of Jewish and Christian Apocalyptic Traditions,* paper presented at Text, Thought, and Practice in Qumran and Early Christianity, International Symposum, Hebrew University of Jerusalem, January 11–13, 2004). In view of the messianic connections I have already suggested for Jesus, Qumran, and Pharaoh Akhenaten, one possible interpretation is that the two prophets are Akhenaten and his high priest, Meryra, who were slain in the holy city of Akhetaten. Jesus and his resurrection

become related to the messianic force that will take vengeance on the forces of darkness at the End Days. Reference to a measuring rod reprises the experience of Ezekiel in being shown around a supposedly visionary temple, which I have elsewhere argued is actually a distant memory of the real Great Temple that stood on the banks of the Nile at Akhetaten. Clearly the city that is spiritually called Sodom and Egypt is not Jerusalem, but has Egyptian overtones as well as the flavor of a Dead Sea–area location.

8. Joseph Zias, "Crucifixion in Antiquity" (Century One Foundation, www.centuryone.org/crucifixion2.html). The discovery at Givat Hamivtar was made by accident by building contractors. Deliberate excavation of a Jewish tomb is forbidden by law.

9. V. Tzaferis, "Jewish Tombs at and Near Giv'at ha-Mivtar," *Israel Exploration Journal* 20 (1971).

10. Nicu Haas, "Anthropological Observations on the Skeletal Remains from Giv'at ha-Mivtar," *Israel Exploration Journal* 20 (1970).

11. J. Zias and E. Sekeles, "The Crucified Man from Giv'at ha-Mivtar: A Reappraisal," *Israel Exploration Journal* 35 (1985).

## Chapter 37: Closing the Circle

1. Norman de Garis Davies, *The Rock Tombs of El-Amarna, Part 2. The Tombs of Panehesy and Meryra II* (Egypt Exploration Fund, 1905).

2. Gwil Owen, "The Amarna Courtiers' Tombs," *Egyptian Archaeology* (Autumn 2000).

3. Beneath the figures of Akhenaten and Nefertiti and the figure taken to be that of Jesus can be seen three important-looking figures. Could these have been the original images behind the legend of the three Magi who came to do homage to the infant Jesus? There are other signs of early Christian activity at Akhetaten, evidenced by drawings of other figures on tomb walls adorned with the sign of the cross. The prayer that Pope John Paul II placed in a crevice of the Western Wall read: "God of our fathers, you chose Abraham and his descendants to bring your Name to the Nations: We are deeply saddened by the behavior of those who in the course of history have caused these children of yours to suffer and, asking your forgiveness, we wish to commit ourselves to genuine brotherhood with the people of the Covenant."

4. Nicholas Montserrat, *Akhenaten: History, Fantasy and Ancient Egypt* (Routledge, 2000).

5. Another inscription, ending in –*eos*, could be that designating Matthew, Bartholemew, or Thaddaeus. Analysis of the plaster and pigments used in the wall reliefs at Kom el-Nana showed that two different yellow pigments had been used, one probably yellow ochre and the other a paler yellow crystalline-structured pigment, possibly orpiment or jarosite. The first yellow was used more extensively in depicting the gold cloaks, whereas the paler yellow was used only in a single area. The pale red, used for cloaks and between figures, was derived from a single color, probably madder, rather than from mixing red and white. The red coloring was not based on red ochre, the normal choice in pharaonic times, but possibly ver-

milion or realgar. Significantly, the pigments used in Panehesy's tomb when it was utilized as a church showed plaster and painting techniques similar to those at Kom el-Nana ("Tell el-Amarna, 2001–2," *Journal of Egyptian Archaeology* 88, 2002; 89, 2003).

6. Report of the 2001/2 season by the Egypt Exploration Society, London. See also Gillian Pyke, "Church Wall Paintings from Kom el-Nana," *Egyptian Archaeology* 22 (Spring 2003).

7. "The Impact of 3D VR Reconstructions: Amarna," www.digitalegypt.ucl.ac.uk/3d/impact_amarna.html.

8. Robert Feather, *The Mystery of the Copper Scroll of Qumran* (Inner Traditions, 2003).

9. 2 Kings 2:11.

10. A full discussion of the significance of this relief, which Psalm 104 of the Bible effectively paraphrases, is given in Robert Feather, *The Mystery of the Copper Scroll of Qumran* (Inner Traditions, 2003).

11. Barry Kemp, of Cambridge University, the Egypt Exploration Society–backed resident archaeologist at Amarna, describes a monastery at Kom el-Nana near Amarna as dating back at least to the fifth century C.E. Recent excavations are reported by the Egypt Exploration Society. The monastery was apparently abandoned some two hundred years later. There are numerous examples throughout history of prominent figures who have recognized the ongoing significance of Egypt to Christianity, from Giordano Bruno, a great sixteenth-century Hermetic Italian thinker, originally a Dominican friar, who came to the conclusion that ancient Egyptian religion preceded Christianity, to more modern scholars like Professor Karl Luckert, who sees Christianity's roots in Egypt (*Egyptian Light and Hebrew Fire,* State University of New York Press, 1991).

12. The Amarna letters are collections of some four hundred cuneiform tablets comprising records of correspondence between the Egyptian court of Amenhotep IV (Akhenaten) and vassal states, composed in the mid-fourteenth century B.C.E. They were discovered at Amarna in 1887 (William L. Moran, ed. and trans., *The Amarna Letters,* Johns Hopkins University Press, 1992).

13. Geoffrey Thorndike Martin, *The Royal Tomb at El-'Amarna* (Egypt Exploration Society, 1989).

14. Roland de Vaux, *L'Archéologie et les manuscrits de la Mer Morte* (Oxford University Press, 1961).

## Chapter 38: The Holy Family in Egypt

1. S. H. Steckholl, "Excavation Report in the Qumran Cemetery," *Revue de Qumran* 23 (1968). Steckholl discounts any possibility of the form of burial coming from Egypt at the time of the Temple of Onias IV at Leontopolis, second century B.C.E. to first century C.E., as it "reflects a society far earlier in time and conception than the time when they existed." He notes that a burial system using a recess for the body at the bottom of the shaft together with an air pocket over the corpse covered by bricks was particularly prevalent in Egypt as early as 1500 B.C.E. There are, in fact, also examples of deep-shaft burials at Akhenaten's holy city in the

northern hills of Amarna, although the nobility were predominantly buried in spacious cave tombs. Another highly intriguing aspect of Steckholl's work was his finding that seven of the eleven skeletons he dug up had red staining consistent with a high intake of madder root, possibly for medicinal purposes (S. H. Steckholl, Z. Goffer, H. Nathan, and N. Haas, "Red-Stained Human Bones from Qumran," *Israel Journal of Medical Sciences* 7, no. 11, 1971). A brief reference to the chemical content of the cemetery bones appeared in a book by E.-M. Laperrousaz entitled *Qumran L'Établissement Essenien des bords de la Mer Morte* (A. & J. Picard, 1976). See also E.-M. Laperrousaz, *Qumran*, vol. 2, *Archéologie, Dictionnaire de la Bible* (Paris, 1979), edited by H. Leclercq. The article was referred to by Gloria Moss in her treatise "Religion and Medicine: The Case of Qumran," *Faith and Freedom: A Journal of Progressive Religion* 146 (1998).

Professor Rosalie David, Egyptologist at the Manchester Museum, has encountered similar red stains on mummified remains from ancient Egypt but has yet to report an analysis of her findings (Robert Feather, conversation with Dr. Rosalie David, Egyptian Cultural Centre, London, February 10, 2000). Similar red staining was noted in the Kurth collection of bone material, but it was concluded that it resulted from soil deposition rather than from ingested vegetation (Röhrer-Ertl, Ferdinand Röhrhirsch, and Dietbert Hahn, "Über die Gräberfelder von Khirbet Qumran die Funde der Compagne 1956. 1. Anthropologische Datenvorlage und Erstauswertung aufgrunde der Collectio Kurth," *Revue de Qumran* 73, June 1999).

2. C. Clermont-Ganneau, *Archaeological Researches in Palestine*, vol. 1 (Palestine Exploration Fund, 1899).

3. Robert Bauval, *Secret Chamber: The Quest for the Hall of Records* (Arrow, 2000).

4. Mamdouh El-Beltagui, *The Holy Family in Egypt* (Egyptian Ministry of Tourism, 1999). According to local traditions, the Holy Family stayed in Egypt for three years and eleven months; Coptic Christians celebrate their journey each year on June 1 (see Christian Cannuyer, *L'Égypte Copte*, Gallimard/IMA, 2000).

5. Ibid.

6. Barry Kemp exploration of Kom el-Nana, Amarna, www.digitalegypt.ucl.ac.uk/3d/impact_amarna.html.

7. Ibid.

8. Norman de Garis Davies, *The Rock Tombs of El Amarna*. Part 2, *The Tombs of Panehesy and Meryra II* (Egypt Exploration Fund, 1905).

9. Hartmut Stegemann, *The Library of Qumran* (Eerdmans/Brill, 1998); K. Schubert (*Die Qumran-Essene: Texte der Schriftrollen und Lebensbild der Gemeinde,* UTB, 1973). Rainer Riesner ("Jesus, the Primitive Community, and the Essene Quarter of Jerusalem," in *Jesus and the Dead Sea Scrolls*, James H. Charlesworth, ed., Doubleday, 1992), has also suggested that many members of the primitive Christian community were Essenes.

10. Phylacteries (Hebrew, *tefillin*) are small containers with leather straps that are attached to the forehead and arm by devout Jews during daily prayers. Some thirty phylacteries were found in various Qumran caves, most containing biblical

texts that varied from those in modern phylacteries, which include Exodus 13:1–16 and Deuteronomy 6:4–9 and 11:13–21.

11. See chapter 20 of Robert Feather, *The Mystery of the Copper Scroll of Qumran* (Inner Traditions, 2003).

12. Maurice Cotterell, *The Tutankhamun Prophecies* (Bear & Co., 2001).

13. David Christie-Murray, "Speaking in Tongues," *Mysteries of the Church—Miracles of Holy Mysticism*, ed. Peter Brookesmith (Orbis Publishing, London, 1984).

14. Giovanni Filoramo, *A History of Gnosticism* (Blackwell, 1991).

15. Jan Wilhelm Drijvers, *Helena Augusta: The Mother of Constantine the Great and the Legend of Her Finding of the True Cross* (Brill, 1992).

16. Michael Grant, *The Emperor Constantine* (Weidenfeld and Nicolson, 1993).

17. Cyril E. Pocknee, *Cross and Crucifix: In Christian Worship and Devotion* (Mowbray, 1962).

18. Carsten Peter Thiede and Matthew D'Ancona, *The Quest for the True Cross* (Weidenfeld and Nicolson, 2000). It has to be borne in mind that no murals showing the cross have been found in early catacombs of Christian burials. Also, the evidence presented by Thiede and D'Ancona is intended to buttress their theory that the Titulus of the Cross (headboard above the crucified person), preserved in the Church of Santa Croce, Gerusalemme, Rome, is a genuine relic of the original cross on which Jesus was crucified. A very early date for the cross as a Christian symbol would help confirm their theory about the genuineness of this relic. On this latter aspect, I believe the authors are barking up the wrong tree. Nevertheless, the authors' scholarship, together with the findings in the tomb of Panehesy showing the extreme age of the cross as a symbol, is overwhelming evidence in favor of a very early dating of the use of the cross as a Christian sign. That the plain cross existed in early decorative imagery can be seen from the example on a pot (now in the Cairo Museum) found in the tomb of Yuha and Tuya, grandparents of Akhenaten, which carries a red cross on a white background—the Cross of St. George!

19. Other examples of the SATOR palindrome, a word that reads the same forward and backwards, have been found in Italy at the Church of St. Peter, Capestrano; at the Cathedral of Siena; and in a circular version at the Cathedral of St. Orso, Aosta (Anna Giacomini, "Il Sator de Sant'Orso," *HERA*, February 2003). Other examples have been found in a rubbish heap in Roman remains at Manchester, in England, and on the wall plaster of a house in Cirencester, England (Carsten Peter Thiede and Matthew D'Ancona, *The Quest for the True Cross* (Weidenfeld and Nicolson, 2000). Another early monogram of letters indicating the name of Christ combines the Greek letters *chi* and *rho*—an X with a P set vertically at the intersection of the arms of the X. A Jewish document bearing this sign was found near the Dead Sea at Wadi Murabba'at, just south of Qumran; it is dated to around 135 C.E. (P. Mur, P. Benoit, J. T. Milik, and R. de Vaux, eds., "Les Grottes de Murabba'at," *Discoveries in the Judaean Desert II*, Oxford, 1961). This finding has been a puzzle for scholars, as it appears to place a Christian symbol within a Jewish text. Perhaps it is not such a puzzle, bearing in mind the connections that

have been made to early Christianity and the Essenes and the connections others have made between Qumran and Murabbaat in the finding of related scrolls. The text was written on leather, a preferred holy material for the Qumran Essenes. It includes a Greek *delta* two letters to the left of the *chi-rho*, which has been associated with a sign possibly meaning the Holy Trinity.

20. F. Strickert, *Bethsaida: Home of the Apostles* (Liturgical Press, 1998).

21. Bargil Pixner, *Wege des Messias und Stätten der Urkirche* (Brunnen Verlag, 1996).

22. Carsten Peter Thiede and Matthew D'Ancona, *The Quest for the True Cross* (Weidenfeld and Nicolson, 2000).

23. The Bodmer Papyri (see table 8) contain three examples of the ankh sign in the Gospel of Luke.

24. One of the earliest examples of the cross incorporating a sun sphere can be seen in the Victoria and Albert Museum, London. The colored-design cross headed by a sphere is embroidered on a piece of linen fabric found at Oxyrhynchus, Egypt.

## Chapter 39: The Qumran Essenes' Presence at Amarna

1. That Ezekiel was a figure of major importance to the Qumran Essenes is underlined by the belief of Professor Ben Zion Wacholder, of Hebrew University, Cincinnati, that Ezekiel was the founder of the movement.

2. Cyril Aldred, *Akhenaten, King of Egypt* (Thames and Hudson, 1996). The word *repoussé* means hammered into relief from the reverse side; *gesso* is a backing made from gypsum, a naturally occurring hydrated form of calcium sulfate, often referred to today as plaster of Paris; *faience* is decorated and glazed ceramic material. Despite mentions in the Hebrew Scriptures of the thousands of chariots supposedly owned by King David and King Solomon, no remains of such chariots have ever been found in Israel.

3. That it was customary for kings to go forth in a chariot to conquer their enemies is illustrated in a number of ancient Egyptian reliefs—for example, that showing Tutmoses IV, grandfather of Akhenaten, shooting down Asiatics (found in the tomb of Tutmoses IV) (Cyril Aldred, *Akhenaten King of Egypt*, Thames and Hudson, 1996).

4. The chariot depicted in the Sepphoris mosaic has six spokes per wheel with thin wheel-rim design, as seen on wall reliefs at Amarna showing Akhenaten riding his royal chariot beneath the blazing Aten sun disk. Chariots were introduced into Egypt by the Hyksos in the sixteenth century B.C.E.; subsequent designs down to the end of the fifteenth century had four wheels. By the fourteenth century B.C.E., six-wheel design came into use and remained popular to the time of Ramses in the thirteenth century, when eight-spoke wheels started appearing in Egypt and Assyria. By Greek-Roman times eight-spoke wheels were the norm (Zeev Weiss, "The Sepphoris Synagogue Mosaic," *Biblical Archaeology Review* 26, no. 5, 2000). Interestingly, one of the earliest depictions of Christ, in St. Peter's in Vatican City, shows him as Helios mounted on a chariot. Zeev Weiss is not the only scholar to be nonplussed by the use of imagery specifically forbidden in the Mishnah, a confusion confounded by the traditional Jewish prayer to the sun,

*Sefer Harazim* (see Lee I. Levine, *The Ancient Synagogue*, Yale University Press, 2000). This prayer paraphrases many of the themes in the Great Hymn of Aten.

5. John J. Collins, *Apocalypticism in the Dead Sea Scrolls* (Routledge, 1997).

6. Examples of this imagery can be seen on the walls of the Osiris temple at Abydos and in the tombs of Ramses VI and Ramses IX. The Theban recension of the Book of the Dead explains that there were seven halls in Sekhet Aaru that had to be passed through by the deceased. Within the halls were ten secret gates, each guarded by a named gatekeeper, which had to be negotiated until the Field of Offerings or Field of Reeds could be reached and everlasting bliss attained (see, for example, E. A. Wallis Budge, *The Book of the Dead,* Gramercy, 1995).

7. R. T. Rundle Clark, *Myth and Symbol in Ancient Egypt* (Thames and Hudson, 1978).

8. Scrolls 4Q521, 4Q427, 4Q471; 1 Enoch 108:12; Matthew 19:18; Luke 22:30; Revelation 3:21, 20:4; Isaiah 9:24. Scroll 4Q471 is considered to be part of the War Scroll, which in itself is replete with references to ancient Egypt. See Geza Vermes, *The Complete Dead Sea Scrolls in English* (Allen Lane/Penguin, 1997).

9. John J. Collins, *Apocalypticism in the Dead Sea Scrolls* (Routledge, 1997).

10. 4Q186 ascribes physical characteristics of a person with thick hairy fingers and thick thighs and short thick toes, as eight parts in the House of Darkness and one part in the House of Light. Long and lean thighs and toes, by contrast, endow six parts in the House of Light and three parts in the House of Darkness. Egyptian overtones are not hard to detect, and the image of the predominantly good person with elongated limbs may well be based on the classic depictions found at Amarna, showing Pharaoh Akhenaten with exaggeratedly long thighs, fingers, and feet.

11. There are constant references in inscriptions found at Amarna to King Akhenaten and his teaching—"Oh my servant who harkenest to the Teaching"—and to the superintendent of the Treasury of Golden Rings: "Take the High Priest of the Aten in Akhetaten and put gold around his neck to the top of it, and gold around his ankles because of his obedience to the Teaching." On the walls of the tomb of Tutu, chamberlain to the king, we find: "I was a servant favored by his lord; his teaching and his instructions are in my inmost heart. . . . He rose early every day to teach me because of my zeal in performing his teaching." From Ay, head of the Companions of the King: "My lord taught me and I do his teaching."

## Chapter 40: Conclusions and Significance of the Discoveries

1. Burton L. Mack, professor of New Testament, Claremont School of Theology, a scholar heavily involved in the Jesus Seminar debate, goes further in his book *The Lost Gospel: The Book of Q and Christian Origins* (Harper, 1993). He maintains the followers of Jesus did not believe he rose from the dead, or was the son of God. The majority of Christians, and especially Catholics, believe in the bodily resurrection of Jesus; and according to William Lane Craig (professor of philosophy at Talbot School of Theology, La Mirada, California), an increasing number of scholars of the Christian Scriptures would defend the historicity of the empty tomb of Jesus ("The Historicity of the Empty Tomb of Jesus," *New Testament*

*Studies* 31, 1985). The idea that Jesus's resurrection was spiritual, rather than bodily, is evident in Paul, the earliest chronicler of Jesus. Nor does Mark detail an appearance of Jesus in bodily form. Although the other three Gospels detail a bodily resurrection in their witnesses, they also depict an inherent spiritual afterlife in which Jesus has ghostlike characteristics. Jesus's bodily appearance to Peter is now seen, by people like Elaine Pagels, of Barnard College, Columbia University, as a means of endorsing Peter's authority as heir to the leadership of Christianity, a legacy taken up by the popes throughout history as their legitimization (Elaine Pagels, *The Gnostic Gospels,* Random House, 1979). In fact, the early Gnostic branches of the followers of Jesus, as recorded in the Gospel of Thomas, denied a bodily resurrection.

2. John Dominic Crossan, *The Birth of Christianity* (HarperSanFrancisco, 1999).

3. The author is aware that many of the early workers at the École Biblique and members of the Vatican were hugely disappointed that proof of Jesus's existence did not emerge from the early Dead Sea Scrolls texts.

4. R. Bultman, *Jesus and the Word* (Scribner, 1934).

5. Ernst Käsemann, "Das Problem des historischen Jesus," *Zeitschrift für Theologie und Kirche* 51 (1954).

6. E. P. Sanders, *Jesus and Judaism* (Fortress, 1985); Gerd Theissen and Annette Merz, *The Historical Jesus: A Comprehensive Guide* (SCM, 1998).

7. N. H. Taylor, "Stephen, the Temple, and Early Christian Eschatology," *Revue de Qumran* 78 (December 2001). That Stephen was promulgating the Qumran-Essene preference for the Mosaic priestly line centered at Shiloh, Samaria, rather than the Aaronic priestly line centered at Hebron, is indicated by his statement that the tombs of the patriarchs were located in Shechem, rather than in Hebron (Acts 7:16, Gen. 33:19). The closeness and unique nature of the views of the early followers of Jesus and those of the Qumran Essenes toward the temples is yet another confirmation of the very tight links that initially bound the two groups. Their joint attitude toward the illegitimacy of both the First and the Second Temple, and the exclusive holiness of the Tabernacle of the Wilderness, also reprises the argument previously rehearsed, that there was a separate line of priests with their own view of God's laws, outside those of the mainstream Temple priests, which stretched from the wilderness of 1200 B.C.E. right down to the Qumran Essenes of 150–68 C.E.

8. The modern process of reconciliation between Judaism and Christianity probably commenced in 1948 with the work of Jules Isaac, a French historian who, while mourning the memory of his wife and daughter in Auschwitz, wrote a work entitled *Jesus et Israel* that documented the systematic anti-Semitism propagated by Christianity through the ages. His work came to the notice of Pope John XXIII, who in response penned a most powerful prayer: "We see the sign of Cain written in our faith. For centuries our brother, Abel, has been lying in his blood shed by us. Forgive us the curse we uttered against the name of the Jew. Forgive us that in their flesh, we crucified You again." One of the first acts of John XXIII on becoming pope in 1959 was an instruction for the removal of offending passages about "perfidious Jews" from the Catholic liturgy for Good Friday. In his convocation of the Second Vatican Council, there was an intention unambiguously to

declare the rejection of anti-Judaism. When Pope John XXIII died in 1963, his dream had not been fulfilled, but under Pope Paul VI, 2,222 Catholic bishops approved a statement in Latin condemning anti-Semitism and the deicide charge against the Jews. It was the beginning of a proactive campaign to reform and enlighten Catholicism's own churches and seminaries, which in turn inspired similar statements and actions from Protestant and Orthodox churches around the world. *The Irish Times,* May 29, 2000, by Dr. Racelle R. Weiman, director of the Israel branch of Temple University, a Philadelphia-based global dialogue institute, and a lecturer in interfaith relations and Holocaust studies at the University of Haifa, in Israel.)

9. Solomon Shechter, *The Chosen People* (Cambridge University Press, 1901).

# Appendix 1

1. Alexander Jannaeus officiated as high priest and, according to Josephus, was despised by the people. The Pharisees plotted to call on the help of the Seleucid King Demetrius III circa 88 B.C.E. The attempted coup failed, and Jannaeus had eight hundred Pharisees crucified. This act is alluded to in 4QpNah 1, which mentions Demetrius King of Greece, and the passage is interpreted as referring to "the furious young lion (Jannaeus)" who executes revenge on those who seek smooth things (interpreters of the law) and hangs men alive.

While I do not agree that Alexander Jannaeus (102–76 B.C.E.) was the Wicked Priest, as he was not a contemporary of the high priest Onias IV (175–164 B.C.E.), whom I take as the Teacher of Righteousness, it has long been the standard model of Qumranology that the Essenes were adamantly opposed to the Hasmoneans. King Jannaeus would therefore have been persona non grata to them. To say that a fragment known as Eloge du Roi Jonathan (4Q448) caused consternation among Dead Sea Scrolls scholars would be an understatement. Virtually everyone agreed that its title should be translated "Homage to King Jonathan" and that its thematic content was one of praise of this king as a hero of the Qumran Essenes. They also agreed that the Jonathan being referred to was Alexander Jannaeus. One dissenter, Geza Vermes ("The So-called King Jonathan Fragment: 4Q448," *Journal of Jewish Studies* 44, 1993), identifies the figure as Jonathan Maccabeus (161—142 B.C.E.), but he was never a king, and the idea finds limited support. The editors of the translated fragment, Hanan and Esther Eshel, of Bar-Ilan University, Israel, try to get around the problem by suggesting the offending passage is not sectarian. Others, like Professor George Brooke, of Manchester University, sit on the fence and say that this king cannot be identified with certainty.

What almost everyone does agree on is that 4Q448 is a most important and significant document, so critical that three eminently respected American scholars decided to ditch the standard model of hostility between the Qumran Essenes and Jerusalem, built up over generations, and conclude there were, at least in the time of Jannaeus, cordial relations (Michael Wise, Martin Abegg Jr., Edward Cook, *Les Manuscripts de la Mer Morte,* Perrin, 2003). This conclusion calls in question the entire previously accepted standard model of the evolution of the community and its writings. In my view the basic progression of this concept results from a complete misreading of the wording and sense of the fragmentary texts.

The difficult semicursive script read as "Jonathan" is already removed in translation from the usual name of the king in question, Jannaeus, or Jannai, but in looking for a king there is nowhere else for the translators to go than someone known by the name of Jonathan contemporary with the period of the Qumran Essenes. The Hebrew letters that are read on bronze Prutah coins struck by this Hasmonean king give his name as "Yehonatan Melech" (Yehonathan the King). On the reverse side is seen, in Greek, "Alexandroy Basilewc" (of King Alexander). The Lepton or so-called widow's mite coin of the Christian Scriptures bears a similar "Yehonatan" (Hebrew, *yntn*) inscription. The 4Q448 text, however, is rather different from this formulation, the name of Jonathan being obtained from *ywntn* (*Discoveries in the Judaean Desert* XXV, edited by Émile Puech, Clarendon Press, 1998). Robert D. Leonard Jr., an expert numismatist who has looked at 4Q448, noted that the name claimed to be that of King Jonathan on the fragment was not spelled in the same form as on coins of his period: "4Q448 has Yonatan, but a plene spelling [grammatical form given in Masoretic texts as corrections of the defective forms that appeared in ancient Biblical texts] with an 'o' sound that is lacking on the coin version" (e-mail communication from Robert D. Leonard Jr., October 21, 2003). What 4Q448 does show are root letters that could well be read as "Aten." In fact, it fits very well with the reading of the name Uaenaten, a version of Akhenaten, seen on an inscribed piece of glass dated to the Amarna period in the collection at Alnwick Castle, England (cited in Feather, *The Mystery of the Copper Scroll of Qumran,* Inner Traditions, 2003). The name YHW NTN in fact appears on numerous seals from ancient Israel and is generally read as meaning the name of God coupled with the Hebrew verb for "has given." These and the formulation in 4Q448, however, might better be read as "God related to the Aten."

When the three-column text is considered as a whole, the broad flavor is one of similar adulations to the heavenly Aten, king "of the heavens and the deep sea . . . thy name be blessed," as seen on inscriptions at Amarna. Column 2 of 4Q448 refers to the "Holy City" of the king. Jerusalem can hardly have been considered by the Qumran Essenes a holy city at the time of King Jannaeus, nor is its name mentioned in the 4Q448 texts. For them it contained a temple that they despised and would not enter. Looked at in the context of the immediately preceding passage to 4Q448, a version of Psalm 154, there are telltale signs of the setting being in the time of Jacob; and the exact same phrase that appears in one of the Amarna letters addressed to Pharaoh Akhenaten is seen in the last line, where the pharaoh "chooses to set his name in Jerusalem for ever." As Robert Eisenman and Michael Wise note (*The Dead Sea Scrolls Uncovered,* Penguin, 1992), references to "visiting" and "joiners" in the text are problematic in the context of King Jonathan, as they seem to relate him to the first messianic figure of the community and the presence of God-fearing Gentiles in a final war.

Underlining the antipathy of the Qumran Essenes toward the Hasmonean regime, not one single fragment of any of the pro-Hasmonean Books of Maccabees has ever been found at Qumran. In fact, King Jannaeus was known to be a devious, secular king who would not have had much in common with the religiously devout Qumran Essenes. One is hard-pressed to understand how the standard model can be so readily jettisoned on the strength of virtually one sole apparently anomalous textual word in the face of the other, overwhelming evidence that the Qumran Essenes rejected the Jerusalem Temple and those who were not Sons of Light. The standard model, as far as it goes, still holds.

# Scroll and Texts Glossary

This is not a comprehensive list; it includes only sectarian and other material pertinent to the content of this book.

## The Dead Sea Scrolls

Consisting of scrolls and fragments written on parchment, papyrus, leather, and copper, the Dead Sea Scrolls were recovered from eleven caves in the hills behind Qumran between 1947 and 1967. They are considered to have been written or copied between the fourth century B.C.E. and the first century C.E. and comprise biblical texts, sectarian texts, and Jewish apocryphal and pseudepigraphic texts. The more important and larger items are kept in the Shrine of the Book, Israel Museum, Jerusalem; Rockefeller Museum, Jerusalem; and Archaeological Museum, Amman, Jordan. Smaller items are at various universities (Chicago, Manchester, Heidelberg); at the Bibliotheque National, Paris; with the Syrian community in New Jersey; and in private collections.

**Books of Enoch (Cave 4)** Previously known from the Book of 1 Enoch in versions from the Ethiopic Church, the Books of Enoch are dated to the mid–first century B.C.E. They include a Book of Watchers, a Book of Astronomical Secrets, a Dream Book, and Enoch's Epistle. Embedded in the Epistle is an Apocalypse of Weeks, which measures the history of the world in forty-nine-year periods. The texts stress the origination of sin in heaven, predestination, and the need to follow a solar calendar. The works appear to have been considered of great importance to the Qumran Essenes.

**Community Rule (1QS and fragments from Caves 4 and 5)** Originally known as the Manual of Discipline, the Community Rule (also referred to as the Rule of the Community and the Rules Scroll), dated to around 100 B.C.E., was found in Cave 1 and has eleven columns. It contains descriptions of religious ceremonies and blessings, instructions on truth and dishonesty, descriptions of the struggle against the forces of evil represented by Belial and the forces of good represented by the Sons of Light, initiation and behavior within the community, organization and rulings for the council of the community, discipline and punishment, the religious duties of the community leader and his hymn, and seasonal ceremonials.

**Copper Scroll (3Q15)** Dated to the first century C.E., the Copper Scroll comprises three thin sheets of copper riveted together and then rolled into a scroll measuring about eight feet in length. Engraved in an ancient form of Hebrew with interspersed Greek letters and Egyptian numbering units, it lists some sixty-four locations where treasure related to a temple was hidden. Since the scroll's discovery in 1952, none of the treasures had been found, until the identification, in 1999, of some of the items as coming from excavations in Egypt.

**Damascus Document (Caves 4, 5, and 6)** The Damascus Document, dated around 100 B.C.E., is sometimes referred to as the Cairo-Damascus Document to reflect its similarity to two complete copies of the document that were discovered in the late nineteenth century (see *Genizah Texts,* page 430). There are also what seem to be later versions that were developed at Qumran. The texts refer to an original Interpreter of the Law and his associate Prince of the Congregation. They demand that the righteous understand the history of their foundation and acknowledge the authority of the Teacher of Righteousness, founder of the renewed Covenant in Second Temple times. All those who would harvest the fruits of the coming encounter with the forces of evil are enjoined to observe the word of God and God's laws. There follows a series of statutes that must be followed relating to swearing of oaths, offerings, the ten judges of the congregation, purification by water, the Sabbath, community settlements, and rules for the congregation regarding monies.

**Greek Fragments (Cave 7)** The Greek Fragments have been said by several scholars to contain examples of the Christian Scriptures writings of Mark, 1 Timothy, James, Acts of the Apostles, and 2 Peter, but these claims have now largely been discounted by the majority of those who have investigated them.

**Habakkuk (1QpHab)** Habakkuk is the longest of a series of biblical commen-taries. Dated to the late first century B.C.E., the text elaborates on hidden meaning in the biblical version in the form of an expansion and explanation (Hebrew, Pesher). The prophecies deal with a threat from the Kittim, and with the future Teacher of Righteousness as the defender of goodness and a Wicked Priest, together with a Man of Lies, as the perpetrator of evil. The Wicked Priest is said to pursue and attack the Teacher of Righteousness in his place of exile.

**Halakhic Letter (4Q394–99; also known as 4QMMT)** Dated to around the middle of the first century B.C.E. and thought to be a letter written by the Teacher of Righteousness to the Jerusalem authorities, the Halakhic Letter sets out legal views on ritual purity and holiness and condemns the practice in the Jerusalem Temple that allowed offerings and sacrifices to be made by Gentiles.

**Heavenly Prince Melchizedek (11Q13)** Heavenly Prince Melchizedek is sometimes known simply as Melchizedek. Dated to the mid–first century B.C.E., it describes a heavenly deliverer who combines the qualities of the first-ever high priest and a king, history in terms of ten blocks of jubilees, and salvation for the Children of Light through a temple ritual on the Day of Atonement. On that day it is said that Melchizedek will execute the judgment of God on the holy ones and those of Belial (the evil one).

**Jubilees (Caves 1, 2, 3, 4, and 11)** Previously known from eighteenth-century discoveries of versions held by the Ethiopic Church in Abyssinia and dated to the latter part of the first century B.C.E., Jubilees deals systematically with periods of Israelite history in blocks of forty-nine years, from creation up to the time of Mount Sinai. In stressing the need for obedience to the Law of the patriarchs, it implies that the Law was fully developed before Sinai, as several other Dead Sea Scrolls report, and that Levi, Jacob's son, was appointed to the priesthood long before the time of the construction of the Tabernacle by Moses. It emphasizes requirements for the proper observance of sabbaths, feast days, and a solar calendar.

**Messianic Apocalypse (4Q521)**   Also referred to as the Resurrection fragment and dated to the beginning of the first century B.C.E., the Messianic Apocalypse speaks of a messiah who will liberate the captives, restore sight to the blind, straighten the bent, heal the wounded, revive the dead, and bring good tidings to the poor.

**Messianic Rule (1Q28a)**   Originally called the Rule of the Congregation, the Messianic Rule is dated to the mid–first century B.C.E. It was intended as instruction for all the congregation in preparation for the last days and a messianic war against the forces of evil. In that time the priest and the messiah were expected to come and join the heads of the congregation in a meal of bread and wine.

**Nahum Commentary (4QphNahum)** One of a number of commentaries (Hebrew "Pesharim") on biblical texts, dated to the mid-1st century B.C.E. It mentions a Greek Seleucid king, Demetrius, probably Demetrius III, and probably refers to an incident when Pharisees elicited his help to try and take control of Jerusalem, in 90 B.C.E. The Hasmonean, Alexander Jannaeus (the "Lion of Wrath"), is thought to be the king who

took revenge on the Pharisees (the "Seekers of Smooth Things") by hanging 800 of them alive—confirming the contemporary practice of crucifixion by suspension, rather than the Deuteronomic requirement of hanging the body on a tree after stoning to death.

**New Jerusalem Scroll (Caves 1, 2, 4, 5, and 11)**   Dated to around 10 B.C.E., the New Jerusalem Scroll is thought to be a detailed visionary description of a holy temple and its holy city that would be built in the eschatological age. The measurements, in reeds and cubits, define a vast city, far larger than Jerusalem, with broad streets paved with white stone, marble, and jasper; regular blocks of houses; and towered structures. The scroll never mentions Jerusalem, however.

**Paean to King Jonathan (4Q448)**   The Paean to King Jonathan, also dated to around the middle of the first century B.C.E, is thought to be a prayer for the welfare of the Hasmonean king Alexander Jannaeus, but there is little agreement as to whether it was to him or some other king. It has caused endless controversy, as the consensus view has been that the authors of the prayer, the Qumran Essenes, were opposed to the Hasmoneans (see appendix 1, note 1).

**Pierced Messiah (4Q285)**   Also known, together with 11Q14, as the War Rule, and the Rule of War (Hebrew, Serekh ha-Milhamah), the Pierced Messiah scroll is a six-line fragment written in Herodian-period Hebrew and dated to the early first century C.E. It refers to a Prince of the Congregation, a descendant of Jesse, and a "pierced messiah" or possibly a "messiah who pierces," and a priest of renown. The pierced messiah has erroneously been identified as Jesus.

**Phylacteries (Caves 4 and 5)**    Strips of leather containing passages from Exodus 12:43 and 13:16 and Deuteronomy 5:1, 6:9, 10:12, and 11:21, the phylacteries (Hebrew, *tefillin*) were used in ritual prayers. They date from the mid– to late first century B.C.E.

**Rule of the Congregation (1Qsa)**    Dated to around 100 B.C.E., the Rule of the Congregation covers many aspects of requirements for behavior and communal meals. In describing a congregation that includes women and children, it appears to be more concerned with the wider community of Essenes outside Qumran that was governed by the priests and council of Qumran.

**Scroll of Instruction (Caves 1 and 4)**    Also referred to as Wisdom texts and Sapiential works, the Scroll of Instruction is dated to the early second century B.C.E. and comprises an older stratum of wisdom admonitions supplemented by apocalyptic discourses. The admonitions provide guidance on family relationships, financial matters, dealing with superiors and subordinates, and agriculture. The apocalyptic sections deal with divine mysteries and the restoration of the righteous in the final days. The author looks to universal judgment in heaven and on earth during God's final intervention. Authority for the instructions and revelations is dependent not on the Torah but on the mystery to come (Hebrew, *raz nihyeh*), God's comprehensive plan for creation, history, and redemption. These divine mysteries have been revealed to the community, which is described as God's eternal planting, the nucleus of the future restored Israel.

**Son of God Scroll (4Q246)**    The Son of God Scroll is a fragmentary text also known as the Aramaic Apocalypse. Dated to about 10 B.C.E., the scroll fragment refers to a Son of God who appears to have messianic characteristics and, as such, has been likened by sensationalists to Jesus and passages in the New Testament. The setting, however, is one of carnage relating to kings of Egypt and Assyria and cannot be a direct reference to Jesus.

**Songs of the Sabbath Sacrifice (Caves 4 and 11)**    Songs of the Sabbath Sacrifice (Hebrew, Shirot 'Olat ha-Shabbat) is also known as the Angelic Liturgy. An example of the fragmentary manuscript was also found at Masada. Dated to the mid–first century B.C.E., it contains a section for each of the thirteen Sabbaths of the year in a solar calendar cycle. It describes praise by cherubim (winged figures with a human head) and princely angels of the King of Glory before the image of a throne-chariot, above which is a fiery vision of the most holy spirits.

**Temple Scroll (11QT)**    Largest of the nonbiblical scrolls, the Temple Scroll is thirty feet long and is thought to have been copied in the latter part of the first century B.C.E. It sets out a comprehensive guide to religious laws, often different from the biblical versions seen in other texts. It describes in detail a huge temple and a holy city that is far larger than Jerusalem and sets out how the Israelites are to behave when they enter the Promised Land. Written as if God were speaking directly to God's people, it defines a religious solar calendar, sacrificial and purity rules, legislation for political and military behavior, and the role of the king, but it never mentions Jerusalem.

**Testament of Levi (Caves 1 and 4)**  The Testament of Levi, also known as the Aramaic Levi Document and Aramaic Testament of Levi, was previously known from a Greek version from the eleventh century C.E. found in the Monastery of Koutloumous, Mount Athos, Turkey. Dated to the early part of the first century B.C.E., the text, in the form of a prayer to God, describes Jacob addressing his priestly son Levi before the appointment of priests by Moses as described in the Bible.

**Thanksgiving Hymns (from Caves 1, 4, and 5)**  Sometimes called the Hymns Scroll or Psalms of Thanksgiving (Hebrew, Hodayot), they date from the mid– to latter part of the first century B.C.E. They comprise a series of hymns that develop the theme of God's glory in relation to humanity and the certainty of predestination. Often they seems to refer to the Teacher of Righteousness, recounting his exile from his homeland and then his founding of the Qumran community.

**Therapeia (4Qtherapeia)**  A small fragment dated to the first century C.E., Therapeia was at first translated as the report of a traveling physician. It is now thought to be nothing more than a scribal practice sheet.

**War Scroll (1QM and other fragments from Caves 1 and 4)**  Dated to between mid– and late first century B.C.E., the nineteen columns of fragmentary text of the War Scroll describe preparations for the final war against the Kittim (thought to mean the Romans, although the setting clearly attests to a period at least one thousand years earlier). The scroll gives details of battle strategies, the role of the infantry and mounted soldiers, the duties of the priests and Levites, battle and victory prayers, a thanksgiving ceremony, and the final battle led by the high priest and supported by the Prince of Light against the forces of darkness led by Belial.

# Genizah Texts

The Genizah Texts are Jewish texts and codices recovered from a storage Genizah in the Ben Asher Synagogue, Fostat, Cairo, between 1896 and 1898. (The storage Genizah was literally a hole in a wall, high up on the first floor of a synagogue, which served as a place of storage for old and worn prayer and Bible material that could not be destroyed because it may contain the name of God.)

These texts date to between the seventh and nineteenth centuries C.E. The main collection, now in the Taylor-Schechter Library, University of Cambridge, England, holds about 140,000 fragments (75 percent of the total known to exist).

**Cairo-Damascus Document**  Originally referred to as the Zadokite Documents, the Cairo-Damascus Document exists in two nearly complete versions dating to the tenth and twelfth centuries; these have been identified as later versions of the Qumran Damascus Document.

**Wisdom of Ben Sirah**  The Wisdom of Ben Sirah is known as Ecclesiasticus in the Catholic canon. It is similar in content to scroll material found at Masada, which is thought to have originated at Qumran.

# Masada Scroll Fragments

The Fortress of Masada was captured by Jewish Zealots in 66 C.E., led by Eleazar ben Yair, rebelling against Roman rule. Reconquered in 73 C.E. by the Roman's 10th Legion, under Flavius Silva, virtually all of the 960 defenders committed suicide rather than be captured. Jewish texts from scroll fragments discovered during excavations carried out from 1963 to 1965, under the leadership of Professor Yigael Yadin, showed that some of the refugees from the destruction of Qumran in 68 C.E. must have fled to Masada, bringing with them some of their sectarian scrolls.

**Book of Deuteronomy—part of the Hebrew Scriptures**   Hebrew fragments of the final chapters of the book.

**Book of Ezekiel—part of the Hebrew Scriptures**   Hebrew fragments of chapter 37.

**Book of Genesis—part of the Hebrew Scriptures**   Hebrew fragments of chapter 46 verses 7–11.

**Book of Joshua—part of the Hebrew Scriptures**   Hebrew fragments dated to c. 170 B.C.E.

**Book of Jubilees—prior to Qumran finds, previously only known through Greek, Ethiopian, and Latin versions**   Hebrew text consistent with Hebrew versions found at Qumran.

**Book of Leviticus—part of the Hebrew Scriptures**   Hebrew fragments of chapters 8–12.

**Psalms**   Fragments in Hebrew from Psalms 81–85 and 150 of the Hebrew Scriptures.

**Songs of the Sabbath Sacrifices—view of worship in the heavenly temple**   Fragments identical to scroll contents found in Cave 4 at Qumran.

**Synagogue Area**   Fragments found in a Genizah pit within an open-air synagogue at the top of Masada.

**Wisdom of Ben Sirah**   Greek translation included in the books of the Apocrypha, and known as Ecclesiasticus. Also previously known from Syriac versions and from a Greek version found amongst the Cairo Genizah texts. Dated to the first century B.C.E., the Hebrew fragments are consistent with the Hebrew version found at Qumran.

# General Glossary

**Ain Feshka** Essene settlement about two miles south of Qumran, where fresh water was available. Evidence of parchment manufacture and crop cultivation indicates it was a source of materials, food, and potable water for the Qumran Essenes.

**Apocrypha** Sacred "hidden" (from the Greek *apokryphos*) Jewish texts written in the Second Temple period and up to 35 C.E., which are additional to the thirty-nine books accepted as part of the Hebrew Scriptures. They are known from the Greek Septuagint version of the Hebrew Scriptures and were accepted as canon by the Catholic Church, but excluded from the canon of the Protestant churches at the time of the Reformation. They include the Books of Judith, Tobit, the Wisdom of Solomon, and Ecclesiasticus. (Ecclesiasticus is not to be confused with Ecclesiastes, which is part of the Catholic, Protestant, and Hebrew Bibles. In the rabbinic period of the Middle Ages, rabbis tried to suppress Ecclesiastes, as it counsels behavior on the basis that human life is preordained and oppression and injustice have to be accepted. They nevertheless felt obliged to accept it as part of the canon because of its attribution to Kohelet, son of David, although modern scholars now think it is probably third-century B.C.E.) Other biblical-related Jewish texts, rejected by the Catholic Church, are called Pseudepigrapha.

**Akkadian** A Semitic language originating in the Tigris-Euphrates region in the third millennium B.C.E. It was in use at the time of Akhenaten in Egypt, and as the diplomatic language of the Levant, until it was superseded by Aramaic.

**Aramaic** A Semitic language dating back to 900 B.C.E.; it was the lingua franca of the Persian Empire and was used extensively by the Jews after they returned from the Babylonian exile. The cursive script replaced ancient paleo-Hebrew for secular writing and holy scriptures.

**Assyrians** Semitic tribes of ancient western Asia that dominated the Middle East in the eighth century B.C.E. and into the late seventh century. They conquered the Northern Kingdom of Israel around 722 B.C.E. and laid siege to Jerusalem, in the Southern Kingdom, in 701 B.C.E.

**Babylonia** See *Mesopotamia*.

**B.C.E.** Before the Common Era, taking year zero as the date of Jesus's birth.

**Boethians** A group named after Boethius, the father-in-law of Herod the Great. Boethius's son, Simon, was an Egyptian priest from Alexandria and appears to have been buried in the Hebrew cemetery at Leontopolis, the site of a temple built by Onias IV. The likelihood that Onias IV was the Teacher of Righteousness of the Qumran Essenes would help explain an apparent connection between an ongoing movement known as the Boethians, who are referred to by later rabbinic sources, and the Essene movement.

**Books of the Dead**   Egyptian funereal incantation texts, dating back to 2700 B.C.E., found in pyramids and coffins. First consolidated as some two hundred chapters at the beginning of the New Kingdom around 1540 B.C.E., the spells, hymns, litanies, and magical formulas constitute rituals and procedures for the dead body in its state of afterlife and include a description of the last judgment of the deceased. In this procedure, the heart of the deceased is weighed against *maat,* or truth and cosmic order, symbolized by a feather. Judgment of a person's moral behavior, to decide whether the person could enter the land of the dead, was delivered by forty-two judges and the god of the underworld, Osiris. Texts were written in Egyptian hieroglyphic, hieratic, or demotic characters on papyri; extracts were inscribed on amulets and incorporated into the coffin with the mummified body. One of the best-known examples is the Book of the Dead, prepared for Ani, a royal scribe, dating from the Theban period of 1420 B.C.E. The twenty-six-yard-long papyrus is housed in the British Museum, London.

**calendar, Christian**   Hellenic astronomers of the Ptolemaic Egyptian period, c. 250 B.C.E., added the missing quarter-day to the Egyptian calendar (a true year is 365 days, five hours, forty-eight minutes, and forty-six seconds) by adding an extra (leap) day every four years. This approach was eventually adopted by the Romans under Emperor Julius Caesar in 46 B.C.E. The only mod-

ification to the Roman, or Julian, calendar was made in 1582 C.E. by Pope Gregory. His astronomical advisers suggested dropping the leap year whenever the year ended in two zeros, giving us the Gregorian calendar, which is in use throughout the world today.

**calendar, Egyptian**   Year based on the coincidence of the helical rising of the star Sirius with the rising of the sun, and made up of twelve periods of thirty days (approximating months) with five intercalary days added at the end of each year.

**calendar, Jewish**   Essentially lunar-based, dating the creation of the world from year zero; for example, the year 5757 was between the autumns of 1996 and 1997. Prior to about 360 C.E., the beginning of the Jewish month was marked by the first sighting of the new moon. With the threatened demise of the Sanhedrin (the ruling Jewish religious authority in Palestine) and the need to coordinate timings with communities dispersed after the destruction of the Second Temple in Jerusalem, Hillel the Younger introduced a calculated calendar. This rabbinic calendar was modified up to about 850 C.E., and from then on remained essentially the same as that used by Jews all over the world today. Calculations to predict the date of a particular festival or event are extremely complicated and are based mainly on lunar and partly on solar movements. The Jewish year comprises twelve lunar months, normally of alternating lengths of twenty-nine and thirty days, but to keep in line with solar-dominated agricultural festivals, the lunar year of 354 days is augmented by adding a full month seven times in a nineteen-year cycle.

**calendar, Muslim**   Purely lunar, each month closely following the moon's movements; as a result, it cycles through all four seasons during a period of thirty-three years.

**calendar, Qumran-Essene**   Solar-based (although the Qumran Essenes took note of the times of the new moon), relying exclusively on the sun's movement, giving them a year that contained 364 days. This was divided into twelve periods of thirty days (approximating months), and one of four extra days was added at the end of each three-month period. It also seems likely that they practiced a form of intercalation to retain the sabbatical character of their solar calendar.

**carbon dating**   Use of heavy carbon-14 isotope for dating materials containing carbon by radioactive decay measurement. The half-life of carbon-14 is about 5,730 years. Recent developments using accelerator mass spectrometry allow testing with only a few milligrams of material, and accuracies of plus or minus twenty-five years are achievable.

**Cathars**   Gnostic Christian religious movement centred in the Languedoc region of southern France. It probably emerged out of an earlier Eastern gnostic tradition associated with the Bogomils, a sect that flourished in the Balkans and Bulgaria between the tenth and fifteenth centuries. The first French Cathar bishop was appointed in 1149 in northern France, and the movement, variously called Manichaeanism or Arianism, subsequently spread to southern France and Lombardy in Italy. Gnosticism's dualistic philosophy and ascetic disciplines, denial of the incarnation of Christ, the Eucharist, and baptism inevitably brought it into conflict with the Catholic Church. The Cathar movement came under increasing criticism and persecution, and at the instigation of Pope Innocent III, the so-called Albigensian Crusade (named after the town of Albi in southern France) was launched in 1208, culminating on March 2, 1244, with a massacre of the Cathars at their final stronghold, at Montségur Castle, near Rennes-le-Château in Languedoc.

**C.E.**   Common Era, after the birth of Jesus, dated as year zero.

**circumcision**   For Jews, the ritual ceremony takes place when a male child is eight days old; for proselytes it occurs at a later age. The practice of circumcision has also been adopted by the Muslims, who follow many of the teachings of Moses (Quran, Suras 2, 20, 26, 28, etc.) and acknowledge Ishmael, the son of Abraham, whose circumcision was taken as a sign of a covenant with God, as the founder of the Arab nations.

**Council of Nicaea**   Called by the Roman emperor Constantine, some 250 Christian bishops (according to Eusebius; see *Eusebius*) attended the Council of Nicea (modern Turkey) in 325 C.E. The bishops agreed that Jesus was divine, but those favoring the Alexandrian line said he existed with God before the beginning of time, whereas those following the line promulgated by Arius of Antioch claimed he had been created later and was subordinate to God. Emperor Constantine ruled in favor of the Alexandrian line and required inclusion in the creed (established by Eusebius, bishop of Caesarea) that Christ was *homousion,* "of one substance" with God.

**Dead Sea** Formed 1.5 million years ago following a major earthquake, the Dead Sea is the lowest point on earth. Water evaporation, particularly over the past century, has markedly reduced the volume of the Dead Sea. In the last fifty years the surface area has decreased by 30 percent and the level by about fifty feet. At the present rate of evaporation, the Dead Sea will fall another three hundred feet over the next 120 years and shrink in size by 66 percent. The rate of evaporation, however, will decrease as the surface area decreases and the concentration of salts increases. A return to a "wet" period with flooding of the Jordan River could reverse the shrinkage process. The sea is currently 1,330 feet below sea level, compared to Death Valley, California, which is 280 feet below sea level. Jerusalem is 2,700 feet above sea level and Masada 1,500 feet. The concentration of salts in the Dead Sea is ten times greater than in average seawater levels, approaching 35 percent by weight (compared to 25 percent in Lake Utah), and this prevents any living creatures, even bacteria, from surviving in it. The chemical composition is approximately 95 percent magnesium chloride and 25 percent sodium chloride, with a balance of calcium chloride, potassium chloride, magnesium bromide, and trace elements. The pH is approximately 5.5 to 6.0. The pH is a level of acidity or alkalinity in a liquid, measured in terms of the logarithmic concentration of dissociated hydrogen ions. The range of pH values extends from 0 to 14; pH values under 7 denote acidity; and over 7, alkalinity.

In the Hebrew Scriptures, and in modern Israel, the Dead Sea is called Yam Ha-Melah, Salt Sea, and to the Greeks it was known as Lake Asphaltites because of the bituminous deposits that are occasionally thrown up. The Romans knew it as Mare Mortuum. Christians in the Middle Ages referred to it as the Devil's Sea. In Arab literature it is called The Overwhelmed, referring to Lot, Abraham's nephew, and to the cities of Sodom and Gemorrah, believed to be in the vicinity. It was also known to the Arabs as the Sea of Zughar, relating it to Zoar, a city that escaped destruction in the Middle Ages. Today it is referred to in Arabic as Bahr el-Lut' (Sea of Lot).

**Dead Sea Scrolls** Collection of scrolls and fragments discovered in the caves above Qumran on the Dead Sea, generally thought to have belonged to a community of Essenes who lived there between around 250 B.C.E. and 68 C.E. (The term is sometimes used to include any ancient scrolls found along the shores of the Dead Sea.) The first scroll material was discovered in the spring of 1947 by Bedouins and subsequently, up to 1956, ten other caves yielded further examples. The scrolls include items from every book of the Hebrew Scriptures except Esther, apocryphal and pseudepigraphic material, and other works written, copied, or collected by the Qumran Essenes. To date some 50 percent of the material has been translated and published; this includes all the major works.

**Didache** A Christian work thought to have been composed in the late first century. Alternatively known as the Teaching of the Twelve Apostles, it is referred to in ancient texts but came to light only in 1875 as a codex dating to 1057, when it was found in the patriarchal library of Constantinople. It describes ethical instruction and regulations on baptism, fasting, the Eucharist (ritual partaking of bread and wine as a symbolic union of Christians with the body and blood of Christ), and welcoming visitors into a community, as well as development of the early church.

**Dion (c. 40–112 C.E.)**    Dio Cocceianus, Greek philosopher and orator, born in Prusa, Asia Minor, a city in Bythnia (mentioned in 1 Peter 1:1). He was known as Golden Mouth (Greek, Chrysostomos) for his powerful orating ability. He lived in Rome under Emperor Vespasian and was banished by Emperor Domitian. He returned to Rome in 96 C.E. He appears to have known about the Essenes and is mentioned by Synesius of Cyrene (c. 370–415 C.E.): "Elsewhere he [Dion] praises the Essenes who have their own prosperous polis [settlement] near the Dead Sea, in the middle of Palestine, not very far from Sodom."

**DNA**    Each human cell has forty-six chromosomes grouped in twenty-three pairs (except ova and sperm, which have only twenty-three chromosomes). Aligned in single file along each chromosome are thousands of genes. Genes are short strands of DNA (deoxyribonucleic acid), a molecule that carries coded heredity details. It is found in the nucleus of almost every cell of all living organisms, except some viruses. It consists of two double-helix chains with instructions for the body on how to make structural proteins or enzymes that control the body's biochemistry, including the production of new copies of DNA.

**Ebionites**    A Jewish-Jesus group, thought to be related to the Essenes, who rejected the virgin birth, were hostile to the Temple cult and sacrifice, practiced ritual baptism, adopted vegetarianism,

and had a dualistic outlook on good and evil. They are believed to have lived in Transjordan in the region of Batanaea, and a Gospel of the Ebionites is attested to by Iraneus (c. 180 C.E.).

**Ephesus**    City in the Roman province of Asia (in modern western Turkey) located on the estuary of the river Cayster. The city's vast Temple of Diana was one of the seven wonders of the ancient world. Straddling an important trade route between East and West, it had a population of about three hundred thousand at the time of Paul, including a large settlement of Jews. Paul is believed to have lived in Ephesus for over two years and to have written his letters to Corinth and possibly his letter to the Philippians at Ephesus. When Paul left Ephesus, Timothy remained behind to help develop the Christian Church.

**Eusebius of Caesarea (c. 264–340 C.E.)**    Theologian and scholar, known as a father of the church. Eusebius was probably born in Palestine; he became bishop of Caesarea in about 313. He wrote numerous works, some of which are extant, largely in support of Christianity, and attended the Council of Nicaea as head of the moderate party, which was averse to discussing the nature of the Trinity. His *Ecclesiastical History* recorded the main events of the Christian Church up to 324.

**Hellenism and the Hellenistic period**    An ancient culture centered on what is now modern Greece and parts of Asia Minor, whose origins stretch back beyond the time of Pythagorus (c. 580–500 B.C.E.) to at least the eighth century B.C.E. With the conquests of Alexander the Great from 336 to 323 B.C.E., Greek philosophical ideas, enunciated by great thinkers like Socrates, Plato, and Aristotle—together with revolutionary concepts in monarchy in the style of Alexander, political thinking, architecture, city design, astronomy, mathematics, art, and lifestyle—spread across the civilized world. After the demise of Alexander, Hellenism continued to prove attractive to the emergent Roman Empire and subsequent cultures, although, in one sense, the Hellenistic period ceased with the coronation of Octavian under the name of Augustus, the first of the Roman emperors, in 27 B.C.E. As Hellenism's ideas continued to spread and Greek became the common language in the Mediterranean and Asian areas, Judaism, with its strict moral and religious convictions, resisted its polytheistic views and epicurean hedonism more than most cultures, culminating in the successful revolt of the Maccabees around 170 B.C.E. Nevertheless, the newly established Jewish Hasmonean state was not immune to other persuasive aspects of Hellenism.

**Hippolytus (c. 170–222)** Christian writer who became Presbyter in Rome and possibly the "anti-pope" to Callistus from 217 to 222. He mentions the Essenes and their daily routines of "girding themselves with linen girdles . . . taking their seats [for breakfast] in order and in silence . . . conversing quietly [for supper]" (Hippolytus, "Refutation of All Heresies," in *The Essenes According to the Classical Sources,* ed. by G. Vermes and M. Goodman, Sheffield, 1989). Hippolytus was a fierce opponent of Gnostic Christianity and the School of Valentinus.

**Hyksos** Semitic invaders from the East who dominated most of Egypt from about 1640 to 1538 B.C.E. They made their capital at Avaris in the Delta region of the Nile and worshipped Seth (Set), Anat, and Astarte. At the beginning of the war of expulsion, legend has it that their king, Apepe, endeavored to make Set (Sutekh) sole god. The biblical personalities of Joseph, Jacob, and their families are wrongly attributed to the Hyksos period.

**Josephus, Flavius (37–100 C.E.)** Jewish historian who became a Roman citizen and wrote extensively, inter alia, about the Essene community and its settlement on the Dead Sea and about Pontius Pilate. Born into a wealthy priestly family, he spent the first half of his life in Jerusalem. As a general commanding the Galilee area during the Jewish uprising of 66 C.E., he fought against the Romans, but after being captured gained favor with the Romans by correctly predicting that the commander of the Roman army, Vespasian, would become emperor. After 70 C.E. he settled in Rome, continuing his friendship with the new emperor and subsequently his successor, Titus. He wrote extensively on Roman-Jewish history, including *The Jewish Wars,* describing the period 175 B.C.E. to 74 C.E.; and *Jewish Antiquities,* covering the period from the creation of the world to 66 C.E. He mentions the Essenes, John the Baptist, Caiaphas the high priest, Pontius Pilate, James the brother of Jesus, and Jesus, although this latter reference is thought to have been augmented by later copyists.

**Kabbalah** Jewish religious belief based on hidden revelations, dating from the time of Christ. Kabbalah was codified by Shimon bar Yohai in the Zohar in the thirteenth century C.E. in Spain. It claims to give the true meaning behind the Torah in two forms, one basic and the other secret. Its teaching was prohibited until the sixteenth century, but parts of its doctrine of mystical piety and concentration on the presence of God were absorbed into Hassidism (a branch of Orthodox Jewry) around the eighteenth century. Some elements of the Kabbalah philosophy are that the Torah contains a secret code and that the Zohar can unlock the code; that Judaic astrology can throw light on the meaning of the universe; that meditation can enhance praying and human potential and elevate consciousness; and that the Messiah will come through study of Kabbalah. In the ten levels of attainment before oneness with God is achieved, there are some similarities with the teachings of Buddhism, Confucianism, and Indian religious ideas of inner awareness. There are also overtones of Egyptian mythology in Kabbalah's theories of the visible and invisible aspects of God, and of the judgment of the soul after death and its allocation to paradise or hell, or its transmigration into animal or other human form where restitution may be sought. Mysticism, magic, divination, and sorcery were and are today severely frowned upon in rabbinic teaching. Nevertheless, after the Exodus, residual beliefs lingered on in superstition and folklore and eventually found expression in the form of Kabbalah, which can be traced back as far as ancient Egypt. Akhenaten, however, shunned Egyptian magic and mysticism; Kabbalah was also strongly resisted in ancient Judaism, and is still looked on with reservation by many rabbis.

**Karaites**    Jewish movement, initially known as the Ananites, established by a Persian Jew named Anan ben David around 750 C.E. He advocated a return to strict Hebrew Scriptural Judaism, to the exclusion of other rabbinic teachings such as the Talmud and Mishnah. After his death the movement spread throughout the Byzantine Empire to the Holy Land and became rooted in Egypt. One of the main surviving works of the Karaites is the Cairo Codex. Written in Tiberias in 895 by Moses ben Asher, it contains the books of the prophets written in Hebrew; as such, prior to the finding of the Dead Sea Scrolls, it contained the oldest Hebrew version of the Hebrew Scriptures. It is now kept in the Russian State Library, St. Petersburg. The Asher family also compiled the Aleppo Codex, an eleventh-century version of the Hebrew Scriptures, found at Aleppo in Syria in the fourteenth century C.E. It is incomplete, having suffered fire damage, and is now kept in the Shrine of the Book in Jerusalem. These Hebrew versions of the Hebrew Scriptures were the basis for the development of the modern Masoretic Hebrew Bible used today. Karaite historians believe that the movement looked to the Essenes for spiritual inspiration and were familiar with the Damascus document, among other Dead Sea Scrolls texts.

**Knights Templar**    On November 27, 1095, Pope Urban II called for a crusade to, among other aims, assert the power of the Roman Catholic Church in the Near East. As a direct result, Jerusalem, occupied by Muslims since 638 C.E., was stormed in July 1099. The Templars came into existence in the aftermath of the First Crusade as the Order of Poor Knights of the Temple of Solomon, ostensibly to protect pilgrims journeying to the holy sites in Jerusalem. In France,

Bernard of Clairvaux backed the formation of a similar order, the Knights Templar, in about 1118. A secret order behind the Knights Templar evolved as the Templars, variously known as Prieure de Sion (Priory of Zion) and by other names. The order is suggested to have tendencies toward the Johannite Mandaean heresy, which denounced Jesus as a false prophet and acknowledged John the Baptist as the true messiah. Within two centuries the order, centered in the Languedoc region of southern France, where the Catholic Cathar movement flourished, had become so wealthy and powerful that it was seen as a threat to the French king and the Catholic Church. On October 13, 1307, King Philip IV of France, known as Philip the Fair, backed by Pope Clement, had all the Templars arrested on grounds of heresy. They were subsequently tried and put to death. The Order of the Temple, formed in 1118, is seen as a forerunner of the Masonic movement.

**Maccabees** Jewish priestly family whose head was High Priest Mattathias, whose son, Judah, led a successful revolt against the Greek Seleucid leader Antiochus Epiphanes in 167 B.C.E. and reoccupied Jerusalem in 164 B.C.E. His rededication of the Second Temple at Jerusalem is now remembered in the celebration of the festival of Hanukkah.

**Mandaeans** Gnostic-influenced early Christian movement that incorporated a form of dualism and a veneration of John the Baptist. Compilation of references to John the Baptist in the Book of John, based on legend and teachings of John that support gnostic themes, is thought to have been developed in the eighth century C.E. There are still followers of the religion in parts of modern Iraq, primarily in Baghdad and Basra, and in Iran.

**Manichaeanism** Gnostic, mystical religious movement founded by the prophet, painter, and poet Mani (215–277 C.E.) in Persia. Mani taught that prophets such as Buddha, Zarathustra, Jesus, and himself were not uniquely supreme but part of an ongoing line of messengers of God. Born in Ecbatana, he traveled widely, spreading his teachings as far as India, China, the Balkans, and Europe, and his church had a strong presence in the Rome of the fourth century. He was executed in 277 C.E. by Zoroastrian rivals, who crucified him. His teachings of learning, moral purity, and kindliness, in a world divided between good and evil forces engaged in a predestined cosmic war, were taken up by the Cathars of Languedoc; residual pockets of his beliefs still survive in this region, as well as in parts of Bulgaria.

**Mesopotamia, Sumeria, Babylonia**
Sumeria was composed of city-states that emerged about 3,400 B.C.E. in the region of the Tigris and Euphrates Rivers, generally referred to as early Mesopotamia (modern Iraq). Babylonia was a kingdom in the southern portion of Mesopotamia formed under Hammurabi around 1790 B.C.E. Its capital, Babylon, was about fifty miles to the south of today's city of Baghdad. Biblical references to these areas are few and sparse in detail. Abraham sends his servant (probably Eliezer) back to Nahor to find a wife for his son Isaac, but there is little description of the place or its inhabitants. Nineveh is mentioned in the Book of Jonah as "an exceeding

great city" he is called to redeem from its evil ways. Nineveh also features in the minor Book of Nahum, in which it is similarly berated by the prophet for its evilness as he describes its destruction. Apart from these relatively uninformative passages, there is little else. References to Babylon, to which the Jews were carried off in 597 B.C.E., are similarly very few, and geographic descriptions are vague and generalized.

The city of Ur, located in Mesopotamia (modern Iraq), was overwhelmed by a flood in about 4200 B.C.E. but reestablished its importance to became capital of Sumeria around 3000 B.C.E. The Temple of Uruk testifies to the wealth and advanced construction, building, and craftsmanship of the people at this period. One of Ur's main trading partners was Dilmun, modern Bahrein. Ur was sacked in 2000 B.C.E. but soon recovered its regional trading position, only to start going into decline around 1800 B.C.E., as Babylon to the north took over the lucrative trade with Persia. By the fourteenth century B.C.E., Ur was somewhat restored to its former activity. As part of the region's cultural development, numerous mythological stories emerged, one of the best known being that of the king of Uruk, Gilgamesh. In the *Epic of Gilgamesh* he sets out on a quest for eternal life and encounters a Sumerian Noah. Conventional exegesis of the early stories of the Hebrew Scriptures relate creation, Noah and the flood, and the lives of the patriarchs, as well as episodes from Babylonian (the southern portion of modern Iraq) and Assyrian (the northern portion of modern Iraq) records. This tracing holds true only for limited parts of the early Bible and soon becomes problematic as the major influence that takes over is Egyptian.

**Midrash**   See *Torah*.

**Mishnah**   See *Torah*.

**Oxyrhynchus Papyri**   Mid-second-century and later papyri found at Oxyrhynchus, near the Faiyum area of central Egypt, by Bernard Grenfell, a student of the pioneering archaeologist Professor W. M. Flinders Petrie and Grenfell's colleague Arthur Surridge Hunt. Fragments of papyrus were later attributed to the noncanononical Gospel of Thomas, including previously unknown sayings of Jesus. *Oxyrhynchus* means "sharp-nosed fish," a fish that was held to be sacred by the ancient Egyptians. Known in the dynastic period as Per-Medjed, Oxyrhynchus became prominent under Egypt's Greek and then Roman rulers. It was the hometown of the sophist Athenaeus. Later it became famous for its many churches and monasteries, and today the village of el-Bahnasa occupies part of the ancient site. It is located about a hundred miles south of Cairo on the river Bahr Yusef (Joseph's River), a branch of the Nile that links Amarna, ancient Akhetaten, and Lake Moeris in the Faiyum region. Other finds among what was essentially a rubbish dump for the ancient city include songs of Sappho, plays of Meander, and elegies of Callimachus.

**paleography**   Form, style, and shape of the letters and symbols used in writing.

**papyrus**   Writing medium made from papyrus plants, found growing mainly in the Delta marshes of the Nile in Egypt. Earliest examples date back to 3035 B.C.E.

**parchment**   Animal skin, usually goat or sheep, specially prepared and used for writing. Used in Egypt from 2000 B.C.E. and Judaea from about 200 B.C.E.

**Pentateuch** The first five books of the Hebrew Scriptures: Genesis, Exodus, Leviticus, Numbers, and Deuteronomy.

**Persians** People from the area of modern-day Iran who drove out the Babylonians from the Holy Land and conquered Egypt around 525 B.C.E. under King Cyrus and dominated the Middle East for about two hundred years. They allowed Jews exiled by the Babylonians to return to the Holy Land and generally acted benignly toward them. The biblical story of Esther is generally thought to have been enacted in Persia.

**Philo, Judaeus (c. 20 B.C.E.–c. 40 C.E.)** Jewish-Egyptian philosopher and Greek scholar, born in Alexandria. He worked at Alexandria on Bible commentary and law and mentions the Qumran Essenes in his writings.

**Pliny the Elder (23–79 C.E.)** Gaius Plinius Secundus was born in Como, Italy, to an aristocratic Roman family. After a term in the Roman army, he later devoted himself to writing historical treatises on, for example, oration and the history of Rome. A friend of Emperor Vespasian, he died during the volcanic eruption of Mount Vesuvius in 79 C.E. He wrote about the Essene community by the Dead Sea.

**Pliny the Younger (c. 62–113 C.E.)** Nephew and adopted son of Pliny the Elder, he was born in Novum Comum and became a renowned orator and Roman author. In correspondence with Trajan, he recorded the denigrating attitude of early Romans toward Christians

and how the Christians "sing a hymn to Christ as to a god."

**Plutarch (46–120 C.E.)** Greek historian, philosopher, and biographer whose works included forty-six portraits of great characters who preceded him.

**Pseudepigrapha** Jewish biblical texts not canonized by the Catholic Church, and those considered to be written under a false name or attributable to biblical characters. (See *Apocrypha*.)

**Ptolemies** Greek rulers of Egypt who followed the Greek Macedonian period of rule by Alexander the Great, his half brother, and his son, from 323 to 310 B.C.E. The Ptolemaic period of Egypt lasted from 305 B.C.E. until the demise of Cleopatra VII in 30 B.C.E.

**Romans** Dominant power in the Middle East and Mediterranean region from the middle of the first century B.C.E. to the fourth century C.E. The Romans conquered the Holy Land around 44 B.C.E.; Octavian Augustus appointed himself pharaoh of Egypt in 30 B.C.E.

**St. Jerome** Previously known as Eusebius Hieronymus (c. 342–420 C.E.). Born in Stridon, Dalmatia, he studied in Rome; after being baptized a Christian, he became a priest at Antioch and traveled to Rome, where he became secretary to Pope Damasus. In 386 he settled in Bethlehem, where he wrote the first Latin translation of the Bible, known as the Vulgate, from the Hebrew.

**Sinai, Mount** Mountain in the southern part of Sinai where the Bible relates the Ten Commandments were give to Moses by God. There is some evidence that the mountain of God was Jebel Madhbah in what was the land of Edom.

**Suetonius, Gaius Tranquillus (c. 70–140 C.E.)** Roman biographer and secretary to Emperor Hadrian. His major work, *De Vita Caesarum* (Lives of the Caesars), covered the lives of twelve emperors, from Julius Caesar to Domitian, mentioning Christians in his coverage of Emperor Claudius (41–54 C.E.). He also wrote biographies of Roman poets.

**Sumeria** See *Mesopotamia.*

**Synoptic Gospels** A phrase coined by the German scholar Johann Griesbach, writing around 1774 C.E. He grouped Matthew, Mark, and Luke as Synoptic (meaning "same view") Gospels written earlier than the so-called Fourth Gospel of John.

**Tacitus, Gaius Cornelius (c. 55–120 C.E.)** Born in Narbonese Gaul, Tacitus studied rhetoric in Rome and became an eminent lawyer. He married the daughter of Agricola (the conqueror of Britain) in 77 C.E. and wrote extensively on the history of Imperial Rome in his *Historiae and Annals,* in which he mentions Jesus.

**Talmud** See *Torah.*

*tefillin* Phylacteries, or small leather containers with leather straps, strapped on the left arm and on the forehead during daily prayer recital by Orthodox Jews. Today they usually contain a piece of leather inscribed with sections of Deuteronomy (6:4–9 and 11:13–21) and Exodus (13:1–10 and 13:11–16). The forehead tefillin contain the same biblical citations, but they are written on four separate leather rolls secreted in four separate compartments. Tefillin found at Qumran also contained the Ten Commandments and their context in Deuteronomy 5:1–6:9, and an extended passage relating to "circumcision of the heart" (Deut. 10:12–11:21). Some thirty phylacteries were found in various Qumran caves, most containing biblical texts that varied from what is found in modern tefillin.

**Templars** The century following 1134 saw the Templars, centered in southern France, become extremely wealthy and powerful, building five hundred abbeys and eighty churches across Europe. Eventually the French king Philip IV, known as Philip le Bon ("the Good"), allied himself with Pope Clement V and set about destroying the Templars and their strongholds and confiscating their wealth and property.

**Torah** The Torah, in its narrowest sense, comprises the Five Books of Moses (the Septuagint) of the Hebrew Scriptures. In its wider sense it encompasses the whole of Jewish teaching. Together with the Ten Commandments given to Moses on Mount Sinai, Orthodoxy holds God gave Jews 603 other commandments, the basis of the Torah, and an oral commentary explaining the rest.

**Valentinus (c. 100–160 C.E.)** Gnostic teacher born near Alexandria, Egypt, who tried to combine Hellenistic, Oriental, and Christian ideas. As a disciple of Theudas, who was a disciple of St. Paul, he claimed secret knowledge of Paul's teachings. Moving to Rome around 136 C.E., he established a considerable following there until his excommunication by the orthodox community around 155 C.E., when he is said to have retreated to Cyprus.

## Terminology Relating to Jewish Religious Teachings

### Torah*

Comprises the Pentateuch of Genesis, Exodus, Leviticus, Numbers, Deuteronomy (according to fundamental tradition given to Moses on Mount Sinai c. 1200 BCE). Torah contains 613 commandments, including the Ten Commandments.

### Oral laws

Made up of Mishnah and Gemara to comprise the Talmud (a handbook of Jewish observance)

| Mishnah | Mishnah |
|---|---|
| (Based on oral traditions) | (Based on oral traditions) |
| Laws, stories, moral instruction (Aggadah) | Laws, stories, moral instruction (Aggadah) |
| (by Tannaim—rabbis pre–200 C.E.) | (by Tannaim—rabbis pre–200 C.E.) |
| + | + |
| **Gemara** | **Gemara** |
| Discussion of the Mishnah | Discussion of the Mishnah |
| (by Amoraim—rabbis living from 200 to 500 C.E.) | (by Amoraim—rabbis living from 200 to 500 C.E.) |
| ↓ | ↓ |
| **Palestinian Talmud** | **Babylonian Talmud** |
| (Written in Hebrew and Western Aramaic) | (Written in Hebrew and Eastern Aramaic) |
| Compiled from pre–400 C.E. works | Compiled from pre–500 C.E. works |
| (Earliest complete text now in Leyden, Holland, | (Earliest extant text, 14th-century codex |
| 1st printed version, Venice, 1522 C.E.) | now in Munich) |

### Posekim (Codifiers)

The numerous sources of Mishnah were edited by R. Judah Ha-nasi and written down c. 200 C.E. The Palestinian and Babylonian Talmuds both use Ha-nasi's Mishnah but different Gemara. The work of codifiers (Posekim) of the law ( Hallachah), such as Maimonides (1135–1204 C.E.), Isaac Alfasi (1013–1103 C.E.) on the Babylonian Talmud, and Asher ben Jehiel (1250–1327 C.E.), were collated by the Sephardi scholar Joseph Caro (1488–1575 C.E.) into a work called Shulhan Arukh. Moses Isserles (1525–1572 C.E.) added to this work the views of Ashkenasi scholars, and the supplemented code has become the accepted authority for Orthodox Jewish Law. Where the supplements differ from main text, the Sephardim Orthodox (Spanish and Portuguese traditions) follow Caro's interpretation and the Ashkenasi (German and French traditions) follow Isserles.

### Midrash

Homilies usually based on Bible texts. One "Collection" of Midrashim was arranged in Bible order in Yalkut Shimoni in the 13th century C.E. based on 0–10th-century-C.E. homilies, interpretations, and commentaries on the Scriptures.

| Midrash Rabbah | Shoher Tov | Pesiktot | Other Midrash |
|---|---|---|---|
| Commentaries on the Pentateuch and five Megillot (Song of Songs, Ruth, Lamentations, Ecclesiastes, Esther) | Commentaries on Psalms | Commentaries on special sabbaths and festivals | On ethics, morality, conduct, and history |

*Torah is also used in a wider sense, meaning the whole of Jewish teaching.

# ── Index ──

# Books of Related Interest

**The Mystery of the Copper Scroll of Qumran**
The Essene Record of the Treasure of Akhenaten
*by Robert Feather*

**The Way of the Essenes**
Christ's Hidden Life Remembered
*by Anne and Daniel Meurois-Givaudan*

**Gnostic Secrets of the Naassenes**
The Initiatory Teachings of the Last Supper
*by Mark H. Gaffney*

**The Gospel of Thomas**
The Gnostic Wisdom of Jesus
*by Jean-Yves Leloup*

**The Discovery of the Nag Hammadi Texts**
A Firsthand Account of the Expedition That
Shook the Foundations of Christianity
*by Jean Doresse*

**The Brother of Jesus and the Lost Teachings of Christianity**
*by Jeffrey J. Bütz*

**Jesus the Rabbi Prophet**
A New Light on the Gospel Message
*by Jacques Baldet*

**Gnostic Philosophy**
From Ancient Persia to Modern Times
*by Tobias Churton*

Inner Traditions • Bear & Company
P.O. Box 388
Rochester, VT 05767
1-800-246-8648
www.InnerTraditions.com

Or contact your local bookseller